A Love Story and a Riddle

Reading this book is like discovering a lost Edith Wharton novel or anticipating an upcoming season of "Downton Abbey." Set between 1929 and 1944, the book is an intriguing and delightful window onto an amazing love story, set forth both through narration and an exchange of letters between South Africa and America.

Part of the interest in the later letters is the role (and frequent plight) of women during the Great Depression and WW II era. Despite her respected skills as a secretary/stenographer in her male-dominated work environment, Helen's advancement and pay increases are hard fought for and slow in coming. The general expectation is that, as a wife and mother, her primary duties are to her household, her children, and her husband. Helen proves herself both capable and vulnerable as she attempts to master both worlds, taking minutes of important war-related meetings by day, sewing, for her children at night, and eagerly anticipating infrequent week-end visits from her husband who is in training for deployment.

Helen's story is full of joy, humor, struggle, life, and love; but, above all, it is heroic and singularly heartrending.

Ed Higgins, Ph.D., literature and religion

***

The letters of Helen Dixon Evans, responding to news from home during the period spanning the late-1930s to the mid-1940s, provide rare and vitally important glimpses of life back in East Tennessee. Her comments help us recover the words, ideas, and lives of those now lost to us, the common people whose remarkable experiences appear in far too few original documents. The letters also enable us to see how Appalachian society in the early decades of the twentieth century shaped Helen Dixon Evans herself. Rich details and perceptive comments about her growing family, women's roles, life in South Africa, the Second World War, and much more, reveal the values that nurtured her youth and young adulthood. Evans, marveling in June 1939 at her five-year-old daughter Eve, wrote, "If they could only see her in Elizabethton." Scholars of Appalachia have long wanted to see another "her"—women such as Helen—in communities such as Elizabethton. With these evocative letters, we now have a fresh chance to do just that.

David C. Hsiung
Charles and Shirley Knox Professor of History, Juniata College

Robin Lawton combines the historian's craft with the novelist's creative and intuitive skills in telling the love story of her mother, Helen (of Tennessee), and her father, Wilfred (of South Africa). Astute interpretation of family documents as well as others made available through extensive research allow her to painstakingly solve the riddle so dear to her heart: how such an improbable union of souls could withstand family reservations, world events on three continents, geographic separation from her parents, health problems, and other obstacles, and find happiness. But Robin Lawton had me early on when she wrote of her mother: "She was a reserved woman and shy to a fault, but the day after the party she walked up to Wilfred, who was sitting on the beach, knelt down beside him, and kissed him."

Robert E. Hamilton, Ph.D., African history and anthropology

Collected and Edited by
ROBIN MYFANWY LAWTON

A Love Story and a Riddle

The Life and Letters of Helen Hunter Dixon Evans

Dating from 1929 to 1944

CREATESPACE
INDEPENDENT PUBLISHING PLATFORM

Copyright © 2015 by Robin Myfanwy Lawton
Newberg, Oregon

Library of Congress Subject Headings

Lawton, Robin M. "A Love Story and a Riddle"

Topics: Letters, Women, Daughters, Mothers, Prejudices
Form: Letters, Biography
Geography: Tennessee, East; South Africa—History—1909-1961; Germany—History—1918-1933
Chronology: Great Depression, World War II
LCCN: 2014920589

While every effort has been made to gain permission to use some of the photographs in this book, the only permission that has been received is from North Carolina State University. NCSU kindly granted use of content excerpts, quotes, and photos from its 1929 *Agromeck* yearbook.

All rights reserved, including the right of reproduction in whole, or in part, in any form.

ISBN# 978-1507817940

Dedicated to my mother,
Helen Hunter Dixon Evans,
and to my father,
Wilfred Victor Collingwood Evans

A Love Story and a Riddle

Helen Hunter Dixon, Elizabethton, Tennessee

You will not forget me—will you?
I have no one but you.

~ *Joyce Carol Oates*

Contents

Preface	1
Hearts in Hiding: The Story (1929—1937)	3
Finding the Letters	29
The Letters: At Home (1931—1933)	35
1. Safe in Their Alabaster Chambers	37
Apr. 1931—Aug. 1933	
2. Forsaking All Others	49
Aug. 1933—Sept. 1933	
At Home in America (1933-1937)	59
3. I Hail the Superhuman	61
Oct. 1933—Sept. 1937	
(No letters during this period)	
The Letters: Abroad (1937—1944)	69
4. And Indeed There Will Be Time	71
Sept. 1937—Aug. 1939	
5. I Dwell in Possibility	213
Aug. 1939—Apr. 1940	
6. A Vale of Soul-Making	267
May 1940—Feb. 1943	
7. Affairs are Now Soul-Size	437
Mar. 1943—Oct. 1943	
8. An Open Boat	483
Oct. 1943—Dec. 1943	
9. Sailing to Byzantium	497
Jan. 1944—June 1944	
Afterword	521
Timeline	523
Map of South Africa	527
Family Tree	528
Map of Sophia's Journey	531
Acknowledgements	532

Preface

My mother and father were Helen Dixon and Wilfred Evans. The story of their love unfolds against the backdrop of the late 1920s through the early 1940s: the Wall Street crash; Tennessee during the Great Depression; farming in the heart of Africa; student life in Munich during the dawn of Nazi Germany; boom and bust times in South Africa; and the beginning, middle, and end of World War II.

After her marriage in 1933 and four searing years in America, Helen, in letters to her parents, friends, aunts, and uncles, describes her daily life in South Africa between 1937 and 1944. She reflects back on her life in Tennessee and shares her successes in building a home for her family in Africa: her joy in looking after her beloved children, her love of her husband, her devotion to her parents, and her daily tasks of shopping, cooking, sewing, and working outside the home—all in a new country and culture that she gradually learns to embrace. She also conveys her pleasure and pride in supporting her husband's successes in various business endeavors and as a Captain in WWII.

This book may be viewed not only as an exotic love story, but also as a compendium of the kinds of challenges women—and men—faced in the first part of the twentieth century. Above all, Helen's letters are a tribute to the moral fiber of a courageous woman whose truthfulness and delightful sense of humor could leaven even the most difficult moments.

Those who knew Helen Hunter Dixon Evans in person are fading in number, but the most prominent of those who remain are her much-loved cousin, Kathryn Hall, and her adored children, Eve, Robin, and John. For these, and their descendants, the gift of her letters is as immense as is the burden of their poignancy.

Robin Myfanwy Lawton
Newberg, Oregon
February, 2015

Hearts in Hiding:

The Story
1929-1937

HEARTS IN HIDING: THE STORY
(1929—1937)

"I have always been sorry I did not marry Wilfred when I first met him, and he feels the same way." (Helen Dixon Evans, August, 1943)

My parents' marriage is both a Love Story and a Riddle: "How is it possible for two people to continue to love one another for fifteen years, despite finding themselves living apart for eight of those years, suffering through four more, and happily settled for only three?" The answer to the riddle lies in the letters that follow.

My mother, Helen Hunter Dixon, and my father, Wilfred Victor Collingwood Evans, met at a house party at Nags Head, North Carolina, in July 1929. Both were twenty-two. Their meeting led to an extraordinary love affair set at the peak of the high-life affluence of the late 1920s, only two months before the Wall Street Crash and America's descent into the Great Depression.

Helen and Wilfred's meeting at that house party was unlikely since they were both vacationing at Nags Head, North Carolina, for only a week, and their homes were at the opposite ends of the Earth: Helen's was in Tennessee, and Wilfred's in South Africa.

Helen Hunter Dixon, 1929

Their motivations for being at Nags Head could not have been more different. While Wilfred was there to celebrate his graduation from North Carolina State University (known then as the North Carolina College of Agriculture and Mechanic Arts), Helen was there probably attempting to assuage her grief over her brother's death. Three months earlier, Robert Edward Dixon, a United States Marine, had been killed in

Nicaragua at the age of twenty. Having heard that his father was ill, Robert received permission to leave camp and travel to the coast to get a boat back to the United States. He was murdered at some point during his journey. Who killed him, and why, is a mystery that was never solved.

Nags Head was a lively destination point for young people of means in the 1920s. For Helen, meeting Wilfred at a party in the small resort was love at first sight. Wilfred was a handsome young man, six feet tall, with blonde hair, intense hazel eyes, a lithe, athletic physique, and a dynamic and confident personality. Helen was lovely, with a sensuous mouth, soulful eyes, and radiant skin and hair. She was a reserved woman and shy to a fault, but the day after the party she walked up to Wilfred, who was sitting on the beach, knelt down beside him and kissed him. Shortly before her death, Helen recalled the week of their meeting as "the most wonderful week of my life; the only time I have been absolutely happy. For a week I did not know the time of day, nor the month of the year."

Helen and Wilfred's relationship was filled with drama from the first. Not only did their meeting occur three months after Robert's death, but also shortly before Wilfred was due to return to South Africa. From there he was to travel to Marandellas, Southern Rhodesia (now Marondera, Zimbabwe), where he had secured the job of establishing the first tobacco research station in the area. While tobacco had been grown in Southern Rhodesia for some years, Wilfred's charge was to help put the industry on a more scientific footing.

Clearly his degree in Agriculture, with a specialty in tobacco farming, put Wilfred in a strong position for the job. When he graduated at twenty-two as an Agricultural Specialist with honors, his prospects for the future were bright.

Wilfred, right, and his close friend George Frederik Papenfus, a fellow South African and graduate of North Carolina State University, 1929

Note: Wilfred's love of challenges had been in evidence at NC State where he had been on the staff of the Wautagan, Copy Editor of The Technician, a member of the N.C.C.P.A, and the Pullen Literary Society. He was also a member of the Blue Key and The Golden Chain, a senior honor society that recognizes etraordinary contributions to the university.

As their infatuation with one another grew, love took hold in the few days that followed. Helen and Wilfred found that they shared many of the same life experiences. Although born on different continents, both were born in 1906, only six weeks apart. Both were from affluent families. Both had attended expensive private high schools as boarders: Helen at Stonewall Jackson in Virginia, Wilfred at Kingswood College in South Africa. Both had attended college in America: Helen at Mary Baldwin College in Staunton, Virginia, and Virginia Intermont College in Bristol, and Wilfred at North Carolina State University in Raleigh. Both had lost a beloved sibling: Helen had only recently lost her younger brother, Robert; Wilfred had lost his younger sister, Thelma, some years earlier. Both had traveled abroad and had been deeply impacted by their experiences in Europe during their formative years. Helen later remembered her travels as "something very special that no one can ever take from me."

In 1928, a year before meeting Wilfred, Helen, at twenty-one, had gone with some of her friends on a "Conducted Tour of Europe" with the Frank Tourist Company. Starting on June 10, 1928, she spent two-and-a-half weeks in New York visiting places of interest. On June 30, she sailed on the *S.S. Arabic* for France. The tour included two days in Paris, two days in Avignon, four days in Nice, a three-day tour through the French Alps, two days at Chamonix, Montreux, Interlaken, Lucerne, Munich, Nuremburg, Dresden, Berlin, and Frankfort. From Frankfort, the participants sailed down the Rhine by steamer to Cologne for two days. From there they traveled to Amsterdam for three days, returning via The Hague, Brussels, and London. The six weeks of travel cost in excess of $13,500 in today's currency.

Wilfred had also traveled widely both as a child and as a young man. He had been educated mostly in South Africa and, sporadically, in Wales, and, most recently, as a young adult, in the United States.

While each immediately knew they had found a soul mate in the other, it was not clear how they could proceed with their relationship. Helen had grieving parents back home in Tennessee; Wilfred was committed to a new job back in Africa. Their options were limited by youthful inexperience, by a sense of obligation to commitments already made, and by having only a few days to get to know each other.

In a move completely out of character for someone so shy, Helen, after knowing Wilfred for only three days, invited him to Elizabethton to meet her parents. It seems that in the fun-filled spirit of their friendship, Helen and her best friend, Mary Walker, who had witnessed the fateful meeting on the beach, had prevailed on Helen's parents, Sophia and Harlow Dixon, to extend an invitation to "the man from Africa." So, before embarking on the long journey [continued pg. 10]

WILFRED V. C. EVANS, A Γ P
BLOUERFAUTEUR UNION, SOUTH AFRICA

Agricultural Specialist

Golden Chain; Blue Key; *Watauqan* Staff, Editor, 4, Managing Editor, 3; *Technician* Staff, Copy Editor, 3; Member N. C. C. P. A.; Pullen Literary Society.

"BILL"

"Bill," or that "Bally Englishman," was a familiar figure on the campus; he really needs so eulogism, for we all knew him for what he was—a gentleman. "Bill" straightway became interested in the publications of the college, and because of his ability and capacity for work, ended up as the editor of our literary magazine, at the same time gaining for himself the title of "the most energetic senior at the college."

"Bill" never said a great deal, but his laconic observations and long "a's" were a treat. Even though you are an Englishman, we must hand to you that you have a sense of humor. Because of his extensive travel and wide experience, "Bill" is quite a philosopher. And indeed at one time proved to be a guide, philosopher and friend to all the freshmen on his hall. Despite his many interests "Bill" still managed to graduate with honors.

We wish you all of the best, "old top," and unreservedly pronounce you the most popular foreign student we have had on our campus. Oh! I nearly forgot, for the "love of Mike," don't worry about your hair falling out, it's what's under it that counts.

This article about Wilfred appeared in the 1929 North Carolina State University Agromeck yearbook.

Wilfred (Bill) Evans was nicknamed "that *Bally Englishman*" and declared "the most popular foreign student we have had on our campus."

Note:
As a result of a proofreading error or an act of mischief, the heading shows Wilfred as a resident of "Blouerfauter Union, South Africa." This should read "Bloemfontein, Union of South Africa."

Page Fifty-one

Agromeck yearbook North Carolina State University 1929

Wilfred "Bill" Evans was widely admired by his classmates while he was a student at North Carolina State University in Raleigh

journey back to South Africa and from there to Southern Rhodesia, Wilfred visited the Dixon family in their lovely home on "G" Street in Elizabethton, Tennessee.

I intuit that my grandmother, Sophia Dixon, felt an intense wariness toward Wilfred, seemingly from their first meeting. He acknowledges as much in a letter written four years later, on August 3, 1933: "I was happy to learn from your letter that I had your respect and hope someday to win your affection too. I left your home with the firm idea that I had in no way gained your regard . . ."

Guessing at Sophia's state of mind, several factors come into play. It was probably too soon after Robert's death for her to assimilate her daughter's overwhelming joy and total infatuation with this foreigner. In all likelihood, Wilfred was considered unsuitable by Sophia since he represented the threat of another loss should he take Helen, her remaining child, to Africa.

This home on Riverside Drive in Elizabethton was built by Dr. E.E. Hunter, Sophia Dixon's father. It speaks to Sophia's pride in her heritage.

Further, Wilfred was not American. For a woman like my grandmother, who considered herself American aristocracy,[1] this man from the Dark Continent—despite his good looks, careful manners, and intellectual prowess—was an unwelcome suitor. In letters written eleven years later, as she tries to justify her love and admiration for Wilfred, Helen gradually gains the courage to confront her

---

[1] The Southern sense of what it meant to be American was just as pernicious as the English class system. Helen's friendship with Mary Walker would be compromised by this notion every bit as much as Wilfred's relationship was with Sophia. Of course, this idea of class was not restricted to America and England. It was, and is, alive worldwide, including South Africa in the 1920s, 1930s, and beyond, where being of European descent automatically conferred privileges upon an individual, whether earned or not.

family on their prejudice and hostility. Her pain from her family's treatment of him is clear.

But, in the summer of 1929, with the warm sun playing down on them, Helen, Mary, and Wilfred basked in delicious youth. Mary Walker later related an amusing incident. While the three of them were together at the "G" Street home, Helen suffered the embarrassment of having the elastic on her bloomers snap, allowing the cuff to peep out from beneath her sun suit. Attempting to soften her embarrassment, Wilfred coined the phrase "Jannie Langbroek" (a South African Afrikaans phrase meaning "Little Johnny Long Pants"). This title amused all three of them, and so the moment and the days they spent together passed happily.

In my grandmother's mind, Wilfred might have had a charming sense of humor and impeccable manners, but to her they were the formal manners of a well-bred Englishman, lacking in soft Southern charm. And then there was Wilfred's rather headstrong and conceited personality. In his mind, he was golden: educated on three continents, he had graduated from college with honors at the age of twenty-two and was destined for a leading research position in the heartland of Africa. For Sophia Dixon, having just lost her only son in the jungles of Nicaragua, the thought of losing her daughter to this foreigner from South Africa, however handsome and well educated, was too much.

Probably hardest of all was the fact that Wilfred was only a year and a half older than her beloved Robert, and was very likely in her mind no match for him. Ironically, having watched his own mother grieve the death of his little sister, Thelma, Wilfred was deeply conscious of Sophia's agony, possibly unbeknownst to her. Four years later, in a letter written to Sophia on August 3, 1933, he says, "I oftimes wished to talk to you, for I was struck by your quiet sadness and wished to say I understood, for I had seen my own mother bear the same sorrow." But even as they continually failed to find common ground, every character in this drama would, as the years unfolded, have reason to soften and mature.

For now, in the summer of 1929, while young Helen and Wilfred fell more deeply in love in the few short days before he was due to leave America, Wall Street jitters were making Sophia's life even harder. Sophia had repeatedly pleaded with her husband, Harlow, to get out of the stock market, but he had persisted with what she considered his "risky investments."

Since Harlow had come from considerable wealth, he probably found it hard to conceive that his financial stability could be compromised. Although traditionally rooted in Baltimore and Cumberland County, Maryland, the Dixon family owned large forested acreage in the mountains of East Tennessee.

Sophia was only nineteen in 1905 when she married Harlow Dixon, a hardworking man of twenty-eight. As a young man, Harlow rode his horse, Doc, up to thirty-six miles a day or walked as many as nine miles a day across the vast acreage owned by his family to estimate the number of board feet of lumber available for harvest. Once harvested, the lumber went by rail to the family-owned Dixon Furniture Factory located in Elizabethton, of which Harlow was eventually president. The Dixie Chair Company manufactured Windsor-backed chairs for Sears, Roebuck.

In the final months of 1929, when Harlow and Sophia had been married for twenty-four years, Harlow had the satisfaction of being able to count on his own hard work and on the Dixon wealth, which was substantial. It was so substantial that Sophia could not in good conscience accept the Hunter family inheritance when her father died ten years earlier. She refused on the grounds that "Harlow has more money than we can ever spend" and suggested that the money be given to other family members more in need. I still remember my grandmother recounting the joys and perils of going on vacation in the family-owned railroad car, and Helen, in one of her letters, mentions the car her parents had given her.

With all the utopianism of the late 1920s, it is little wonder that Harlow Dixon had been so optimistic about settling in Elizabethton. He and Sophia were amazingly blessed through the Dixon wealth and the Hunter family pedigree. Sophia's grandfather, Dr. Abraham Jobe, and her father, Dr. E. E. Hunter (Dr. Jobe's son-in-law), had been distinguished physicians in the area. Dr. Jobe was a "personal and intimate friend" of President Andrew Johnson and physician to the president on his deathbed. Along with Sophia's seven siblings, this created a rich family heritage with deep roots in Elizabethton.[2]

But in October 1929, little more than a dozen years after refusing her inheritance and within the space of four months, Sophia and Harlow lost their son, witnessed their daughter fall in love with a man from Africa, and watched as Harlow's fortune vanished almost overnight. With the Stock Market beginning its downward spiral, Sophia's world, at age forty-three, was rapidly shifting from fairytale to nightmare.

HELEN'S LIFE IN DEPRESSION-ERA AMERICA

Helen, meanwhile, was the ever-dutiful daughter. Even as she bore her own grief, she recognized the deeper grief her parents were suffering from the loss of their son. She also was mindful of the mounting financial losses they were facing. So, instead of following her heart and going to Africa with Wilfred, she took a job as a secretary at The American Rayon Corporation in Elizabethton and stayed home to help Sophia and Harlow with both moral and financial support.

---

[2] See *A Mountaineer in Motion: The Memoir of Dr. Abraham Jobe 1817-1906*. Tennessee State University Press, Knoxville, 2009. Sophia was also proud of her D.A.R. status: through the Tiptons on her mother's side and through the Hunters on her father's side.

Her support was all the more keenly needed since, to add to her burdens, Sophia was gradually assuming responsibilities as the primary caregiver of her mother, Mollie Jobe Hunter (Mama Hunter), and her mother-in-law, Mrs. Virginia Dixon (Mama Dick). Both women were in their late seventies and did not like each other. Sophia would later recount with wry amusement how each would glare at the other from their respective beds, which, of necessity, were in the same room.

Despite the challenges she faced, Sophia Hunter Dixon was a woman to be reckoned with. She never gave in to self-pity or hysteria. She was smart and emotionally steady. As a student, she had shown mathematical talent and had tutored young men applying to West Point Military Academy. She had a sharp mind and something of a sharp tongue. Once asked by an acquaintance how old my thirty-something-year-old sister was, she replied, "She's fine, thank you. How old are you?"

On another occasion, when the church asked for suggestions as to how it might help the poor multitudes of Africa, she responded with, "Send them the pill." Sophia was a capable seamstress and a great organizer who ran her home meticulously. She was also loyal, pragmatic, unsentimental, and unafraid of hard work—a blessing considering what she was facing and would still have to face.

Somewhere between June 1932 and July 1933, after suffering major losses on the stock market, the Dixon family moved from the house they had built on "G" Street to Broad Street, a cheaper side of Elizabethton. There they had a house large enough to eventually include Sophia and Harlow, Helen and Wilfred and their first-born child, baby Eve, and later Sophia's mother and mother-in-law, and, subsequently, boarders. Sophia managed the establishment with aplomb. Later, when Helen was living in South Africa, she tried to persuade her mother to hire domestic help, but Sophia refused, probably out of necessity. She may have lost her house on "G" Street, but Sophia Dixon never lost her pride or her sense of self.

If the years following the Wall Street Crash were hard on my grandmother, they were equally hard on Helen. Helen had also suffered through the loss of her brother, Robert; she had watched her mother and father grieve his loss; and she had met the man of her dreams—only to have him return to Africa. Now twenty-three, she was faced with the task of helping to provide financial support for her stricken family. From the age of twenty-three to thirty, between 1930 and 1937, during the early years of the Great Depression, Helen worked first at the North American Rayon Corporation on the outskirts of Elizabethton, and later in Nashville. Fortunately for the family, Helen's strong shorthand and typing skills qualified her as a top-flight secretary.

It was against these developing complexities in the summer of 1929 that Wilfred—with his heart in Tennessee with Helen, but with his dreams of his life back in Africa still intact—left America for his future back on the continent of his birth.

The Vanishing Dixon Family Fortune: Repercussions of the Great Depression

The house on G Street in Elizabethton (above) was built by Harlow Dixon for his wife and children. Helen moved here as a teenager.

After suffering major losses in the Stock Market, the Dixon family moved to this house on Broad Street (below) in a less affluent part of town.

HELEN AND WILFRED, WORLDS APART: AMERICA AND AFRICA

The surviving letters do not fully reveal the nature or quality of the four-year correspondence that followed between Helen and Wilfred after Wilfred's return to Africa in 1929. What is clear is that it was at times sporadic and given to misunderstanding, as shown by my father's letter written on April 22, 1931. In this letter, Wilfred is concerned that he has not heard from Helen in at least five months and hence is driven to write to Sophia and Harlow in a bid to re-establish contact. Also evident is that some understanding of Wilfred and Helen's love for each other had been decided upon before they parted in 1929, and, even as it waxed and waned during their separation, it somehow survived the four years until they were reunited in Germany in 1933. Ten years later, in a letter written on August 11, 1943, Helen confessed, "I have always been sorry I did not marry Wilfred when I first met him, and he feels the same way."

In the meantime, as she intimates later, Helen was pressured by her family to date other men. During this four-year hiatus, Helen became engaged to a doctor and possibly to another man to whom she alludes in her letters. For unknown reasons, she called the engagement(s) off. It would appear she had decided that Wilfred was, after all, the only person she really wanted to marry—in spite of the vast distance and lifestyles that separated them.

So it was that, early in the decade of the 1930s, Helen's life was structured by work and bound by conservative Southern values. She was living, at best, a half-life: tethered to her secretarial job at the rayon factory in order to help with the family finances, unmarried and therefore obliged to live at home in accordance with the strict social conventions of life in the South, and in love with a man half a world away.

But for now, having a job during the Great Depression in the U.S. was a godsend for Helen and her family. A photograph taken in 1930 in front of the Personnel Office at the North American Rayon Corporation in Elizabethton shows dozens of men and women lining up in search of work. So, without complaint, between 1929 and 1937, between the ages of twenty-three and thirty-one, Helen worked to support herself and her family, first in Elizabethton and later in Nashville. The truth of Helen's feelings about her work at the plant emerged only later, when she was finally free to reflect on that time of sacrifice. Like her resilient mother, Helen was never one to give in to self-pity, even while she grew to feel increasingly ambivalent about the close-knit community of the factory and the confines of the little town of Elizabethton. It is possible that, with a wider horizon seemingly within reach, Helen began to find the community of the plant and Elizabethton stifling, with their tendencies to small-town gossip and narrow-mindedness. In a letter written from Africa in 1940, she confesses to her parents: "I really think it would kill me to live in Elizabethton again."

WILFRED IN MARANDELLAS, SOUTHERN RHODESIA

Wilfred's life in Africa, meanwhile, was infinitely different. Back then, Southern Rhodesia was rather loosely bound by British good form, sunshine, clear air, wild animals, hopeful farmers, opportunity, unbounded freedom for the in-coming settlers, and, of course, all the advantages of racial superiority if one happened to be white.

Wilfred returned to South Africa on the eve of the Wall Street Crash of 1929, and then traveled into the heart of Africa to Marandellas in Southern Rhodesia (now Zimbabwe), where he worked conscientiously at his dream job of establishing the first tobacco research station in the area. With the help of the local people, he orchestrated the building of a modest residence and tobacco sheds, and planted fields of tobacco. While there,

Wilfred with his parents and sister Bert at the Tobacco Research Station in Marandellas, Rhodesia, 1930

he was visited by his mother and father, and by his sister, Bert. All the while, his heart was with the wonderful young woman, Helen, he had met back in 1929 before the world, as they knew it, had turned upside down.

For more than two years, Wilfred worked steadily and proudly to build the research station before succumbing one terrible day in late 1931 to the dreaded blackwater fever, a severe complication of malaria. Its symptoms—chills with rigor, high fever, jaundice, vomiting, rapidly progressing anemia, and dark red or black urine—were, back then, most often a prelude to death. While treatment today cures fifty to seventy-five percent of cases, there were no ready cures in 1931. However, since symptoms declined in winter, doctors were convinced that the best treatment for Wilfred was to find a cold climate that would aid in killing the parasites.

WILFRED IN ESSEN, GERMANY

One can only imagine the sense of urgency that ensued as the Evans family back in South Africa sought a safe, cold-climate environment for their dangerously ill son who was living a thousand miles away in Southern Rhodesia. Since it was summer in southern Africa, the only choice they had was to send Wilfred into the winter of the northern hemisphere. Fortunately, a friend of Wilfred's had previously stayed with a Professor Vriesen in Essen, Germany, in preparation for his studies at Oxford University. The Vriesen family was duly contacted, and in February 1932, Wilfred sailed for Europe. He moved into the Vriesen's home to live with Professor Gustav Vriesen, his wife Gerda, and their three sons in early April 1932.

Upon his arrival in Essen, Wilfred was surrounded by political turmoil and his first exposure to Nazism, a stark contrast to his life back in Africa. After all, for more than two years (late 1929 to early 1932) he had been sequestered in what was then considered the back of beyond in Southern Rhodesia. He had, as he put it, "only scant news through the agency of English newspapers," and letters from the United States to Southern Rhodesia in those days would have taken between a month and six weeks to deliver.

Now Wilfred was in Essen, a large, industrial city in northern Germany. There he became aware of Nazism and the emergence of Hitler, who was well on his way to becoming Chancellor of Germany. Hitler was no stranger to Essen, home base of the munitions giant, the Krupps family. On April 8, 1932, Hitler gave a speech in Essen intended to rabble-rouse and gain support for his candidacy for the position of Fuhrer. I do not believe that Professor or Mrs. Vriesen expressed sympathy for the Nazi movement; however, their son, Kiki, and his brothers were later drafted into the German army. Ironically, Wilfred ultimately found himself fighting against the very people who had helped save his life.

Wilfred, now twenty-six, quickly acclimated to his new environment and culture, and kept busy mastering German. He took a position as secretary to the Reverend Right Honorable Count von Korff, and, true to his studious nature, was fluent after studying German for six months. By the fall of 1932, Wilfred traveled south to the University of Munich to study philosophy, and to enter fully into Germany's academic and cultural life. Little did he realize that he was also entering the birthplace of the Nazi Party.

WILFRED MOVES TO MUNICH AND DISCOVERS NAZISM

In leaving behind the quiet, scholarly home of the Vriesens in the fall of 1932, with their honorable, conservative Christian values, Wilfred was also leaving behind Essen, which lay at the heart of industrialized Prussia with its centuries-long association with the Krupps family and its gigantic armaments factory, soon to be funded by Hitler. Ironically, it must have been a proud moment for Wilfred as he anticipated his graduate studies in Munich with its illustrious place in culture, guaranteed by its many museums, galleries, and places of higher learning. It is doubtful that Wilfred could have had an inkling that Hitler was at that self-same moment plotting to establish his headquarters within walking distance of the University of Munich, where Wilfred had decided to study.

Wilfred's sojourn at the University of Munich in 1932 and 1933 was marked not only by serious study of philosophy but by outings to the theater, to concerts, and to the opera. Dressing for the opera was a serious business. Top hats and long white silk scarves were *de rigueur* for gentlemen. My sister, Eve, remembers, at the age of nine, seeing Wilfred's magical top hat spring to life when it was taken from the thin flat box in which it had been packed for more than ten years. Programs at the concerts and opera were printed on black paper with white lettering so they could be easily and quietly read in the dim light. Completely silent attention to the performance was expected. On one occasion, Wilfred, who was congested and breathing somewhat heavily, incurred the wrath of his neighboring theatergoers, who did not appreciate his violation of their enjoyment of Wagner.

The exterior of the library at the University of Munich

The University of Munich was founded in 1472. Today, home to thirty-thousand students, it survives in its original buildings on Ludwigstrasse, commonly called "the most beautiful boulevard in Munich." While Wilfred's leisure hours included more frivolous pursuits, such as beer drinking with his newfound friends and trips to the Alps to ski, his studies at the university consumed most of his time, for he was anxious, once again, to prove himself. But crowding in were other considerations, such as his three-year-long correspondence with Helen; his growing awareness of the grip of Nazism on the German people; and the upcoming visit of his sister, Bert.

Bert with fellow passenger and officer en route to England and Germany, 1932

Although she was four years older than her brother, Bert, now thirty, was young at heart. Forbidden by her conservative father to work at a paying job, she, her father (who was now retired), and her mother sailed from South Africa to England, arriving in Southampton on August 22, 1932. They lived in London where Bert began her studies in massage at Guy's Hospital in London. Over the Christmas break, Bert traveled to Germany, first to Essen, where she was hosted by Prof. and Mrs. Vriesen who were now like family. In the evenings, she was wined and dined by one of the Vriesen's sons, Kiki. She then traveled south to ski in Bavaria and find amusement in the city of Munich while Wilfred was in class. But, with Nazism taking hold, Wilfred became increasingly fearful of Bert's happy-go-lucky attitude. One day before setting off for class, Wilfred said to her, "Do not leave the apartment today! There is an election. The polling booth is downstairs, and they are expecting trouble." Surprised by Wilfred's seriousness, Bert complied. During the morning, she heard two shots ring out. Shortly afterwards, Wilfred returned to check on her. "Thank God you are alright! We heard that people had been shot at this polling booth." With a growing sense of horror, Wilfred and Bert began to realize that civilians were being shot by the Nazis and that, once again, the world Wilfred was creating for himself was at risk.

Other incidents foreshadowed a bleak future for Germany. One day when out for a walk, Bert and Wilfred found themselves outside the Brown House, Hitler's newly acquired headquarters. Bert mistook the Brown House[3] for a museum and, even as Wilfred remonstrated with her for her boldness, she entered the building and headed for the grand marble staircase. Intrigued by what she supposed were waxwork soldiers lining the stairs, rather like the waxworks she had seen at Madame Tussaud's in London, Bert placed her foot on the first step. The frozen figures sprang to life, lunging forward in unison, barring her way with crossed bayonets. Badly shaken and with a deep sense of foreboding, Bert and Wilfred hastily retreated. On returning to their apartment, they found themselves served with an order to appear in court.

On the appointed day, they were ushered into the courtroom where they were faced by a judge with an impressively waxed moustache sitting on his raised dais. The people waiting to appear before him sat on little benches. At the height of six feet, Wilfred found his knees under his chin and his sense of dignity badly compromised. Bert, meanwhile, still in her lighthearted vacation mood and thoroughly enjoying the absurdity of the occasion, nudged Wilfred and whispered, "Take a look at those handlebars!"

Wilfred, none too pleased to be in this situation, responded, "Be quiet! You've caused enough trouble already!"

The judge ordered Bert to stand before him. After looking at her passport and then looking at her, he reached forward, took her by the ear, and roughly pulled

---

[3] The Brown House was destroyed by Allied bombing in 1945.

her head to one side to examine her in profile. Wilfred, who had something of a quick temper, could barely contain his rage. The upshot was that Wilfred and Bert were ordered to register every move they made from that moment on. Visits made to other people required them to record the names of those visited, as well as the location and time of the meetings. Since Wilfred was a tall, blonde foreigner who spoke German fluently, the Nazis probably thought he could be a spy or a threat to Hitler's life, so they pursued him doggedly.

Meanwhile, other events persuaded Wilfred and Bert that they were living in a tinderbox. They witnessed at least one of Hitler's massive rallies involving thousands of marching soldiers, mock battles, and armored tanks. On that particular day, there had been a great deal of rain during the morning, and the ground at the entrance to the demonstration field gradually became impassable. The unintended "climax" of the battle occurred when the tanks, mired in mud, rammed into each other and collapsed before their eyes. It turned out that the entire battle scene had been staged, with all the props made of wood. The thought of what this mock drama[4] might represent for the future of Europe filled them with horror.

Shortly after this event, Bert left Germany to return to England where she continued her studies at Guy's Hospital in London, leaving Wilfred behind to continue with his studies in Munich.

If Wilfred had any doubts about Hitler's intentions, they must have been dispelled by the May 10, 1933, infamous book-burning at Konigsplatz. The book-burning ceremonies were planned with meticulous attention to detail, offering a glimpse into the future Nazi assault on Germany's intelligentsia. Enthusiastic crowds witnessed the burning of books by Einstein, Freud, and Mann, among many other well-known intellectuals, many of whom were Jewish. Invitations posted around Munich described the upcoming celebrations as follows:

> Invitees must arrive at the designated area at precisely 11 p.m. At 11 p.m. the torchlight procession of the entire Munich Students Association will be arriving.
> 1. The united bands will play parade music.
> 2. The festivities will begin at 11 with the song 'Brother, Forward!'
> 3. Speech by the German Students Association Kurt Ellersiek.
> 4. Burning of the nation-corrupting books and journals.

---

[4] Readers who want to know more about this period in history should read *In the Garden of Beasts*, by Erik Larson. In reading Larson, I was gratified to discover that his account matched precisely the accounts given by my father and aunt some seventy years ago.

    5. Group sing-along of . . . songs.

The seeds of Wilfred's commitment to fighting Nazism eight years later were clearly germinating at this time. These events had a deep impact on him, and, it could be argued, were to cost him and his future family dearly.

THE MARRIAGE OF HELEN DIXON AND WILFRED EVANS

Despite juggling an active social life with his new university friends, studying at the university, and worrying about being suspected as a spy, Wilfred continued writing letters to Helen. In June 1932, Mrs. Gerda Vriesen, aware of Wilfred's longing for Helen, had written to Sophia Dixon, Helen's mother, inviting Helen to spend time at their home in Essen, but Helen did not make the visit. It took another fourteen months for them to reunite.

Through the mail, Helen and Wilfred planned a reunion and a possible wedding. It was agreed that Helen would sail from the United States to Bremerhaven, Germany, and that they would marry in Essen at the home of Professor and Mrs. Vriesen, who by then thought of themselves as surrogate parents to Wilfred.

Helen and Wilfred's relationship was, however, somewhat fraught and undecided, at least on Helen's part. Not only had they known each other for only a week during the summer of 1929, but, to add further complexity to their relationship, the social status for each had shifted radically. Wilfred had lost his research job, his savings, and his health, and was only a year into his graduate studies. Helen, meanwhile, had watched her father lose most of his money and had helped the family move from upscale "G" Street to the less affluent Broad Street. While she had been weathering the Great Depression in America, supporting her family by working for the North American Rayon Corporation in Elizabethton, Wilfred, now supported by his father, William Evans, must have looked as if he were living the high life of an affluent graduate student. But even after a sporadic four-year correspondence, and against all odds, Wilfred and Helen set a marriage date: August 26, 1933.

I believe that Helen's first thought was to marry in Elizabethton. However, as leading citizens of this small Southern town, there were certain social lines that were simply not to be crossed. One of these pertained to Helen's closest friend, Mary Walker. Although Helen and Mary had been best friends since they met in Sunday school at the age of five, and although Sophia liked and respected Mary, Mary's family was apparently not part of the Dixon social circle. From the Dixon's point of view, it was impossible to think of including Mary in the wedding party.

However, from Helen's point of view, it would have been unthinkable for her to marry in Elizabethton and *not* include her best friend in her wedding party. After all, not only had she and Mary been best friends since Sunday school days, but Mary had witnessed the enchanted meeting between Helen and Wilfred at the party and on the beach at Nags Head and had, most likely, played a role in bringing Wilfred to the Dixon home back in the summer of 1929. Helen's only other option was to marry Wilfred in Germany.

There may also have been some appeal for Helen in this plan since she and Wilfred had not seen each other for four years, and Helen often wondered out loud if she were making a mistake committing herself in marriage to a relative stranger. As she told her mother, "When I see him, if I find I still love him, I will marry him."

The letters that follow, first to Sophia by Wilfred's mother, Eva Evans, from Cape Town, South Africa, on July 4, 1933, and later by Mrs. Vriesen and Wilfred from Essen, Germany, on August 3, 1933, attest to the flurry of activity resulting from Helen and Wilfred's decision to marry. Doubts about Wilfred's suitability for Helen seem to have been harbored only by those who did not know him well, but those doubts were to hinder their happiness for the next four years.

In the meantime, despite obvious difficulties and knowing she could only be away from her secretarial work for six weeks, Helen sailed for Germany with a Mr. Kramer, possibly a co-worker at the rayon factory. From her modest salary, she had managed to save for her wedding clothes and for a passage, steerage, which she describes in one of the letters. Meat, bread, and potatoes for dinner were standard fare, and Helen did not grumble since thrift, determination, and common sense had become hallmarks of her character. In the same vein, either out of a shortage of fine clothes or in defiance of convention, Helen wore her wedding dress to a dance on board.

Helen and Mr. Kramer en route to Germany, 1933

Helen boarded the *Bremen* in New York on August 17 and landed in Bremerhaven, Germany, on August 22, 1933, giving her three days to decide whether she still wanted to marry Wilfred. The rather stiff and silly postcard (transcribed in the letters that follow) written by Helen, Wilfred, and the Vriesens on the day before the marriage is evidence of the strain of the meeting.

It is worth noting that in the postcard to her parents from Germany dated September 4, 1933, nine days after the wedding, Helen does not mention the wedding ceremony. One can only speculate from this total absence of sentiment that she may have been at first disappointed in her decision to marry Wilfred, or that she was deeply hurt by the failed plans for an American wedding, or a combination of the two. Only when they were settled in Assmannhausen on the Rhine, twenty days after the wedding, does Helen mention the "beautiful wedding supper" and the "gift from Wilfred."

Sadly, Helen also alludes in her letters home to their ill health: one of her "bad colds," or, more likely, asthma, from which she suffered throughout her life; and Wilfred's recurrence of a malarial attack. So the honeymoon, which Helen refers to as a "holiday," must have carried with it many tensions. They barely knew each other, for one, and Helen was almost immediately facing a solitary return to the United States with its privations—the job at the rayon factory and the yet-to-be revealed prejudice against her new and now absent husband.

But there was also clearly joy on their honeymoon, however fleeting. On September 3, 1933, Helen and Wilfred "climbed the Lorelei." It seems almost certain that my sister, Eve, was conceived within days of this event since she was born almost nine months later to the day: June 6, 1934. Helen subsequently told her friend Mary that, "Wilfred and I made love in a field of flowers. I hope that was where Eve was conceived."

Wilfred and Helen leaving for their honeymoon on the Rhine

For now, Helen returned to the United States alone, possibly unaware that she was pregnant. I do not know what plans she and Wilfred had for a reunion. Since Wilfred had not known whether or not Helen would marry him, he did not book his passage to America until after the wedding. And then there was the fact that he was still enrolled at the University of Munich, while Helen was on leave from the rayon factory and committed to return to her job in Elizabethton. Whatever the understanding between them on Helen's departure, Wilfred left Germany months later in fear of his life. The family story is that he escaped from Germany on a fishing vessel bound for England. Once there, he went to the Foreign Office in London and begged them, in vain, as so many others had before him, to listen to his fears about the future of Germany and Europe.

In a letter written later, it becomes clear that Wilfred had borrowed money from the Vriesens to pay for his passage to America, a debt he was able to repay only four-and-a-half years later.

MARRIED LIFE AND PARENTHOOD IN DEPRESSION-ERA AMERICA

If Helen and Wilfred thought that their lives to this point had been hard on account of their separation, the Dixon family's losses, Wilfred's illness, and the Great Depression, they were in for a new series of shocks once they were reunited in Tennessee. In spite of knowing about the altered circumstances of the Dixons, coming home to the house on Broad Street, rather than to the lovely home on "G" Street, must have been something of a shock for Wilfred. Although his mother-in-law's dislike of him continued, Wilfred and Helen were forced for financial reasons to live with Sophia and Harlow, and Helen was pregnant—which meant she was tired after a day at work.

A further sadness came in the form of what must initially have looked like a bonus. Because all of the senior management at the German-owned American Rayon Corporation, where Helen was secretary to Mr. Funcke, were highly educated Germans who had been separated from the events occurring in Germany, it was only natural that Wilfred sought out their company. Sadly, he found himself in double-jeopardy: shunned by the locals who saw him as a foreigner, and slighted by the Germans at the factory who made no attempt to hire him, perhaps associating him with current events in Germany.

Years later, Helen, on hearing of the death of a co-worker at the rayon factory, wrote, "By getting away from it all, I saw how much of the suffering I went through directly emanated from B.S. and P. The news [of the death of B.S.] only gave me a queer feeling of vacancy, of no longer having that person to hate. When I see how Wilfred outstrips every other person in every group he is put in, and how quickly he masters different subjects with distinction, and they did not give him a chance at any time to fill the openings that were always occurring, I am simply made sick that I kept Wilfred in Elizabethton all that time and that I was foolish enough to think always that there was something wrong at our end, and not to realize that there was a definite force working against us."

Although Wilfred was a cosmopolitan man with broad experience of the world, it was almost as if a vendetta had been declared against him. He found it impossible to get work of any sort. He could have written professionally. He could have taught languages or science or farming techniques. He could have worked in a research lab. He was a capable carpenter. But in 1934, there was little work to be had, and southern parochialism firmly locked him out of the few opportunities that might have presented themselves. Instead of being able to put his talents to work while Helen went off to the factory every day, Wilfred found himself at home with Sophia.

On June 6, 1934, the family celebrated the birth of Helen and Wilfred's baby daughter, Helen Eve Collingwood Evans. Helen later described it as an easy birth, both joyful and portentous, since baby Eve was born with a "caul"—a thin membrane veiling the head that only one in 80,000 infants are born with. The caul was purported to signal good fortune or a special destiny.

But there was no time to linger over her new baby. Helen had to return to work almost immediately while Sophia continued to have her hands full with running the house; caring for her mother-in-law, Mrs. Virginia Dixon; caring for her mother, Mollie Jobe Hunter; and now caring for little Eve. In letters written to her mother years later, Helen confesses to her sadness at having to leave Eve at home while she continued to work.

Since Wilfred had no money of his own to contribute to household expenses, proven by the fact that he was already in debt to the Vriesens, the first three years of marriage were a deeply dispiriting experience for both him and Helen, as her letters home years later attest.

At this point in his life, Wilfred was universally despised and regarded as lazy. Ironically, this was the same man who had been nominated only five years earlier "the most energetic student" in his graduating class of 1929 at North Carolina State University, and who later would distinguish himself through his business acumen and wartime record. One can only wonder at the toll this took on his self-esteem and his marriage, let alone his standing with the rest of the family. One of the family's mantras was "How is it possible that a man who can speak five languages cannot even find a teaching job?"[5]

Helen's Uncle Edwin, Sophia's much-loved younger brother, was apparently particularly hard on Wilfred, as a letter from Helen written two years later, in April 1940, reveals. As a side note, somewhere around 2005, Eve and I met a centenarian who knew our mother and father during those years. I asked her what she remembered about my father. She answered bluntly, "He didn't work."

Added to the distress of being unable to find work was the shock of moving from university life in Munich in 1934, with its stable economy, cultural wealth, and historic place in world events, to the depression-ridden Elizabethton where he was known as "the foreigner."

By 1936, the Dixon-Evans family was in crisis. Sophia's mother, Mollie Jobe Hunter, died. Harlow Dixon had to face the liquidation of the Dixon Furniture Company, the only company with which he had ever been associated, and Wilfred, completely fed up with his unemployment in Elizabethton, looked elsewhere and finally found employment in Nashville (some three hundred miles away). Helen, having worked at the rayon factory for four years, followed him shortly thereafter.

In Nashville, Wilfred took work as a janitor/porter at Sears, Roebuck and Company, while Helen became a secretary in the state welfare department. They

---

[5] Wilfred spoke English, Afrikaans, and German, and, in all likelihood, Tswana and Shona, since he had lived in Bloemfontein in South Africa, and in Marandellas in Southern Rhodesia. (Southern Rhodesia, now known as Zimbabwe, has sixteen official languages.)

left little Eve with her Mama Sophia and Papa Harlow and returned to Elizabethton to visit them whenever they could. With the new expenses they incurred as a result of leaving Elizabethton, Helen and Wilfred were desperately short of money, even going to bed hungry for several months during one period. But at least they were finally together as a couple, and Wilfred was working and gaining self-respect. One of the complicating factors in their finances was the fact that, some years earlier, Helen had purchased a house in Johnson City through a program set up at the rayon factory to encourage investment and savings. This house, which they rented out to a Mr. L., was to cause them endless financial stress as the years unfolded.

IMMIGRATION: A NEW LIFE FOR WILFRED, HELEN, AND EVE

The move to Nashville, however spartan, proved fortuitous. In an extraordinary turn of events, in September of 1937, the head of Sears International (an entity separate from Sears, Roebuck) with headquarters in Chicago, visited the Nashville branch of Sears. In conversation with the Nashville manager, the CEO mentioned that Sears International was going to open a branch in Johannesburg, South Africa. Naturally, the Nashville manager thought of the South African, Wilfred Evans, who by then had worked his way up to Manager of the Refrigerator Department.

The head of Sears International asked to meet Wilfred and would have been, I imagine, rather taken aback by this urbane former janitor. He asked Wilfred where he would recommend locating Sears International in Johannesburg. Wilfred thought a moment and gave his answer. It turned out that the modern building in Johannesburg that he identified as the best image for a burgeoning company was where Sears International had already decided to locate. This confirmed for the CEO the value of this young man. Within the hour, Wilfred was offered the job as the South African Representative of Sears International in South Africa.

After eight miserable years in depression-ridden America, Helen was about to return to some of the privileges she had enjoyed while growing up. And, after three and a half years of humiliation in Tennessee and poverty in Nashville, Wilfred was about to be given the opportunity to prove himself once more—this time in the realm of business and management and, gloriously, back in his beloved Africa. Although South Africa had suffered considerable hardship between 1925 and 1933, by 1937 its gold production was protecting it from the worst of the Great Depression. Building was booming, and growth in the "City of Gold" was exponential.

While only fifty years old, the center of Johannesburg was, in effect, a miniature New York. It had tall buildings, a gracious city hall, a large library and art gallery, modern apartment blocks, manicured parks, glorious homes with generous well-tended gardens, and a fabulous art, music, and dance scene nurtured by artists fleeing Europe for the safety of a civilized country far from the unfolding horrors back home.

On September 27, 1937, a week after meeting with the Sears CEO, Wilfred took a train to Chicago, where he underwent training. Nine days later, after clearing out their apartment, selling their car, and saying farewell to her parents in Elizabethton, Helen and little Eve caught the train for New York, where they reunited with Wilfred. They sailed immediately for Southampton on the *Queen Mary* and, from there, sailed on the *Winchester Castle* bound for South Africa: First Class.

This brings me to the end of the story of Helen and Wilfred's meeting, their marriage, and their early years together. The letters that follow go back in time to 1931, with Wilfred writing from Marandellas in Southern Rhodesia to his future mother-in-law, Sophia Dixon.

Sadly, Wilfred's condescension toward black Africans is in evidence from the start, as is Helen's and Sophia's. Such attitudes were ingrained in both South Africans and in Southerners from birth, so one must reluctantly accept them as part of the culture of the time.

The rest of the story unfolds in Helen's own words as she writes home, from 1937 through 1944. It is a story of the daily joys and travails of an immigrant wife and mother in South Africa at that time. It tells of extraordinary happiness and unimaginable suffering. It covers Eve's discovery of South Africa at age three, my birth in 1938, our father's enlistment in the army in 1940, and our brother John's birth in 1943. It concludes with our mother's illness in 1943 and Sophia's remarkable flight to Helen's bedside—even as the Battle of Normandy raged below.

Editor's Note: The letters that follow are transcribed exactly as written, except for minor punctuation adjustments for ease of reading and a few, brief omissions of highly personal lines of text. Likewise, initials have been randomly assigned to protect the identity of certain individuals named in the letters.

Finding
The Letters

FINDING THE LETTERS

While the first part of this story has always been part of family lore, the family letters, written between 1937 and 1944, came to light only after the death of our grandmother, Sophia Dixon, in 1984.

While cleaning out a hall closet at Sophia's home in Durham, North Carolina, my sister, Eve, found seventy-five letters. Most were written by Helen to her parents, Sophia and Harlow; others to various aunts and uncles. Eve was entranced by this opportunity to find out more about our mother and took the letters home to read. Sometime later, she sent copies to me and to our brother, John. I kept them to one side, wanting to read them, but knowing that I lacked the maturity to deal with them. I was forty-six years old at the time. On the eve of my fiftieth birthday, in 1988, I locked myself in my bedroom and finally found the courage to face my mother's death by reading her letters. The first was dated September 1937, the month Helen and Wilfred left the United States for their new life together in South Africa.

A second set of letters came to light six years after the first collection was found. In the summer of 1990, Eve and I decided to clean out the garage at Sophia's house. After sorting through the usual debris, we came across an old trunk. Looking at each other, we both felt the kind of excitement described in children's books when an old trunk of great import is discovered in the attic. We were not disappointed. Reverently, we opened it. Laid out before us was a range of items, neatly folded and arranged with great care. It soon became apparent that the trunk had been packed around 1937 and not opened until that moment—fifty-three years later. It appeared to be a personal family time capsule. We were thrilled but apprehensive. Our family's history had been dramatic and traumatic. What would we find that would further illuminate or darken the story?

The trunk seemed to hold everything that my grandmother might have found too painful to have around her. An ornate Yale lock key with the inscription "Duplicate 833 Hotel Times Square N.Y.C." was placed beside three antique fountain pens. An old pink and gold ornamental porcelain dish, with "R.S. Prussia" stamped on the back, was possibly a gift to my grandmother from her son-in-law, Wilfred, after he moved to the United States from Essen, Germany, in 1934. There was a velvet jacket we recognized from a portrait of our mother that now hangs above the mantelpiece in Eve's dining room at her home in Durham, North Carolina. Nestled next to a black velvet V-neck, long-waisted dress, with four-inch bands of gold lace set into the skirt and a reversible black and ivory silk vest, was an exquisitely designed handmade jacket, the result of my great grandmother Virginia Dixon's talent with tatting.

But there, under the clothes, lay the most precious treasure of all—a store of letters and postcards, some written by our parents and some by people who had a profound impact on their lives. Dated 1933 and later, they were the precursors to the letters we had already read. Our excitement was unbounded. Eve and I had grown to adulthood with an overwhelming desire to know more about our mother, who died when Eve was just ten and I was five going on six; now we had written proof of her life before marriage. What might have been a trunk of painful memories for my grandmother was for us a treasure trove from the past that we were eager to explore.

The third and final set of ten letters emerged in 2014, just as I was preparing this book to go to print. They were tucked into a box along with pamphlets my mother had saved from her 1928 grand tour of Europe.

People often ask me what has been the most important discovery I have made from delving so deeply into my mother's past by reading and analyzing the more than one hundred letters she wrote to her parents, relatives, and friends. Overwhelmingly, it is respect—the respect I feel for my mother, my father, my

father's sister, Bert, and my grandparents on both sides of the family. Their commitment to one another and to their extended family is impeccable. Somewhat surprising to me is the awe I feel for my maternal grandmother, Sophia Dixon, whose words, ironically, are absent from the correspondence until the very last pages, which document her memorable journey across Africa to be at Helen's bedside.

Since only their daughter Helen's letters have survived, along with a sprinkling of others, we are left to intuit how my grandparents must have responded to each letter. Always clear is the love that each member of the family felt for the other and the emotional and material generosity that flowed among them. All of this despite deep hurts that continued to scar each of them to the end.

A final note about family records from the past: In early 2013, as I was tidying up papers that had lain around for far too long, I came across Sophia's account of her journey in 1944 from America to Helen's bedside in South Africa. This account is included at the end of the book. How this remained hidden for sixty-nine years I will never know, but it serves as a fitting finale to an extraordinary story.

The Letters:
At Home
1931 ~ 1933

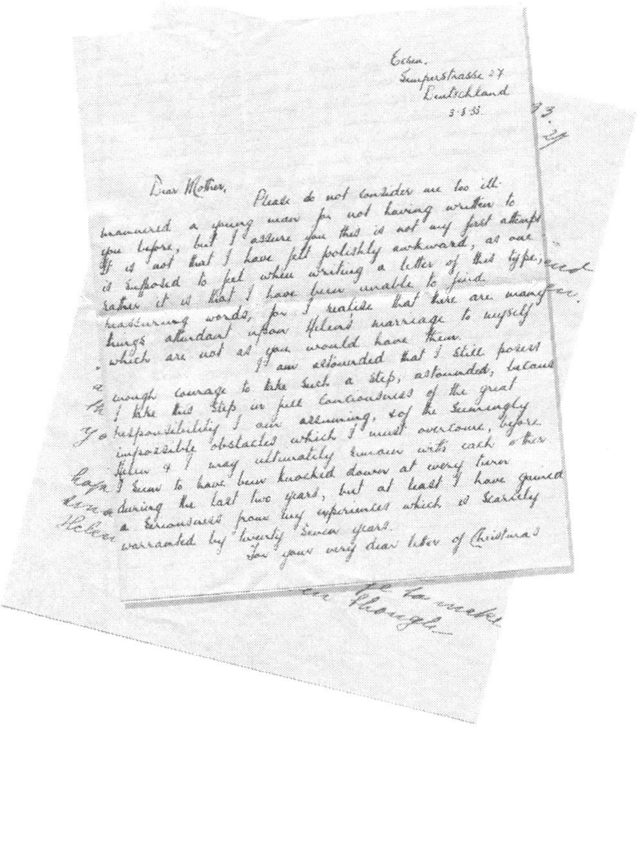

A devoted Helen with her parents

Safe in their Alabaster Chambers

April 1931 ~ August 1933

Safe in their Alabaster Chambers –
Untouched by Morning –
And untouched by Noon –
Sleep the meek members of the Resurrection,
Rafter of Satin – and Roof of Stone!

~ Emily Dickinson

1

From what must have been two hundred or more letters written in the four-year period between Wilfred's departure from America in 1929 and his reconciliation with Helen in 1933, only five remain—two from Wilfred (first from Southern Rhodesia and later from Germany); one from Eva Evans, Wilfred's mother (from South Africa); and two from Mrs. Vriesen (from Germany). Since these letters were addressed to Helen's parents, Sophia and Harlow Dixon, they survived. Those that Helen and Wilfred wrote to each other have been either destroyed or lost.

I believe that if one were able to speak to Helen and Wilfred about the years between 1929 and 1933, they would describe them as The Wasted Years. They were deeply in love, but apart. This was a time when neither of them, but particularly Helen, was truly alive—a terrible waste, considering that these were the years between the ages of twenty-three and twenty-seven, the time in life when one should be fully alive and productive. While the world went on around them, Helen and Wilfred, like the so-called "dead" in Dickinson's poem, were seemingly incarcerated—Helen at home in Elizabethton and Wilfred in Southern Rhodesia and later in Germany.

In her poem, "Safe in their Alabaster Chambers," Dickinson challenges the biblical injunction: "Blessed are the meek, for they shall inherit the earth." Instead, Dickinson characterizes the "meek" as the living dead, watching the world go by from the safety of their coffins.

The entire moral arc of Helen's life is her struggle to escape the confines of reticence—of meekness—and to pursue what she believed in. Ironically, Wilfred, while less meek in affect, did not take the risks that the shy Helen took. Years afterwards, both agreed that they should never have allowed their separation to happen.

Why Helen did not accept the kind invitation issued by Mrs. Vriesen (see her letter, June 1932), I do not know. Perhaps the proposed trip was considered too daring or too expensive, or perhaps hurt feelings played a part. Or perhaps this was the time when Helen had already accepted a proposal of marriage from another man. Or maybe she stayed close to her parents out of a sense of obligation since they had lost both their son and their fortune. In any event, fourteen more months elapsed before Helen, in August 1933, abandoned the safety of home in Elizabethton, sailed to Germany, and married Wilfred in the home of Professor and Mrs. Vriesen in Essen.

As an aside, Wilfred's August 1933 letter to Sophia, his future mother-in-law, is heartbreaking in its sincerity and meekness—or what his mother, Eva, called his "ultra-conservatism." This letter stands in sharp contrast to his first letter to Sophia, written in 1931, which reflects a man who believes he knows who he is and who is unafraid of his opinions. However, after being "knocked down" by blackwater fever and its attendant challenges, Wilfred, like Helen, is beset by doubt even as he tries to reassure his future mother-in-law. His words almost prefigure what fate holds in store for him and his beloved Helen: years of grind, disappointment, galling dependency on those who could ill-afford to support him, and unwelcome proximity in the confines of the Dixon home. Now twenty-seven, erudite and well-educated, Wilfred has only two years of well-paid employment behind him, and, unbeknownst to him, is facing three years of unemployment and merciless scrutiny from people who do not wish him well—before the world once more gives him the opportunity to prove himself. His frustration manifests itself later in an almost obsessive desire to succeed.

Safe in Their Alabaster Chambers (Apr. 1931—Aug. 1933)

To: Mr. and Mrs. H. S. Dixon from Wilfred Evans, [age 24]
"G" Street
Elizabethton,
Tennessee, U.S. of America

Tobacco Research Station
Marandellas, Southern Rhodesia
April 27, 1931

Dear Mr. & Mrs. Dixon,

 I wrote to you at Christmas time, but as yet I have received no intimation—either from Helen or from yourselves, that the letter ever arrived. It is highly probable that the letter was never posted, as I have comparatively recently discovered that one of my boys, whom I sometimes employed as a runner, was by way of being a philatelist. It hardly seems credible that any person would steal a letter for the monetary value of the stamps affixed to it. When one considers, however, that the postage rate to America is equal to a day's pay, one realizes the feasibility of such a theft. One is apt to become prejudiced with regard to the blacks and make sweeping adverse criticisms and generalizations about the race as a whole when incidences such as this do occur. I have found numbers of them who are remarkably honest and loyal; they are, I fear though, in the minority. Most of them are alarmingly deficient in distinguishing between mine and thine. Their thefts or pilferings are of such a petty nature as a rule, though, that one is actuated more by a sense of pity than anger when one discovers it.

 I have been considerably distressed to hear from Helen of the persistent misfortunes that have befallen you during the last eighteen months. One must, I suppose, bear misfortune with fortitude, lest those very misfortunes become an obsession, obscuring the hope of surmounting the difficulties. Some persons are apt to regard their misfortunes as a visitation of divine wrath for past sins. Whether that be so or not, I cannot say, but personally I prefer to regard it as a phase in the compensating law of the balance of things. We humans are apt to regard ourselves as something apart from nature. That is why, I think, we understand so little of ourselves, and the translated forces that actuate us. Nature can undoubtedly be kind but mostly, I think, is rather cruel. The same fundamental laws of life obtain for man, animal, and plant. Tread upon, or be trodden on. Kill or be killed. Remain firm or be swept aside. I see this happen almost every day with the lower forms of life, and, stripped of sentimentality, life presents a very similar aspect to me. I fear I am becoming metaphysical—a dangerous pastime.

 America as a nation is going through a very severe and strenuous period, it would seem. I receive only scant news of the true economic condition through the agency of English newspapers. It would appear that there is a considerable body who are advocating that the government become paternalistic. It is indeed to be hoped but some more healthy remedy will be brought forward. It is not difficult to trace much of England's industrial depression to paternalistic experiments. The cry was once against the idle rich, but the dole is producing something infinitely more dangerous, namely, an idle poor. There are literally thousands of young men in England today who have never done a day's work. They have arrived at the age when government insurance provides for them as unemployed.

Since childhood the word America always seemed synonymous with prosperity to me. During my stay there I became rather interested in American prosperity, and persistently endeavored to arrive at the cause of it. I fear I was not very well equipped to go into the matter very deeply, but after a very superficial survey, several things seemed to be all wrong and contrary to sound economics to me. I met a rather wealthy New York banker while he was traveling abroad, and subsequently visited him in America. I was permitted to see something of the operation of American business methods through this man. I supposed that some of the methods must be sound, but I could not help feeling that some persons were making hay while the sun shone, and that the very making of the hay would subsequently cause the sun to stop shining. Credit and marginal buying on the stock exchange, it seemed, must inevitably bring about a general financial debacle at some time. It surely is incomprehensible that a country that legislates against betting on horse races should countenance marginal buying.

Credit was obtained remarkably easily, I found. A friend of mine in Raleigh who was always dabbling on the exchange, and in fact lived on the proceeds, once remarked to me that most of it was done by credit. From the figures available, it did not appear that business growth at that time was very marked, and yet the supply of credit seemed to be taking prodigious leaps. From what I had seen in my own small circle, I was forced to conclude that the credit was being used for speculative purposes, and not for the purposes of production—or, in other words, sound business.

Observation of movements on the exchange showed that prices were soaring above reasonable figures. Banks could sell illimitable amounts of money at high rates when such profits were to be made, but sound business concerns surely could not pay that price for money. The law of saturation, too, would be bound to operate, and finally the speculators themselves would not be able to afford it. With the cessation of credit, the marginal buyers would be caught out, and the ball must inevitably start down the other side of the hill.

Credit is for the use of stable business, I should say, and not for wildcat speculating. My economics might be faulty, but it seems reasonable to suppose that business conditions should be in direct ratio to credit rates; it also seems reasonable to suppose that when credit becomes too expensive for business then there must undoubtedly be some misuse of money somewhere.

Safe in Their Alabaster Chambers (Apr. 1931—Aug. 1933)

Wilfred, age twenty-three, at his first appointment after college as head of the Tobacco Research Station in Marandellas, Southern Rhodesia, 1931.

I suppose these armchair theorizings form quite the most popular indoor sport in America at present. I found American politics and American financial practices to be a wonderfully interesting study, and, being an outsider and disinterested, I was oftimes tempted to think that I saw what Americans as players in the game did not see. That America is in an extremely precarious position there can be no doubt, but that the keenest financial brains of the world are in America is also not to be doubted. It is to be hoped that those businessmen will dominate the politicians and bring the country through onto firm ground once again.

This country has recently had a most disastrous setback in the form of an outbreak of foot and mouth disease. One company has recently been forced to destroy 16,000 head of cattle. The effect on the cattle business is, of course, ruinous, but unfortunately it does not stop there. All exports that have to be packed in straw have been stopped. One hears of tales of woe on all sides while the capital is like a deserted village. The legislators, of course, are pounding away at the government—the opposition, of course. I sometimes wonder if governments were not perhaps invented so that the malcontent politicians might have a handy scapegoat. It seems to be their chief function at the present day.

At least we can be joyful about the weather and the benefits connected with it. The rains have ceased and the thermometer is behaving reasonably. The mosquitoes have stopped singing and biting. One does not really mind the singing type, however. It is the malarial anopheles that are dangerous, and they never sing; they simply bite one without as much as by your leave or here I come.

I had better say cheerio now, as I have a band of warriors outside who are waiting for me to lead them to fields of glory—white-washing a big shed I have recently built.

I sincerely hope your misfortunes are ended, and that the future holds something of its sunnier treatment in store for you.

Sincerely yours,

Bill (Wilfred)

To: Mrs. Sophia Dixon from Mrs. Gerda Vriesen
West "G" St.
Elizabethton, Tennessee, U.S. of America

Semperstrasse 27
Essen, Germany
June 30, 1932

Dear Mrs. Dixon,

As the mother of Helen, of whom I have heard so much, I write to you, inviting your daughter to spend a holiday at my home. As a mother, I can fully appreciate your feelings in a matter of this sort, but I give you every assurance that Helen will be cared for as though she were visiting Wilfred's own mother.

Essen seems to have gained the reputation of the German Pittsburgh, therefore is deemed not healthy nor yet beautiful. Wilfred, who seems to have been everywhere, and who is an indefatigable walker, seems to find the environs of our city very lovely though.

Our home is, I fear, very quiet, and, outside of the opera and conventional sports, we have little to offer by way of entertainment. I imagine, though, that Helen will find ample compensation in the company of Wilfred.

Wilfred has been with us for two months, though we heard of him years ago, through his lifelong friend who stayed with us before entering Oxford. Despite this short acquaintance, and a discrepancy in language and nationality, he is considered as a son by both my husband and myself.

In the light of my standing with Wilfred, I extend to your daughter Helen a most cordial welcome to visit us for as long as she finds it congenial.

Sincerely yours,

Gerda Vriesen

To: Mr. and Mrs. H. S. Dixon from Eva and William Evans
814 Broad St.
Elizabethton, Tennessee, U.S. of America

7 St. Claire Court
Highveld Road, Sea Point
Cape Town, South Africa
July 4, 1933

Dear Mr. & Mrs. Dixon,

On behalf of my husband and myself, I feel it my most pleasant duty to write to you as the parents of our future daughter-in-law, and were it not for the ultra-conservatism of my son, I would have written to you long ago.

With a forethought, which has always been in advance of his years, Wilfred preferred I did not write to you, or Helen, until it was definitely established that nothing could come between their mutual affection.

It was a wise thought, perhaps, that they should conduct their affairs quite after their own fashion, as they both appear to be young people of most reasonable and intelligent natures.

Wilfred confided to me only a few days prior to my departure from England of Helen's proposed European trip, but I only heard definite news [via] this mail regarding the marriage, which is to take place August. The exact date I shall know later. From many (or most) points of view, this is a most auspicious time for their marriage. Fate seems to have dealt these two dear children many undeserved blows, and we cannot but think that, if this step will tend to their happiness, then, for that reason alone, the marriage of Wilfred and Helen deserves our unqualified approval.

If it has appeared that we have held ourselves aloof, and conveyed the idea of tacit disapproval, please accept our apologies, but you will understand why it has so seemed.

My own admiration for your daughter Helen is quite unbounded, and my husband joins me in his approval of Wilfred's choice, and we consider him a very fortunate young man in having won the love of your daughter.

You will both feel very sad to know that you will not be present at their marriage. We shall also share your feelings in that respect, but we are happy to know that Helen is going to a home in Germany where she will have parental love bestowed on her by Mr. and Mrs. Vriesen.

Our children love them both very dearly, and we are very happy to know that Wilfred met such wonderful people. He has been in the environment of Christianity and love since he has lived in their home, and I am sure that everything that is in their power will be done to further their happiness. "Mutti" (as Wilfred calls her) will be as excited as if they were her own children, and we are sure that their affection will never be erased from Helen's memory.

With our united good wishes, we remain yours very sincerely,

Eva and William Evans

To: Mrs. Sophia Dixon from Gustav and Gerda Vriesen
814 Broad St., Elizabethton, Tennessee, USA

Semperstrasse 27
Essen, Germany
August 3, 1933

Dear Mrs. Dixon,

I wrote to you last year, inviting your daughter Helen to spend a holiday at my home here in Essen. Helen is only now accepting the invitation, and her visit is to be coupled with a quite momentous step, namely: her marriage.

I can quite appreciate the feelings of a mother placed in your circumstances, and for that reason I now write you giving you assurance that I will attempt the impossible task of taking your place at Helen's wedding.

Mr. Vriesen joins me in the hope that we may in some small manner manage to make Helen feel happy, even though the circumstances call for the presence of Helen's mother and father. Please accept our sincere good wishes.

We remain, very sincerely,

Gustav and Gerda Vriesen

Safe in Their Alabaster Chambers (Apr. 1931—Aug. 1933)

To: Mrs. Sophia Dixon from Wilfred Evans [age, almost 27]
814 Broad St.
Elizabethton, Tennessee, U.S.

Essen, Semperstrasse 27
Deutschland
August 3, 1933

Dear Mother,

Please do not consider me too ill-mannered a young man for not having written to you before, but I assure you this is not my first attempt. It is not that I have felt foolishly awkward as one is supposed to feel when writing a letter of this type; rather, it is that I have been unable to find reassuring words, for I realize that there are many things attendant upon Helen's marriage to myself which are not as you would have them.

I am astounded that I still possess enough courage to take such a step; astounded, because I take this step in full consciousness of the great responsibility I am assuming, and of the seemingly impossible obstacles I must overcome, before Helen and I may ultimately remain with each other. I seem to have been knocked down at every turn during the last two years, but at least I have gained a seriousness from my experiences which are scarcely warranted by twenty-seven years.

For your very dear letter of Christmas time, I must thank you now. It came at a time which I shall never forget: at the end of the blackest year of my life, wherein I had lost the little money I did have, my health, and my faith in all things. I was happy to learn from your letter that I had your respect, and hope someday to win your affection too. I left your home with the firm idea that I had in no way gained your regard, and was oftimes most unhappy in the thought. I oftimes wished to talk to you, for I was struck by your quiet sadness, and wished to say I understood, for I had seen my own mother bear the same sorrow.

I wish you had sent me the letters you wrote, for I think the knowledge of your hardships would have helped me keep my balance, and thus have spared Helen the pain which I caused her before Christmas.

Please know, dear mother, that although the way seems very steep at present, yet I will do all in my power to preserve Helen's happiness, and I ask that you send her to me with your blessing.

Sincerely, your Son,
Wilfred

2 Forsaking All Others

August 1933 ~ September 1933

"Helen Hunter Dixon, will you have this man to be your husband: to live together in the covenant of marriage? Will you love him, comfort him, honor and keep him, in sickness and in health; and, forsaking all others, be faithful to him as long as you both shall live?"

"I will."

"Wilfred Victor Collingwood Evans, will you have this woman to be your wife; to live together in the covenant of marriage? Will you love her, comfort her, honor and keep her, in sickness and in health; and, forsaking all others, be faithful to her as long as you both shall live?"

"I will."

"Will all of you witnessing these promises do all in your power to uphold these two persons in their marriage?"

"We will."

~ Book of Common Prayer

2

The time-honored vows from *The Book of Common Prayer* were spoken by the Count von Korff, the man to whom my father had been secretary, as he bound Helen and Wilfred in holy matrimony in Essen, Germany, on August 26, 1933. The music played during the ceremony was Handel's *Largo*.

Witnessing the marriage were the kind and generous Professor Gustaf and Mrs. Gerda Vriesen, who had opened their home and their hearts to the young couple. Helen's parents were in the United States; Wilfred's parents were in South Africa.

The irony, of course, is that within seven years, South Africa, and later the United States, would be in mortal combat with Germany, and Wilfred would be risking his life and Helen's health and happiness on Germany's destruction.

For now, this is all shadow. Helen's ever-present common sense prevails as she writes prosaically, maybe defensively—or even evasively—to her parents, who disapprove of the marriage. This is Helen's fourth stand against meekness. The first, of course, was kissing Wilfred on the beach at Nags Head four years earlier. The second was inviting him to her home in Elizabethton after knowing him for only a few days. The third was traveling in the company of a Mr. Kramer (who may have been a co-worker at the factory) and deciding to wear her wedding dress to a dance on board the *Bremen*. The fourth was arriving in Germany and marrying a man she scarcely knew and of whom her parents disapproved. She later muses that while her actions may have been "headstrong," she was proud of the fact that she had finally taken charge of her own destiny.

To: Mr. and Mrs. H. S. Dixon from Helen [age 26]
814 Broad St.
Elizabethton, Tennessee

Hotel Pennsylvania, New York
August 15, 1933

Dearest Ones,

I suppose you want to hear about the bus trip first of all. I do not believe I was much more tired from the bus trip than I would have been by the train trip. I stood it extremely well. Coming by bus, I saw many interesting things I would not have seen otherwise. For instance, in Washington, the beauty and size of the new government buildings cannot be described, and there are so many under construction that it looks like they are rebuilding the whole city. To me, it was somewhat unnerving to see so much money being spent.

Yesterday, Mr. Kramer and I got everything attended to which was necessary for sailing. I got my visa. Today is free for whatever we like. I have an appointment for 10:30 at Emil and Paul's for a trim and shall have a shampoo in the hotel here, so I can dry my hair in my room.

Last night we had dinner on the roof of the hotel and danced, as they have a very good orchestra, then to bed as we were rather tired and wanted to do a round today.

It is delightfully cool in New York just now. I wore my brown knit suit yesterday, and it was not too warm.

If I mail a card from the pier, I cannot say anything intelligent on it, but just know that it is from the pier.

Hope you are all well.

Lots of love to the whole family.

Affectionately,

Helen

To: Mr. and Mrs. H. S. Dixon from Helen
814 Broad St.
Elizabethton, Tennessee

Norddeutscher Lloyd Bremen
Dampfer *Bremen*
August 20, 1933

Dearest Ones,

I promised a diary of my trip across, but it would necessarily be, first day: eating, sleeping, sitting in deck chair, and ditto for each succeeding day. I must, however, tell you about Third Class because, no doubt, you are afraid that I am not finding it so good, but it is much to the contrary. My cabin is spotless and most comfortable, since I have running hot and cold water and fresh ice water twice a day. I have a large closet, equipped with hangers for my clothes, a shelf for hats and plenty of room for shoes. It has not been damp, so far, so I have washed and dried all of my soiled clothes, even to a slip. The food, on the whole, is good, though some meals it is meat, bread and potatoes, which makes it hard for me to adhere to my diet. I have my orange juice every morning so am not terribly upset.

My deck chair is on the open deck, and I have had some nice sun but am not burned except for my forehead.

The dining, smoking and reception halls are certainly nice. The furniture is the color of dark maple and the draperies are rose, as well as the upholstery. Our table in the dining room is for four, but there are only three of us seated there: Mr. Kramer, myself, and a German business man, who has been living for the past three years in Canada and speaks English very well.

The people, as a whole, are naturally of the lower strata of society; most are Poles and Hungarians and one South African Negro, who has been studying in the States. He is a well-mannered and natural-acting young man. I hope to have some conversation with him.

Mr. Kramer told me the man in the cabin with him, who is nice, told him that everyone was saying that we do not belong in this class, meaning Mr. Kramer and me. Some people do stare at us terribly because of our clothes.

I have been sick only one morning, but I am sure I would have been sick had I been on dry land. I ate two very large dill pickles for supper, and ham, and it all felt quite heavy the minute it hit my stomach. When it came up the next morning, it was just as I had swallowed it. The sea has been very smooth, just a rather pleasant roll for the past two days.

I have been sleeping a great deal, sometimes a nap in the mornings, and one in the afternoon too. I lost a great deal of sleep for three nights, however, the night before I left—about two hours sleep in all on the bus, and then the noise in New York kept me from sleeping much there.

Mother, I got your letter Tuesday night when I got on and was so glad to see it. Mr. Umbach's[6] letter was certainly nice. Tell him I appreciated it a great deal. I had a telegram from Arno and roses from an unknown donor.

Today, we had the unexpected opportunity to go over the liner and see First, Second, and Tourist Class. First class is beautiful. The walls around the swimming pool are of mosaic wood, green, red and yellow. There is a small bar in this room in a Chinese red, which is a most effective thing to look at. In one reception hall, there are many panels of exquisite inlay and other rooms with hand-carved panels. These panels are pictures of, perhaps, Egyptian, slaves, etc. The panels above the

---

[6] Mr. Umbach was the pastor of the Presbyterian Church that Helen and her family attended in Elizabethton.

bookshelves in the library have carvings in every language. The Wintergarten has lovely palms and the largest hydrangea in a variety of colors that you ever saw.

There is a perfectly equipped gym for this class and decks broad enough for an automobile to drive down. It was far beyond the *Leviathan* in appointment, and far beyond anything I could imagine.

Second Class is very nice in every way, but it is just over the engines and shakes you nearly to death. It is no wonder Mr. Funcke[7] is always sick. Tourist Class, which is $20 more each way than Third, is no nicer in rooms and furniture than Third and is still rougher than Second.

Third class is as smooth sailing as First, and now I know I would only use First or Third on a large liner. I was glad to have the tour of inspection, for I am perfectly satisfied with my choice now.

Last night we passed the *Europa*, the other large liner of the North German Lloyd Line. It was lighted from top to bottom, and they played colored lights out over the ocean. It was an impressive sight. We are passing liners, freighters, fishing boats, both power driven and sail, all the time now. Tomorrow morning at five, we get into Cherbourg, and I want to be up for it, as I landed there in '28.

By 10:30, we will be in Southampton, and the next morning at 7:00 a.m., Bremerhaven. The trip has been very short. Mr. Kramer has been perfectly wonderful to me and has meant everything to my enjoyment of the trip. He finds out everything and sees that I get to take it in. I would never have known about the tour of inspection this morning if it had not been for him.

We have picture shows every other night and dancing every night. The music isn't so hot, but we have a very good time. Last night, at our table during the dance, five different countries were represented and everyone speaking English as the common means of communication.

They only had church today for the Catholics. They must think the rest of us don't need it, or are simply heathens and wouldn't go if we had the opportunity.

There is a concert every morning and afternoon.

There is a French woman in this Class who is the most beautiful creature I ever laid my eyes on. I hope I shall always carry a picture of her in my mind. I have not tried to talk to her for fear of being disillusioned. I am afraid she is dumb, for her husband is not so much, to my way of thinking.

Mr. Kramer addressed this envelope for me, so it wouldn't be in my handwriting.

There is a girl in our crowd going to Finland to be married, but she is staying there. She is Finnish herself and very nice. She has been in the States for the past twelve years.

---

[7] Mr. Funcke was Helen's boss at the Rayon Factory.

Forsaking All Others (Aug. 1933—Sept. 1933)

My feelings are quite mingled as I near Bremerhaven.
Lots of love to all,

Helen

To: Mr. and Mrs. H. S. Dixon from Helen
Postcard picture of D. Bremen
814 Broad St.
Elizabethton, Tennessee, U.S.
August 22, 1933

Have just landed and feeling great. Am waiting for lunch at hotel here in Bremen and leave at 1:53 p.m. for Essen. Will be there a little after 5:00 p.m. Got with an awfully nice crowd for the last two days.

Love,

Helen

To: Mr. and Mrs. H.S. Dixon from Helen
Postcard picture of Zur Platte, Essen-Werden
814 Broad St.
Elizabethton, Tennessee, U.S.A.

Zur Platte
Essen-Werden, Germany
August 25, 1933

[Helen's handwriting] This is a lovely place. We are having coffee, only my coffee is ice cream, [Wilfred's handwriting] while my coffee has turned to beer. [Gustav's handwriting] A German friend and German beer and American young ladies sends his best salutations. Yours G. Vriesen. [Gerda's handwriting] We brought Wilfred and Helen to this place the day before their marriage to make them forget their sad feelings about taking leave from happy days of freedom. Most sincerely, Gerda Vriesen. [Gustav's handwriting] Kind regards and many happy returns of the day!

Gustav Vriesen

To: Mr. and Mrs. H. S. Dixon
Picture postcard of Cologne Cathedral[8]
814 Broad St.
Elizabethton, Tennessee, U.S.A.

St. Goar A/R
September 4, 1933

Your letters to Wilfred were rec'd by us here this morning, and we were so glad to get them. From Koln we went to Koblenz, and then here for three days. Tomorrow, we go to Bacharach for a while. We were there this afternoon, and it is lovely. The Rhein Valley cannot be described or painted. We climbed the Lorelei yesterday and investigated the Ruin Rheinfeld the day before. Love to Mama Hunter and Mama Dick and all the family.

Helen

To: Mrs. Harlow Dixon from Helen
814 Broad St.
Elizabethton, Tennessee, U.S.A.

Assmannshausen
Am Rhine, Germany
September 15, 1933

Dearest Folks,

I received your letter this morning, mother, and was of course delighted to get it.

We are continuing to spend rather lazy days on the Rhein [Rhine]. We like it here at Assmannshausen so much, as our landlady is charming and our accommodations are excellent. Besides this, we are near so many interesting places.

Wilfred has had malaria one night since we have been here, so I have been introduced. It is terrible to think he will most likely have to endure it for life.

I have had one of my colds for about ten days, and I do not hope to get over it, as the evenings are so cool that I get thoroughly chilled going to bed. We have had wonderful sunshine through the days, though.

I will sail the 26th of September or the 5th of October. I am waiting on a note from Mr. Funcke. Mr. Kramer may be sailing on the 26th but I am not sure. I can manage alone quite all right, though Mr. Kramer did a great deal for my comfort.

---

[8] Cologne, or Koln (one of Germany's oldest cities), must have made a deep impression on Helen, since, a year after she visited the city, she had a prophetic dream about its lying in ruins.

I have so much to tell you about the beautiful wedding and wedding supper Mutti had for us.

Wilfred gave me the most beautiful silver comb, brush, and mirror for my wedding present. I got many other lovely presents too, which I shall of course bring home with me.

I had a letter from Tootsie this morning too and was so sorry to hear about her mother. If you see her, thank her for the letter and tell her how sorry I am. I am not going to start writing cards, as there is no end to it.

Wilfred has been wonderful to me in every way, and we are having a happy holiday together. Love to all,

Helen

Wilfred and Helen wedding photo, 1933

At Home
in America
1933 ~ 1937

Wilfred in Tennessee

I Hail the Superhuman

October 1933 ~ September 1937

A mouth that has no moisture and no breath
Breathless mouths may summon;
I hail the superhuman;
I call it death-in-life and life-in-death.

~ William Butler Yeats

3

The poet Yeats predicts that each of us, if we live long enough, will at some stage become extraordinary. Whether the catalyst is war, poverty, depression, sickness, or loss, we will face the moment of having "no moisture and no breath," the moment when, by our mere survival, we become "superhuman." What marks these moments, for Yeats, is the sense of "death-in-life and life-in-death." On the one hand, there are the moments when everything around us seems to have died but, unaccountably, we continue to live. On the other hand, there are moments when life is going on all around us even as we sense that we are dead or no longer have the capacity to live. So it is with Wilfred and Helen during this period.

After their marriage in Germany in 1933, Helen and Wilfred returned separately to Elizabethton. Helen returned first, followed by Wilfred, some months later, in time for the birth of their daughter. He had not booked his passage since he did not know for sure whether he and Helen would be married. On arrival back in Elizabethton after a four-year absence, Wilfred must have been shocked by the changes in the Dixon family circumstances. When he had last visited the Dixons in 1929, they were living in one of the finest homes in the best part of Elizabethton. Their new home, a rental on Broad Street, while adequate, must have been a constant reminder of what had been lost.

By the time of his reunion with Helen in Elizabethton, Wilfred and Helen had spent one month together in the four years since their first meeting. Their living circumstances were far from ideal for a young couple trying to get to know each other, since the whole family—Helen and Wilfred, Sophia and Harlow, together with Sophia's mother, Mollie Jobe Hunter (Mama Hunter), and Harlow's mother, Virginia Dixon (Mama Dick)—was living under one roof. For this reason, there are no letters to document their responses to what was going on around them on a daily basis. But the pressures for Wilfred to succeed in this hostile environment must have been overwhelming. Helen's emotional turmoil over the unkindness of the residents of Elizabethton is documented in the letters that follow.

Mollie Jobe Hunter, wife of Dr. E.E. Hunter—mother of Sophia and her seven siblings

Clearly of vital importance during these years was the birth of Helen and Wilfred's darling little daughter, Helen Eve Collingwood Evans, on June 6, 1934. Her birth added a fourth generation to the family on Broad Street.

Between 1933 and 1936, Wilfred did everything in his power to get work in Elizabethton (population 10,000), but to no avail. Not only was he jobless, he was actively discriminated against, suffering (due in part to to his English heritage) as Helen later writes, "every humiliation known for three years in Elizabethton."

The year 1936 must have seemed at the time like a final insult to the Dixon-Evans family. Harlow liquidated the Dixon Furniture Company, which had been the primary source of family income for a generation or more; Sophia's mother,

Pictured here are members of the four generations living on Broad Street between 1933 and 1937: Harlow Dixon; his mother, Mrs. Virginia Dixon; Eve; and Helen. Also living in the house were Sophia; her mother, Mrs. Mollie Jobe (pictured on previous page); and Wilfred.

Mollie Jobe Hunter (pictured on page 63), died; Wilfred, after three years of desperation, continued jobless; and Helen labored on exhausted at the Rayon factory, seldom able to spend quiet time with Eve or private time with Wilfred in a house bursting with the competing interests of four generations. Finally, desperate for a change in their circumstances, Wilfred moved to Nashville where he found work as a janitor at Sears. Later, Helen also found work there, giving them their first moments of privacy. They made the three-hundred mile journey to Elizabethton as often as they could to visit the family and little Eve.

No letters were exchanged during this period, or, if they were, none remain.

I Hail the Superhuman (Oct. 1933—Sept. 1937)

Forced by unemployment into idleness, Wilfred would, on occasion, visit the home of Sophia's brother, Edwin Hunter and his wife, Lennie Hunter.

Their children, Kathryn (left) and Helen, took great delight in Wilfred's ability to hypnotize the rabbits in their garden.

Nine months after their marriage in Germany, Helen gave birth to Eve on June 6, 1934.

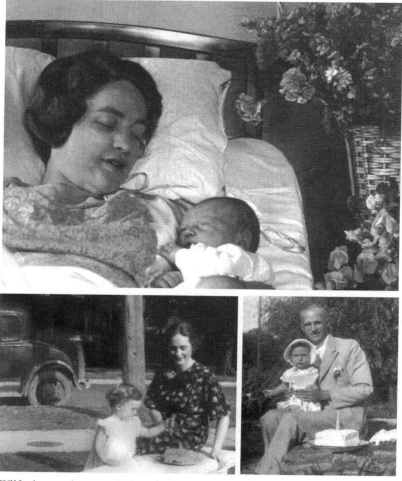

Wilfred, meantime, was isolated by his joblessness. He tried to fit in with the four-generation household but felt dispirited and alone, wanting nothing more than to find a job or return to South Africa with its more robust economy.

I Hail the Superhuman (Oct. 1933—Sept. 1937)

Between 1930 and 1937, Helen worked as a secretary for the North American Rayon Corporation in Elizabethton. She is pictured here in the upper right hand corner with her colleagues at the plant, her youthfulness and luminosity seemingly gone.

"I will always have a soft spot in my heart for all the office crowd at the plants that I was so closely associated with."

Helen Dixon Evans, 1942

The Letters:
Abroad

1937~1944

Bert and Helen, Johannesburg

4 And Indeed There Will Be Time

September 1937 ~ August 1939

> Time for you and time for me,
> And time yet for a hundred indecisions,
> And for a hundred visions and revisions,
> Before the taking of a toast and tea.
>
> ~ *T. S. Eliot*

4

We are now halfway toward solving the riddle: "How is it possible for two people, to continue to love one another for fifteen years, despite finding themselves living apart for eight of those years, suffering through four more, and happily settled for only three? At this point in the story, Helen and Wilfred have lived apart for four years and have endured another four years of pain in depression-ridden America.

After eight years of the extraordinary—the loss of her brother, the loss of autonomy, the loss of the house she thought of as home, as well as marriage in Germany to a man she barely knew, the birth of her child, the unforgiving rigors of work during the Great Depression, the diminution of the husband she loved and admired—Helen, with the stroke of a pen at Sears International in Chicago, had almost everything restored to her. Like any other woman of means in those days, she was now free to immerse herself in the ordinary. The offer of responsible and meaningful work for Wilfred with Sears International and the excitement of immigration to Wilfred's homeland in South Africa made her journey to Africa (from New York to Southampton, and from there to Cape Town) a pure delight.

For some years now, it has been a source of joy for me to know that I was conceived at this happy moment in my parents' lives—on the Atlantic—somewhere between America and Africa, my two homelands.

After settling into her new life in Johannesburg, Helen indulged herself: looking after three-year-old Eve; playing bridge; buying furniture; hosting dinner parties; preparing at leisure for the birth of her second child; and getting to know her father-in-law, William Evans, and sister-in-law, Bert. As with each of us, once they are restored, ordinary moments seem as if they will last forever. Easily deluded by the notion that "indeed there will be time," we become complacent.

What is special about Helen and Wilfred's story is the number of times they were roused by the extraordinary and just how precious, therefore, the three years of the ordinary were to become. That is, if one can ever consider as ordinary emigrating from America to Africa, encountering an international financial scandal, giving birth to a baby in a foreign land, and moving five times in two years.

To: Mr. and Mrs. H. S. Dixon from Helen [age, almost 31]
814 Broad St.
Elizabethton, Tennessee

1229 17th Avenue S.
Nashville, Tenn.
September 27, 1937

My dearest Mother and Father,

    I've put Wilfred on the train Thursday night for Chicago and got a telegram from him this morning saying his new job is Representative in the Union of South Africa for Sears International, separate yet associated with Sears, Roebuck. We must sail October 6th from New York on the *Queen Mary*. I know our leaving the U.S. is going to hurt you as it does me, but this is our big opportunity. My days of working in an office are over, and that means a great deal because, for the first time, I can really know my little girl. I have tried to hide these three years how much it hurt to see her only in the evenings, after I was tired from the office. There is always a sacrifice to make in every joy that comes, and my sacrifice is leaving you two.

    Wilfred's job is a very big one; his rise in the firm is something unheard of. He will be responsible for a million dollars' worth of trade. We shall live in Johannesburg, and that will be nice for us, with Bert and Mr. Evans there. All our travel expenses will be paid by Sears International. I did not dream we would be going so soon and expected to spend about three to six weeks with you, at home. I worked my last day today, but I must sublease my apartment and sell the car before I leave. I shall try to finish up here on Wednesday and come home Thursday. I shall wire you when to expect Eve and me. We'll come as soon as possible. Let us be as happy as possible the few days I can be at home.

    Nannette and I had lunch together today, and I am sending this letter by her.
All our love and kisses,

Helen and Eve

Hotel Pennsylvania, New York
October 6, 1937

Dearest Ones,

    Eve was a perfect traveler on the train. It was really a very easy trip, as our waking hours were taken up by eating dinner and breakfast. When I got in, there was no sign of Wilfred, but [that] did not really worry me because the train was so long it was easy to miss each other, so I had a red cap carry my baggage to the Pennsylvania Hotel, but I did start worrying when they told me W. Evans was not registered. They also handed me my telegram to him and a letter for him. I took a

And Indeed There Will Be Time (Sept. 1937—Aug. 1939)

room, found Sears Roebuck in the telephone directory, and asked Sears for the manager. I only got the assistant manager, but he had me connected with Sears International, which was not listed, and, from them, I found out Wilfred was in the city and registered at the Pennsylvania Hotel as D. Evans, Room 206. I went down and asked to see the registration card of D. Evans. They brought it out, and it was Wilfred's signature; they had taken his "W" for a "D." Mr. Sobels at Sears International told Wilfred he must have a very smart wife to trace a thing down like that in ten minutes in all.

We got Eve's coat at Macy's. It is a pretty blue with hat and leggings to match.

Eve is eating huge meals and having normal actions even though she is traveling.

Must start packing now for the boat. By the way, I found my Kodak, thank goodness, so you will be getting some pictures.

I got a pair of I. Miller evening slippers in silver and black. The other stores couldn't begin to fit me; in fact, I was told at Macy's I couldn't get a fit in New York. I asked where, in all the world, could I get a fit in evening slippers then.

Lots of love and kisses from Eve and me,

Helen

Cunard White Star
R.M.S. *Queen Mary*
October 9, 1937

Dearest Ones,

The *Queen Mary* is certainly not a disappointment. I was afraid she would be because I had read so much about her. She is just as large and larger than I expected. We have a beautiful cabin in A Deck, about the middle of the ship. It is in the best location you can possibly have. I had been assured it would be nice, but when I walked in and found it looked like a cabin one sees in the picture show, my breath was taken away. I tried to control myself until Mr. Sobel of Sears left; then I investigated everything. The cabin walls are of curly maple, there are three beds, not bunks, two dressing tables with lots of drawer space, two closets, indirect lighting, electric fan, heat to be turned on at will by a button, but best of all a private bath with tub and shower, hot and cold salt water, hot and cold fresh water. There are gorgeous thick rugs on the floor and beautiful chairs. Everything is done in a very modernistic design.

Eve went in the swimming pool today with Wilfred. I am going to spend some time in the gym tomorrow. Eve played in the playroom some but had rather be on deck with me. She has not been at all sick; however, there has been no reason for sea-sickness as the sea has been so smooth. The boat is just starting to roll tonight. Eve has taken everything in stride, and even the great whistle they blew as they pulled out of New York only made her jump once. Eve has had a good appetite for the most part, and she does enjoy having ice cream so much.

There is a good motion picture every afternoon. Yesterday, it was Robert Montgomery and Rosalind Russell in *Night Must Fall*, and today, Leslie Howard and Bettie Davis in a film, but I don't recall the name of it.

It took a lot of pushing in New York for us to make the boat. We didn't have more than a half hour from the time we arrived at the pier until we sailed.

When Wilfred told me silk hose are $3.50 a pair in South Africa and those are Sears 79-cent hose, I bought fifteen pairs to supplement what I got as presents in Elizabethton. I have already started washing them out and drying them, which is not hard with heat in my cabin.

We have five days between boats, and we are spending the time in London. Please do not write Mrs. Vriesen that we have so long between boats, as she would be very mad that we did not come to Germany.

I want to do some shopping in London, however, as my evening slippers and Eve's coat were all I had time for in New York. I also want to see some of the good shows one can always find in London. I am terribly thrilled about having this much time there.

There is so much to do on board that I regret it takes only five days to cross. There is dancing and Keno in the evenings, and the pool and gym, besides the deck games during the day.

The trip on down to Cape Town does not take as long as I thought, as we arrive there November 1.

Mother, I wish you would buy a hat or dress material for Mama Dick and take it out of the rent money. I simply had no time to select anything in New York. I want to give it to her on her birthday and wish you a happy birthday.

Going up on the train, Eve said a smart thing. She looked at the sky, which was very blue next morning, and said, "When the sky is blue like this, it looks like the river."

I have seen Tommy Farr several times. He is the Welshman who fought Joe Louis. His face is very battered up, but he looks like a kid.

We shall have a maid for Eve in London, so don't worry we will be leaving her alone.

Eve talked about you all today, like she might be a little homesick for you.

And Indeed There Will Be Time (Sept. 1937—Aug.1939) 77

I'll add a P.S. if anything of interest happens before we land. Must go down and take a look at Eve.

Best love and many kisses from Eve and Helen

Sunday

P.S. Yesterday was our only rough day, but Eve did not get sick. Today is nice again, and we sight land at five o'clock this afternoon. There is a party this afternoon, at four, for the children. Eve is thrilled over the prospects. She is eating an apple and standing beside me while I write this.

THE Swimming Pool, above, is both a social and a sportive rendezvous. On the wide balcony as well as right beside the gleaming pool are tables and comfortable chairs where refreshments are served. Indirect lighting reflected from the mother-of-pearl ceiling is restful and pleasing. And after a round of dives and plunges down the chute, the Turkish Baths alongside invite you to expert massages, infra-red or violet-ray treatments.

Queen Mary Brochure

Union-Castle Line
R.M.M.V. Winchester Castle
October 15, 1937

Dearest Mother and Father,

It is only about an hour before sailing time and everything is in a rush and scramble on the boat, but I had to get a line off to you before my long journey. We had a fine five days in London. We stopped at the Grosvenor House in London. It is one of the two best in the city, just beside Hyde Park. One night we went to an Austrian restaurant, so we could hear some German waltzes again. The dinner was wonderful. Eve went to the zoo yesterday with the governess of the children of the London representative of Sears, and I drove all day with his wife through the quaint villages of Surrey County. It was a marvelous opportunity. One night we went to see the stage performance of *Victoria Regina*. We had wonderful seats, and were so surprised, as we took two of the last four seats in the theatre.

We have two cabins with private bath on this steamer. The boat seems so small after the *Queen Mary*, but it is very nice, as it is only five years old. It is the second largest of the Union-Castle Line.

Eve is very blasé now. Last night, after she had had supper, she said she was hungry. I asked her what she wanted, and she said, "I don't know, just *order* me something." This morning she said she liked the boat better than the train.

This is only a rough outline of our activities. I shall try to write the whole trip in an interesting manner, so you can pass it around to those who are interested. We are the proud owners of a portable typewriter, so that will make it easier for me.

Lots of love to all,

Helen and Eve

Union-Castle Line
R.M.M.V. Winchester Castle
October 17, 1937

Dearest Ones,

We are off the coast of Portugal tonight, and our ship is rolling considerably; however, we have been lucky, as the Bay of Biscay was very calm, and it is usually rough. I am writing this so that I can post it from Madeira. We only have four hours there, and I want to spend every minute sightseeing. We will be there from 6:00 a.m. to 11:00 a.m.

Eve has a big appetite and almost has to be stopped, she eats so much. She has had roses in her checks all today and her hair rather curly. She doesn't look like the same child. She did not look so well on the *Queen Mary*. She has gradually been looking better and has had a better appetite since I took her off of milk. I believe she was bilious from milk.

Everyone seems to be going to Johannesburg. We have met a very nice couple, whose home is there. They have just been in London for a visit, and touring the Continent. They have a little girl who is fond of Eve and wants to look after her, but Eve continues to be a mama's baby and stays right with me.

We shall be in the tropics after Madeira. We reach Madeira day after tomorrow. There it is sunny all day and very warm, even in the evenings. Eve can wear her sun suits, and I shall have to get out summer clothes. Right now, we are still wearing coats all day.

I wish I could have news from you. Mail takes nine days from Capetown to London, as it all goes by air now whether you use an airmail stamp or not.

Have I yet mentioned that I got your wire to the *Queen Mary*? We had several. Lots of love,

Helen

Union-Castle Line
R.M.M.V. *Winchester Castle*
October 24, 1937

Dearest Mother and Father,

Today we cross the Equator. Usually it is a torrid day, but we are fortunate in having a cool breeze from somewhere. We have had only one really hot day.

October 29

Eve interrupted me, and I am just now getting back to my letter, as so much has been happening. First, I must tell you about the Fancy Dress Ball on last Monday evening. Up until noon on Monday, I said I wasn't going to dress in fancy dress; then the thought struck me, why not go as Mae West since my black velvet evening dress is just the style she wears. I had, fortunately, not worn the dress on this ship. I borrowed a large black hat from an elderly lady, which I put on at a daring angle; my hair I did in the style of 1900, with curls on my forehead. I wore a borrowed black ostrich feather cape, a great deal of jewelry with a black velvet band around my throat, and one of my dress buttons on the front of it. I carried my large white beaded evening bag and smoked a cigarette held in a long gold holder.

For the whole evening, I swaggered around with my hand on my hip. When I passed in front of the judges (all women) I said, "Come up and see me sometime." Lady Stanley, the wife of the Governor of Southern Rhodesia, was one of the judges. I thought I had no chance with ladies judging—I knew the men liked the costume—but they must have been a broad-minded group, as they gave Mae West first prize for the most original costume made on the boat.

My next victory came last night, when I played off the finals in the bridge tournament, and won. Yesterday morning in the tournament, I had the best player on the boat as my opponent. She wanted stakes on the side, and I let her set them and took her money. She didn't like it a little. I haven't played much bridge on board except in the tournament, since the first game I was invited to the stakes named were as expressed: "The usual stakes, a pound a hundred" ($5.00 a hundred). I excused myself with a headache. I have never seen so many people before with so little regard for money; they must have so much that it doesn't need to mean anything to them. Tonight, they present the prizes won on the voyage, and I shall be up for two. They will be checks for about $2.50. I know it will thrill the bridge players of Elizabethton to hear that their weakest member won the tournament among a lot of high-stake players.

I am enclosing snaps with explanations written on the backs. I think our first efforts with my new Kodak are very good.

Wilfred is leaving the ship at Capetown, but Eve and I are staying on to Durban. The extra boat fare was the same as rail fare from Capetown to Johannesburg, and it gives us a chance to see East London, Port Elizabeth, and Durban. (It also means our meals for another week. Wilfred will get a place for us to live, so we won't have a big hotel bill in J'burg. We are on our own expense as soon as we reach J'burg.) Eve repeats over and over to herself: "All the way to Africa."

You would be quite proud of Eve if you could see her in the swimming pool, as she is not at all afraid of the water and lets Wilfred and the Life Guard swim any place with her just holding around their necks. She goes in nearly every day. She eats such huge meals that our punishment now is she can't have her next meal if she isn't good. For lunch today, she will eat a bowl of soup, a large piece of meat, a vegetable (green), a potato, bread and dessert and then some fruit. When she does have milk, she drinks a glass full in one gulp. There is never any coaxing about food. If she does have a light meal now and then, I know she can afford to have it and that she just does not feel like eating. She often speaks of you two and asked Wilfred a good one the other day. She said, "Why didn't you bring Mama Sophia along?" He answered that he didn't know why he didn't, and she said, "Didn't you have enough money?" We thought it very smart of her to realize that it takes money.

Madeira was not a disappointment. We had a beautiful drive up the mountain and saw such gorgeous formal gardens at the Belmonte Hotel. The natives, begging you to buy, rather spoil one's visit in the town itself. We drove around by car, but many still use the oxen and sled, like the one we stand in front of. That used to be the only means of transportation in Madeira. I found them too smelly.

It is quite cold again. It was not until this trip that I could appreciate the first lines of Kipling's poem:

        On the coast of Mandalay
        Where the flying fishes play –

And Indeed There Will Be Time (Sept. 1937—Aug.1939) 81

We have seen the flying fishes on the warm days. They are very small but come up out of the ocean in large numbers. They look more like humming birds than anything else.

Eve is getting restless now, so I must close. She has been very quiet and patient during this long letter.

I am anxious to hear from you and know how everything is at home.

Lots of love from us both.

Eve sends kisses and hugs.

Helen

Hotel Majestic
New Line Marine Parade
Durban
November 10, 1937

Dearest Mother and Father,

We arrived in Durban Sunday morning and are leaving this afternoon for Johannesburg. We will arrive there tomorrow morning about 9:00. I have enjoyed Durban, as it is beautiful, and we are right on the beach; but, by now, I am getting anxious to really unpack my bags and have a place to hang my hat. I would never take a trip around the world. I have already seen more of South Africa than many South Africans have seen. The towns are all very clean and all the buildings are very substantial, no "joints" as we have along our main street. East London is the same population as Elizabethton, but the impression is one of a much larger place.[9] They have a wonderful snake garden

Durban's Marine Parade, overlooking the Indian Ocean, was lined with luxurious apartments and hotels.

---

[9] The British influence in South Africa was in evidence everywhere. Large, ornate public buildings, city halls, museums, libraries, perfectly tended gardens, a fine rail system, and a well-ordered educational system (for Europeans) had been built in the fifty years between the discovery of gold and diamonds (1886-1887) and 1937, when Helen first arrived. The exploitation of cheap labor accelerated the growth.

and museum of stuffed animals and birds, including a rhino and a giraffe, also the skeletons of two whales.

On our train trip, we shall pass native kraals this afternoon. I had a native girl for Eve Sunday, but let her go on Monday, as she could not understand anything I said to her, and Eve complained that she smelled bad, which she did. Eve has made up with all of the rickshaw boys dressed up in feathers, flowers, and ribbons, also the women dressed in bright colors on the streets, but her native girl did not have such fine clothes and was too prosaic for Eve. Why she was not afraid of their wild appearance I shall never know. I'll send some more pictures shortly.

Much love to all and xxx from Eve.

Helen

Zulu man with rickshaw

Note: After their move to South Africa, through letters to each other, Helen and Wilfred continued their friendship with Mary and Knaffl Walker. Some eighteen years later, Mary became famous as Mary Starr of the WETA TV station. "Mary Starr," a cooking show, was one of the most popular TV shows in Knoxville in the 1950s and 1960s. Always poised and confident when on the air, Mary has since been called the Martha Stewart of her day.

To: Mary and Knaffl Walker from Wilfred Evans

210 Killarney Court
Johannesburg, S. Africa
November 27, 1937

My dear Mary and Knaffl,

I'm sorry that I never let you hear from me before leaving the U.S.A., but, as Helen most probably told you, I have been simply rushed off my feet ever since I reported to Chicago.

We had a most pleasant journey out here, and are finally located in the town of my birth. We moved into our apartment yesterday, and are simply delighted with it, though the rent is confoundedly high ($125 without heat or light).

It is midsummer out here, of course, but Helen has been shivering since her arrival. The town is 6,000 feet above sea level on great plains, though I have an idea that if Helen sat out on a porch in Hell for an evening she'd be cold.

And Indeed There Will Be Time (Sept. 1937—Aug. 1939)

The sight of Cape Town with its really magnificent background of Table Mountain is one that has inspired poetry and prose. We arrived in Table Bay at eleven o'clock at night, and Cape Town looked like a fairyland, millions of twinkling lights overshadowed by the dim outline of that forbidding mountain. I had been on deck for hours watching the approach of the mountain and the lights, and when we dropped anchor in the placid bay that mirrored the dancing lights of the Cape of Good Hope, I rushed below to call Helen. Helen did say it was beautiful. She then said she was cold, and after a long silence remarked, "I think we'd better all have an early bath tomorrow morning." I should have let out a . . . piercing scream; instead, I used the good old iron control and finally tottered off to the bar and had a stiff whiskey. If I had not known her rather intimately for some four years, I would definitely have pushed her quietly overboard.

Can you believe it? I am homesick for America! Though a small American town peopled by very small people nearly made of me a gorgeous case of dementia praecox, yet an American firm gave me a job as a partner and was not afraid to let me climb. I may sound horribly sentimental, but know this, that I cherish the friendship of you two above any other human relationship that has ever come my way in this bedizened world—Sears, Roebuck and the Walkers signify America at its best.

Eve is the delight of the community with her East Tennessee accent. She is full of "Yes Siree's," "I'll say's," "Honey's," and "Aint's." I am enclosing a picture of her taken by a woman on the boat. The woman in question had first taken a walk around the deck and had left a box of candy in her deck chair. When she returned, she found Eve behind her deck chair devouring the candy, and she, fortunately, had a camera at hand to record the thieving inclinations of our offspring.

I had intended giving three spears to Joe—the ones we had over there. Helen tells me, however, that she promised one to the Tipton twins. Why she would promise spears to that wild bunch I can't think:

> The Assyrians came down like a wolf on the fold,
> Their cohorts all gleaming in purple and gold.
> And the sheen of their spears was like stars on the sea . . .

Well, I hope they get their spears into some of my pals around the village. In any case there is—or will be—one left. The Tiptons are not to receive their hardware until I say, "Go," so first pop around to Broad Street next time you are up there and select the best one for Joe.

Have you heard this one? An American lay brother got a job in the Vatican, his job being to awaken the Pope every morning. He would knock on the door and solemnly announce, "Good morning your holiness. It's seven o'clock and the sun is shining." And the Pope would always answer, "I know it, and God knows it." This went on for months, and the American was beginning to get pretty damned sick of his job. One morning, after knocking, he delivered his formula: "Good morning your holiness. It's seven o'clock and the sun is shining." And the Pope answered, "I know it, and God knows it."

"Oh ho," snarled the American, "Coupla wise guys, huh? Well, it's six o'clock, and it's raining like hell."

Can you really believe that I do know a parlour joke!

Give my regards to Joe, and tell him that, if I should run across anything in Zulu daggers, I'll send one over.

To you two, all the luck in the world and the sincere appreciation of a one-time "furriner"[10] in East Tennessee.

Wilfred

Note: Helen's seeming indifference to their arrival in Cape Town—an extraordinary moment—becomes understandable later. Had she stayed to savor the moment, however, she might have learned from Wilfred some of the facts known to almost every South African schoolchild: that, in 1580, Sir Francis Drake, while circumnavigating the world, called the Cape of Good Hope "The Fairest Cape in all the World," and that, in 1652, the first multinational, megacorporation in the world—the Dutch East India Company—needing to replenish its ships en-route to the Dutch East Indies (called Indonesia after World War II), established vegetable gardens and built a castle on the southern tip of Africa. The grand harbor in Cape Town is perfectly balanced by the massive outline of Table Mountain, inspiring, as Wilfred says, "poetry and prose." Indeed, Table Mountain inspired the brilliant South African scholar and general, Jan Christiaan Smuts, to write and publish his book "Holism and Evolution" in 1926. And, years after Wilfred and Helen had died, views of the mountain would inspire Nelson Mandela to unimaginable feats of inner heroism during his eighteen years of imprisonment on Robben Island in Table Bay. (He spent nine more years in other prisons.)

---

[10] The word "furriner" became something of a wry family joke. "Furriner" was an exaggeration of the way the residents of Elizabethton pronounced "foreigner"—a term widely used in reference to my father because he spoke with an "upper-class" British accent. Labeling him for three years in this way appeared to give the residents of the city the power to exclude Wilfred from everything that might have helped him find a job or happiness. It appears that Mary and Knaffl Walker were among the very few residents of Elizabethton to offer friendship to Wilfred and Helen as a couple. My father also clearly liked Helen's grandmother, Mama Dick, and must have felt liked by her. These observations are not meant to imply that Wilfred and Helen were themselves free of prejudice. As it is for all humanity, moving beyond prejudice takes time and effort, involving a deep and constant struggle for self-awareness.

And Indeed There Will Be Time (Sept. 1937—Aug. 1939)

To: Mr. Harlow and Mrs. Sophia Dixon from Helen

210 Killarney Court
Johannesburg, South Africa
December 1, 1937

Dearest Mother and Father,

Eve is standing by me, and I asked her what she wanted me to tell you all, so I will give you her message first. She said tell them I have been a good girl, and tell them we have a new apartment. Of course, she was bragging a little in her first remark.

I know it is terrible that I have waited so long to write, but I have been so busy trying to get settled, and the altitude has left me with very little endurance. I find I must lie down quite often and must sleep a great deal. Asheville, N.C., always made me sleepy, but the altitude there was nothing compared to this place. Coming up on the train, I thought my head would burst.

We had a small flat in town, where we knew we would not stay, and that unsettled condition, for the first ten days, made me feel terribly homesick. I am feeling much better now, however, as we have a really beautiful flat in one of the best places in town. It is completely furnished, and we have it for six months, with the option of keeping it longer if we like. It is the flat of a stockbroker, so you can imagine that it is nicely furnished. I am enclosing a plan of it. We pay $125 a month for it. This place is like living in New York City when it comes to rents—and everything else, in fact. Everything is new, all the stores and the many, many apartment houses, and everything is most modern in design, and everything was built with the idea that everyone has money. Bert is living with us, and I am very glad to have her, for she is a lovely person, so very kind and thoughtful, and a very cheery person too. Her pictures do not do her justice, as she is one of those persons whose coloring and general make up mean so much.

I have an excellent native girl, or colored girl, as we would call them. I hope nothing happens to her, as she is a treasure. I have only had her four days, but what a different aspect life has taken on in those four days. She is an excellent cook. All I have to do is have food in the kitchen, and she brings a good meal to the table, served faultlessly. I do not plan the meals unless there is something special I want to have. She does her dusting and tidying of the bedrooms without a single direction from me. She does not have to bother with the floors or scouring of the bathroom, as that is done every day by a native boy, and by that I mean to say my floors are waxed and polished every day of the week. Every flat in Johannesburg is a service flat, and that is the service given. My floors are all parquet, so you can imagine that they look quite lovely. All of this service is naturally a joy, except for one thing, and that is that one never knows when one has privacy, for the native boys work so quietly down on their hands and knees (no shoes) that you think you are quite alone, and then you find you have company in a corner you hadn't looked in. I go snooping around my flat the whole time.

I have been invited out several places. The Bob Cades had us to a cocktail party. He has a big firm of accountancy here. Wilfred knew him in Bloemfontein; he is also financial adviser of Sears International. He serves in that capacity for a lot of American and English firms doing business out here. We also had tea and dinner with a family by the name of Rennie. He is one of the wealthiest men in Johannesburg. He is on the stock exchange. Wilfred made a friend of him on the ship coming out. He has a large family, seven children, and it was wonderful being in a real home like that one, just after getting here, and when we were so unsettled ourselves. A Mrs. Butler I met at the Cades has had me for tea. There are some Hollanders I knew quite well on the ship living in Killarney Court too, and I was there for tea yesterday afternoon, and they are coming for tea with me this afternoon.

Believe it or not, but tea is served this many times in my home: seven in the morning Bert has tea in bed (this is a general custom here), at eight we have it for breakfast, at eleven o'clock Ellen (my cook) appears with tea again. Ellen also appears again at four in the afternoon with tea. Frankly, I go into another room quite often, as I can't stand to see it so often. I have to manage the afternoon tea, as one usually has it with guests, or is invited out for it. Ellen rescued the tea cozy Bert sent me from Eve's head and now it always appears on the teapot. Eve can't understand its new place of prominence in the family—neither can I. [11]

I was very sorry to hear about J. K. It is a shame she couldn't pull herself together when she got married and could have had a decent life. I knew she was pretty fargone when I was associated with her at Alexander's.

I hope you will buy something for Mama Dick for me right away, as I am afraid she will not last much longer, and I want her to have a present from us before anything happens. I am sorry I did not leave the radio for her and Uncle Hunter, [12] as I cannot use it out here; also my electric iron is useless.

---

[11] A "tea cozy" is a cover for a teapot. Made in the same shape as a winter cap, it serves a similar purpose—only, in this instance, to keep the tea hot. While still living in America, Helen had received a tea cozy, hand-knitted by Bert. Eve had worn it as a winter hat until they found themselves in South Africa where that simply wasn't "done," and the tea cozy was restored to its original purpose. A note here: a tea cozy has an opening on one side for the spout of the teapot and on the other side, an opening for the handle. Helen had always wondered why openings were left for the child's ears when the purpose of the "cap" was to provide warmth.

[12] Helen's grandmother, Mrs. Virginia Dixon, "Mama Dick," had two sons: Harlow, who was Helen's father, and Hunter, who, by coincidence, shared the name "Hunter" with his in-laws.

And Indeed There Will Be Time (Sept. 1937—Aug.1939)

A great many of my nice things were broken. It will not help your feelings for me to enumerate, so I won't. I don't want to buy a thing out here to cart back with me in three years. I shall probably leave here in two-and-a-half years, as I want to take a long trip back through the Mediterranean, and Wilfred wants the quickest trip over, as he is seasick nearly all the time.

The summers here are cooler than at home; in fact, I am too cool in the house most of the time. All places are built of solid brick, so it is always cool like Aunt Hattie's house at Hampton.[13]

I was glad to hear all the news about Roberta's wedding and that you have such a pretty new dress.

About my income tax report. I interviewed the Tax Collector at the plants when he was there, and he said there was no need for me to make out a return, as I owed no tax. I gave him the exact income of Wilfred and myself for the year, and it was far below the $2400 or $2500 allowed for a married couple with one child. If it is necessary to make a return, you can get my income for 1936 from the plants and Wilfred's from Sears, Roebuck in Nashville, if you write and explain what it is for. Value the house at $12,000 showing taxes paid per year on it, monthly payments to the loan company, and insurance.

I suppose this will reach you in time for me to wish you all a very Merry Christmas and to let you know I would certainly like to spend it with you. It is impossible for me to get the Christmas spirit here in warm weather. I have had no time to shop for anyone, as I have so far been buying little necessities for the house only. I do not have much inclination to shop either, as everything is about twice as high as at home.

Do not waste your money sending me Air Mail letters, as all letters come to South Africa from England by Air Mail letters anyway. That is the only way they come, and Air Mail letters are not flown across the Atlantic anyway, so the only advantage you would have (a doubtful one) would be that it would be flown from Bristol to New York. The plane trip from Cape Town to London takes nine days. I met quite a few people on the ship who had made that flight. [Flights between South Africa and London only became commonplace during the early 1960s.] Wilfred may come back that way.

Give one spear to Joe Walker in Maryville and one each to the Tipton boys. Suggest to Nannette that she hang them up for them, as they will otherwise break them in a day or so.

---

[13] Large and gracious, Aunt Hattie's "house" at Hampton, which still stands, could be more aptly described as a mansion. Hattie, Ruth, and Mollie (Sophia's mother) were three of Dr. Abraham Jobe's twelve children. See *A Mountaineer in Motion: The Memoir of Dr. Abraham Jobe. The University of Tennessee Press, 2009.*

I must stop and take Eve out for a walk. She looks so penned up in the flat, even though the rooms are very large.

Best love to all the family, and a cheery greeting to everyone who inquires. Eve has grown a great deal and seems very grown up.

Love and kisses from Eve and me,

Helen

To: Mrs. John T. Dixon
[Helen's paternal grandmother, Virginia Dixon]
Alexander Apartments
Elizabethton, Tennessee

210 Killarney Court
Johannesburg, South Africa
December 24, 1937

My dearest Mama Dick,

Eve has just now done something that has reminded me of you so much that I had to sit down and write you. What Eve did was this: I have just put her to bed for her afternoon nap, and when she noticed her pillow had a fresh slip on it, she refused to lie on it—said she didn't want to mess it up. She laid it carefully aside and said she didn't mind sleeping without a pillow. I laughed and said she was just like Dicky, and that made her laugh too.

It is very hard for me to realize that tomorrow is Christmas, even though I have a big turkey in the refrigerator and a plum pudding, because one buys flowers to decorate with since there is not a sprig of holly or mistletoe. It is really pitiful to see the imitation mistletoe for sale in the stores. We are having a tree, but a rather sad one compared to some in the past, as they cost a great deal since there are no native forests. When one sees a forest, one will notice immediately that it has been planted, as the trees are in very straight rows.[14]

I have been thoroughly enjoying the counterpane you made for me since I have been here. I have had it on my bed ever since I settled in this flat, about the 25th of November. Everyone thinks it is beautiful.

Mother writes that you are still not well, which I am certainly sorry to hear. Wilfred is always as distressed as I am to hear you are not well and sends his best love.

---

[14] Helen later became aware of the indigenous forests around Knysna, an area on the south coast of South Africa that gets summer and winter rainfall. The "forests" in the Transvaal and Natal, however, are usually comprised of trees that have been planted—often for use as pit props in the mines.

I have only the last two days felt well since arriving in Johannesburg. The high altitude affects nearly everyone at first. Many people have told me it took them three months before they felt well here. For one thing, I have never been so cold in my life, even though it is the summer season now. There are strong winds so much of the time, with no mountains to stop them, and the walls of the houses are solid brick, so that what heat there is from the sun never penetrates the houses.

Eve went to kindergarten for two weeks before the holidays and she simply loved it. She had to leave at 8:00 every morning. I think it rained every day she went, so she looked just too grownup in her raincoat, galoshes, and school satchel, starting out early every morning. The teacher reported her "very self-willed."

Lots of love and kisses from us all,

Helen

210 Killarney Court
Johannesburg, South Africa
January 4, 1938

Dearest Mother and Father,

I think I've had six letters from you since my arrival, and I am glad to learn that my letter mailed in Cape Town has reached you, but I am afraid I have been a very poor correspondent since then, as this is only my second letter to you. Today, I am feeling better, but this altitude simply got me, and so it is with everyone about the first three months.

On my maid's night out, I am simply exhausted after getting the dinner. You know that is very little for me to do considering what I once could accomplish. I feel about a hundred years old, having to lie down so much, and feeling so little interest in anything. I simply accomplish nothing all day long. I have thought perhaps some of it comes from this being my first opportunity in years to let down, but I must say letting down, to the extent I have, is no pleasure.

I must also say that I have come nearer freezing here than any place I have ever been; I was amused when you wrote that you hoped I could stand the heat. I have worn mostly my winter dresses so far. When one is right out in the sun, it is hot, very hot, but not the kind of heat that makes you perspire. At night, I usually sit in my lounge [living room] with a coat on. On the other hand, I walked to the Zoo the other day, which is about a mile from us, and nearly had sunstroke from it. What worries me from feeling so cold during the summer is that, be it winter or summer, I only have an electric heater in the lounge and nothing else. It has just managed to warm me up some during this summer. I have wondered if this place is not a wonderful opening for furnaces.

The trouble is that it is hard to change these Englishmen. The way they have always lived they consider good enough to continue. Here they build the most modern-looking blocks of flats, or apartment houses, as we call them, but there isn't a central heating system in the lot; furthermore, there are no screens in the windows. You do not need to be afraid to repeat this, thinking that perhaps I do not live in a good place, because I live in the very best. The flat next to mine rents for $150 per month, unfurnished. An elderly lady and her husband occupy it, and she told me it was so cold that her doctor told her she could not stand it another winter. Can you believe it? On the other hand, she has everything else for her comfort, a houseboy (native, colored, boys are used as much as or more than native girls as servants because they are considered better than the girls) for her cooking and her dusting, and a chauffeur and car at her disposal. I can't have a boy for my work on account of Eve.

My girl is a trained servant and very satisfactory most of the time. She knows how to do, but is just lazy at times and has to be called down. She knows how to set a table, which is much more complicated out here than at home, since there are fish knives and different forks for fish, and a fork as well as a large spoon for most desserts; in fact, I never feel sure of myself when I set the table. She knows how to serve the tea at all the different hours and goes about her work in a systematic manner. I do not have to go in the kitchen at all unless it is to show her how to prepare some typically American dish. I have given up, however, and my beans are always those underdone green things you abhor. Having Bert here, I have to think of her, and she won't eat my kind of beans at all.

A Negro is always a "boy" or a "girl" no matter if he or she is sixty years old. And an Indian from whom one buys fruit and vegetables at the door is a "Sammy." Ellen, my girl, always calls me "Madam" and Wilfred "Master." When one goes calling, one asks if Madam is in, not if Mrs. Evans is in. There is a lot like this to learn if one does not want to always be spotted as a foreigner.

I suppose you have seen Mama Dick's letter and know, by now, about Eve's two weeks of school. She adored it, and looked so grown up every morning as she left with her school bag, which contained only an eleven o'clock lunch, except when Eve slipped some plaything in. The teacher said she was one of the most self-willed children she had ever had but is anxious for me to send her back. I am not sending her back, however, as it is a long way from us, and Eve had to walk one way every day.

We are also joining a club very near us where Eve and I can go swimming every day, and be out in the open, which I think will be better for her than the school, as I felt sure the children were not in the open much. Eve certainly is not afraid of the water, as she went in the children's pool at the club with a little friend of hers while I sat by having morning tea, and while she was in, she stood on her head in the water.

I'll have to tell you something she said the other day. A little boy about five years old, named Douglas, who lives in a flat near us, came in to play with Eve's

And Indeed There Will Be Time (Sept. 1937—Aug.1939)

Christmas toys. They were alone in the lounge for some time and, after Douglas left, Eve said to Wilfred, "Douglas is not a gentleman."

Wilfred was naturally immediately anxious to hear more after that startling statement, so he said, "Why isn't Douglas a gentleman?"

Eve said, "Douglas acts like a gentleman, but he isn't a gentleman. Douglas kissed me like a gentleman, but he's just a little boy."

Five dollars per hundred points is what the stakes of some people were on the boat when playing bridge. I figured what I could lose in an evening and naturally stayed out. One day, a man paid more for his tickets on the ship's mileage than he won. They bid on the tickets ten over and ten below the Captain's number for the day; that was the Captain's guess on the knots run for the twenty-four hours, and quite often over $15 was bid for a single ticket. Money was nothing to most of those people.

Wilfred gave me a beautiful evening coat for my Christmas. It is Chinese and is reversible. One side is white fur and the other is embroidered on white satin. It is knee length and, I think, very lovely. I saw it in town and admired it is how I happened to get it. It came as a surprise, however, on Christmas morning. Bert and her father gave me a lovely pink and apple-green quilted bathrobe. It is lovely and warm, and they gave it to me because they knew how I suffered from the cold. Your package has not arrived yet, but I am sure it will. Bert has her flat rented to a girlfriend of hers who takes care of our mail for us.

Eve liked her Christmas fine, but it sounds more like a boy's Christmas than a girl's. She got a Mickey Mouse that runs on a railroad track, a battle ship that runs on the floor, blocks to build a house with, a beautifully-illustrated book, which she does not appreciate yet, as she colored two of the pictures with crayons before I discovered what was happening. She got a telephone that talks to her when she takes the receiver down and also has a bell on it for her to ring when she gets ready to dial it. There were lots of other little things that entertained her as much as these nice things.

Eve informs me, every once in a while, that she doesn't like this place as well as Mama Sophia's, and today she said it again. I don't think she will forget you before we get back, but I don't want to make her unhappy by talking about you all too much. I had a twelve lb. turkey for Christmas dinner and it was delicious. I supervised it closely. We had a very good dinner with plum pudding to end on. I missed having cranberries as usual, but you can't get them out here.

Wilfred's father has Sunday dinner with us every Sunday, and all holiday meals. He likes me very much, and that is perhaps because he only sees me about once a week. On Christmas night, he and Wilfred were down at his club, and he told Wilfred he wanted to give a toast to the finest thing that had ever happened in Wilfred's life: Helen.

Bert has had flu for the past week. She was taken sick Christmas eve and was in bed all through the holidays. This rather dampened our Christmas spirits. Today is her first day back at the office. Bert and I are still fond of each other and get along just fine.

Eve does not have a different accent yet, but some expressions from Bert, such as frock instead of dress, etc.

We got your wire on the *Queen Mary*. I am sorry if I never mentioned it. So much has happened that I am apt to overlook something when I write, even though I have it in mind to mention it before I start my letter. The picture of the three of us on the *Queen Mary* was made as we sailed out of New York but was not mailed until Southampton, of course.

I shall be awfully glad to get *The Reader's Digest*[15], as we buy it out here every month anyway. We also buy *Time*, even though it is a month old when we get it. The newspapers here are very local in their news. I get mad every time I read one, as I don't care a rap about the things they cover the pages with.

Eve is still feeling fine and still has a big appetite. Her breakfast usually consists of a glass of orange juice, a large bowl of oatmeal (porridge), bacon and egg, and a slice of bread. No one has to stand over her either. This is a larger breakfast than is consumed by anyone else in the family. For the rest of her meals, she eats either as much or nearly as much as any other grown person at the table. She is not fat but pretty and plump, and has grown quite a bit taller. She has had no sick spell since arriving in Johannesburg. She was a little upset the last day or so of the boat trip. I was very well on the boat and only felt bad after arriving here.

I knew Art Spencer and am very sorry to hear of his death. Pneumonia is the great danger here in Johannesburg, and I am scared to death of it, and always have been. It seems to me that everyone I talk with has had it at some time or other, or some member of the family had it during the past year. It is supposed to be from the dust from the mines. However, we live as far from them as it is possible to live, and I do not notice the dust being bad here; in fact, no worse than in Elizabethton. I am going down in one of the mines, perhaps this week, and will let you know all about it. Do you know that, although Johannesburg is 6,000 feet above sea level, some of the mines go below sea level?

I am sorry to hear things are so slack at home. They are not considered good here, but I am sure they are not that bad. There is still a great deal of building going on here, and, of course, there is little industry anyway, apart from mining. I had much rather be in America than here. A person may like to visit other

---

[15] Published in seventeen languages at this time, and with the highest subscription rate of any magazine, *The Reader's Digest* was considered by Americans, and others sympathetic to American ideals, to be a reputable source of news. Even though the content varied somewhat from country to country, the core values remained.

countries, but they usually like to live in their own country; but I feel very thankful that we are out, as Wilfred would have been worried continually about his job there with a depression on, and I wouldn't have felt good about mine either. (There isn't much chance for more than our salary for some time here, and it is worse than trying to live in New York City on it.) I can really think of nothing, but a few fresh vegetables, that is cheaper. Canned goods are sometimes as much as twice as high as at home. It is no wonder that this government is not in debt, as nearly everything must be imported, and they get a good slice out of everything that comes in.

I am very sorry to hear about Mrs. A.C. and Mrs. N. If Ruth gives in to Mrs. N., she has endless trouble on her hands for years. She had better be a little cruel now, dismiss the nurse, as nothing is wrong with her mother, and refuse her Luminol. If there is no one to wait on her, she can't stay helpless for long. See what I would do to you if you pulled that on me? I heard from Leone and Mary at Christmas time, also Aunt Lula,[16] and Uncle Earle, and Gladys. Gladys sent Eve socks, and Mary sent her two hair ribbons as well as an evening handkerchief for me.

I do not seem to have my big picture of Eve with me. Please let me know if it is at home. I would feel terrible if it is lost.

If you should ever want to cable me, just cable *Searsell* Johannesburg, as that is Wilfred's cable address. You know, in a cable, you have to pay for each word of the cable address, so it means quite a saving to have a cable address. This was necessary, of course, because he gets so many cables from Chicago.

Eve and Helen, 1937

---

[16] Helen's mother, Sophia Hunter Dixon, had six brothers. This meant that Helen had six uncles on her mother's side: Walter (wife, Lena; daughter, Hildred); Fred (unmarried); Earle (wife, Lula; daughter, Gladys); Charlie (wife, Elizabeth; son, Charles Harris); David (wife, Nellie; son, Eugene); Edwin (wife, Lennie; children, Helen, Kathryn). Sophia's only sister, Nellie, had died at the age of twelve. Helen also had two great aunts: Hattie and Ruth (their sister, Mollie Jobe Hunter, died in 1936). Helen's father, Harlow Shaw Dixon, had one brother: Hunter Dixon (wife, Kate; children, Gordon, Thomas), which meant another aunt, uncle, and two cousins for Helen. (See Family Tree at end of book.)

If this letter is disconnected, it is because Eve has been singing the whole time, or asking me questions. She is never quiet, but must be singing or talking always as she plays.

Eve needs bedroom slippers, as she has come completely through the ones she has. We were getting her some for Christmas, but your letter arrived on the day we intended buying them.

How is Uncle Charlie? I believe he was in the worst health of any of them when I left. I hope you won't hold anything back from me about any of the family. There is always something wrong with some of them, so I want to know who it is now.

I saw *Victoria the Great* yesterday. You must see the film. It seemed strange that it was to her grandson that we should all stand and pay homage to, just after the film is finished. At the end of every picture, one stands while a picture of the king is flashed on the screen and the national anthem is played. Did you know I am considered a British subject now? I couldn't help it, and I am wondering what trouble I am going to have when I am ready to come back to the U.S. Of course, I didn't have a change of sentiments,[17] but Great Britain just claims anyone in my position, and so it was written in my passport: "Landed as a British subject." I was afraid to make a fuss about it, as every country acts as though they aren't going to allow you to land anyway.

I am sure there is a lot more to write about, as I think of so much every day, but I have been writing all afternoon and feel quite tired.

Lots of love to all,

Helen

210 Killarney Court
Johannesburg, South Africa
January 22, 1938

Dearest Mother and Father,

The Christmas package from home arrived a few days ago, and we were delighted with it. Eve, for the first day or so, had to wear her blue slippers nearly all the time she was in the house, and I was so in need of panties I could hardly wait to get into my new ones. The package was beautifully done up and had not

---

[17] As her correspondence proceeds, it becomes clear that Helen was, in fact, deeply conflicted about her identity and her allegiance to America and Great Britain. The fact that she chose to adopt the English way of spelling—even when writing home—speaks to her ambivalence. And now, even as she proclaims her loyalty to the United States, she must have been wrestling inwardly with the seeds of her disaffection, which she only fully expresses six years later.

And Indeed There Will Be Time (Sept. 1937—Aug.1939) 95

been torn to pieces by the customs inspectors. I believe you asked me to let you know what I paid on it—I paid 2/3 or two shillings, three pence—in other words about 50 cents. Most of the charge was for inspection and clearance, just a few cents for duty.

Socks for Eve from Gladys, sent in an envelope, arrived duty free, also handkerchiefs for Eve from Aunt Lula and a handkerchief from Mary to me. If it is anything you can send in an envelope, do so, even if it is a large envelope. We also had the package from the Johnson City folks yesterday, which was very Christmasy and contained presents for all of us, and things we were delighted with. We only paid 4/- on it—that is, about $1.00.

I did not mind that things arrived after Christmas because it just made Christmas last longer. I think it was most thoughtful of all of them in Johnson City to send us a package. Katye Wray [who was married to Helen's first cousin, Eugene] seems to have done the compiling and mailing. She is always so full of holiday spirit.

Yesterday, I went to Pretoria with Wilfred, as he was going over on business. Pretoria is the capitol of the Union and is only about thirty-five miles from here, but this was my first trip over. The government buildings are beautiful, and the grounds perfectly lovely. They are terraced, and each terrace bordered with different flowers; one border was pink and blue, as far as the eye could see. It was terribly hot there, so hot that my legs shook under me while I climbed the many steps. It is one of the hottest places in the Union, much hotter than Johannesburg, because it is in a valley, whereas we are on a plain. The rest of the town is not much. Johannesburg is the only real city in the country.

I am writing on Wilfred's stationery, as I thought you would be interested in seeing it. I do all of Wilfred's correspondence, as Sears International is not what Sears, Roebuck is financially. They do not know I do it. They think Wilfred is doing it himself, which is impossible with all he has to do. He is going to tell them he cannot keep it all up, and try to get a small salary for me, say $30 per month. If I get this, I intend to save it so I can have a trip through Egypt, see the Pyramids, etc., on my way home. I think I just won't be able to stand it if I have to pass this by when my boat will be taking me so near to it all. In any case, I am coming back by the East Coast and shall see Madagascar and many other places; in fact, the boat makes so may stops that it takes six weeks to make this boat trip. Eve will be old enough to get quite a lot out of it too.

Tell Tootsie that she had better write to someone in India for a tiger-skin coat, as there are no tigers in Africa except in zoos, where they are quite a curiosity to the populace.

Eve is as brown as a berry from going in the baby pool at the club near us. She loves it there. I get no satisfaction out of bathing her now, as she looks the same after as before the bath. She eats everything, and quantities at that, and nothing seems to disagree with her. She ate a big slice of watermelon last night, and, when I looked up, she was into the rind. I was sure she would be sick, but she didn't have a pain, she says. The other day she said without any prompting, "I'll tell you how to get back to Mama Sophia. You get on the *Winchester Castle*, and then on the *Queen Mary*, and then you get on the train and then on the bus, and you are at Mama Sophia's." I think it is remarkable how she reversed the journey, boats and all.

I was awfully sorry to know that Eugene has been sick. Why don't you suggest water from Craig Healing Springs? I think it would be a good thing if you and Father drank plenty of it for a while too. Water at home is too free of minerals, I am afraid. I am glad Mama Dick feels like a new hat again and happy she is pleased with it. Tell her not to try to write me—to just give a message to you,[18] because I know what a terrible effort it is for her.

I sincerely hope you get rid of the termites in Johnson City. Be sure that any old wood taken out of the house is carried away to the back of the yard and burned. I think all requests of Mrs. L. are warranted. If we go into your debt over Eve's account in the bank, let me know, and I will send some money.

I shall send home to you for my shoes, as in all of Johannesburg there is only one pair that fits me, and they aren't so hot and are over $10. I haven't a foot that should live abroad. I'll try to make up my mind as to what I want in plenty of time to get it. Of course, the seasons being reversed makes it difficult too. I have seen Rhythm Step shoes here imported from America, and they are no more what they sell in America than if they weren't Rhythm Step. Much cheaper leather, and short vamp, which is the style here. Silk is much cheaper here than at home, and, if I could really sew, I would be O.K. They use silk for many things that we use cotton for because it is cheaper than cotton. America should do something about that. They must not have a competitive tariff compared with silk.[19]

For one thing, the infant dresses are all made of silk instead of batiste, and infant dresses happen to be of interest to me just now. I have been so sick that we are sure it must be a bad little boy on his way. I hope you won't feel upset that we decided we wanted a family instead of one spoiled little girl.[20] I feel just as well now as I did with Eve, but that is very recent, and you have had to suffer long silences from me just because I couldn't even write a letter. It wasn't that I was nauseated every minute, but, as well as being nauseated most of the time, I was

---

[18] Mrs. Virginia Dixon, Harlow's mother, was then ninety-one years old.

[19] After years of work at the Rayon Factory in Elizabethton, Helen had a keen interest in fabrics, while her interest in different woods and furniture had its roots in her father's previous occupation in lumber and furniture-making.

[20] This is typical of Helen's indirect way of broaching subjects that will have a big impact on her life and on the lives of her parents.

And Indeed There Will Be Time (Sept. 1937—Aug.1939) 97

very depressed, and I knew it would show that in anything I wrote. Now that I feel well again, I am perfectly contented that I am living here, and we really have a good time; but, for a while, Wilfred thought he would have to send me home. He offered to do it, but I had enough sense to know it was a temporary condition.

I found I was greatly relieved after I got a girl and had no responsibility. I could not stand for anything to depend on me. I was afraid I was getting a complex on that one thing, and that it might go too far with me, but now I am eager to be up and doing again. I really hope we have a boy this time. I have one of the best doctors in Johannesburg. I hear his praises from all sides. I have also had him look Eve over, and he says she is perfect. I have struck an epidemic of babies here, as every second woman one sees on the streets is expecting one. I have never seen anything like this at home. I must engage a room right away at a nursing home, as I understand many have been turned away because they could not accommodate any more. Sometime in August will be the birth date, I think. I do not want this broadcast, because I think it will make a nice surprise, and I hate things being whispered around anyway; so please keep this to yourselves.

Everything is sky high over here, so I want all useful things for Eve sent to me. Diapers are $5.00 per dozen; so, if there are any diapers worth having left, I would like to have them. In the parcel of second-hand things, do not enclose anything new, as they will be likely to slap a duty on the whole thing. Do not try to put anything over on them by washing something new, just strictly used things. After I get this parcel, which should include those shoes of Eve's in the attic, I can then tell what else I want to have you get for me in America. Write on this package: "Not dutiable, second-hand or used clothes." I would like for you to get these things off to me as soon as you can get them together.

I shall try to do much better about my writing now, but I do have a lot to do, doing Wilfred's work as well as running the house. My days seem to fly by, so I must be happy. I have no draggy days at all. I have a lot of other personal letters to write within the next week.

I think you made a big mistake by not going to Florida. One must have changes just to live. I may arrive home with the same clothes I left with, but I shall see some things before I get back. I suppose it would be a unanimous vote that I need to care a little more about clothes.

I am enclosing two pictures of Eve, taken by a lady on the *Winchester Castle*, and which I consider to be the best made on the trip of her. She is sitting just outside, or rather on the steps of what was known as the pavilion, or, at least, I think that was what it was called. Anyway, one could sit there in the open, at tables, and write or have tea, etc. This is the teddy bear I bought Eve with my prize money; it plays a nice tune.

I hope you are both well and that Father's business has not been affected too much by business slowing up. I am so sorry to learn that things are bad in America again. They are not supposed to be any too good out here, but these people do not really know what a depression is.

Eve says she wants to send you both love, and so do I.

Devotedly,

Helen

Postcard To: Reverend and Mrs. E. M. Umbach
Main Street
Elizabethton, Tennessee

Johannesburg
February 10, 1938

This photo will give you an idea of the rolling plains I am living on six thousand feet above sea level. This view was taken from a tearoom I visited last Sunday. Wilfred has been in Cape Town for the past ten days, so Eve and I are trying a new country quite alone. However, we find it a most friendly place. The Presbyterian Church here reminds one of its origins, as everyone in it is from Scotland. Kindest regards to all the family.

Helen Evans

210 Killarney Court
Johannesburg, South Africa
February 24, 1938

My dearest Mother and Father,

I shall try to write long easy letters at least every week or two, but I am afraid it will usually be two weeks between letters because a week passes so quickly, and sometimes there is really nothing to write about. You have the advantage of me since I know everyone at home and am interested in the happenings of the community. But here, we have no mutual background. Please do not worry about me, because I promise you, that in case of something going wrong, you shall be informed immediately. I think that is only fair on both sides, and it is the only way to be relieved of worry.

I had a good cry over Mama Dick [Helen's grandmother, her father's mother, pictured in her old age on page 64], and I do hope it isn't cancer. I suppose one must go with something at her age, but she must not be allowed to suffer. I have always said I could be reconciled in the death of an old person, but somehow she isn't old to me. It is because she has such a joy in living and a keen interest in everything. She has always been wonderful to me.

Indeed, I am shocked about K.R. Mr. and Mrs. R. have had more than their share with their family, it seems to me, and they should be a lesson in courage for the rest of us. K. must have drunk himself into debt, because I cannot think how else the money was used, as they lived in a most economical way, it seemed. If he had lived soberly, they could have lived well on his salary, having their home. Did you attend the funeral? I am sure you did. It must have been a very difficult one to conduct. I do feel very sorry for R., as it seems to me she has had nothing out of life for years, except terrific worries.

The bombing of the Gouge house in Hampton was a terrible thing. I suppose it has been nationally reported on.[21] I am anxious to see what those men get in our local courts—not what they deserve, I am willing to wager. It must have frightened Aunt Hattie, not to mention Aunt Ruth, to death. I take it they were in Hampton at the time since you say in your last letter that you were up to see them.

I should like very much to have the address of Mrs. Harry Miller's niece here in Johannesburg, and be sure to tell me all you know of the Harry Millers, as I don't know which ones they are. I haven't met any Americans, so far, though the town is full of them. Somehow, I feel no closer to Americans than South Africans, unless they have some connection with home—that is, Elizabethton, Johnson City, etc. You know how at home we feel with a New Yorker . . .

I attended the first meeting of my book club this morning. It is just like the one at home, and I feel that I am very fortunate in being asked to join such a club so soon after my arrival. The membership is limited to ten, and I found them all very congenial women. I have been exceptionally fortunate so far in the people I have met, since they are all people one would want to cultivate, and not a person yet that I must try to escape. I got into this club through the wife of the manager of a large firm of shippers here, with whom Wilfred is associated in a business way. We like both Mr. and Mrs. Wilson very much. It is their eight-year-old son who says he is going to marry Eve when he grows up. He has confided this to his mother, father, and sister separately. I am really sorry to discover Eve attracts them so early, and one so much older than herself is amazing. He is not the one who kissed her.

She is looking much prettier than she ever did at home because her face is very full now and she has a good color from playing out so much. She is many shades darker than you have ever seen her; in fact, I think she is much too dark for a blonde, but there is nothing to do about it. She started improving greatly when I started putting her to bed regularly at 7:00 in the evenings. She has a rest of an hour or more during the day, whether she sleeps or not. Eve plays the complete

---

[21] On January 6, 1938, as a result of a long-running business dispute, the home of Harmon Gouge of Hampton, Tennessee, was blown up. Harmon was not at home at the time, but his wife, Pauline, was seriously injured and their three little girls were killed.

weekend, that is, all day Saturday and Sunday, with a little friend who goes to school during the week, in the child's garden at her home. They have a wonderful big garden with a shallow pool with bridge across it, and here the two of them make mud pies the whole day long and have their lunch served to them outdoors, picnic-style. I visit there a great deal myself, where I must have coffee in the morning with cakes, lunch, and then tea in the afternoon. One finishes up such a day by mincing something a little each time, but never really enjoying a real meal the whole day because you have no appetite for lunch or your dinner in the evening. I must tell you that many of them also have tea just before going to bed at night.

To give you an idea of the life of ease lived here, even by the servants, I shall tell you what happened to me yesterday. The day before I had told my girl, Ellen (unfortunate, since I am Helen), to wash the curtains in my bedroom, two windows is all, and to get them back up as soon as possible since there was no privacy in that room without curtains—there is not a window shade in the whole country. She said she could wash and iron them the same day. That night, I found them lying in my room on the chair, clean. Yesterday, I was extremely busy all day typing for Wilfred, and it was after five in the afternoon before I had time to look round my flat to see how things were. The first thing I noticed was that my curtains hadn't been hung, so I went in to tell Ellen to hang them. She said, "Madam, I will have to get Jack (he is the flat boy who does the floors and the bathroom everyday) to put them up."

I said, "Why Ellen, because it is too high?"

She answered, "Yes, madam."

I went in for another look at the height of my windows, got up on my dressing table bench and easily took down one of the curtain rods. What I had to say after that made Ellen get the curtains up in the next ten minutes without Jack.

One must be everlastingly on the alert for such shirking of duty. If I had waited to let her get Jack to hang those curtains, she would never have been able to hang a curtain for me, or if I had become energetic myself and done it, which I could easily have done, I would have lost prestige immediately. If I go into the kitchen to cook something I want to do myself, she deserts the place and leaves the whole thing for me. There is a great deal of psychology in knowing how to handle them successfully, and even some people born in this country cannot manage them and have white help instead.

Mrs. Wilson, for instance, says she cannot get along with them and has a white woman as housekeeper, a wonderful person whom the children love like a mother, and a young white girl who does the cleaning. She is fortunate in having a house large enough to accommodate a white staff. She does keep a native boy for the garden. Every house here has a two-roomed house on the grounds for the natives. When you employ a native boy or girl, they must live on your premises, and if the

And Indeed There Will Be Time (Sept. 1937—Aug.1939) 101

boy wants to leave your premises at night, he must have his pass, signed by you for that night, or he is apt to land in a "gaol." That is the way it is spelled here, and tires is spelled "tyres." A dress is a "frock" and a living room a "lounge." It is such words as these that Eve has taken up, but there is no change in her accent.

In speaking of money, she uses the English denominations, such as shillings and pence. In speaking of towns in her play, she uses Cape Town, Durban, Bot River, etc. She often says we did so and so or said so and so in America. She asked me to stand as doorman at the entrance to her "club" today. Every day I see the influences of her travels in her play, things she couldn't have known about if she had not had this trip. She now uses a knife and fork when eating and has taken up the Continental and English way of manipulating them. Since she has started imitating the grown-ups, she has fits when she must put her serviette in the neck of her dress. I had to break myself of saying napkin immediately upon arrival, as that only means what is used on a baby's bottom.

I have finally succeeded in having a cold, and it was a bad one. Now I am sure most of my trouble was in the order of hay fever. I am almost over it now. Wilfred had a bad cold at the same time. Strangely enough, he caught his on the train coming up from Cape Town, and I met him at the train with mine. Fortunately, Eve did not take one.

Eve wrote the "E" for you all. I showed her the "E" in the typewriter and now she comes to me with E's in the magazines all the time. She gets such a thrill when she sees one. I also showed her the "V" but that does not occur often enough in print for her to find it. She wrote an "E" and brought it to me without my ever showing her how. She takes great pride in them now.

I have many letters to write but feel that so much is expected of a letter from me out here that I put them off for that reason.

I am glad the family in Johnson City are getting along very well now.

I got a letter from both of you in one day, so even though they are not written the same week they often arrive together. I appreciate it that you write me often, and please do keep it up, even if I don't always do so well. I especially appreciated the letter from father, as I know how difficult it is for you to write.

We are reading *Turning Wheels* just now ourselves. You can't buy it now, but we got it from Mrs. Wilson. It is a book club book of the club I have just joined. It was discussed this morning, and the South Africans there considered it authentic. A cousin of Stuart Cloete[22] was in the boat coming out from England. She is Lady Stanley and the wife of the Governor of Southern Rhodesia. We thought she was a

---

[22] Stuart Cloete, author of *Turning Wheels* and other books about South Africa, was a famous South African writer who lived in Hermanus in the Cape Province for many years. He was the author of fourteen novels, twelve collections of short stories, and eight collections of non-fiction.

sister but have found out since that that is incorrect. She was one of the judges of the fancy dress ball on the boat.

It is too terrible about the Elssner baby.

Eve wears sunbonnets to play in. The children out here still wear them, and they look so cute.

I shall have to give you another insight into the minds of these natives. When Wilfred went to Cape Town, he told Ellen to take very good care of Madam, and he would give her something extra, and he told the flat boy to watch after Madam and watch the flat, and he would give him something. He naturally had only my safety and my comfort in mind when making these requests. When he got back, he asked Jack if he had looked after Madam, and with that, Jack motioned him into a room where they wouldn't be heard and said, "Master, no other boss has been here while you were away, because I went in the early morning when she wouldn't be expecting me, and no man was ever there." Of course, it made me mad enough to die, but everyone else thinks it is choice and simply kill themselves laughing. I hope you all will see the funny side of it too.

Of course we have electricity and everything you have in America. At home voltage is 110, I believe; here it is 210/220. There can also be the difference of direct and indirect current to contend with, so when you go abroad to live, leave your electrical appliances at home, as in all probability they won't carry the correct voltage. If I should attach my iron or radio, they would just explode. Since I can do nothing with them for three years, I have thought of doing that, just for the excitement.

Much love to all the family and especially Dickie, with the greatest love and affection for yourselves.

Devotedly,
Helen

To: Mrs. David Hunter from Helen
Gump Addition
Johnson City, Tennessee

210 Killarney Court
Johannesburg, South Africa
March 15, 1938

My dearest Aunt Nellie,

I am so sorry to type a letter to you, but I know I will write much more this way than with pen and ink. The reason I have not written sooner is that I wanted to make it a real letter when I did write. Knowing that mother reads all of my letters to you all, I must have something new before I can write to one of the family, and

And Indeed There Will Be Time (Sept. 1937—Aug. 1939)

things do not happen so thick and fast, even in Johannesburg, which is supposed to be rather that way.

First of all, I want to thank you all for the beautiful box of presents sent us. Eve is enjoying her necklace very much and I my pin of initials. Wilfred's handkerchiefs were just what he likes, plenty of color, and he will write a note at the end of this letter. The customs officials had been most kind and had not torn all the packages to pieces, so they were still in their beautiful and artistic wrappings. I recognized the wrappings as either yours or Katye Wray's. We all want to thank you for being so thoughtful of us.

I must tell you that I served your chocolate ice cream and squash recipe at the first dinner I had my father-in-law to. He thought both dishes delicious. In fact, they were the only two things he commented on. They rather got me into trouble, as he has come around for every Sunday dinner since. He is really very lonely, as he lives quite alone; so, of course, I am glad to have him. [Eva Agatha Hudd Evans, William Evans's wife, pictured on page 16, had died some years before.]

Sunday, we took our picnic lunch and drove about forty miles out of Johannesburg to the Vaal River. That is the nearest river to us. This is a most uninteresting country for drives; one must go three hundred miles to reach another town of any size, and, in between, there is nothing but flat plains and scrub trees. To me, the most interesting thing on the drive was when we passed the mine dumps of the Robinson Deep Gold Mine, the deepest gold mine in the world. This is just as one leaves Johannesburg, but it is was the first time I had been close to the mine. They look very pretty at some distance, as they are so white and symmetrical.

We saw some funny sights near the compound of the mine.[23] The natives were enjoying themselves, as it was Sunday and a holiday. We passed one group dressed in skins only, and with bright plumes waving from their heads. They were dancing along to the rhythm of a perfectly wonderful big drum. They, no doubt, all owned an interest in that drum. Further on, we passed two native boys on bicycles, their ankles swathed with tails from some animal, their loins covered with leopard

---

[23] A "compound" in this context means a male-only dormitory, or series of dormitories, where black men from all regions of South Africa and beyond lived while employed on the mines. While leaving home and traveling to Johannesburg provided these men with work, it also destroyed the families and the cultures of the indigenous populations. While dreadfully exploited, the black population of South Africa has been spared the indignity of slavery. However, South Africa has known a slave trade. In 1653 the first slave, Abraham van Batavia was brought by the Dutch East India Company from Indonesia to the Cape. Others followed—from Mauritius, Madagascar, Angola, and Guinea. The indigenous people of the southwest tip of South Africa, the Hottentots (Khoikhoi), were also, in smaller measure, bought and sold into slavery. In 1806, Britain occupied the Cape, and in 1807 it ended the external slave trade. By 1834, Britain had put an end to the slave trade within the Cape Colony, a move that spurred the exodus of Afrikaner farmers from the area.

skins and one had on his head the crown of a woman's straw hat with a brilliantly pink plume waving from it. I must start carrying my camera with me, as one sees very funny sights even on the principal streets of the city.

This city is a paradox between the old and the new. These people pay about twice as much for a car here as we do in America, but they have them just the same, and I have never seen so many cars chauffer-driven any other place, unless it is New York. But still they must often poke along behind an ox wagon. Johannesburgers think this is the only city in the world. They are very conceited, and perhaps they have a right to be, because the place only started fifty years ago and most of the growth has been within the last four years. But still, I have to argue with them that they have the most wonderful climate in the world. I have nearly frozen all summer, and it is always cold the minute the sun goes down. I have never slept without a blanket and sometimes a comforter too.

Another thing that they refuse to take any notice of, and a thing I must bear in silence when it happens, are the earth tremors. I have felt the most terrible ones when I would be out for tea (the favorite way of entertaining), and not a soul would mention it. There is one cinema house here that I try to stay away from, as I have felt the most terrible tremors nearly every time I have been there. The first time it was so bad that hundreds of people ran out of the theater. I am sure they were not Johannesburgers, as the locals claim these tremors are merely caused by the framework in mines, no longer worked, caving in. Personally, I do not believe a word of it because I live three miles or more from any of the mines, and I have had to hold onto furniture here in my own flat. They are quite foolishly building tall buildings now, and their pride may cost them a lot one of these days.

My maid is leaving me tonight. I have had her a little over three months. She does her work well and is very clean, but she doesn't want to do much work, and that is what we came to blows about. It got to the point that she was spending two hours every morning out of the flat, and from three to four hours every afternoon. You see, there are native quarters attached to every apartment house, and one must rent a room for one's servant, as none of them are allowed to go home at night.[24] In any case, it would be too far away from where we live.

I had another girl call this morning about the job, but am going to try to do without one for a while at least. I feel like I want to try my hand at the cooking and see if I can become a good cook. I know I am the slowest thing that ever got into a kitchen, anyway. We shall perhaps put Eve in a kindergarten if I do my own work, so that I can get out occasionally. I already belong to a book club that meets every Thursday morning. My book just now is *Madame Curie*, a wonderful book.

---

[24] Even prior to the apartheid era, which began ten years later, in 1948, the movements of black workers outside the workplace were strictly controlled.

And Indeed There Will Be Time (Sept. 1937—Aug.1939)

Eve really needs a school now. As she is rather advanced for her age by her travels, she is also not easy to control, and perhaps someone who has made a study of children would do a much better job than I am doing. She is the greatest know-it-all that I have ever known. Already, she is of the opinion that her parents know nothing. I expected this with adolescence but not so soon as this. By her dresses, I can see that she is at least two to three inches taller than when we left home. She has filled out some too.

I have just finished making a silk dress for myself. It doesn't look too bad, even if I did make it. It should look all right, as I took infinite patience and did all the basting and pressing and notching that one is supposed to do as I went along. If one can sew well, there is no reason not to have clothes, as silks are much cheaper here than at home, but the ready-made things are sky high. This is true of everything, since practically everything is imported and these merchants won't think of less than 100% profit or, rather, mark-up. This is not an exaggeration, as we are in the business and know.

Mother has written me that Eugene and Katye Wray are in Mexico on a vacation, which Eugene needs very much. I am afraid Eugene will always overwork, but I do hope this trip will do him a lot of good. The small taste we had of Mexico has made me ever since want to really see that country. I hope they have gone to Mexico City, as I believe that is very beautiful. The altitude there might do Eugene some good. It may take a while to become acclimated, but I think to go to a higher altitude is very invigorating. I did not feel well here, at first, but I am feeling quite well now. I shall write Katye Wray and Eugene soon, and you can forward it to them, wherever they may be. I shall send it to your address instead of to their apartment.

Wilfred has taken up golf again, but it is taking him some time to get back into the game he once played, as that was a very good one.

Last night I had quite a thrill, as Wilfred talked to Chicago from our flat. He had a cable in the morning from the president of Sears International saying that he would call Wilfred at a certain time. We were excited somewhat all day, wondering just what the call might be about, and we were wrecks by the time it was over, as Wilfred could not hear any too well, and the call lasted ten to fifteen minutes. I wish they had sent us a present of the money expended for that, as it wasn't any too satisfactory anyway. We were sure it would clear up a certain matter about a dealership, but it didn't. It made me feel a little nearer home, for a while, anyway.

This is a letter for all, of course, and I send it with much love and affection. Eve's message is, "I love you Aunt Nellie, I send my love to you."

Helen

P.S. From Wilfred: I am enjoying the handkerchiefs tremendously. I have a suit to match every one of them—many thanks. Helen, I believe, is very happy in this country. What with bridge, book clubs, and the Country Club, she really spends a very full life.[25]

Regards,
Wilfred

March 20, 1938

My dearest Mother and Father,

We have just received your letter about poor Mama Dick and are all so sad that she has gone away, with us so far away that we do not even know about her passing for over a month afterwards. It is better that I did not know anything by cable because there would have been a whole month to wait for the details. Your letter told me everything that I would want to know about all of the circumstances, except the date of the funeral. It is so good that she went quickly and did not have to face death for a long time.

I got your letter yesterday morning when Eve and I were alone in the flat, and she was as comforting as she knew how to be. I was sitting in the lounge reading your letter and crying, and she came to me and asked me what was wrong and I told her. She said, "I will take care of you, honey." She left the room and next appeared with the little pillow off of her bed and put it behind me and told me to lean back and put my head on it; then she sat down in the chair beside me and asked me if I wouldn't like for her to tell me a bear story. I thought it was awfully sweet of her. I, too, am awfully thankful I had written Mama Dick from here; I was just planning to write her a second letter when your letter arrived.

Helen's Grandmother, Mama Dick, as a young woman

Where will Uncle Hunter live now? That is the question we have been asking

---

[25] If Wilfred's tone seems forced, it is because of his need to impress upon Helen's family that, given the opportunity to forge a career for himself, he is able to afford an extensive wardrobe as well as a leisurely life for Helen. Wilfred softened his tone considerably as the years went by.

And Indeed There Will Be Time (Sept. 1937—Aug.1939)

ourselves for a long time. I do hope Thomas will come to the fore better than I think he will.

You need not worry anymore about my health because I have now become acclimated and feel just as well as I ever did. In fact, I feel well enough to do my own work, which would have been impossible a short while ago. Last Tuesday, my native girl walked out on me. I could have made her give notice, as we would have had to give her a month's notice if we had been discharging her, but I know how they act if they are forced to stay on, so I paid her to date and had nothing to say. She was staying out of the flat for five or six hours every day, about two hours in the morning and three to four hours every afternoon, and I was paying her fifteen dollars for this.

My washwoman wasn't any good, so I decided to have the clothes washed by the laundry and let her iron them here, to give her something to do. I offered her a small raise of $1.25 for this extra because I thought she was getting enough anyway. This she refused, and so we had the parting of the ways. On top of this we had to pay $2.50 a month for her room. They eat so much bread, potatoes, and sugar that you simply can't keep in these items. When she first came to me, she would carry out to her room anything and everything left from a meal, no matter how much it was. This I very soon stopped. I now have the flat boy wash my dinner dishes as well as do the floors and bathroom every day. The second day after my girl left, I had ten ladies coming for tea, and this I managed alone very well too. Eve behaved like a lamb, played in the bedroom the whole time they were here.

I play bridge once a week, just one table. How I am to manage that and the book club every week in regard to Eve I do not know, for, unfortunately, I do not have a Dickie[26] to come in. It will be awfully hard coming to Elizabethton and not finding her there; I can't imagine the place without her.

I'm so glad to think the winter at home is nearly over. You have no idea how many times I have thought of you firing the furnace all winter through. You must not do this another winter, as I am absolutely sure it is much too hard for you and very injurious to your health. If you want a smaller place, take it, because Eve and I will feel at home wherever you may happen to live when we arrive back, as you were always able to make any place seem like home, even the rooms over Simerly's store.[27] I have thought of that often, since I have been out here, and feel that I do not have that knack at all. Perhaps one reason is that I scarcely have

---

[26] Mrs. Virginia Dixon, Harlow Dixon's mother, was also known to the family as "Mama Dick" ("Dickie"). Dickie had been a great help to Sophia while she was raising Eve.

[27] I can only assume that the Dixons stayed over *Simerly* store in Elizabethton at the time of their transition from "G" Street to Broad Street.

anything of my own around. It is really terrible living with other people's furniture all the time, as one continues to feel like one is living in a hotel. I would feel no different if I bought furniture, however, as it would all be new to me, and there would be no feeling of permanency about owning it, because, when we leave here, we would naturally have to sell everything.

I have made a tour of the maternity homes here, and it was most discouraging. I went first to the Queen Victoria, considered the best, and they were booked up through next October. I have heard that people booked there a year ahead, which seems ridiculous, since one only knows nine months ahead, but now I believe it is nearly true. I then went to the Clarendon, which was too terrible for words. The woman who runs it informed me that she put the babies out of doors winter or summer, on the second or third day, and took me out to see her babies. They were sleeping in their baskets on a screened-in porch, with a dog sleeping under them in his basket, and another dog wandering around. Two young children wandered around looking at them too. The door leading to the porch had no screen and led off the hallway just before the door to the kitchen, where there was the usual noise from pots and pans. They also had no way of heating the rooms, even when bathing the patient. She also told me that the patient was hauled out of doors herself, as soon as possible. Since I shall be going during the worst of the winter out here, I decided my constitution could not take it, so we thanked her and left.

We were feeling very dejected when we discovered a perfectly gorgeous nursing home still under construction. It will be open by the time I shall want in, and it is too beautiful for words, with air-conditioning and heat in every room, installed and general electric. They have incubators, etc., so you can get an idea of how modern it is. It is terribly expensive, but at that, only ten dollars more a week than the one I last described. It is very conveniently located too, coming out from the city toward where we live. It is certainly needed here and should coin money.

I have made my own maternity dress and did a very good job on it. The only trouble is that it makes me look bigger than my ordinary dresses do. The ready-mades in town looked even worse, however, so I should be satisfied.

Canned goods are so expensive here that I don't know what we are to do this winter when the green vegetables are no longer coming in. I think the best thing to do would be for you to have shipped to me, right away, the following:

24 cans asparagus
24 cans chili con carne
24 cans baked beans

Of course, if you can possibly manage to get them wholesale, that would be splendid, but even retail I'm sure I will come out much better, with duty and freight, than I do as it is. I can send a draft for the amount when I know how much it is.

I shall be writing you to get me some little dresses for the baby, as the dresses here are not what we are used to at all, and I can't imagine using them; furthermore, they cost five dollars and over for a decent-looking one. They put infants in silk dresses, and I think it is too tacky for words. They use flannel dresses for the winter, which is no doubt necessary, since they have no heat. I wish I could make up my mind as to just what I had better get, but, so far, I have not been able to do so.

Did Dickie look younger, like Mama Hunter[28] did? I am sure she looked very pretty and sweet. I know you did everything very well. Anyone who does things is always criticized by someone. The only way to avoid criticism is never to do anything.

Worlds of love and kisses,

Helen

210 Killarney Court
Johannesburg, South Africa
March 28, 1938

My dearest Mother and Dad,

It seems that the more I have to do, the more energetic I become, as here I am writing a letter for the very next mail boat; one week is all we have.

Such a ten days as I have had. There has been an epidemic of small pox in South Africa, with quite a few cases in Johannesburg, several hundred Natives in one compound, so everyone has been vaccinated, Europeans and Natives (whites and negroes, we would say at home). It has been considered so serious that no one from South Africa was allowed to land in England, the Continent, or America without having a recent vaccination. Naturally, we felt that Eve must be done, so she was done ten days ago. Such a sick child as she has been—ever since the third day. She has been in bed twice with the doctor to see her.[29] The first time she ran a very high fever of 104 and had a bad throat. This time (she is still in bed) she does not have a fever, but she has a bad throat and a lump on her side, as she was done on the leg. I think she will be able to get up tomorrow. She has been in bed three

---

[28] My sister, Eve, remembers, as a three-year-old, seeing the casket of Mollie Jobe Hunter under the window in the living room in the house on Broad Street. She recalls being lifted up to see her great-grandmother. Since Mama Hunter looked as though she were asleep, Eve reached out her hand, wanting to open her eyes, but was held back.

[29] Doctors in South Africa made house calls routinely during the 1940s and later. Some still do.

days this last time. She is rather beginning to like the idea of her invalidism, and often refers to her "sickness."

On top of Eve's "sickness," Wilfred has been in bed four days with the worst cold I have ever seen him have. He hopes to get up tomorrow too, as he is much better tonight. Of course, this spell of sickness would hit us when I have no maid. I have run with trays and answering calls from morning to night all this time. They have been in separate rooms on account of Wilfred's severe cold. If I could have made them into a ward, it would have been some easier. Fortunately, I was not vaccinated. I intended to be done the same morning Eve was done, but since I wanted it on my leg, my doctor refused because of my condition. There is nothing to worry about in Eve's condition now, and she is safe for seven years. In this country, one must simply be vaccinated for small pox, as epidemics are always breaking out among the Natives, and one's cook sits in the Native buses, etc., so there is always the danger of infection.

I have just finished reading *Madame Curie*, which is the book I bought for my book in the book club. It is a wonderfully inspirational book to read, and I hope you will get the opportunity soon. Try to get it. I know you must have been disgusted with *Turning Wheels*. I read a little of it, but it was so nauseating that I did not bother to finish it. I thought if I had to learn about Africa from it, I would just remain in ignorance. Nearly everyone here thought it was a vulgar book.

We are having beautiful weather now. Since the first of March, the days and nights have been perfect, just like our summers in Elizabethton. Next month is supposed to be a beautiful month; in fact, it does not get cold until June, so you don't need to worry about me until then.

If I prepare something to eat that Eve considers good, she will invariably say, "This is marvelous. Mama Sophia cooks good things too." Or, if it is something she has had at your place, like asparagus soup, etc., she will say, "I used to eat this at Mama Sophia's." She certainly hasn't forgotten. If we go walking, she will say, "Papa Harlow and I used to go walking." I know you miss her terribly, and it makes me feel bad that we cannot share her.

I wish you would send me your recipe for hot rolls. I want to educate these people. I give them hot biscuits now, and they like it.[30] Be sure to tell me everything, as I am not an expert cook, you know. I have an electric stove with a register on the oven, so tell me at what degree to bake them. I also have a Norge refrigerator, so you see I have a very modern kitchen.

---

[30] Helen's use of "these people" and "they" is typical of the immigrants' view of their new country as different, "foreign," or "other." It is informative to watch Helen's transformation from stranger or foreigner into identification with her new country and her slow move toward viewing the United States as "foreign" or "other."

And Indeed There Will Be Time (Sept. 1937—Aug.1939) 111

Bert is packing up at her old flat tonight. She has had it sub-leased furnished, but the girl is giving it up at the end of this month, so Bert must put things in storage. She will be with us for another two months, and will then go back to a flat of her own as we will have enough family of our own by the time the baby arrives. She is a wonderfully sweet girl and very helpful in the house since I have no help; however, yesterday she did the unbelievable. She, of course, knew that Wilfred and Eve were both sick in bed. She left the house at nine o'clock to play golf and returned at one-thirty with her young man at dinner. He came as a complete surprise just as I was taking out dinner. I had two trays to fix and then dinner to serve. I could have understood a nineteen-year-old doing that but not someone thirty-five. He then stayed the whole afternoon and until ten o'clock last night. They went out for a walk about seven-thirty, and when she came back, she saw me making sandwiches (there happened to be only two, one for Wilfred and one for myself). She must have thought I was trying to martyr myself, for she said, "Julian doesn't want anything to eat; don't fix any sandwiches."

My reply was, "It's a good thing he doesn't; these are for Wilfred and myself." Don't mention this in any letter when you write back, but I can tell you I was irritated. I believe whenever you run a home you are apt to be ringed in a time or two like that, but I shan't limply accept my fate often, because I can say, if necessary, there is nothing to eat here today. If she were in the habit of doing such things, I would have been very rude, but, as I say, she is such a help to me that I naturally kept quiet for this one time.

We are now paying 64 cents a dozen for eggs; in fact, we have been for some time. Butter and eggs are always high. Speaking of groceries, I find I can save one pound, that is, $5 a week, on my grocery bill by doing the work myself. It was actually a difference of $9 last week, but I do not think it will average a saving of more than $5 a week. If a servant only cost their wages, one could afford to have them, but I am sure my Ellen cost me $35 to $40 a month. The reason I did not get another girl right away was that I wanted to find out just how much they cost in all. If I keep well, I intend to do without, until June anyway, and save that much. It wouldn't be so hard if everyone were well and things were running normally.

Did E. J. ever go to live with her husband? I just happened to think of her last night. Isn't there any gossip or scandal? Of course, you and I never heard it until it was practically dead anyway.

Must close and go to bed, as Eve wakes me a time or two through the night, and I must get my sleep in some way.

The bedroom slippers you sent Eve are almost too small already. She can't wear any of the shoes she had when she left America. She has a pair of black patent leather ones now that she thinks are wonderful—just because she never had black before.

My first copy of *The Reader's Digest* has arrived. It is a most welcome gift every month. I always enjoy it thoroughly. They have no good South African magazines, and the English ones copying *Time* and *Reader's Digest* do not come up to the American editions. The newspapers are so local in their reading matter that we get practically nothing there, so we are always behind with our news, so we wait on *Time*.

Lots and Lots of Love from your little girls,

Helen and Eve

210 Killarney Court
Johannesburg, South Africa
April 13, 1938

My dearest Mother and Father,

Today, I received mother's letter telling me of her eight days' illness. I do hope your throat is entirely all right long before the writing of this letter. I am so sorry you have had such a bad spell. You must be run down; perhaps the winter firing of the furnace was too much, as well as the attendance at the trial. Please let me know how that comes out, and who the lawyers in the case were.

We, too, have had our bout of sickness. After Eve's first illness I wrote you about, she was back in bed for two weeks with sore throat, earache, eyes hurting, and a lump in her side. She is up now, but I watch her very closely and make her rest a great deal. If I had known she would have had so much trouble with her vaccination, I would never have had it done. The scabs just came off yesterday, and she still has the lump in her side. I had to put hot fomentations on her vaccination for days, and the other day she informed me that she was glad I didn't have to put "hot-tations" on her leg anymore.

During the whole of Eve's sickness, I had Wilfred sick in bed; in fact, he was in bed much longer. He had terrific pain from his sinus after having flu. He has been examined by the best specialist in Johannesburg for that particular trouble, and has been X-rayed. Dr. Campbell has told him that he must have an operation as soon as the present trouble has cleared up, or it may mean his death one day. He will go into hospital a week from today. They must straighten the bone in his nose, caused by his automobile accident several years ago, as this is what has started the sinus trouble. They must also open up the sinus. He is dreading the operation a great deal, and we all know it is very painful.

One good thing is we all have great confidence in his doctor. We had the family doctor with Eve three or four times, and Wilfred had his eyes examined, as well as his nose, by another doctor, so we shall have some nice doctor bills, all of which come at a most unfortunate time, as we need to be saving for other things. I can tell you, I have had my hands full with the two of them sick and doing all of

And Indeed There Will Be Time (Sept. 1937—Aug.1939) 113

my housework myself. Wilfred had to be in a dark room for three days on account of his eyes, as the nerves in his eyes were terribly inflamed.[31] The eye specialist also found that his present glasses are too strong.

Thank you very much for the pretty linen handkerchief enclosed in your last letter. I also received the box of baby clothes yesterday and find much that will be of value to me and save me some money. I did not have to pay any duty but the usual inspection fee. Remember that it is always better to make up one large package to me than to send several small ones, as the most expense comes in the inspection fee for each package. Thanks very much for getting all of these things together for me. I have the slipcovers for the down puff Mrs. Vriesen made.

I hope Uncle Hunter [Harlow's brother] gets a job in Cincinnati, as it would mean so much to him as well as to the whole family to get him located. I am not at all surprised by Thomas's attitude [Uncle Hunter's son]. I believe Thomas would even leave his father in the streets hungry before he would do anything for him. Thomas is so stingy he will not even enjoy his own money but lives on perhaps $50 a month out of what he makes. He is a born miser and cannot help it. [On his death, years later, Thomas Dixon left all of his money to the church.]

I am glad you are getting the house and walk fixed up for Mrs. L. Do you think they will lease it for the next year? I hope so, as I hate any change, and one is sure of the rent from them. If you have any reason to think, by other rents in Johnson City, that I have a chance to get $65 this next year, try to get it for me. I wish that house were in Johannesburg. I would get $150 a month for it. That is no exaggeration, so you can see what we are up against. We were offered a three-room house for $62.50 not long ago, but we must have another bedroom or we would have jumped on it.

I shall tell you the following in strictest confidence. It was reported in a trade journal in America that Sears International would perhaps liquidate in June. This was denied to us by the Vice-President of Sears International. However, a very big New York banker has just been to Johannesburg, and Wilfred met him because of his connection with Sears, and this man told Wilfred in confidence that such a thing must happen to Sears International. Well, you can imagine how up in the air

---

[31] Wilfred was in all likelihood suffering from iritis, a painful inflammation of the iris of the eye. Its symptoms are excruciating pain, sensitivity to light, and blurred vision. Left untreated, iritis may lead to blindness or glaucoma. Iritis can be a symptom of untreated gluten intolerance, its most severe form being celiac disease, a condition resulting from a genetic intolerance of wheat, barley, and rye. Ingestion of these foods robs the sufferer of essential B vitamins, which leads not only to inflammation of the intestines, but to anxiety and depression. Since Wilfred was hospitalized for two weeks in 1942 with colitis, an inflammation of the large intestine, it is possible that he also suffered from untreated celiac disease or inflammation of the small intestine, a condition that affects five of his descendants.

we feel, since Wilfred's contract is subject to immediate cancellation. They must bring the whole family back to America, however, so that is that much. Their prices are too high on everything except radios, and, with all that, Wilfred has written them, giving them other landed prices of refrigerators, in particular. But they simply say they cannot lower their prices.

For instance, in America, Norge sells at a much higher price than Coldspot refrigerator, but it lands out here much lower than Coldspot; in fact, Coldspot lands at a price as high as General Electric and Frigidaire, and they are advertised here as extensively as in America, but, of course, Coldspot isn't. What chance do they think they have with such a set-up?

Since I write all the correspondence, I am right up with the whole thing, and I can tell you it is impossible to get an answer from them on any important decision. But they send us more junk in the way of literature on everything imaginable, as well as business leads that would, perhaps, mean the sale of three refrigerators a year, whereas Wilfred has the chance to make a connection with one firm to take 2000 refrigerators a year if they will get their prices right. He also can get a huge radio contract for the whole Union and the Rhodesias if they will make a radio with a thirteen-meter band and a lowboy model, which is the popular style out here. On these two big deals, he has been waiting over two months for a decision, and they even called him from Chicago to ask more questions. But no decision is forthcoming, and it is simply distracting, as one cannot hold people indefinitely; there are too many people after the business.

Competition is just as keen here as in America, as every large business is represented. Most of the automobiles are American, and all of the refrigerators are American makes. You cannot mention any of this, but do not be surprised at what may happen. It was, perhaps, a very bad move on our part that Wilfred took this job, as it is hard to prove that you are not to blame in the least for bad business. I think worry has brought on a lot of Wilfred's trouble, but it does little good to say, "Don't worry!" when he knows what he does. Due to my fortunate disposition, I am not worried. I am sure I have father to thank for that in my make-up.

I have told Eve where Robin is—that is what we have all started calling the new baby. She asks me any time of the day if he is kicking, and dozens of other questions. She decided, all by herself, that he is coming out of my mouth, and remarked that my mouth was quite large enough for that but that it would be too bad if he had to come out of Wilfred's mouth. When Eve wants to be real chummy, she calls me Helen and her Daddy Wilfred.

I can tell you that Bert is not larger than me; in fact, she is a very small person, wearing a number 8 stocking when she can find one, tiny shoes, etc. She is much shorter than I am and smaller across the shoulders and hips, and everyplace, in fact. She is a very pretty girl and most vivacious and attractive. Men, and women too, always notice her and admire her. She is very capable in every way and the

And Indeed There Will Be Time (Sept. 1937—Aug.1939) 115

quickest person I have ever known in everything she does. No one can keep up with her and what she can accomplish.[32] She is extremely fond of Eve, and Eve loves her. Mr. Evans is very fond of Eve, but Eve is hardly ever nice to him. She called him "Old ugly face" the other day. I have heard from the outside that he has left her a nice sum in his will, so I do wish she would be nice to him, as, if there were not the blood tie, I am sure he would feel like cutting her out of his will. She has a terrible name of being cheeky around the flats.[33] Even the superintendent's wife said it to me. She is not more like I was at her age than anything, and it seems to me we shall have to send her to school to get some of this out of her.

Wilfred's sister, Bert

Eve watched me wash out my sink in the kitchen today, and she said, "I never saw a Mother wash out a sink before—that is for a maid to do." I can tell you she is a real South African in her ideas on that subject. My friends send me maids all the time and think I am going to kill myself doing my work. The women simply do nothing out here but try to manage a large staff of servants. I think they would nearly all qualify as generals in the next war.

I am sorry to hear of Aunt Lula's bad turn and also of I.'s and C.'s trouble. I am sure he leads her a devil of an existence. Has Bill Jenkins ever married?

Eve and I miss you all terribly sometimes, and are always conscious of our loss that we cannot be with you, but it seems my life was not patterned to run along a smooth, straight course, near family and friends.

I have been kindly received here, my best friend being a Mrs. Vanzalingen, whose husband is director of Phillips Radios and Lights in South Africa. He has an organization of seventy-three men working for him, and this means a very big job, of course. They have everything they wish for. I am spending the day with her tomorrow and know I shall enjoy it, as she has a large garden to sit in and a little girl to play with Eve. The little girl is not her own, but by his first marriage, and she is expecting a baby the first of August. You need not expect any word from me along that line until July 15. I think it will more likely be in August. I cannot give

---

[32] Years later, I remember our Auntie Bert making two dresses in one morning—one for Eve and one for me—to wear to a matinee at the local movie house which she owned and managed at that time.

[33] A "flat" is the English term for an "apartment."

you any more definite time. I was gaining too much before I started doing my work, but have stopped gaining now, and I think I am just about normal size. I keep well and have no more sickness.

Do you know how Knaffl is getting along? I have not had an answer to my letter to Mary, and, if I do get one, she will not say anything about business.

You may get tired of typed letters from me, but I could not find the time nor the strength for such long letters if I wrote them long hand.

Worlds of love and kisses from Eve and your Helen

210 Killarney Court
Johannesburg, South Africa
April 27, 1938

My dearest Mother and Father,

I hate to miss a week writing to you, but my weeks are so full that it seems I can't help it at times. At least my whole family is up and well again. Eve is looking healthier than ever and has grown so much that I don't believe you could ever fit her in clothes, as you could have no conception of her size. I received the two pairs of socks for her, and they will barely go on; they should have been a size larger. The blue striped one is so pretty. I shall let her get as much wear out of them as possible right away.

Eve asked me to do something special for her tonight, and I said, "Oh, I can't do that."

She said, "Be a good sport."

To her, a "dress" is now a "frock," and she is always asking me if I don't think she is "clever," whereas we would say "smart." She even came in and pronounced one of the little boys in the flats as being a "silly ass." You will notice a decided English influence in her speech. She is now very taken up with painting in watercolors. I can hardly get her out of the house since Easter, when she received this set. She has been writing an E and an H for some time now, but just two days ago she came to me with her complete name printed EVE. She felt terribly proud of herself. She shows great interest in learning, as long as you do not push her; then she refuses to do a thing. Left alone, she picks up such things.

I was so sorry to hear about little Joe Baughman being struck, and I hope he has received no permanent injury. I shall write him a card from Eve or write Elizabeth. I was also sorry to hear about W.D. I always knew they couldn't live as they did on his salary. How foolish people are to make life easier for themselves for a while, and then have to pay so bitterly for it all. I suppose M.'s trip was their last fling for her. I hope nothing too serious develops for him from it all. How in the world did V.J. get the job? I am glad enough to see him get it, for she has worked so hard all these years. I shall write the E. girls about their father.

And Indeed There Will Be Time (Sept. 1937—Aug.1939)

Since my last letter, giving a rather discouraging picture of our business out here, we have had a cable from the president of Sears International, Mr. Artamonoff [who was, apparently, the son of the famous Russian General Artamonov], saying he will be here the middle of May, which is only a little over two weeks off. We are delighted, for he can then see conditions for himself and make some decisions so necessary for the business to go on. He made this decision to come after talking to Mr. Appleby, the banker, who has just been out here.

I shall certainly be looking forward to the box you are sending me for the baby. I am glad you wrote me what you are sending, as I shall not duplicate. I was just getting ready to make some gowns but won't need to now. I went out to play bridge this afternoon, and one of the ladies presented me with a lovely knit sacque and two pairs of bootees that she had made herself. I thought it was awfully nice of her, as I have only played bridge with her about five or six times. It looks like I am going to have to buy very little outside of a bassinet. I must give a very nice present to my Hollander friend who is going to have a baby shortly after me, as she has offered to keep Eve at her house for the two weeks I will be in hospital. I think it is one of the biggest things I ever heard of anyone doing.

Do not worry about our expenses, as for once we are well fixed in that respect. It has certainly been impossible for us to save any money so far out of Wilfred's salary, but, the first of May, Wilfred comes into some money, about $500 left him by his mother. This will take care of my hospital expenses and the many doctors' bills of Wilfred and Eve's. Out of it will also come the money that Wilfred still owes Mrs. Vriesen. Mrs. Vriesen's son, in Bloemfontein, is going back to Germany in May and will take the money with him. I shall be very happy to see this paid. Wilfred's father informed him that he had done nothing to deserve this money, that Bert should have it, but I did a little informing myself, and said I had had it hard long enough and this was my chance to have proper attention in a good hospital and not have to worry about bills, and I intended to have it. If we had plenty of money, I too think Bert should have it, but not under the circumstances, when Wilfred's mother wanted him to have it.

Bert is leaving the end of this month and taking a room in a block of flats in town.

I would write more, but I want this to get off on this mail.

Lots of love,

Helen

P.S. Send me the formula and the schedule we used for Eve, if you have it or can get it, and what condensed milk we used for her.

210 Killarney Court
Johannesburg, South Africa
May 2, 1938

Dearest Mother and Father,

I know you will be glad to get the enclosed snaps. I shall make a few comments on each:

1. Is a picture of Killarney Court. I have marked the windows of my flat with an "x." There is still another window on the other side, as this building is built around a back court; in fact, all of the apartment houses are built that way. Our porch is a very nice size, as you can see. The flat just in front of mine on the corner rents for $150 a month unfurnished. All on that corner do. All that you see is Killarney Court. Perhaps Mrs. Gilliam would be surprised to know that we live in such a swank place. I have to laugh every time I think of her exalted opinion of the Alexander Apts.

2. Is a picture of Eve. The way it happened was that she was playing just there one afternoon, and I thought what a cute picture it would make and snapped it. The bird is hers, a gift from her Auntie Bert. His name is Peter. He is a budgery, and although he is small, he is of the parrot family. If kept away from other birds, he can be taught to talk just like a parrot. Ours has too many birds around him in the other flats so cannot talk.

3. Is of Eve and Mickey Vanzalingen taken in the garden of the Vanzalingen home. Eve is invited there every week for the day. Yesterday, she spent the day there with two other little girls, and they have home movies in the afternoon, which Wilfred and I went to see too. First, a picture about the Dionne Quints[34], and then the *Life of Edward VIII*. I think I have written you that Eve has been invited to stay with these people when I am in hospital. Mickey is seven years old, but Eve holds her own very well.

4. Is a picture of Eve when she was out on a picnic with Bert and some of Bert's friends at Eastertime. She had a wonderful day, I understand.[35]

Eve had a very exciting Easter this year. Wilfred and I gave her a very pretty green flannel bathrobe, which she needed badly, as you remember. You will wonder why I bought green when she had new blue slippers from you, but it was the only color they had in her size. I selected a rose one at first, but it was too small for her. Bert gave her watercolors and a painting book, and her grandfather

---

[34] This is a reference to the famous Dionne Quintuplets, born May 28, 1934, in Ontario, Canada—the first quintuplets known to survive infancy. They became world-famous and a significant tourist attraction for Ontario; at least two movies were made about them.

[35] Since many of the photographs have not survived, the pictures that appear in the text do not always correspond with those promised in the letters.

And Indeed There Will Be Time (Sept. 1937—Aug.1939) 119

gave her a chocolate egg. Easter Sunday afternoon she went to the Vanzalingens for an egg hunt and came home with beautiful things—rabbits, chickens, eggs hand-painted and chocolate ones, an egg cup and a mug, and I don't know what else. Just a day or so ago, your very lovely Easter card arrived for her, and I read her the little story. I had never known that one could buy such an appropriate card for a child. She likes it very much. On Easter Monday, Eve went on the picnic with Bert for the whole day. People seem to like to have her, as she is so sweet and good. I think she is better away from me.

I don't suppose I have written you that we must move the first of June. We will always be moving because we have no furniture. We could only have this flat for six months, and this month is our last month. I am not at all sorry because the rent is too steep, and Bert is not here this month to help out with the $35 she paid us. That did not amount to much on the amount we are paying here, however.

Bert moved the last day of April into a flat of her own in town. We have found for ourselves a lovely furnished house, and we are delighted. We will have a lounge, dining room, kitchen, and three bedrooms and bath for eight months. It is in a good section of town; in fact, the approach to it is beautiful. We are near the largest park of the city in which they have a lake and boats and a swimming pool. It is just a nice walk from our new place, but then we won't be terribly interested in the park as we shall have a bit of ground of our own.

The place is a bargain for Johannesburg, and I can't understand them renting it for that price—$80 a month. We thought we would have to live in a dump if we found something at that figure. I had decided that we would—before I again paid the rent we are now paying. We shall be much more comfortable in the house than in the flat we are now in, as Eve will have a yard to play in, and the house has two open fireplaces, one in the lounge and one in the dining room. We are buying two electric heaters for the bedrooms.

One of the nicest things about it is that one bedroom is furnished for a little girl—it is in green and just the right size of furniture for Eve—bed, dressing table, wardrobe, and chairs. She is going to be thrilled to death with that. We needed three bedrooms, but I never dreamed I could have them at the price we could afford to pay. The large bedroom has twin beds, which is so much nicer than the double bed we have at present. The third room I shall use for the nursery. The bathroom is tiled and all fixtures are in green. It is one of the prettiest ones I have ever seen. There is an automatic electric hot water heater as well as a GE stove and a Crosley refrigerator.

Everything is furnished but the linens, and I have some myself and shall buy some more. I can't blame anyone for not wanting those things used for eight months. I shall perhaps take over the native girl who is staying there. She is a Zulu and they are the most honest of all the natives and, too, she hasn't been down long from Zululand, which is an advantage in many respects as when they are city

Negroes they are usually too fresh. I must have a girl as soon as we go into a house, as I shall have no one to do the floors there, and you have no idea how floors are kept in this country—done with wax every day. Too, I must know I have a good, reliable girl before I go to the hospital.

Bert continued to impose on me. She had her young man here three weekends straight running for Saturday night supper and Sunday dinner and Sunday night snacks. This was the three weeks I had both Wilfred and Eve sick in bed. She did not ask me one time if she could have him, just brought him in. I was determined that I would say nothing, as she was going into a place of her own June 1st anyway, and she is a marvelously sweet girl, and I like her very much, but the whole thing was too much for Wilfred. He could see I was worked to death; in fact, anyone should know that I was, with two sick for so long and all the cooking and cleaning to do myself.

Bert got awfully mad when Wilfred called her down about it and reminded her that she did not bring guests in unannounced on her Mother, so why should she do it with me. Her boyfriend had never even so much as taken us out to a meal. He had sent some flowers to Bert, me, and Eve during the sickness, but that was all he had ever done.

So much feeling sprang up over the whole thing that she moved a month early. This is the last time I shall ever try to live with anyone else, unless dire need makes it necessary. I don't believe it can be done because I certainly liked Bert, and she is really a wonderful person, and I can't imagine why she was so inconsiderate of me. I was not out of the house for three weeks, and she played golf those three weekends and came in on me for meals for the two of them.

I shall be glad when I have a cook again, as I believe cooking makes one feel like the biggest martyr in the world. A meal you spend two hours preparing is eaten up in half an hour and not a murmur from anyone about it being good. All you have to go by are the clean plates you carry back to the kitchen. I can understand you better now and sympathize. Everyone takes the housewife too much for granted and seems to think that she should be satisfied with her pots and pans. I can turn out a pretty good meal rather easily now, and I get a lot of personal satisfaction out of that, but it was something I always felt I couldn't do. If you mention any of this in a letter, write it on a separate sheet of paper that has no connection with the rest of your letter.

I am delighted with the things you have bought for the baby, and I can think of nothing else that is needed. I am making two pinning blankets myself.

I am keeping Eve's ring all right, as I wear it all the time. I know of no better way to safeguard it.

It is too crazy for words that they got an appointment for West Point for Bob C. He can't possibly pass his exams, and they should know it. They will only make his inferiority complex worse by such things.

It sounds like you have some pretty clothes for the spring. You once asked me what I bought in London. It was so little that it was hardly worth writing about. I bought a black lace dinner dress for about $8.00, which is surprisingly pretty. I also bought a black and white linen dress for about $10, and a black felt hat with veil. That was all for me, as Wilfred had to have a dinner suit with accessories before he could get on the boat, and our expenses were pretty heavy.

It is not easy going from a small job to a rather big one, as one's wardrobe is not equipped with even the necessary things for the new life. Eve had plenty of clothes and was complimented quite often. I felt all right in what I had too. My silk underclothes and wash silk dresses have fallen to pieces. I don't know whether it is the change in climate, the voyage, or age, but I must have quite a lot as soon as I am going out again. Now no one expects much of one in dress. I have all I can do socially now in the way of bridge and shows.

I must close, as I have an appointment with my doctor for this afternoon. I don't know when I shall have time to write everything—all that Eve says and such things.

I love you both, and you will find it won't be long until we are reunited. Don't worry that I shan't be able to get home on account of war, as there are about four different ways for me to come, and I am sure one of those ways will be safe at that time.

Helen

Note: This is Helen's first mention of the possibility of war, although the idea was scarcely new to her or to Wilfred, who had witnessed first-hand the buildup of Nazism in Germany in 1932 and 1933. Both were incredulous as they watched Prime Minister Chamberlain dither in the face of German atrocities. The visit of Kiki Vriesen (one of Gerda and Professor Vriesen's sons) must have added to Helen's fears since he had been questioned by the South African police in regard to his having photographed major installations in South Africa during his stay in the country. Nevertheless, Helen, as always, plays a cool hand when confronting her parents' fears. She doesn't mention Vriesen's brush with the law or exaggerate the possibilities of war that will involve South Africa or its potential consequences, but Kiki's visit was obviously a catalyst for her concerns. Kiki was especially fond of Wilfred's sister, Bert, and once asked her whether, in the event of a war between England and Germany, it would come between them, to which Bert answered with an adamant, "Yes!" It was obvious that, with the annexation of Austria in March of 1938 by Nazi Germany, war could eventually spread to Great Britain and hence to South Africa. The American papers were full of dire predictions.

210 Killarney Court
Johannesburg
May 23, 1938

My dearest Mother and Father,

I feel quite ashamed of myself, for I find I have three letters and a box in the post office from home since I last wrote. I just got the notice about my box and shall go in tomorrow to get it, as I am so anxious to see all of the pretty little things.

I have really been busy, as on last Thursday I had to read an original article to my book club. I wrote on Joseph Pulitzer. It was really interesting and seemed to be enjoyed by everyone. I was glad to get my turn over with. Wednesday night Mr. G.L. Artamonoff, president of Sears International, arrived. I had him for dinner on Sunday with Mr. and Mrs. Van Zalingen, Mrs. Van Zalingen's sister, Ida, and the little girl, Mickey. I had the girl in that I intended to hire when I go into my house. I found her very thorough but slow with her cleaning and simply at sea in the kitchen and serving. I cooked everything myself and explained beforehand what they could expect when it came to the serving. I will tell you what I had, and I can tell you everything was delicious. I had tomato soup, followed by my main course of leg of lamb and mint sauce, cauliflower, roast potatoes, French peas, tomato casserole (a new dish with me which was highly successful), and, for dessert, homemade ice cream, then coffee in the lounge. I had toast with the soup, as you can't buy crackers over here, and only sliced bread with the rest of the meal, which is all anyone serves. I can make gravy nearly as good as yours. I wasn't in the least nervous, thank goodness, but it was no small undertaking with a new and inexperienced girl.

Eve was coached for several days to say, "How-do-you-do, Mr. Artamonoff," when she saw him. She went around singing it for days, and I was afraid she would do the same when she saw him. Then she said she wouldn't do it, so I had to threaten to give her no ice cream unless she did; so, on Sunday, she came running in from play and asked if he was here, and when I said yes, she dashed into the lounge where all my guests were assembled, and in a very big voice said, "How do you do, Mr. Artamonoff." Unfortunately, she wasn't looking at him at all, but she got it said. No name seems to stump her, as that name is rather difficult, I think, and also "Van Zalingen," but she says them both perfectly.

We went for a drive after dinner and then to the Country Club for tea. The Country Club is a beautiful place and very exclusive. We went as the guests of Mr. Van Zalingen, as it takes a year or more to get in. Mr. Artamonoff is a most charming man. He is a Russian, you know, and an ex-Count, I suppose you would call him. He is about thirty-eight but does not look it. [Helen is now thirty-two and seven months pregnant.] He is a very handsome man with blue eyes, black hair, tall, but, best of all, he is so well informed, and the conversation on Sunday was really worthwhile. I found I had more to say being with people who know so much. Mr. Van Zalingen is a widely-traveled person too, having lived some time in the Near East. Mr. Artamonoff gave a description of language, which I thought was very true (he speaks five himself). He said that Phillip of Spain once said that he spoke Spanish to his friends, Italian to his mistress, French to his diplomats, English to his business associates, and German to his enemies.

Mr. Artamonoff is charming but not an easy man to do business with. If I should tell you how absent-minded he is, you would throw up your hands, as I have done. For one thing, Wilfred's letter of credit was stolen, and, at the end of this month, it will be four months without any salary—$1200. Wilfred said to Mr. Artamonoff that he needed some money, and he said, "Why, are you in debt?"

Wilfred said, "Don't you know about my letter-of-credit?"

He said, "Oh yes, it was stolen from you. We had a cable and a letter from you about it."

"Well," Wilfred said, "it will be four months that I have had no pay at the end of this month."

"Oh, we'll get a cable off," said Artamonoff.

Wilfred had to explain that he could not wait on cables but made him give him what he had in his pocket. Can you imagine why they did not attend to such a matter immediately? You must not mention it, of course, but they attend to everything the same way in Chicago. We have never had an answer to a single important question that we have written them about. It has nearly made a nervous wreck of Wilfred.

He finds it practically as difficult to make Mr. Artamonoff see the urgency of these different matters now that he has him here. I am afraid he is a Russian dreamer. His father was one of the great Russian generals during the World War. Mr. Artamonoff escaped from Russia by joining the Red Army and changing (or rather escaping) to the White Army. He was evacuated from the Crimea with the rest of the White Army when it became apparent that they would be wiped out, and was taken to the Philippines. His sister is still in Russia and can never get out. She teaches languages in the University and is called up by the police every three months. It cost him $500 to get a passport for his mother. He was only able to get her out a year ago.

From now on address your letters to me to 20 Chester Road, Parkwood, Johannesburg.

We move the 31st of this month and, since we are going to be in a house, which is most comfortable. I am going to have the baby at home and have a trained nurse for three weeks. I already have her engaged. A trained nurse is $25 a week, and my room at the nursing home would have been $60 a week, so you can see I am very glad to stay at home. I don't feel that I shall have any trouble, as I am not so large this time as I was with Eve, and so far there is no swelling of my ankles, etc. I buzz around like anyone else and nearly die when extra pillows, etc., are brought out for me. It is too funny when Mrs. Van Z. and I go out together—it looks like we have infected each other. She is much larger than I am though she is expecting hers after me. I am sure she is going to have twins.

I played bridge again this afternoon with the three I play with so much and won again. I have never lost playing with them; in fact, I think I am always the biggest winner.

I am always interested in the clippings you send, especially the one of Dot Siemen's engagement. I suppose Mrs. Siemen is full of it. Give Dot my best wishes when you see her.

Eve had a letter from Joe Baughman for her birthday. I thought it awfully sweet of Elizabeth, and Eve was thrilled to death, as she has never forgotten Joe. I shall write for her and will send him something from S.A. as soon as we get our money. He wrote about his broken leg, and I heard Eve *bragging* to her playmate, Sonya, shortly after I read the letter, that her sweetheart in America has a wooden leg. She did not appreciate it when I corrected her. She will have a small party on Sunday the 5th of June. They will enjoy themselves, as Wilfred will take them rowing on the lake nearby our new house. I shall make some pictures to send you and shall look for the negatives of her other birthdays that you do not have.

If you have this letter before shipping the canned goods, do not send the cans of chili but merely send me chili powder, and I shall make my own because the freight will be considerable on all of that stuff. You should be able to get it wholesale. In any case, declare it at the wholesale price.

I should like a pair of black dress shoes—that is, afternoon shoes. I can't wear a pump in comfort, or I would say a black kid pump. I must have a strap or elastic with bow on top or something to keep it on. I want a medium heel, as I can't stand the very high. My size is 7 ½ AAAA. Do not let them send anything else. I do not want cloth again. I also want a pair of white and brown shoes with medium heel—sport type. I can get nothing here in the way of shoes, so you will always have to send them. I prefer that they have a strap rather than lace, but I must leave it to you. I also want these in leather and not cloth. Declare these at original price less 1/3, as that is about their mark-up. Try to get a sales ticket showing the wholesale price instead of your purchase price.

What was W.D.'s shortage? It must have been pretty big. I am awfully sorry for them. Do you have any idea what he plans to go into? Will he now be prosecuted?

I shall have an article written before I get home, as I suppose I shall be called on at least once for something about my life here. They don't need to expect me to be a second Olive Allen, however. Unless I have an interesting trip back, there won't be much to tell anyway.

I didn't know Eugene was building until your letter of April 16th. I should like a rough plan of the house and would like to know whether it will be brick or frame, etc. I am very happy for them that they are to have a home of their own. I hope he will not find the paying for it the load that the rest of the family has felt with their respective homes.

I can imagine Mrs. Miller's niece, age nineteen, would love taking children to America. She would want her whole passage for it and would deserve it. Anyway, I am coming much in advance of Wilfred. I am traveling on a Dutch or German boat next time where you can get the services of a nurse for a small amount.

Mrs. Vriesen's son, Kiki, visited us a week ago for the weekend. He sails for Germany June 1st to serve two years in the army. We think he enjoyed his stay. Anyway, we did what we could for him. [See Note, page 121]

The news from the plants sounds very exciting. I would like a letter from someone on the inside, but you can't get any of them to talk. Keep me posted on what you hear.

Artamonoff has our typewriter, and I nearly have writer's cramp, so I must close whether I am through or not.

Worlds of love and kisses from Eve and me to you both,

Helen

P.S. I don't know about Eve's I.Q. Her education will be difficult, I know, as so far she cannot be taught but picks up all kinds of things herself. She is intensely interested in the alphabet and writes a great many of the letters, but, the minute you try to teach her more, she becomes a mule.

20 Chester Road
Parkwood, Johannesburg
May 31, 1938

My dearest Mother and Father,

Although I have moved today to my new house, I must write a short letter to you tonight to get off on this week's mail because, since my last letter, I have the box of baby things and Eve's dress. I was terribly thrilled with everything, and they were just the things I needed to finish out my layette. I don't need another thing now except such things as safety pins, soap, and powder, etc. Eve and I both loved her dress, and I was so happy over the baby dresses, as you can't get such dainty ones here. Thanks so much for all of these lovely and practical things.

Indeed, I am lucky in this house as it even has a baby bed and bath. Here we have a lovely new radio too. I am not so tired as you would think after the move. I had my new native girl come and help me at the flat this morning and then sent her over here on the dray.[36] I don't know yet how she will be—I am afraid slow, but honest, and not fresh, which is something. You should hear me talk to natives now. It is really true that you have to call them all kinds of names and treat every little thing they do wrong as a major offense. I don't like it, but it is all they know and understand. [Helen's confusion about how to relate appropriately to the native people of South Africa haunted her for years.]

Eve spent today and will remain through tomorrow with the Van Zalingens. She spent Saturday night up there and never mentioned me. In fact, I had a hard time getting her to come home with me on Sunday afternoon. I am terribly lonely without her.

I like my new house so much that I feel more satisfied than at any other time since my marriage. I feel like we have really established a home.

I must close and get to bed, for I was up quite early this morning.

I have bought two lovely new blue blankets and two sets of pink sheets and pillowcases. I must have still more, of course, as such things are not furnished here.

Many, many more thanks for my box of pretties.

Love and kisses,

Helen

20 Chester Road
Parkwood, Johannesburg
June 7, 1938

My dearest Mother and Father,

I had a letter from you today dated May 5, which is not bad since it was forwarded from Killarney Court to my address here. It is the letter containing the handkerchief from the Mary Cameron Bible class party. You should have kept it yourself, but, of course, I appreciate your sending it on to me. I am glad you went to the party. Mother's Day is not known out here, so I forgot it completely. [Ironically, Helen is now eight months pregnant.]

At last I am more or less settled in my new house, but not without some upsets. The native girl I first took started work last Tuesday, and on last Thursday she fainted in my arms. She had not been overworked, as we hadn't had a meal in the

---

[36] While Johannesburg in the 1930s and '40s was a modern city, with cars, buses, beautifully designed buildings, and hard-topped roads, remnants of its more primitive beginnings remained. It was common, for example, to have one's luggage or pieces of furniture moved from place to place in a rickshaw pulled by a man. Unlike the elaborately dressed rickshaw men in Durban (and some in Johannesburg), these hard-working men pulled goods for a living, often dressed in little more than rags. It was also commonplace for horse-drawn carts to deliver milk and other items within the city.

And Indeed There Will Be Time (Sept. 1937—Aug.1939)

house. She had only had cleaning to do. She asked me to telephone her mother. On arrival, her mother decided a hex had been put on her daughter by the native girl who had lived here before and who had wanted to work for me. She wanted to leave her daughter with me for three days until she had consulted a witch doctor.[37] I told her I couldn't look after her daughter, as I needed someone at this time to look after me. I made her leave and was glad to have an excuse to send her away, as she was the dumbest girl I have seen out here. She had said she could cook, but I left some dried beans cooking and went to town and told her to take them off when they were done. She let them cook from ten o'clock in the morning until three o'clock in the afternoon (the time I got home and discovered them).

On Friday morning a strong-looking girl came by wanting work, and, after investigating her reference, I took her and so far she is excellent, except she can't cook. I only pay her £2.10 a month, or about $12.50, and she does my washing and ironing. I was paying half that amount to have my washing and ironing done every month, so you see she isn't costing me much in wages. By doing the cooking myself, I can watch that side of the thing very easily.

I had a birthday party for Eve on Saturday, June 4. I only had two little girls and the mother and auntie of one of the children. We knew others to ask, but they were much older, and I thought it would be hard to keep them entertained. Bert and Mr. Evans came for the party too. Bert gave Eve two pretty white serge skirts and a red hand-knit sweater and a blue one. Mr. Evans gave her a lovely silk and wool dress and is giving her a pair of shoes as soon as I can go to town for them. One little girl brought her a nice doll and the other brought watercolors, a coloring book, and plasticine [playdough]. We gave her a watering can and shovel for the garden. There were lots of balloons, a parasol for each little girl, and a false face for each, which frightened Eve. I had a lovely birthday cake baked in town with lots of rosebuds on it and "Eve" written across the cake. I made chocolate ice creams according to Aunt Nellie's recipe. The ice cream you buy here is terrible. I also made cookies in the shape of ducks, pigs, cats, and birds, which delighted the children. We had lemonade too, and Mr. Evans brought lots of candy. I used the little pink rosebuds and candles you sent, and Eve blew the candles out in one very long puff. She was delighted with everything and fully repaid me for my small efforts. It wouldn't have been an effort at all if I hadn't moved only four days beforehand. I took some pictures, which I will send if they turn out to be any good.

---

[37] This belief in the healing powers of native African healers (or what the white population called "Witch Doctors") persisted, even at the governmental level, under Prime Minister Thabo Mbeki (1994-2008) who, throughout the AIDS epidemic in South Africa, refused to believe in the viral theory of AIDS and banned antiretroviral drugs in state hospitals, thus contributing to thousands of unnecessary deaths. Thabo Mbeki was Nelson Mandela's successor.

My trained nurse was here this morning, making up some things for my confinement, and I am sterilizing them now. I like her very much. There is no doubt that she is most capable. I am very glad to be staying at home. Our expenses won't be so great, as the nurse is $25 a week, and my doctor is only charging $50 for his services. I know a woman who is in the Clarendon Nursing Home, the terrible one I wrote you about, and she is receiving the most awful treatment you ever heard of. If it were me, I know Wilfred would have me taken away in an ambulance. Here, all the nurses make you sit up for the first three days. They think binding useless and terribly old-fashioned.

I think it just as well that you don't send the canned goods, as I only pay about half again the price of the same thing at home. Toothpaste and many such things are the same price as we pay at Taylor's Drug Store or Harry Burgie's. I would like the chili powder so I can make chili myself, as I have a recipe. If you want to improve Brown Betty, use grape nuts on top instead of breadcrumbs. I got your recipe for rolls and shall try my luck very soon.

Mr. Artamonoff tells us that the U.S.A. is practically back to the worst of the Depression times.[38] Father must take care of his job, as I know he will, because I don't know how you all could live through times like we once knew. Frankly, I had rather be dead than to go through it again, but death does not come at such opportune times. I think of many of my friends and relatives who must be affected. I am wondering if you know anything about Mary and Knaffl's finances, or the Holden's, as I have not heard from Mary even though I wrote her about my baby. I am afraid she is too despondent to write. You may tell who you like about the baby, as it will only be a matter of a few weeks after the arrival of this letter that Robin will arrive.

I had a very peppy letter from Helen Hunter[39] and shall answer it as soon as I have a day that I feel young enough to reach her enthusiasm for life. Her letter made me feel just one hundred years old. I

Kathryn, Aunt Lennie, Uncle Edwin, and Helen Hunter, circa 1938

---

[38] While economists disagree about its cause, the 1937-38 Recession in the U.S., which occurred during the Great Depression, resulted in industrial production dropping almost 30%, while unemployment jumped from 14.3% to 19% during that period.

[39] Helen Hunter and her younger sister, Kathryn, were Helen's first cousins.

am writing Millicent Bitter right away and shall explain why I haven't answered her letter sooner.

The weather here at present is just like late fall at home. We are keeping warm enough, so don't worry. The sun is warm all day, and I have an open fire in the grate in my lounge every evening.

I now pay about 60 cents a pound for tea and even the native girl must have it. They would all have their tea out here if it were dollar a pound. I still pay 75 cents a dozen for eggs.

Don't ever apologize for your letters, as they seem as good to me as mine seem to you. I'm sure you have to guess in many places what I mean, as I never read my letters over.

Don't let any of the family send me baby things, as they have given me quite enough without my being able to return anything. I have all I can use anyway, and it would just mean paying for duty. If you run across someone who must do something, suggest a dollar and open a bank account for Robin.

I am happy for you that you are getting so much done to the house. I would surely love to see it.

Mrs. Van Zalingen's mother is arriving Friday from Amsterdam to be here during her confinement. I surely do envy her.

Eve and I send all our love and only wish we could see you both now.

Devotedly,
Helen

20 Chester Road
Parkwood, Johannesburg
June 20, 1938

Dearest Mother and Father,

It is quite cold here today. In fact it is the coldest day I have felt. We even had a little snow a while ago, and we have been having short rainfalls for several days, which is quite unheard of for this time of year. I am very glad not to have it so dry. I have the coldest bathroom on two continents, and the other morning I woke up determined to do something about it. There is no heat in it and, on top of that, I found that there were two outside ventilators and one inside one that could not be closed. You could even see daylight through the things. I had my girl stuff them up with rags, and that has helped. Then I determined to install an electric heater, though that is strictly against municipal regulations, and terrible things would happen to me if they found out. There being no wall plugs, of course, in the bathroom, I had the girl up on a step-ladder and attached it overhead (all ceilings here are 9 feet or more), then I moved a cupboard in and put the heater on top of it, as it would not nearly reach the floor.

The heater will not heat the place, but, when it is turned directly on you, there is a nice hot blast that feels good. Although I have three bedrooms, I shall have to take over the dining room (which has an open fireplace) when the baby arrives. Last year nine-hundred people in Johannesburg died of pneumonia; and it is easily understood, as the weather is most treacherous and the people will not have heat, even in a bathroom. I do get terribly annoyed over that one thing, and everyone thinks I am a fool, except Wilfred. He had learned to appreciate furnaces in America. Our health is excellent, as I am very careful, and I think I have only had one cold since I have been here. I am convinced that my trouble at home came from the low altitude and conditions peculiar to that section. I know now that I am no more susceptible to the ordinary cold than the average person, or not as much so.[40][41]

Of course I have written you about my friend, Mrs. Van Zalingen, who was expecting a baby about two weeks after me. She has put me in the shade completely by producing twin boys this past Saturday, June 18. They were born at about 7½ months, which is fortunate for her, for she was huge. The first one weighed 5 lbs. and the second 4¾ lbs. They are doing very well for such tiny tots. They arrived before the doctor, with only her mother and sister there. Fortunately, her mother is a nurse, but she had intended having a Holland's nurse from Cape Town all the time. This nurse arrived this morning. We kept Mickey Saturday afternoon and night, and all day Sunday. They are going to do the same for me. I am expecting mine around the 18th of July and expect nothing like what has happened to Mrs. Van Zalingen.

I have made a sweet basinet for my baby, almost exactly like the one I made for Eve. It will cost me just around $5.00, and, as I remember it, that is what Eve's cost. I had a very hard time finding a cheap basket to work with. I finally found one imported from America at $2.50. Everything made over here was nearly $5.00 or more. I saved on the silk lining, ribbon, and net, however, as such things are cheaper and better over here.

My health is perfect, and I am not so very large this time and still have no swelling whatsoever in my ankles and feet. I have seen the doctor regularly, and

---

[40] Located inland in northern South Africa, at an altitude of 6,000 feet, Johannesburg can be bitterly cold and dry in the winter. Built on the wealth of the gold mines that made it a center of affluence, Johannesburg is the largest city in the world not located on a body of water.

[41] Helen's constant concern over colds and pneumonia is understandable when one considers that antibiotics first came into limited use only a year later, at the start of World War II, but were still years away from general use.

And Indeed There Will Be Time (Sept. 1937—Aug.1939)

he anticipates no trouble whatsoever. There is nothing to worry about. My nurse is a most efficient person and very particular about everything. She has been here twice making preparations. I like her very much.

I made the rolls up according to your recipe, and they were excellent. They were as light as a feather; the only thing wrong was that they perhaps needed a little more salt, or so it seemed to me. Such things are a waste of my time, however, as only Eve and I enjoy them especially. They aren't as much trouble as I thought they would be.

There is a good dish I fix occasionally and one that would be cheap this summer with you. I butter a Pyrex dish and line the sides with slices of hardboiled eggs, then slice ripe tomatoes, about three or four, and fill up the center of the dish. Over this, I pour a white sauce to which I have added about ½ cup of grated cheese. Cover all with buttered breadcrumbs and bake in moderate oven for twenty minutes. Everyone I have served it to likes it very much. I make lots of baked dishes.

I am having my book club for the second time on this Thursday. I shall be glad when it is over, as my girl is no cook at all and the whole thing will be on me. The next week I am having four for lunch and bridge, and after that I shall do nothing, as I find such things somewhat of a strain at the last minute.

We have a radio now, but, even though it is a good make, it is most unsatisfactory out here. The atmospheric conditions are not conducive to good reception. All that I can get at all well is Berlin and Dutch programs out here, which do me a lot of good, and, when I do get England, I can't understand them any better than Berlin, so it is a washout as far as I am concerned.

I'll bet if you should investigate that you would find that Mr. M. is sending money to his family in Germany under pressure from the German government and not because his family needs it. Why don't the U.S. and England wake up? They could save themselves a lot if they would clamp down now on Germany.

I am enclosing a match-folder for Pat Dungan. We seldom get them is the reason I have not sent more.

Thanks a lot for offering me money, but we have plenty for all of our expenses. I shall take care of myself properly, so don't you worry.

I am terribly worried about Uncle Hunter. If you all take him in when and if he comes back from Cincinnati, you will have him the rest of his life, for Thomas will never come forward unless forced to. Thomas will not, of course, think of keeping house with his mother [Kate], as to keep house would mean an outlay of $100 a month compared to the $25 he spends now. He cares for nothing but money. There is not one spark of sentiment in him. I am very sorry to learn of Aunt Kate's illness. Give her my love.

I must stop now and get dinner for my hungry family.

Eve has just said, why don't we go back to Mama Sophia's? It is much nicer there. She really has a wonderful place to play here, as far as that goes, but she misses you all, just as I do. We'll stay with you about a year when we do come, so you will have quite enough of us. I really don't plan to stay three years before coming back, but only two to two and a half years. I think it can be arranged all right.

Lots and lots of love from Eve and me,

Helen

20 Chester Road
Parkwood, Johannesburg
June 26, 1938

My dearest Mother and Father,

While my family sleeps I shall try to write you a letter. We all ate such a big dinner today that we were quite drowsy, so all went to bed for a nap. It is now six o'clock, and Wilfred and Eve are still fast asleep. Eve needs all the sleep she can get, as she has had a very bad head and chest cold for about five days, and her coughing has kept her awake at night a great deal. The cold is mostly in her head now, which is disagreeable but much safer than in the chest. She has been kept in bed most of the time but has been up for a while today. The winters here are like our most treacherous spring weather, and everyone has colds just now.

Eve has the best underwear I can buy for her—all-wool combination suits under the trade name of *Chillpruff*. Over here, that has the same meaning as *Vanta* at home. I paid $3.00 a suit, so you know they are good. She is made to put on a sweater when she goes out of a heated room into the cold part of the house.

Eve has looked and looked at the snaps I am enclosing. Yesterday she came to me with the one of the false faces and her crying. She said, "Are you going to send this one to Mama Sophia?"

I said, "Yes."

She said, "You know, I am four years old in that picture."

I said, "Yes, I know you are."

"Well," she said, "you mustn't send that picture to Mama Sophia because she mustn't know I cried when I was four years old."

So I really must not let her know I have sent it to you, for she mentioned it several times during the day and seemed much perturbed over it.

I was very sorry to hear that Aunt Ruth has had another stroke. Old age in our family seems to be anything but pleasant. Please give my love to her and to Aunt

Hattie.[42] Ask Aunt Hattie why her postcard was so specifically to Eve. I hope we haven't offended her in any way.

I had my book club this past Thursday and got through the tea all right. I made a pineapple-upside-down cake, olive sandwiches, and tomato sandwiches. That is all we are allowed to serve for tea—I mean, only two or three things. I used my crocheted doilies given me by Mama Dick[43] and had roses and carnations from my garden as the centerpiece of my table. It looked very pretty indeed. I am going to a bridge party tomorrow given by Mrs. Wilson, president of the book club. She is entertaining for her two sisters from Cape Town. I am having her with her two sisters for lunch on Friday with bridge afterwards. I expect to let this end my social activities until after the arrival of the baby, as I can keep myself quite busy here at home attending to many small details since I am having the baby at home.

I think it was awfully sweet of you both that you planned to send me $100. I am glad it is not necessary, and I hope it will never be necessary for you to help me again, as I am anxious for you to save up for yourselves, and I, personally, have been quite enough expense on the family. I think children should not be kept as children so long but be put on their own quite early. Most of us have to grow up sometime, and the longer it is delayed, the harder it is on us.

I shall never have higher praise given me than that my own mother thinks I am the best woman she ever knew. No better epitaph could I ever have. If you believe this to be true, little credit can come to me, for the credit must go to my good heritage. The way I have acted in all matters was the only way I found possible to act. I had no fights within myself, no inclination to take an easier road.

Mr. Artamonoff has left and continued his trip around the world by airplane. While he was here, he lowered the prices on the Coldspot (the electric refrigerator) so that it was possible to close a very big contract for a distributorship. Wilfred got the firm interested in acting as distributor for the Union of South Africa. He made all financial investigations about the firm, and worked up all price comparisons with Norge, GE, Westinghouse, etc., which had to come through friends as the information was confidential, and Artamonoff made a trip out here to say Sears International would come down to the prices suggested by Wilfred. That cinched the deal, but why they did not write or cable the information we do not know. Since Artamonoff proceeded on around by India, Philippines, etc., we take it that

---

[42] Helen's great-aunts, Aunt Hattie (born in 1856; now eighty years old) and Aunt Ruth (born in 1864; now seventy-four years old), were both sisters of Mollie Jobe (Hunter) Sophia's mother, who had died before Helen left the United States. See portrait on page 63. (All three sisters were the daughters of Dr. Abraham and Sophronia Jobe.)

[43] Harlow's mother, 'Mama Dick,' was renowned for her talent in crochet and tatting. (See picture of her wearing one of her jackets on page 64.) The jacket that Eve and I found in the trunk in Sophia's garage had been made by her.

he merely wanted a trip, as they have no representatives in the East, and the trip that way takes weeks longer and is many times more expensive. How long they will last this way we don't know. Artamonoff did not do one other thing while out here except see the Game Reserve. Enough of that.

I must close, as my family is now awake and I must fix some supper.

Lots and lots of love,

Helen

[To: Mary Walker from Helen]

20 Chester Road
Parkwood
Johannesburg, South Africa
July 10, 1938

Dearest Mary,

I was indeed glad and relieved to hear from you. I was beginning to think that perhaps something dreadful had happened to you and that everyone was keeping it from me. Hearing that conditions are what they are in America, I am not surprised to hear that Knaffl's business is not so good, but just the same I am terribly sorry to hear it, and just wish it were possible for you all to not feel this present slump in business. Although you do not say it, I know from experience that it is none too easy to work and keep house, but you know I admire your spunk. You do have the advantage of knowing how to cook and make a house run smoothly, which I did not have. I have certainly been taking advantage of the last few months, however, and have been educating myself along these lines. I shall never let a daughter grow up in ignorance of such homely things, as I do not know but what she might have to face the same thing as I did. I am not a good cook yet, but I don't mind preparing a meal for company, so you can guess what strides I have made.

I hope you are better at making change than I am. I should never be able to hold down a job as a cashier. You can imagine what I go through with now that I must handle English money. I didn't lose any time learning the money when they tried to shortchange me by $25 in London. Since things are so slow at the plants, I have been wondering about David and Elizabeth. Have they been getting only part-time? These things worry me, as I know the holding of the home place depends on their jobs, and I feel it would be too terrible for anything to go wrong there. Please let me know everything.

I am surprised to hear that H. and his wife have adopted a baby. I think that is mighty fine of them, and maybe it will make H. more interested in home. Tell them I will furnish them with any other babies that they might want. Any more, and I shall have to start placing them.

And Indeed There Will Be Time (Sept. 1937—Aug.1939)

Going on your recommendation, I bought *Madame Curie* as my book for the book club I belong to. It has been praised more than any other book in the club, but how else could it be? I started doing my own work, so I could learn to cook immediately after reading the book. I simply felt I must accomplish something, and, although cooking may be a very simple thing to most people, it has always been a big bugbear to me. Somehow the book did not stress genius but rather made one feel that he or she could accomplish just as much if we would stick to a certain job. I am reading *The Rains Came* now. What they read here and what we read at home is rather different, however. You know I gave an article on Joseph Pulitzer, and only one in the club seemed to know who he was and anything about the Pulitzer Prize.

Business is not good all over South Africa and hasn't been for six months or more. Wilfred managed to make one very big deal for Sears International, however, which will hold them for a while.

I think I shall have to take Eve to see *Snow White,* as I have told her the story so often, getting the details from the write-up of Walt Disney's production in *Time.* She is able to stand my description of the Witch, so I think she will hold up during the movie. Wilfred has listened to me telling the story and said he never heard such a bloodcurdler used as a nightcap.

How sporty the Trammels are to have a cabin cruiser. I hope you get to enjoy it several times during this summer. I know how thrilled Joe must have been to steer it. Yes, I can see his grin. It is a very delightful one, but don't tell him I said so, or he might not speak to me the next time I see him.

My event is due the 18th of this month, so of course I imagine things all the time and just hope and hope that each day will be the day. I should know from past experience, though, that I shall hold out to the last. I have been very friendly with a girl I came out on the boat with since we were both in the same fix. She expected her event about two weeks after mine, but on the 18th of June she produced twin sons. Of course, this was a little embarrassing for her, as she only married on her arrival November 1. Her husband seems perfectly satisfied, however. As he is a rather conceited Hollander, he doesn't think anyone else could have given her twins anyway. Please do not take it that I am saying any of this in a catty way, as I have never seen anyone more circumspect than she was on the trip out. I am quite sure I wouldn't do so well myself.

I am having the baby at home and shall have a trained nurse for two weeks. We moved into this house the first of June with that in mind. I like having a house infinitely better than an apartment under the circumstances. Of course for you, now, an apartment is the only thing. We have a living room, dining room, kitchen, pantry, three bedrooms and bath all on one floor. It is as well-furnished as our apartment was and is in as good a section of the city, but we are saving $35 a month in rent.

Of course, I have a native girl now, but she costs me less than the one I had in the flat and does my washing and ironing too. The ones in the flats know too much about what each other gets. Even with this move, our expenses are none too light. I must say vegetables are very cheap here, and it will kill me to buy them at home when I get back. I shall have to have my own garden until I have forgotten. Yesterday, I picked four-dozen lemons off my lemon tree. They are lovely ones. Wintertime is hardly the time for lemonade, but lemonade we shall drink. Eve loves it, so it makes no difference to her whether she consumes by an open fire or on the front verandah with palm leaf fans waving.

Wilfred and I plan to have our last celebration this week before the baby arrives. We shall have dinner at the Criterion in town and then go to see *Jezebel*. Mary, you would love the Criterion. It is one of those quiet but gay-looking small places with just the right atmosphere and the best food in Johannesburg. I usually take duck or something like that that I do not fix at home. The chairs are all done in a gay, red plush. Maybe red plush doesn't sound good in this day and age, but it can have an atmosphere. Everything is so very modern in Johannesburg that this Old World atmosphere is a relief. Of course, I am anxious to see *Jezebel*. I suppose you have already seen it long ere this.

Wilfred would like a letter from Knaffl, but I can see Knaffl trying to get down to writing it. Tell him to do it if he can. Better late than never.

We had a few minutes of snow yesterday and have had some rain this week, which is very unusual as this is the dry season, and usually it doesn't rain for eight entire months. June, July, and August are our winter months. Here it is the middle of the winter, and I have only used a half a ton of coal. I'd use more if they gave me more places to burn it. I have toughened up considerably as far as standing the cold goes.

We shall let you know how things go with me. I am expecting an easy time and hope I am not disappointed. I want a boy and Wilfred wants a girl, so one member of the family will be satisfied anyway. Eve wants a little sister. She told me that she saw a little baby boy at Killarney Court, and he looked so terrible that he scared her.

Wilfred has gone this afternoon to see the Rugby match between England and the Transvaal. Wilfred once played rugby himself, so of course he is interested.

Lots of love to you all,

Helen

And Indeed There Will Be Time (Sept. 1937—Aug. 1939)

20 Chester Road
Parkwood, Johannesburg
July 12, 1938

My dearest Mother and Father,

    I have so much news for you that I hardly know where to start. I shall never be able to tell the whole thing in a letter, but, as far as I can see at present, I shall be with you very soon, anyway. Ever since the 28th of May we have known that we were out with Sears International, but I saw no use of telling you until we had some definite plans. To tell the story shortly, after the big contract for refrigerators was signed with Finbro Furnishers, Artamonoff told Wilfred that he was transferred back to Sears, Roebuck in America. A clause in our contract said it could be cancelled immediately. Wilfred said to him that it seemed too bad that such a thing should happen just when his commissions would be starting ($10,000 a year), and his reply was, "Oh, I am afraid there would be nothing for you since we have reduced our prices so much."

    The whole thing is that Wilfred worked up this deal for $250,000 worth of refrigerators per year, for a period of five years, and, after a thorough investigation of Sears' other lines, he had to tell them that they were completely out of line in price, or did not have the proper merchandise, such as the Silverstone Radio. Every radio out here had a 13-meter band so that Daventry, England, will come in during the day, but Sears will not manufacture specially for this country, even though Wilfred could have placed their radio with one of the biggest distributors in South Africa, and their radio sales would have been fourth in radios in South Africa.

    However, the market did not look big enough to them (that was, $100,000 a year). Wilfred even found that some of Sears International's lines were already in the country; that is, the manufacturer of the particular line, such as their pianos, already had a sole distributorship. Wilfred went into Mackay Brothers to try to interest them in pianos, and there he recognized his own piano, and they informed him that they had had the sole distributorship for years. Sears International didn't even know this, but this is only one small thing they do not know about their business. It is the most loosely run concern I ever came in contact with. The only two men in the home office of Chicago with authority to do anything, the president Artamonoff, and the vice president Kearney, spend most of their time traveling from one country to another.

    For instance, Artamonoff's present trip keeps him away from May to August, and the only thing he accomplishes by it is being here in person to sign the one contract with Finbros. He paid $500 more to have all of his trip back through the East by plane, but he only gets home two days earlier. They have no representatives in the East and do not plan to have any. He is General Wood's curly-headed boy, and that is why he is getting by with his present methods. So much for why Wilfred is out.

It may interest you to know that, since it happened to us, we find that it always happens when a big order is landed. Since South Africa is an importing country, except for gold, the place is full of manufacturers' representatives, and most of them came out here first for one firm, as Wilfred did, and when they landed a big order that established the business in the country, they were let out, and then they established agency businesses of their own. The man who brought Neon signs out to the country had the same experience and now is opening an agency and has invited Wilfred to join him.

Some other friends of ours, the Reppetos, have been in this game for ten years; and, in ten years, he has changed firms six times. Just as he saw he was going to be let out of one, he would tie up with another. They are now left out here without passage money home. We wouldn't go with any American firm as a representative, no matter what the salary and promises of commission might be, as you can't get any place with them. Wilfred has had several long talks with the American Trade Commissioner here in Johannesburg since this happened, and he told Wilfred that such cases come to their attention all the time and that they are doing everything they can to show American firms that this is poor business and that Americans are not trusted in business at all out here. They break contracts all the time and pull "slick deals" that might pass unnoticed in America but get aired out here where business is still done on English lines, which means that a verbal agreement is just as binding as a written agreement.

We have not been left in bad shape, as we got Wilfred's back salary, passage money home, and salary until the end of August. But, to get this, I shall have to tell you another story of interest. When Artamonoff told Wilfred that his job was over out here (they are not sending anyone else out but are doing away with the job entirely), he offered to settle by paying him his three months back salary. I may have written you once that it was four months, but it was three. Of course, that would have left us in fine shape, as we had naturally had to borrow to finance ourselves during that time.

We now know why they did not reissue our letter of credit and left us more or less stranded for three months, hoping we would be so glad to get that that we would let them off for nothing more. Owing all of that, we were not thrilled pink with just that amount, so Wilfred told him that the only fair settlement he could see was the back salary, passage money home (same amount as it cost to bring us out here), and salary until the end of August, since I could not travel before that time. Since this came to $3,000, Artamonoff naturally bucked and went off to Cape Town without leaving us a cent. During this time we could imagine our fate at the very darkest.

And Indeed There Will Be Time (Sept. 1937—Aug.1939)   139

Wilfred went to the best lawyer in Johannesburg and showed him his contract and told him the whole story. The lawyer said he had seen so much of this business with American firms that he would take the case home and study it that night, and if he could find any way of fighting the thing for the commissions accruing for the three years of the contract or at least for passage money and salary until the end of August, he would take the case. The next morning he had to tell Wilfred that there was not a thing he could do with Artamonoff, as the contract made it only possible to sue Sears International in America.

However, he gave us the advice that got us the $3,000. He said to Wilfred that he should use bluff on Artamonoff, so this is what happened. When Artamonoff got back from Cape Town and was making all of his plans to fly from here back to Egypt in about three days, Wilfred told him that he was not leaving the country, as he was having him held here for a court case. He told him he would not settle for less than $3,000, and that it might take nine months for the case to be settled, during which time he could be held in the country—that he would also see that the American Press got the story of the president of Sears International being held by one of his representatives for salary and passage money, and he thought the press would love the story. This was all Wilfred's idea, I should have said, and, when he presented it to the lawyer, the lawyer told him to try it.

Artamonoff looked startled and said, "Oh, you can't do that, Evans!"

Wilfred answered that all he had to do was go to the telephone and call his lawyer, and the whole thing would be started. He said either that or we go to the bank and you pay me $3,000.

Artamonoff thought about two minutes and said, "Let's go to the bank." There, Wilfred got his money and deposited it to his own credit. He and Artamonoff separated for about two hours, and, when they met again, Artamonoff was furious and said, "Evans, why did you tell me you could hold me in this country when you know you can't?" He went on to say, "You know I can hurt you with Sears, Roebuck when you come back."

Wilfred then said, "Artamonoff, if you hurt me with Sears, Roebuck or any firm when I ask for a letter of recommendation from you, I'll go to Chicago and show General Woods where you dropped over a thousand dollars of the firm's money because you didn't go to see a lawyer, and that won't look well for you."

After this last thrust, Artamonoff became even friendly because he had to admit he had just been out-smarted. To use such methods to get something not due me, I would be the first to frown on them, but when we only saved ourselves from being virtually stranded in this foreign country, then I do nothing but laugh that we were able to outwit them. In any case, they were doing us out of enough for the next three years.

Wilfred does not want to go back to Sears, Roebuck, as he was done out of commissions in Nashville even. They told him that they would give him 1½%

commission on all increase in sales in his department and, when it amounted to nice money, they told him they had said ½ of 1% and that is all they ever paid him. We see no future there, so Wilfred is not going back but is going to take his chances out here.

He has been offered a connection with the firm of Hendy & Farquharson, who are manufacturers' agents. They are well established here in Johannesburg, and they want Wilfred to open up a Cape Town office for them. He will be paid purely on a commission basis, so of course he is taking a chance, as it all depends on the business he can bring in for them. However, they will furnish him with an office and a stenographer, which is more than he had from Sears. They defray all expenses, such as cables, stamps, stationery, etc. There is small chance for commissions to start coming in for from six to nine months, however; so until that time, we must be very careful.

Wilfred is agreeable to my taking passage money and coming home instead of using it for living expenses in Cape Town, and then he can allow me a small monthly amount. Using so much for passage home, I don't believe I could give you more than $25 a month for myself and the babies. If this would not be enough for the increase in the grocery bill, please cable me, because I do not want to be a burden. We have to finance ourselves for nine months at least, we figure. Wilfred does not like the responsibility of using up my passage money for living expenses and not knowing how long it would be before he could afford to send me home for a visit. You see, it is rather a matter of having the cash in hand now, and we all know how hard it is to get that amount saved up.

If anything has happened at home that makes this plan unfeasible, please cable me immediately; otherwise I plan to sail September 11th on the *S.S. West Cawthorn*,[44] which makes a straight trip from Cape Town to New York, Trinidad being the only port of call. I would land the 10th of October in New York. This is a small boat carrying only ten passengers, but I think it suits my purposes better than one via England or Gibraltar, as I would have to change boats and have a five-day wait either place.

Please do not be upset by this news, as we now know it was something that would have happened sooner or later, and the sooner we know that we were in a very insecure position, the better. Please do not mention any of this to anyone. Of course, you can say I am coming home for a visit, but no one needs to know that Wilfred is changing his business. I emphatically do not want this mentioned to anyone, as I have had my affairs discussed too much in Elizabethton, and I do not intend to live under any such strain there again. If I found out anyone knew this, I

---

[44] Some eighteen months after Helen made these plans, the *S.S. West Cawthorn*, an American cargo ship, was torpedoed.

And Indeed There Will Be Time (Sept. 1937—Aug.1939)

would leave, because I really can't stand to think of ever again going through having my affairs discussed by everyone as they have been in the past.

Eve is completely over the cold that she did have and is looking quite well again. I am feeling and keeping perfectly O.K. The doctor paid a visit to me here at the house day before yesterday to have a last look at me, and my nurse came by yesterday to see how I was and give me last instructions.

Wilfred has made $50 this month selling radios for a firm, and it looks as though he might make $200 more this week. Eve made her first money today. She came to me with a penny (2 cents) and said she gave a native boy two bottles, and he gave her the money. I miss two vinegar bottles she has been playing with. I was terribly amused. Stewart Hampton has nothing on Eve. I shall have to watch my things now.

Wilfred's father is here and will take this letter into town for me, so I must close, as he is waiting on it. Wednesday is the day I must mail my letter to you.

Lots and lots of love from both Eve and me,

Helen

20 Chester Road
Parkwood, Johannesburg
July 20, 1938

My dearest Mother,

Just a short note to tell you some of the things about my confinement that I know you are anxious to know. Of course, it was natural for me to want a boy this time, but we got a perfect little girl, and, since she is perfect, we can ask for nothing more. She weighed only 7½ lbs., for which I am very thankful. She is just as strong as Eve was, already able to lift her head and look around at everyone. She has a beautifully-shaped head, which Eve did not have. Her eyes are blue, of course, and her hair about as Eve's was. Her name is Robin. If we had had a boy, the name would have been Robert Kevren and, while small, we would have called him Robin.

As to my confinement. Well, it was so easy that I can hardly believe it. It was about one tenth of what it was with Eve. Of bad pain I did not have more than two hours. I got the nurse here in plenty of time, as I had pain at long intervals from about six o'clock in the morning of July 16th. She came at nine o'clock, and the doctor came for a few minutes at eleven. Things were very slow at that time, but shortly after my castor oil and enema, things started rushing along. Things came along so fast in the last hour that the nurse was caught unawares and did not call the doctor soon enough, so that we found ourselves at the last minute with no doctor. The nurse was actually holding the baby in for ten minutes, waiting on the doctor, and I was saying some pretty strong things and insisting on her letting the baby come.

My doctor never did arrive until after the baby was here, but his assistant got here in time to catch the baby. That was actually all he did. I have been through it without an anesthetic and without a tear, and I must say it makes a difference in how you feel afterwards. I felt marvelous immediately. If one must suffer through hours of labor pains, one had might as well go through the whole thing without an anesthetic. The last is no worse than the others. My nurse is excellent. She is a midwife herself and could have delivered the baby. The doctor was entirely unnecessary. My milk is in and is very rich. The baby is doing fine on it.

Eve is a little jealous, but we are making a fuss over her so she won't be. Wilfred has bought her the most beautiful doll you ever saw.

I was so thrilled to get a letter from you yesterday and the lovely blue hanky. Lots of love and kisses,

Helen

20 Chester Road
Parkwood, Johannesburg
August 9, 1938

Dearest Mother and Father,

This letter will be a week later than it should have been if I could have found time to write it earlier today. I know you can imagine that my time is well filled these days. I naturally have complete care of the baby as well as Eve, and must do most of the cooking, as my girl is no cook. Today my day started at three a.m. with only one hour's sleep this afternoon. An hour's sleep, and I feel quite refreshed, though.

I was so happy to receive your cable. I had thought that you must be just receiving my letter saying I was coming. Since writing you, Wilfred has secured a position with Westinghouse here in Johannesburg at a set salary of $200 per month plus commissions. We are naturally elated over this good fortune, as the other was so uncertain. Wilfred starts work on the 15th of this month. Westinghouse is putting stores in all of the important towns in South Africa, and Wilfred will be Assistant to the Vice President, who is the general manager of all the stores. The head offices are here in Johannesburg. Wilfred will be here most of the time but will make trips occasionally when Mr. Sours cannot make them.

Wilfred is so pleased to have an office and a stenographer and to be able to conduct business in a business-like way, with regular hours and all that. It will be good, too, to be selling a product that one has confidence in. We are happy over the change, and I think it certainly speaks well for Wilfred to be able to get such a good job so quickly. The people who wanted to have him open an office for them

And Indeed There Will Be Time (Sept. 1937—Aug.1939) 143

in Cape Town are very upset, but we could not turn down a certain salary with a firm like Westinghouse for something that it would take months to realize anything on.

I suppose I am still coming home, though, of course, this is my chance to buy my own furniture and rather settle myself. To own our furniture would save us quite a lot of money too, as we could get unfurnished houses at about $50 per month. However, if I spend the money on furniture, I don't know when I would ever be able to save up enough money to come home and, of course, that is most important to us all. If I should find a furnished place at a reasonable rent, I would take it for six months and then come home, as it would be much easier traveling when the baby is a little older, and I would feel much safer taking her later.[45]

She is really doing beautifully. She is looking lovely and fat, and every time I turn her on her stomach she tries to crawl and actually makes a little progress. She was lifting her head on the second day, just like Eve did. She is just as wonderfully strong as Eve was, but she has missed having thrush, and I missed bealed breasts [mastitis] because we have been well cared for all along. She has been registered as Myfanwy Evans. Myfanwy is pronounced Mavanwee. This is a pure Welsh name and is beautiful when pronounced correctly. We continue to call her Robin, however.

Eve is quite full of the idea of coming home and will be very upset if we don't go at this time. I have two people begging me for my reservation. It is not easy to get on one of those small boats making the trip from Cape Town to New York. Wilfred had given Artamonoff's booking through the East to Parry, Leon, and Hale, traveling agents, which amounted to $1500, and they got my reservations through pull because of that.

I am registering Myfanwy at the American Consulate, which will enable her to travel on my Passport. It also gives her a chance to select her own country. At the age of twelve, she can decide whether she wants to be a British subject or an

---

[45] Helen's relationship with furniture was complex. While she frames her indecision primarily in terms of the money she could save by buying her own furniture, Helen was in fact on a quest to belong—somewhere. Where, ultimately, is her home? As she gathers her furniture around her, Helen increasingly feels at home in South Africa. Her rather offhand treatment of her first view of Table Mountain can be better understood if one considers that Helen felt she had been evicted from the United States and that, in fact, she belonged nowhere. Because she is so homesick for her parents, Helen at first feels ambivalent about South Africa, but as she becomes more identified with her new homeland, she feels freer to state her feelings toward the United States, finally, in 1943, blurting out the truth about her sentiments: "I really hate the land of my birth." To the end, one can only say that Helen remained deeply conflicted in her loyalties: Did she want to be in the United States, the land of her birth, with her parents and many close relatives, or in South Africa, her adopted homeland, with her husband, her children, and her true blue friends? In the end, her actions speak for themselves.

American citizen. I think this is a very good idea, as it delays matters a number of years.

I am enjoying taking care of Robin, and for this first time I realize how little I ever had Eve as a baby. This is just like having my first baby.

I have already had to give up breastfeeding her, and she is now taking the formula we used for Eve of cow's milk, water, and Dextra-Maltose. That is the favorite food out here for babies. If we come home now, I shall have to put her on canned milk, of course, before we leave.

I must close and feed Robin. She can certainly make herself heard if you are late with the bottle.

Tell Uncle Fred that Eve asked me to write to him for her the other day. She said to tell him that she had broken one of her Teddies but not the one he gave her, but that an eye was missing. She also wanted to say that she loved him a lot and wanted to see him. I had to tell her I wrote him, but I just did not have time to do it.

I haven't received the box yet, but it was lovely of you to send me such a wonderful box of things. You do not mean that the shoes are a present too, do you? I think that would be too much. Duty is not high on what I have received so far. On the baby's box I paid about $1.50, I think.

Do not say anything about Wilfred's change for a while yet. People always think you haven't done so well by yourself, so it might be just as well to let them think he is still with Sears. We can talk it over later anyway and decide.

Lots and lots of love from Eve and me to you both

"Castlewellan"
No. 2 Eighth Avenue
Parktown North, Johannesburg
August 24, 1938

Dearest Mother and Father,

Your marvelous package has arrived at last, and Eve and I had a wonderful time opening it and admiring our new things from home. My housecoat is lovely. Bert said she had never seen me look so good as when I was wearing it on Sunday. My white shoes are simply too good-looking. I never selected so well when I was buying for myself. I like the black shoes too, very much. They are more or less the type you see over here, but for the white shoes, you couldn't even buy them in this country. Bert has me show the white ones to everybody who comes in, for she has never seen anything like them. As for styles in dresses, hats, etc., it is no different here than at home, except perhaps they wear more fancy things than we do now at home.

Eve loved her pyjamas and panties and brings out her pyjamas every night to ask if she can put them on, but I still have her in woolen nighties. My slips are so pretty, and I shall shorten them as soon as I have time. I think you can't beat the Barbizon slips. I already had one, and it feels so good on. My panties fit perfectly and are just what I like. Thanks ever so much for these lovely presents. The duty came to about $4.00, which I considered very reasonable. They are much more reasonable here about duty than at home.

I suppose you have already noticed my new address at the top of the sheet. I do not move until the first of September, but I wanted you to know it as soon as possible. Of course, this means that I am not coming home just at this time, but that is much the best since the baby is so young and considering I have only been away one year. Since I can't be running back and forth every other year, I had rather save my trip until I have been away the three years. I shall come when I promised, that is in two more years, God willing.

I tried the baby on powdered foods, but she cried the whole time I had her on them and was never satisfied. When she got back to cow's milk and Dextra-Maltose she was perfectly satisfied again. Of course, it is impossible to get cow's milk (fresh) on a boat, and tinned foods are the only thing. Myfanwy is getting along so beautifully that I couldn't bear to upset her. She really looks lovely, so nice and fat and so very strong. Too much strength for the sense she's got. She can't even be left on a bed, and she is only five weeks old. She is very fair as far as her complexion goes. Her eyes are blue, of course, and her hair and eyelashes are looking very gingery, so I shan't be surprised if she turns out a redhead. I know you don't like blue eyes and red hair, but she didn't have a chance to have anything but blue eyes, and she had a big chance to have red hair, since it is in both families. I know you are going to be disappointed that we are not coming, but I know you had rather have it spaced a little better.

The house we have taken is unfurnished, and now, for the next week, I shall be ever so busy buying enough to at least start housekeeping. We are saving a great deal by getting our own furniture since we are paying only $45 a month for the house. We shall also be able to save a great deal on the furniture since we can buy for cash, and Wilfred can get good discounts several places because he is in the retail business himself and also because of his former connection with Sears. I know it is much better that we take our money and get furniture so we can start living on an economical basis. I can then save every month for my trip home. If I came home now and spent all our money, then, when I came back, we would still have to pay big rents and have absolutely no chance to save anything to buy furniture with.

I wish you could see my new house, which is an old house. I looked at quite a few places, but for $45 to $50 you must usually take something in a poor neighborhood where the houses are jammed right up against each other, or the sewage is outside only. My house is in a fair neighborhood, but in any case I am in large grounds with a very, very high hedge all around it, so neighborhood doesn't make a great deal of difference to me. The grounds will not be too hard to keep, as most of it is in fruit trees. I shall have a lot of things to can, which was another consideration. My house is stucco and consists of lounge with open fireplace, two bedrooms (both with open fireplaces, which was certainly a consideration with me) and a third room, which I shall use as a sewing room, etc., as one must pass through it to the bathroom, kitchen, and pantry. The kitchen has a coal range, which I am glad of as one simply freezes in these electrified houses. In this house, I can be perfectly comfortable in the coldest weather they get out here. It never gets as cold as at home, but just how cold it gets I cannot say.

    We have had a very mild winter this year, and August is the last month of winter. Our spring starts with September. We shall have our meals in the lounge, which is a large room. I shall furnish the place simply; however, I want rather good things in the lounge since that is the room my guests will see. I have quite a few callers all the time, and I must live decently. I must write you a list of all the baby things given me by friends when I have more time. I am surprised at how many friends I have already. Mrs. Rennie, whose husband has a seat on the stock exchange and is buying seats for two of his sons, is kindness itself to me, as well as her eldest daughter. They have seven children in all and are one of the wealthiest families in town. She brought the baby a beautiful knit coat.

    Wilfred is delighted with his new job. One reason being that they seem so delighted with his work. He does not have to sell (which he always loathed), but he travels to Pretoria and Springs and gives sales talks to the salesmen, and he gets out a weekly sales letter to all their stores. Yesterday, he gave them his ideas on merchandise control, and the heads were delighted with the system he had worked out. His training at Sears, Roebuck is proving invaluable. Of course, writing and talks are just what Wilfred enjoys. He is like a new person since he is doing work that is congenial to him.

    As to the tire retreading business that Father is considering, I have no advice to offer, but I feel I must pass on to you what Wilfred learned about it in Nashville and here. He told me when I mentioned it to him, and I remember he had told me before, that the big rubber companies, like Goodyear, go around to garages handling second-hand cars, for instance, and say, "How much will it cost you to have these tires retreaded?" When the owner gives the retreading price to them, they say, "All right, we will give you new tires for that price." The American companies even do it out here, where there is a big price to pay for tires. They make a canvass of this sort so many times a year. Walter Wiley's brother was in this business in Johnson City. You might be able to find out something there. I hope Father will investigate thoroughly before going into this venture and be guided by what he finds out. I know it takes a lot to dampen his enthusiasm once it is up. You may not hear of this locally just because the rubber companies have not been given enough competition around Elizabethton and Johnson City, but this is what they do in other places, and you know you can't fight the big companies.

That was a dreadful thing about Mrs. F. killing her son-in-law. I don't see how they can let her off scot-free, as there were other ways for her to have handled the situation. She could have called the police or a neighbor, and in the meantime have knocked him down with a chair or something else. If she had killed him by striking him with something, then she shouldn't even have a trial, but it looks to me like she just wanted to kill him. Perhaps she had always hated him. Of course, everything depends on O.'s testimony. It is a sad situation for O. at any rate. Is there any talk of his having been a Sadist?

Don't be surprised if you do not hear from me for two weeks, for I have a great deal to do.

Eve is awfully well and looks fine these days, and I am feeling perfect and have not overdone myself since I got up. I have such a good girl that there is no need for me to.

After I am settled, I shall try to write every week. I think I must have a writing day. I have had a letter from Virginia Lovette and Leone, and a card from Dr. Roesel. All were enjoyed and appreciated. I hate to think of Virginia having to work and especially with such early hours. She is too pretty and should have an easier life. Has she left F., or do you know?

Lots and lots of love from Eve, Myfanwy, and me. You will enjoy Myfanwy more in a year or so than you would just now. She looks almost just like Eve did at that age.

Helen

"Castlewellan"
Parktown North, Johannesburg
September 12, 1938

My dearest Mother and Father,

I hope the fact that Wilfred has a good position and is assured of a steady income will compensate for my not coming at this time. I would have cabled you in a day or two that I was not coming, so it is too bad that you had that extra expense. I simply had not had time to do so, as every day I was attending auction sales trying to buy all of my furniture that way, and I had such a short time to get even the bare necessities so that we could move in. I managed that much, however, but we are still lacking many things; but I am buying gradually and saving a lot of money as well as getting things I like. I am really enjoying this bidding very much. The first sale I attended I spent over $125 that day. I bought two lovely pieces of stinkwood, which is the best you can have here; one is a desk, the other a chest of drawers. Both will go in my lounge.

We have a beautiful new Westinghouse refrigerator, 5' box. We got it at landed cost, plus 10%. I have teak furniture in my dining room and shall have my bedroom all in teak when I can find what I want. I so far have only a Scotch chest of drawers and two good mattresses (new, of course). It is really lots of fun getting one's own furniture, and especially this way. When the house is completely finished, I shall describe each room for you.

I think you will agree with me that it is much better that I come in two years time instead of so soon after leaving. I am afraid only you two have missed us so far after just a year's absence.

Saturday, Wilfred had to go to Pretoria and Springs as Westinghouse has stores in both places, so he took Eve and me along. We went in the company's car, which is a new Ford V8, and the trip took us right along the Reef where three-fifths of the gold of the world is located. The skyline is mine dumps. When we came through one mining area, the natives were just leaving the mines, and there was a continual stream of about five abreast coming for a mile. Eve loves the mine dumps and gets so excited when she sees one. I did a bit of sightseeing while in Pretoria. I went to see Paul Kruger's home. He was President of the Transvaal Republic during the Boer War.

We weighed Robin yesterday, and she weighs ten pounds. She is really a beautiful baby and so wide-awake. She smiles at us if we are giving her all the attention she wants, and she does her best to sit up, but of course that isn't allowed. She has the prettiest-shaped head I ever saw on any baby, and great big eyes like Eve's. I have some pictures of her that I will send to you as soon as they come to light. Much that I have is still packed up.

I had such a nice letter and two pretty bibs from Mrs. Richter. I thought it was awfully nice of her. I also had a letter from Virginia Lovette, and cards from Edna Edens and the Mary Cameron Bible Class. Of course, I have heard from Mary Walker too. I shall write them all as soon as I am a little more straightened up.

Eve was very disappointed that I gave up the trip to America; however, she was torn between two places, as she didn't want to leave her Daddy but she did want to see Mama Sophia and Papa Harlow. I must get this off today to catch the mail boat. I have so little time for writing.

I enclose a picture snapped of me the other day downtown. I was on my way to see the Agent who rented us our new house, as all my water pipes were leaking. I was as mad as I had ever been in my life. It looks like the man behind me is laughing at me.

Lots and lots of love,

Helen

And Indeed There Will Be Time (Sept. 1937—Aug.1939)

"Castlewellan"
No. 2 Eighth Avenue
Parktown North, Johannesburg
September 27, 1938

My dearest Mother and Father,

    I am enclosing a map of the town showing the different places we have lived. I thought you might be interested in getting some idea of the layout of the City of Gold. I know it pretty well now since I have managed to live in several different localities myself. We are now on a hill that overlooks a lot of the city, and it is really beautiful at night. I like where we are now better than any place so far; it is the most perfect place for children you can imagine, with large shade trees, a high hedge all around about an acre of ground, etc.

    We certainly don't feel any too good about conditions in Europe. I am enclosing a clipping of an incident that happened here on the 24th of September. I am wondering if Hitler may not make a point of it. This paper does not mention it, but what started it all was that the car with the five men in fascist uniforms knocked down a native boy and then stopped and got out and started beating him up. An ex-soldier of the World War noticed it and pitched in, and this started a free for all. This happened on the busiest corner in the city.

    Robin and Eve are just fine. Eve is already as brown as a berry, and Robin is having her sunbaths every day—but not much, as she is very fair, and I am afraid she will freckle easily. Eve has a permanent wave, which improves her a great deal. It is so dry here that her hair was as straight as a stick. She thinks she looks like Shirley Temple and told us she would really be Shirley Temple if she had an automobile and house of her own. She said a quaint thing the other day. Bert gave Eve a budgie, a bird you see a great deal out here, and Wilfred bought Eve a French poodle some time back. The budgerigar (Peter) got out of his cage and flew away, and the poodle stayed with us only one night. It has been two months since we have had either pet, but the other day Eve said, "Myself is withering for Peter and my little dog." Another thing she is always saying is that she can't bring her Shirley doll outdoors because her eyes are "flavoring." Her dolls are always ill, according to her.

    I don't think I have told you that I had three nurses during my confinement. The first one I had for five days, and she was excellent. Her next case called her on my fifth day, and, being big-hearted, I let her go. The next nurse (she got her for me) was what is known out here as "Dopper Dutch." The lowest class of Dutch and the most irritating person I ever ran across. I kept her one day. The next nurse was just out from England, but she was mental, I should say, and talked me to death about her recent illness. The Dutch nurse left a dummy [pacifier] in the baby's mouth all night to keep her from crying. She and I were at dagger points the whole twenty-four hours she was with me. She also said she never used disinfectants since it was foolish. I told her she would use them with me. She said she was taking the chance if anything went wrong. I told her it so happened I would be the one to suffer and who would get the blame, so it would not make much difference if anything went wrong. I could write volumes on her, but I find myself getting mad all over again.

You can tell, if you like, that Wilfred has left Sears and gone with Westinghouse because he found out that Sears International was none too firm financially. Sears International is quite separate from Sears, Roebuck, and Sears, Roebuck refuses to go into the exporting field in any way themselves, except agriculture implements. Wilfred is crazy about his new job and thinks his boss is perfect. I have never seen him so happy. He has to work hard, and we have very little time together, but we are both delighted that he is with Westinghouse because we think he is going places with them.

I am feeling as strong as ever; in fact, I don't know when I have felt so well. I weigh 140 lbs. and, since that is less than I have weighed for some time, I look much better. It has also helped my looks that I do not have to work so hard anymore. Of course, I have quite a lot to do with two children, but I can lie down whenever I want to, and I don't have to keep going like one has to when you go to an office every day.

What is wrong with Aunt Kate? You just wrote me that Kate is still in the hospital at Abington and that is all. There are so many people I would love to write to, and she is one of them. I have no time for writing just now, so please give her my love.

Strangely enough, the day before I got your letter telling me of Mr. Barney Thompson's death, I thought of him and said to myself, I wonder when I will hear of his death. The Whiting girl was such a pretty girl the last time I saw her years ago. I know she has been an invalid, but I don't know just what the trouble was. Do you know? I would like to know.

Wilfred goes to Pretoria and Springs about three or four times a week, and I can drive with him whenever I have the time. I have been twice and it makes a nice outing. We took Eve one time and took a picnic lunch. She had a grand time, of course. I am sure I am writing some of these things for the second time. I should make carbon copies of my letters, as it is so hard to remember just what one has written about, because I often have a lot of things in mind to say in a letter and just don't have time to write them and think I will include them in my next letter.

I must close now and get busy bathing Eve for the night and helping with dinner, etc. From five o'clock in the afternoon on is a very busy time in this household.

With lots and lots of love from your devoted children,

Eve, Robin, and Helen

Note: In 1938, South African Europeans, both those of British descent (i.e., the English) and those of Dutch, German, and French Huguenot descent (i.e., the Afrikaners) were still at loggerheads with one another over various British interventions in South Africa. Still fresh in the minds of many Afrikaners were the memories of England's abolition of slavery in the early nineteenth century and of British atrocities during the Second Boer War, when 26,000 Afrikaner women and children were incarcerated and died of diseases and starvation in British concentration camps. At this point in time, the British were the source of the Afrikaners' rage, but black South Africans were also a target for their anger. Later, with the advent of fascism in Europe, this latent prejudice evolved into the idiology of "apartheid," or the separation of the races. In spite of the fact that the Facsists in Europe lost world War II, by 1948 the hostility to those who were not of European descent (70% of the population) had grown into extreme prejudice in South Africa. The Afrikaners referred to "Non-Europeans" as "Die Swart Gevaar" ("The Black Threat"), and the Nationalist Government began the task of dividing people of color into separate groups based on language and appearance. They called this ideology "Separate Development." By the early 1990s it became clear that "Separate Development" had failed. On May 10, 1994, Nelson Mandela (of the Thembu tribe), after twenty-seven years of imprisonment for protesting white rule, was inaugurated as South Africa's first democratically elected president.

"Castlewellan"
No. 2 Eighth Avenue, Parktown North
Johannesburg, South Africa
October 4, 1938

My dearest Mother,

    Such a stew as you have worked yourself into. Please don't do it again. Can't you imagine that letters may have gone astray? I have not waited eight weeks to write you, so some letters have gone astray. Did you ever receive any letters postmarked from London, England? I sent you some letters Air Mail through Hendy and Farquharson which would have been postmarked from London. All mail from here to England goes Air Mail, so Hendy and Farquharson had an arrangement with an English firm to forward mail for America for them by surface mail, thereby getting Air Mail service for regular postage. You may not have received those letters. You may still get letters postmarked London, as Westinghouse has a similar arrangement with a London firm.

    I am returning your money order as the cable I sent only cost me seven shillings, about $1.75. I could easily afford that. It is thoughtful of you to send it, but you must not do it again. To send money is quite expensive, as one always loses on exchange. I hope you can get your money back all right.

I haven't written you often during the last two months because I have been so busy trying to get my furniture together cheaply and take care of Robin too, but Bert remembers that I gave her a letter to mail to you about the 20th of August. That was the letter thanking you for the wonderful box of clothes for Eve and me. Then I have written you at least one letter in September, since I moved to my new place. I know that isn't much, and I can do much better from now on, but I was simply too busy for more at the time. After my nurse left, and I had sole care of Robin, I only averaged four hours sleep in twenty-four, for two or three weeks. I nearly went crazy for sleep. Now our baby sleeps from six at night until 6:30 or 7:00 in the morning.

When we found a house we could afford at $45 per month, which decided one to stay, I had to start buying furniture. I hardly have a new thing in the house, as I have bought it all at auction sales. I have my place furnished very nicely now at a surprisingly low figure. One must have patience to furnish this way cheaply, as you often must let things go by that you want because you know that no doubt the next week at another sale you can buy it at half the price. I have two vases that cost $10 each (they match) and I paid $1.25 each for them. They are the willow pattern. My dining room table is teak oval with plate glass top, and I only paid $10 for it.

As our house has no closets, which is the usual case over here, I had to have a wardrobe, so I bought a good teak one, with dresser and tallboy to match for $35. The wardrobe had a full-length mirror inside one of the doors. I even bought my dishes, glasses, silver, and cooking utensils this way. I bought Robin's bed new. It is like the one Eve had but in Robin-egg blue and has solid ends. The sides slide, of course. We got it wholesale, however. If we had had to pay retail prices for new furniture, it would have cost us several thousand. As it is, I think it cost around $1,000. I'll write you when I figure it up. I am into making curtains now. They don't come cheap, I find, but I want them new. I don't like the usual taste in curtains out here.

Wilfred was put in charge of personnel at the store starting today. His real job, however, is Assistant Supervisor of the Transvaal—therefore he travels a great deal every week, but he can always be home at night, as Pretoria and Springs are only thirty-five miles from J'burg. He also writes sales letters now and then, which are sent all over the Union of South Africa. He is very busy, as you can see, but he is crazy about his work and his boss. He played golf on Sunday with his boss, the accountant of Westinghouse, and the J'burg store manager. He came out with low score.

Robin is simply beautiful. I would give anything if you could see her. If she turns out to look as I think she will, she will be a knockout. Mr. Evans worships her. He has no ears even for information about Wilfred's progress when he is here, as he just sits with Robin in his arms. Bert cries over her every time she sees her. Eve is looking pretty, too, with her eyes as big as ever. I am going to investigate a kindergarten nearby and, if I like the teacher and children, I shall start Eve, as I haven't the time for stories, etc., that she wants and should have now. She still prefers boxes and string to any toys. She does clever things with them. If you haven't disposed of her toys that we left, don't, for she remembers everything and wants to go back to them. They will do for Robin when we get back.

By the way, Eve has a letter for you, which I shall mail if I can find it. I don't know what is in it, as she handed it to me sealed.

I mustn't write more, as I shall try to send this Air Mail through Westinghouse.

I'll let you know when to worry about me, so, until proper notice, just keep calm. Wilfred or Bert would always cable or write if I couldn't.

Lots and lots of love and kisses,

Helen

"Castlewellan"
No. 2 Eighth Avenue
Parktown North, Johannesburg
October 11, 1938

My dearest Mother and Father,

I got your letter yesterday saying you had heard from me. Since you knew I must be having a busy time, I do not think from the 20th of July to the 9th of August was such a long lapse of time between letters from me. I can tell you that your letters have made me feel terrible recently, and I am just as happy to have this last letter from you as you were to receive my letter of August 9.

You need not worry about my investment in furniture, as nearly all of it was bought second-hand, and, if I wanted to sell it a year from now, I could get what I put in it and more on some pieces. I have everything but my living room rug, and we are having that covered completely with green carpeting. I need some small rugs for my two bedrooms and curtains all over the house. I know this will add up, but we still have the money for it, so I am not worrying. Wilfred's family—that is, Bert and Mr. Evans—only have enough for their two flats, as they disposed of the rest when Mrs. Evans died. I am using a few things of theirs, such as a clothesbasket and a kitchen bin, also some linoleum.

Mr. Evans plans to sell his stocks when the market here is again normal and build Wilfred and me a home. We will pay the rent we can afford to pay and live in a nice place. I know Mr. Evans and I will disagree on a thousand points, but, so help me, I intend to have the house the way I want it. The only way I know of to do this is to say that, if he builds what we want, we may, when we are able, start buying it from him. Of course, I want a furnace and screens throughout the house and the commode in the bathroom and no ventilators in the house, etc. All of these things are unheard of, and, before I have finished, I suppose I shall have a few run-ins with the municipal inspectors. Once they get a way of doing things out here, there is no changing them. Of course, a lot of money will have to be sunk in building the house of solid brick, as they think anything else will topple over one fair day. No doubt this is even a municipal regulation, as they will not allow a frame house to be built in the city limits.

    I have been so wrapped up in my own affairs that I am afraid I have forgotten to wish you, Mother, many more happy birthdays. I spent my birthday quietly at home, as my girl has Sunday afternoons off, and Wilfred did not have the car from Westinghouse that weekend. We often have a car over the weekend and about three nights a week so that it is just about like having our own car except we have no investment and no expense. I call that pretty good. It is like an extra $25 on Wilfred's salary. If we did not have the car, we could never get into town to shows, as we are so far out that it takes half an hour by bus, when you finally get a bus, for they do not run so often out this way. It is nothing to wait half to a whole hour on one.

Helen and baby Robin

    Did I ever write you about the scare I had over my best furniture? At the first auction sale I attended I bought the best furniture I have, two pieces of stinkwood among the lot. I turned it over to a native boy to deliver, and he did not turn up with it until the next day. All the afternoon and night of the day of the sale I was sure it had been stolen by him, and I did not know his name or his number. We reported it to the police, and they sent a sergeant to take my statement. The next morning we went to the main police station, and the man in attendance gave me a long lecture on what I had failed to do, such as take the boy's number (cart number). He finally annoyed me so that I told him in no uncertain terms that I had not come in for a lecture from him but to see if he could assist me in finding my furniture, which I now doubted. Wilfred was so surprised at me that he nearly dropped over. He then gave me a lecture outside that I certainly went about getting assistance in a queer way, by making the man mad.

And Indeed There Will Be Time (Sept. 1937—Aug. 1939)

I suppose I controlled myself in Elizabethton for so long that that is the reason I go on a spree now and then here. The other day at an auction the auctioneer asked for a starting bid on a wardrobe and a dresser. They were very good furniture. There was not a sound from anyone although he repeated his request several times. Finally, since I wanted to bid on it, I said four pounds, $20.

He turned to me and said, "Madam, what are you bidding on, may I ask?"

I said, "I am bidding on what you are trying to sell, now go on with the bidding."

He saw he had gotten fresh with the wrong person, so he said, "Thank you madam, a very good bid." And he went on with the bidding. Wilfred's father was with me and he was well amused, as well as everyone else.

We have a boy cutting the hedge today. It will be about a four-day job, he says, and I don't doubt it because it is completely around the property, and our lot is as big as the L's. By the way, do what you think is best about the shades. I know it is an expensive job if they need new shades all over the place. There are so many windows there. Let me know how the accounts stand on the property. I suppose you can see the house is not a good investment, and I hate to have the drag of it since I shall never get to live in it. Wilfred's business will never take him to Johnson City, and, if we should ever be fortunate enough to retire, it would not be in Johnson City. That house would rent for $125 over here, and then it would be a good investment.

Wilfred gives me $150 per month to run the house on and keeps fifty for his own use—lunches, bus fare, amusements for both of us, etc. I am anxious to see how I come out. I was terribly nervous at first, writing checks in pounds, shillings, and pence, but I understand it all now and have only had to stop payment on one check. The firm is foaming at the mouth, but let them. They tried to get tough with me over a bed I bought for Robin and did not want and never even had it in the house, so I just stopped payment on the check I had given for it. Here, if you once hand out some money, you need never expect to see it again. For instance, Wilfred and I both paid the same telephone bill a month ago and we are still trying to get the money back, even though it is run by the municipality.

I wish I could make the drive to Blowing Rock at this time of year. It must have been beautiful. We do not have a single pretty drive around here. The other evening we drove to Northcliff, the highest point outside of J'burg, and had a wonderful view of the city, or rather of the lights. Below us were thousands of lights, just as far as one could see. There is a tearoom at Northcliff, also some very lovely big homes.

Robin is doing so well; she sleeps from six o'clock at night until six or seven in the morning. She does this every night now. Last night at six, she threw up her milk, and I expected to have trouble with her during the night, but not a sound until this morning at six. She seems all right today, so I don't know why she threw it up. I gave her Cod Liver Oil just before it, and I thought perhaps that had something to do with it. She likes Cod Liver Oil and orange juice. Next month, I start her on Pablum[46] too. I do wish you all could see her, as she is so pretty. She smiles at all of us when we talk to her, and she looks around from one to the other and guides her bottle to her mouth and holds on to it for dear life. She has also started cooing, which I think is so sweet. Robin is the first baby I have ever had. I didn't have Eve until she was three years old. When I used to come home from the office, I could never get into the way of doing things for Eve. I never felt she belonged to me. I suppose you often wished I did feel some responsibility.

Eve was delighted with her cards from you, Mother, and Uncle Fred. Did you two make the trip alone?

Eve is now at the age that she has just started asking for toys, and she can think of more things that she just must have. For Christmas, she wants a big dollhouse, a real motor car like Shirley Temple's, a pram for her doll, a kitchen "cabin," etc. Today she called a vase, a "vah." She is really comical striving for the broad "a."

I did a good job yesterday shortening a dress at the waistline two inches. I also shortened two princess slips. I have Bert's Singer sewing machine out here. It is a hand one, though, and that makes it a little difficult to do a good job, as one hand must be occupied with turning the wheel.

I have bought *The Running of the Deer* as my next book for my book club. I have ordered *The Importance of Living* for the one after that. They are so slow about getting certain books out here. They are always stocked with books by local authors, which I have decided are no good, just like their local bottled and canned goods. Why they can't make good vinegar or good pickles in this country I do not know, but I always pay the higher price to get the imported goods.

Poor Uncle Hunter. I was afraid he would not get a job in Cincinnati. Who is paying his board at the Southern Hotel and where is that? How is Aunt Kate now? Is she going to take up her job at Intermont? As for M. and Mrs. D. going to Florida for two weeks, I suppose you will hear little about it since no one expects any better than that from either of them. People can get by with more in Elizabethton and still go around than any place I ever heard of.

This is washday, so I must stop and get busy around the house, as I must do the work on that day and do quite a lot the following day when Lizzie irons. Lizzie went home this past Saturday and Sunday, and I had to get along alone. It wasn't

---

[46] Developed in 1931, Pablum is a dry cereal known for its ease of preparation. Up until that time, babies in industrialized nations were, on account of various nutritional deficiencies, susceptible to rickets. Pablum made it easier for mothers to be sure that their babies were receiving the nourishment they needed.

too bad, but I can tell you I never stopped until Sunday afternoon. (Sketched map of new home enclosed.)[47]

Love and kisses,

Helen

> "Castlewellan"
> No. 2 Eighth Avenue
> Parktown North, Johannesburg
> October 25, 1938

My dearest Mother and Father,

The rush of the morning is over, as it is now 10:30. From 7:00 until 10:30 is a very busy time in this household, as the milk must be made, the bottles washed and boiled, and the baby bathed, fed Cod Liver Oil, orange juice, and a bottle of milk. She loves them all. She has started gargling her oil, which is too funny. I would give a great, great deal if you both could see Robin and Eve. Robin is lovely and fat and has rosy cheeks. She has done so well all along. Eve looks very pretty now, as her hair curls beautifully and is so fair. I think the sun keeps it that way.

I played bridge yesterday for the first time since Robin's arrival, and I was rotten. I had nearly forgotten the game, it seemed.

Wilfred will be made assistant manager of the Transvaal (officially) at the end of this month. He has been that in reality for a month or more. He still likes his job just fine. We feel more settled than we have ever felt before—that is, as far as business goes.

As for my house, well, I hope to move again at the end of this month. The place we want to take is $60 per month, but, if you pay less, you can't live in a decent place. To think that I now pay as much as you do, and the house is so poorly built that the whole thing shakes every time the bus or a truck passes. In quite a few places the planks in the floor give way until you think you are going through. The inside commode does not work, so we have to use the outside one with our native girl. I have Eve use a chamber all of the time. I have to keep Jeyes Fluid in the inside one to keep the odor down, as it is choked right up. Of course, we did not know there would be anything like the commode out of order, and we did not know the house would shake.

When I asked that the commode be fixed and the leaks stopped, the agent said, "You are not living in Parkview and paying £18 rent." Parkview is a good suburb.

---

[47] The sketch has not survived, but Helen loved to draw plans of the homes she lived in. As a young woman, she was a fine artist with a flair for working with watercolors and oils. Only four of her paintings survive.

I said, "No, I am not living in Parkview, and I know it only too well, but I <u>am paying</u> rent, am I not?"

There are about three different kinds of woodwork in each room, etc. It is simply a jerrybuilt place. We have spent so much on painting two rooms and the floors and cleaning up the grounds that we want to get out without paying this month's rent. Whether we can or not, I do not know. The other house is really nice. There is a large lounge with open fireplace, dining room, three bedrooms, kitchen, pantry, bath, garage, and servants' quarters. The yard is small but large enough without a garden boy. It is in a good locality—a bank manager lives next door. I just haven't let anybody come to see me here. You can continue with my present address until I know, as I will leave my new address at the post office here.

These stamps came through unmarked, so I am sending them back to you, as I can't use them.

I am surprised at C.B. marrying A.R. He may come from a good family, but I had never thought of him as her social equal. She is a good friend of J.B. Have you heard anything about her? I expected to hear of her marriage to N.J. before now. Do you hear of Mr. Smith going with anyone?

I hope to go over to Pretoria this week, as this is Jacaranda Week and Pretoria is famed for its trees. It is a gorgeous purple bloom, you know.

I must get busy on shortening some of my summer dresses. This is our rainy season, but we have many hot days now.

Lots and lots of love,

Helen

"Castlewellan"
No. 2 Eighth Avenue
Parktown North, Johannesburg
November 5, 1938

Dearest Mother and Father,

I have letters from both of you this week, which is so unusual that I feel you should each have a letter from me, but then I would be repeating myself in the two letters, and I know you don't want repetition in my long epistles.

You all had might as well let me know in advance about tonsil operations, etc., for I know there is something up, but I am mystified as to why I am worried. Just about the time Father had his operation, I felt worried about him. I know tonsil operations aren't supposed to amount to much, but every operation is dangerous to a certain extent. I am glad it is all over now, and I do hope Father took enough time off from the office to fully recover. I remember I felt bad for several weeks after mine were taken out.

I know you will be glad to get the two snaps I am enclosing. We took these last Sunday, and they are real good, I think.

November 9th

I was interrupted at this point and am just now getting back. Unfortunately, I have developed a bad cold and do not feel like writing the long letter I had intended to write. I must mail this today to catch the mail. I am in bed today, as that is about the only thing to do for a cold. It is wonderful that I have a good girl and can stay in bed when necessary. I hope to be up tomorrow. We missed getting the house we wanted, but don't worry about us where we are, as it is livable. We must have something better, however. We shall never get it, however, under $62.50 per month. Note how Lizzie keeps my porch and steps polished. Eve loves to have her picture made, as you can see from her pose.

Lots of love,
Helen

"Castlewellan"
No. 2 Eighth Avenue
Parktown North, Johannesburg
November 5, 1938

My dearest Mary,

I have thought of you every day, I suppose, and all the things I wanted to tell you have gone back and forth through my mind a million times. I knew when I wrote it would have to be a long letter, and there just hasn't been time for a long letter, so I have waited and finally a day has arrived in which there promises to be a few free hours. Since this is Guy Fawkes' Day[48] and the English celebrate it as we do the Fourth of July, I am expecting nothing less than a bomb any minute to interrupt my serenity.

To begin with, let me thank you for writing so often during MY LAST DAYS of Preg. I appreciated that a great deal. I am wondering if you have heard all about it from Mother. I had my easy time, all right, and was talking about another one just a few hours afterwards. Really, it was next to nothing. I had no chloroform or ether, and my nurse held things up a good twenty minutes waiting for the doctor, so I nearly had no doctor. I wish he hadn't arrived and we would be in ten guineas.

---

[48] Guy Fawkes' Day originated in England as a way to celebrate the foiling of a plot to assassinate King James I in 1605. Guido Fawkes and his fellow-conspirators had planned to blow up the English Parliament and kill the king. This, they hoped, would pave the way for the reinstatement of Catholicism in England. Every year, the detention and death of Fawkes is celebrated on the 5th of November with bonfires and the burning of Fawkes' effigies.

Robin is a lovely baby and has done so well all along. She has rolls of fat and rosy cheeks, and a big appetite. She laughs and makes gorgeous noises—such cooing, gurgling, crackers, etc. Really, we are terribly happy over having Robin. She has blue eyes, of course, and we aren't sure, but maybe red hair. Robin is just her baby name, as she will be christened Myfanwy. Correctly pronounced, that is a beautiful name; maybe you heard that Leone said it spelled "My fanny" to her. No doubt it will prove a dangerous name to have in America.

Well, what a busy time I have been having. It wasn't enough for me to give birth to a child, so, six weeks afterwards, I was buying furniture and fixing up a house, as I wanted it. Really, I was so sick of other peoples' taste that I didn't know what to do. Also, for the first time, I feel settled here. I haven't much, but thank goodness it is all paid for, and, not having much money to do it on, I had great fun finding bargains. Everything was bought at auction sales, and what I have came from some of the best homes in J'burg. I felt a bit like a scavenger, as my bargains came from someone else's misfortune, such as death or loss of money. I have never known such a place for auction sales in my life. Of course, at first I sat and listened and tried to understand just one word the auctioneer was saying. It didn't sound like anything but a mumble at first; then I caught on and spent $125 at my first sale. I have two very nice pieces—a stinkwood desk and a stinkwood chest of drawers. It is to me the most beautiful wood I know. It is very valuable, as it grows only in a restricted area in the Cape and nowhere else in the world. It takes over six hundred years for the trees to mature. The other possession I am proud of is my Westinghouse refrigerator.

My Westinghouse brings me to tell you of Wilfred's change. He is no longer with Sears International but with Westinghouse Electric. We kept on hearing that Sears International was going to close up, not from the organization itself, of course, but from bankers, etc. Sears International actually wrote a letter to all their men denying the reports; however, we did not feel too safe, so when Wilfred was offered a job with Westinghouse, he took it. Westinghouse is new out here, just since last February, so Wilfred is in on the ground floor. He is assistant superintendent of the Transvaal and must travel between Pretoria, Springs, and Johannesburg. He likes it many times better than his connection with Sears. I go with him when I can. However, due to so much business at home, I have only been to Pretoria twice and to Springs once. The last trip to Pretoria I made to see the jacaranda in bloom. All the streets are lined with these trees, so it is just one avenue after another of purple. In the morning it is a light shade, more lavender, but in the evening it is a real purple.

You know, of course, without my saying it, that I am terribly sorry that you all are having a more or less difficult time now. I suppose you all had hoped that the mill would be able to support two families by the time Mr. Walker went out of office. If you felt you must work, I am so glad you are doing something you really

And Indeed There Will Be Time (Sept. 1937—Aug. 1939)

like. It seems to me that during the last few years America has been a very hard place in which to survive. I don't believe I could have stood it all any longer, as I had such a big dose. Conditions are much better out here, and I do wish South Africa was not so far away, and I would say for Knaffl to come try his fortunes out here. The only thing Wilfred could help him get into is selling on commission, and you know how unstable that is. Too, it costs so much to get out here. Anyway, Wilfred wants to know if you all would consider coming here. If you say "yes" to this, be sure to let us know what Knaffl's prospects are there, so we would know better what would be the wise thing to do.

Knowing how much you have read (and, having read, then dreamed) about distant lands, I think you would find it a kinder fate if you never get to travel a great deal, for, from the bit I have seen, I must say that, often, to travel is to be disillusioned. For instance, I had always wanted to see Madeira. I have looked with longing at it a hundred times on different maps, and then I saw Madeira. Madeira itself is beautiful, but it is ruined by the beggars on the streets. They drive you crazy; in fact, I had to go to bed when I got back on the ship because they had exhausted me. The only thing to do is to go quickly through the town and take a drive up the mountain, which we did. The view is magnificent looking out over the harbor. Then too, one knows that many of the men rush to the famous whorehouse of Madame Jesus. Such blasphemy is too dreadful, but that is the name of it. As for South Africa, and what I have seen of it, Cape Town is beautiful, but there is nothing to East London, Port Elizabeth, and Durban, and you can't imagine a more uninteresting place than Johannesburg. When we take a drive, about the only thing I can think of that I want to see are the mine dumps. To me, they are beautiful, but then everybody else here thinks I am crazy.

The gardens to the homes here are, I imagine, about the most beautiful in the world. On my street is a house and garden too lovely for words; it looks like a fairy castle set back in the loveliest garden imaginable. When I was a child I never dreamed of a lovelier place, and you know what a child's fancy is. I want to take pictures of it, but I am sure they would be disappointing. The house is built of rondavels;[49] each room is round, and each one seems to be on a different level, and it is thatched. It is a place that stirs your imagination. You wonder what is around that side of the house, and what is behind that wall, or that shrub. What I have just tried to describe seems to contradict completely what I set out to prove—that to travel is to be disillusioned.

---

[49] Rondavels are a westernized version of the cylindrical one-roomed African hut. They may be simple structures serving as a single guesthouse or garden room, or they may be large and linked together in interesting patterns for the affluent homeowner, the results of which can be stunningly beautiful. Rondavels, in the areas of the city that were reserved for Europeans, were covered with expensive thatched roofs harking back to the European roots of their owners while melding with the simpler indigenous thatched-roofed huts of rural South Africa.

I am much thinner than you have seen me in a long time; in fact, I should say I am just about the right size for me. You know I don't look well too thin. I had my hair cut just this week and wear it in one of those very modern modes of rolls and ringlets. I had to have it cut without Wilfred's knowledge since he insisted that he wanted me to have long hair, but now, of course, he likes it ever so much better. I am, therefore, looking a bit younger than I have looked in years, although my hair is turning quite grey. It has turned much greyer this past year, and if I come home in two more years, you may see it white then. I had rather have it white than streaked, as it is.

Try to get *Lust for Life* to read. It is the life story of Van Gogh. No doubt you have already read it long ago. Have you read *The Rains Came*? I finished it in bed after Robin arrived.

I have written a long letter, but what I need is a long talk with you, for there is heaps more to be said. Anyway, I must buzz off and do some other things right now.

We all wish the best of everything for the three of you. Mary, please give my love to your mother and Elizabeth.

Lots of love,

Helen

"Castlewellan"
No. 2 Eighth Avenue
Parktown North, Johannesburg
November 14, 1938

Dearest Ones,

I have to write my letter in such a hurry, usually, that I am sure I don't answer your questions as I should, but tonight, with Wilfred back at the office and the children asleep, I hope to answer a few things in the letters spread around me.

Today, I got your letter with the very nifty pair of hose in it. They came through without any trouble at all, but it won't pay me to buy them that way, for they are just about the same price here. People here are under the impression that hose are cheaper in America, and they are always grumbling about what they have to pay, but it is no more than we pay. I haven't bought a pair yet, but I am right at the end of my supply now, and these you have sent will look very smart with my white shoes and the new London tan dress I bought to wear with them.

You know, I weigh just about 136 now, and, in this new dress, my figure looks very good indeed. I am just the size now that we always agreed was most becoming to me. And this reminds me that I haven't told you that I have had my hair cut, and I wear it with a roll in front, a roll in the back, and curls on the side. It is a great improvement. Unfortunately, I continue in turning grey, and I have a

And Indeed There Will Be Time (Sept. 1937—Aug.1939) 163

great deal of simply white hair. I hope I shall at least look distinguished one day. They charge $10 to dye your hair, and then you must have it touched up every six weeks at $5 a time, all of which I can't do. I forgot to say I have a perm, but you must have guessed it. It isn't frizzy, but I paid top price for it at the best place in town. It cost $10.

You ask what all Robin got. She got about eight sweaters and about eight pairs of booties, a handmade blue woolen dress made by a friend of mine, a pink woolen dress, white kid shoes with fur around the top (Mrs. Days shoes), a pretty pink linen cover for her cot with beautiful embroidery on it, a pair of knit panties which are very nice when she goes out. She has about six sweaters she has never had on. She also has a blue cape that was given to her that she looks too cute in. I had beautiful flowers too. Everyone was lovely to me, and I have been so torn up [about the house] since the baby's arrival that I have been anything but sociable.

Since I found this house so unsatisfactory, I haven't bought curtains or rugs. I have only bedroom curtains. In my room, I have the green ones Bert sent me with the green silk bedspread. In Eve and Robin's room, I have pink ones with a white dot. Bert made them, and they are awfully pretty with a frill all around. Bert made the prettiest blue sheets for Robin's new blue bed. The top sheet is tucked with two rows of lace insertion. We have material for a pink pair too.

The only thing you might send Robin for a present is a pretty lace cap. I do not like the caps she has on her. That is the only thing I can think of. I mention this because you seemed to want to know of something. I shall be glad to have the sun suit for Eve. She has already been able to wear one a day or two this spring. Some days are very hot, even this early. I think they look cute in sun suits. How about that yellow sun suit that Eve has? If it is O.K., I would like it for Robin. I always loved it on Eve. I shall be most happy to get my wash dress. I am wondering if you made it. The green housecoat is much too large for me now, but Bert and I are going to take it up, which won't be hard to do. The dress I bought was a 16 [English size], so nothing had to be done to it. It was simply a perfect fit.

I would love to have seen the Presbyterian Church all decorated for Dot's wedding. I hope Mrs. Siemen appreciated what you all did. I am sorry you are having so much trouble with L., but anyone who deals with him will have trouble. Now you will better appreciate the spats that Father, Wilfred, and I had with him. I am glad you got $65 out of him, but no doubt the taxes take it all. That is, the increase in taxes takes the increase in rent. For $65 I can't even get a place with three bedrooms and an inside toilet. If you ever get a chance to sell at $10,000, for goodness sake, do it, because it is never going to be worth anything to us. With $4,500 to $5,000 capital, I could be assured of a trip home every three years on just the interest.

I wish we could be rid of L. too, because I really hate the man. There were four or five months before we went to Mrs. Alexander's to board that there was never a day that Wilfred and I had enough to eat in our effort to meet the payments on that house. One month we lived on $40, which I consider something of a feat in any country. The plants thought I would lose that house and they'd have it back for the amount of the mortgage. I thought this when I was in the middle of the stew, and I hold the same opinion now that I am out of it.

I know Dad is tired of all this about clothes, etc., and wants something about this country and the customs. Well, it is about as different from our section of the States as Texas is. That is, just about all the people here remind me of the people in Texas. They have an awful lot of money, but they can remember when they didn't, and, when they think back on the lean years, their faces light up as though those were the best years. Of course, one meets those who haven't anything and were born social climbers, and they are just as unpleasant out here as at home. Unfortunately, most of these are Americans.

Helen's investment house, Johnson City, Tennessee

One day I must take my Kodak to town with me and snap some pictures. Some of the things I take for granted now might seem queer to you—such as a native boy in the heart of the city delivering a large tray of tea at eleven in the morning by riding a bicycle with the tray balanced on his head. Then there are the delivery carts that one may hire for delivering parcels four or five miles away. These carts are pulled by a native boy dressed in ceremonial robes, it would seem. They wear heavy blankets on the hottest day, feathers, beads, etc.

Then there are the native girls carrying their babies on their backs. Of course, here a negro woman is called a girl all of her life, and a man is a boy all of his life. Eve often carries Joan (one of her dolls) on her back, held on by a piece of material tied around her. The natives always talk together in their own dialects. They manage to understand each other even though they speak different dialects. They must always have a little conversation too. Every delivery boy stops for a chat with my Lizzie. Fortunately, Lizzie is married and apparently faithful to her husband. Her husband stays here too and is a wonderful worker. He has done a lot for us in the evenings.

Nearly everybody I know goes out or entertains with bridge or tea every day in the week, and they book up for two weeks ahead. Of course, I haven't time for all of that and try to keep it down to three times a week. They also play a lot of golf and tennis. Every woman can play tennis, it seems, and they are at their prime when they are Mother's age. I do not know anyone who would consider working as you have always done, and Aunt Lennie, and Aunt Nellie, Aunt Lula, etc. Not many of them have such nice homes as you all are living in, or have lived in, and their husbands keep the car all day, but they tea it up and take it easy. I am gradually calming myself down. I catch myself burning garbage or covering it up now and then, and, as soon as I realize what I am doing, I come in and content myself with a book. There is definitely more grace in living here.

Yesterday, Mr. Sours, president of Westinghouse in S.A., and Mrs. Sours and daughter called on us. I nearly died when I saw them at first, but later was glad of their visit, for he may decide we need more money to live even decently. I had met her before, but not him. He is a very witty man, and I enjoyed him. The children both looked clean, and so did I, as well as Bert, her father, and Wilfred. The house was clean but bare, so he should know whose fault that is.

Personally, I think we have given so much to Hitler that one might as well give him his colonies back; that means Southwest Africa. They pick diamonds up off the ground, but otherwise it isn't worth anything.[50] I must to bed.

Lots of love,
Helen

No. 2 Eighth Avenue
Parktown North, Johannesburg
November 29, 1938

Dearest Mother and Father,

This will go Air Mail, so I must make it short so my letter won't be overweight.

The Ocean and Accident Insurance Co. is bonding Wilfred, so Father may get a letter of inquiry from them about Wilfred. You may not get a letter at all, as they may only write Sears International and Sears, Roebuck. If they do write, however, you need only testify as to his honesty. The wife of the assistant general manager

---

[50] Of course, Helen is being ironic here. She and Wilfred were deeply concerned about England's failure to confront Nazi Germany and the losses that could accrue from a war. Helen could also have mentioned that Southwest Africa, now known as Namibia, had not only diamonds but huge designated wilderness areas for lions, giraffes, rhinos, elephants, and other animals, making it one of the largest protectors of wildlife in the world. The Germans had surrendered Southwest Africa in 1915. In 1919, General Smuts (and Louis Botha), eager to broaden South Africa's influence, argued successfully for a formal mandate over Southwest Africa by the Union of South Africa.

of this insurance company is in my book club. They have invited us over this week for cocktails. I like her very much, and Wilfred likes him. I haven't met him yet. She is very literary, so I am sure she and Wilfred will enjoy each other.

I did worry a bit when I did not hear from you last week, and then thought how foolish, for I know how busy I am some weeks. I was glad to find it was only a good time that kept you from writing.

I don't know whether little girls over here wear long party dresses or not. I haven't seen any. Bert is making Eve a party dress for Xmas. What Eve needs most is a lightweight coat. Do you think you could make her one? I think I would like it in pink or tan. Her winter coat is blue. I had thought of trying to make one myself.

Wilfred is building a lovely doll's house for Eve's Xmas. Of course, she knows nothing about it, but her one big wish is for a doll's house. Sunday she was very rude about something, so Wilfred told her that Father Christmas [Santa Claus] had said he wouldn't bring her a doll's house if she were rude. Instead of this making her meek, she merely said, "I don't care if he doesn't bring me a doll's house, I'll buy one myself." Wilfred asked her where she would get the money. She said, "Oh, I'll sell the beer bottles out the back porch."

The other day she said to me, "Daddy will have to get an aeroplane and take me up to Heaven, so I can ask God to send some rain because the heads of the poor little flowers are drooping," and she demonstrated how they were drooping. I told her an aeroplane was not necessary, as all she had to do was ask God from down here, and he would hear her. I went out that day and, while I was gone, Eve went out in the yard and simply yelled up, "God, put the rain on," and that night we had the first rain in months. She didn't forget she asked for it and is still taking full credit.

Robin is doing beautifully. She is the happiest baby I have ever known. She actually laughs out loud now. She looks exactly like "Dopey" in Snow White. She wants to sit up, but I am keeping her down until she is six months old.

Eve has not forgotten you two. Hardly a day passes that she does not ask me when we are going back to Mama Sophia's. She asked me if I remembered when Papa Harlow used to take her to the river and tell her stories.
I hope to start saving the first of the year to come home, and I am counting on it not taking more than two years to save enough. I certainly hope not anyway.

Try to read *We the Living*. It is an excellent book on Russia.

I hope you have a very merry Christmas. We shall be with just the family. Everyone I know is going away for six weeks at that time

Lots and lots of love,

Helen

And Indeed There Will Be Time (Sept. 1937—Aug. 1939)

No. 2, Eighth Avenue
Parktown North, Johannesburg
December 13, 1938

My dearest Mother and Father,

    I like writing you all on Tuesdays since your letters arrive on Mondays and the mail boat goes on Wednesdays. I had never realized before what a perfect day Tuesday is for writing. I shall try to reserve it for you. It is usually a very busy day, however, since it is ironing day. Today, however, it was washing day since I had guests last night for supper and of course we did not try to do the washing. Anyway, the washing and ironing are going to be much more simplified since we will have a washing machine by next week. Wilfred helped a German woman get her furniture stored for nothing, and she is letting us use her washing machine until she needs it. I expect to have it a year, and maybe by that time I can afford one myself. I wish I could afford to send my clothes out, for, at best, it is an effort at home. The wash girls here are none too good, though, and they lose and tear so much, and the laundries are still a luxury.

    Last night we had Mr. and Mrs. Gott for a Chili con Carne supper. Fortunately, she is very fond of hot things. I had celery soup then a big plate of Chili each and my three-sectioned dish with salad—radishes, cucumbers, and lettuce and tomatoes. Believe it or not, but I love cucumbers and radishes now. My taste seems to have changed completely. I then had that lovely chocolate ice cream of Aunt Nellie's and coffee and mints. It was all easy, so I enjoyed it myself. I insist on enjoying my own parties, and the only way to do it is to have it simple. I used my pretty lace tablecloth that Mary gave me and had a ring of red and white flowers in the center and the red candlesticks at each end. On my buffet, I had lovely red gladiolas in my tall silver vase that the Vriesens gave me.

    This reminds me that I am nearly out of Chili powder, so will you please send me two more tins of it—Bee Brand is what I have now, and it is good. You cannot get it in Johannesburg, and it is something different to serve. Also, I would greatly appreciate it if you would send me about six tin pan lids in three sizes—big for skillets, etc., medium size, and small. You simply cannot buy a lid that is separate from a pan in the whole town. They pick you out for a "damn American" the minute you ask for one. These things you must put down on my account, and, when I come home I will settle it, or, if it gets too big I will settle before, as Wilfred has some money coming to him from Sears, Roebuck, as they put aside so much of his salary in their profit-sharing fund.

    Since you will be sending a parcel to me, I wish you would include a pair of white pottery vases for ivy, as such things cannot be found in the 5c and 10c, called Bazaars here, but are in the other shops and would be at least $1.50 each. I am badly in need of something for my mantle, and I think that would be lovely. The mark-up out here is 100% after importation.

We know people who have lived practically all over the world—England, Europe, China, and Philippines, and they say Johannesburg is the most expensive place they have ever lived. The people here are used to it and look at you in amazement, and, I am sure, feel a little peeved when you complain about prices. Fortunately, we get a lot wholesale too. Our refrigerator only cost us $140. We got Robin's cot wholesale too. It is a lovely one in blue, with the sliding sides. We are also getting a white enamel table for the kitchen wholesale. Retail they are $25. If we didn't have to buy things for the house all the time, we could live all right on Wilfred's salary. But it is amazing all the things one needs to keep a house. There is really a fortune invested over the years.

There was a write-up in the papers here about the broadcast that so upset the U.S. I enjoyed having the clipping from home, though. What I want to know is: Did you hear it? Or did they get all excited in Elizabethton?[51]

I'll bet Marguerite was glad to get her new position in Washington, for she was so tired of the plants. She had been there since the beginning of Bemberg. If I were still there, I have no doubt that I might have had the vacancy. She was Dr. Wadewitz's secretary. Thank goodness I am not still there. I had quite long enough of it myself.

Robin has already started a Dixon failing. I have her propped up in the corner of the settee here in the room with me, and I just now looked over there and found her sound asleep. Park benches are no trial for us.

The other clipping you sent about the sausages and pancakes no doubt refers to the Voortrekker celebration when they passed through Johannesburg.[52] This is the 100th year since the Dutch trekked up from the Cape Province, and it has been celebrated by their descendants trekking again. They started three months ago from Cape Town and have been joined along the way by other good Dutchmen. They have traveled in covered wagons, and the men have all grown beards and the women dress as they did then. Even the Dutchmen not trekking who are descendants of the Voortrekkers have a three-months' growth of beard. They look too terrible. Many of the bus and trolley and tram drivers are Dutchmen, and they look too funny with these beards.

The English have not been asked to join in any of their celebrations, so I have seen none of it. All their notices, etc., are printed in Afrikaans, so I haven't

---

[51] Helen is referring to the Orson Welles' radio dramatization on October 18, 1938, of H.G. Wells's *War of the Worlds*. The program set off a massive panic in the U.S. since many believed that the country had indeed been attacked by Martians.

[52] The Voortrekkers were Afrikaner farmers of Dutch descent who, in 1838, traveled in covered wagons with all their possessions in search of freedom from the harsh droughts of the Eastern Cape Province and from the British, who had abolished slavery in 1833 and who had insisted that the Dutch farmers of the Cape Colony do the same.

bothered to find out anything about them. The big final celebration takes place in Pretoria on Friday, which is a public holiday, as it is Dingaan's Day. I think that is celebrated because the Dutch killed a lot of natives on that day.[53]

Just now I am trying to find some green furnishing taffeta for my living room curtains, but there aren't ten yards in one piece in all of Johannesburg, as the Voortrekkers bought it out for their dresses. You should hear Eve pronounce "Voortrekker." She has heard it so much from Dutch people living next door to us that she gives it the real Dutch pronunciation.

Is Ruth Piercy able to work again and is she back at the plants? I do hope she is well again and can take up a normal life. If you see her, give her my love. If you see Donna Perry, tell her I received her Xmas card and think it was sweet of her to think of me, and that she shall have a card from me one of these days. I have also just received an Xmas card from Leone. She sent one to Eve too, all to herself, and Eve was tickled with it.

Mr. Evans says now that he will not build, but buy. This does not thrill me so much since few of the houses appeal to me, as there is so much wasted space in most of them. Anyway, he hasn't sold his house in Bloemfontein yet, and property is not moving over there just now. Another thought that has come to me is that, if he owned the property, I could perfectly understand it if he wanted to build a rondavel for himself on the place. Lots of people have an extra room outside that way. Then, the next thing would be that he would want to have his meals with us, and that just would not do.

He is going down to Cape Town for three months, as he says he finds Johannesburg too expensive for him. This really isn't true, but no doubt he wants to put his money in something that he is saying nothing about. He pays $35 for his flat—one room, kitchenette, and bath. He cooks some at home and takes the rest of his meals at his Club, which is close by. He is very close, just between us, as he did not give Robin a thing when she arrived, yet he is simply crazy about her. He

---

[53] "Dingaan's Day," December 16, 1838 (also known as "The Battle of Blood River," "The Day of the Covenant," or "The Day of the Vow"), was a day when the Boers (another name for Afrikaner farmers who were trekking in search of land free of British rule), although greatly outnumbered, fought and defeated the Zulus, who, they believed, had betrayed them. The Boers' victory can be attributed to their superior weaponry, to their extraordinary courage and determination in the face of seemingly overwhelming odds, and to their faith in God. Four hundred and seventy Trekkers armed with guns faced an estimated ten to fifteen thousand Zulus armed with spears. Three Trekkers died, while an estimated 3,000 Zulus died. If blessed with a victory, the Boers promised to build a church and to honor forever December 16 as a holy day. After apartheid ended between 1990 and 1994, it was decided to include the entire South African population in honoring December 16 by calling it "The Day of Reconciliation."

finally, after about a week, arrived with a bunch of flowers for me. If he gives us anything at Christmas time, it is because Bert has told him to, and goes and gets it and makes him pay for it. On the other hand, when Bert's holidays arrive, I throw out big hints to him that he should give her some money for them, and last year he gave her $50.

I think Eve, poor thing, has inherited this miserly instinct from both sides, from me and from Mr. Evans, and really she is too funny. She hordes the candy Bert brings her. Last night I was serving her ice cream and started to give her another spoonful, and she said, "Don't give me any more." I naturally asked why, and she said, "I want to save it." The things she likes the best, she always eats the least of, thereby losing out entirely, for the rest of us eat it up. Having to spend so much running the house, I find that I am getting completely out of the habit of saving.

The package for Christmas has not arrived yet, but I feel sure it will arrive in time for Christmas. I am awfully glad you are continuing my subscription to *Reader's Digest,* as I would feel completely lost without it now, and when the December issue arrived, I was just bemoaning the fact that it was my last copy. They are excellent people to be receiving a magazine from, as every time I have moved they have sent a duplicate copy to my new address. I am glad you sent the quilt Mama Dick gave me, as it will be most useful. I can also use a housedress very nicely.

I was awfully glad to get the picture of you taken in Smoky Mountain Park. I am sorry to report that Eve did not recognize you all and simply insisted that that wasn't Papa Harlow. I can understand that because there was such a glare on his glasses, and she couldn't realize what that was, of course, and no doubt thinks they are his eyes. Nearly every day, though, she asks to go back to Mama Sophia's.

How is Ellen Sutton? You mention going there for bridge. I hope she has pulled through all right. Speaking of bridge, I am almost burnt out on it. The other day I went to a bridge party at the Orange Grove Hotel, given by a friend of mine who lives there. It is a swanky place. At my table, they wanted to play for 5c a hundred, so I proceeded to lose $2.50 during the afternoon. What killed me was that I lost it to this woman who was talking about her cook boy and chauffeur, etc. Money goes to money. I really believe that. Another American woman and I lost 1400 [points] on one hand, and that was all her fault, as she went way up in her bidding without a chirp from me. I don't think she could afford to lose it any more than I could.

Mrs. Tiedeman, the wife of Wilfred's boss, has just had a baby, so I called on her while she was in the nursing home and took a jacket to the baby. This was their third girl. We also sent flowers to her. She and I had a good old gossip together, and I shall run over to see her at home when the baby is a bit older.

Did I tell you that Wilfred has moved his office for the Johannesburg store to Maritime House, one of the largest office buildings in Johannesburg? In Maritime House, they have the central offices of the whole organization. Wilfred says his is the busiest office in the whole place, and he is thrilled to death with the way everything is going with him.

I think to run a home well is the hardest job I know of, and I am going to have my two girls learn cooking and sewing and management young. Not starting in on any of it until after thirty has not been easy at all. I suppose a reason of mine for starting them young is that mother can have a rest from it all before they are married. I have already decided to be another Lena Whittaker.

Maritime House in Johannesburg, home of Wilfred's Westinghouse office

This is a dream for the future, but just now I must come back to realities and that Robin is crying for her Pablum.

Lots and lots of love to you both from us,

Helen

No. 2 - 8th Avenue
Parktown North, Johannesburg
January 3, 1939

My dearest Ones,

There is so much to write about in this letter, and I am getting such a late start in the day that I don't know where to start.

I hope you all had a nice Christmas and did not think too much on what it could be if I were there with Eve and Robin. I also hope my little gifts arrived in time. Your box got here at a perfect time, just about three days before Christmas. We got a big thrill from it. The Christmas dresses for the children are too lovely. It is good you sent Eve the party dress, since her Auntie Bert did not have time to make the one she planned to as she had so much night work. She gave Eve a new red bathing suit and beach hat instead. The panties for Eve always come in handy, as she is so hard on them,[54] and I can't find what I like here. I haven't had time to shorten my dress and take it up in the waist, but I shall enjoy it as soon as I get that done. I, too, loved the little dress you said was from Elizabeth Hunter. That will be Robin's first real grown up dress.

Thanks ever so much for the money order too. I have bought a pair of golf shoes with that. Having an expensive foot, I had to add a bit to it, of course. I was awfully glad you put in the quilt. I had forgotten it. It is such a pretty one, and of course I can make good use of it. Thanks ever and ever so much for all the things. I must mention here that the bath towels arrived in the other box. The boxes never look like they have been opened for inspection. It is disgraceful the way they do in America—send the package to you with the contents falling out. I paid about $1.75 duty on the Xmas box.

Enclosed are pictures taken over Christmas. I think Eve is beautiful in the one taken in her sun suit. Bert is crazy about her sun suit and wants her to wear it on all occasions. They don't get things like that out here for some reason or other. The hat Bert gave her goes with it perfectly. Eve had the thrill of her life when she saw her doll's house. You can see the doorknob and knocker in the picture. The knocker is a lion's head. Just above the door is the electric light, and there is a light in each room inside. I think I could wire a real house after the struggle we had wiring that doll's house. The furniture is too cute for words. You can see some of it outside—a table with sun umbrella attached, a chair for baby with potty underneath and tray that moves up and down.

In the picture of the house, you see Robin with one of her usual smiles. She has the most marvelous smile I have ever seen. Eve and Robin both have their swings in the backyard, as you can see. Grandpa Evans gave Robin her swing for Xmas. In the other picture you see Robin in her bathtub. It is a nice one, as it is made all in one piece. Bert gave me the tapestry seat, and Dad[55] is having a stinkwood chair made for it.

Wilfred and I did not give each other anything, as we have had too much to buy, and the stinkwood desk is counted as my present. We did something most sensible, I think. We treated ourselves to three days at Vereeniging over New Year's. There is a lovely, very modern hotel there—the Riviera—on the Vaal River. It is the prettiest spot I know of around here—thirty miles from Johannesburg. Bert kept the children for me and ran the house with Lizzie's help. We got back last night, and I have accomplished so much in the house today just

---

[54] Little girls always wore dresses in those days, and, as a matter of course, they played outside in the trees, the sand, and the mud, so the fact that "panties" did not hold up under these circumstances is understandable.

[55] This is the first time that Helen refers to her father-in-law, William Evans, as "Dad."

because I was rested. While we were away, I stayed in bed every morning until eleven and had breakfast on my balcony.

There was a big supper dance on Saturday night. We played golf and went speed boating for the rest of the time. Monday, before lunch, we drove to the Vaal Dam, the largest in South Africa. The water falls 120 feet and, since we have been having a lot of rain, it was tumbling over beautifully with mist rising from the valley below. I played golf and am about to decide to take it up. The nice thing about learning golf is that you only hurt yourself when you play poorly. Wilfred and Bert both have nice clubs, so I wouldn't need to invest in that, and I have my shoes now, so it is just a matter of green fees and caddy and a few lessons. We had a beautiful room at the hotel on the first floor up with a perfect view of the river. It was furnished in the most modern furniture, allover carpet, etc. On our balcony we had a canvas couch for sunbaths, as no one could see you on the balcony. I had a new evening dress for the dance, a dark blue (not navy, however) with sequined flowers on the bodice and a few on the skirt. It is a Viennese frock. They are considered in the same way as a French frock. You will see it when I come home. I looked quite smart in that and my white fur evening coat.

Don't use our cable address now, as the year is up. You didn't avail yourself of that saving before, so I don't suppose you will now. Are you suspicious of cable addresses or what is it?

I got the Chili Powder you sent me. I am enclosing a dollar bill I found among our things to take care of the expense of the lids, Chili Powder, etc., I asked you to send me.

We had such good news just before Christmas that our holidays have been perfect. Wilfred was told then what to expect, but today is his first day as Divisional Superintendent of the Transvaal. That is his previous boss's job. Mr. Tiedeman is now Merchandise Manager for Africa. Wilfred now reports directly to the President, Mr. Sours.

Wilfred is direct head now of all operations in the Transvaal. They are opening two new stores this year in the Transvaal—one in Bloemfontein and one in Pietersburg, and I hope to go along with Wilfred when he has to go, as he will be driving. They call the car Wilfred's car now, and we have had it for the last ten days, day and night. From the first of February his salary is increased by $50 per month; that will make it $250 per month. That is a pretty nice jump in six months. They would like to raise him now, but it is company policy not to give an increase in less than six months.

Wilfred now comes under the New York Office and is no longer of the local staff office—that is, Mr. Sours, Mr. Tiedeman, Mr. Clark Hunt (Comptroller), and Wilfred. They have certainly complimented Wilfred highly on his work, and he loves every minute of it.

I haven't been to his new office yet, but he and Bert tell me that he has, from his balcony, one of the most beautiful views of the mine dumps along the Rand[56] that they have seen. They both said it was a perfect place to take a visitor to the city. He is on the 9th floor of Maritime House. If you ever meet anyone from Johannesburg, that will mean something to them.

I simply must stop now, as I have had many interruptions with the children and so it is now dinnertime—seven o' clock.

With all kinds of good wishes for the New Year and best love from us all.

Helen

No. 2, 8th Avenue
Parktown North, Johannesburg
January 10, 1939

My dearest Folks,

I am so worried about Father's fall. He should take a taxi to work on slippery mornings—it is economy in the long run. Let me know how he is feeling now. I must say in looking back that I think we looked after the pennies a bit too carefully and easily gave up our dollars. I am breaking my habit of doing that as fast as I can, and I enjoy life much more. I haven't many dollars to look after, you see, so money doesn't worry me at all. I believe it about necessary to go to the other side of the world to get a good perspective on how you have lived your life. The main thing I have learned is to take it easier. Everyone here, no matter how poor, takes at least a two-week holiday, and, when it comes, they go some place too. I must say they know the art of living better than we do, but still not so well as the Chinese. I am reading *The Importance of Living* now and am finding out how we Americans look to other people.

It was awfully nice of the Maryville Hunters to send the children $2.00. I shall write them all (Gladys also) right away—no doubt this afternoon. I think the best thing to do with it is put it in the bank to Eve's account. I do not think of anything they need just now. We are buying a pram for Robin right away but shall finance it ourselves. I am getting one that will fold, so I can take her on the trams if I want to go visiting with her.

---

[56] "Rand" is an abbreviation for the name given to the Johannesburg area, "Witwatersrand," whose literal meaning is "Ridge of White Waters." The mine dumps are massive heaps of tailings from the mines. Reposing in relief on the seemingly endless length of the flat ridge, they create a dramatic landscape. At sunset the pale dumps, the color of beach sand, turn pink against a sky red from the dust in the air. The allusion to "white water" is to the white lakes formed by the water pumped from the mines, accumulating in the adjoining valleys. Now, some seventy years later, owing to improved extractive techniques, these dumps are themselves being mined for small amounts of gold.

And Indeed There Will Be Time (Sept. 1937—Aug.1939)   175

You certainly have my permission to send L. the letter you enclosed to me. I can see nothing wrong with it. If you have any kind of a lease, he cannot move to the other house you mention anyway. When and if another lease is drawn up with L., I want this put in it—that he give two months' notice in case he vacates—that is, even at the expiration on the lease. In other words, if he wants to leave at the end of his lease, he must notify you in writing two months in advance. That keeps you from wondering what he is going to do and gives you time to advertise it for rent. Most people must give one month's notice to leave a house, so if you know two months in advance, then it gives anyone interested in the property time to give their month's notice. I have missed several places here because I did not know about them until after the first of the month, and they were let before I could finish out the current month and give the month's notice. All the best places here require two months' notice. Make him pay up the whole rent of $65 per month at least before the end of the year. If you are easy with him, he thinks you are afraid of losing him, and his demands will never cease.

Bert was holding Robin in the chair, and I took the picture. My hair didn't look nice that Sunday, and that is why I didn't want to be in the pictures. Yesterday, I had part of my permanent re-done, as some curls did not take. I believe he did six curls yesterday. He cut a lot out too, as it was very heavy again. I have it rolled away from my face all the way around now. It looks very good.

I enclose a drawing of Eve's. This, so she says, is a little girl. I guessed that on seeing it and think I am pretty clever. I must tell you a good one she got off. I hope I haven't already written it. The other day she was drawing, and when she finished she asked me to guess what she had drawn without a look at it. I guessed a bird, a flower, a frog, and all kinds of things until she decided to give me a few hints, so she said, "It is something you get money from." I first thought of a cash register and then a bank, but I knew she would never think to draw either, so I had an inspiration and said, "Daddy!" She said that was right, and then she produced a drawing which looked a great deal like the one I enclose except it was minus the hair. I saved it to send to you, but someone has thrown it away.

Write me your guest list for the supper you gave. I am interested. I wish I could have been there to help you. I would really be of some help now. I am afraid, though, when I get back with you, I will be afraid to trust myself and again lean on you in all such matters.

I don't know whether it was in your papers or not, but we had quite a quake here last week, Saturday to be exact. It shook the whole Rand, and it is the first one I have seen get headlines in the local papers. I am very glad I am in a one-storey house and not in a block of flats. Bert and Dad said it was terrible in their buildings. I was shampooing Eve's hair in the bathroom, and Lizzie had just come into the bathroom to say she was home from taking her little girl to the station when it happened. Lizzie and I just looked at each other with big eyes. You hear it before you feel it. There is a rumble like thunder underground, then the whole house shakes.

I have found a new way to economize. There is a meat market in town with very low prices, cash and carry, and they give exceptionally good prices—if you buy, say, half a sheep—which is just what I did last Wednesday. I bought half a lamb for $2.00 or rather just under that. That has done us an entire week, and we have had variety too. We of course have had the chops, then the shoulder, and for Sunday, the leg, and a meat pie from the shoulder. All of the meat was excellent, and I am going to continue with them for my meat. You buy the whole thing as it hangs, but they cut it for you any way you want it. I know you wish you could buy your meat so cheaply. I must have meat every night for Wilfred, so I would have a terrible bill if I had to pay what you do. Lizzie also had her meat from the part you stew.

I have found a very nice house for $52.50 with electric stove, but it will not be vacant for five months yet. I know the people, and they are building and have a lease on the place for that long. It is in Parktown North too, but in a better neighborhood than I am in now. Parts of Parktown North are all right. There is a nice size yard there but not a huge one like I have here to keep up. I shall certainly be glad to have an electric stove again. There is a small room for Robin too. I know she disturbs Eve sometimes, as she growls and grunts or coos in the night, but never cries. I can't think of any way to get in all of the milk that my government book recommends for babies, as Robin will only take four bottles a day and has for ages now.

Robin is getting her two lower front teeth now but is not cross about it. She weighs 16½ lbs., which is average for her age. Wilfred's father thinks I take wonderful care of her, and he is wild about her, so I think I must too. If he is well-satisfied, then anybody would be. She now sits in her swing for an hour every afternoon and looks too cute. Wilfred is so crazy about Robin that he says there should always be a baby in the house. We have really had so much pleasure from her.

We have had such a cool summer that I forget it is summer. Do send me your recipe for pepper relish and full instructions as to how it should be made. My peaches came just at Christmas time, and I didn't put any of them up, as I had too much to do, and I wasn't going to wear myself out for a few jars of peaches. However, I have two more trees coming on now. My fig tree isn't going to do much, but I don't like figs anyway. The pomegranates are doing beautifully, but they have too many seeds to fool with them.

I must stop and get supper organized.

If you want to vary your hash, try a stew I make. Cook your round steak as usual, then cut it in squares and put it back on and add several pork sausages and cook for a while, then add two or three skinned tomatoes and, when they are stewed to a sauce, thicken. I use no potatoes in the stew, but it is nice to have boiled potatoes with it. The sausages certainly give flavor.

Do tell Mr. Umbach that I appreciated the picture. I thought it was very good of you, but I did not recognize Mrs. Umbach. I thought at first it was Mrs. Siemen.

Lots and lots of love to you both,

Helen

No. 2, 8th Avenue
Parktown North, Johannesburg
January 14, 1939

Dearest Mother and Father,

I enclose the picture of Mrs. Sours, as she is the wife of the headman in Westinghouse out here. We are calling on them tomorrow afternoon, as she has been to see me twice.[57] We think she will not come back to South Africa, as she hates it here, and Mr. Sours has told Wilfred that he will not be here longer than a year more himself. Mr. Tiedemann, whose job Wilfred got the first of the year, is getting Mr. Sours' place, that is Vice-President. The President of the export company is in New York, and the headmen in the different countries are Vice Presidents. I left the bride's picture attached to show the prominence of Mrs. Sours' picture.

Wilfred has asked me to write you all and say that he would like to forget the bad feeling in the past. He thinks it best to have no apologies and no rehashing of the whole affair but just to consider that we were all in an impossible situation,[58] in which the best would have broken down. He would like it if you all would feel like visiting us sometime. I could not recommend the long and expensive trip to South Africa for what there is to see, but we may not always be so far away. Let us hear how you feel.

---

[57] Helen had been brought up in the Southern tradition of visiting with neighbors and "owing" them a visit if they had dropped by previously. I remember experiencing this custom, years later, when living with my grandmother Sophia in North Carolina. As a South African, I found it tedious to get dressed up to "drop in" on friends who had "dropped in" on us and having my grandmother feel the constant burden of keeping count of what was owed and to whom.

[58] Despite his willingness to "forgive and forget," Wilfred's 1933 letter to Sophia remains his only conciliatory letter to her. It would appear that, since the strained feelings had originated with the Dixon family in Tennessee, Wilfred sought to prove his worthiness for Helen by his actions rather than by further verbal protestations. It is worth noting that, at this stage, Helen discourages her parents from visiting South Africa, possibly because the pain of their past interactions with Wilfred are still too raw.

Today a parcel came from Katye Wray with lovely panties for Eve and a sweet pale pink dress for Robin. I have just finished a letter to Katye Wray. I have also written Aunt Lula and Gladys.

I may go to Salt Rock, about an hour out of Durban, for three months the first of March. I can get a nice house here June 15, and I really feel I can't stay on where I am, as we do not want to spend any money on it, and it would take a lot to have it livable.

Thanks a lot for the offer to sew for the children. I shall take you up when they need something. I have a Singer machine myself, though. It is Bert's. Must stop and make some cookies.

Lots of love,
Helen

173 Louis Botha Avenue
Orange Grove, Johannesburg
February 7, 1939

My dearest Ones,

At last we have found a house and are moving the last of this month. I give the new address at the top of this letter. I was so disgusted with this place that, in a sudden fit of anger and despair, I told Wilfred to give notice the first of the month even though we did not have another place to go to. I thought if I found nothing during February that the children and I would go down to the Coast for a few months until Wilfred found a place. That would have been a big expense, so I am very thankful we have found a place. We are delighted with our next home, and, since it becomes vacant at the end of this month, we could never have had it if we had not taken a chance and given notice here. I can't wait to send you pictures of the new place since it is built of rondavels and has a thatched roof.

It has lovely vines, trees, flowers, and grass and is so typical of the tropics and South Africa. There is a

Helen with Eve and baby Robin, 1939

And Indeed There Will Be Time (Sept. 1937—Aug. 1939)

very large lounge, 18 to 20 feet long, and at one end of that is an entrance hall, and at the other a small dining room. Then at each corner is a rondavel, which gives us three bedrooms and a kitchen. At the back of the lounge is the bathroom and pantry. Outside, of course, every wall is curved, but the way it is built the lounge has, for the most part, straight walls. There is an entrance step straight into the lounge and a side porch or verandah leading into the entrance hall. It will be the prettiest place we have lived in, and at the surprising price of $55. It is on the best trolley route in town since at least four different lines pass the door, so you can catch one any minute. We will be just four miles from town there, whereas we are five and a half miles where we are, with only one bus passing us.

Unfortunately, we will still have a coal range, but you can't have otherwise at the price we will pay. We can well afford the increase in rent with Wilfred's nice increase in salary. I shall only be half a mile from the Orange Grove Hotel where I often play bridge with friends. It is a place we certainly will not be ashamed of, and I can't say that for where I am now. It will be so nice having a room for Robin and one for Eve.

Thank goodness this is a short month. The present tenants were trying to save the place for some friend of theirs and told us it was rented, but we investigated for ourselves and took it the minute we found it was still to let. No doubt the other people were trying to get out of the place they were in before obligating themselves for this place. There are some beautiful homes on Louis Botha Avenue, so it certainly is not a bad address to have.

That is enough for our house, as this morning we had great excitement of another nature. When Lizzie went in to give Robin her early morning bottle, she found the young miss of six months standing straight up in her bed, naturally holding onto the sides. She has been getting up on her knees for the last few days, but I didn't dream she could get up on her feet. I presume, since she has done it herself, she is strong enough to stand on her legs. However, I shan't encourage her.

I know I have not written for some time, but I have had so many letters to write to the family and different ones, and I knew you wouldn't worry about me if letters were coming to them.

I cannot be sure whether or not I have written you since receiving the beautiful blue scarf with the world on it. It makes me feel very young and snappy when I wear it. I wish I thought I could do a good job of it and I would embroider in Johannesburg. I wear it with a white linen dress on which I wear a novelty belt of the same shade of blue with a white anchor as the fastener.

You have really been awfully good about letters. I had two long ones from you last week full of news.

I don't think you need worry about my passage money home, as I think Wilfred can manage to save that up, but you may have three hungry mouths to feed for about six to eight months when we come, as I am afraid it will have to be purely on a visit, as I must save for my return trip while I am there. It takes about $500 each way. That would include everything: railway passage, tips, etc.

If I can possibly afford it, I want to make one trip by the East Coast. The other trip I would make straight from New York to Cape Town via Trinidad. I think the nicest time of year to get home would be April or May, so my present plans are to leave here the first of March or first of April 1941. Eve will be big enough then to be of some help with Robin, and Robin will be through her most trying period. I don't anticipate so much trouble with them. Eve now takes her own bath, dresses and undresses herself, feeds herself, naturally, goes to the lavatory and attends to herself there quite alone. So she is no trouble at all. Since she is not at all timid, she will enjoy herself thoroughly on a boat trip.

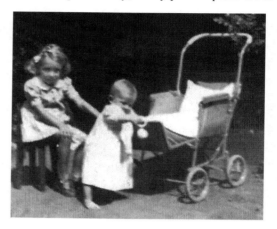

Eve and Robin

She said something so cute Sunday. Robin was taking her bottle, but every time Eve moved around in the room Robin would stop and look at her, so Eve said, "Robin thinks she is a Mommie, and I am a baby." I asked her what made her think that Robin thought that. She said, "Because she keeps an eye on me."

I am glad the presents to the different ones arrived before Christmas. I wish I could have sent more drums, but, though not expensive, they were too much for me to send to all the little boys in the family. The one I sent Joe Baughman came to about $2.00, including the postage. Of course, that is most reasonable for such a thing, I think. It was reduced to me because I was buying quite a few things that afternoon. I am so glad the Baughmans liked it. You didn't say what Joe thought of the drum. I had a hard time sending it, as Wilfred wanted it himself.

By the way, the toilet here has been fixed for some time. Why I didn't report it to the municipality, I do not know. We should never have stood for all we did. The "To Let" sign has been on the house since the first, but only one person has been here. It is a paradise now compared to when we moved in. We had to stay a while because we had spent so much money on it ourselves, painting the woodwork and walls in two rooms, having the hedge trimmed, which extended over half a block one way and a quarter of a block another and a quarter another, burrying rubbish, and digging the yard, etc. The man across the street told me I had lived here longer

And Indeed There Will Be Time (Sept. 1937—Aug. 1939)

than anybody. Everybody is attracted to the grounds, and it is a place that gives one the urge to try to do something with it. However, the outlay would be endless on it.

We were all very sorry to hear that Roosevelt had not said that France was the U.S. Boundary. We all rejoiced when we read that and thought it would do more to stop war than anything. From the weak way England and France are acting, I would not think it wise for the U.S. to pick a war, for I doubt if they would get any support from either nation. On the other hand, they would expect help from the U.S. if they got into a scrap with Germany and Italy.

We have just read of the insults in the Italian press to Roosevelt. I am disgusted that England, France, and America are taking so much off of those two nations. I know the Germans very well, you must admit, since I was associated with them so long, and though I have some good German friends, and would not have you repeat me, on the whole they have mean natures and force is the only thing they understand.

Unless we keep our armaments and army and navy and air force at such strength that they will be afraid of us, we will always have a source of danger from them. Might is all they understand. As for the Italians...we could fix them up quickly. I think we get all the news of most importance in our papers; however, Wilfred subscribed to *Time* yesterday, as we both love it so—even if we do get it a month late.

You say I never mention flies, Well, I can tell you I had more flies than you ever saw when I moved in here. Every day I closed up each room and sprayed it with Fly Tox and picked up every fly and burnt it. I nearly went crazy since there is only one screen in the house. We could not even get the owner to order the city to collect the garbage for six weeks, and the city would not take the order from us. The owner is an Italian, so the collection of garbage was of no importance to him, of course.

I am so glad you mentioned that you were making a coat for Eve, for I had forgotten that I had written that she needed one and was just ready to buy the material and make one myself. I don't think Eve can wear her blue coat again this winter. It was small last winter. While we are on the subject, I must mention that thin dresses, sun suits, etc., are of little use here. Even though we have so much sunshine, it is nearly always cool.

I love the sun suit you sent Eve, but she has worn it very little. I think it will be necessary to put Robin in woolen dresses and Eve also this winter. Everybody else wears woolen clothes, and they heat accordingly, so it drives one to wear woolen things too. I saw lovely thin Shirley Temple dresses at ridiculously low prices the other day in town, but I did not even consider them because you can count the days that children could wear them. The houses, being solid brick, are always cool, just like Aunt Hattie's place at Hampton. I wish you would send that redingote[59] of mine, and I will have a dress made for it. It is just the sort of thing one needs here.

I feel very chatty this afternoon and could go on indefinitely, but I am going to Bert's this evening, as she is having a few in, and I must do my nails and have a bath, etc. I rolled my hair up this morning. I am getting very clever at that and can do just about as well as the beauty parlor. That means something in my pocket since they charge $2.00 for shampoo and set. You don't know how lucky you are. When I get home, I think I shall have my hair done once a week just because it is cheap.

I would love to send you some almonds from my own trees, as I have worlds of them, but they would weigh so much that it would be foolish.

I have not been able to find the issue of *Time* that has the picture that looks like Robert [Helen's deceased brother]. Do you think you might be able to get it from someone? I would like to see it. What was the accompanying article?

I am glad you are over your entertaining by this time. I must have a few little things when I get settled in my new place.

I have had nice letters from Helen and Kathryn. I shall write Helen shortly. I had a lovely lot of things from Aunt Nellie, Uncle Fred, Katye Wray, and Gene. I have written all of them.

I am so glad to hear that Father is feeling all right again since his fall.

Lots and lots of love to you both,

Helen

P.S. Eve knows the days of the week now and counts perfectly to five and imperfectly to ten and higher. She doesn't like to be taught anything, however. She does not like Sunday school over here. The reason is they have them all in one room, and one man gets up and talks to all of them. Of course, she can't understand a thing. One Sunday, she said she was ready for Sunday school (a little girl was calling for her), and I said, "Eve, you can't go with your hair looking like that." She always tries to escape having it combed since it is fine and tangles terribly. She said, "Oh, the teacher won't see it. He never looks at us." That has always tickled me, for I can just picture rows of untidy children sitting, waiting for some man to finish something they can't understand and something in which he is so engrossed that he doesn't know they all look like little waifs.

---

[59] Redingote: A full-length, unlined, open-fronted woman's coat, revealing a decorative skirt underneath.

And Indeed There Will Be Time (Sept. 1937—Aug.1939)

February 12, 1939

My dearest Mother,

Your letter about Uncle Fred came yesterday. [Helen's Uncle Fred was Sophia's second oldest brother. He was never married.] Unfortunately, I got my mail just before getting on the bus to go to town, and I read it there. I shall never take that chance again. This comes as a great shock to me, and I do not mind saying it means the loss of my favorite uncle. What a shame I never told him that. Was Uncle Fred's death a complete shock? Your letter sounds as though Aunt Nellie watched him rather closely. I suppose he went the way we could have expected it, as for years he has complained of his head.

Eve has just said a sweet thing, as I waited until this morning to tell her. She said, "When will God make Uncle Fred another time? If he doesn't make him another time, I'll cry."

Quite late yesterday afternoon, about six o'clock, I went to Mr. Evans's flat and had a cup of tea with him, Bert, and a friend of Bert's mother. Bert said, "Let Mrs. Williams read your tea leaves, Helen."

Mrs. Williams looked in my cup and said, "I see the letter 'F,' do you know anyone by that initial?" I said yes, thinking, of course, of Uncle Fred.

She said, "You will receive two letters from home and one will make you cry."

I received two letters from you just before seeing Mrs. Williams, and one was about Uncle Fred. I then told her what I had just heard.

In my cup she also saw money just on my doorstep, so I hope that means everything will work out all right with Wilfred, as your other letter was about that. Your idea is as good as any about him closing out the business as managing salesman. Let us know the minute you hear from Wilkes, if you do. Also, let us have a copy of Father's answering letter. The bonding has been given to another company from the one who wrote for the information about Wilfred. Also, all bonding matters are handled by Wilfred. Wilfred can furnish Westinghouse with a bond, all right, as one of his best friends is in the business, but Westinghouse requires that it all come through one company. I feel he will come through it alright. Mr. Tiedeman and Mr. Sours have both told him several times that they did not think they could have found another man in South Africa for the job, that they were just sending to America for a man. Wilfred has about 180 employees under him. I think that is the figure. He has every chance for a very big position one day at very big money, so we must hope that nothing will go wrong.

I do think the post office was too dumb for words. You would think the Dixons hadn't lived there all their lives. We are not losing any sleep about it, so I don't want you to. I shall write you as soon as we get reactions at this end.

I certainly feel sorry for Aunt Nellie, as Uncle Fred was the one who was companion to her. I hope Uncle David will do his part for her now, but I don't think there is much chance of it. I hope you will go there more often, as I know that will help, and maybe you can get her to spend a few days with you.

I do hope they will not put an outsider in Uncle Fred's place in the oil company. I certainly think it is the best thing they have, and if it means Uncle Earle or Edwin giving up their present business and going over to the oil business, I think it is the thing to do. Uncle Earle could turn over his work in Maryville to Cy and give him a chance there. No doubt Cy could handle it as well as he does, and Uncle Earle would no doubt be a great asset to take the oil company. I believe those two hold the controlling stock, and I hope they will look after it. Maybe, being at a distance, I see things more clearly than those close by, but this idea is very strong upon me. Of course, if they are giving up the position to Uncle Charlie, that is splendid. They must keep it in the family, though.

I hope we are at the end of our sorrows, and that there will be nothing else to mar my homecoming in two years.

Frankly, I think of Uncle Earle for the Houston Oil, as I think he, of the three—Uncle Charlie, Uncle Edwin, and himself—has the best chance of a long life, and if he goes in now, and stays at the helm of the business, it will mean a lot to all families concerned. Later on, he will be just too old to make such a change.

Thank you for writing me in detail about everything. I am glad that everything was so nicely done, and I am sure that Uncle Fred always had many more friends than he realized. We all continue well. Robin has her first tooth. It came through on the 10th of this month. Eve has done a bit of drawing and lettering for you.

Lots of love to all,

Helen

173 Louis Botha Avenue
Orange Grove, Johannesburg
Union S. Africa
March 1, 1939

Dearest Mother,

I can only write a note, as we have just moved and there is so much to do, but I didn't want you to not have word from me this week. We moved on Sunday, Feb. 26, as the people were already out of our new place, and, on Sunday, I could have the assistance of Wilfred and Bert. They really did the whole thing, and I wasn't even tired at the end of the day.

Your marvelous box has arrived. I don't know that you have sent a nicer one. All the things are there, and the duty was only $1.50. Eve's coat is just the smartest thing I have seen. I have never seen her look better than in it. It is all right for winter here with a sweater for colder days. The fit is perfect. I shall send her measurements later. The blue dress was so pretty too and is a perfect fit. Eve is a good four years. She is much larger than most children her age. My shoes are lovely and fit very well, a bit loose but OK. Believe it or not, a narrower one would be better, but I am afraid they don't make them.

We are simply entranced with our new house and garden. It is one of the most romantic places I have ever seen. I wish you and Father could visit me here. I shall send you a lot of pictures of it and us as soon as we are settled. We are having to spend about $150 more on furnishings, but our place will be lovely then. Even Robin seems to love it here. I think I can easily rent it for $70 per month furnished when I come home.

Please keep books on what I owe you for shoes and clothes, etc., and we shall settle when I get home. It is such a help to get the things you send. We loved everything, but I can't go into detail now. Off to work, straightening up.

Lots of love,
Helen

173 Louis Botha Avenue
Orange Grove, Johannesburg
March 8, 1939

Dearest Ones,

I have had letters from both of you this past week and shall answer them by next mail if possible. We like our house better every day. It is one of the prettiest small places in Johannesburg.

I played bridge yesterday with the wife of the American Consul, also the wife of the Vice Consul. I only lost 25c at 5c a hundred, for which I was thankful.

Eve has an upset stomach today. I think it came from eating cookies from the party yesterday. I was entertained by a Mrs. Adam, an American, and she sent Eve some of her very rich cookies. Mrs. Adam is very popular here in Johannesburg and lives near me.

I must mail this, then roll up my hair and manicure my nails for tonight. I can do wonders with my hair myself.

Lizzie wants me to get another servant to help her. I am afraid it will have to be me. The people next door have three, and I think that is what is wrong with her.

Best of love to you both,
Helen

Sunday Morning
March 20, 1939

Dearest Mother and Father,

Wilfred was delighted with your letter, and, of course, I was too. It is so foolish for a family to let such things go on year after year. Wilfred is out playing golf this morning, or he would write a line too. He is playing a good game again and is thrilled to death over it. The fact that he is playing golf this morning and that we are invited out for lunch today and also for tea this afternoon accounts for my having time to write a letter this morning. Usually such activity is going on here.

I doubt if I have written you that Wilfred's father is in Hermanus in Cape Province. He thought he was going to have a nervous breakdown, though I thought he was just working himself into one. He likes it so well there that he says he is going to stay. Everyone is pleased, since he is rather difficult and demands so much of Bert's time.

This past Thursday night I had Mr. Sours, the head of Westinghouse, for dinner. Since Mrs. Sours is in America, I had a newspaper woman as his partner. I also had Mr. and Mrs. Gott. I had a formal dinner—oyster soup, entree of peppers stuffed with tuna fish, then fillet and mushrooms, pear and potatoes au gratin, and ice cream and cake, coffee. It was all good and served very nicely by Lizzie. I never once got up from the table.

Mack, Lizzie's husband, and Eve have just passed the window. He is trying to teach Eve to ride her tricycle. Eve reported she could ride, but I discovered it was a false alarm. We are sending Eve to a kindergarten only two blocks away after the Easter holidays. I am anxious to see her development. She is going to be quick, but lazy, I fear.

Mr. Sours was enchanted with the house and furnishings. He pays $225 a month for his furnished flat in the most exclusive place in Johannesburg. It is just around the corner from Killarney Court where we lived. He said if he had seen this first we would never have had it, and he meant it too. I have been to his place, and it simply doesn't compare with what we have. All the rest of the party thought it a dream place too. I shall send pictures of the outside in my next letter. Have I written you that I belong to the American Women's Club of South Africa? I shall find out exactly, but I think there are about two hundred members. I am a charter member. There are many branches to it—a cooking class, needlecraft, literary, and what not. We have clubrooms in the Carlton Hotel, the best in Johannesburg. There is a library there, and one can always have tea there and take four guests a month. I am hostess the afternoon of the 31st of this month at the clubrooms. I must introduce myself to everyone coming, take care of the library, and serve the teas. I shall perhaps be a wreck before it is over.[60]

I do hope Eve's hat turns out well. I am holding off buying one until I get the one you are making. I simply love her coat. She does too, except for the white collar; for some reason that annoys her. I don't know whether to take it off or not. I still remember some of my agony over being made to wear things I didn't want to.

I am having my book club on this coming Thursday. They have heard me talk about my other terrible place so much that I am sure they too are going to be pleasantly surprised. By the way, you should read *Rebecca* by Daphne du Maurier if you haven't already. It is strictly a woman's book.

I am having a black chiffon afternoon dress made. I hope it turns out well. I have a very snappy new sports hat in a greenish blue felt with brown band. It is one of the most becoming hats I have ever had.

I hope you will not discontinue your social activities for long because those things help one over such sad times. I think you should certainly have your friends in for a table of bridge right along.

Does Aunt Lennie seem a bit queer when I am mentioned? Don't ask her if anything is wrong, but I am sure she has feelings against me. She sent us a Xmas card and did not write a word on it, and that seemed more than strange since she had never acknowledged Robin's arrival. Of course, to me the card was more of a snub than if I hadn't received one at all. [In the original, this last sentence has been crossed out]. In any case, of the whole family, Elizabeth Hunter [one of Helen's maternal aunts] was the only one who promptly acknowledged Robin's arrival. The others, only at Xmas time. However, I am really too happy these days to give

---

[60] Being a married American woman in a large cosmopolitan city like Johannesburg was an enormous social asset for Helen, as she was immediately part of a circle of like-minded women. Outside of the club, she and Wilfred had access to other young married American couples who were in Johannesburg on business, permanently or semi-permanently. The fact that they had all been sent to South Africa by American companies meant that these couples had a common bond and all fell into a high-income bracket. Whereas in South Africa membership in the group derived from a common bond in business, in Elizabethton—despite the fact that Helen's family had been wealthy and among its founding settlers—Wilfred's being a South African placed both of them outside of all social groups. In spite of the lingering effects of the Depression, the mid-1930s in Elizabethton had been a time of gaiety for young couples who met and danced at the Lynnwood Hotel, which, according to a local historian, had "for three decades been a social hub of the town." It seems possible that, even though Helen and Wilfred loved socializing and dancing, they had in all likelihood been excluded from these events. Adding to their confusion and misery must have been the fact that Dr. E.E. Hunter (Helen's grandfather) had been a founding member of the Lynnwood Hotel Company in 1906, the year of Helen's birth. Helen does talk of dancing as something that helped to alleviate her depression during this period, but, in all likelihood, she and Wilfred danced during their stay in Nashville rather than in Elizabethton.

it much thought, so please don't let it worry you by thinking I was particularly hurt. I must say, my newfound friends have been kinder than most of my old ones, so I can hardly be blamed for loving South Africa. [This line, too, has been crossed out.] The hurt about Robin is gone, or I would never have mentioned it, so forget I have mentioned it. Ask Aunt Nellie to re-mail her letter that was returned and give her my love.

Lovingly,
Helen

173 Louis Botha Avenue
Orange Grove, Johannesburg
South Africa
March 27, 1939

Dearest Mother and Father,

I am so glad I have some pictures to send you in this letter. I believe they will give you an idea of what a pretty place we have. There is not a window in the house that does not look out on beauty. The trees you see are on our property. I even have a willow. You will also see that the children and I are looking well, and so we are.

Eve's hat arrived this morning, and it is very sweet on her; I think you were terribly clever to make it. It will do her all winter, and she will look very smart whenever she goes out. She feels very dressed up in it. She wanted to tie the streamers down the back under her chin since they have always been that way, but I finally managed to explain their usefulness down the back.

Father asked what a pram is. A pram is a perambulator. I am very thankful there is a short word for it. South Africans are great on shortening words. A refrigerator is a fridge. If one calls a pram a carriage, they merely stare at you blankly, so one just never does call it that but once. My vocabulary has undergone quite a change. Just how much, only you all will be able to tell me when I get home. Americans with an American accent now sound very funny to me. Even though I belong to the American Club, I am mostly with South Africans or English people.

I was delighted to find a bank balance on the L. house. I think quite enough has been spent on the place for the time being. I cannot understand why either bathroom had to be painted since Wilfred painted both of them. Why was it necessary? When the insurance comes due again, renew it for another three years since one saves so much on it. There will no doubt be a refund on the old policy at that time.

And Indeed There Will Be Time (Sept. 1937—Aug.1939) 189

When Mrs. Sours left for America, I asked Eve if she would go along, but as much as she wants to see Mama Sophia and Papa Harlow, she would not go without me.[61]

Mr. and Mrs. Clark-Hunt leave for New York on the 31st. He has been here setting up the accounting dept. The employees gave a big supper dance for them last Friday night. It was very pleasant for me to be sitting at the head table with Mrs. Sours and only the headmen and their wives. I could not help but think shortly over the past and how quickly Wilfred had put me in such a position. They made moving pictures of us. If they are good, and I can get some stills made, I shall send them.

Ruth MacDonnel, a friend of ours, is selling out her household things on Friday. She gave me a beautiful lamp yesterday in green for my lounge, also a flower bowl and candle sticks in orange. Two of the pictures I am sending were made at her house. Glen Baine is her little boy by her first marriage. The house is already sold. They are going to board, as they are trying to get a transfer to Cape Town on account of his heart. Elizabeth Hunter's letter came today, and I certainly appreciated it and shall answer when I can.

I am, of course, very glad to hear that Uncle Fred left you some of his insurance. I certainly feel the right persons got the money: you and Aunt Nellie. I know you all miss Uncle Fred terribly. It is something I try to keep out of my mind. I believe I am more ready to accept these losses than any of you could be because of one experience—and that experience was going to the other side of the world to live. So often on that voyage I was impressed by my own insignificance in this world, how foolish that we are shocked when death comes. I am saying this very badly, I realize, but do you understand that living in one place all of your life has given you a false feeling of security and importance? Perhaps you guessed that it was not unkin to dying for me to leave you all for so long and go to a country different from my own.

I was indeed depressed to hear about Mrs. Umbach. Couldn't she go up to Richmond? I wish you could let the furnace go and do that for her. I hope you understand that I consider life important, but we should not be surprised when it goes, but rather surprised that it is ours for so long. I hope you are wrong about Anna Lu Burnette, but she always looked delicate. One feels so helpless in the face of both T.B. and cancer.

---

[61] I find this willingness to send Eve halfway across the world, at the age of four, surprising. I can only assume that parents back then had a higher opinion of their children's sense of autonomy than do parents today. This notion seems to be borne out by the practice of sending young children to boarding school or leaving them in the care of others for days or even weeks at a time.

Wilfred's father is back from the Cape and as nervous as ever. When I think of all you and Father and what we went through, and he hasn't a worry but has a nervous breakdown, well, I just get fed up. He has always had an easy and secure life. Bert is the only one with any sympathy for him, but she is just that way. He plays billiards and bowls all the time. He can have a job if he wants it, or he has enough to live the rest of his life wherever he wishes, yet he breaks down and keeps the whole family upset.

Must close, as it is getting bedtime for the babies.

Lots of love,

Helen

Note: Helen's anger is understandable given the hardships back in America from which she was still emerging. However Wilfred's father had not in fact, always had an easy life, since he was born in Wales in 1872, a year before the beginning of the "Long Depression," which, by some estimates, lasted in the United Kingdom from 1873 to as late as 1896. Owing to these difficult conditions, William grew up working on his grandparents' farm in Wales. Later, he was a coal miner, a quarryman, and a platelayer for the railways in Wales. He and Eva Agatha Hudd (a school teacher) married in 1898. In 1902, in response to the hardships they had endured in his homeland, they immigrated to South Africa. There, William worked in management for the South African Railways. Through hard work and careful investing, he and his family led privileged lives, allowing them to pursue their interests in the arts, education, and travel. They returned to Wales every few years to visit relatives.

Years later, while Helen and Wilfred were still living in Elizabethton, Eva died. By the time Helen is writing this letter, William, at age sixty-seven, is a widower, retired and alone. I believe that, as much as anything, Helen is responding to William's obvious preference for Bert over Wilfred and to his seeming miserliness even as she extended hospitality to him.

It is interesting to note the parallels between William's and Wilfred's lives. Both had fled to South Africa to escape the horrors of Depression—William, at age thirty; and Wilfred, at age twenty-nine. Both of their wives were pregnant during the voyage to South Africa: Eva with Bert; and Helen, some thirty-five years later, with Robin.

173 Louis Botha Avenue
Orange Grove, Johannesburg
April 2, 1939

My dearest Ones,

It is hardly fair for me to send this picture, as it is a good one of me but not of Bert. She was looking very tired out the day it was snapped in town. Haven't we a lovely background? It is hard to get any other, however, since there is so much building in J'burg.

And Indeed There Will Be Time (Sept. 1937—Aug. 1939)

My dress looks like a bag on me because it was made for me when I weighed about 150 instead of 134, as at present. I suppose I have never told you that a great deal of that came off my hips. I have very small hips now. In fact, I get plenty of compliments on my figure.

I have finished my duties as hostess in the American Club rooms. I was there on Thursday morning, March 3^{1st}. I really enjoyed it and met lots of people. My first visitor, an American, was most interesting because she was born in New Orleans but is now an Italian Countess. Her name is Countess Caraccioli. She is living at the Carlton Hotel so was actually waiting for me to open the clubrooms. She has lived many places and loves to talk, so you can imagine how interested I was. She is forty-five to fifty years old and only arrived in South Africa two weeks ago. I met many more Americans during the morning, but you can hardly call them Americans because nearly all of them have been away from the States for years and have lived all over the world. To be a traveled person in Johannesburg is nothing—everybody is. I need an atlas to talk to some of them because they have been in such out-of-the-way places that you are not quite sure you know what continent or which hemisphere they are talking about.

I am joining the cooking and sewing classes of the club. One club member who lives just around the corner from me came to see me yesterday. She took Eve home with her to play with her little girl during the afternoon. Now Eve can think of nothing else but going back to play. Eve is looking very pretty just now. Robin is as strong as an ox and should have been a boy. She has very broad shoulders, so broad that even the yellow and blue dress Elizabeth Hunter sent her is too tight across the shoulders. She has such a big appetite all the time that I am sure she is going to be a fatty like I was.

Wilfred's dad has moved into a boarding house and gave me his pots and pans and crockery, also the use of a wardrobe, which is most needed for Eve's room. I now have all the furniture I need, except some rugs for the bedrooms. They will have to come later, however. Among Dad's things, I acquired two beautiful ebony elephants with ivory tusks and nails. They are very heavy. They look simply wonderful in my house because of the style of the place.

Father is always wanting to know of different customs, so he tempts me to tell him something that some friends of mine told me. Unfortunately, the world is becoming the same all over, so one must look very hard to find a difference in custom, but here is one. These girls are Hollanders and were brought up in the Dutch East Indies. I have forgotten the name of the place. In any case, there they did not have toilet paper; no one did. Instead, the procedure was thus—a pitcher of water was kept in the lavatory and a towel for each member of the household. One merely poured some water over oneself and wiped with a—towel, it is hoped. Just how one satisfactorily pours the water over oneself, I have never fathomed, and I have given it considerable thought. Now there's one for you, Father.

Have I ever told you our financial arrangement? Wilfred gives me $200 a month, and I run everything. He has $50 for his own use and our amusements. I think it a splendid arrangement. I have my own bank account. If I save anything, it is mine for a trip home, so it is up to me.

I do hope you two will take a nice vacation together this year. If Mother doesn't, it will be the most foolish thing in the world. Do it in a nice way, whatever you do. Please do this.

It is still lovely weather here. It is only cold during June, July, and August

I must stop now, for there is plenty to do. I shall try to write Aunt Nellie this week. Give her my love.

Lots and lots of love,

Helen

173 Louis Botha Avenue
Orange Grove, Johannesburg
April 17, 1939

My dearest Mother and Father,

I am sitting here in my rather lovely garden with my typewriter on a card table. Robin is beside me in her new playpen, which Wilfred built for her. It is so sturdy that it takes two people to move it and looks like it had been built for a bull and not a baby. Eve is still at her lunch since it still takes her an hour or better per meal. Robin, on the other hand, quickly devours everything offered her. She, for that reason, is now much fatter than Eve ever was; in fact, she is very fat. I am afraid she is going to be like me in that respect.

I am very pleased indeed that you are going ahead and making a dress for my redingote, as, with so much to do, I do not seem to be making much headway with a winter wardrobe. However, I am afraid you will pay much more for the material than I would here. I bought four yards of lovely woolen material for $1.25 the lot. I also got four yards of beautiful black chiffon for $2.25 the lot. I have had a very pretty afternoon dress made of it. I am going to try to make the wool myself.

I certainly did recognize the picture from *Time* as being the one you thought looked like Robert. I think it is just exactly like he was. I want to know if you have a copy at home; if not, I want to send it back to you.

Bert is now away for three weeks on holiday. She went to St. James this year, a resort, which is really a suburb of Cape Town. She seems to be enjoying herself.

We are putting Eve in a kindergarten nearby, only two blocks away. I think I shall start her tomorrow. They must wear uniforms, which are in brown; and, of course, Eve is going to look terrible. All the private schools have uniforms, and all of them are ugly. I actually feel sorry for the girls having to look so terrible. I like the teacher very well at this school, and all the children are nice. It will be $3.00 a month, but I am sure it will be well worth the investment.

This past week I got off a few social obligations. I had a table of bridge on Thursday and one on Friday afternoon. They play mostly one table here or not more than two. I like it much better too. Yesterday afternoon I had people for tea. And then for a chili supper. They didn't seem to like the chili, which was unfortunate since that was all I had. I have told Wilfred it is dangerous to invite people for chili since they don't know it and may not like it. However, he likes it so much that he thinks it is the ideal way to entertain. Since the guests didn't eat the chili, he ate so much that he made himself sick, so today he thinks perhaps chili is not such a good idea.

Wilfred has made a really nice bookcase to fit one wall space perfectly. Our living room is rectangular, you know.

I had a letter from Katye Wray and she also told me about Eugene's large Bible class and the improvement in Uncle David. I am pleased about both, of course. I do hope it lasts. Aunt Nellie has not had an easy time of it. I would love to hear all about Kayte Wray's furniture and the colors used in the different rooms. I think I shall draw the plan of my house in this letter and show the furnishings.

I do wish you would send my black satin coat to me, as they use such things here, and it would go well with my chiffon dress. I plan to have a cape made out of my old fur coat. It is impossible as it is.

Mr. Sours had us to dinner at his flat last Tuesday night. We went to a movie afterwards and enjoyed ourselves very much. A movie here is quite a treat since they are so expensive. We are going out to dinner on Wednesday night with the MacDonels, friends of ours. They are at a large boarding house here, and the food is supposed to be excellent, so I am looking forward to it. They are the ones who ate chili with us last night. I suppose they want to show us real food. Bert may go to live there in June. She is quite lonely in her room in town where she must have her meals in restaurants.

I must close now if I am going to draw the house for you. I hope you are both feeling very well now.

Lots of love from us all,

Helen

173 Louis Botha Avenue
Orange Grove, Johannesburg
April 23, 1939

Dearest Dad and Mother,

I haven't had a letter this past week, so hope there is one tomorrow. I do hope you are both well and that everything is all right. If you don't hear from me, it is just that I have too many irons in the fire and can't get everything done.

Eve's started kindergarten on Tuesday of this past week. She loves it, of course. She is there from 9:00 until 12:00. Her school is known as the Linksfield Kindergarten and Preparatory School. She must dress in the school's uniform of brown. Of course, that is not going to look good on Eve, but all the uniforms are pretty terrible here, and all the schools insist on a uniform. From now on until she is through school or has left S. A., she will be in dark blue or dark brown or green. The only improvement I see so far is that she is more affectionate because she sees less of me.

Today I have kept her in bed because she has a bad cold. I hope she will be well enough for school tomorrow. Robin is getting along beautifully and has five teeth. She says "Mama" now. She has lovely rosy cheeks. We have never tried to economize on her food. She has had Mead's Dextri-Maltose No. 1 in her milk for nine months and has just now started with plain milk. She gets Mead's Pablum, 6 Tbs. a day now, an egg a day, orange juice every day, and mashed vegetables. I gave her Cod Liver oil while she was little, but I have stopped that since she plays out in the sun so much of every day. I can't understand the different ones at home trying to economize on their babies' diets since I have had to pay much more for those things than they would have to pay. I have regulated Robin's diet the whole time myself, just as you did with Eve. Of course, I remembered quite a bit from Eve.

Wilfred was quite lucky yesterday, as he won $16 on the horse races at Germiston, just outside of Johannesburg. We did not go to the races. He placed his bet because he had a tip. It was his first bet since we have been here. We are going to celebrate tomorrow with dinner at the Criterion and a movie—*Idiot's Delight*.

I don't believe I have written you that we have a Westinghouse radiogram. It is their biggest model, and it is wonderful. We have no aerial on it and yet we get England, Germany, etc., anytime. Of course, Germany is so powerful you can hardly get any other station. By not having an aerial we do not get static, and that would be very bad where we live since we are right on the electric trolley line. We get to exchange this every time a new model comes out, and it doesn't cost us a cent but the license. That is about $10 a year. You can feel thankful you don't have that. Automobile licenses are also terribly expensive, something around $30, I think.

The Alexanders must feel very proud of Thad. Have they heard from Margaret Sells yet? I didn't know she was in China.

I had already read the article about young children using the typewriter. Eve has been able to write her name on it for a long time. I have never dyed Eve's hair or used anything at all. I think it is sun-bleached.

I shall write Helen Hunter and Aunt Nellie, especially, when I can. Just now I have so much sewing to do, getting ready for the winter. Must close now, as I hear Wilfred coming in, and Sunday nights I must get the supper—bacon and eggs it will be. He has been up to see his Dad.

Lots and lots of love,

Helen

P.S. Eve is maternal with Robin. In fact, when she gets mad with me, she tells me Robin is her baby and that, if I am not good, she won't let me touch Robin.

173 Louis Botha Avenue
Orange Grove, Johannesburg
May 16, 1939

My dearest Ones,

I know it has been a long time since I have written, so I am sending this Air Mail so as to even things up. In other words, you will have my explanation of my silence before the period of no letters arrives. I am so thrilled to hear that you can get an Air Mail letter from me in two weeks. If it is not overweight, it is only 1/- (i.e. one shilling, or 25 cents, in your language). Funny, now, if I think money, I think in English money, even if I must convert U.S. money into English money.

The package with the dresses, etc., has arrived, and I am so thrilled with everything. Your black velvet dress looks wonderful on me, and just fits, and the hat is most becoming. When Wilfred saw the hat, he said, "Well, when Bert sees that, she will more than likely lay an egg." She did almost—as she loves feathers, etc. She has already asked to wear it, and it looks very good on her too. The redingote and dress just fit too, except they are a little long. I wish I could sew like you, as the dress is beautifully done. The material is so pretty too, and I can bet it was expensive. The apron is dear, and Bert plans to copy it to give some of her friends as a Christmas present. Eve got busy with her crayons and book right away, and Robin seems to love her doll. By the way, Robin is saying "Mama" to me and "Nannie" to Lizzie these days. We do appreciate the box and are now quite set up as far as the winter wardrobe goes.

The reason I have not written is that Eve and Robin have been very sick with colds, and I feared whooping cough, as the little girl next door had it and they were both exposed. However, they are better, at least Eve is, and I do believe it is nothing more than colds. They both have had a cough.

On top of this, Wilfred had £32.30 stolen from him. I am sorry to say that it seems to point to Lizzie, but we could prove nothing and have not accused her. It happened the first of the month, when he had it in his pocket to pay some bills. We went out to dinner that night and took the manager of the Pretoria store and his wife. When Wilfred paid the bill, he had £32.50 left in bills and some change. That night he came to bed after me, so undressed in the lounge and left his clothes in there, supposedly with the money in the pants pocket. The next day after Lizzie had cleaned up, Sunday about noon, Wilfred looked for his money as he was going to play golf, and he found all the bills were gone and all the notes there.

It was most upsetting to lose that amount in one month, but we have managed. Then, on Monday morning, Lizzie gave notice that she was leaving. That added to my suspicion about her, but, as I say, there was no good to be had in accusing her. She leaves at the end of this month. She now says she only wants a holiday and wants to come back. She is good but sulks a great deal, and I shall never be able to forget about the money, so I don't know that I shall take her back. I now have a wash girl, and Lizzie does not have the washing to do, but she objects to doing the floors. She thinks I should keep a boy for that. In other words, I think she is too high folooting (don't know how to spell it) for me. I have taught her so much, she thinks she can go out as a cook, now, I suppose, or a nurse girl. People here spoil them terribly. I get so annoyed with the lot of them. My so-called friends think I am a slave driver, but you know I could never be that. They think you must keep two to three servants. I am the only member of the book club with one servant, and some of them are only husband and wife.

You see why I haven't felt much like writing. It is often just a succession of petty annoyances that keeps me from writing.

Wilfred, Bert, and I went to the Empire Theatre on last Saturday night to see the ice show. It was really wonderful, as they had the leading skaters of England and Canada. It was hard to remember that they were on skates and not just dancing.

Eve is back in kindergarten and struggling with 2's. She naturally wrote her 1's very well, but the 2's are rather dreadful. Her teacher says she has a keen sense of humor since she is always laughing out in school. She is also *demanding*, according to her teacher.

I was so sorry to learn that Father had had flu. You should have told me at the time instead of only writing me afterwards. It was nice getting a letter from Father. He told me a lot of things you hadn't, or gave me a different angle on the thing.

I am so pleased to hear about Katye Wray and shall try to write her. I must get something off to her for the little one [Kay].

And Indeed There Will Be Time (Sept. 1937—Aug. 1939)

One of my best friends, Blanche Butler, left Saturday afternoon with her husband and daughter for a holiday in England. Unfortunately, when they get back, they will be in Salisbury, Southern Rhodesia, as he has been transferred there, as a manager, by his insurance company. She was always sweet to me, and doing things for the children. We played bridge together a lot, and I shall miss her very much. People in Johannesburg never seem settled. The whole atmosphere of the place says, "I am only stopping over here for a little while."

There has been a lot of sickness, as we had a drop in temperature of over 30 degrees in one night. It was at that time when Eve and Robin started with their colds. It has warmed up again, so don't worry that we are suffering from cold. We have an open fire in the lounge, the kitchen range, and an electric heater to transfer back and forth in the bedrooms.

Against Mother's advice, I have put Robin in everything woolen, as one really must here. She has lovely new undervests, flannel petticoats, and fine woolen dresses. All her things are most expensive. The material for her dresses is £1.00 per yard, and it takes a yard and a half.

I have had my fur coat made into a cape, and it looks very nice. Everyone is doing that here. This climate is well suited to capes, but they would not do one much good in Tennessee. My black coat that Father bought me ten years ago looks as stylish as anything just now. I have just had it relined and shall wear it this winter. It has been a marvelous coat.

There are three holidays in the month—the 18th, 24th and 31st, and everybody gets them. We are going on a picnic on the 18th. We are taking Robin, even. She is wonderful when she is out.

I got a hanky from you in a letter, for which I want to thank you—also the hanky to Eve in her Easter card. She appreciates those things so much and looks at them a long time. This will be overweight if I write more.

Love & kisses,

Helen, Wilfred, & Babies

173 Louis Botha Avenue
Orange Grove, Johannesburg
June 7, 1939

My dearest Mother and Dad,

It is just six thirty in the morning, but I thought it might be the most uninterrupted time I would have for a letter to you. Eve [now age five] is sitting beside me dressed in her new school clothes, a present from Wilfred's Dad for her birthday, and she is endeavoring to knit with her new knitting needles from her Auntie Bert. Well, she really looks quite grown up in pleated brown skirt and tan blouse, very tailored. I am amused. If they could only see her in Elizabethton.

You are certainly good on timing things, as she received her lovely little red bag on the 5th, and is she thrilled with it—perhaps we should have it in her own words. I have just asked her what she wants to say, and she has assumed the usual self-conscious look of a letter writer stumped for something to say. She says, "Send her my love from my bag." The Afrikaans influence has her a little mixed up with her prepositions. Anyway, it is a pretty bag, and she looked very smart yesterday when we went to town, as she wore the coat and hat you made her, the white gloves from Ann, and carried her red pocket book. Please thank Mrs. Alexander and Ann for the gloves. I will write a note when I can. It was most thoughtful and most unexpected. They fit perfectly.

June 12, 1939

I am just now finding a minute to get back to this letter. It is really terrible. Just as I stopped the preceding paragraph, I had a chance at a very high stepladder for a couple of days, and I started house-cleaning, which is something in this house. We swept all the thatch inside the house, and the peak of the ceilings can just be reached from the top of a high stepladder with a broom, and those peaks were full of spider webs, which I have been crazy to reach. It meant moving everything out of every room as it was cleaned. This brings to mind something queer. Over here they call the broom we use at home an "American broom," and it is usually used only in the yard. The rugs are swept with a more-or-less soft brush, which leaves much dirt behind it, but you must grin and bear it. To be happy in a foreign country, you must do as everyone else does.

We were all so pleased to get the pictures of Papa. They are very good of him, I think. One is rather stern-looking, though, and makes us think we had better all be good girls.

L. should take care of the shrubs and trees himself. I am thoroughly disgusted with him, and if I ever have the money, the first thing I will do will be to tell L. to get out. If you must do it to take care of the planting, do so, but do not fail to tell him it is his place to take care of such things. You are certainly getting a lot of things out of the C's on the house you are in. It is a very different tale from the time Mrs. L. owned it. Whatever happened about the lawsuit on it?

They are trying to sell the place we are in, and that makes the landlord very indifferent about doing anything. We intend to hold them to our lease of one year if that is at all possible. I don't think I could stand to try to find another place and all the moving. We will never be satisfied again anyway, as this place is so unusual and that it is a show place. Everyone who comes just can't help but comment on it and the furnishings.

I don't doubt that the story circulating about S.B. is correct. What disgusting things go on. What he wrote in the papers was most amusing. One can hardly believe it possible for a man to make such a fool of himself as to write in that vein.

And Indeed There Will Be Time (Sept. 1937—Aug.1939)

I am always glad to get suggestions on children's diets. I go chiefly by my U.S. Government book. Robin gets a cereal now, since I stopped Pablum about two weeks ago—either Sago, Semolina, or Malted Mabela. I don't suppose you know any of them, as I had never heard of them until getting out here. I could eat the Mabela myself, it is so good. It comes from Natal.[62] You can get the canned vegetables out here, but I have never bought even one tin. I find it so easy to prepare her vegetable when the vegetables for the rest are cooked. She gets peas, beans, carrots, and pumpkin mostly, along with an egg every day. She is lovely and fat and has rosy cheeks. She would be beautiful if she only had curly hair, but it is perfectly straight. She is inclined to overeat on her vegetables, etc., and is lots of times not able to take all of her milk. She is not as active as Eve was, and I think that is why she is so fat, or vice versa.

Bert has made Robin a beautiful pink knitted dress and a knitted cap in bunny wool. She looks too lovely in them. They must be saved, however, for her party. Eve will wear the pink dress you all sent her for Xmas. It had to be lengthened before she could wear it.

I am sorry to say that I have feet like yours, Mother, and really, it is terrible. The only comfortable shoe I have that I can really walk in with complete comfort is a pair of golf shoes. The heel is just right to take the weight off the ball of my foot, and the crepe soles are comfortable too. They cost me over $10, but I wear them to do my housework. I would advise you to try this in a pair of really good ones. While I think about it, don't buy me another pair of Rhythm Step shoes, as the supports in them seem to hit me in the wrong places, and they are most uncomfortable.

My new girl is getting along rather well. You know Lizzie left on the first of the month. Over here, you must give a servant one month's notice, and they must give you the same. This girl is dying to learn to cook, so Saturday night I had the dinner on cooking, and was in the lounge talking with Bert. I called Agnus and told her to slice some tomatoes in the glass dish and put vinegar over them. "Yes, Missus, I understand." Bert was a bit doubtful that she understood, and told her to "cut" some tomatoes, saying to me that Agnus would not understand "slice." Bert went out to see how things were coming along and found that Agnus had put them in the Pyrex dish with vinegar and put them in the oven. That is how much idea she has of cooking. I have to take them raw like this, however, and get them to clean the floors; otherwise you must keep two, one for floors, the other as cook. Lizzie had learned too much from me to continue doing floors.

---

[62] Natal was one of the four provinces of South Africa at that time. The other provinces were the Cape Province, the Transvaal, and the Orange Free State. The largest cities in each of these provinces were Durban in Natal, Cape Town in the Cape Province, Johannesburg in the Transvaal, and Bloemfontein in the Orange Free State.

I played bridge this afternoon and won two pence, about four cents. We were only playing for a penny a hundred. I play with them quite often because they won't play for more than that, and that suits me perfectly.

I would like to come home whenever we have to leave this house if I can have the money by then. That is rather doubtful, however, since I see no way to save a penny for several months yet. I wouldn't like to sell any of my furniture even though I would get just as much as I paid for it, but I don't know when I could get it at such good prices again, and nearly everything we have is just what we want. I wouldn't want to buy any clothes until I got home, as you are naturally ahead of us in styles. We are necessarily a season behind.

I haven't contacted Miss Doak yet, but I will. No, Kensington is not considered a good residential district, but it isn't bad, for there are many new and comfortable houses there. It is just considered the wrong side of town. Lots of business girls live there, however, and men.

I shall give you the list of "Raymonds" out of the telephone directory, and you may give it to Mr. Wolff if you like. I really don't know how I would ever find the right one without writing to them all, and that would be a little silly. He may write if he likes, giving the man our address. Wilfred is not keen on doing anything along the line, as he thinks Wolff could have helped him get in the plants and he didn't. We can't forget what people in Elizabethton put us through. Thank goodness, somehow or other we kept on believing in ourselves, and now we are capable of making good just as well as other people.

You asked about Wilfred's position in case of war. He was called up to register, and he would be in the first line of reserve in the Royal Air Force in case of war. All we can do is hope we won't have war. If I were you, I would read the papers less, for the newspapers keep one in a continual turmoil.

I hope there is no more trouble about Father's job. I think it was most unfair of the bus company to threaten him with losing his job if Uncle Hunter succeeded in his enterprise. It looks like they won't let Uncle Hunter make a living in Elizabethton. I do wish he could get something to do.

Wilfred, Eve and I are going to spend this weekend in Pretoria with the manager of the Pretoria store and his wife. They live on a farm out from Pretoria. Bert is going to keep Robin here at home. It will be a break for me. These people have a little boy just about Eve's age, and they play awfully well together. Pretoria is 1000 feet lower than Johannesburg, and even that drop is a help now and then.

I must stop now and have a look into cutting out a skirt to wear with the new cardigan Bert has knit for me in green Bouclé.[63] I am making a brown skirt.

---

[63] Bouclé is usually a three-ply yarn with one thread looser than the others, producing a rich, nubby, textured fabric.

By the way, I have beautiful roses in bloom all around my house just now. We are very protected by our high hedge and being a bit below the level of the street. I have over twenty blooms on my poinsettia. You would pay $1.50 per bloom in pots at home. I wish I could sell them at that. I also have violets in bloom just now and quite a pretty lily. It is most mild tonight. We do not even have a fire and are comfortable.

Wilfred has been devouring the *Reader's Digest* while I have been writing this letter. We look forward to it each month and read it from cover to cover.

I wanted to send *Our Land* for Father's birthday on the 30th of this month, but I have not been able to get the cards to finish it. You will love having the book when I can send it, as it will give you such a wonderful idea of the country. The pictures are perfectly marvelous, as I can judge by the ones of Johannesburg and Cape Town that I know myself. These books sell for $7.50 in England as they can only be compiled by collectors in South Africa. I lack five pictures now, so maybe it won't be long. Anyway, I want Papa to know we thought of him on his birthday and wish him many happy returns of the day. It won't be more than one more at the most until we spend it with him.

I hope you all are going to the World's Fair in New York.[64] I shall be very disappointed if you don't, and really annoyed, so please do go and see everything and really enjoy yourselves. Take plenty of money along so you can. Don't you wish you could have seen the King and Queen? I hope they will come to South Africa in the next year or so.

I am giving the children a birthday party on the 15th of July, being a Saturday. I hope to have it very nice indeed. Eve will have some children from school and other friends she knows outside. It is always made very difficult because of the mothers who come along. I must serve tea to all of them. I suppose we will get through it.

We are going to a Symphony Concert tomorrow night at the Town Hall. Bert worked up the party. Leslie Henson is here with his London company in *Going Greek*. We are going to see it since he is perhaps London's best comedian. We do get some very good things here now and then. They are not much more expensive than a movie, either. I shall certainly be ready to take in all the shows at 25 cents a time when I get home. We must pay from 80 cents to a dollar a seat for a movie.

---

[64] The 1939-1940 New York World's Fair, which covered 1,216 acres, was an attempt to ameliorate the some of the devastating effects of the Great Depression by promoting the notion of a middle class and a more affluent future for all. Over the two years that it was open, some forty-five million people attended. Among the commodities being promoted were television, cars, street lighting, and electricity for all. New products included nylon, air conditioning, color photography, and electric typewriters. Although the United States did not enter World War II until the end of 1941, the fair provided a window into the troubles already developing in countries like Poland, Czechoslovakia, and France.

I really must stop now. I know I have written a lot of little things, but I am just feeling talkative.

Lots and lots of love,

Helen

>173 Louis Botha Avenue
>Orange Grove, Johannesburg
>June 19, 1939

Dearest Ones,

This past weekend I had a complete rest from the babies by spending Saturday and Sunday in Pretoria with Mr. and Mrs. Phayn while Bert took charge here. Mr. Phayn is manager of the Pretoria store, and they live in the country about seven miles from Pretoria. On Sunday we drove out to the Premier Diamond Mine, about twenty miles from Pretoria. This is where the Cullinan Diamond was found that is now in the Crown of the King—that is, parts of it, as it has been cut up. The Mine was disappointing as it is closed down and has been for five years. We could not get close to anything because it was all wired in. Cullinan has a beautiful home out of Pretoria. The dumps of the diamond mine are bluish, whereas the gold mine dumps look just like sand.

Isn't it about time for the insurance on the house to fall due? Be sure to take out a three-year policy and see what dividend is due at the time. I hope you are going to have money for it when it falls due.

By the way, Bert was exhausted when we arrived back. It doesn't hurt for them to see what I have to do. I was exhausted when I left on Saturday.

We have conclusive evidence that Lizzie took Wilfred's money. Last Tuesday night we were dressing to go out to hear Cecelia Wessels, who is going over to sing in the Metropolitan Opera Company, and I went to get some of my evening clothes out of a drawer in the lounge. There in the corner was a £5 note ($25). I simply stared and then shook everything hoping to find the rest—£1.10, but the £5 was all that was there. Evidently Lizzie, being a Native, got afraid of having such a large note, so gave it back before she left. Wilfred absolutely had not put it there. Also, we had searched every drawer in the room the day we missed the money, just to have some place to look. It had been there at least thirteen days. We were certainly glad to get that much back. Also, Lizzie must have taken sugar all the time, as I will use 10 lbs. less this month than any of the time Lizzie was here. This girl manages to eat about one third of what Lizzie took out. Lizzie rode me well, it seems. She was very capable and could get through a lot of work, but she cost me plenty. I have to work very hard for this new girl to get through.

I did not have a letter from you this past Saturday, which is the day I usually hear. I do hope you are both well. Please let me know if you are not.

And Indeed There Will Be Time (Sept. 1937—Aug.1939)

This will bore Father, but I am so annoyed over having a beautiful hand ruined for one this afternoon that I must tell you about it.

I had:

        ♣ A K Q 10 9 8 3
        ♠ A 4
        ♦ A 8 3
        ♥ 8

My partner had:

        ♣ 6
        ♠ Q J 10 8
        ♦ K Q 10 8 3
        ♥ 10 7 2

I opened the bidding with 2 clubs, pass; my partner said 2 diamonds. I knew she was not showing me an ace, for I had that, so took it she had the king. I then bid 2 spades to show my ace. She said 3 spade, so I took it she had the king. I then said 4 clubs to give her a chance to bid the ace of hearts if she had it. She says 4 spades. Taking it that she did not have the Ace of hearts but feeling sure I could make 6, I said 6 clubs; she denies this with 6 spades. I then knew she thought I had a good spade suit as well as club suit. To save myself, I said 7 clubs, knowing I couldn't make it but having every reason to think it would be better than 6 spades, and I collapsed. I have never been more annoyed at a bridge table in my life. I couldn't restrain myself from saying, "You have ruined my hand."

We were doubled, of course, and went down 2000. If you think I did not bid correctly, I would like to know. We could have made 6 clubs, as it turned out, which was all I ever dreamed of bidding.

Tomorrow is the general monthly meeting of the American Women's Club, and our speaker is a Dr. Sung on China. We may each take a guest, so I am taking a lady who has had us for dinner. She does not play bridge, so it is a way to entertain her. It is always a nice tea at the Carlton Hotel. The following afternoon I must keep the clubrooms again. I do not mind, since I have been initiated.

Eve has been a bit broken out from eating too much fruit but looks better now. Robin is doing splendidly.

The enclosed photo was taken by Bert of Sir Abe Bailey's house in Cape Town. It was just next to her hotel. He is one of the richest men in South Africa. I sent it because I think it is a rather lovely example of the Cape Dutch Architecture, which I like very much. Sir Abe has had both of his legs removed since I have been in S.A. Bert met two of his nurses and had dinner with them at his home.

I have a beautiful sweater in bluish green bouclé that Bert has just finished for me. I made a brown skirt to go with it and have a very smart outfit, all for $4.50.

My black chiffon is very pretty and cost about $7.50. I made my skirt so well that Bert wants me to make one for her.

Wilfred has an upset stomach and isn't feeling a bit good. He is already in bed.

I really must close and go to bed too, as I must be up by six-thirty in the morning if I am to go out for morning tea.

Lots of love and kisses to you both from us,

Helen

July 6, 1939

Dearest Mother and Father,

Wilfred is staying over in Pretoria tonight, as the store manager there is sick and he must take his place, so I have a whole evening to chat with you all. I would feel a bit lonely with the children in bed and Wilfred away if I didn't have you for the evening.

There are lots of things in your letters to answer, so first I want to say that I have never received Aunt Nellie's letter with pictures of Uncle Fred and the Clems enclosed. Why her letters go astray I do not understand, unless she does not write plainly or unless she only puts my street address and not the suburb. Unless you put Orange Grove, I cannot possibly get it, as each suburb has its own post office, stores, town hall, etc., and they are really all little townships within a big one. The same was true of Parktown North, Parkwood, etc. I too am very worried about not receiving it since I would so love to have the pictures. Perhaps it will be returned. I think you had better address the next letter. Could Uncle David have forgotten to mail it or have put too little postage on it? You sent me one letter with only a 3c stamp on it, but I got it all right.

As to the present for Katye Wray, I am already in the middle of making a pair of sheets in pink for the baby. I am not putting any embroidery on them, only lace, and she should not have to pay any more than 25c on duty. If it is more, they are highway robbers. Tell her to let them return them to me if they want more than 50c duty. I see perfectly beautiful embroidered ones in town, but she would have to pay 90% duty, and I do not want to put her in that position.

I'll send the pictures you want for enlargements when I am not sending by Air Mail. I am so thrilled that you can get letters in two weeks that I am tempted to send all my letters by Air.

Your latest box arrived in due course, and we all went into ecstasies over Robin's dress. Of course, it will be her party dress when we celebrate on the 15th. It fits her perfectly already. She is very large, as the one-year-old dress Elizabeth Hunter sent her is too small. Her baby undervests didn't cover any of her when I discarded them. Eve can wear the ones for Robin now, and they fit one of them just the same as the other. Robin is a shy baby and hides her eyes behind her hands

And Indeed There Will Be Time (Sept. 1937—Aug.1939)

when she meets strangers. She also blushes a fiery red and ducks her head onto my shoulder. It is too cute for words now, but I do hope it doesn't stick with her. I haven't forgotten my days of agony yet.

You were very sweet to send me your coat, but, as you say, I do not need it, as I have so much of my own. Now what am I to do? I am waiting for instructions from you before posting it back to you, as I want you to inquire about the duty and see if there is any way for it to be sent so you won't have to pay any duty on it. I only paid 75c myself on the whole package. I shall be able to make use of the scarf, as I have a brown skirt and a green sweater known as a cardigan over here. It is of bouclé. I am finishing the petticoat up for Eve. She can make good use of it. Thanks very, very much for everything. You must not send your green dress to me, as I really have plenty this winter and you can make good use of it yourself next winter.

No doubt you now understand from my subsequent letters that we only lost $32.50, not $162.50, as you think. I must have converted the pounds into dollars and then put a pound mark in front. I am very sorry to have misled you and have you so worried. It would have been tragic if we had lost $162.50. Also, you have misunderstood the price I pay for material for Robin's dresses. It is $1.50 per yard (One dollar and a half). Robin does not need any more winter dresses, and for summer I have a big supply of Eve's old dresses for play, and all she needs is a dress-up dress or two. The one you have sent will do for that for a long time. I really don't believe any sewing need be done for her or Eve just now. If you were only here, there would always be something, of course. I have about a dozen things now on hand: a dress to shorten, bedroom curtains to make, a cover for the steamer trunk, etc. I shortened my light blue dress at least 1½ inches, also the redingote. I also took out an inch on each side seam, cut out the back of the neck to make it fit better, and changed the shoulder seams. It really fits me for the first time now. I can remember the back of the neck never looked right.

I am glad you have gone away for a visit to Mrs. Chambers and that you will have such good company. Those are three of your friends whom I could always enjoy thoroughly myself. They are all just good sports and will never grow old because there is so much fun in them.

It would be too bad if my name had been in the guest list of the Caudills' and Evans' party when I wasn't there and not even invited. I would have made a public announcement in the newspaper that I wasn't there. You won't know me when I get back, for I haven't had anyone to say "No" to me in a long time. You know Wilfred wouldn't. When I occasionally do something *terrible*, he is only highly amused.

I did something lovely and rude at the Consul's cocktail party on the 4th of July. There is a Mrs. Hastings here, an American woman about my age, Chairman of the Entertainment Committee of the American Women's Club, who has been very rude to me on three occasions (the only three times we have met). She is this way to nearly everybody until she decides to accept them. Financially and socially she is on a plane with me. I first met her at two tables of bridge and, since she was going my way in her car, I asked her for a lift. She said she thought I could get there quicker by bus.

The next time I met her was at the general meeting of the Women's Club, and the lady I was with asked her if we could sit with her and another. She said no, another was joining them. The lady said, "Well, we will just move our chairs over to your table," since she was a very wealthy woman and couldn't believe she was being snubbed. We went over, and Mrs. Hastings never addressed one look or remark to us. I thought kindness would finally win, so the next time I saw her just the two of us passed each other in the hotel corridor and I said, "Hello Mrs. Hastings." She said "Good morning," as though she had never seen me before. With that, I swore I would make her remember me at least, so at the cocktail party she was one of the hostesses and naturally had to be nice, so up she comes to our group. Someone said, "Mrs. Hastings, do you know Mrs. Evans?" She said, "I believe I do." I said nothing but turned my back immediately and started talking to someone. I then turned to the group again and said, "Excuse me," and joined another group. Mrs. Hastings then came up to me and said, "I believe you turned your back on me just now." And the only satisfaction she got was "Yes" from me, and I turned my back on her again. She may always hate me for this, but she didn't like me before, and I like myself a lot better after doing it. Wilfred was there and got the shock of his life, as he thinks I just wouldn't go that far with anything.

At the date of writing, the children are both very well. They don't even have colds, which is unusual around here in the wintertime, since it is hot one day and cold the next. Eve went to a little friend's birthday party today. The people there were all Americans and there was a crowd. The most interesting lady I met was down here on holiday with her husband and three children from Bechuanaland Protectorate. They live on the edge of the Kalahari Desert and must go 350 miles across it to reach home from the nearest railway. It takes them three days and two nights to make this journey, as the roads are so terrible. Of course, there is hardly a road at all. Her husband is a medical missionary among the natives there, and theirs is also the government hospital. She was very homely-looking but a good sort and had something interesting to talk about.

It looks like the city wants to jump from the frying pan into the fire to turn Crawford Alexander out and put Banks in. They are always in turmoil there. You know, it is a rest—and a wonderful rest at that—not to care about civic problems.

Do not worry about us throwing our money away on horse races. The race I wrote you we won on was a mistake. To show you how little we know about it all, we took the height of the horse as the odds in the paper. We lost about $3.00 on that sure bet. No, Wilfred is less of a gambler than I am. Please don't mention

Idiot's Delight to me, as the money we spent to go to see that dreadful show hurt us more than the $3.00 we lost on the horse.

I had forgotten that I did not know until a year and a half ago that I did not know what a radiogram was. A radiogram is a radio and gramophone combined in one cabinet, and the gramophone has a wonderful tone coming through the apparatus for the radio. We have the biggest and best thing put out by Westinghouse and a wonderful selection of records from Bert.

The army planes are droning overhead tonight. They have night maneuvers over Johannesburg some night in every week—in fact, twice a week, I think. The police force of the whole Union has been doubled, and of course the army and flying squad have all been increased. As I see it, our best protection is the size of the country in miles, not men. I refuse to have the newspaper jitters every morning, so I am saving my energies until something does break loose, which it looks very much like it will. Wilfred and I think Roosevelt was the only person who did anything constructive during the recent crises, and that Chamberlain acted a doddering old fool. Of course, this opinion cannot even be expressed in the family without sending Bert into tears and Dad into a fury. Everyone here thinks Chamberlain has been too marvelous.[65]

That was dreadful about B.D.'s wife. I feel so sorry for him. Such a thing one could never get over, as the circumstances are so horrible. I hope he didn't find them himself.

Please let me advise you not to buy the property you are in. You do not know how soon the day will come when you will not feel up to looking after a big place like that, with roomers; and, if you have to keep a servant, where are you? The plot of ground it is on is much too small, and the neighborhood is poor. Do not clutter up your life again with obligations. Isn't it much nicer having just so much and knowing what that will be and living within it? I only have $100 outstanding against our furniture, but neither of us can hardly stand it until we get that paid off. Wilfred cannot bear debts. He worries foolishly over them, as no one has been pushing us at all.

I think you can forget the matter about Wilfred's bond since he is bonded now. From all we can find out, they merely accepted his Johannesburg references. We aren't worrying about it. He got his job even though Westinghouse was never able to get one word about Wilfred from Sears, Roebuck. Wilfred finally told Mr. Sours the whole story, and he thought it a huge joke and never worried anymore about hearing from them. They still hold about $100 of Wilfred's that was taken out of his salary every month from the time he started with them. He has written

---

[65] It took another ten months before backbench fury in the British Parliament over the inaction of Neville Chamberlain led to the installation of Winston Churchill as prime minister of a coalition government in England on May 10, 1940.

and written about it. We would let Eugene [Helen's uncle, who was a lawyer] take it up, but we don't want to air the whole thing to the family or anyone.

Eve said a cute thing yesterday. She came in from school and said, "Mommy, you know little Carl cried at school today because he lost his temper." She said, "Now that wasn't anything to cry over, was it?" Wilfred asked her if he ever found his temper, and she said no. And he assured her that little Carl was much better off for it.

Lizzie's people have been here time and again looking for Lizzie, as she came back to Johannesburg from her home about ten days ago and simply disappeared. Her sister told me today that Mack, who lived here all the year she was with me, was not her husband but her sweetheart and that they were to have been married in August. Lizzie stole the money, we know, but, since she returned $25 of it, we would not prosecute her even if we knew where she was, as she was a marvelous girl and a hard worker. I have another good girl now, but I am keeping her down. Lizzie had a fine opinion of herself because we praised her so much, but I will never do that again. I dish out the bread and milk, etc., to this one. I saved 75c this past month on bread and used 10 lbs. of sugar less. I pay her $2.50 less a month, and she does the washing and ironing, which Lizzie did not do at the last.

I am cooking a leg of springbok Sunday. It was sent to Dad from the Free State [one of the four provinces of the Union of South Africa]. It is venison, of course. I am having an old friend of the family's from Bloemfontein here for the dinner.[66]

Well, I have been writing so long that I don't know what I have said. I shall perhaps wake up tomorrow morning thinking how I forgot to say this and that. I must close, as just now I fell off to sleep at my typewriter. By the way, this is airmail stationery.

I do hope you are both in the best of health and that you will know there is nothing for you to worry about so far as we are concerned.

Lots and lots of love from us all,

Helen

July 31, 1939

My dearest Ones,

I have been getting a letter from you each Saturday, and you know how welcome they are. They make me feel quite bad, though, that I do not write so

---

[66] Springbok, the national animal of South Africa, is an antelope of medium size that is a very fast runner. Wilfred always referred to American-born Eve and Helen as "The Yankees," even though they came from the South, and to himself and Robin as "The Springboks," since they were both South African-born. The meal, therefore, must have been accompanied by a great deal of laughter.

often. You must admit that I write a lot when I do settle down to it. I really can't write anything decent unless I am in the humor for it, and I hope you two will not worry about me but just know if anything is wrong I will let you know it immediately and otherwise I am merely waiting for the muse.

Thanks a lot for the pretty yellow handkerchief. You keep me supplied with such fine ones that I can't find anything to blow my nose in.

I am so sorry to hear that Mr. Mayr is leaving and wish I were there to find you somebody else. I feel very guilty that you merely keep that big house running so you will have it when we come home. I am sure it is a burden. It isn't so long now until we will be on our way. I am determined to stay away three years so I will really be missed, and I would like to be home during the good weather. Bert talks of going to England next June. If she does, I shall see if Eve wants to go along and come on over to you and stay until I come. I think she might do it with Bert. She can safely cross the Atlantic alone if it is a boat with a child's nurse aboard. You could meet her in New York.

I am sending you by this mail, also pictures of Eve and Robin's joint birthday party. Wilfred had these made especially for you all. It was raining the day of the party, and we couldn't take pictures outside, so he had a photographer come and take them. I am so glad you will get some idea of my house inside too. The picture of the big group is not very good, but I know you all will enjoy it. It is taken in the living room looking into our little dining room. Eve's teacher is on the extreme right, just past Bert and Robin. Wilfred looks silly, and I look like the care-worn mother of all the children. The couple to Wilfred's left are very good friends of ours. Sonia Beaton, Eve's best friend, is to her (Eve's) left. Sonia's mother has the flower on her shoulder. You will recognize table and pictures. You can also see the covering of my suite of furniture. I think you will see a write-up of the birthday party in the Elizabethton paper before you get this letter. We did it as a surprise for you all. I enclose some drawings Eve did for you. The amusing part is to have her explain the pictures.

Bert has just sent all of her old furniture to the auction mart to be sold and has moved into a lovely new flat and refurnished. I have been after her for a long time

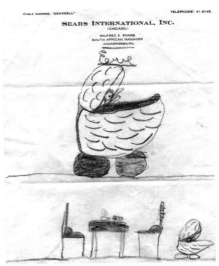

Eve's drawing of Robin in pram

to do it, and it isn't going to cost her more than $50 to have lovely new things. She had a small suite I had bought at a sale reupholstered, and I have never seen anything prettier. It cost her less than half if she had bought it new, and it is just like new now. She has a plain plum-colored rug, 9 x 12, and new divan bed covered in plum-colored cloth. The suite is covered in linen in Jacobean design. She has an attractive bookcase that Wilfred made for her, a tea wagon, which I had sanded down from a plain oak finish and that will be painted the same as the bookcase. She has also bought a dropleaf table from me that I first used as a dining room table before I found my lovely black teak one, and that will be ducoed.

She really had old and unattractive things, half bedroom, half living room. Now her place is furnished completely as a living room, and there isn't a more beautiful room in Johannesburg. Her curtains are gorgeous and cost her $50 for two windows, but they give a rich air to the whole place. They are Velasque Blue, which is a greenish blue, and are a knobby, satiny material that I really can't describe because I don't know what it is called. She had the best decorator in Johannesburg do the flat. She is so thrilled over it, and I am so happy that she has it. On top of her new flat they have a very large swimming pool with palms, deck chairs, etc., around it. It is right in town.

The children and all of us are well. Eve is getting fat and has more color than usual.

Spring is already here, it seems. We have had some very cold days in July, but not many. You can know that since I only burned one ton of coal during July, and I do all my cooking with it. My roses have never stopped blooming. You must simply learn to dress warmly. I think you should cut down on your heat and wear more clothes. I couldn't afford the coal bill I know you have.

You know I would be so glad to have a picture of Robert. I would like the one made when he was about thirteen or fifteen. I do not want the one in his uniform, as that one hurts too much. Eve often mentions him. She remembers so much of her time with you. [Robert died five years before Eve was born, but he was seldom out of the family's thoughts and conversations.]

Helen's brother,
Robert E. Dixon, at age 15

I must close and mail this as I fetch Eve from school. Everything—bank, post office, school, all kinds of shops—are within two blocks of me.

I was so sorry to hear about Gladys. I shall try to write her.

Lots and lots of love,

Helen

[To: Sophia Dixon from Bert Evans]

P. O. Box 1167
Johannesburg
August 15, 1939

Dear Mrs. Dixon,

Helen has asked me to write and tell you that they have been transferred for six months to Durban, and that she will be writing you as soon as she arrives. Wilfred left today by car and Helen, Eve, and Robin leave tomorrow afternoon by train. They are delighted about the transfer, as it will be a delightful change after being upcountry for so long, and I personally think the change down to the coast will do them a lot of good.

Until you receive their address, will you send your letters to Helen, care Poste Restante, Durban.

Please excuse brevity, am anxious to catch the mail.

Yours sincerely,
Bert Hudd Evans

Robin, Helen and Eve

5 I Dwell in Possibility
August 1939 ~ April 1940

I dwell in Possibility –
A fairer House than Prose –
More numerous of Windows –
Superior – for Doors –

~ Emily Dickinson

5

This seems to have been Helen and Wilfred's big moment, a moment to dream of endless possibilities. Frosty dry Johannesburg is in the past, and Durban unfurls itself—a lush, humid paradise with endless beaches and endless possibilities for advancement. Wilfred has been ordered to spend six months breathing life into the Durban branch of Westinghouse, and he is succeeding.

Life is opening up for them, and Helen is hoping for a long-overdue rest. They have a car and the joy of visits to the ocean. At the same time, they both suffer ill health. Helen has bronchitis and asthma, and Wilfred has a bad back and colitis, brought on, seemingly, by the stress of the infighting at Westinghouse.

The mood of the Dixon-Evans family on both sides of the Atlantic is tempered by the news of the beginning of World War II. Wilfred knows he will have to serve if the war starts to engulf South Africa. Even though he does not shrink from a fight, he loses weight as the pressures within Europe accumulate.

August 1939 is the tenth anniversary of the meeting between Helen and Wilfred and the sixth anniversary of their marriage. This is Helen's third year away from the stresses of the Great Depression back home, and Wilfred continues to work hard to protect his little family. With more time on her hands, Helen finds herself caught between missing her family back home—"it was not unkin to dying for me to leave you all for so long"—and relief at no longer being in Elizabethton—"I really think it would kill me to live in Elizabethton again."

With the thought of a family reunion in America receding as the war in Europe gathers strength, and as she falls more deeply in love with her husband and her new country, Helen tries to persuade her parents to come to South Africa, where she feels sure that she can find work for her father, who is now fifty-two.

Helen's optimism will soon fade, however, as Britain enters World War II on September 3, 1939. And South Africa follows suit three days later, on September 6, 1939.

To: Helen's parents from Helen [age 32]

> The Echoes
> Durban
> August 22, 1939

My dearest Ones,

I am sure it is quite a surprise for you that we are in Durban. The transfer had been in the wind for some time, but we weren't sure, so I thought it best to wait until it was definite before writing about it. The Durban store has never done well, and, since all of Wilfred's stores in the Transvaal are leading the Union in sales, he has been sent down here for six months to see what he can do for this store. The manager has been fired, and Wilfred is, for the time being, manager and in charge of the warehouse, which is their biggest one, since everything is landed here except merchandise from Cape Town.

We are very pleased to be here for a while, since it makes a fine holiday for all of us. We are spending this first week at a hotel, The Echoes, right in Durban on the beach. However, on Thursday we move to Isipingo, thirteen miles south of Durban. Isipingo is one of the most beautiful spots in the world, I think, and I have seen quite a lot. We shall live at a small boarding house situated on a sixty-foot bluff overlooking the Indian Ocean. Straight below us stretches the beach, which has a natural pool in the rocks for the children to bathe. The boarding house is a cottage just renovated, and the people running it are a retired couple from Johannesburg. She has six daughters and three sons but is still pretty and, you can imagine, motherly. I shall have a young native girl for the children and laundry (to be done each day). I plan to have a marvelous rest, for I haven't had a real rest in years, you know.

In order to live so far out, we have bought a car. Don't get a shock, because it isn't extravagant. It is a De Luxeford V8. We got it for the balance of the installments. It is a 1939 car selling for £450 ($2,250) over here. We bought it for £190 ($950). The man owning simply wanted to be relieved of any more monthly payments immediately, and we know him well, so we got it. It costs us $50 a month to carry, but we only pay $100 a month board, which we could never get in Durban. It is $140 a month where we are, and other places we tried were $200 per month. We have let our house furnished to some new people with Westinghouse from England. We got $20 a month out of that. Not bad, eh?

I hated to leave my little place, as all the trees are coming into bloom just as we left, and it looked too beautiful. However, I think we are very lucky to get this change under such auspicious circumstances. There is so much to see down here too. We shall drive into Zululand one weekend and see the natives in their natural habitat. Eve and Robin are eating with tremendous appetites and are looking so well. They are having a great time. I have a nurse girl for them who does everything, so my rest has already started.

The family in our house consists only of man and wife and daughter of eighteen, so I know it will be well taken care of. They kept my native girl on too. They can look after it even better than I could with two children.

I was most happy to receive two letters from you down here, forwarded from J'burg, also the August *Reader's Digest*. Just before leaving J'burg, I had a splendid letter from Father too, which I so much enjoyed.

Johannesburg was cold and rainy when we left, but we have had perfect weather here for bathing until today, which is overcast and windy. Father would love it here, and I do wish he could enjoy it with us. I know Mother isn't so keen on the ocean, but perhaps a view over it from a verandah 60 feet up would be appealing. From the station at Isipingo to the beach, one drives two miles down an avenue of trees, which form a perfect arch over the road. Can't you chuck it all in Elizabethton and come over?

Bert certainly hated to see us leave J'burg. However, she can come down for Xmas. Don't worry that having a car will keep me from saving enough money to come home, for in a year from now we can sell it for as much as we have paid for it. I shall come even if I have to sell my furniture.

I am wondering how things are with Katye Wray. I have been delayed on the present I am making, as I had so much sewing for the children at the last minute. I also had to make curtains for one bedroom that I had never curtained. I enjoyed the letters from Mrs. Clem [Katye Wray's mother] and Munna [Katye Wray's grandmother]. I think Munna wrote a remarkable letter for a person her age. Did she look very old? I have not been able to get any trace of Aunt Nellie's letter at this end.

The swimsuits you have sent Eve will come in well this summer. We are practically in the tropics in Durban, you know. Sunday we took a lovely drive, which took us through the sugar cane and overlooked the sea on one side and the Valley of a Thousand Hills on the other.

I really must stop, for I must do some shopping before leaving Durban. Eve has just told me she doesn't remember Dicky and Mama Hunter. It hurts me that she has forgotten them. She does remember you all, however.

Lots of Love,
Helen

Ocean View
Isipingo Beach, Natal
South Africa
September 2, 1939

My dearest Mother and Father,

My thoughts have been almost constantly with you two since we got the war news yesterday, for I know how you feel about my being so far away at such a time, and I feel the same way myself, since, if it gets as bad as we expect, there may be periods that we cannot even get letters back and forth. However, you have nothing to fear as far as our safety, for we are just as safe here as we would be in America. There will be a lot of fighting in Europe before there is any here.

Prices have shot up overnight; gasoline jumped up 12 cents on the gallon because it is all imported, and there is the possibility of not being able to get it. Foods went up 50% overnight. No doubt the same has happened in America. You will be glad to learn that Wilfred is now classed in the third line of reserve instead of the first. I suppose you know, however, that South Africa is the only colony not to stand behind England, but they can make her, if necessary. That is, the Dutch influence out here. They have complete control of the government.[67]

We had quite a misfortune yesterday, as Wilfred lost a letter of yours to me before he could get it to me. He remembers putting it in his inside pocket when he was sitting at his desk, but he simply can't find it. I naturally feel a bit upset about it.

Wilfred is very happy with his work down here, but we are afraid that war will completely wreck the business. Such things we may have to suffer, but we can be thankful that we are all living in out-of-the-way places. A Man-O-War has just passed down the coast, patrolling, I suppose, but I think they are only doing it to feel that they are in things. It is the first I have seen pass. The portholes of all the Mail Boats are painted black so that one only sees one light as they pass at night. Only a week ago they were a merry blaze of light when they passed.

---

[67] Helen wrote this letter at a moment in time when history was being made. On September 3, Britain declared war on Germany. On September 4, the South African parliament decided to depose General Hertzog and promote General Smuts to prime minister. (Since 1934, South Africa had had a coalition government between the National Party—under the leadership of General Hertzog, a conservative Afrikaner who made a plea for siding with Germany or, at the least, for neutrality—and the South African Party—represented by General Smuts, who was pro-British.) On September 6, 1939, the new party, known as the United Party, formally declared South Africa at war with Germany and the Axis. Smuts had foreseen that South Africa, with its ports situated halfway between West and East, would inevitably be drawn into the conflict, and he understood the imporance of supporting the Allies. (See Helen's letter of January 14, 1941 for further details.)

I Dwell in Possibility (Aug. 1939—Apr. 1940)

We have been at Isipingo Beach only ten days, but what a time we have had. Wilfred went down with lumbago [backache] the afternoon we arrived and could not move at all for four days. For two days, we could not even get him under the covers of his bed the pain was so bad. He is now back at work, however, but has the worst cold I have ever seen him have. I, for my part, have had bronchitis and now a runny cold. For three nights, I sat up all night gasping for breath and actually spent the third night in the car outside. I now have some very powerful medicine, which gives almost immediate relief. I also found a tick on Robin, and she started with a cold today.

I am afraid we are too near the sea and just can't stand the dampness. Unless we all improve, we shall look for a place about seven miles inland. It is beautiful here, and I should hate to leave it, but you can't enjoy anything if you are sick. Eve is the only one thriving on it, and she is eating her head off and looks marvelous. Robin is looking well too, but her cold may pull her down a little. Wilfred has lost 12 lbs. in two weeks and only weighs 150. I am afraid I would have a hard time finding another place at the price we pay here of $100 per month, all-inclusive. To get that rate, we must stay three months. The place just opened up under new management, and things are extremely quiet with them, so that is the reason they are anxious to have us even at such a low price.

We are very comfortable with two rooms, and ours a very large room. We also have a radio out from the store, and our reception is excellent since we are in this small village on the coast. We get our news direct from London and Berlin. It makes it nice for us that Wilfred knows German. We have not had America yet, though we tried, and other people here get it about six o'clock in the morning. One certainly wants a radio during times such as these; it is the first time I have cared about one.

Bert has been sick for the last fourteen days, so her father has written. They say it was a chill, but I am sure the main cause was our leaving Johannesburg. She is highly strung, like Wilfred, and could actually get ill from being sad. The weather is most changeable there, and it isn't easy to keep well, but I find it harder to keep well here. The weather is changeable here too; one day you can go bathing and the next you must wear a coat all day.

EVE   EVE   EVE   EVE

Eve has just done her name for you. She doesn't have to be shown. She knows the E and the V on the typewriter.

Our Land went off today to you. I do hope it arrives safely.

Someone re-posted the letter Wilfred lost, so I finally got it, much to my relief. It was such a cheery letter about ordinary things to receive during a time of stress. It was marvelous getting it. Wilfred says he too has thought so much about you since war broke out and knows how you would love to have the children and me with you, but I wouldn't travel the seas at this time for anything.

I do wish America would come into the war now. That would end it in a hurry. I believe that, as it is, it will drag on as the World War did until she will finally have to come in. It is to her interest too that Hitler be stopped. I feel very sorry for the many Germans that we know in Germany, which reminds me, is Julia Brewer still in J.C.? If so, I suppose she is very upset about Richard Haumann. I believe a lot of the Germans who went back were told to come home. I feel very sorry for the Richters and Funckes. The Vriesen boys must all be in the service. She never answered my last letter from over here.

I shall get your coat off right away. I am wondering if these things will arrive.

This morning's paper gives accounts of rioting in Johannesburg and on the Rand in general. Any German business, or even people with German automobiles, seem to be in danger. There are a lot of Germans there, and the Dutch and English would like to make this an excuse for a good fight. Here in Natal, it is practically all English, so we won't have any trouble.

Yesterday's paper said the prices of automobiles will go up in the Union. When they do, we shall sell ours if we can make a nice profit. We considered it an investment all along.

I must close and write to Bert, as her birthday is tomorrow. [Helen's letter evidently took several days to write; the last part of the letter was clearly written on September 5, one day before Bert's thirty-seventh birthday on September 6, 1939.]

Lots and lots of love,

Helen

P.S. The postage on a book is much less if you slit the parcel so the inspector can see it is a book. I paid only 14c on the book to you; otherwise, it would have been 75c.

SEPTEMBER 3, 1939
BRITAIN DECLARES WAR ON GERMANY

SEPTEMBER 6, 1939
SOUTH AFRICA DECLARES WAR ON GERMANY

To: Helen Evans from Elsie Arridge
[Renter of the Orange Grove house]

173 Louis Botha Avenue
Johannesburg
September 4, 1939

My dear Mrs. Evans,

It was so nice of you to write, and I was delighted to hear from you. I do hope that you and your husband are both better; nothing is worse than to be away from home—it makes one feel quite desperate. I have had, and still have, a most frightful cold, which, combined with terrible anxiety over my dear old parents over in England, has made me most wretched. In reference to my frenzied cables, they removed from London into the country, and are now out of the worst danger zone, but of course they will miss all their very comfortable home-comforts, and it is hard lines at seventy-odd years to have to do that. My brother is a captain in the Royal Engineers and is by now, I expect, in the active service.

I simply love the Rondaval, and the fact that I am living in such a dear little place and that you have shown perfect taste in its furnishing compensates for a good deal. Johannesburg, on the whole, appears to me as dust, concrete, corrugated iron, wire, and general untidiness. We have Freddie, Mrs. Sours' driver, and he sweeps up and keeps the garden nice in the mornings. I have put some fresh wire on the gate, and he is going to paint it all green tomorrow. I went down to the City Hall and got the sanitary people to remove garden cuttings, but first of all we extracted all the big branches and made an interwoven screen to hide those dustbins belonging to the flats next door. I shall try to grow some creeper up it.

The agents called here about the rent, and I reminded them of the repairs to the thatch; also, I went in on Friday and told them if it is not repaired I shall have to get an estimate for them to submit to the owner. However, I am quite charmed to be here, leak or no leak. I should hate a flat, having always had a garden to wander in. The blossoms are falling quietly, but the little bush opposite the dining recess window will soon be like a giant snowball. Your birds visit us regularly, and we feed them with seeds and crumbs.

Agnes is quite good and tries hard. She spends a remarkable amount of time in her "kya" and, when I first came, was visited by schools of "brothers" and "sisters." It was quite disconcerting to have such a large family about the place, so I firmly but kindly told her *no* brothers until Mrs. Evans comes back! And only one mother and one sister to visit! They will probably have a glorious reunion when you return! By the way, what about those undies belonging to your baby, shall I post them to you? She will have grown out of her sleeping suit!

It must be lovely for the kiddies to have the sea and beach to play with, and will do them worlds of good. I do hope you will be able to stay at Isipingo; it sounds most delightful. We went to Vereeniging about forty miles away yesterday on the border of The Orange Free State. The river, with its lovely green weeping willow trees and sloping fields, was more like my own dear country than anything I have yet seen here, though of course I love the mimosa groves and glorious sunsets in Africa.

It has just been announced on the radio that the Germans have sunk the liner *Athenia*. What a nightmare world! I suppose the Union will keep out of it all as long as possible; everybody appears very self-centered here, but war is so destructive one can hardly blame them.

I was so glad to find Mm. Curie here to be able to re-read!

Let me hear from you when you have a few minutes to spare.

With kindest regards to yourself and husband.

Very sincerely yours,

Elsie S. Arridge

Verehurst Hotel
Isipingo Beach, Natal
South Africa
September 27, 1939

My dearest Ones,

We have moved to another hotel here in Isipingo. The Verehurst is considered the best here and, strangely enough, we pay no more for the best than we paid for our other accommodation. I am glad I moved before I became confined to my bed, for Mrs. White, the proprietress, has been wonderful to me, and at the other place I suppose I just couldn't have gone to bed. I have been in bed three days and am expecting the doctor today. I started with a bad spell of bronchitis, but that is much better. Now I have a bad pain on my left side, which may be pleurisy or may be only soreness from coughing.

Anyway, I must know which, so I shall know how careful to be with myself. We had two days of solid rain, which didn't help me any. It was also cold, and we have no means of heating the room. I have a native girl for the children. She is fair but needs much supervision, which I am hardly able to give. I would give anything to be at home where I could hand the responsibility over to you for a week, and know I could get well. I haven't felt well, even one day, for a month now. It shows what a perfect climate J'burg is for me. I shall let you know what the doctor has to say. Don't worry, for I shall take care of myself, as we can't afford a long illness.

Robin is walking everywhere now and only started some three to four weeks ago. She eats too much, I think, but she screams if she doesn't get it. Eve also eats a tremendous amount but does not gain in weight.

I enclose a letter from Mrs. Arridge, who is living in our house. I thought you would enjoy hearing from someone else about our place. Mr. Arridge is a big shot sent out from England as Sales Manager of the Union. He speaks of taking us back to J'burg, but he says he must have our house, as it is the only thing in J'burg his wife likes. They brought their Packard car with them, so they are used to things, and yet she thinks so much of my house. It would be hard to go back and not have the house, but it is let for six months anyway, and then, no doubt, it would be the diplomatic thing to do to let them keep it on.

Wilfred is dying to have a house again so as to eat my cooking and to have more room for the children. He cannot bear boarding, but it is restful for one. If I had been well during the month I have boarded, I would no doubt be ready to go back to housekeeping, but so far I have had no benefit from it.

Tell Elizabeth Swan that I never received her letter and that I am crazy to have a letter from her with all the news from the plant. She had better let you address it. For some reason I only get your letters, it seems. What is wrong with Mr. Smith that he must go to hospital? The files are very complicated, and I am not surprised that they are in bad shape with so many changes in the office. I'll bet they have wished for me several times. Did Ethel Brumit lose her job in Nashville or just leave? How is the new Governor?

I have August 21st *Life* and two August *Time*s to read, which Wilfred brought over last night as well as lovely pink carnations with some mauve flowers and baby's breath.

We seem to get so little news of the war. I wonder if there is so little going on or if a lot is suppressed. It seems to me England has done nothing so far. I suppose it is rather tense in Elizabethton with so many German families with relatives in Germany. I feel sorry for the Richters getting back just in time to get into it all. This will wreck Mr. Funcke's nerves completely. I do hope the German people will take this opportunity to get out from under Hitler's yoke. I guess you are glad now that I didn't marry H. or any other German. Don't repeat this to anyone and don't mention it when writing back to me. Life is full of changes; one is on top of the stack one year and on the bottom the next. It does seem to be as changeable as that—year by year.

Must stop so this will catch this week's mail boat.

Lots and lots of love,

Helen

Verehurst Hotel
Isipingo Beach, Natal
Union of S. Africa
October 3, 1939

My dearest Ones,

I thought of you two many times yesterday, being my birthday [this was Helen's thirty-third birthday], and all you have done for me. I celebrated it by getting out of bed but am back in again today. During my poor health down here, I have thought so much of all the nursing Mother has done for me, and I wish I could have it now. I do not have pleurisy. My severe pain comes from so much coughing.

I only wish I could be well down here, as Wilfred likes it so much better than Johannesburg. He has already doubled the turnover of the store for the two months he has been here over their previous months, and all of his salesmen are 100% behind him. His personal sales have been higher than any one of his salesmen, even though he knows no one in Durban and has all the detail work of managing the store.

My trouble today is that I have completely upset my stomach with so much medicine. I shall get up for a while this afternoon, I think. We shall more than likely move inland to a place called Fairydene on the 23rd of this month. It is 1100 feet high and twelve miles from the sea. Wilfred says the hotel is nice and has running water, which one cannot find on the South Coast. Durban, of course, has water; but the small resorts down the coast have only salt-water baths and rainwater for drinking and sponging off in the washbasin in your room. The lavatories, although water-born, are all outside. Few South Africans have been convinced that it is sanitary to have them inside.

When we first arrived here, Wilfred said, "You should have your mother come over; she would love it here." I said, "Father would love it, but not Mother."

I shall now confess that I also had an outside lavatory for my dear rondavel in J'burg. The new houses, or at least most of them, have inside sewerage. Even the American Consul has it outside, as he lives in an old place.

Eve has been in bed two days with sore throat and high temperature, but is out today with a normal temperature and throat O.K. I thought she was taking flu, there is so much about.

My box hasn't arrived yet. Of course, it must be readdressed from J'burg. I am so anxious to see what you have sent and so glad you have sent me a dress. Do you know the children and I have practically done in the clothes you had sent us. There just hasn't been any money for clothes because of furniture. We only owe $35 more on our furniture and then that is clear, but now we have a few doctors' bills, and so it goes. Clothes will always come last with me. I get so many compliments on the redingote. It is my best street dress.

We usually pay 50c for a packet of oranges, which is many, many dozen, and they are lovely ones, without seeds and very sweet. I have seen them for 25c since being down here. Such things are very cheap. Only apples are expensive, but then you only see selected ones each wrapped in tissue paper.

I am still working on the present for Katye Wray. I would have had it there in time if I had not had this move and then felt so rotten. I hope everything goes well, and I do hope they keep her sitting up the first three days and nights. Maybe they know to do it every place but the St. Elizabeth.

You have never told me how much Aunt Hattie got for her house. I wish they had some imagination to use the money they now have.

Yesterday we went to see the *Shirley Temple of Zululand* dance and sing. It was pitiful. She sang Shirley Temple's songs and danced (or tried to dance) her dances. Poor little picanin had arms like brown sticks and huge hands that hung down inches below her knees.

Robin, as dressed by the maids at The Verehurst Hotel

Robin with fishing pole at the cottage at Ocean View

You forgot to enclose the picture of Judy Harlan's child. I didn't know she had one. It must be by her second marriage. I enclose some pictures showing Robin's first efforts at walking and showing Our Cove where we like to bathe. The one of Eve pouring water is so graceful, we think. In one, Robin is walking down the garden path of Verehurst Hotel. It is a *very* pretty path. You see how native girls dress them when Mother is sick? The other one of Robin with her fishing pole shows our cottage at Ocean View, the first place we lived. We think this one is cute enough to enlarge.

I also enclose a clipping of Intambo and Mafuta, meaning "thin like a string" and "the fat one." This will give you an idea of the town native girl and the one from the kraal. You see them in native dress, as in this picture, especially here in Durban. When we walk along the beach and I can't use the baby carriage, I let my girl carry Robin so on her back. It is much the easiest way. Naturally, the outlines are exaggerated. Here in Natal we have so many Indians that I shall never want to go to India. One section of Durban has only their shops and market, etc. We pass a mosque between here and Durban.

I do hope you will have someone to fire your furnace this winter. I think you should help unemployment to that extent. I am trying to put your back up now. Did Mr. Myer go to Germany? Robin is so popular with the children here at the hotel that I wouldn't need a girl if I were well. There were three in her room as she had supper last night.

Lots of love,
Helen

Verehurst Hotel
Isipingo Beach, Natal
Union of S. Africa
October 10, 1939

My dearest Mother and Father,

The perfectly wonderful birthday box has arrived, and three little female hearts were gladder by new clothes. I love my two dresses, and I wondered if you really made both of them, but it didn't take me long to find out you had, for I found basting threads in both—a sure sign. They fit me as perfectly as if I had been there for fittings. There is nothing to alter in either, not even the length. I shall have a lot of good out of the sports dress down here. I have a wide white belt to wear with it. It is such nice material. I hope there will soon be an occasion for my long flowered frock. The children's coats look very nice on them, and they too fit so well. The dress you sent Robin is a darling. I hate to use it, for they are never the same after they are washed.

Wilfred wants me to thank you for the hanky you included for him. I thought it most thoughtful. After all, it was only my birthday. The sheet and two pillowcases will come in nicely when we get back to our house. Eve is already busy with her books. It was a great treat for us all, and we all send many, many thanks. I know what a lot of time you spent on those two dresses for me. They are beautifully made. It reminded me of school days when I would come home from boarding school and find a new evening dress.

I wish to goodness I could send you some embroidered gowns and luncheon sets. They have such beautiful Chinese work here, and so reasonable. If anyone I know well enough goes over to America, I shall send you some things. Otherwise, there is so little to send.

Yesterday and today I have felt much better. I hope I shall be alright now. Wilfred is again having trouble with his back. He strained it lifting. He went yesterday to a chiropractor for treatment, and he told him he would always have to be careful about lifting now that this has happened. It seems now the other was not lumbago but a bad strain.

They want Wilfred back in Johannesburg as soon as he can find the proper man to put in as manager of the store here. We can't go back too soon to suit me. It is only from a health point of view that I am anxious to go back, because it is beautiful country here and there is no scenery around Johannesburg. I would like to come home now, while my house and furniture are in good hands and we are on the loose, but Wilfred is not willing to let Robin go, as she is just entering the cute age. Eve is not so pretty now, as she is losing her teeth.

I am enclosing a letter received from my first native nurse down here. The first Sunday I had her she wanted off to attend a party they were giving for her father, who had been dead just three weeks, she said. The second Sunday I got this note. I had to let her go, as she had been to a mission school and was always referring to herself and the wash girls, etc., as ladies. She also stole. Mission boys and girls are always the worst about that. I wonder why that is.

I am anxious to hear from Katye Wray.

I have so many letters I should write and so much sewing to do. I intend to busy myself a great deal for a month.

Did you have a nice trip with Miss Espey? I am sorry Father is so confined. It is too bad the arrangement with Uncle Hunter had to be terminated. He needs a long holiday each year. They should have a man to relieve their regular men for a holiday period each year.

We get our *Time* magazine regularly. I enjoyed the copies of the *Elizabethton Star*. I see Gordon [Helen's cousin] is a traffic cop. Did he have a State job up until that time? Don't have my *Reader's Digest* changed to this address. They forward it from J'burg.

I hope you have a nice birthday, and I am sorry you did not have a nice box from me for your birthday.

Lots and lots of love,

Helen

Verehurst Hotel
Isipingo Beach, Natal
Union of S. Africa
October 17, 1939

My dearest Ones,

I am so happy over each letter I get, as I was like Father and feared all communication might be stopped. I know you were glad to hear I had received the box. It would have been too dreadful to think such a box had gone astray. I do hope your coat will reach you, also *Our Land*.

Our bad luck continues, as Robin scalded her hand badly the past week but has gotten along beautifully. My girl had brought a jug of nearly boiling water to the room for Robin's bath and set it down on the floor. Robin was walking around and, while I had my back turned, put her hand down in the jug. She screamed for 1½ hrs without a break and kept hitting the burnt hand with her other hand. She was most annoyed with the hand that was hurting her. I put Vaseline on first thing, then butter and soda, then some Carron oil given me by a guest of the hotel. She would not keep a bandage on, so it has healed without much of anything on it. The rest of us are better these days.

I think it will be some time, if ever, before Wilfred will be called up, for S.A. is only going to defend S.A. If he should be called up, we would be ruined financially because the British soldier is paid practically nothing. I would have to get a job if it came to him going.

I came out with the bright idea yesterday that if the Germans would stay away from the Western Front there would be no war. What a shame they haven't thought to do that.

Where are Dr. Roesel's parents now? I thought they were coming to Elizabethton. What about Katye Wray? I hope to have good news this week.

Hope you enjoyed your trip.

Lots and lots of love,

Helen

P. S. Eve drew the pictures quite alone.

There is simply no excuse for food prices to go up in America. They have come down here, and everyone who raised them was fined for profiteering.

October 24, 1939

My Darlings,

Your letter of Sept. 8 has just arrived, and it seems that all letters are coming thru as regularly as ever, for which I am more than thankful.

Wilfred and I were both distressed about the $24 stolen. I wonder why Father doesn't use the night depository at the bank since it is so close. I suppose it would cost something each month, but the security of his cash would certainly be worth it. You will, I hope, get your new dress and hat a little later.

I am wondering if the house account had the full $130.95 for the taxes. Let me know. I do wish the place could be sold, as we shall never live there.

I am sorry to hear that Uncle Hunter has had to have an appendix operation. I hope everything goes well. I hope you visited him while he was in hospital. We are invited to an Indian wedding this Sunday. If we go, I shall write you all about it. In any case, I shall send you the wedding invitation we received.

Robin did such a cute thing yesterday. I knew she was sleepy, but it was an hour before the time for her morning nap, so I didn't put her to bed. She went over and got a blanket off of Eve's doll's bed and came back and put her hand on her bed, then sat down beside her bed, put her thumb in her mouth, and pulled the blanket over it—her only way of going to sleep. I couldn't resist that, so I put her to bed and she was asleep in two minutes. She is simply a darling now.

I didn't know that I hadn't written you about the Van Zalingens. About five or six months ago they were transferred to Budapest. They had to sell out all of their lovely new furniture and go to such a dangerous spot. I feel so sorry for them. Her home, Amsterdam, is no safer, and they were always saying how thankful they were to be out here and safe. I did not mind seeing Mickey off, as I found her to be a very naughty child and had to refuse to let Eve play with her, and, furthermore, had to tell them why. I was very annoyed when I found out they knew all the time what type of child Mickey was and yet they invited Eve, much younger, to play with her.

The uprisings in J'burg were nothing but the work of hooligans. They are always having such trouble in J'burg. We were down here when it happened, but Bert saw it all, as it happened at the back of her block of flats. The biggest mob was at the club, where they smashed windows, etc. They also turned over DKW's, a German make of car. They smashed the windows of German firms in town.

The picture you sent of General Smuts must be twenty years old, as he doesn't look like that now. He is quite old. I do not believe Wilfred will be called up unless the war lasts a long time. I think he would perhaps be in the intelligence dept. then, with his knowledge of Germany and the German language. They were very interested that he knows Essen so well, the Krupp town. They have this information about him, and he might be called for a special service, but let us hope not. Wilfred cannot get over them letting Hitler go so far without checking him. It looks to me like it is a poor battle they are fighting now. We saw fighting on the Western Front in the *March of Time* last night at the bioscope.[68]

I am glad you have received the picture. The one I sent Helen Brading for the paper is a much better picture just of the children. She has been so long in putting it in, tell her not to bother, but to please let you have the picture. I sent her all of that Air Mail, and it cost me $1.00 to send it, and you got yours surface mail before she published it. I should think she would be glad to brighten up her social column. I shan't trouble myself again.

I am feeling much better the last three days, and the rest of the family is well. Love from us all,

Helen

P.S. I hope to have good news from Katye Wray next post. Don't change the address of our *Reader's Digest*.

Attached page: These pictures were done by Eve quite on her own. She says she has written the name of each girl below the pictures. Those round things below the skirts are their panties, she says. The one in the lower right-hand corner is holding a sunflower in one hand & an umbrella in the other. [Unfortunately, these pictures have been lost.]

[To: Mary Walker from Helen]

Verehurst Hotel
Isipingo Beach, Natal
South Africa
October 27, 1939

My dearest Mary,

I have been such a long time in writing that I am sure you will expect too much of this letter. I wish I could hear you say, "Just do the best you can, don't bother too much."

Mother and Father have both written me that Knaffl is traveling for a chemical company. I do not know what company it is, nor where it is located, except that he gets up to Elizabethton now and then. Please let us hear all about it and how he likes it, etc. We do hope that he is in something he likes, and in which he can do well.

I believe you have had a second trip to New York at the store's expense. They must think a lot of you. I am so pleased that you are doing so well. I know you

---

[68] Bioscope: South African term for movie theater, no longer in use.

have wanted to get into business for some time. It is good for any woman to know she can make her way if necessary. I wouldn't take anything for my years in business, even though they were hard at times.

I guess you are wondering about this changed address, unless you have already heard from Mother or Father. Two months ago Wilfred was transferred from Johannesburg to Durban as Manager of the Durban store. The store in Durban has never done well, but it is doing well now, so we feel quite pleased and so does his boss. Wilfred likes Durban much better than Johannesburg and is anxious to stay down here. I, on the other hand, have been sick ever since coming to the coast. I have had bronchitis for two months, and colds. My bronchitis is very bad. I have been a little better the last few days. In Johannesburg I did not even have my old colds, so you can imagine that I am rather anxious to get back to what is "the land of the living" for me.

It is so pretty here, and so barren in Johannesburg, that I want to try to live here. We are living twelve miles out from Durban at this little beach, the name Isipingo meaning "the place of adultery" in Zulu. It is beautiful here. The breakers are so big. Of course, the Indian Ocean is a bit wilder than the others. Much of the coast is rocky, which gives it character, and yet there is a beautiful little cove which is quite safe for bathing, and also a spot known as the River Mouth, where the ocean backwashes into the river. This is not just a resort place, as there is a fixed population of about 700 souls; however, only one general store is allowed, and that is why I am using this wonderful stationery.

If we forget to get a thing in Durban, we have to take what they have in the general store, and they hardly cater much since they have no competition. They are lovely and independent, like some of the general stores in the mountains at home. Isipingo is up one hill and down another, and, on the slopes to the sea and those not under cultivation, one sees masses of tropical growth, wild banana trees, and flowering plants typical of tropical parts of Africa. We live at a very nice hotel with lovely grounds, and I am taking a very good rest and no doubt have the name of being the laziest woman in Isipingo, as I keep a nurse girl for the children. It is really the first time I have thoroughly relaxed since I was twenty-three, however, and that is ten years ago, so I hardly think I need worry what my reputation is. I am taking every advantage of it. However, I seem to invariably read something that makes me feel I am simply a rotter since I don't do my own washing, etc., such as *Wilderness Wife*.

I am going to be very busy sewing now, as Wilfred made such a good figure in the store that they promised to give me an electric sewing machine if he made it. He set the figure for himself and they thought he couldn't do it, but he more than did it. I am terribly anxious to get it and see what I can do, for I really do have a lot of time on my hands. I have a lot of things to do over for the children.

Wilfred is in Johannesburg on business, and I knew a letter to you would make me forget I am lonely. I am sitting in his room, writing. I have the two children in a room with me. Wilfred calls it the "Girls' Dormitory."

Well, of course we all think the war is awful and wish to goodness something would settle the whole thing before any more nations are ruined. Wilfred is listed as a Reserve; his badge, etc., arrived in the mail today. He is in the third line of Reserve, however, since he has a family, and I hope it will never be necessary for that class to be called up. Mother seems to be much fuller of the war than people out here. She thinks you all are getting more news than we are, but I hardly think so; in any case, Wilfred and I read *Time* when it does get out here.

Robin is walking now, and is such a fat little thing, much heftier than Eve ever was. Eve is losing teeth and looks a bit funny. They are both good little things, and sweet. Eve can be very cheeky but is very sensitive, and a good talk can put her in tears in a minute. If you tell her she has been rude, she is distressed to death.

How is Joe? Tell him I never met a nicer boy than he is. I often wish I had you next door to help me with my child problems because I think you have first-class judgment in such matters. I wish you were next door for more reasons than that, old dear.

You know the only way one can stand to be a nomad is not to think too tenderly of any one person or any one place, so enough of that. The only way for my kind to be truly happy is to think a disgusting lot of one's self. I think I perhaps manage it by thinking of nothing.

Eve asked me the other day, "Mommy, why did God make mosquitoes?"

I said I didn't know.

"Well, why did God make flies?"

Same answer from me.

"Well, Mommy, why did God make Hitler?"

Then Mommy came to life and laughed, but still had no answer good enough to give.

Oh, by the way, I am going to a big Indian wedding on Sunday. I do wish I had waited with this letter to describe it. Our invitation is too quaint for words. I am sending it to Mother and shall write her a description of it. I hope to take some pictures too. There are 120,000 Indians in Durban and only 100,000 whites; there are another 100,000 natives. Some of the Indians are very wealthy, and I understand these are. However, they feel very honored if a white person accepts an invitation and comes to their weddings. I feel terribly squeamish about eating anything at the reception, for I have seen their sweets displayed in the Indian Market and never have I seen anything any more poisonous looking.

We have rented our place in Johannesburg, furnished, to people who have come out from England to join Westinghouse. They are lovely people, and I know they will look after my things even better than I could, for they are three grown-ups. She is keen on gardening, and, I believe, is doing a lot to it. It is a lovely garden in any case, but she is planting in the few places not already planted. We get $20 a month rent on our furniture. Not so bad, is it?

I am reading *Dr. Bradley Remembers* just now. Do you still find time for some reading? I am sure you do somehow, for you are so fond of that pastime. I certainly hope you do anyway.

This has become a long letter, and now I must close.

Give my love to your family in Elizabethton when you write or see them, and tell Elizabeth I am so disappointed that I never received her letter and that I do hope she will write another letter giving me all the news at the plant.

Our best love to you and Knaffl and Joe. Wilfred so often says, "Gosh, I'd like to see Knaffl and Mary."

Ever yours,
Helen

Verehurst Hotel
Isipingo Beach, Natal
Union of S. Africa
November 1, 1939

My dearest Ones,

It is such a relief to find that we can still get letters as quickly as ever from each other. This will only stop if America goes into the War, and let us hope that will not be necessary.

Poor Ruby, I suppose she now realizes that it is impossible for Mayr to get back—unless, of course, he could come by Italian steamer. Let me know what happens. Of course, he can't get out the Northern route. Is he still a German or has he taken out American citizenship papers? If he is still a German, the English or French would intern him the minute they got their hands on him. Of course, a lot of prominent Germans in this country have already been interned in Pretoria. Wilfred is so thankful he did not take any of the jobs offered him by Germans some time ago. It was hard to resist the offers, for none were at less than $50 more than he is making. What does Aunt Lennie think of Hitler now? She thought he would never gain much power, nor be an influence in the world.

I am enclosing $2.00 with which we want an account opened at the bank for Robin. It should be in the name of Myfanwy Evans. This is our last U.S. money except for some very small change.

You are quite right about Christmas this year. Everything sent might be lost because the ship was sunk, or America suddenly went into war, or a million and one things.

I must tell you one thing that Eve said. We had tongue the other day for lunch and she said, "Why does this taste so much like tongue? It tastes like it is still in the animal's mouth." She likes big words and said this morning, "I just feel like collapsing on the bed." She also likes to think she is speaking some foreign language and has picked up a lot of Zulu words and Afrikaans. Mrs. Graddock told me that when Eve and her child play together they use more than 50% Zulu. Practically everyone here gives instructions to the natives in Zulu. I therefore have an extremely difficult time with the natives.[69]

I also enclose the invitation to the Indian wedding. We went, and I found it very interesting. It was held at the bride's home under a big canopy. The bride and groom were seated in the middle under a specially decorated canopy; the guests were divided on either side, male on one side, women and children on the other. The women were dressed in the lovely pastel shades of silk worn by Indian women in toga fashion. The men have adopted Western clothes; since these Indians were not Mohammedans, they did not even have the colorful headdress that so many Indians wear, except for the groom, and he wore a very elaborate turban.

The ceremony was conducted in their language, so I didn't get anything out of that. There was much sifting of rice through their hands, those of the bride and groom, and at one time I thought they were going to smoke the bride out completely. The ceremony started at eight o'clock in the morning and we didn't get there until nine thirty, so the bride and groom were looking pretty spent already. We stayed until eleven, and they were just about ready to pronounce them man and wife. We were served tea, cakes, and sandwiches about 10:30, as well as the other guests, but this did not interrupt the ceremony. Girls danced around the couple at one time and, when they had finished, they were presented with white leather pocket books.

It was such a mixture of their customs with our setting that the effect was spoiled. We were the only Europeans there. The wedding must have cost about $500. One of the most interesting things was that they passed wooden bowls of beetle [betel] leaves, the beetle kernels, and a white paste. They, the women, each took two leaves, enclosed some of the kernels, and took a dab of paste with their fingers and spread them over and put the whole in their mouths and chewed. This makes their teeth very red, in fact the teeth of the old women are permanently stained. If you have read any books on India, you will have heard of this beetle. I read one long ago which mentioned it. I am not sure I have spelled it correctly.

---

[69] While South Africa at that time only had two official languages, English and Afrikaans, years later, after apartheid ended, the country recognized eleven official languages and scores of unofficial ones.

I would have liked a clipping of the children's party picture and the accompanying article. I am very suspicious that something was wrong about the whole thing, or I am sure you would have sent it. We have looked forward to that for such a long time.

I am so sorry to hear of Mr. Toncray's death. Really, I think the funeral was awful, having a loudspeaker, etc. He led such a retired life for years that I am sure he would never have wished the funeral that was given. Changes continue year by year.

Would you all be afraid for me to come home now on an American boat? I wouldn't want to do it if you feel it is too dangerous. I had so planned on coming at the end of three years that I hate to give the idea up. If Father could come out here, I would insist on you all coming here for the visit, for the trip would mean so much to you, whereas another voyage means little or nothing to me. I have had my share of all such things, I feel. I have little curiosity left about the rest of the world. It is a dreadful way to get.

I must close now so that I can get the children ready for supper and bed. They have supper together in their room and go to bed at six. It works very well.

We are all quite well now, and we all went to the beach this morning, as it was lovely for a change. Not even a wind blowing and no rain. Most unusual for this place.

Lots and lots of love from us all,

Helen

Verehurst Hotel
Isipingo Beach, Natal
Union of S. Africa
November 8, 1939

My dearest Ones,

My, what a lot of rain we have been having—it rained four days and nights without a break, and, since these people would never dream of a fire, and since there is only a fireplace in the lounge, you can imagine my predicament with Robin's napkins. I almost spent the day keeping her on her pottie, so she wouldn't run out of napkins. We just made it, and what a washing I put out on the 5th day. Unfortunately, I had no girl at the time, but one arrived the next day, and I am more or less free again; at least, I do not have the responsibility of the children every minute of the day.

Address your letters from now on to me at Westinghouse, Durban, as we plan to move into Durban either on the 23rd of this month or the 1st of Dec. However, the lease for the flat has not been signed, and I never take anything for granted, so it is no use giving you that address until all is settled. The main issue just now is that I won't sign until she promises to furnish crockery and cooking utensils. I naturally don't want to buy a second supply of such things since I have all of that in Johannesburg. Also, I want a $5.00 reduction in the rent, as I have looked at other places and find we are overpaying about that much.

 The place is a flat in a private home, first floor, consisting of living room, three bedrooms, breakfast room, kitchen, trunk room, (private bath and inside lavatory—hurrah!) and fifteen-foot veranda. We also have our own grounds and are practically next door to a lovely park. It is in the best section of Durban, high up on the Berea, overlooking the town and harbour. For this furnished, and that is in very good taste, with garage, the owner wants $62.50. I find I should only pay about $57.50 for it, and I intend to hold out for the lower rent. These prices are so much lower than J'burg that we can't get over it. We looked at an unfurnished flat in a beautiful old world building at $47.50. In J'burg it would be at least $87.50. It is on the best residential street in Durban too. Our place is the next street up, so naturally very good. We are getting good money for the use of our furniture, so we can't afford not to get it.

 In any case, we have signed a lease. It is being beautifully cared for too. If Durban becomes permanent with us, we shall finally have our own things, no doubt. However, furniture is much cheaper in Durban, so I imagine we shall sell up in Johannesburg and buy here. Railage over here is almost prohibitive, and, if sent by truck, it would be jolted to pieces since the roads are so bad. I wouldn't sacrifice anything, though, and I really don't think it would be necessary to do so.

 We have decided to go into town, as twenty-four miles a day is a lot of unnecessary travel, and we find it most inconvenient to ever go to the movies, etc. There is nothing here but the beach, and we have been promised a very wet year by the native prophets,[70] so the beach won't do us much good. Wilfred uses $20 in gas just going back and forth, besides the wear and tear on the car. He also has long hours and must do night work whenever he has a long report to write, so it is most inconvenient being out here, and he has to buy so many meals in town. I also find two rooms and two children very trying on rainy days.

 Wilfred also likes for me to help him with his reports. I have worked for him two days at the office already. One big factor is that he got fined $25 this past Monday for driving thirty-eight miles per hour on the highway between here and Durban where the limit is twenty-five mph the whole way. Of course it is nothing less than robbery, and since then he has been creeping in at twenty-five mph. Because he knows the Mayor, he got it cut down to $10, but, even so, one can't

---

[70] With few people owning radios, most South Africans relied on the wisdom of the indigenous people to forecast the weather.

stand that drain often. Wilfred is such a good driver and so careful that I feel too annoyed for words because the big majority over here drive like fools.

I suppose America is greatly annoyed about the "Flint."[71] They don't quite seem to know what to do about her. The war seems to be at a standstill. This is what we've been expecting.

The native girl I have now is very new and doesn't understand a word of English. I am now trying to learn enough Zulu to give her instructions. I find, since I must, that I really know more than I thought I did. I love speaking it. "Lala" means sleep. Doesn't that make sense though? "Lala panzie," stay where you are. "Zula" means keep quiet. "Scoff" is food, and "Chesa Manzie" is hot water.

I must stop now so this letter will go off today. Miss Duncan, the postmistress, lives at Verehurst, and I shall send it by her at noon.

Robin and Eve are both well and seem to have a marvelous time. I enjoy them so much. Robin has had two dry nights by being taken up when I go to bed. I am very proud of her. She always likes the natives, but Eve doesn't at all and will not stay with them. Eve has so much imagination that she is always busy and never asking, "What can I do?" She amazes one every day with the things she thinks up. I am determined that this gift shall not be killed by routine. I want to start dancing lessons as soon as we are in Durban. There is

Westinghouse, Durban, 1939

also a kindergarten nearby us, I understand. Robin, so far, is one of those easygoing people who is very fond of eating and sleeping. She has a marvelous smile and is very pretty these days.

I hope you are both well and that all is going well.

---

[71] Helen's mention of "The Flint" refers to the U.S. Merchant Marine ship, SS *City of Flint*, which was the first American ship captured in WWII. Ironically, it had first become involved in the war when it rescued two hundred survivors of the torpedoed British passenger liner SS *Athenia* on Sept. 3, 1939. In October 1939, *City of Flint* was carrying a cargo of tractors, grain, and fruit to Britain when a German battleship seized it, declaring its cargo to be contraband and the ship a prize of war.

How is Uncle Hunter? I hope everything is O.K. by now. I do not blame you for not paying any of the bill. Thomas makes a big salary and only has himself, and he has his youth. He will end up a more or less rich man, I imagine, but he will never get anything out of life.

I am anxious to have good news from Katye Wray.

Did Helen Hunter go off to school this year? You haven't mentioned that.

Lots and lots of love from us all,

Helen

P. S. I am playing a lot of bridge these days, or rather nights.

November 14, 1939

My Darlings,

How are you? I'll bet you are both reading the papers entirely too much and keeping yourselves in a stew about the War. Wilfred has his National Service badge and number. It is very good that he signed up voluntarily[72] at the first, for now it is compulsory and you don't get a badge, so you are rather marked as a slacker. We are dying for *Time* magazine and can no longer get it over here. I know it has been banned in England, but just what is wrong out here I do not know. In any case, I wish you would start a subscription for Wilfred right away. It is to come as an Xmas present from me. Please pay for it out of the house funds. That will be the first penny I have ever taken out of the house, but certainly not the first I have put in. I hope there is enough for the subscription. I hope they will put an Xmas slip in the first copy.

November 15th

Last night we went to see *Confessions of a Nazi Spy*. There is a full house every night. I think 11,000 people saw it in Johannesburg. Really, America is much too free when you see what we have allowed to go on. Well, there is plenty of trouble in Germany since the bombing. I only hope it continues. Too bad they didn't get Hitler and his big men with that bomb, though.[73] There are plenty of Nazi sympathizers among the Afrikaners out here, and some of them don't see

---

[72] South Africa had 334,00 volunteers of all races during World War II—of these, 211,000 were European; 77,000 were Black; and 46,000 were Cape Colored (people of mixed heritage) or Indian (descendents of indentured workers from India). Only the Europeans were allowed to serve in combat. Blacks, Cape Coloreds, and Indians served in the medical corps, food services, etc.

[73] It is likely that Helen is referring here to the Nov. 8, 1939, failed assassination attempt on Hitler, in Munich, at his Beer-Hall Putsch.

why they should fight for England. They haven't forgotten the Boer War, and they say, "Should the Czechs fight for Germany?"

The answer is obviously "No."

Then, "Why should we fight for England?"

It is possible for us to have plenty of trouble here if Germany makes any headway.

We have our furnished flat in Durban for $57.50 per month, only $2.50 per month more than we paid for our unfurnished house in Johannesburg. It will be a much easier place for one to run too, as I have an electric stove instead of coal range. The inside lavatory will make such a difference with the children too. Furniture has advanced 40% out here, so I am very lucky to have bought. The refrigerator we paid $137.50 for we can now sell second hand for $200, but, even so, we don't intend to do it. My two pieces of stinkwood have doubled in value, and just now people are buying mad. Wilfred is having wonderful business.

Eve was looking at a map of Europe the other day and wanted me to point out Germany, so I did. She then pointed to Italy and said, "Germany has a shoe on." She is most observant.

There are always people down from Johannesburg. We have someone out for a meal every week. It will go hard on me when I keep house. Just now the MacDonnels are here. They are the couple to the left of Wilfred in the group picture we sent you. They are coming out today to play golf. We have one of the best courses in S.A. here in Isipingo. The South African golf champion has been playing here a week.

What is the news from Katye Wray? I have finished making the sheets for the baby, but think I will wash them before sending them. I have worked on them so long that they need it in any case.

I must stop now and get ready for my guests.

Love and kisses,

Helen

Verehurst Hotel
Isipingo Beach, Natal
December 3, 1939

My dearest Ones,

I have been a long time writing this time because Bert has been down visiting us for the past ten days and only left yesterday. She has been sick so much during the past three months, and her nerves are in such bad shape, that they sent her down here to pull herself together. She was better when she left, but she could have done with another week of sunshine and quiet. Bert is so highly strung that she very easily goes completely to pieces.

For myself, I am getting a lovely tan, more than ever before, and Eve is as brown as a berry all over. Robin looks well but is not so brown, as she sleeps so much during the mornings, and the afternoons are usually overcast.

Wilfred is feeling so good this month, as the Durban store came first in the Union for November. This is the first time the Johannesburg store has been beaten. In three months, Wilfred brought the store at the bottom in sales to first place. His sales were £5,400 and he made £80, as he is on a commission and salary basis now. His salary is £35 per month, and the rest depends on sales. We are terribly bucked up, of course.

I have been to Durban this afternoon looking for a place to live, as we didn't get the flat I wrote about. The owner refused to keep up the stove and refrigerator, and Wilfred refused to keep them up because he knows the stove and says the plates are always burning out. They cost quite a bit to replace. She was furious about the whole thing and said I wasn't a lady, but a hard creature who tried to beat her down on price, and that Wilfred wasn't a gentleman. Wilfred finally got annoyed after she had said this about three times, and told her she was an old fool. Just the same, I wish he hadn't been so exacting, for I find it isn't easy to get located on short notice, and they can't keep me on here except until the 14th, as they are booked up after that.

I am only looking at places on the Berea so that I shall be high up from the sea. So many places don't take children, especially babies like Robin. I can get in one hotel at a rather high figure—£27.10.0, twenty-seven pounds, ten shillings, and no pence, but—it's two rooms and only one other using the bath. There is a private balcony, which has the most glorious view, exactly the one in your book which says "Durban Harbour from the Berea," or something like that. I do not have the book myself. I was never able to get a complete second set of cards. Bert did not like my flat for some reason or other; she expects things rather perfect. I look to comfort with the children more than appearance.

My last girl has left me; she is the third in three months. She left because I accused her of taking some money. However, she is good riddance, as Mrs. White (the proprietress here) found her the other night while I was out—using my toothbrush and paste to clean her teeth. I am afraid she has done it before, but that can't be helped now. I threw my brush and Eve's away and took out of her pay for the new ones.

I find myself going to sleep over this letter so will answer your questions next time.

Lots of love and kisses,

Helen

P.S. I am so glad Katye Wray's baby has arrived, and am sure they are pleased to have a girl this time. [Little Kay's older brother was Gene]. Please give her my love.

P. O. Box 276
Durban, South Africa
December 18, 1939

Dearest Mother and Dad,

It has been two weeks since I have written, and as long since I have heard from you. I suppose mail will be irregular from now on. I have been very busy, as I had to get the family located since we couldn't stay on after the 14th of this month at Verehurst, as they were booked up.

We are now in a furnished house of friends who are away on holiday until the end of the month. We are so wonderfully comfortable here that I don't know how I stood the inconvenience of the little resort place for so long. This house is exceptionally convenient, as there is even an electric hot water geyser [tank], inside lavatory, four bedrooms, and sleeping porch, etc. I have their cook boy and my girl, an excellent girl from the Catholic Mission, for the children. I simply have nothing to do in the house, which is a very good thing just now, as my time is completely taken up with doctors. I have a growth in my nose caused by excessive sneezing. My doctor tells me I do not have bronchitis but asthma again, combined with hay fever. You can imagine my condition.

I had no care at Isipingo, but you can rest assured that I am now in good hands. I have the two best doctors in Durban. I have a nose specialist for my nose and a physician giving me the different injections to see what I am allergic to. I have a terrible reaction to household dust. I am now sleeping on the sleeping porch, and, since doing so, I have had my first nights of sleeping straight thru in months. He has told me I must always sleep in a bare room, no rug, no curtains, etc. These two doctors keep in touch with all the latest methods in America and Europe, and Dr. Savage is a personal friend of some of the big noises in medicine in America. I hope they can cure me and that it won't cost too much. He hopes to reduce the growth in my nose without an operation.

We have had great excitement here in Durban with a British battleship, a British cruiser, and a British aircraft carrier all in the harbour at one time—the names *Gloucester*, *Cornwall*, and *Eagle*. I was walking out of a hotel on the sea front with Wilfred when the three ships were seen coming toward the harbour. Everyone was excited, and we dashed down to the docks to see them come in. The town is full of sailors, and it seems a shame that there aren't enough girls to go around. It is good that the *Admiral Graf Spee* is accounted for now at the bottom of the sea.[74] The Germans seem great on scuttling their own ships.

Going from the serious to the frivolous, I have been spending a lot of money just on Helen. Wilfred simply made me get busy on myself. Your expenditures were modest when you hear mine. I have really worked at spending so much money during the past two weeks. I have a new perm, and it is a beautiful one. It cost $10. I have two new dresses, one a blue and mustard tailored dress in a linen material for town, the other cyclamen georgette for dinner. They came to $37.50 for the two. I have new white shoes, $15, and they are nothing but Rhythm Step. I must not be caught short again on shoes. New beach sandals in red, white and blue, $2.00; a blue straw hat, $4.00. That is very inexpensive for a hat here, but it is what I wanted. A new corset, $11.00 (a "Gant" or "Le Gant"). A white coat, very good-looking, $16.00. A pair of gloves in natural doeskin, $1.25. I now need a hat for my dinner or afternoon dress, and a white bag, and I am fixed up.

It has certainly made a difference in the way I feel to be really smartly dressed. It killed me to spend so much money, but I suppose it was all absolutely necessary. I have my dinner hat picked out. It is of white feathers with two birds in three different shades of cyclamen. I would wear a veil with it if I buy it. It is a very tailored model. It is over $10, so you can see why I hesitate.

I am glad to get these things before the doctors' bills come in. I am so glad you are pleased with your new outfit. One should get at least two nice outfits a year, and then you can build up a fairly decent wardrobe. Wilfred is so pleased with me in my new clothes. I don't think he thought I would spend money on myself like I have. The nice thing is that I paid cash for everything. Wilfred has a very good-looking new suit, blue with white and red stripe, new shoes and hat, also a supply of underwear and socks, ties and handkerchiefs.

---

[74] The *Admiral Graf Spee* was a heavily armoured German battleship designed to outgun any cruiser fast enough to catch it. Within a four-month period (from Sept. – Dec. 1939) it had sunk nine ships before being confronted by three British cruisers at the Battle of the River Plate, on Dec. 13, 1939. Convinced by false reports of superior British navel forces approaching his ship, its commander ordered the vessel to be scuttled—a significant loss for the Nazis.

I Dwell in Possibility (Aug. 1939—Apr. 1940)

Robin and Eve must have new shoes, and then the Evans family will look very presentable.

Robin had such a bad accident to her hand today. Eve slammed a back door on her fingers. She will lose two nails, the little fingernail and the one next to it. We had a terrible time getting her quiet, but she finally went off to sleep after half an aspirin.

Eve is getting a nice Xmas this year—a doll's carriage, doll, cleaning set with carpet sweeper, duster, mop, etc., and dishes. I wanted to make a wardrobe for the doll, but they have sold out of patterns for doll's clothes. She is an 11" doll that wets herself. I'll have Bert try in J'burg for a pattern. If she can't get it there, I'll ask you to buy a McCall's doll pattern for me. Bert is going to knit for the doll. I haven't much for Robin but have an idea she will enjoy Eve's cleaning set.

We just wish you all could be with us here in Durban for this Xmas. I am sure you would both love Durban. It is packed this year for Christmas and the month of January. People can't take their usual cruises and their long leaves to England, so they are coming here, and to the Cape too, I suppose.

It is 9:30 and Wilfred hasn't come in for his dinner. He is at the office waiting on a long distance call to J'burg to Mr. Arridge. They are trying to palm a fellow off on Wilfred here for credits who has just made a mess of things in Port Elizabeth as manager, and he wants to scotch it right now, before he is officially told he has the man on his staff. The man simply will not work but is a squash friend of Mr. Sours.

The Arridges do not want our furniture after the end of January, so we must know by then what we are doing so that we can bring it down here or go back to J'burg to it. We know nothing so far. Wilfred will make another $400 this month, or very near it.[75]

The package from Aunt Lennie and the one from Elizabeth Hunter have arrived. I haven't opened them, as I like surprises for Xmas too, but I am dying to see Eve's dress since you wrote me about it.

We are so very happy, and things are better for us financially than they have ever been, that it hardly seems right with the war causing so much suffering and sorrow.

Love from Wilfred, myself, and babes.

Devotedly,

Helen

---

[75] Four hundred dollars in 1939 was worth approximately $6,600 in today's currency.

P.O. Box 276
Durban, South Africa
December 31, 1939

My dearest Folks,

    I have been trying to ring Western Union all morning to send you a cable to relieve your mind, but there is no answer, and I suppose they just aren't open on Sundays and no doubt won't be open tomorrow either, it being New Year's day. Most places are to be closed Tuesday too, so I can't be sure of getting a cable off before Wednesday. I know this seems amazing to you all, but nothing must interfere with an Englishman's holiday. Since you are so worried, I do wish I could relieve your mind. I do wish you wouldn't worry this way, as Wilfred would always cable you if I were very sick. You can depend on that. That is the only sensible arrangement to have, and I hope you will give me the same assurance from your end. I do not hear from you for two to three weeks now, and then I get two letters. I am sorry if I don't write often enough, but there is now no regular mail day, and I can't bear to write and say nothing. Unless I have news, I can't write. With the assurance I have just given you, I think you should be able to take it easy until you do get a letter.

    Well, I can't thank you enough for the big Xmas you sent us. We are doing with that money exactly what you would most like us to do—putting it on time deposit as the nest egg toward a trip home. Now that I have a start, I am sure we can add to it every month. The start always seems hard to make. Please do not think of sending us anything else, like a box, because there is really nothing we need, as the children got so many nice dresses for Xmas from the different ones at home and Bert; and, as I have written you, I have just spent a lot of money on myself for clothes. We have never been so well off in that respect since we started our family.

    My health is much better since I have some care. If I follow the doctor's instructions, I get along fine, but if I break ever, I get in bad shape immediately. The instructions are simple, and it is good to know I can just watch a few things and be very well. My only internal medicine is potassium chloride, and I must deny myself most of my salt for it to be effective. I can't eat chocolate without dire results, and I think of all the cocoa I have drunk. I am a blood case, which means my system is highly sensitive to certain things.

    Anyway, I can live here now, which certainly pleases me, as Wilfred wants to stay here. He made £80 again this month, and also won the cup again by making 140% of his quota. His store is by far the best paying store in the Union. Wilfred had a wonderful Xmas present from his staff—a pocket watch, and the inscription on the back is "From a Happy Durban Staff, Xmas 1939." I think that says a lot, and to think he has only been down here four months. He was so pleased with the watch and especially the inscription. The staff gave more than they could use for the watch, and the rest was given to the War Fund in Durban. Wilfred is having great difficulty in getting used to having a watch and is always letting it run down or is asking someone else the time. Wilfred gave me money to put toward a trip home, which pleased me more than anything else could have.

The children had a nice Xmas. The toys were given to them together. A doll for each, Eve's wets itself, and Robin does double duty for her doll. They got a very nice and expensive doll's carriage, a set of dishes, and a set of cleaning things, carpet sweeper, broom, dust pan, mop, and hand mop. Robin loves these things. I was happy with my selection, as they aren't junky things that you want to throw out in a week's time. Then they were very thrilled with the clothes sent them. Bert gave Eve a new kimono and Robin a bathing suit and blue silk bonnet.

Your Air Mail letter mailed on the 4th of Dec. reached us on the 30th. The time made was nearly as good as ever. In the same post was your letter of Nov. 17th. That took quite a long time, as you can see.

I feel very worried about Uncle David. I haven't received Father's letter yet, giving me full details. I am sure the family is scared to death. Isn't it just the same as Uncle Fred and Mama Hunter? I do hope something can be done, since he is going to have the very best care. I am sure Aunt Nellie will be quite lost if anything happens to him so soon after Uncle Fred's death. I do hope for favorable news about Uncle David.

We have enjoyed having a house during the holidays. We entertained all the Westinghouse staff Sunday before Xmas at a cocktail party. We had over thirty here. Everything went off nicely, and I found it no worry or trouble. Of course, I have so much help, a good cook boy and a good girl for the children. Xmas evening we were invited to the Majestic Hotel for dinner and dance. The Majestic is where we stayed when we first came out to S.A. Last night we celebrated New Year's at Caister House, the best hotel in Durban. We were in a party of six very congenial people. The orchestra was good and the food excellent. Caister House is high on the Berea and overlooks Durban and the harbour and sea. There were balconies leading off the dance floor from which one got this glorious view, which was mostly neon signs and street lights and certain of the tall buildings illuminated.

January 1, 1940

Well, just one year has passed since I started this letter. I am really getting bad about writing. A Sunday morning caller interrupted me.

By the way, Johannesburg is 483 miles from Durban, and the road is far from perfect, as part of it is dirt, and in the wet weather it has been terrible—one hundred cars were stuck on it this past week at one time. Now you know I would simply adore for you to come out here to see me, but you wouldn't have me cross the ocean at this time and neither would I have you. It isn't safe anywhere. Things are too lively around our coast. Yesterday we went down to see a submarine, which is in the harbour. We are anxious to go on board but so far haven't managed it. This particular sub has been at sea twenty-one days according to the sailors we talked to. We are getting more war news than you think we are, I believe, as I have known all the things you have sent me clippings of. I just don't mention things about the war because so much has happened in between the writing of such things and the receipt of the letter.

Wilfred was highly amused about your dream of half packed boxes in my bedroom, as that is the way we are living just now, also that you couldn't tell whether we were moving in or out.

I am surprised to hear that you all are receiving mail from Germany.[76] Of course, such a thing is impossible over here.

We have been bathing in the sea twice today. The most fun is with the surfoplanes [small air mattresses]. I had some beautiful rides in on the waves today. Eve is very good on them too, manipulates by herself. She has her head under the water most of the time and doesn't mind at all. Robin also can take a dousing and never murmur.

Tell Anna Lee Burnett that I will see about a doll, but I don't know just what she wants. There is a black baby doll sold here which is dressed in beads like the native children in the kraals; however, it may even be made in England. I really don't know. Then there are the wooden dolls carved by the natives, which I would consider the real South African doll. The black baby is by far the cutest. Neither will be expensive, so there is no question about price; just let me know which to buy. I am perhaps going into

Helen and Robin on the beach

---

[76] I can only assume that the "mail" from Germany is from Professor and Mrs. Vriesen, but I have no proof of how long the relationship with the Vriesens continued. In any event, this is the last possible reference to the family that had been so extraordinarily kind to Wilfred and Helen. I do know, however, that Kiki Vriesen's rather strange behavior in South Africa back in 1938 had strained the relationship for Helen, Wilfred, and Bert, and that Helen had decided not to share her concerns with her parents.

Zululand in a week or so and will visit native kraals. If I see some attractive doll there, I shall take a chance and buy it. Tell Anna Lee that I can buy beautiful Viennese dolls over here.

I must really stop here, as I have gone to sleep several times. We have been keeping late hours.

Many, many thanks again for the scrumptious Xmas present.

Lots and lots of love to my dear ones,

Helen

To: Mrs. C.H. Hunter [Elizabeth Hunter, one of Helen's aunts]
90 King's Store, Johnson City, Tennessee

P.O. Box 276
Durban, Natal
January 9, 1940

Dear Aunt Elizabeth,

I must thank you for the darling bloomers you sent Eve and Robin. They are the prettiest I have ever seen, and Robin simply looks too cute in hers. Eve has always loved to dress, so you hit her weak spot. It was so sweet of you to send them.

I did not get the Christmas spirit this year and made no preparations for the occasion, but when the holidays did arrive we had a very nice time; in fact, our very best Christmas—that is, for Bill [Wilfred] and me. Durban is such a beautiful place, and we love the bathing. Beside that, we had some nice dinners out with friends at some of the large hotels and went to several dances. I was feeling quite well for the first time in over three months. Really, I have never been so miserable as during that time when I had asthma and hay fever combined.

How are Harris and Uncle Charlie? I do wish you would send me a snap of all of you. I wish the whole family would do that.

We are to stay in Durban permanently, it seems, and shall bring our furniture down from Johannesburg the first of March. I am crazy to have it again and feel settled. Just now we are boarding and have it as comfortable as possible, but still it isn't a home. We have an

Durban Post Office, 1939

apartment of three rooms, living room, two bedrooms, private bath and balcony, and take our meals in a central dining room. It would be perfect for anyone who worked. Do you still keep house? I don't know how you do it all.

Wilfred and I both wish you and Uncle Charlie all the very best for 1940.

Much love,

Helen

January 15, 1940

Dearest Mother and Dad,

I am so thankful you have at last had a letter from me. I have found out that all mail to America was greatly delayed at the time you were not hearing from me; however, we got mail out here fairly regularly. All the Americans I know have had to send reassuring cables home. It was most unfortunate that the last letter you had from me before that period of delay said I was ill. I am happy to report that I am like a new person now, and the treatment is simple. I take potassium chloride before each meal and then have very little salt on my food. If I become wheezy at night, I take a Felsol powder, not a drug, which relieves me immediately. I am about to start believing in medicines. You know what I have always thought of them.

I feel so worried about Uncle David. I wrote Aunt Nellie this morning, and it was such a hard letter to write, for I don't know what has happened. It is dreadful being so far away.

Wilfred didn't strain his back at the store, so Westinghouse can't pay the doctor's bills. He doesn't have to do any lifting there because he is the big shot. I can't even carry my parcels in his office if I have been shopping. One of the native boys always comes running to meet me and carries them. The store here won the cup again for the month of December making 140% of quota. The trouble now is they don't have the stock to sell, so we are expecting a lean period. It is not the fault of the war, but bad merchandising. Wilfred is fed up because he can make good money if he has the stuff to sell. It's his first chance to really make some money.

We have no shortage of gasoline in South Africa. We can get as much as we want. A blockade of South Africa would only affect us so far as gasoline and such things are concerned. We have plenty of food, wool, coal, etc. My feet would also suffer, as I can't wear local-made shoes. Most things are manufactured here now, but they are inferior to the imported products, so that is why there is still a big import market here. They even make electric stoves here.

Please extend my congratulations to the Roesels. I am sure a child will mean a lot to them because I think Dr. Roesel feels a bit excluded from local society. The

Germans were not nice to him, and you know he was a bit hard for us to understand.

We have been told we are to stay in Durban, but we can't take that as absolutely settled, as there is plenty of trouble in the company just now. Several of the big shots are trying to cut each other's throats. We asked to come to Durban because of the politics up there, but we said it was for Wilfred's health. It simply became too dangerous up there. It was the wisest thing we ever did. The company has been frightfully mismanaged, but we doubt if the new man from England (Arridge) would be any better. Mr. Sours, the present president, doesn't know one thing about the organization; he is only interested in women and drink. He came down here New Year's for a week, supposedly on business, and was in the office two hours in all. Wilfred begged him to personally investigate prices, etc., but he wouldn't. Mrs. Sours left him a year ago and went back to America; she said she knew when she wasn't wanted.

I am so glad Aunt Kate is so happy in her position at Intermont. I can imagine that the girls are crazy about her. It must be nice to be appreciated. I can imagine how little her wit was appreciated by Uncle Hunter, Thomas, or Gordon. They considered her the cook and housekeeper.

Why don't you get a fur coat? I really think you need it in Elizabethton.

Eve pulled a good one the other day. She told me a girl said to her that her mother shouldn't let her cross the street by herself. (Our flat is across the street from where we take our meals.) Eve said, "I gave her such a look she shivered." She can do it too. She has cast a few of them at Wilfred and me.

The picture of us in the rickshaw is very good of the children, but I don't like it of myself. My hat is really cock-eyed. The native boy's headdress is of course much too heavy for him to pull a rickshaw around. His wives made it for him, and you pay him to have your picture made with him. He told Wilfred he was soon retiring to his kraal, and that he had enough money to buy a lot of cattle, which is their wealth.

I don't know whether I have already asked it or not, but I would like to know the exact amount still due on the loan on my house in Johnson City. Since things are so good in your section now, isn't there a chance of selling the house? If you sold it and sent the money over here now, at the present rate of exchange we would gain about £150 on the exchange alone. That alone would give me my trip home. I do not want to hold the house if there is any way to sell it. Please let me know what you are doing about it. I think L. is still a prospect. I'll bet he has the cash necessary.

   I am enclosing New Year's letters to Wilfred from Mr. Sours.
I haven't received Father's letter yet. I wonder why. I hope the post is regular from now on.

Wilfred came home just as I was finishing this letter and brought Father's letter. It had been opened by the censor. I'll enclose the envelope. The first one I have had opened.

Lots and lots of love from all,

Helen

P.O. Box 276
Durban, South Africa
January 28, 1940

Dearest Mother and Dad,

Yesterday I received Mother's letter telling me of the very serious condition of Uncle David and Uncle Charlie. I felt all the time that there was no hope for Uncle David, but I am shocked to hear what you have to say about Uncle Charlie. It does seem they are leaving us while they are much too young and should have years more. There is much too much sorrow with a large family.[77] I am mailing a book of Native Studies to you all, which I want given to Uncle David. You understand why I am not sending it direct to Uncle David. If it got there too late, then nobody would ever enjoy it.

As much as I enjoy Father's letters, I think it is too much for him to try to write. I had rather for him to rest or be out doors during any spare time he has.

We see in our papers that Tennessee, Georgia, Kentucky, and Alabama have had a terrible cold spell with over three hundred deaths and many places snow bound. I do hope you two have taken care of yourselves. I know how determined Father would be about getting to the office regardless of weather, and that worries me. I also think about all the coal Mother will feed that furnace.

I continue to be so much better here in Durban than I was in Isipingo. I am about four miles from the sea and about as high as one can get in Durban. It is a crime that we stayed in Isipingo so long and I suffered all that time.

I am sorry I failed to enclose some of Eve's drawings, but I can't enclose them now, for I have no idea where they are or what they were. She hasn't been doing any lately. This morning I started her in the Presbyterian Sunday school about four blocks from us. She enjoyed it because the teacher told them a story and then let them make things of plastercine that were mentioned in the story, arrange these in a sand box, etc. I am glad to have found a place where the Sunday school is really conducted for the children. There is no class for the grown-ups even though it is a big church. That just isn't done over here. Only church for them.

---

[77] Between her mother's and father's siblings, their spouses, and chidren, Helen had something like twenty-four aunts, uncles, and cousins, four of whom died while she was in South Africa.

I am enclosing a clipping about how bad the sharks are here. I hadn't read this and went bathing at this very spot the next morning. Eve got badly stung by blue bottles, a blue jellyfish which follows the sharks. We rather quickly took the sting out with the pulp of the aloe. We shall be most careful from now on.

Would you all even consider coming out here to live if Wilfred could get something for Father at about $150? I know Father would love Durban, but I wonder if you would be so well satisfied away from Elizabethton. Personally, I much prefer living here to my life at any time in Elizabethton. I really think it would kill me to have to live in Elizabethton again. That, of course, isn't a nice thing to say about one's hometown, but I can't help it.

Mother's letter with a few bright comments about the English and tea drinking, etc., was opened by the censors, but nothing was marked out. There is still great freedom of speech in this country, as you will see from the enclosed clippings. A great part of the country here is pro-Nazi, and I shouldn't be surprised to see civil war. The Negroes are even taking the thing up and say the Germans are coming and will give them their lands back. Every night a German station broadcasts in Afrikaans to the Afrikaans people in South Africa. They don't know which side the army would fight for if called into action. They can't even locate all of the armaments that have been landed in the country, and the Dutch[78] say they are keeping them for an emergency.

This last may be idle talk. Anyway, Durban and all of Natal is very English; the real trouble will be in Johannesburg and all along the Rand. The Rand is the gold reef, with mine after mine, and built up with small mining towns. You can imagine the rough and ready type there, and the cosmopolitan crowd. (Eve is so busy talking to me that I can hardly write.)

I am so glad Gordon won the $1000 in the newspaper contest. Did he really get the money? I am also pleased about Mrs. Alexander.

I have already written Aunt Nellie. It was a hard letter to write, but I think I handled it all right.

Your Xmas card was so appropriate and was appreciated, even though it was late.

Lots and lots of love from us all,

Helen

---

[78] The Afrikaners, European immigrants of Dutch, German, and French descent, were often referred to as "The Dutch." Unlike the Dutch of the Netherlands, Afrikaners who had trekked from the Cape to the Transvaal and Orange Free State were often aligned with the Nazis in their ideologies. Their extremism was due to the hardships they had faced during their migration north, including their searing encounters with the Zulus and the British.

P.O. Box 276
Durban, South Africa
February 5, 1940

My dearest Ones,

Wilfred has just telephoned me that the Arridges are leaving our house on the 13th of this month and that we can get the furniture any time after that date. I shall go up perhaps on the 14th and send it down immediately and hope it is here for the first of the month. We are anxious to feel settled once more. I am not bringing everything, as I can sell in J'burg and get my money out of it and buy again down here. I have already bought my dining room table; it is rosewood and perfectly round with the leaves out. I have eight extension leaves for it, so you can imagine the size of it full out. I never use them all. It is really lovely. It cost $100 new; I paid $17 for it. I shall have it refinished. I also bought a little oak coffee table for $2.50. They use low odd tables so much over here. Now I am afraid I shall have to pay too much for chairs to match my dining room table. I hope the trip to J'burg may be beneficial to me. I think I thoroughly mistreated myself when I first arrived down here. Perhaps with a new start from J'burg and care, I can be all right. I am taking dust injections, which are very expensive—$20 for the medicine alone.

We shall have the president of the South African branch of Westinghouse and his wife in Durban for two days this week, so I must be busy getting my hair and nails done, etc.

Love and kisses,
Helen

P.O. Box 276
Durban
February 22, 1940

Dearest Ones,

Here I am back in Johannesburg, enjoying a little holiday with Bert in her lovely flat. I had to come up and see about my furniture, as the lease is up. The best of it is on its way to Durban, and the rest is at the auction mart here to be sold. Railage is very expensive, and I hated to ship things that I really wanted to replace. In any case, Westinghouse is paying for the move.

I am selling my dining room table and chairs, my bedroom suite of teak, consisting of a wardrobe, dresser, and cupboard for chambers, to be specific. Such a suite was all right in the rondavels, for they are rustic, but I have taken a modern flat in Durban, which has five built-in closets, thank goodness. So, for my bedroom, I am buying a mahogany chest of drawers from an antique shop, very old piece, and am having a mahogany draped dressing table. I am keeping my same divan beds but am getting new covers for them. I have already replaced my teak dining room table with one in rose wood, which is perfectly round when closed up but has eight leaves and is banquet size when extended. I have sold Eve's bed and desk, which were in oak, and I hope to have ducoed furniture for them in blue, as Robin's bed is blue. I shall have to spend some extra money, but I am anxious to have my flat very nice. I am also selling my garden tools, wheelbarrow, hose, etc. My move was naturally easy, as the packers did everything.

Bert and I have been enjoying ourselves, as there has been a round of bridge for me, teas, dinners, concerts, and now, tonight, the biggest thrill of all—for at last I am going down in the Robinson Deep gold mine, the deepest in the world, 9,000 feet deep, and I am going to the bottom. It is 3,000 feet below sea level. I hope to be given a sample of ore, which I shall send to you, and shall write a description of our trip in my next letter. I am out of paper. Here's some of Bert's come to light.

I have left Eve and Robin with my native girl; their meals are prepared by our boarding house, and Wilfred is there in the evenings. Wilfred said over the phone yesterday that everything is going fine without me—Eve hasn't cried once, and that was what we were afraid of. Wilfred took them to the beach over the weekend, and took Eve out to dinner Sunday noon. I am feeling very fit again up here, and shall try to look after myself when I go back down to Durban.

I plan to go back by train Sunday, Feb. 25, getting into Durban Monday morning. I will have had ten days up here by then. I came up from Durban in a car to save money—you know how I am. Wilfred was opposed to the idea, but I wouldn't do it, and now there is a very big laugh on me. I contacted this man thru a travel agency, but never actually saw him until 4:30 of the morning we left. He was rather dreadful looking, and, when I saw the rest of the occupants, I knew I had let myself down rather badly. Anyway, I enjoyed the trip as far as the scenery went, but it is a long trip, 450 miles, and some of the roads are bad. In any case, the driver showed decided preference for me and wanted to drive me back to Durban, but I said I could make no plans.

This past Sunday evening, Bert and I went to a concert given in aid of the Red Cross. Bert sold flowers with the social elite of J'burg, and we therefore were invited to the party for the participants afterwards. A Mrs. Manning offered to drive us home, and when we went out to get in her seven-passenger Cadillac, who should be her chauffeur but my friend. It was the same car as I had driven up in. I nearly died but managed a look when I got in the door, which he held open.

While I was writing this letter to you, a letter from you arrived, redirected by Wilfred. It contains the one returned to you, which has the picture of the children's party. I am so glad to finally get that. I shall paste it in their snapshot book. I was so glad to hear from Uncle David too, but sorry that the news is no better. I do wish I could go to see him, as Gladys has done.

I am relieved to know that the robes have arrived. There were other things I would have preferred sending, but the duty was too high. I shall have to bring them when I come home.

Things are more settled in Westinghouse now. We have had a terrible strain playing politics. It became a fight for power between Mr. Arridge and Mr. Sours. We knew this would happen, and that is why we maneuvered a transfer to Durban, so that we wouldn't have to take either side; but even so, Wilfred did not escape, as both men asked Wilfred for written reports which would be damaging to first one and then the other side. Wilfred had to comply in some cases, as it all became rather personal. Each report he read to me, and we discussed it, and he had my consent to send it. I thought he was most thoughtful of me, as he risked nothing without my consent. Now Mr. Sours has been fired and Mr. Arridge is in. We liked Mr. Sours, but he did no work at all, and the company was completely disorganized with no one to appeal to. If Mr. Sours had stayed, we would have still been in, for we had played our cards well. It has been a terrible strain on Wilfred for six months now, and he is going away for a holiday next month just on his own.

He is going up in the Drakensberg[79] Mountains where he will have hiking, fishing, golf, and plenty of sleep. He must also come to J'burg on business, but I hope that won't take long. He will see some of his pet aversions in the company dismissed, the biggest pet being a man by the name of L.C. Fairey, Credit Manager. Wilfred always called him Elsie, which was amusing because the man was so effeminate.

Fairey and Wilfred disliked each other because of a social engagement Fairey broke with Bert; he had the nerve to appear with a married woman at this dance, knowing we would be there. Wilfred offered to punch his nose for this, but Fairey would not accept the challenge; since then he has always wanted to do Wilfred a dirty turn in some sly way. The thing Fairey tried to pull was to make it appear that Wilfred was so anxious for business in Durban that he was *forcing* the Credit Manager, Mr. Thompson, in Durban, to pass credits that were not good. Fairey, therefore, suggested to Mr. Sours that Mr. Thompson be put in as manager and have charge of credits too, suggesting that Wilfred could not be relied on for any

---

[79] Peaking at eleven and a half thousand feet, the Drakensberg Mountains are the largest and highest in South Africa. The range runs north to south, thereby dividing the country into two geological and political areas: Natal on the eastern seaboard, and the Transvaal, Orange Free State, and Cape Province in the west. The mountains are rich in flora, fauna, and anthropology, with up to 40,000 examples of Bushman (San) art, possibly dating back as much as 23,000 years.

position with responsibility. Wilfred intercepted this letter that gave a full outline to Thompson.

Apparently, Thompson also said that, in a letter of Wilfred's, he had the tool to strike Wilfred with by quoting a paragraph that was a bit ambiguous. Wilfred opened this letter because his typists had told him that Fairey was writing damaging things about him to the head office. We had to expose the letter because it would show Fairey's animosity toward Wilfred and discredit anything he had said. We hit upon the scheme that it was addressed to Wilfred instead of Thompson by mistake, or rather the kindness of someone in head office. This went down very well, and now Fairey is on his way out. For it to be necessary to do such things to hold one's position actually puts years on one in a few days. If we hadn't intercepted this letter, what the story would be now I do not know. Thompson is not supposedly Wilfred's friend. He is a manager of Pietermaritzburg under Wilfred's supervision. Must stop.

Love,
Helen

New (and I hope permanent) address:
Minley Court
Manning Road, Durban
March 2, 1940

My very dearest Ones,

I have again staged a move and am attempting to settle down and feel at home in a place I never saw until three weeks ago. It is amazing how many places I must call home, but I truly hope I am settled here for a long time, as I am sick to death of moving.[80] You may address letters to me at the above address or continue with P.O. Box 276.

Today, I received your fourth letter in the New Year and have received all the ones previous to it; some were reversed in the order they were received; in other words, No. 3 arrived before No. 2. I am glad you are getting letters from me now. I received finally the newspaper clipping of Eve and Robin's birthday party. I was embarrassed that they published my letter verbatim. If I had thought they would do that, I would have read it over more than once before mailing it, which was all the time I spent on it.

I had my trip down the Robinson Deep Mine, and it was quite an experience. I want to try to write it up properly and send it to you for publication in *The Star*. Because I am going to make a real effort on it, I shall not go into detail now, and

---

[80] By now, Helen and her little family have moved eight times since first arriving in South Africa in 1937.

would prefer if you don't mention anything about my going down until the article appears. I shall send you a sample of the one called "Rand" before the article comes out, and Father will have it at the Bus Terminal to show to those who mention it.

I may be a bit slow in getting these things done, as there is so much to do on this flat I am in. Not a curtain I had will do here, and my rugs are a great disappointment here. I must also have two more rugs, and I dread that expense. My curtains will also cost a pretty sum, for my windows are huge, but each one is a beautiful picture in itself. The windows are completely across one end of each room. The two front rooms (lounge and dining room) look out over the harbour, the two side bedrooms over a beautifully kept garden with a lovely tree, so large that it shades the two bedrooms and kitchen. I selected this flat for the views and the quietness mainly, but it is very modern also. White tiled kitchen, bathroom and lavatory (inside). My kitchen looks so very nice with my new Westinghouse electric stove and refrigerator (brought from J'burg). I also have a Westinghouse electric sewing machine, but I haven't tried it yet.

The reason I didn't write you about it is that we thought we did have it, and then we thought we didn't. Mr. Arridge said he was giving it to Wilfred; then, when we asked for it, he said his wife was using it, and that it would be left with our furniture. He is full of promises, so we thought this would be the last we would hear of it, but sure enough, it was left with our things. Closed, it looks like a walnut table with drawers. It is very pretty, but Mrs. Arridge never got it adjusted so it would stitch well. However, I shall soon give it a try. Mrs. Arridge didn't like anything out here, however.

I am glad Uncle David is not suffering so much. It must be terribly depressing for you all to see so much suffering and know of so many deaths—for instance, Mrs. Hedgepath's. I am sure that was a great shock to you.

March 5, 1940

It seems impossible to get back to this letter once I was interrupted.

I don't believe I have mentioned that I found Eve and Robin perfect on my return; they only needed fingernails and toenails cut, and Eve needed one of my haircuts. I always cut her hair. She has been to a barber once since we have been out here. Robin still doesn't talk, but she has her own way of asking for water. When she drinks water, she drinks so fast that she makes a funny sound in her throat; now, when she wants a drink, she comes to me and makes the same sound in her throat. Eve, on the other hand, does not lack for words. The other day she said, "You don't need to do it that way; you could *arrange* it this way," and gave a detailed explanation.

Wilfred gets in this evening from J'burg, and I know he will be dog tired, as he will be driving all the way back himself, and it isn't a road like we have at home.

Yesterday, I bought three antique chairs—[including] a stinkwood slave chair[81] for the tapestry Bert made for me Xmas before last. I have been looking all of this time for a chair I liked and could afford. One quote from a new stinkwood chair for the tapestry was over $45. I paid $10 for this one, and that includes putting the tapestry in. The other two chairs are rosewood and are for my bedroom. One I shall use in front of my draped rosewood dressing table.

Regarding the bad check, I would tell Mrs. M. that you were having L. arrested if it bounced, and I would do it too. He should have been pulled up long ago. I only feel sorry for the two children, for they are just the nicest young boy and girl that I have ever met.

Eve remembers you all and often talks about you. The other day I complained that she ate so slowly and she said, "Well, Mama Sophia eats slowly too, so I guess that makes it all right."

I must stop and see to supper for the children.

I am so glad you were pleased with the robes and they were a surprise.

Lots and lots of love,

Helen

P.O. Box 276
Durban
March 15, 1940

My very dearest Ones,

I was so grieved to hear of Uncle David's true condition. How helpless we are in the face of such disease. May I hasten, however, to reassure you about myself. I saw my doctor yesterday and told him about Uncle David and asked if he thought the growth in my nose might be cancerous. He said that it was only a polypus,[82] a swelling of the mucous membrane from sneezing, and that he did not for a minute consider there was any chance of it being cancerous. He said that if there were any doubt in his mind when he removed it, he would have it microscopically examined. He said for me to tell you that cancer does not run in families; it is a matter of vitamins, so you all should see that you eat a well-balanced diet.

The doctor's own mother died of cancer, the growth of which she kept concealed from him until it was too late. He said, however, that he was not at all afraid of dying of the same thing. I have the best medical attention available in

---

[81] There was a thriving furniture-making trade in South Africa during the early 18th century, utilizing slave labor. Two centuries later, these handcrafted pieces became highly collectable.

[82] Polyp and polypus have the same meaning: an abnormal proliferation of tissue.

Durban, and I am sure it compares with what one would receive in large cities at home. My condition is so much better, just as good, in fact, as when I lived in Elizabethton. I have started with my dust injections and hope they will be beneficial.

My native girl has been to school for five years, I believe, and is supposed to understand English, but she usually does just opposite what I tell her. You should see her Zulu Bible. She goes to the Church of England every Sunday afternoon so dressed up I can hardly recognize her.

I was sorry to hear of the death of Annette's mother. What was wrong with her? Did she have T.B.? I have this impression.

Wilfred has received the two copies of *Time* from Father and certainly appreciated them. The night of the day they arrived, he sat up until two o'clock in the morning reading them from cover to cover.

Wilfred is exhausted from work and must get away for a holiday, but it seems he has nobody to hand responsibility to. I am really worried about him if he doesn't leave soon and have a complete rest. He has so many problems every day—the seasonal affairs of his staff as well as the business.

Downtown Durban, 1939

Mr. Tiederman, who leaves next month for the U.S. with his wife and three children, has promised to visit you all on a long weekend and give you firsthand news from us. He was second in command out here. Do not be afraid you will not have things nice enough, for everything is, and they will only be interested in scenery around in N.C., etc. They do not care for bridge or dancing or drinking, so don't worry about any of that. They are very straight-laced. I just hope the family will be in a position to have them for a [?]; it would be nice for them to see [?]'s house. Of course, I know you will do all you can for them when the time comes.

Must get the babies to bed.

Love and kisses,

Helen

March 20, 1940

My dearest Ones,

    We are approaching our Easter holidays, at which time everyone gets four days off. I wish this time of the year meant the same for Father. I often think of his long hours, and I have continually kept my eyes open for any opening out here that might be profitable for him.

    There is one business I am sure he could make a success of here if he learned it well before coming over, and that is the filling and sanding and waxing of floors. I wrote you once that the floors are beautiful, and so they are, after two or three years of natives polishing, but that is rather long to wait. The only thing they do to new floors is *oil* them, and I have been in beautiful new homes that had terrible dull oiled floors because there hadn't been time for the daily polish to take. And as far as light floors go, they don't even know them. Now, you can't teach them anything about heating, but they would take to anything beautiful in floors. This is something that could be your own business, and yet your investment should be small. There has been considerable building out here, but that has slowed down; but, in any case, old floors are just as good a market, and people spend money out here, as I am sure you have never seen it spent except in New York City.

    Wilfred's business continues good—$30,000 this month. He could be of help, as they sell floor polishers, and his salesmen could suggest the floors be completely refinished first, etc. Let me know what you think of this idea of mine. I would so love to have you all out here with me. I am sure you would love Durban.

    I am sending you a sample of the material I am making my bedspread of. The heads of the beds will be padded and covered with the same. There is no footboard, so these covers fit all around with a very full ruffle all around, put on with cord of the material. They are called French beds out here. The pillows are to be put in a long, round puff I am making. I finished one spread today, and it is beautiful. Each bed is costing me about $8.00, but if I had had it done, it would not have been less than $25. I don't blame them either, because I have worked for three days on one cover. I did most of it by hand, all the hems, which no one else would have done. I know it is made better than if I had had it done. My sewing machine is marvelous.

    Wilfred is so happy and contented since we have a home again, and he is eating about twice as much as he did.

    I wish that I could hope for some good news from Uncle David, but I know that isn't possible. I should write him, but I don't know what to say. Give him my love, and tell him I always ask about him.

    Lots of love to all,

Helen

4 Minley Court
Manning Road, Durban
March 25, 1940

Dearest Mother and Dad,

I am just sending a few things along in this letter that I found in my move, and thought they might interest you.

I feel very sorry for little Eve today. When she found her Easter basket of chocolate eggs, she immediately wanted to ask some friends in, and made up little nests of candy for each, which made it about two pieces of candy to each, as her present from the bunny was very modest. She said she wanted to cut the pieces of candy up into dynamites, meaning diamonds. I tried to discourage her because she had so little to offer, and I didn't have any cakes or anything, but she must do it. She said Easter should be a happy time, and you should have your friends around you, so I let her go ahead and ask three children.

I heard great laughter very soon from all but Eve, the two nannies, native girls, included. Eve was in tears and heartbroken. They wouldn't even accept what she had made up for each, which was well done for her age, and laughed and said she asked them to come for two sweets. I almost kicked them out I was so annoyed. They were children I did not care for anyway, but they were the only ones we know so far in Durban. Eve is very sensitive and very original, and few children can understand her because she thinks heads above them. She will only be held back because she is lazy. She watched me making my bedspreads and said, "I wouldn't do all of that work." And that is only too true.

It has rained continuously during the holidays, but we needed it. Wilfred left yesterday afternoon for Pietermaritzburg with Mr. Arridge for a store dinner, since they won the cup last month. They haven't come back yet, but should be in any time now, as it is after eight. Mr. Arridge is down here for a week's holiday, and we have been entertaining him. It is really quite a strain at times.

Mother, I wish you would send me a pair of brown and white sports shoes, with military heel. I take a 7½ AAAA, you remember. I can wear Rhythm Step all right now. I believe I once wrote you they were not comfortable. I paid $15 for a pair of Rhythm Step out here. They can only fit me, as it is a toeless number. I could use a pair of nice black shoes too, if you find something on sale very nice. I think you had better pay for these out of Eve's money and keep account, so I can pay her back when we come over. The exchange is too bad just now to send the money. Do not think of paying for them yourself, for I am quite able to buy them myself.

I am in love with my Westinghouse stove and am beginning to think I can cook. My, but the work is easier with one. You see, for a year I have used a coal stove. We are enjoying a Westinghouse Radiogram too, which we can have out on demonstration. Yesterday afternoon we had San Francisco, California, coming in as plain as you could get it. It was most thrilling. They read a lot of letters to people in South Africa from people in America. I waited for mine, but it didn't come up.

Goodnight, and a kiss for each of you with my love.

Helen

P.O. Box 276
Durban
April 10, 1940

Dearest Ones,

I was going to write a very long letter on my typewriter, but it seems to be locked, and I simply can't discover how to unlock it. They have been using it at the office. I really feel peeved. It is a Remington, and I have never understood the thing.

I suppose none of us can think of anything much today except the invasion of Denmark and Norway. I do wish the U.S. would come in now, as I think the moral effect on Germany would be most beneficial to the Allies. I do not think it would mean the loss of American lives, as the Allies have enough men, but it would mean stopping shipments to Germany, which big business does not want to do until the last minute. What a loss of lives and property because of greed, because America doesn't dare let Germany win this war. Can't you talk our cause up? How do you feel about it, really? I am anxious for the news today. We have one Danish and one Norwegian family living in our apartment house. There are only six flats here. Wilfred's assistant is also a Dane, and of course all are very upset.

I enclose a bit of Robin's hair to show you how fair it still is. I hope you will like these pictures of the children, also their black nanny. She has a real African face, hasn't she? I love the one taken on the beach of Eve and Robin. Robin's suit is yellow; Eve's is green. They look sweet in them. The other pictures were taken in the park near us. I shall send Aunt Lennie one of them at the beach. I can't very well dress Eve in the dress Aunt Lennie sent, as she has worn it too hard and it wouldn't look too good.

The man-killing shark is still about, so we aren't going bathing these days. He got the last victim only about five yards out. They are planning to enclose the bathing area if the cost is not too great. I think six have lost their lives so far.

I was surprised about N.B., and M.G. is very cold-blooded and likes social position. I suppose money was a very deciding factor since it was all so sudden. P.D. used to drink a lot. Of course, I don't know how he is now. I hope it turns out happily, but I am afraid he will make a very indifferent sort of husband. I think we have heard the old tale long enough about no man being good enough for J.N. I know plenty as worthy of good husbands. Most of them are already married to husbands not so good.

Robin is already trained and wears little panties. Of course, there are accidents now and then.

Thanks for the information about the house. I don't want the property put in an agent's hands, as the L.'s will only be annoyed. However, if you hear of a likely prospect, you could write them and let them know the house can be bought. My price is $10,000, no less.

I have just had a $40 doctor's bill from the doctor called in by my specialist. I am feeling very fed up, for I still have my polypus. There are a lot of bloodsuckers, especially out here.

I have a new solid-blue Wilton rug 9x12 for my bedroom. It looks lovely with the pink spreads and draped dressing table. I also have my curtains up and shall enclose sample. They are so heavy because we do not have window shades over here, as we have casement windows.

I am so sorry about W.L.'s romance being broken up. The girl must be out of her head. We are all so foolish when we are young, though, that it is a wonder we don't wreck our lives. She will see the day she would be glad to have a religious husband.

Robin has no scars from her two accidents to her hand and is perfectly all right now. She saw your picture, Mother, for the first time this morning. I had to have the frame repaired and am just now getting it up down here. I took her over to it and said, "That's Mama Sophia."

She said "Mama, bubba" (a term of endearment) and then kissed it. I thought that very sweet. Also, she said "pretty" the other day, looking at you-all's Xmas card.

Time is coming regularly, and I almost feel like I am back in America. There are so many things we find we didn't know. For instance, we didn't know Douglas Fairbanks [a famous action movie hero] was dead.

I am so glad you have a fur coat, especially since you have had such a severe winter this year. We are expecting a cold winter, as the Drakensberg Mountains are covered with snow already, first time in thirty-five years, I believe.

Must stop and start lunch. You would die if you could see what I have to cook for lunch every day since Wilfred comes home. Anyway, he is gaining weight, so I am pleased. Then, a fair dinner at night.

Worlds of love to you both,

Helen

I Dwell in Possibility (Aug. 1939—Apr. 1940)

P.O. Box 276
Durban
April 25, 1940

My dearest Ones,

I have letters from both of you to answer today, which makes this a <u>very</u> special occasion.

Well, I am really surprised at Dad for thinking it too late to make a change. I am really afraid Mother has done the thinking there. Westinghouse is still too unsettled, however, for me to want you to join them. Although the company showed a big profit, they had to write off $2,000,000 loss in South Africa. It could pay, but they have had fools running it. Wilfred's store has shown a profit several months as a store, but that has been swallowed up by the overhead expenses in Central Office, so his figures are now in the red. Our commissions have been cut in *half* and we are now on a profit-sharing basis, but I doubt if there will ever be any profits. Do not worry about this, however, for our living is still good, and much over Johannesburg—we should always have over $300 per month. I suppose you will think still less of my floor proposition; I would like for you to find out exactly how they fill and wax new floors, for I am very keen to try the business myself. Wilfred doesn't agree with me, but I still think I am right. I have tried using an O Cedar Mop on my floors, and it is perfectly useless. The girl must get down on her knees every day and go over them with a brush.

The nasal douche is all right, according to my doctor. However, he will only allow one to use bi-carbonate of soda in warm water, as he says salt water must be of a certain strength or it is injurious; however, the soda cannot hurt. A teaspoon to a glass of water is what I use.

Gone with the Wind is showing in Johannesburg now and will be here in a few weeks, we think. The seats have doubled in price for it. We pay nearly a dollar per seat, now, for every show we see. There is no reduction on return pictures at the small playhouses either. The only cheap movie is a morning movie for Eve. I take her to see Shirley Temple sometimes, but she is usually dissolved in tears the whole time. I bought her a book of all the old favorite fairy tales when I was in Johannesburg, but she cries so over them that I hate to read them. *Beauty and the Beast* was almost too much for both of us. She even got sympathetic with the Beast.

Eve has had such a thrill receiving the doll-clothes dress, rubber panties, socks, and slippers. The socks for Robin were a perfect fit and greatly appreciated. I love my pot lifter. It is good fun getting these things and having them around. I was just trying to remember to buy a pot lifter. By the way, I would love for you to send me the picture of *Blue Boy* Aunt Nellie made for me in Baubola, also the *Madonna and Chair* Mama Dick gave me. I get so homesick sometimes, and to get some of my little things I left behind now and then would help. Also, I am wondering if

Eve's pink doll's carriage is still there. It would suit Robin fine. She and Eve are always scrapping over Eve's new one. This would be the best birthday present you could send Robin if the postage isn't too much. If it's over $1.50, I had better buy over here; however, I had to pay about $7.00 for Eve's carriage for Xmas.

I am so glad you got the money from L. and don't care a bit that you took the action you did, for he is no good. This will preclude him ever bothering you all again.

I still have the growth in my nose but shall perhaps have it out in the next few days. It means only twenty-four hours in hospital. I don't mind the op but hate the expense. They are bloodsuckers here.

I am glad you are off cigarettes, since they continued to make you cough, but it looks like you'll have to watch your weight. I am not so fond of sweets anymore myself. I think it's Wilfred's influence.

Since you won't consider coming over here, I have a business proposition that you might do something with in America. I shall send you a model of an invention by a man in J'burg. He has it patented in South Africa.

I enjoyed the clipping of the Elizabethton matrons so much. It was most interesting.

By the way, Mother, I do wish you would not ask Uncle Edwin [Sophia's younger brother] to do anything for me. I had rather pay higher taxes than be under any obligation to him. He owes me an apology, and, until he sees fit to give it, my feelings toward him shall remain as they are. I will not hurt you by describing what they are. Must see about lunch.

Lots of love,

Helen

P.S. Wilfred keeps forgetting to take this letter and mail it, so I have opened it up to enclose a sample of my living room curtains. The velvet comes from Italy, and I am wondering if the thread was made in Dr. Staltenhoff's factory. No doubt it was.

I am also enclosing pictures of Bert's flat in Johannesburg. It is a shame you can't see the colors, for that is one of the loveliest things about it. Wilfred made the bookcase, and it is beautifully finished in duco. Bert's rug is a deep burgundy, and that color is also in the linen design on her suite of furniture. The draperies are a beautiful blue. Bert bought the suite from me, also the drop-leaf table. She, of course, had the suite re-upholstered, which I would have done had I kept it. It was too small for us, we thought, but perfect for her. That is a bit of tapestry done by Bert in the stool. The vase with gladioli is Royal Doulton and very valuable. She let me use it when I was in Johannesburg. The picture is an autographed photo of

Pavlova[83] given by her to Bert when she toured this country. She was very impressed with Bert's dancing.

Bert furnished her flat complete for $250, but it would have cost the average shopper twice that amount. Bert gives Wilfred and me credit for having it, as we insisted she sell up her old fashioned things and refurnish. I helped her a lot because I had experience in where and how to buy. The tea wagon she already had in very dull oak. Ducoed, it looks another thing. I was the one who told her not to sell it but have it ducoed.

I went to tea this morning and met a lot of Americans and the American consul's wife. They were all very nice.

Bert's flat on the eighth floor of MacKay Mansions, Rissik Street, Johannesburg.

---

[83] Anna Pavlova, who created the role of the Dying Swan, was one of Russia's greatest prima ballerinas. She was the first ballerina to tour the world with her own company.

Helen, Robin, and Wilfred in Durban, South Africa

6

A Vale of Soul-Making
May 1940 ~ February 1943

I say 'Soul-making.' Soul as distinguished from an Intelligence. There may be intelligences or sparks of the divinity in millions, but they are not Souls till they acquire identities, till each one is personally itself.

~ John Keats

6

The notion of life being a "Vale of Soul-Making" was the poet John Keats's spirited and poetic response to the Christian notion of life being a "Vale of Tears." Keats's bravery in the face of his imminent death puts me in mind of Helen's response to South Africa's entry into World War II in September 1939, and her response to Wilfred's departure for camp on July 4, 1940.

Later, on October 2, 1940, facing financial ruin and being alone to care for her two children, Helen tells her mother and father, "Please don't ever think of my life as a sad one because I do not consider it so, as I still get a big kick out of everything, and whatever happens is just a broadening experience."

With Westinghouse closed for the duration of the war and Wilfred over four hundred miles away at army camp with only occasional visits back in Durban, Helen finds work, first as a filing clerk, and later as a secretary in the Ministry of War Supplies in Johannesburg. In Durban, she shares a house with another woman whose husband has also signed up, and finds happiness everywhere—in her children, in those around her, in her new jobs, and in planning for a new future. Well-served by years as a top-flight secretary and able, finally, to put her shyness aside, this is Helen's moment to acquire her identity, to become "personally herself."

Helen's journey into selfhood is marked not only by her role as a working mother of two in wartime, but also by the number of times she feels forced during this period to move—six times in all: to a nice apartment in Durban; to a shared house in Durban; to a boarding house, Kya Lami, in Johannesburg; to a shared house at 4 Reform Avenue in Melrose, a beautiful part of Johannesburg; and finally to a house, at 8 Reform Avenue, that really feels more like home. During these years, Wilfred is at camp and in training for combat, which means that, after Helen moves to Johannesburg, she and Wilfred are able to be together on most weekends. She is once more in a quandary about "coming home," back to America, but she decides to stay.

Memories of Elizabethton and its residents and the treatment meted out to her and to Wilfred have given Helen the courage to stand up for herself. In a letter to her friend Mary she says, "Mary, I must be happy. I had too much at one time in the past to bear, and I let it make me thoroughly miserable, and it broke my spirit so completely that I have been nursing that spirit back to health for three years in Africa, and only in Africa, or some other place ten thousand miles away from Elizabethton, could I have succeeded in my struggle to be a normal soul again, instead of a cringing, frightened pup."

But even as she continues to develop joy in her own competence, by 1942 Helen faces hospitalization for sinus surgery and exhaustion.

To: Helen's parents from Helen [age 33]

Durban
May 10, 1940

Dearest Mother and Dad,

Today has been a very sad day for me, as well as many others, and a depressing day for all the world.[84] Today made it quite clear to me that we shall become more active here in South Africa, and, of course, we must face the fact that Wilfred will have to go—something he is most anxious to do. I would not stop him going, even if I could, because it isn't in Wilfred's nature to stay out of a good fight. There is a lot to be done, and the task will take the wholehearted support of every man and woman.

As soon as Wilfred is called away on active service, I shall make an effort to come home with the children—if we consider it safe enough, and if we can raise the funds. I could not bear to sit alone with the kiddies here in South Africa and wait for news from the front. I would have a visit with you, and, if the war still continued, I would want you to keep Eve and Robin so that I could be free to go into some branch of the service myself. It would be the only way to endure the ordeal, as I see it. In any case, you would have two lively youngsters to keep things moving for you all. It would make me happy to think I was giving you all some happiness by having them with you. I had more or less just settled down and thought how easy my life was going to be with enough money to live comfortably—this for the first time in years and years—and now a world war is breaking that up. It seems I was not destined for an easy life, and no doubt it would bore me to death anyway. I shall keep you posted about us as developments come.

Wilfred and I are just back from a five-day trip to Johannesburg. We went up in the most terrible rain and snowstorm of the year. I shall enclose clippings showing the road we traveled. We were fortunate enough to secure accommodations for two nights on the road. Many sat in chairs at the various hotels all night, or in railway stations. Most of the road from Durban to Johannesburg is under construction, so you can imagine the condition of it in bad weather. We could never have got through without chains. Eshowie, a place in Zululand, not far from Durban, had twenty-three inches of rain and is still cut off by road and rail. The street in front of our place here in Durban (that is, our block of flats) was so flooded that cars could not travel on it. It also simply soaked through my walls. It did not come in any of the windows, but soaked through the

---

[84] May 10, 1940, saw the successful German invasion of France and the defeat of the French forces as well as the forces of the Low Countries.

walls terribly. The place looks a mess. It also got on my new velvet curtains in the living room. We saw at least twenty-five cars off the road on our trip, and many people wouldn't travel at all.

I was rather surprised to hear that Gordon had married again. I hope it will be more successful this time. Please congratulate him for me when you see him. Tell him Bill and I wish him all the best. Has he ever offered to take Ann? What a shame she doesn't live with one or the other of her parents. I am glad that Virginia is so happy. I think she was a very wise girl to take things in her hands as she did. I'll never forget when she ran away and how Mrs. Alexander tried to get her back. She had made a mess of things in Elizabethton, and a fresh start was evidently what she needed.

I am enclosing some of Eve's work that she has brought home from school. At last she is learning something, it seems. I am quite satisfied with her progress now. She recognizes all the letters she has written, knows what they spell, etc. She also knows that she left an "i" out of kitty.

I left the children with my girl for the five days I was gone, but friends of ours came in two and three times each day to see how they were. Everything went off all right.

Wilfred had to go to Johannesburg on business. Wilfred was apparently successful in what he had to see to, but we are not at all satisfied with the way the firm is run. Instead of an improvement with the changes made, I do believe there is more unrest and uneasiness than ever before. They have closed the store in Port Elizabeth and, from all indications, will close the one in Cape Town. Durban continues to be their best store. Wilfred is very proud of his record and will put this on file in New York when he is called up for service so that he will have a chance to join the company in America when he comes out of the war.

I am invited to play bridge at Mrs. Corrigan's on Monday, the 20th of May. Mrs. Corrigan is the wife of the American Consul and very nice. Quite by accident we met at the cinema this afternoon and sat together. It was just this morning she had invited me to bridge. Quite a few of the Americans have called on me, and I could enjoy myself socially here, I am sure, if I did not have so much to worry about just now. It seems to me that I always have something to keep me from being frivolous and enjoying myself, drinking tea and playing bridge like other women do. I wonder if they have just as much as I, but just go ahead and appear lighthearted.

Uncle David's condition simply hangs over me. I believe I have already asked you to let me know how Aunt Nellie is holding up. You have not mentioned her at all. I am anxious to hear if the loan company succeeds in selling their house for the loan on it. If they do, I know I can sell mine. As I see it, they had no equity in the place. Do not tell them I said so, but that is my opinion. I am surprised that you ever thought Eugene should come in and save it for them. What was there to save?

Thanks for the cheese biscuit recipe. I shall try it right away. I planned to make them for a table of bridge I was having on the Monday I went to Johannesburg. I have put that off, but shall invite them very soon now.

We found Bert quite well, and Wilfred's Dad. Bert has a new job in the Gold Fields and is very enthusiastic about it. They are delighted with her work in the new department. Wilfred's secretary was thrown from her horse the last day of her holiday and now has a broken arm. I must help in the office now and then with dictation, as the other two girls are none too good on it.

While in Johannesburg I broke loose completely and bought four new dresses. They are cheaper up there than down here. I got an Angora two-piece suit, two very pretty sports dresses, light weight, as we have so many warm days in Durban during the winter it is like Florida, and a white evening dress that simply looks marvelous on me. It has a halter neck, no back, and is very full and sweeping. I went to a dance the other night and danced with so many good dancers that I became enthusiastic about dancing again. That is why I have a new evening dress. Now I feel so depressed that I shall perhaps never use it. With a good dancer I really can dance, if I do say it myself.

I do hope the invasion of Holland will tend to bring about a united front in South Africa.[85] If it does that, it will have accomplished something.

I would like to go through your last letters and mention different things, but I am very tired and must get to bed. My health continues very good indeed. I find that I must keep away from the seafront at night, and take a few other precautions, and I keep very well. Eve and Robin are the picture of health, and Wilfred would be all right if he did not have so much to worry him just now. I find myself letting him take all responsibility for the family and do all the worrying. When I relinquished the harness, I seem to have done it completely, and often feel ashamed of myself that I am now so dependent on him for everything. I know I often ask him to attend to matters that I could attend to myself. Responsibilities start again for me, however. Please do not worry overmuch about the news contained in this letter. I suppose this was inevitable from the start, but I was optimistic, and never thought it would come to us.

Love and kisses,

Helen

---

[85] Although anti-British sentiment remained strong among those white South Africans of Dutch descent who had left the Cape between 1835 and 1846 (The Great Trek), a contingent of more liberal Afrikaners who had remained in the Cape helped sway the parliament in favor of joining Britain in the war against Hitler. Helen saw Germany's invasion of the Netherlands (Holland) as an opportunity for healing between these factions. However, since the lines had been drawn between the English and the Afrikaners more than a hundred years before Helen wrote this letter, this did not happen.

P.O. Box 276
Durban
May 23, 1940

My dearest Mother and Dad,

I have just received your letter of April 8th which tells me how near death Uncle David is, and I have no doubt that he has now found a much needed rest from his sufferings. I am anxious to hear how Aunt Nellie is [Uncle David's wife], and I hope you will try to be cheerful and thereby help Aunt Nellie and Eugene [Uncle David's son]. I am glad Eugene has such a nice home for his mother to go to, and whatever he does for her now can't be enough, for she has given and given as far as both Eugene and Katye Wray are concerned. She has always been wonderful to all of us, as far as that goes.

Uncle David was always such a cheery one that he will certainly be missed in the family. I am quite sure that he had the best philosophy of life of any member of the family—he did not deny himself the simple pleasures he so loved: fishing, baseball, and football games. I really think you deny yourselves too much. We should make the most of our lives and get the most enjoyment out of them that we possibly can.

Well, the war news is terrible. The only thing that could make Wilfred or me really happy would be to be called to perform some useful service. We are not financially able for him to join as a private, as that means five shillings a day for the family to live on, which, of course, is impossible. He has tried so hard for a small commission so that the allowance for the family would be enough for us to live on, but the latest news is that they are not training any men over thirty to be officers. It seems a foolish decree to me, for surely a man over thirty, who is used to handling men, is better qualified than a man under thirty, who has perhaps only held a clerical position in civilian life.

Business is at a complete standstill as far as our line goes. So much is also coming back from people who have been called up. I did not tell you, but our income was cut by one third some time back—about two months ago—and now it will be a bare existence, and how long we shall even have that, I do not know. I do not think for long, as they were seriously considering closing the company before things got as bad as they are now. We are now making an effort to turn what we have into cash; the first thing to go will be the car, of course, then our furniture. It will perhaps all have to be sacrificed, as so many people are just where we are and are also trying to dispose of their possessions.

It breaks my heart to sell my furniture, for I like everything I have so much, and, after this experience, I doubt if I'll ever try again to own anything. I have little to grumble about, though, when I think of the real suffering in Europe. We have invested just over $1000 in furniture, and, of course, we must be prepared to take a loss. In any case, I hope we shall clear enough to pay our passage to

A Vale of Soul-Making (May 1940—Feb. 1943)

America—that is, for Eve, Robin, and myself. It is impossible for me to get a job here, and, in any case, I could not go to business every day and leave the children with a native girl. They must be with you if I work.

Our passage will cost us twice as much now as it would have before the war, which is a blow, but it can't be helped. I do not want you all to offer me one penny, as that help might be needed after I arrive. I want to see what Wilfred's father will do. He is so terribly patriotic but also so terribly stingy. In any case it is up to him if the worst comes to worst. He can afford to help, and he has never done a thing. He gave us no help in America when you all did all you could, so please refrain from mentioning sending us money. I really feel like I should like to have to sit down on him for about three months just to see how he would take it. So far the only thing we are trying to sell is our car. I shall keep you posted as to what we are doing. I am determined not to worry this time, like I did during the Depression; it only makes me ugly and bad company. I don't want you to worry either, but just rather be happy that it may not be so very long until you will have us with you. That is the silver lining to this cloud—and what a silver lining.

I was so sorry to hear of Mr. Nick Miller's death. I am sure it was expected by the family; nevertheless, it is hard to bear. Please extend my sympathy to Mrs. Miller and Elizabeth.

I am so glad Mrs. Umbach is at last back home. Seven weeks in a hospital means she had a very serious time and it will take her a year or more to feel normal again. I do hope Mr. Umbach will keep this in mind, as I think he expects too much of her.

I am glad to hear the Clems [Katye Wray's parents] came up. They are such nice people and so cheery. I am sure they will be a help.

Please send my letters to P.O. Box 276, and not to Minley Court, as we cannot possibly stay on in this flat with our income cut to the bone. It will be even less than we had when we started with the company, so you have an idea of the economies necessary. Fortunately, one can find decent cheap places in Durban—if we find it is best to stay on here; in other words, if Wilfred does not go to war. You remember we are paying $60 rent; well, I think we can get something that will still be decent for $40. This, minus the expense of our car, will make quite a difference in our living expenses. I am sorry all of these economies must come now if we do stay on in S.A., for I am meeting such very nice people just now. I played bridge yesterday with people that you would have liked so much and would have felt so at home with them, mostly Americans. I played the best bridge I think I have ever played. I have never done so many smart things in one afternoon.

I think the joke about Dr. Hofmann is just too good. We have had a big laugh out of it. I do wonder how much trouble they are going to have now that a portion of the plant has fallen into a cave. I know they must be worried to death about it. I should think Arno would have something on his hands now.

It was terrible that you did not remember Mr. Smith, but I can well understand it. I don't suppose you had even thought of him for ages. I am sure the same thing is going to happen to me when I come back. Faces will be familiar, but it will be so long since I have thought of the person that I won't be able to place them.

While I think of it, Leone and Frances sent me a lovely pink satin nightgown for Xmas. I am sorry I have failed to mention it to you. I have written to both of them.

Perhaps your newspapers have mentioned the rather severe earth tremor we had in South Africa. It was felt from Durban to Johannesburg and was very severe in Zululand. You will be glad to know that I did not feel a thing. It was bad on the beach but was not felt up on the Berea. I have been looking for a letter from Bert about it, as she is on the 8th floor of a large building right in the city, and I understand it was felt badly in those tall buildings, and that people dashed from them into the streets.

We are receiving *Time* and *Reader's Digest* very promptly. *Time* sometimes does not come for two or three weeks and then we get two or three copies, but we can't expect better just now. We had a notice from *Reader's Digest* that our subscription was up, but we wrote them that we thought they were mistaken, and we have received a copy since we got the notice. It comes from London now instead of the U.S.

I am surprised to hear you have three boys rooming with you. I thought there was only Winder Lane. I hope it won't prove too much trouble giving breakfast. I should serve it downstairs instead of in their rooms. I think they would like it better, and I am sure it would be easier on you. I am wondering which you are doing. I wouldn't mind breakfast too much, especially to young boys who do not expect the thickest cream, etc. We have done a lot of humoring in our day, and I pray it is not the lot of the world in general to have to do just that sort of thing for the rest of them. We had such a lovely cake yesterday baked by our hostess, and, during tea, we were talking about the war, naturally, and taking a rather gloomy outlook on it, so I said to my hostess, "Well, the Germans like their cake, you know." This got a big laugh from everybody, but we wouldn't laugh if it really came true.

What is Lem Reece doing in Washington? I suppose Carrol has fixed him up in a Government position.

I must close now and bathe the children. They are sights by the end of the day. I suppose the more dirt on them the more certain we can be that they enjoyed the day. When I said I was writing you, Eve immediately got busy, and I enclose her contribution, notable mostly for the word KITTY she has printed on it. I find she thoroughly understands all she is reading in her reader, as she writes the words and even sentences from memory, so it shows she really knows the words.

Lots and lots of love to you both and the family,

Helen

To: Mrs. W.V. Collingwood-Evans
From: Edwin Hunter [Helen's uncle]
c/o Mrs. Harlow Dixon
Elizabethton, Tennessee

P.O. Box 276
Durban, South Africa
June 11, 1940

Dearest Helen,

Even before you left to make your home in Africa, I intended to offer you an apology for the remark I made to you in your home in Elizabethton that certainly took away any spark of affection you might have had for me, but it seemed I never had the opportunity, and most assuredly I planned a hundred times to write you concerning it but neglected it until today, and the importance of it was impressed on me by a remark your Mother and Father made to me at my home on Sunday when they said you felt I owed an apology to you. There certainly was no denial on my part, and I do hope you will forgive me. However, in defense of myself, I wish to assure you it was simply an error of judgment and motivated by my love for you and yours. Subsequent events have proven how wrong I was, but I doubt if anyone other than you and your immediate family have gotten more enjoyment than have I over the progress that has been made.

We all enjoyed so much your nice letter to Helen, which she received some months ago, and she seems to have followed your advice in applying herself in college as she should. The school has improved her, and she liked it very much. By going north, she had an opportunity to see how the other half live, but, in spite of their ample financing, she came home unchanged and seemingly with a deeper love than ever for all of us. This, of course, was worth the "price of admission" to Lennie and me.

Your mother and father are fine, and we, of course, see them frequently. You should write them a little more often, as they naturally long for a word from you. A postcard each week would bring so much extra joy into their lives without much added burden on you.

Business in this country is improved, and ours seems to be no exception. How sustained it will be is beyond me to foresee, but I am enjoying it while it lasts.

Tell Wilfred how happy I have always been over his splendid achievements, and I only hope that he will make even greater advances in the days that are to come. Give the children my love and tell them how I long to see them.

It might be of some little interest to you to know my health is improving with each passing year, and I can now do at least part of a man's job. It has turned out about like Mayos predicted, in that it would take from four to six years for me to recover.

Lennie, Helen, and Kathryn are fine, and we all seem to continue our love for each other, which makes for added happiness and a joyful home.

With worlds of love to you all, I am,

Devotedly,

Uncle Edwin

4 Minley Court
Manning Road, Durban
June 13, 1940

Dearest Mother and Father,

I have had Mother's letter about Uncle David's passing, and also the letter enclosing the newspaper clipping. I hope they have done the right thing in taking Aunt Nellie to Dallas, but I can so well understand that she would have preferred staying in Kingsport and keeping house for Eugene. After the strain of the last half-year, I don't think the solitude would have hurt her; she needs just that to pull herself together. I know how insistent the Clems can be, though, and of course they think they are doing the right thing. Too, I am sure Aunt Nellie would have loved some time alone with Eugene.

I have waited so long this time to write because I have expected each day to be able to give you a sailing date for myself and the children, but now that is ruled out. Westinghouse has folded up for the duration of the war, and Wilfred and I seem to be the only members of the organization who were not surprised. They are closing entirely all the small branches and keeping two to three men in the others as debt collectors; in other words, just a skeleton organization to receive payments, etc., on what has been sold. They do not want to make any further sales because of the unsettled state of affairs in this country.

Naturally, it is work for clerks at £25 to £30, so Wilfred has had to resign. He has an excellent record behind him, though, to start again after the war. He left for Johannesburg and Pretoria tonight to see how he can best serve his country. It seems the war really started only a few weeks ago for us. Do not be alarmed at what has happened here so far; the man who did the bombing of the Italian ships one hundred fifty miles out of Durban is a friend of Wilfred's. We saw the planes coming back the morning they did it. We feel like we are really in the thing now, but still we feel safe here.

I have my passage money in the bank in case things get really bad[86] and it seems advisable for us to leave. Wilfred's father gave him a cheque for £220 for this purpose, and I would most likely be sailing the 16th of this month if he had given it with more grace, but we didn't like the way he did it even though he knows he can have it back in about three months from money Wilfred has coming to him, so Wilfred prefers that I wait until his money comes in and not use his Dad's, but we are keeping it for the time being in case of an emergency.

However, I am making all plans to remain here and shall start looking for a stenographic position. Bert and Dad asked me to come to Johannesburg and all of us share a house there, but I could see that Dad would take all the credit and say he had made a home for me when the truth was that he was willing to put in £10 [Pounds] per month, merely board for himself, and I know what it takes to run a house in Johannesburg, and I also knew Bert would expect to put in £7 to £8 per month and the rest would be for me. Dad also said he would have to have a girl for the house and a boy for the garden. Well, that can't be done on less than £35 per month, and I don't know whether it can be done on that. Bert wanted a house in the best part of J'burg, as she is very proud. I could see myself upsetting their lives, as they are now running, and all the time they would think they had done so much for me, but I would bear most of the expense and not even have money for stockings and tram fare. So I have decided to stay in Durban on my own and take all credit or blame unto myself. Durban is so much cheaper than Johannesburg, and people are more friendly. Johannesburg is as heartless a city as you would find any place.

Bert and Dad have been down for a week, and, frankly, I couldn't live with them under the best circumstances. I feel very guilty saying this, as Bert really loves me, but she spoils the children and has her way with them every time unless I get unpleasant, and you know how I hate to do that. Then, she is most untidy, like I was when I was single, and I can't stand that now since I keep house. She is highly strung, which makes me feel like a lump of dough. On the other hand, Dad completely takes the life out of me as well as everyone else. You know those killing people. Of course, you must never refer to any of this in a letter. For some unknown reason, if I say a word against either Bert or Dad to Wilfred, Wilfred tells them. Is this always true in families? I never make this mistake now, even though he may be saying all kinds of things himself.

Going back to the intended trip home, it would have been via Australia, New Zealand, Pago Pago, Tonga, Hawaii, and San Francisco. Three days before we went in to book, the fares went up 1/3 and had previously gone up considerably. It is impossible to get passage just now from Cape Town to Trinidad to New York,

---

[86] On June 22, 1940, eight days after German forces overran Paris, Adolf Hitler forced France to sign an armistice.

or via Buenos Aires. This route is booked up to next January, I understand. I could have come on a cargo boat, but we went down to look at it, and, with all my nerve, I couldn't go for that. It was too terrible for words. To begin with, the rails were so far apart that both Wilfred and I could see both the children overboard before we were well on our way. I would also have been the only woman on the boat and the children and myself the only passengers.

I have already sold some of my things, thinking I was leaving. Now I would like some of them back but suppose I can't ask for them. I sold my two lamps, also my bridge table, some odd dishes, pots and pans and knives and forks. The bridge table is the only thing I would really like to have back.

Durban is still warm like summer. The climate here is like Florida, so you need not worry about us being cold.

Robin is beginning to talk a little, and we get a great thrill out of that. She still has a terrific appetite.

I am looking forward to getting my black shoes. They should be pretty.

I must close now, as it is getting late; also, I have a flea on me and can't wait to get into a hot tub of water. Every time I am around a dog, the fleas leave it and come to me.

My letters will be forwarded to me all right, so use this address. I am not sure of my number at the house.

Lots and lots of love from us all,

Helen

4 Minley Court
Manning Road, Durban
June 26, 1940

Dearest Ones,

There is so much to write but so little time for writing that I must make this brief. First of all, the box arrived with my beautiful white and tan shoes, also the darling dresses for Eve and Robin. They were very thrilled. Please keep books on what I owe you for shoes, etc. I expected the black ones first, but they haven't arrived.

I started to work on Monday, June 24th, for Dunlop Tyre Co. in Durban. I am a filing clerk in their head office. They have their South African factory here. It all reminds me a lot of North American Rayon. It is run on the very same set up. Of course, I hate filing, but it was the only opening, and I make £15 a month, which is considered good out here. It isn't nice getting back to the routine again.

Wilfred is in Pretoria, and I still don't know which branch of the service he will be in. He is trying out as a gunner in the Air Force. Of course, he couldn't have selected a more dangerous place. I do my best to just not think at all. Everybody I know is going, so Durban is going to be a town of women and children.

You would be very happy if you could see the charming girl my own age that I am going to live with. She is the daughter of American Missionaries to China and has lived in China all her life. She is married to an Englishman, and he is going on Active Service, so she and I have taken a house together from the first of July. She has two little girls the same ages as Eve and Robin, so we should manage famously together. We have found a sweet place for £9.9.0 or $47 per month. It has a beautiful garden for the children and is a safe place for them. It is a bit inaccessible, but Edith has a car, which is to be for the use of the family. She thinks she is lined up for a job in the American Consulate here. I hope so, for it

Helen (right) on her first day at Dunlop Rubber Company

will be such a nice place to work. She reminds me of Gladys and makes wonderful pies, etc., so I shall enjoy that and perhaps get fat.

[Section marked out of text by censors.] I am a perfect fool and want to cry every time I see a uniform.

Mother, thinking of the problem of what to do with your hair, I would suggest the style I use for mine. It starts in a roll over the ears and continues completely around the head in one continuous roll to the other ear. The front bit is cut off short enough to make a roll across the head, not straight up from the forehead, but a wave or two across and then the roll. The hair must be practically down to your shoulders for a proper roll. You would also need yours thinned out. You shouldn't let it grow out and do it up. I know I wouldn't know what to do with long hair.

I must tell you that Robin really takes a size three in a dress. She has broad shoulders and has just managed to squeeze into the size two you sent.

I am sorry I have been so upset that I forgot to even send greetings for Dad's birthday, which is now only four days off. It is better late than never, I suppose, so I shall now wish you many, many happy returns of the day. I did want to send a present, but we are just managing to live now; however, we have nothing to grumble about.

Love and kisses from us all,

Helen

Please address me:
c/o Dunlop Rubber Co.
Sydney Road, Durban
July 9, 1940

Dearest Folks,

Thursday, July 4, Wilfred left for training camp at Voortrekkerhoogte in the Transvaal. They do not keep them there long, about a month, and then they are off to unknown destinations. Wilfred is in "Q" Services, which is Supplies, Ammunition, etc. He is starting out as a sergeant, which is good, and means about twice as much money per month for me—£20 per month. I get £15 at my work, so we have enough to live on. I shall not go into how I feel about it all, for I am writing in the office during the noon hour, and to think too much about it all would be just too upsetting for such a public place. Wilfred spent three weeks getting in as sergeant. He is very good at getting what he wants, though, by sheer plugging away at it and leaving no stones unturned.

If all of this had not come up, I am sure Wilfred would have become a rich man within the next few years. He has great business ability, it seems, and usually is the man to get ahead wherever he is. Perhaps you will find this hard to believe, but it is quite true. One of his competitors told him after he had left Westinghouse that he was certainly glad that he was out of the electricity game in Durban, as they simply didn't have any business while Wilfred was with Westinghouse and that, before, they had simply laughed at Westinghouse. Wilfred told him that he knew he didn't have any business because he had all the first-class salesmen in town working for him.

Poor little Robin has grieved so over her Daddy being gone. All day Friday she made Alice, the native girl, carry her around, and she cried and called for Daddy. Friday night she was restless but slept some.

Saturday Edith Broadbent had her out for the day, playing with her little girl, but Saturday night she did not sleep at all the night through but called for Daddy, and "Where Daddy lala?" meaning, "Where is Daddy sleeping?" And, "I want my

Daddy." Of course, this made it terribly hard on me. Thank goodness it happened on a Saturday night and not a weekday night, when I would have had to come to the office next day. She seems happier this morning, and slept soundly last night. Wilfred is crazy about Robin and she about him.

I had three letters from Mother in the same post, and were they welcome, for they came on Saturday after Wilfred left. They are dated May 15, 22, and 28. I have also been most unsettled in my household, having moved the 28th of June into a house, which I was to share with Edith Broadbent. After Wilfred saw the house and its situation, he said we could not stay there, as we found it was on the edge of "Coolie town" (Indians) and, of course, is not the safest place in the world, especially since we are preparing for blackouts, etc. So we went house-hunting again and found a very nice new bungalow in the right section of town, near where we were on Manning Road and just a few doors from the boarding house where we stayed. It is near Eve's school and also near Susan Broadbent's school. I am moving there again on the 16th of this month.

Wilfred and Robin, 1940

Of course, I am not even trying to fix up the house where I am. I am alone there and find it very dreary, but I am so tired every evening that I have been in bed by 7:30 each night. Saturday night I got the full benefit of the Indian music from my neighbors, and there is no music more doleful in the world. So far, though, they only entertain themselves on Saturday nights by playing. The house has a beautiful garden, which was the undoing of Edith and myself, for the place is most inconvenient to work and the children's schools. There is a fishpond, birdbath, and poinsettias completely around the garden, and they have grown much taller than I am. They are in full bloom now and are beautiful. I suppose they are larger than any you have ever seen. I have the red and the pink.

I think Leone's sending you a present for Mother's Day is just the sweetest thing I have ever heard of. I shall write her. I don't know when I have ever appreciated anything so much. She is so thoughtful and sweet. I hope you will entertain her during the summer at bridge. I want you to start going out. One should become more active after a sorrow, for the main thing in life is to try to be happy. We all have our sorrows, but I do not intend to give up to mine.

The strangest thing happened when Wilfred left; we said good-bye looking out over the harbour, and there was a wonderful rainbow stretching across it. When we met in Germany, there was also a rainbow when I stepped off the train.

I shall send you some of the pictures taken of the family the day Wilfred left. They are just snaps, but some are rather good. I have sent the first prints off to Wilfred.

I know of home after home that has been broken up just as mine here in Durban, but the people of Durban are wonderful and are making it as easy as possible, and offer all kinds of assistance. I think the Germans have their nerve having a Victory celebration in America. It is time you all put a stop to some of those things. I don't think I could have managed to live at home during this time on account of them. I realized that when I considered coming. I hope they will have occasion for different feelings not too far distant. They have always said the British were their enemy; well, they are right. They are just now meeting their real enemy. Durban and vicinity alone have raised £185,000 for aeroplanes. They are raising £35,000 more, and that will buy a squadron. People are giving their money, time, their husbands and sons, and they will win.

I must go to work now.

Worlds of love,

Helen

519 Moore Road
Durban
July 17, 1940

My dearest Mother and Dad,

I think you can consider the above address as permanent, but I wouldn't dare say anything was permanent during these times. Anyway, I am in the house I expect to share with Edith Broadbent. She is coming in next week. It is a new bungalow and is most conveniently arranged. There is a large living room, large dining room, nice kitchen and pantry, and three bedrooms, lavatory (inside), and bath. These are separate, that being a great South African custom. There is a nice garage and native quarters. I shall take some pictures of the place one of these days.

Eve is as happy as a lark, as she has her best friend next door and they are together all day. The child is eight and the most carefully supervised child I ever knew, outside of the Everett children. Do you remember them? There is a reason in this case, though: the child has an enlarged heart, and they must keep her quiet. Eve has a terrible crush on her. I am afraid Robin is a bit lonely, though, but she won't be after the Broadbents move in. I feel so much better about being away from the children when I know they are happily playing with other nice children. My native girl is more or less intelligent, and I think she takes care of their physical needs fairly well.

I had a letter from Wilfred today, and he is very cheerful. He has gained six pounds in two weeks and says his colour is good and that it is wonderful not having any worries. He had more than his share during his years with his last employer. I don't know how he stood it. His nerves were so bad, and I am sure having just manual labour will be a perfect cure. If it only didn't have to be followed by war, it would be a grand experience for all of our men.

I am enclosing several things in this letter that I think will be a bit interesting to you all. One is Eve's first report, which I considered most satisfactory. I am also enclosing one of the blue "Speed the Planes" tabs. These could not be had for less than Two Shillings (50c) each. They raised a million dollars in Durban and vicinity for this one cause.

Bert is very busy knitting for Wilfred. He has had two pairs of socks given him by a Mrs. Hooper, a friend of his mother's, and Bert is knitting a "Balaclava"— that is a hood, in case you don't know. I now wish I could knit. She is also going to do a pair of mittens for him. Everybody in the office knits during the lunch hour. I have selected a beautiful wristwatch for Wilfred, and it is being engraved. It has the luminous dial and is waterproof. He is so keen for this. I shall send it off tomorrow.

Wilfred's dad is back at work for the railroads and is so thrilled. I had a letter from him today enclosing a cheque for 10 shillings for Robin's birthday. I shall get her bedroom slippers and a sweater with it. These two things are her crying needs just now. Wilfred sent her a dress and bloomers. I must close now and get to work, as I am at the office.

Lots of love,
Helen

To: Mr. Edwin H. Hunter,
c/o General Shale Products Corp.
Johnson City, Tennessee

519 Moore Road
Durban, South Africa
July 21, 1940

Dear Uncle Edwin,

Your original letter and copy have both been received, even though there was an error in the address of the original. Need I say that your letter gave me a great deal of joy? There remain many things in my memory that took place during my last three years in Elizabethton that I would like to forget, and now I can forget and forgive one of them. This one hurt most of all because it was between you and me, and that is why I wrote Mother that I would like a letter from you, for I knew that only then could I regain my old affection for you.

I am so glad to hear that your health has improved. It has certainly been a long battle for you, and I am sure it was most discouraging at times. When we have good health we can face a lot of things that are mountains to us when we are ill.

Thank goodness I have the health and the courage to face the fact that Wilfred has gone to war. He is now in training at Robert's Heights, near Johannesburg, and, in a few weeks, will leave there for parts unknown.[87] They are never allowed to say where they are when they go off. This is rather hard to bear, but I am only one among a thousand others in Durban faced with the same thing. Wilfred, through sheer determination not to leave me too badly off financially, managed to enter the forces as a sergeant. He is attached to the Air Force but has a ground job. He wants to become a gunner in the Air Force, but I have asked him not to because we all know how slim one's chances are then of ever coming back.

To make my income sufficient for myself and the kiddies, I have had to start out in business again. I got a job within a week after I started going after one, and am now with the Dunlop Rubber Company. They are marvelous people to work for. You would be amused if you could drop in at ten-thirty in the mornings and three-thirty in the afternoons and see us all drinking tea (furnished by the company).

I believe a short resume with figures of Wilfred's four years in business might be of interest to you. I consider it a splendid record, and he was always known as a square shooter. He started with Sears-Roebuck as a porter at $15 per week, and was raised to $20 per week at the end of his first week with them. He was trained in the Stock Room, then was made manager of their warehouse, then manager of the Refrigerator Department, all within one year. At the end of that year, he got the job as South African Manager for Sears International at $300 per month plus commissions. They never paid the commissions, so he left them to join Westinghouse and had promotion after promotion, and when he left them he was making from $500 to $750 per month. He was on a commission basis, so it varied between the two figures. Durban was a store they were ready to close because sales were practically nil, but in three months Wilfred had its sales up until it led all of their other seven stores. It seems his success came from his ability as a salesman and as an executive.

I feel that I owe it to Wilfred to let others know these things because he suffered every humiliation known for three years in Elizabethton.

---

[87] Because he became an instructor in the army, Wilfred only left for Egypt and Italty some thirty-four months later.

I am glad to hear that Aunt Lennie, Helen, and Kathryn are fine and that Helen has done so well in school. I hope Helen will write to me again; I am afraid my letter full of advice scared her off of me. Tell her I won't do it again.

The middle of this week my American friend is moving in with me. She is seeing her husband off on Tuesday, and she too has two little girls practically the same ages as Eve and Robin. In this way we hope to fight loneliness and also reduce our living expenses. We have taken a very nice new bungalow with three bedrooms. She has lived most of her life in China. She thinks it the only place in the world to live except for the Japanese trouble, which made them leave, as her husband was in shipping.

My love and all kind thoughts to each of you,
Affectionately,
Helen

519 Moore Road
Durban
July 30, 1940

Dearests,

I have received your letters offering me unlimited sums of money, a home, and just about everything, but I think it better to hold on here for the time being. I would give just anything to come home and spend this time with you two, but I don't think it is too safe sailing the seven seas just now, and Wilfred still has a chance to see us again, perhaps, and so we must do what we can to make him happy. After the war, one can't see just how things will be, but I don't want to make it too long before you see some of us, so I don't see why Eve can't come over to you for a year. I am willing to make this sacrifice, for I know what a sacrifice you all made when you gave her up to me. She is a loveable age now. For a while she was very fresh, but she is getting over that stage.

I do appreciate all you have offered. It meant a lot to me to know all of that was behind me if I needed it.

I am enclosing pictures of the family taken the day Wilfred left. I am so glad to have them. I am also enclosing odd bits that may be of interest to you.

Edith Broadbent has moved in, and we are getting ourselves straightened out pretty well. The children are enjoying each other so much, and it is a cheery household. It couldn't help but be, with four children. There are naturally complications, but everything has gone off as well as could be expected. Edith has told me so much about China that my aim is to visit China if the trouble ever clears up over there. The life is so easy, and who doesn't enjoy that?

My job is coming along all right. It isn't as boring as it was, as I have been given more to do. You know this is an English company, not American. Naturally, it differs in little ways from what I have known before, but it is not fundamentally different.

Wilfred has had the funniest experience. He has been moved to another camp and has been put in charge of filing and all correspondence for the officers. His last letter is to tell me that they couldn't find anybody in the office who could type, so he took a crack at it and is now the typist. He typed his letter to me and it was *perfect*. I am wondering how many times he did it to make it that way. Anyway, this is more interesting than lots of other things might have been, though of course he is fed up with the turn of events. I suppose you remember when he learned to type the touch system in Elizabethton. He has been most considerate and has only written me cheerful letters. It makes one feel much better.

Robin is talking quite a lot now. I am sure it is her association with little Helen Broadbent. The other day, Edith said that Helen hit Robin and Robin said, "I go tell my Mommie." She did come to me, but only did a lot of jabbering.

Since our move in together, I have had to sell my dining room table, as there was no room for it. Wilfred thought I would never get my money out of it, but I have sold it for just what I paid for it. So far, in all of my buying and selling, I haven't lost on a single thing, but for the most part have made. I would love to have a second-hand furniture store if I could get a little more experience in it. That is something that would really interest me, but Wilfred thinks I don't know enough about it and that the idea is a little crazy. I asked him if he would finance me back when I thought he would be able to. It is hardly very elevating socially, but I love the idea. Let's say Antique Shop instead of second-hand furniture.

The operation on my nose still hangs heavy—heavy over my head— and I realize I must have it done in the next week or two. The condition is getting worse. I shall let the municipality pay for it, under the present conditions. It will no doubt be done just as well. Edith, being a trained nurse, can look after me, so everything should be easy. Don't let it worry you for a minute.

I have had a letter from Aunt Nellie and Uncle Edwin, both of which I appreciated so much. I have answered Uncle Edwin's and shall write Aunt Nellie when I can give it some thought.

Love and kisses from us all,

Helen

519 Moore Road
Durban
August 22, 1940

Darlings,

I have had more and more letters from you both; that is, the letters from the Shipping Companies to Dad. I am sorry you have gone to so much trouble about getting information because, of course, living in a rather large Port there are stacks and stacks of Shipper's representatives here, and we can get all kinds of information. We also had the help of the American Consul. It is quite true that one cannot get accommodation via South America until 1941. The only accommodations to be had, and those are few, are via Australia, and of course that is even more expensive than the other trip. I believe we have done the best thing in not spending all of that money at this time. Wilfred must have a start again after the war, and it takes money for that. The only thing is I can't help but think what a good time to be with you two. It is hard, though, to think that Wilfred might be wounded and sent back to Durban and have no one here. There are so many things to consider.

Have I told you my income, so you will not worry about our finances? I get £20 per month from the Government, and £15 per month salary, so we can live nicely. However, the Government pay has not come through yet. I should have had a cheque the end of July, but there must be some mix up. Anyway, I have had enough to go on while those matters are being straightened out.

I have so little time between the office, the babies, and social obligations. I don't know what has happened, but I have more to do than ever, socially. Last Saturday night, Dr. van Rippen, a friend of Wilfred's, had me for dinner and a show, and on Sunday night he took me to play bridge with friends of his. Perhaps you don't approve of Sunday Bridge, but I wanted to meet these people, as he is head of Lever Brothers, big soap manufacturers. Such contacts can't be ignored. I have invited them to come to me for bridge this week.

I have two beaux, one sixteen and one sixty. Dr. van Rippen is the one sixty. The one sixteen is rather a tax, but I couldn't hurt his feelings. I must tell you that Dr. van Rippen asked me to wear a Mink coat, or rather cape, and muff on Saturday night. It is too gorgeous for words, and did people look. I don't know whether I liked their looks or not, if you know what I mean. He inherited all of the personal effects of a very wealthy Boston woman when he was at Harvard, and this cape and muff were among them. He had not had it out for twenty-five years until a few weeks ago, but it is in perfect condition and right in style. He wanted it to have an airing, I think, so I accommodated.

On Monday night, Edith Broadbent and I were invited out for bridge, and tonight the two of us are invited for dinner and bridge with Mr. and Mrs. Corrigan, the American Consul here. I am afraid Edith is not going to get the job at the Consulate because she doesn't know typing and shorthand well enough. I think I could have had it had I applied; in fact, I am quite sure of it, but I have already started now with Dunlops, and it doesn't mean more money. I know it would be infinitely more interesting, however. For that reason I would love it. Saturday night, Edith and I are invited to a cocktail party at the Corrigans, given in honour of the Vice-Consul and his wife, who have just arrived. I wish you could be here to share all the activity. You could have bridge every afternoon with the American crowd here.

One of the girls at the office is dressing my hair for all of these occasions, and she is better than any hairdresser I have ever been to. It looks simply stunning.

Must get to work now. Am enclosing a few things that may interest you. Will try to write a long letter soon.

Love and kisses from the little ones and me,

Helen

P.S. Eve knows *The Lord's Prayer* now and can say it without any help. She says it every night and finishes up with a "God bless Mama Sophia and Papa Harlow," etc. She also says the first part of "Now I lay me."

519 Moore Road
Durban
September 2, 1940

My dearest Ones,

I have had so many letters from you, also a *Reader's Digest*. I am afraid I can't keep up the pace at this end, but I shall be very happy if you keep it up. Mother's letter of July 24th was censored and blanked out for five lines. The last sentence before blanking read, "And you must think of the worst possible outcome of the war." Of course, I am dying to know what the rest said, but don't suppose I ever shall. You are right to say it would be hard for Wilfred to get the papers to leave the country now; it would be impossible, in fact. No man of military age can leave. We are all in for it and must just see what we can do. I think we are perfectly safe here in Durban, so you need not worry about that.

We had a big set-to with our two native girls, and now we are without any help. We simply refuse to take just anybody; we have had droves of girls at the door for the past two days, but this time we are picking and choosing. We were definitely dissatisfied with the girls, and I had a girl sent to the house on Friday night to see me about work. When our two saw her, they gave notice while we were at the dinner table and said they were leaving the next day, that being the last day of the month. I said very well. The next day I called them to come in and work, as they still owed us another day, but they refused, so I called the police. I told them I would make them work, and they sure did work when they saw the police roll up; it scared them to death. If you could have seen their leave-taking at nine o'clock that night, you would have thought we are in the wilds of Africa—the procession down our drive way was this: Two rickshaws loaded with boxes and bedding, even one bed, pulled by two rickshaw boys fully bedecked with feathers and fur around their legs, etc.; following were our two girls and one other with huge loads on their heads. It looked like a safari through the jungle.

Yesterday being Sunday, Edith and I cleaned up after the two brutes. We nearly killed ourselves, in fact. We cleaned and washed out the stove, we defrosted and washed out the refrigerator, we changed the linen on the beds, and thoroughly cleaned two bedrooms, even to beating the rugs. Edith has carried on the mad pace today, Monday, and now we have a really clean house. We simply can't bear the idea of just anyone, and it is so hard to get good help. I shall be happy when I am independent of them. Edith is going to school, and is just staying away until we are settled again. It is very lucky for me, as I have been able to continue at the office.

You must not worry about the children too much. Eve is at school all the morning, and Edith is home in the afternoons. Robin sleeps from 10:30 to 12:30 in the mornings, so there are only about two hours that we haven't an eye on them. Still, I do wish you could have them under your wing. Eve and Susan and two of their little friends decided to help too this afternoon, and they cleaned up the yard and did a marvelous job of it. Robin got the fever of helping too, and this was her offering: I left her in the lavatory on her little potty, and she came running in to me in the kitchen and pulled me into the lavatory and pointed to the commode and said, "See, empty." She had emptied her potty in the commode, and it had contained two things in it. This was really carrying helpfulness to a dangerous point.

Wilfred is over his terrible sinus, which he has had for weeks, and seemed in very good spirits in his last letter. He wired me on our wedding anniversary on the 26th of August [Helen and Wilfred's seventh anniversary], and I got a letter there from him on that day. We seem destined to be separated on our anniversary. I don't know how many times it has happened.

You mention trying to buy shoes for the children. I doubt if that is a good idea, as I have a hard time fitting Eve; however, I shall draw their feet on paper and send it to you. One never sees shoe bargains over here. If any money should come our way at Christmas time, don't send it to us this time but keep it there, and I can write you as we need things. I prefer dresses for the children, and socks. The socks over here are cute like they are at home. If the tags on the dresses you sent were correct, the dresses are much cheaper over there. In fact, we don't see anything as attractive as the two dresses you sent them. Everybody spots them for American dresses. Eve still loves clothes as much as ever, and nothing pleases her more. She must have her brown shoes polished every single day for school, her ribbons pressed, etc. I am glad to see her neat; it will mean a lot to her as a woman. Sometimes it wears off, however, as with me. Still, I have become neat again; keeping house myself did it for me.

If you like to send your copy of *Reader's Digest* on to us, you can after you have absolutely finished with it. If you want to keep them, however, I can buy it here, as it has gone down in price since it is printed in England. I have been getting copies all along, as the London office was waiting to see if the subscription had been renewed. I am sending them five shillings for the copies they have sent.

I can't get over the seemingly good marriage J.B. seems to have made. The man must be a little crazy. She isn't even pretty, as well as all the rest that is wrong.

I have had to have three teeth filled within the last two weeks, and there are still two more fillings. Three of the lot are old fillings finally going bad. Some of them have been with me for about fifteen years, though, so I can't complain. I have an American dentist, and he is charging me half his usual fees, so it won't be too bad. He is from Michigan.

Of all the Americans I have met out here, I have only met one person who knows anyone I know, and that is Mr. Hodgson, manager of Coca Cola in Durban. He is from Atlanta, so I asked him if he knew the Sala family. He said, "Do you mean O. J. Sala? He was my best friend." I said I was a friend of Marguerite and O. J. was her brother. He said O. J. was killed in an automobile accident, and that he was one of the most popular boys in Atlanta. I then asked about Weldon. You know, Weldon was the eldest and good-looking. He then told me that Weldon died several years ago. That is enough tragedy for one family, isn't it? Mr. and Mrs. Sala were so wrapped up in their family too. You know that Marguerite has been divorced and married again.

I forgot to mention that the reason I had a girl come to see me about work was because one of our girls had said to me that one day a native was going to knock Edith down. I didn't tell Edith this but just tried to get another girl. When the two gave notice, Edith blamed me, so I told her why I had done it. I have never seen anybody so frightened in my life. She shook and shook. Her mother-in-law has told her so many terrible tales of what natives have done that she was scared to death. I simply couldn't persuade her that it was an idle threat. She is a bit high-strung and hadn't the control over herself that a person should have at her age. For instance, after the whole thing was over, she started on me last night and said sugar wouldn't melt in my mouth when I talked to Alice, the one I had brought with me. She was just annoyed that I could get along with them and she couldn't. I think she will have to improve in her manner if we are ever to have a smooth-running household. I haven't fussed with her yet, but I have told her several times that she has said enough, and I don't want to hear anymore. I suppose that is more annoying than to have a good fuss, but I can't bear a fuss—it never gets either one any place. Edith is surely doing more than her share just now, however, and I do appreciate it.

I must close now, as my eyes are simply going out. By the way, I am rather enjoying my work in the filing department. They are pushing the responsibility on me as fast as they can, and I heard I was going to be made head of it. They surely needed a good person in that department. I have never seen anything like it.

Thanks for the information about finishing floors, contained in Dad's letter. I want as much on that as you can get.

Lots of love and kisses,

Helen, Eve and Robin

519 Moore Road
Durban
September 19, 1940

Dearests,

This will be very short and sweet, but since your last letter suggested post cards, I suppose you won't mind if I can't write much.

Your parcel arrived yesterday, and we were all so delighted. My shoes are very pretty indeed, but evidently the Customs did not believe they cost only $4.00, as they charged me $2.00 duty on the parcel. Eve's dress is simply lovely and fits her perfectly. I remember the dress it is made from. It is just the type of dress I was wanting for Eve, something for town and Sunday school. I am buying her black patent leather slippers tomorrow and new socks to wear with it. Funny, I had promised her a new dress and thought I would have to get busy making it. She has been so sick for a week and still looks bad, and I thought the idea of some new clothes would cheer her up, and it did. The little dress of Ann's is still too large for Robin, and also the boots, but they will be nice for her next winter. I will write Mrs. Alexander. It is so nice of her to pass things on to Robin. I don't know that the red will be too good on Robin, as she is so blonde. She is looking simply beautiful just now, as her hair is curling something like Eve's did for a while. She is also saying surprising things now, her favourite being "I'll kill you," but she does nothing about this but lets Helen Broadbent bang on her all the time.

I haven't heard the final outcome, but Wilfred appeared before his Colonel on Tuesday in regard to a commission as Second Lieutenant. He was recommended for a commission by his C.O. (Commanding Officer) and was notified to appear before his Colonel on Tuesday. I hope all goes well because he will have better quarters and food, and his associates will be of his kind. I shall be very proud of him if he gets this because he has no pull, and it will be purely on merit and hard work. I was very proud that he went in as a sergeant because he got that without any pull, and that is none too easy to get. We have known our ups and downs, but I'll never be afraid of our not getting along as long as Wilfred is at the helm. Since he has been in business and knows what it is all about, he has shown more push than any young man I have ever known. You can see that he has seen that I was well taken care of financially before leaving me this time. We have plenty to live on and shall have more if he gets this Commission.

I am afraid the Broadbents are a bit jealous, as he is still a private and he joined up before Wilfred did, though he was here in Durban for a part of that time. They have a private income, and I have thought how things are evened up, because he remains a private and she is taking a job at £10 per month, whereas I get £15. Maybe the difference is that Wilfred and I know we have to make our own way, and somehow I prefer it.

Thanks ever so much for making Eve the dress. Whenever you feel like converting other dresses into something for the children, they can always be used.

I went dancing last night and had a great time. Charles Broadbent is home on leave, and he and Edith, Bené van Rippen, Mr. and Mrs. Banns, and I went. Bené is an old friend of the Evans family and is furthermore a beautiful dancer. Bené is a Hollander and about Father's age. He swims, plays tennis very well, dances, and thoroughly enjoys life.

Love and kisses,
Helen

519 Moore Road
Durban
October 2, 1940

My dearest Mother and Dad,

I know I am thirty-four today, but, like Mama Hunter, I must mention that it was thirty-five years ago today that I arrived in Elizabethton and started on the adventure of life, a life which has been rather adventuresome at that. I must thank you two for giving me my start, and please don't ever think of my life as a sad one because I do not consider it so, as I still get a big kick out of everything, and whatever happens is just a broadening experience. I should have hated to have been a Miss B. of Chilhowee. Isn't it funny, but I always think of her when something else comes my way, and just thank Providence that my life hasn't been as empty as I think hers has been. If there has been more to Miss B.'s life than I know about, I should like to hear it. Anyway, a kiss for Mother and Dad on my birthday.

I was alarmed at the flood news. To think how quickly it came and the widespread damage done. I remember the lake on Morman's estate. I had a picnic there with Jack Bitter and Millicent and Richard H. and others one Sunday. I am anxious to hear more about the Power Plant. Were you without electricity, and was it completely washed away? I am so thankful that your damage was no more than you reported. I know it was hard to part with some of the things that were stored in the basement, but others have lost everything. Will they sue Morman? Or just what will happen? I read the two newspapers last night and felt like I was back home. My old friend Roy Hathaway looked like he was on his last pegs in the picture. I certainly had a good laugh over Father being out saving a dog while you had to be rescued. The little story was so typical of the two of you that I shall always cherish it.

Wilfred has just come out of hospital from having German measles. He was in Johannesburg in the big hospital and had excellent attention; however, having measles at that time made him miss his appointment as an officer—2nd Lieutenant. He was to appear before his Colonel on a Tuesday and instead was taken to hospital that day. All vacancies were filled on that day, and now he must wait until other vacancies occur, and those come rarely.

He is very disappointed, and so am I for his sake. It naturally meant more money for us too. Every time Wilfred has an opportunity, he becomes sick. It always happened to him in Nashville, but that did not keep him from getting the promotions there. He knew he had measles long before he gave up, but he was trying to keep quiet about it so he could appear before the Colonel and infect him, I suppose. He is perfectly all right now.

I shall only write on one side of the paper now in case they object to something I say. I know the paragraph they cut out and what a long time I spent writing it. It was merely giving you some idea of our long-range view of the war, which is most interesting and exciting at times.

I have on my new black shoes today for the first time, and they are wonderfully comfortable. Thank you so much for giving me the two pairs of shoes for my birthday, but I really can't accept so much for a birthday present. Let's call it Christmas too. This morning Eve presented me with an ex-candy box with bits of paper cut up in it for my birthday. Susan gave me two of her old pocket books, which she said were to keep Robin happy all day long. I think she thought that would be the biggest help to me. However, our Robin is about the happiest baby I have ever known. She is beautiful now, as her hair curls and it continues to be so beautifully blonde.

I am going to tell you what your Christmas present will be. I am having a photo taken of Robin, Eve, and myself as soon as we are all at our best. Just now Eve isn't looking so well. This will also be Wilfred's and Bert's Christmas from us. I am telling you now, as I don't know whether it will get there by Christmas or not. It is also very hard for me to get into town with the children at the right hour. I work out of town and live two miles from the center of town. I shall accomplish it, however.

I must stop now, as it is time for work again.

Lots and lots of love,

Helen

P.S. I was so sorry to hear about Aunt Nellie's trouble. I hope she will look after her health and do whatever is necessary about it. Give her my love. I do wish I could see Kay.

519 Moore Road
Durban
October 10, 1940

Dearests,

    I am just back from seeing Wilfred in Johannesburg. We had a long weekend over the 6th, so I drove up to Johannesburg with some people, and Wilfred met me there. We had Bert's lovely flat, as she was going out of town for the weekend, and we had a marvelous time just together. We were there for the Coster Fete held in one of the lovely parks and enjoyed it very much on Saturday afternoon, as Bert was taking part in it. They raised over £7,000 for War Funds.

    Johannesburg was such a buzz that we couldn't get seats in any of the picture shows for Saturday night. I had to travel from five o'clock Monday afternoon until one o'clock Tuesday morning coming back. I felt very rested, however, as, being a good Dixon, I slept most of the way both going and coming. They all thought it terribly funny, but I am sure they envied me my ability to sleep sitting up. Wilfred is well over measles and has gained about seven pounds since I last saw him.

    Eve and Robin were well looked after by Edith. That is the great advantage of living together, as we can get away now and then and know the other one will look after the children. She said Robin was perfect, didn't cry once while I was away. She really saves her tears for me, it seems. Edith said Bené asked Robin where her fascinating Mommie was and that Robin would pucker up her face and, with a wide sweep of her arm, say, "Mommie gone away."

    Mother, I wish you would try going to a chiropractor, as I have heard of such wonderful cures that they have been able to perform on women your age. You know that you have a slight curvature of the spine, and there is no telling how much trouble this is giving you. The doctors see nothing they can do for you, but I am sure your health could be improved, and I wish you would try this for my sake. I think I shall take Eve to one, as she just does not look well, and yet there is nothing wrong so far as one can see. I have never seen her look so bad, and, even though she eats well, she doesn't gain an ounce. If she looked well, she would be very pretty.

    Edith and I went to see *Pride and Prejudice* last night, the second show we have been to in over two months that we have paid for ourselves. They cost so much that they are a real luxury—75 cents each last night. We enjoyed it thoroughly. I suppose you have already seen it for nothing.

I am feeling better since my trip but was very low in spirits for a good two weeks before it about my health. I don't eat cheese, potatoes, nor bananas any more and that seems to make a difference. I also find curry bad for me.

Eve wore her new dress that you sent her to the birthday party of a little Canadian friend yesterday. Eve and Susan enjoyed themselves thoroughly but took a present together, which caused considerable dissention as to who should carry it. According to their report, there were hundreds of boys and girls there. We are very friendly with the parents, as we play bridge with them a lot.

There are things I would like to write about, as I know you would be interested, but I think it best to limit myself to family matters.

Lots of love from the babes and Helen

519 Moore Road
Durban
October 17, 1940

Dearests,

I was so glad to have your letter of August 24th saying you had my letter written from my permanent address. I know it was a relief to you to know I was settled.

You ask if I have a raincoat and galoshes. No, I haven't, but they are quite unnecessary since I am delivered to work and fetched by Edith, or drive her car myself. My standby in the way of a coat is still the spring coat I bought in my last spring in Elizabethton. It has been relined and looks alright.

Bert is doing so much war work that she has given up knitting for Wilfred, but I have joined the American Knitting Circle here, to which I pay $1.25 per month, and they will furnish what he needs. They have already sent him a pullover and a pair of socks.

Are Carrs putting a disappearing staircase to the attic? From what you say, they must be. Are they also flooring part of it?

How many do you have in your home now?

Bert bought Robin a dress and socks for her birthday when she was down in Durban and thought we were sailing for America. Wilfred sent her a dress and panties for her birthday.

You can rest assured that we are *all* well fed. My income is $75 per month, so you can know we do not want for anything. Food has advanced in price, but it would have to go much higher before we would stop eating well. We have recently been paying 8c per pound for potatoes as well as onions. Other things are up a little in price. This answers your question about food.

As for clothes, I am better off than at any time since coming to South Africa, as I bought things while Wilfred was making such good money.

When I was in Johannesburg during the cold weather with Wilfred, I bought four new dresses, for which I am certainly thankful, two summer sport dresses, a woolen suit, and a white evening dress. The children both got new shoes last month as well as three pairs of new socks each, and they have plenty of dresses with what you have sent. We are able to live as well as most since we have combined our households. It isn't run as economically as it should be, but that is difficult with so little supervision over the servant.

Have I written you that Wilfred has been transferred to another camp where some of his old friends are? It is a very big camp.

We are getting *Time* more or less regularly as well as your copies of *Reader's Digest*.

Yesterday morning at eight o'clock, Eve had four of her big back teeth out with gas, as they were badly decayed. Dr. van Rippen did it for her, and it went off very well. I kept her in yesterday and today, as the weather turned suddenly cold. The day before was scorching hot. I have never seen such changeable weather. Eve has most of her permanent front teeth, and they are huge, like mine.

This past Saturday night I went for dinner and dance at the Marine Hotel with Dr. van Rippen. It was right much fun. I wore foolish blue velvet bows in my hair. They were really Eve's but looked sweet with my blue evening dress, a Viennese frock. Last night we had the Ken Millers for bridge. They are Canadians, and I like them so much. Eve and Susan were to their daughter's birthday party a week or so ago.

I must stop now and have an early night.

I hope you are both well and that you will try to be happy.

Lots of love to all,

Helen

519 Moore Road
Durban, Natal
South Africa
October 23, 1940

My dearest Mary,

Do you have any idea how elated I was when your letter was handed to me? I think it has been a year and a half since I have heard from you except through Mother. I only wish your letter had given me the impression that you are happy, but then happiness seems to be a very fleeting thing. Anyway, you are taking things in a wonderful way, and you have every reason to expect much happiness in the years to come from such a son as Joe. I am more impressed with Joe than any boy I have ever known, and I know how much he is what you have put into his

A Vale of Soul-Making (May 1940—Feb. 1943)

formative years. Please give him this Auntie's love if that is done when a boy is in his teens. I find it hard to imagine him grown.

As you have heard from Mother, I have just readjusted my life. There were many things that tugged hard at the heartstrings, but now I find myself comparatively happy. Mary, I must be happy. I had too much at one time in the past to bear, and I let it make me thoroughly miserable, and it broke my spirit so completely that I have been nursing that spirit back to health for three years in Africa, and only in Africa, or some other place ten thousand miles away from Elizabethton, could I have succeeded in my struggle to be a normal soul again, instead of a cringing, frightened pup. I am the Helen you knew at sixteen and just as giggly at times too. I pray that I have too much sense to ever let circumstances get me again.

Today I had news that made me realize that it will be a very short time now until Wilfred goes up North; and the realization made me dreadfully weak in my knees for a while, but I am not going to dwell on that but on the fact that he gets five days embarkation leave and we are going to a lovely hotel in the Drakensberg Mountains, a beautiful spot I am told, and there we are going to have a few perfect days together. We have planned quite a few holidays together, but none of them have ever come off, so we are at last going away together and cram all those holidays into this one.

Edith, my housemate, is out for dinner and bridge tonight with some other Americans. I excused myself, as we were out last night and are going out for dinner and a show tomorrow night, and I simply was not going to wait any longer for a chat with you. The house is wonderfully quiet with all the four bratlets asleep, the two-year-olds in their room, the six-year-olds in theirs. At this point my peace was rudely broken by warlike screams from Edith's younger. She is the hardest to control of all, so, after a careful inspection to see that there is really nothing wrong, Auntie is allowing her to cry it out.

Last night Edith and I were invited for dinner and bridge with two other American women whose husbands are out of town. We had the most heavenly chicken I have ever eaten because Sylvia is a marvelous cook. It was cut up like we do for frying, then grilled in the oven and a sauce of Worcestershire Sauce, Tabasco, vinegar, salt and pepper basted over it while it was cooking. It was the best chicken I have ever eaten.

Of course, I didn't get to enjoy my meal on the whole, as Edith seems to have spent her life with different people who were diet faddists, and, it seems to me, she is trying to use the whole lot of them on me at one time in an attempt to cure my asthma and hay fever. Every time something was passed to me at the table, she, sitting directly across the table from me, would smile sweetly and lift her hand— you know, just like the cop does when he gives you the stop signal. Of course, it was rather hard on our hostess, and it was damned hard on me. However, living with me would give anybody a Sister of Mercy complex, as the state of my health remains precarious. I need to go back to Johannesburg to the altitude and dryness, but I hate to leave Durban and its beauty. It is the most beautiful place I have ever lived, and to think of leaving it is very painful.

I was so glad you mentioned La. in your letter because I think of her as one of the sweetest and bravest girls I have ever known. She'll always keep all her flags flying. My, how I would love to see the two of you. I wish she would go to Richmond, Va., to that very well-known doctor to really find out how much trouble she has. It is terrible to live with fear gnawing at the back of your mind all the time. Will you write to her and try to persuade her to do this? I hardly know why she sticks to K. if she only sees him drunk. Why will men ruin their chances and their family's chance of happiness by drinking?

I loved the little story about Ruth. I am afraid I hadn't realized her "old coat" was Mink. I am trying to become more feminine under the tutelage of Edith and appreciate the difference between owning a Skunk and a Mink. Really, I don't think I have given such things enough thought, and that is one reason I took to the idea of living with another woman. Oh, I titivate considerably before the mirror these days, and I talk clothes; but somehow my mind wanders most unpardonably to other topics.

Helen (far right) with co-workers at Dunlop's

Incidentally, I am getting a few other lessons, one being how to live with a high-tempered woman. I have been having the first rows I have had in years; at first, I didn't know quite how to conduct one (my method being to keep my mouth shut), but now you should see me in action—I'm hot. She's much quieter. I think this rubbing does me good; I'm a bit afraid to go on my own, for I am terribly inclined to draw into myself, and I don't want to do that.

I have never felt I was better liked than I am at Dunlops with all the girls in the office. They are all South African and English and are a fine group. On my birthday they sent me beautiful flowers. Many of them have their families living in London or along the coast, but they seldom refer to the fact and take it all in the marvelously cool English fashion. For Hitler to claim that he has demoralized the English is for him to claim that he does not know the English, because it would be humanly impossible to demoralize a race of people who take things in the good old even way they do.

I must stop for this time, as I must have a good night's sleep as tomorrow night we are invited to Bené's for duck and a very good show afterwards. Bené is an old friend of Wilfred's, and he has been a perfect dear to both Edith and myself. He is the bachelor of the town and has his apartment full of the loveliest antiques, which he inherited from a very wealthy woman in Boston when he was a student at Harvard. He is a beautiful dancer, and likes dancing with me, so he takes me out for dinner and dancing quite often. Edith is too tall for him to feel comfortable with her on the dance floor. We have him for Southern dinners now and then, and a game of bridge. Bené has a mink cape and muff, inherited from the same woman, which I sometimes wear when we go out. He says it needs an airing now and then, and I certainly don't mind obliging. It is a long evening cape and a beautiful thing.

I am having pictures made of the babies and myself for Mother's birthday. Please give Knaffl my love and tell him I want him to make you happy, for he just doesn't know what he has in you. I am deeply sorry that he is so discouraged in the business way. We must look forward to making another start after the war, and nothing could be much more discouraging than that.

I simply haven't been able to touch on half I want to, but I shall try to read the books you mentioned very soon. Reading all day doing filing makes it a bit difficult for me to use my eyes at night. I wasn't able to get stenographic work to do, you know. Anyway, I got a job in a week after I set out to find one, making what I did when I first started to work. You should be able to head your department when the chance comes again. Give it a bang, anyway.

Helen sends you worlds of love,

Helen

519 Moore Road
Durban
October 27, 1940

Dearest Mother and Dad,

I hope you will like the enclosed snap, as it was made for you. I knew you would like a picture of Edith and that you would like to know what Bené looks like. We are just ready to have the proverbial cup of tea, accompanied by cream scones this time. Edith's picture certainly does not do her justice. My dress is a very well-tailored white serge, made in China. You would get a thrill to look in my wardrobe and see "Made in France," "Made in Vienna," etc., just like we used to get clothes from all over the world.

I hope Father is really happy in his new position, but I am afraid he rather loved his constant contact with people at that other place. Is the Holston Tire Co. one of the family's places? I know the Holston Oil Co. and "Lodge." Will you be

Edith, Bené, and Helen anticipating morning tea on Durban beach

more explicit? I am sure the salary can't be as good as the commissions Dad was getting, but the new contract certainly left him with very little, considering the long hours involved. I wish Dad got Saturday afternoons off too; one needs them. Sunday isn't enough.

Nobody works in Durban on Saturday afternoons. They have such sensible hours in this country, and everybody goes in for sports. I am handicapped because I can't play tennis. There is no time for it now, especially since I must learn. Edith plays on Saturday afternoons, and Bené asks her for Sunday afternoons at the Country Club, but she can seldom go, as both of the girls go off on Sunday afternoons.

I was shocked to see a debit on the house. I trust you will refuse to spend any more until this is caught up. The amount spent during the portion of the year you have [records] for is $73.04. The insurance companies only spend one month's rent on repairs, and I consider that a good thing to hold yourself to. If the B.s want to move, I can pay the rent myself for a few months and would be pleased to do it to be rid of them, so tighten up a bit with this in mind.

You had might as well dismiss the idea of Wilfred's father ever giving us a trip to America. He gave me £200 ($1000), when I thought I would come home, but he was so miserable and afraid he wouldn't get it back that I sent it back to him. Wilfred could have paid him the first £100 almost immediately and the second hundred as soon as the furniture was sold.

The reason I gave you the impression that it would be a long time before I see you was that it definitely looked that way to me, as Wilfred wants me here during the war, and none of us can bluff ourselves about the economic condition of the world after the war. There is one bright spot, though: Wilfred told me when I saw him in Johannesburg that he wants to go back to America after the war and get a teaching post in one of the boys' military academies. He has always wanted to teach. He realizes the pay is small compared to what he could make in business, but he feels the work would be satisfying.

Robin and Eve are both so well just now. I always feel a new person myself when I see them looking rosy. Robin is most embarrassing about calling Charles Broadbent and Bené "Daddy," but this afternoon she capped the whole thing. I took Eve and Robin for a walk, and we passed two young men about twenty-one years. Robin said, pointing, "There's Daddy. There's my Daddy." This was in a very loud voice. She is talking a great deal now.

Edith's last letter from her mother and father in China was written after they had just spent five hours in their dugout because of air raids. I believe four streets of the town were completely destroyed. She hopes they will be forced to leave China by the U.S. Government.

I am still filing but am training another girl in my work, so I may get some stenographic work when the department is on its feet. Just now we are changing the system.

Must close and write to Wilfred and Bert. Bert may come down and spend a week with us.

I am returning the socks, as Robin wears a 6½. She is a three-year size in everything. They are lovely socks, and I would love the same in the size larger. Eve wears an 8½. They have big feet, I'm afraid. By the way, I am a size 16. I had on an American dress in a size 14 in those pictures. It is a bit tight and perhaps made me look large. I really don't want you to sew for us, though, for I know your eyes are not strong, and you should enjoy reading when you have the time. We are all terribly well off for clothes just now. Eve must wear the striped cotton dress you sent her when she isn't in her school uniform; she is so crazy about it. She simply will not wear her other dresses on Saturdays.

Goodnight and sweet dreams.

All our love goes to you,

Helen

519 Moore Road
Durban
November 10, 1940

My dearest Mother and Dad,

I have had Wilfred at home with me for the past week; he just left this afternoon. Also, I have had a letter from you both this week, so it has been a happy time for me. Dad's letter of October 3 arrived one day before Mother's letter of September 20. You can see from that that you can't expect a letter from me regularly each week even though I may write each week. By the way, I have never received *Life* or *Time* from you, but I have received *Reader's Digest*. We still get *Time* on our subscription.

Wilfred came home full of news, as he has just been on an officer's training course for three weeks. One hundred and forty-five were selected to take the course, and twenty-four of them finished it. Day by day they were eliminated for different reasons—physical, mental, and what have you. Each morning when they sat down for lectures so many were handed train tickets back to their different camps. You will be glad to know that Wilfred was one of the twenty-four who took the final examination and that, of the twenty-four, Wilfred and one other man, a mining engineer, finished with Distinguished Marks.

Wilfred says it is the hardest he ever worked, including his university days. They had fifteen Military subjects, and Wilfred had had none of them. Some of the men on the course had been studying at the officers' training school for months. Wilfred's great advantage was that he is a university man and knows how to study, and that he knows map-reading, surveying, and is well grounded in trigonometry. They have not promised those who passed commissions, but I feel sure he will get one, though you can never tell about the army. He will have further training, of course, when he gets his commission of 2nd Lieutenant. It will mean so much to him in comfort and pride, and it will also mean more money to me. Wilfred said his hours were from five in the morning until twelve at night during those three weeks. He lost nine pounds in weight, but he looked very fit when he arrived home and is feeling awfully well. He just ate and slept for a week, and we all had a most happy time.

Last night we danced at Caister House in a party of ten. Their dances are dinner dances, and the setting is beautiful. The view at night from the balconies leading off the dance floor is unexcelled. One looked past the dark outline of palm trees on a horseshoe of twinkling lights far below, and overhead a deep blue sky. The women were beautifully dressed, and the men were picturesque, some being in naval uniforms, some army, and, most unusual of all, the Scottish Army dress uniform consisting of tight-fitting long trousers made of a Scots plaid. Wilfred wore dinner clothes. In our party were Mr. and Mrs. Ken Miller (Canadians), Mr. and Mrs. McCarthy (Americans), Edith and Pat Goodrin, Bené and Mrs. Murray Little, and us.

I must brag a little and tell you that I was told several times by Wilfred and Bené that I was the best-looking woman there, my dress and all considered. My dress was white, very full, made with halter neck—the only trimming being a very pretty rhinestone clip at the V of the neck. Eve told me I was an angel and wanted to see my wings, being quite serious about it. My white fur coat with the white

Mandarin lining looked beautiful with it, of course. Of course, it is quite flattering for a husband of seven years standing to think you are the loveliest creature he has ever seen, even if it is only for one evening. This morning we had a bracing swim. It was very rough, and I had to picture Mother in such a sea.

I really had a strange experience the other night. We were at the Country Club for Sundowners, and it was getting much after sun down, so I telephoned the girl about holding dinner. I found that Eve and Susan were not behaving, so I told the girl to call Eve to the phone. It was the first time I had ever heard Eve's voice over the telephone, and it was just like talking to Mother. Wilfred has often said Eve's voice was like yours, but I had never heard it until our telephone conversation.

I was very sorry to hear about Aunt Jennie Johnson's death. I think they will have a hard time filling her place in the Sunday school. Who will take her class?

I understand now what the Holston Tire Co. is ("Tyre" to me now). What is Dad's work? Books or what? I will let you know what a 6.00 x 16 would cost over here as soon as I inquire. I don't see so much about the retail prices, or at least I don't remember it because we make so many different sizes, and I am still learning.

The head of the Filing Dept left last Saturday a week ago, for eighteen days, and I was put in charge—my helpers being one girl in the dept. for two years and one in the dept. a month. The one with experience walked out on us the second day, taking a job for the Defense. The new girl and I were left to battle, and what a battle we put up. She was marvelous and worked like a dog. On top of everything, an English mail came in, the first in three weeks. For five days, I think, all requests came in threes, and these lasted the day through. Never did just one person ask for a paper, but three different people wanting three different papers immediately. We kept the papers in order but, of course, got far behind with filing. Miss Mayger was very pleased with the way I handled it.

Robin got into the pantry today and, when she was found, four empty banana skins were also found. She is still all right. I wasn't told until tonight. She is the picture of health, all right, and eats as much as a grown up.

Eve and Robin use the broad A naturally. I use it sometimes and so does Edith. One just naturally does after a time. I am taken always for an American, though, not as a Southerner but as a New Englander. Americans are always surprised to hear I come from the South.

Edith and I are invited out tomorrow night by a very nice officer Wilfred introduced us to, and Wednesday night we are invited to the Corrigans for a buffet dinner. I imagine we'll play bridge afterwards.

I have just been told that this will catch the last mail to America in time for Christmas. I hope yours will be a happy one with the family in Johnson City and Kingsport. We can't have it together, but we can be happy in the thought during that day that we are thinking of each other and are accepting what happiness comes our way during the day. It never seems like Christmas here. We shall perhaps spend part of the day on the beach bathing. I shall endeavor to get the photographs from the photographer today and get them off on this mail. Wilfred saw them and was disappointed. They could have been better, but I had to rush so getting down to have them made and did not have enough time to fix the family up; also, I did not feel I could afford to go to one of the best photographers. I think you will enjoy them even if they aren't perfect.

I shall try to explain the English money, as Father seems interested. It was a great puzzle to me for some time. The coins are:

>   Penny—1d = about two cents
>
>   Threepence—3d = about five cents. Pronounced "thruppence."
>
>   (Also called "ticky" in South Africa but not in England.)
>
>   Sixpence—6d (I am showing you how it is written when not spelled out.)
>
>   Shilling—1/- = 25 cents
>
>   Two Shillings—2/-
>
>   Two Shillings and Sixpence—2/6

These are the only coins; after that comes a Ten Shilling note. Next comes the Pound Note—£1.

The confusing thing to me was that up to a shilling you must think in the terms of the clock, that is twelve, for twelve pennies make a shilling, four threepences make a shilling, as do two sixpences. Then, after a shilling, you must think in tens as we do with U.S. money, as there are twenty shillings to a pound. It is very difficult money to add up because of this.

>   £2.7.8
>   Plus   £1.8.9
>   £3.16.5

Now, think: 8 plus 9 gives 17 pennies, so you take 12 pennies (i.e., one shilling) away from 17, which leaves you 5, or fivepence. If I'd had more than 20 shillings in the shilling column, I would have had to deduct the 20 shillings, or one pound, from that column, carrying it over to the pounds.

I hope this makes it halfway clear. If it doesn't, please write and ask any questions. I was always terribly interested in English money too. I never think in U.S. currency now unless it is a large amount.

This is so scrappy because I had to stop using the typewriter last night so Edith could sleep. Then I have just finished at the office today during my lunch hour.

Must stop now and get to work.

Lots and lots of love from us all,

Helen

P.S. Wilfred is always interested in your letters.

519 Moore Road
Durban
November 24, 1940

My dearest Ones,

It is Sunday afternoon and I am acting as a rather glorified nursemaid to Robin and Helen; Eve and Susan are asleep, as well as Edith. The natives over here insist on having Sunday afternoons. They always give the excuse of church, but I am very doubtful that that is the destination of all of them.

While I think about it, so very many of your letters to me are sent to Durham, N.C., first. I wonder if it would help to have a word with Grace Shell about this. I notice you write Durban perfectly distinctly, so there is nothing you can do in addressing the letters to make it any clearer.

You will be surprised to hear I have had Wilfred at home for another week. He left yesterday by train for Johannesburg to see Bert today and on to Pretoria tonight. Well, this is a lot of preliminary to the news I really want to give you. Wilfred has his commission as a 2nd Lieutenant, and he got the week off to get his uniforms, shoes, shirts, etc. He certainly looks good in his well-fitting clothes, and he is so happy over having his commission. Of course, it makes a big difference in his life in the army.

To add to the thrill of becoming an officer, he has been selected to lecture the officer's training school on military surveying. Wilfred has always wanted to teach, and he is so keen on this appointment that he was terribly restless during the six days he was home. His Colonel told him he handed in the *best*

Wilfred as an instructor, second from left

examination paper of all who took it. He knew that he and one other man got Distinguished Marks, but he didn't know he was best. This appointment as an instructor is only for three to six months, but it may become permanent for the duration. We shall wait a while, and, if it seems he is to be kept up there, I'll move up to Johannesburg so he can come home for weekends. He will be very busy doing a lot of studying himself for the first months and perhaps wouldn't have time for the family in any case. I feel he has found himself for the first time.[88] Wilfred as an officer can go to any club in the country whether a member or not.

Wilfred and I gave a cocktail party on Friday evening from six-thirty to eight. We had sixteen people in all, and it seemed very successful. We had Mrs. Corrigan and her daughter, Mr. and Mrs. Strong (Vice-Consul), Mr. and Mrs. K. Miller, Canadians with International Harvester, Mr. and Mrs. Zalreskia, Americans with International A., Mr. and Mrs. Morgan, Canadians, Bené Van Rippen, Mr. and Mrs. Buchanan, a very big mining man. Wilfred has been playing golf with him a long time. Edith, of course, and Mr. and Mrs. Scott, the first people I met in Durban, she is English and he is South African, Wilfred and myself. I had my snacks made by a place here that specializes in those things, so I had not a thing to do. The girls cleaned the house beautifully and got the children to bed and asleep before anyone came. Wilfred and Bené set out the drinks, etc. Afterwards, Wilfred, Edith, and the Scotts and I went to Bené's for scrambled eggs and mushrooms. Wilfred did the cooking, and it was delicious. Mr. Buchanan came with beautiful dolls for all the children, except Robin; he thought she was a boy and so he had bought a train for her. However, he exchanged that by the next day and all is well. Robin's name confuses people, and she is so sturdy looking that, in spite of dresses, they still sometimes take her for a boy. Mr. Buchanan also brought Wilfred a leather cigarette case.

I have just finished three weeks in charge of the filing department. My only assistant was a girl who had been with us three weeks. The other old girl in the dept. left on the second day. We had two big mails from England during that time, and we worked like Trojans. We both have a sense of humor, so we got along all right. I had Wilfred home two of those three weeks, and I was also doing the housekeeping, so I have had my hands full, I can tell you.

There is a parcel at the customs for me. I will get it tomorrow. I suppose it is an Xmas gift sent early to be sure of delivery. If it is, I shall put it away until Xmas, no doubt, just to make it more like Xmas. I really get embarrassed about the family sending me so much Xmas, and I really wish they wouldn't do it. To think of Aunt Nellie's giving Robin $2.00 is just too much. I don't suppose you can possibly give it back to her, but I wish I could because I know the expense they have had, and that she needs it. I haven't written her yet, but I will.

I am getting the magazines you are sending. Our subscription to *Time* has just run out. I hope you will keep sending us your copy, as we want the news whether we like it or not.

---

[88] The army provided Wilfred with the challenges and opportunities he craved—both socially and intellectually. With his strong memory, his ability to write and think clearly, and his talents in mathematics, business, astronomy, geography, agriculture, and languages, he was in his element.

Eve and Robin use the broad A and speak as Wilfred does. There is no trace of East Tennessee in their accents. There is no trace of East Tennessee in mine either. Americans think I come from the New England states, but South Africans say, "Oh, an American."

Lots of love from us all,

Helen, Eve, and Robin

Dunlop Rubber Co.
Sydney Road, Durban
December 7, 1940

Dearest Mother and Dad,

This letter may not look so good, as I must write it without looking at it very much and without reading it over, as I have a badly swollen eye. Edith is out playing bridge tonight with some people I don't know, and I am left to my own resources, and I can't sew or read, so I decided I wouldn't hurt my eyes if I wrote to you on the typewriter.

I have cold in one side of my face, and my gums and jaw have been aching for several days, and now my eye is almost swollen shut. Our weather is so changeable just now that it is hard to keep well. Anyway, I think I am going back to Johannesburg and good health. I am never quite well here, and it seems a little foolish to let the expenditure of say $150 keep me from enjoying good health.

Wilfred expects to be kept as an instructor in the Union for at least six months, and, if I live in Johannesburg, I can have him at home two or three weekends out of every month. I shall hate to leave Durban, as I know lots of nice people here, but then I have many friends in Johannesburg too.

I shall also have Bert up there, and the children mean so much to her. Whether or not she will live with me, I do not know, but, if I live alone, you need have no fears. Durban and Johannesburg are perfectly safe for a woman to live alone. You remember that some people were afraid even to drive through Elizabethton after the newspaper accounts of the strike there; well, the same thing holds true now as to what you have read about internal conditions here.

Wilfred can get a house at the end of January for me at a most reasonable rent. Friends of ours are living in it now, and Ruth is a beautiful housekeeper. The house is not too marvelous except that it is freshly painted, but it is in a good residential district, and also centrally located. It is right at a good school for Eve.

I shall endeavor to get a transfer from Dunlop's here to their branch in Johannesburg. Failing that, I do not anticipate any trouble finding another job as good as the one I have. I would like to stay with the same firm and establish myself as a sticker.

I shall miss bathing in the sea on the weekends. I simply love it and find it such good exercise. I give you my address at Dunlop's to use in the future, as your mail is sure to reach me if addressed to me there in case I do move. Edith will not be keeping this house on alone, so this address is rather useless.

The lovely big box of Christmas parcels has arrived, and I am controlling myself and keeping it for Christmas, as Wilfred will not be here and I expect Christmas to be very quiet, so I shall want the excitement of my presents at that time at least.

I want to make the dress, if my eye permits, and she does need the hat, so I think her wishes will be granted. None of the parcels were opened, and it came thru in perfect order.

Eve and I went to a children's show this afternoon, and she enjoyed herself thoroughly. Unfortunately, Susan could not go as she had measles. Robin and Helen should come down just before Christmas. They are both looking so well just now that I hate to think of them being sick.

We are having them injected with our blood so that they will have a light case.[89] I remember I had a very bad case of measles once, so my blood should be all right.

Edith thinks Robin is looking simply beautiful. I wish I could have had her picture taken now. She is so lovely I simply can't keep my eyes off

Robin, age 2 ½ yrs.

of her. She is going to give Eve a run for her money in looks, and I hadn't thought so at all before. As for disposition, she has the sweetest one I ever saw. I hope she will always keep it. Eve does not have such a sweet nature, but she is not so

---

[89] When a child was exposed to measles, the parent, or any adult who'd had measles, could go, with a doctor's order, to a lab and give blood. The lab would then spin the blood and separate the serum from the cells, after which the doctor would give 10 ml of the serum to the exposed child during the measles exposure period with the intention of offering some protection from the complications of measles. It apparently did not prevent measles, but it did attenuate the complications associated with the disease. This techinque was used when there was a measles outbreak in boarding schools, with reported success. (This information was reported in British medical journals of the period.)

serious as you think. She has plenty of fun and play and laughter in her. If I never pull her up, then I spoil her, and if I do correct her, she is hurt for ages.

Edith had letters from her mother in the Interior and her father in Shanghai yesterday. He wrote in his letter that the Mayor of Free Shanghai had been murdered while he was there. Edith used to live next door to him. From his letter, they are not leaving China because they are in the Interior and evidently feel safe enough. Of course, Edith is hoping they will be made to leave. Edith's only brother is in California University. He is much younger than Edith. Edith and I are the same age.

I shall write everyone after Christmas and thank them. It was awfully sweet of all of you to make it up, and it certainly looks interesting. Eve has made very sane requests for Christmas—a new dress, hat, and sweater.

I wish Dorette could be out here, and I am sure she would take what is happening quite differently. I have lots of friends with mothers and fathers, sisters and brothers in England, on the Kent coast and in London and all of the heavily bombed places, but they are taking it marvelously. Miss Durnford, who works with me, and of whom I am very fond, calling her Ruth and often comparing her to Mary, has the most hair-raising letters from her mother and father. Their gardener has been killed. They use the closet under the staircase as their air raid shelter. Bombs have been dropped simply circling their house. We hear many things I would like to write about, but they might be cut out and you would always wonder what I had written, so I shall refrain. If you read Anne Lindbergh's book, do write me about it. I should like to know what she has to say since he has made himself so unpopular.[90]

Do let me know if Meyer gets home. How he is ever to accomplish that I do not know. I don't know whether I am broadminded enough just now to have a discussion with him. It may be very interesting as a spectator to discuss the pros and cons of this War, but when you are one of the combatants, you necessarily only see one side, and you hate all else and everyone connected with it.

Charles, Edith's husband, gets home the 21st of this month for Christmas. He hasn't been home for three months, though, so I have really had the best of things and can't complain. Anyway, I am going to feel a bit left out at Christmas time.

Robin is pronouncing her Zulu words as distinctly as English, and the native girls are delighted. Of course, one of them cannot speak a word of English, nor can she understand it; the other one reads and writes it well and told us the other day

---

[90] Charles Lindbergh was the American aviator who made the first non-stop flight across the Atlantic. Before the Japanese attacked Pearl Harbor on December 7, 1941, only six weeks before this letter was written, Lindbergh had campaigned against America's involvement in the war. However, after America entered the war, Lindbergh flew many missions against the Axis. (Recommended Reading: *Those Angry Days*, by Lynne Olson.)

that she thought she would take up Afrikaans, as so much was written in it now. Natal has the rawest of Natives and also the well-educated ones. We have the two examples in our own home.

I have embroidered "E" [for "Evans"] on two bath towels for Bert. I think she needs them more than anything else. I am doing the same for Wilfred. I am also giving him a leather case fitted with brushes, razor, shaving soap, toothbrush, etc. He needs such a case badly now, and I am sure will be delighted with it.

Don't worry about my nose operation, as I am not going to have it. It will be unnecessary since I am going back to Johannesburg. It doesn't give me any trouble now, and there is much less irritation, as I seldom have a sneezing spell.

Have I thanked you for the nylon hose? They were beautiful and cost $2.25 per pair out here. Unfortunately, they were 9's, and I really need 9½. Hosiery is most acceptable out here.

I must stop now, as my eyes are very tired and I feel like I can sleep.

Lots of love and kisses from us all,

Helen

519 Moore Road
Durban
January 8, 1941

Dearest Mother and Dad,

I feel full of news but have such a bad cold today that I simply can't write much. I struggled on at the office for two days with this cold but gave up today. The weather is so very hot that it makes me feel much worse than if we had cool weather. Anyway, I have until the end of this month to put up with the Durban climate and all that it does to my health. I leave with the children by train on February 1st for Johannesburg. I am storing my furniture in Durban and shall board for a while with Mrs. O'Sullivan, who runs a big place and whom I know personally. She has had me there to meals, and they were simply marvelous, but no doubt they were a bit extra for company.

Anyway, boarding is much cheaper, and I must watch expenses until I find another job. I have rather taken this move upon myself and feel responsible for making ends meet. However, I am very happy that I have taken the step because it is a bit foolish to have a perfect climate so near and not take advantage of it.

I intend to try to arrange a two weeks' rest before starting on another job. I seem to be very cocky about getting a job, but they are more or less plentiful now with so many men away. Bert is holding down a man's job now.[91]

---

[91] Part of Bert's work at New Consolidated Goldfields involved going underground to take inventory of mining supplies. It gave her a great thrill to know that she was, at times, the only woman doing what had been deemed a man's job some 6,000 feet underground.

We had a most enjoyable Xmas with both Wilfred and Bert here. We had a grand time opening all the lovely things from home; they were all such wonderfully useful things. I had them in use immediately. Many, many thanks for everything, but especially the apron you made. It is quite the prettiest design I have seen, and I simply groaned over all the stitching on it. The stockings are beautiful, and I am using them only for eveningwear. My dress will be very nice as soon as I put the hem up and make a dark slip for it. I can get to that in the next few days. The children's dresses are beautiful, especially Eve's. I don't know when I have seen such an attractive dress.

Bert and Wilfred, Christmas 1940

I think you and Aunt Lennie were vying with each other on pretty dresses for Eve and Robin.

The children had lots of things. Mr. Evans sent them a £1 note, which I spent on instructive toys: a Tinkertoy set and a box of beads for stringing, at $2.00. I felt rather extravagant there, but they are enjoying them. Santa Claus brought them dolls' beds just alike, with pink taffeta bedspreads—naturally made by me. Wilfred and I gave Eve a delightful book, *When We Were Very Young*, by A.A. Milne. We also gave Eve a hat, a special request of hers. It is the same color as the light blue of the dress you made her.

The babes are over measles now, thank goodness. They were just able to get up Xmas day. They both had very bad cases. Robin has such a bad heat rash that she looks like she still has measles.

I shall be living at Kya Lami, 31 Esselen Street, Johannesburg, but I prefer you to address your letters for a while to Bert at 810 Rissik Street, Johannesburg. I shall see how mail is handled first at the boarding house. Kya Lami means "Our Home."

I haven't heard from you for two weeks, but all mail comes direct now, and I suppose we can only expect to hear every two to three weeks.

I have had Bert with me until today, when she left to spend a week or more on the South Coast at Warner Beach.

She has been with me two weeks. I haven't had much time until the end of today to spend alone. I perhaps need this time anyway after so many months of a full house.

I shall be writing to the different ones to thank them for our Xmas as soon as I feel a little better.

Lots of love and kisses from us all,

Helen

Secret letter from Helen to her parents, sent from:
Hotel Lexington,
Lexington Avenue at Forty-Eighth Street
New York City

January 14, 1941

Dearest Folks,

I have a chance to send you a letter uncensored by a Mr. X, a ship's officer, from Georgia. I have been crazy for this opportunity for several reasons. I must tell you especially since the tidbit you gave me in your last letter, that Mr. Z's step-daughter is one of the censors for Durban. I have been very careful therefore in what I have had to say about them and myself personally. To know any member of the Censor Board is a curse. I didn't know Mr. Z had been divorced. I suppose he would get another one if he didn't fear it would ruin him in his career, as Mrs. Z treats him like a dog and it is so embarrassing to be in their home that I had rather not be invited even though she is the social leader of the American Colony here. She can only be described as a hellcat.

What I shall now say is only for the two of you as there are so many Germans in Elizabethton. I do hope that nothing will ever tempt you to even hint at what I am now writing, but I do want you to know what I see of things. I must be living at one of the most important ports in the world just now as we get all shipping to and from India and Australia.

The harbor is so crowded that I have several times counted as many as thirty ships lying out in the open sea waiting to come in. Because of this, we had one very bad wreck, which is still reposing at the far end of our favorite bathing spot in Durban. The anchor broke loose, and the ship was washed ashore in a heavy sea at night and four of the crew were drowned.

My firm ships to places that tickle the imagination; for instance, Angola, Belgian Congo, Greece, Egypt, Switzerland, via Portugal. In all of these—or rather in our Portuguese East Africa dealings—we must first investigate to see that we are not trading with the enemy.

Here I see nearly every uniform of the Empire, as we sometimes have as many as 30,000 troops in town at one time: the Aussies—Australians, who always behave abominably—so that the restaurants, etc. have to close; the Imperial troops who seem to all be perfect gentlemen; our own with their Scottish regiments of kilts and Tam O'Shantas; fifteen thousand native troops at one time, all over six feet and taken from the kraals, no town ones. It is the "uncivilized" native who is brave and can be trusted. We also have had the Indian troops, who were disappointing, as they were dressed in plain khaki.

We are not allowed to mention any of these things in our letters as you can understand it is not in our interests in any way to let it become known that this is such an important port, though I have no doubt that it is known.

Also here we have all the hospital facilities for the wounded from up North. They are very busy on these buildings and have already taken over our general hospital, which is full. When [the wounded] can be taken out, they are, by the townspeople, who have have free passes to shows, etc. We are already seeing too many young men minus a leg or an arm. At first I cried even when I saw a uniform, but that is nearly all one sees now, and I find I can manage to look at the one arms and the one legs without making a scene, but it hurts.

Everyone is cheerful, and they have always been. We have met some evacuees from England who are sorry they left London and the excitement. They are crazy to go back and help and feel like quitters.

I have just finished reading the November 16th issue of *Time* from cover to cover. I imagine they are having a hard time getting it as it is censored in every country.

I hope this has made interesting reading, and I trust you to let it stop with you. Mr. X is just in today and out at 6 a.m. tomorrow, so I have written this quickly. In acknowledging this, only say, we had a visit from your friend Mr. X and enjoyed him very much.

Love and kisses from us all. The babes are OK.

Helen

Kya Lami
31 Esselen Street
Hospital Hill, Johannesburg
February 3, 1941

My dearest Ones,

The enclosed letter may give you some idea of how busy I have been, and therefore why I have not written for some time. When I suddenly received this appointment, I had to ask Dunlop's to release me before the end of January. They gave me nine days, in which time I stored my furniture in Durban, except for a few pieces for my room up here, then the children and I came up, and I have been busy finding a reliable girl for them and a school for Eve. Everything seems very well settled now, as Eve is in one of the best schools in Johannesburg, a very beautiful school. The young coloured girl seems to be kind to the children and reliable. Mrs. O'Sullivan, who runs the boarding house, also keeps an eye on the children, so they should fare very well. This is a big place, and it is well known for its good food.

Now, I suppose you would like to hear about my new position and how I got it. Everybody asks who got it for me. Well, I got it for myself, and I am simply thrilled to death that I am going to be doing work so actively connected with the war. I am secretary to Mr. Kingston Russell, who is Dr. Van der Bijl's assistant (Dr. Van der Bijl being the Director General of War Supplies). By the way, Dr. Van der Bijl is a personal friend of Bené's, but that had nothing to do with my appointment. Dr. Van der Bijl is one of the biggest men in South Africa.[92]

This position was offered to a Durban girl who gave me a name and box number to write to; however, no one could tell me the nature of the work. I wrote, stating my qualifications, and they had me interviewed in Durban. When I was interviewed and took my shorthand and typing test, I had "flu" and was running a temperature. However, I didn't do badly for myself; in fact, I turned out a perfect piece of work and received a letter dated the following day giving me the appointment. Luckily, they were particularly impressed that I had taken the minutes of meetings for years, and they have told me I will be used for that to a great extent. I must now seriously work on my shorthand speed, as I did no work of that type for Dunlop's. It is very nice to get a £5 increase, $25 from my previous job. I had begun to realize I was foolish to work for that with my years of experience.

Escom House, Rissik Street, Johannesburg

You will be interested to know that I am on the seventh floor of the tallest building in Johannesburg. I think it is sixteen floors high. You will also be glad to know that I dressed myself in keeping with my new position. I went to the most exclusive shop in Durban, and I bought a perfectly tailored navy blue coat suit; with this, I have a navy straw sailor, a beautiful new blue leather bag, gloves, etc. I

---

[92] Dr. van der Bijl founded the Electricity Supply Commission (Escom) in 1923, and the South African Iron and Steel Corporation (Iscor) in 1928. He was appointed Director General of War Supplies in November 1939.

sometimes wear a veil with my hat. I also bought a grey, lightweight woolen ensemble. It is the most beautifully cut thing I have ever seen, and it is the most expensive dress I have ever had. I blew a lot of money, but it is the first time I have felt really smart in years.

Wilfred is thrilled to death with his new wife. And, as you can see from this remark, Wilfred is still here and will be for some few months, he has been told. He is still a lecturer at the School of Administration. I did not write Mary or Elizabeth that he had gone North, but merely said that we were going to have a little holiday together before he went North. "To go North" can mean any place in Africa, north of the Union. We never know where our husbands are after they leave, as all letters are simply addressed to the post office, and they cannot say where they are. Wilfred was over for this weekend. He is about seventy miles out of Johannesburg, so I am still not so close to him, but it is at least better than being down in Durban.

My health was so bad before I left Durban that I nearly despaired. I am feeling better already up here, but my nose isn't perfectly clear yet. You will be surprised to hear that I do not notice the swollen tissue in my nose at all, and never have, really. I shall wait to see if it goes back to normal on its own. I have hopes of that happening.

In answer to your letter of Dec. 6th do not worry that Wilfred would ever try for a teaching position around Elizabethton. I am afraid neither of us has any desire to live in the vicinity of Elizabethton. We both seem to fit in much better anywhere but in the limits of East Tennessee. I realize how long I have stood in Wilfred's way by not letting him leave much earlier.

Robin is saying just everything now and is simply full of devilment. When Eve is sick, it is always an upset stomach. That seems to be her weakness. The children are looking very well now, though.

The tags were on the various Xmas presents, and I shall write everyone as I can. I hope they will understand how much I have to cope with for a while, however.

Know that Wilfred and I are terribly enthusiastic about our work in Britain's fight. I have been told I have no hours. I just work, but I don't care at all because I am right in the swing of things.

Love,

Helen

Kya Lami
31 Esselen Street
Hospital Hill, Johannesburg
March 12, 1941

Dearest Ones,

I have had so many letters from Mother since I have written that I am sure I'll never get all her questions answered, but I am going to make an attempt anyway. The reason I haven't written more often lately is because of Wilfred's operation for varicose veins, and, during that time, I went every weekend to see him, which is a trip of one hundred and forty miles there and back, and I felt I had to write him every day and send him little things.

Then he came home on his sick leave, after hospital, and of course my time was taken up entertaining him after office. Then, on the last day of his leave, he got the most awful throat and has been in bed a week with that. M. and B.[93] was the only thing that helped him. His throat was completely closed for a day. He couldn't even get any water down. Thank goodness, he is now better and was able to go back to camp today. In all, he has been out one month with illness.

I know he is glad to get back to his duties. He was run down after his operation, and that is evidently the reason he got this infection in his tonsils. He has certainly had good food here since he was able to eat, so he should be much stronger now. Mrs. O'Sullivan was simply marvelous to him. She nursed him and fed him the very best of everything.

By the way, Bené and Edith drove up from Durban and surprised me last Saturday morning at the office. I was so glad to see them because they are like people from home. They seemed just as glad to see me. They went back on Sunday morning. I have always meant to tell you, but I don't think I ever have, that Edith's mother was a MacAfee from Kentucky. You know MacAfee in Johnson City was originally from Kentucky, and I feel sure it is the same family. Edith said she attended a MacAfee reunion in Kentucky and there were a hundred or more there.

You all seem to have had a busy and happy Christmas, and I am so pleased you did. It can be such a merry time or such a sad time. My big disappointment was a goose that never got tender, and now I know never *could* get tender. Anyway, he is behind me now, and all cooking is for a while. Our food here at *Kya Lami* is really the best I have ever had. Tonight, for instance, we had tomato soup, fish, veal or

---

[93] Produced in 1938, M&B (May and Baker) was one of the first generations of sulphonamide antibiotics to cure pneumonia. This breakthrough was clearly a boon to the public's health. As the reader may remember, Helen's June 20, 1938 letter mentions the nine hundred people in Johannesburg who had died of pneumonia in the previous year.

chicken pie as an entrée, then roast pork or lamb as a meat course, with spinach, peas, and potatoes, followed by ice cream or strawberry mould and whipped cream, then tea or coffee and fruit. All of this is simply delicious too. I am afraid I am spoiled forever for my own fare.

In my room, I have enough of my own furniture to feel at home—my stinkwood desk and chest of drawers, my carved table, Robin's own blue cot for which I have bought a new mattress and new springs, my own pictures, and new blue carpet, also my two English antique chairs.

Of Mrs. Sullivan's things, I only have the wardrobe and two beds and settee and matching chair. She is giving me two divan beds at the end of the month to take the place of my beds, and, for them, I have my own lovely covers, of which I sent you a sample.

You mustn't consider sending me the lovely white quilted robe the roomers gave you, as I had much rather think of you in it than have it myself. Furthermore, Bert and Dad gave me a wonderful pink quilted robe for my first Christmas here, which is still perfectly good; also, I have a new white candlewick robe which I bought for the beach but can only use in the house here.

I was so interested to hear of Funcke's marriage. [Mr. Funcke was Helen's boss at the rayon factory in Elizabethton]. I knew he would only marry if it meant wealth and position. Of course, he had some of both to offer himself. I always thought he was charming but difficult. He was definitely overworked when we knew him.

I am so glad to hear Aunt Nellie is looking well now. I am writing her in a few days, I hope. Will you ask Eugene and Katye Wray for any pictures of their home, both inside and out, as I would love to see them. I am glad one member of the family of my generation has settled down. Gladys [another of Helen's cousins] has written me. She wishes she had known they would be in Rolla so long, for she says if they had bought a house when they first went there, they could have owned it by now with all the rent they have paid out.

It was nice getting Gene's little letter to you all, except that it brought to my mind the whole day I had to spend writing a letter to Mama Hunter every time a barrel arrived from her when we were in Texas. Thinking of those barrels—did she think we were destitute financially or that we were living in such a wild place we couldn't buy anything, or was it just that she had to do something because you were so far away?

Let me relieve your mind—you haven't repeated yourself more than once or twice in all the letters you have written to me. You thought you had told me Funcke was married, but you hadn't.

I was so glad to hear about the money Father has won over the radio. He is so well informed and remembers things so well that I am not surprised that he could spell the words given out. [Harlow was not only an excellent speller but also a Civil War and Bible buff.]

Personally, I have to live with a dictionary at the office, especially with my present boss, who is an ex-newspaper editor and now personal assistant to the head of our organization. He is so particular about punctuation that my heart stands still every time I write a letter for him. However, I usually find if I use my "gumption," as he says, I come out with a perfect letter. He uses a few uncommon words, but between my dictionary and myself, we come out on top there every time too. With all of this bragging tonight, I am sure I'll make some awful "blue" tomorrow.

The other day we were writing the prologue for a film (movie) to be produced, with a description of the montage, etc., and he suddenly asked me how to produce lightning. I said, of course, that I didn't know, so he said, "I thought you said you'd had a year of university work (college over here is different from college at home, so you must say university). "What the hell *do* you know?" This is the way he talks all the time, but I am usually ready for him.

I answered very quietly, "Oh, there's a lot I don't know. That's why I am still interested in living." He seemed more than satisfied with the answer.

By the way, he is a personal friend of Bob Davis, the columnist, and he has loaned me a book debunking Hoover, which Bob Davis took from his own library and sent to him, as it couldn't be bought. Father should read it. How Hoover can get in again on the food sent to Europe after the publication of that book, I do not know. Hoover sold all the food to the Belgians and pocketed the money. He is evidently the most advanced crook of our times.[94]

I get more news out of *Time* than any place else, but not always what I want to read. We get all the newsreels of the burning of London, etc., and also that marvelous film by Quinton Reynolds.[95] We have a long way to go, but, with America behind us, we must make the grade.

So many of the boys Wilfred went to school with have already appeared on the lists, but the fighting up North has been very minor considering what must come.

I saw *Gone with the Wind* while we were in Durban (before Wilfred signed up), and I thought it was wonderful. Of course, Wilfred thinks I am a second Scarlett O'Hara as far as traits of character go, that is. He considers me more like the one depicted in the book than the one portrayed on the screen. I didn't think they did her justice as far as strength of character went, for she was strong. I don't

---

[94] Herbert Hoover's relief work was highly acclaimed worldwide. It seems, however, that Helen's views were swayed by at least one detractor who believed him to be a crook.

[95] Quentin Reynolds was an American journalist who produced *Britain Can Take It!* (1940), a popular film dispatch from London.

say Wilfred considers I am strong, but he said he thought of me all through the book.

My pair of nylon hose did not wear well, but I think it was because they were too small for me. They laddered from top to toe about the second time I put them on. My Christmas stockings wore well. I am buying Holeproof now and am getting excellent wear.

I am crazy to see the dresses you have made for the children. That should fix them up very well now. Robin has the darling little red and the rust dresses from Ann [Eve and Robin's second cousin], too. She can wear the red one this winter.

Eve must wear her school uniform every day, and can only wear her ordinary dresses at home in the afternoons and on weekends. She must have two plain white dresses for school next summer. That is their summer uniform. If you could make those during the next six months, then they would be ready for our summer. You know how hard it is to find attractive white dresses. I understand any design and any material is acceptable, but I wouldn't make them of anything as thin as voile because it is never very hot here. I believe she wants a big sash at the back.

I was interested to have a description of the Roesel child. Did you ask Dr. Roesel where his parents are? I thought they were coming to Elizabethton, but I have never heard you mention them.

I am glad the picture of us has finally arrived. It was sent long before the others. I am afraid the picture does full justice to Eve and me. Yes. I was a bit thin when the picture was made. It is easy to be thin in Durban. I am sure you found me older looking than you had imagined me—and it *was* a bit of a shock. That was the way I felt about the picture, at any rate. Well, I just am getting older, but every age has its compensations. One hears of the "confidence" of youth, but I had no confidence in myself then. That is only coming to me now, and it makes life so much more pleasant that I am willing to sacrifice a bit of youth for it.

I am so pleased to hear that Robin has $7.50 in the bank. We are starting a period of strict economy in order to save enough to come over after the war.

Wilfred wants to go to New York immediately after the war, as he can get the best jobs there in the export field. He feels he can make the best money in that line. He knows it so well now, especially as far as South Africa goes. He will, of course, see Westinghouse people too.

I might have to hold onto my job for a while here, but he will at least bring the children with him and send them down to you all until I can come over. He naturally wants the whole family to go together, but I believe in playing safe. [This, since boats are being sunk by the Axis.] The fares will be greatly reduced after the war, I feel—unless everybody starts traveling just because they haven't been able to for several years.

It seems like old times to hear that Aunt Kate and Mrs. Whittaker have been with you for a bridge session. I would like to have a good loaf with plenty of bridge with some of you at home, but only a month of it, and then I had rather be back here in an office. I think I am back in office work for a long time, as I see it as a way for us to own our own home someplace some day.

I am sorry to hear Mrs. C.'s last days were so unhappy. I think she had a sad life in any case, as she lost her children one after the other and then the only remaining one wasn't good to her.

You seem to be on very good terms with your roomers now. I used to think we were a bit standoffish, but we had some queer ones at times with whom I simply couldn't get on friendly terms. How many do you have now?

Robin sprained her foot the other day, and long after it was all right, at least three days afterwards, she wouldn't walk on it and pretended she had to learn to walk again and insisted on a full audience every time she would even try to walk. She is almost normal again, thank goodness.

I got the *Time*s you sent to Dunlop's. A very good friend of mine is in the post office there.

Well, I must have exhausted you, if I haven't exhausted myself. The house is very still, and I feel sure it is late, but somehow I could just keep writing, but won't.

Lots and lots of love,

Helen

Kya Lami
31 Esselen Street
Hospital Hill, Johannesburg
March 26, 1941

My dearest Mother and Dad,

Well, this week has just been like having Christmas all over again, as the $50 arrived as well as the lovely box of clothes. I think you both know that I appreciate what is done for me, and I can't thank you enough for this, but I have found you far too generous in sending me $50. If you were rich, I would accept it, but I would really have a very guilty conscience if I accepted such a sum under the present circumstances. I am not in need of money on account of my move, as you perhaps know by this time, since I had so much good luck coming right up to a better job than I held in Durban—$25 a month more, and, on top of that, Dunlop's paid me for nine days leave due me, and, *on top of that*, I get my train fare paid by my present employer, so I have been sitting in the lap of Lady Luck.

I have been investigating to see about sending the money back, but I would have to buy at a different exchange from the one you bought at. As far as not accepting it at all, I could get no sense out of the bank. I think they would make it very difficult for me, so I want you to draw the amount of $50 from what the

A Vale of Soul-Making (May 1940—Feb. 1943)

children have, if they have that much. I really want this done, and will not be happy if it isn't done. If I needed the money, I would take it, and you can wait until the day I may have to ask for some money, though I hope that will never be. I could only put it in the bank when it came, and I don't call that fair. I shall always appreciate the kind thoughts that prompted the gift just as much as if I had kept the money. I think you will understand how I feel.

The dresses for the children are adorable. You will be surprised to hear that Eve liked the white dotted lawn the best, but I was not surprised, for I know her taste. Both dresses are lovely on her. Robin's little dress fit her perfectly and is so sweet on her. I have never seen Eve look prettier than in her white dress. She wore a big white hat with it, with a blue velvet ribbon around it, same as on the dress, white socks, and black patent leather shoes. I also had such a pretty white clip for her hair, and she looked rather Greta "Garbo-ish," as she often does. Are the white leggings and petticoat from Ann? The petticoat is too big for Eve; even so, I don't know why it was sent on, for surely it still fits Ann.

Now I am dying to know if the red housecoat was yours, Mother. Have you been stepping out in such bright things? I even feel a bit devilish myself in it. I shall enjoy it very, very much, though, and do so much appreciate everything. I think the green dress of Eve's is a beauty, and Bert thinks it is too lovely. The dresses are all so beautifully made. I don't know when I have seen such careful work.

I am working hard, very hard, but it is work I enjoy, and every day passes quickly. They used to drag on the filing job. I have just finished typing a rather lengthy article for an English magazine, and it looked beautiful. The boss is a scream. I heard him tell a lady caller that his wife had a floating kidney for years and had to wear a most dreadful looking truss. I repeated this to Mrs. Smith, who works with me, and she wanted to know why he didn't scuttle it. He provokes me into using more make-up than I have ever used before in my life; he said my mouth looked like prime cutlet and that my blood-red finger nails made me look like a vampire, as though I had just dipped my hands into a carcass. Mrs. Smith and I get these personal comments every day. She wore a really dreadful looking dress to the office the other day, and he asked her why she had come in her nightgown.

I have received Dad's letter and did appreciate what he had to say about Wilfred. Wilfred has proven himself practical, and he has been very successful in his endeavours. He insists on our saving each month, now, since we are settled here in Johannesburg. We put $25 away last month and should put $50 or more away the first of April, not counting what you sent.

We did get the doll's dress, and I am sorry I failed to mention it in my letters. It was such a pretty one, and the children loved it. They have a few clothes for their dolls, but the dolls are usually à la nude. Eve does not play with dolls but spends her time learning to write just now. She sits and copies from books by the hour. As always, toys are wasted on her, as she only enjoys creating herself. She has got two pennies from her teacher for being the first to obey commands for two days. She also said her teacher said her mother dressed her nicely, which made me feel good. She has a clean house every morning, and her shoes are shined every day, so she should look very neat.

We have had a few cold days this week and can expect cold weather from now on. I have a big open fireplace in my room, which I shall protect before I use it, but it is going to be a big comfort this winter. I also have two electric heaters that I brought up from Durban with me. We should be comfortable this winter. There are other things more interesting that I would like to write about but think it best to stick to personal things.

Wilfred wrote a most amusing thing on army life, but I am afraid I can't send it. I don't know when I have had such a good laugh. He has his portable typewriter at camp, and he is enjoying himself with it. He has a very nice room and office there, and his food is excellent, but, according to his article, he found a few things not to his liking.

I am very tired and must have an early night tonight.

All our love,

Helen

Kya Lami
31 Esselen Street
Hospital Hill, Johannesburg
April 1, 1941

My dearest Mother and Dad,

I have just finished reading Mother's letter and feel that I must answer immediately, for she still seems worried about us.

First, I cannot think of leaving this country unless Wilfred does. In that event, I shall definitely consider coming home, but by that time I hope to have my passage money saved up. There are many boats now coming direct, and I don't think I would have any trouble booking passage on one of them, and they would be much cheaper than the trip through the East.

Now, do not worry about a coat for me as I have just bought an all-round one since coming up to Johannesburg. It is Camel's Hair on one side, and a drill [strong durable cotton] on the other for rainy weather. It also has a hood with it for motoring, etc. It is just like having two coats. Besides that, I can use my black one Father bought me again, and still feel dressed up. I also have my fur cape, which is still good and will be most useful with my navy blue coat suit, which I bought just before leaving Durban. I simply couldn't wish for more warm clothes than I have just now, and, I can assure you, I am looking smarter than I have looked in years. I sent all of my old things to England—those I was tempted to wear but made me look dowdy. They will be useful to them, but they are no longer smart. Working where I do, I must be very well dressed, must always wear gloves to office, summer and winter.

I paid 3/8 duty on the last parcel of clothes—the three dresses, etc. I thought this very reasonable, as it is just between 75c and $1.00. They are usually very reasonable.

Do not make more dresses for Eve, as she must wear a uniform to school every day, so she has very little chance to wear her dresses. What she does need is panties. She does not like the lovely silk ones sent her, and it is nearly murder to get them on her, but she adores some white cotton ones I made her; unfortunately, they are all worn out. I would like to find the pattern and send it on to you if you would make her about three pairs. I usually trimmed the legs in narrow, strong lace. For Robin I should like some flannel petticoats, about three. Her dress was perfect in length if you still have the length of it. The slips should be slightly narrower in the shoulders than the little dress. She has so many dresses she can wear if she has three warm petticoats. It is turning cold now, so the sooner the better for the little petticoats. Unfortunately, I can't buy either of these articles, and I simply have no time for sewing and really no place, as the children go to sleep so early in our room. I can really only read and write or do a little hand work.

The trouble between the civilians and the soldiers has all quieted down now. I wasn't in town that night, but Bert had a good view of part of it from her flat. She lives right in the heart of the city, but I am about one mile out of the heart of town. I shan't get into mobs if I see any. That is the mistake people make. One man here at the boarding house had several ribs broken. You know, of course, it was really the soldiers and civilians fighting the Police and Ossewa Brandwag, the Ossewa Brandwags being the extreme Nationalists who think S.A. should not be in this war—the Pirow-Hertzog crowd, the ones who gave us the bush cart to go against mechanized armies. The whole world knows this, so it is a waste of time, really, to write it.

I am so sorry to hear that B. and J. T. have broken up. Does B. work? I don't think the future looks too bright for her with two children, but she is very pretty and might make a good marriage outside of Elizabethton. I am glad to hear the house is out of the red. I suppose it does need painting.

Father did not tell me to not mention the money you sent me, so I did tell all the family and Wilfred. It made no difference, however, as Wilfred did not feel that I should accept it, and his big thought right now is saving money. He has lately told me he doesn't think I am as careful with money as I used to be. I think it was because I bought some clothes for myself and got good ones while I was at it. This item had always been nil, practically.

The murder of that baby was horrible. How they could let the girl off, I do not know. She is capable of anything, I should think, and is a danger to the community. To let her go free is just asking for trouble from other sources. Why didn't the Linebacks get involved? They were bound to know something.

The green dress for Eve was a perfect fit, length and all.

Robin is well and fat as ever. She now says her prayers and tonight said, "Gawbes Mama Sopia," "Gawbes Papa Harlow," and was all the time keeping an eye on me to see if my eyes were closed. If she sees them open, she stops everything and tells me to close my eyes. She makes up her own prayer from what she can remember of Eve's. I do not force anything on either of them. Eve shows great originality, and I hope Robin will. I let Eve figure everything out for herself. She is memorizing verses now, merely from having them read to her, and she says them perfectly, but I do not make an attempt to teach her. If I did, it would be useless. Eve must go to the dentist again as she has a toothache, and I must also see our doctor about her, as her nose bleeds every day. I think it comes from the rarified air up here, but I must try to do something.

Lots of love and kisses,
Helen

[Attached letter below to Miss Bert Evans from N. Hawkins]

No 104950
5th Field Battery
7th Field Brigade
Army Post Office, Durban
(January 2, 1941)

Dear Miss Evans,

Thanks very much for the parcel I received from you. I think it marvelous of you to send it to one you do not even know. By the looks of things, the war will soon be over and then I might have the opportunity of thanking you in person. Miss Evans, if you could see one's face when receiving a parcel, especially in the wilds, it lightens up. In that verse you wrote, I think it brings more than cheer because one's so happy and excited you cannot open the parcel quick enough. Well, Miss, once again I thank you and wish you the very best of Luck and a Prosperous New Year.

I remain,
Yours Sincerely,
Neville Hawkins

A Vale of Soul-Making (May 1940—Feb. 1943) 327

Kya Lami
31 Esselen Street
Hospital Hill, Johannesburg
April 22, 1941

My dearest Mother and Dad,

    I was very bad and didn't write to you last week, but that was because I went out nearly every evening and, since I was enjoying myself, I am sure you won't mind too much. I am taking advantage of my lunch hour today to write, but I usually go around and look at the shops for relaxation. I have just finished typing a very long circular and could do with relaxation this noon, but there is so much I want to chat with you about that I can't resist staying in and writing. Just because I don't discuss the war, do not think that I do not get the news and have a very clear understanding of the situation.

    Wilfred has been sent to the Military College for a new course, with which he is very thrilled. He is the only subaltern on the course, the rest being captains and majors, so he feels very proud of himself. He is applying himself as usual and hopes to do very well; being of the lowest rank is added incentive to him to try to top the list in his marks. It is a course on camouflage and reconnaissance flying. He is in the air two hours every day now, observing, which is naturally part of the course. He is always so happy when he is learning something new. He likes the Army very much, and I think he would like to stay in some specialized branch of it after the war if there is an opportunity.

    We must live dangerously these days and accept it as normal. Our friend science is our most deadly enemy now.

    It was very interesting hearing about the wonderful offer they had for the Holston Oil Company. I hope they have done the right thing. I rather think they have because where else could they invest that money and be sure of doing so well? You did not tell me why they switched from Shell to Sacony Vacuum. I am curious. I presume it was a better proposition.

    I had such a delightful evening last night. I went in a party of six to hear Gwen Franken Davies on *The Living Shakespeare*. She is considered one of the two (the other being Edith Evans) greatest English actresses of the present day. To begin with, she looked too lovely for words, and for an hour and forty-five minutes she gave first the life of Shakespeare and then portrayed about five of his characters—Juliet, Lady Macbeth, etc. You all would have loved it, knowing Shakespeare as you do. It is the first time I have heard Shakespeare that intelligibly, as she made passages I do not know at all as clear and distinct as if they had been said in present-day English.

    She said that, when she was a little girl, Ellen Terry told her that she had learned her Shakespearean parts by transcribing them into present-day English and, after she was thoroughly familiar with them, she then learned her parts as

Shakespeare wrote them, and in that way she could give her audiences their full meaning. I was quite convinced that Gwen Davies had taken this tip and used it herself.

There was a very large audience, and the proceeds are going to any needy actors in London. It was held at the University here, in their new hall, which is a beautiful place. The seats are done in pale blue, and the floor is completely covered in a rose carpet. You can imagine how lovely a big hall looks done out in such colours. It is the Witwatersrand University and much larger than you can imagine, I am sure. One can have a splendid education at a very nominal cost living in Johannesburg. I hope both Eve and Robin will take university educations.[96]

I had such a nice letter from Elizabeth Hunter and think it was awfully sweet of her to write me, knowing how busy she is. Please mention to her that I have received it. I think I have already mentioned that I had a most newsy letter from Aunt Lennie too, and so thoroughly enjoyed it. I have also heard from Aunt Nellie and was so interested in Eugene's wonderful grounds. I received a lovely hanky in your last letter, which was much needed and appreciated, as I only have very plain ones just now and could use something good. All good handkerchiefs do the disappearing act in this country, so I brought this one to my native girl's attention and told her to look after it. She knows I have it spotted now.

The other day somebody entered my room and stole my clock, the Big Ben I brought from home with me. That is all I have missed and hope it is all they took. I have been after Mrs. O'Sullivan ever since I have been here about burglar-proofing my windows and putting a Yale lock on my door, and now this has had to happen to get her to do anything. In fact, one of my windows won't close, and I am so near the ground that one can simply step in, and I haven't had a key to my door for months. Robin, of course, usually makes all keys disappear. It is a perfect mania with her.

I am afraid I will have to do something about a winter coat for Eve myself, as we didn't think about it soon enough for you to make it and get it to me. June, July and August are our really cold months. I think I shall try to get through with the checked coat you sent her several years ago, and, if you could make her one for next winter, it would be splendid. Never make brown for Eve because she is much too dark—that is, her skin is a bit sallow. I think a green coat might be nice for her. Any colour is all right on Robin, but Eve is going to be a bit difficult in colours until she starts using rouge. However, lately her colour has been much better; in fact, she often has really rosy cheeks now. The children are both well and

---

[96] Low interest government loans made entry into university in South Africa affordable for those Europeans who passed the matriculation "With Exemption." There were no exceptions to this academic benchmark.

happy. I hope to get Robin into a little school as soon as she turns three and can stay awake for a whole morning. She still sleeps from ten o'clock until one every day. She looks marvelous on it too. I don't think Eve has ever slept enough during the day.

My nose is still stuffy, but I do not have any more trouble with my chest, and I have perfect sleep at night. I am going to investigate how I can have this operation without it costing me about fifty dollars. This place is terrible when it comes to doctor's bills, and it makes one put off having medical attention. Will get the bill for Wilfred's illness with his throat, which won't be less than fifteen dollars, and I will also have a dentist's bill for Eve. As soon as these are settled, I shall see about my nose.

Robin is still wearing the little green suit of Eve's, and next winter she can go into Eve's blue coat, which we bought in New York before coming out here. My silk hose problem is not too bad. I do on two pairs a month at about one dollar seventy-five cents each. I buy two pairs the same shade the first of each month. I walk quite a lot, often walking to the office from home, which is about a mile or more, so I think I am getting very good service.

This morning I got Robin to say, "I'm generosity personified," and each time she would say it she would throw back her head and have a good laugh. She makes such a fuss over her "Grandpops," as she calls him, that he stays puffed up all the time. She never forgets Mama Sophia and Papa Harlow in her prayers, and I wish I knew just what those names mean to her. She isn't prompted, you know, as to what she says when she prays. Her greatest concern at this time is that I keep my eyes shut. I must get back to work now, so "cheerio." That word comes very naturally to me now. I sent you the *Outspan* yesterday and hope you will enjoy the article by Dr. van der Bijl.

Lots and lots of love,

Helen

Kya Lami
31 Esselen Street
Hospital Hill, Johannesburg
May 2, 1941

My dearest Mother and Dad,

I enclose this clipping from yesterday's newspaper, as I thought it would be of interest to you since it shows the office building I am in—Escom House. I have marked my window on the 7th floor. You will also notice how near the mine dumps are to the heart of town.

I don't think I have written you since we went to the dance at the Officer's Club on Saturday night. Wilfred and a friend of his were over for the weekend, and I got another lady, and we went dancing. In the Paul Jones, I got everything from a Lieutenant to a Colonel. I got quite a bit of attention; no doubt the white evening dress should have credit for this. The Officer's Club is a very big place and beautifully furnished. They have a dining room and rooms for the officers in from the camps, and everything is most reasonable. They also serve nice teas in the afternoons. We have had meals there before, but this was our first dance, and we liked it so well that we are going again this Saturday.

Bert has mentioned to me that she has been thinking of chucking her job here and going over to America to see you and then working to make her passage back. Do write me what you think of this because, as it is, I do not know whether to encourage her or not. She is so unsettled because she isn't married, but I am so afraid she would expect too much from her trip. If she had a lot of money so she could travel around and see everything worth seeing, I would think it would be all right, but she hasn't enough to do a lot of sightseeing. I think I can influence her either way, so let me hear from you confidentially.

I think you had better buy a pair of navy blue shoes for me with French heel. You remember my size is 7½ AAA. That is perfect for me, and I find Rhythm Step is all right. There is only one shoe in all of Johannesburg that fits me, and it is 65/- or $15. If you see my size on sale in anything—white, rust, black, wine, tan suede—I would like you to buy it. You know I am hard on shoes, and I do a good deal of walking for exercise. The black patent leather shoes you sent aren't very comfortable, but I can wear them if I am not walking much. The ribbons cut the top of my foot. I can always send the money for them, and it will come cheaper to me.

So far you have made me presents of my shoes, but I had rather you wouldn't always do that because it makes me hesitate to say anything about shoes. The stores here seldom have anything more narrow that an A and just never order anything more narrow than AA from America. You know my foot is more inclined toward an AAAA, so you can imagine how they fit me. The one expensive shoe is a very special English shoe and beautifully made.

I haven't had a letter from you for two weeks but had a *Time* magazine day before yesterday, so hope there is a letter going through the censors now.

Wilfred hasn't had the final results from the exams he took on this last course, but evidently the Colonel has, for he congratulated him on his good work. I do hope he at least gets another pip, and another pip will make him a 1st Lt. instead of a 2nd Lt. Wilfred knows he did well because he said he knew everything asked. He had studied hard until he had a sty on his eye. He has a lot of pride and must do better than anyone else, which has always been a great help to his family.

Charles Broadbent, Edith's husband, who joined up at the same time Wilfred did, in fact a little before, has gone up North still a private. It is no disgrace to serve as a private, but you would expect more from an Oxford graduate. We have heard that he was always in trouble at camp by not keeping his place as a private.

By being so headstrong, he has worked a hardship on his whole family. I never hear from Edith direct, of course, as she simply does not write letters. I have written her twice but find it a waste of time since I never get a reply. I owe Bené a letter and shall pour questions to him when I write. I do wish you could know Bené. I am sure you would think him the funniest little man you ever knew, and terribly foreign. He is very good to those he likes but is high tempered and so afraid of being imposed upon. I think he has had a good deal of that in the past.

I must stop now and do a little sewing.

Robin's newest one is that, when she wants to say her prayers, she says she wants to say her "Mama Sophia." Did I mention that Father was right in thinking Robin had been crying before her picture was taken and that is a tear under her eye. I think Cargille might tint the picture of Robin for you and show it up better.

Lots and lots of love,

Helen

Kya Lami
31 Esselen Street
Hospital Hill, Johannesburg
May 13, 1941

Dearest Mother and Dad,

I have had three letters from you within the last two or three days though they were written over a period of three weeks; furthermore, the last one written arrived first, so you must not worry when you must wait three to four weeks for a letter from me. This time I had been three weeks without a letter from you. I was a bit worried, as you are so regular in your correspondence.

I was so glad to hear that Mr. Hari had been to see you and that you could have news direct from me. Now that I am not in Durban, I shan't be seeing him and won't get to ask him all about you on his next trip.

The green socks for Eve are lovely, and she will be thrilled to death when she sees them. Your letter arrived here at the office this morning, re-directed from Bert. You can send all letters to Esselen Street now, and I think it will be quite all right and I will get them sooner. I don't see Bert for days at a time, and there is a day wasted in her re-directing them.

No, I never commented on B.S.'s death, as I didn't think my comments would make you any happier. By getting away from it all, I saw how much of the suffering I went through directly emanated from B.S. and P. The news only gave me a queer feeling of vacancy, of no longer having that person to hate. When I see how Wilfred outstrips every other person in every group he is put in, and how quickly he masters different subjects with distinction, and they did not give him a chance at any time to fill the openings that were always occurring, I am simply made sick that I kept Wilfred in Elizabethton all that time, and that I was foolish enough to think always that there was something wrong at our end, and not to realize that there was a definite force working against us.

You must have read the article in *The Reader's Digest* by Devine on the evacuation of Dunkirk. This Devine went to Kingswood with Wilfred, and Wilfred said it was always a toss-up whether Devine's essay or his would win the competition for the year. One year Wilfred would win, the next year Devine. His name at school was Froggy because he looked like one.

I have attached a stamp that is being sold of Mrs. Smuts to assist the funds of the South African Gifts & Comforts, which she heads. General Smuts says he can hardly get into his home for all the parcels scattered around. It is marvelous how such an old couple can be the leaders at a time like this and that they have such energy to put into everything. [97]

It is good to hear about the work you are all doing to help Britain. A group of girls I know in Durban have just finished twenty-five sets of underwear for adults. The girl heading it is English. She wears clothes that people give her, and spends her money buying wool for knitting sweaters and material for underwear to send to England. She has a very good job at Dunlop's, but you should see the clothes she is willing to wear herself.

It seems to me that you are always after Carr to repair your house. I am beginning to think you are as bad as the L.'s. Now, does that make you mad? This owning a house is hardly a paying proposition. I am so glad you are full up again and that you do so well by it. I think, however, you should have a servant. I know I couldn't make the rounds of cleaning a big house like that. There isn't a woman in South Africa that would even consider doing it, and I don't think you should. I guess it is a good thing I know my work so that I can help out this way if I can't do housework.

---

[97] Field Marshall Smuts, commonly known as General Smuts (1870-1950), was not only a general, but a lawyer, a statesman, a philosopher, a scientist, and an author. His book *Holism and Evolution*, published in 1926, argues that matter and mind should be seen as "emergent wholes, rather than as discrete domains." He was deeply impacted in his thinking by his life on a farm until he was twelve, his hikes up Table Mountain, his training in the sciences, and by his reading of Walt Whitman. After leading the Boer commandos in the Second Boer War, he sided with the British in World War I (after which he was a signatory to The League of Nations) and in World War II (after which he was a signatory to the United Nations). He was the only person to sign each of the peace treaties ending the First and Second World Wars. He was Prime Minister of South Africa from 1919-1924 and from 1939-1948. (The term "commando" originated with the Boers in South Africa. In World War II, commandos were military units trained and organized as shock troops, especially for hit-and-run raids into enemy territory.)

Don't worry about not sending Wilfred a Christmas present. He can only wear khaki in any case—socks, handkerchiefs, and all must be of khaki. He is well supplied with all the small things, and Sunday his dad told him to go to his tailor and have another uniform made up and send the account to him. The officer's uniform comes to about forty dollars, so it was a very nice present. His father is so proud of the way he leads on the courses he takes at the Military College. I can't wait to see him all resplendent in a new barathea.[98]

I am glad you are as thrilled over my new job as I am. I still like it, though I must put up with a most difficult personality. However, he is also an interesting personality and can be most entertaining on occasion.

The health of the whole family seems to be just perfect now, so you have nothing to worry about there. I get plenty of sleep and haven't felt so rested in years. I usually go to bed at nine unless Wilfred is in. He comes in every weekend, as he is only seventy miles away.

I send you these pictures and am trusting you to keep up a book of the children, for I have nothing of the pictures of Robin, as in every case I have sent them to you and have failed to have copies made for myself. So do keep a book up of the children. I shall write on each picture a little of what each is about, and where taken.

I have received the money you sent me. I have written you about it, but just in case the letter goes astray, I shall mention it again. If you don't receive the letter about it, please let me know so I can repeat what I said in it.

I must close now. I have been writing this during my lunch hour, and my time must be nearly up.

I met a very sweet woman last night at Bert's who used to live in Boston and New York, and then in Vancouver. Her husband, a South African, has died and left her out here with a daughter, sixteen. She has had to go back to work, and the daughter also is at work, although she is so young. They are very nice people, you can tell. She is dreadfully lonely, so I shall try to see something of her.

Lots and lots of love to you both from all of us,

Helen

P.S. Yesterday I bought Eve a lovely heavy robe for the winter. It is a deep red silk, heavily quilted.

It was interesting seeing the addition to the church. How are the Umbachs? You haven't mentioned them lately.

---

[98] Barathea is an expensive, soft, woven fabric with a broken rib weave, used to make high-end clothing, including dinner jackets and officers' uniforms.

Kya Lami
31 Esselen Street
Hospital Hill, Johannesburg
June 6, 1941

My dearest Folks,

Last night I had a letter from you when I reached *Kya Lami*, and in the same post I received the copy of *The Reader's Digest* with Anne Lindberg's book in it, or rather the condensation of it. I thought it was lost, as some time ago you mentioned having sent it. I have just finished reading it and think it was beautifully written, and it gave me the impression of much thought and sincerity. I haven't yet read Dorothy Thompson's reply.

I have been remiss about writing the last two weeks, as I had such a bad cold I had to go to bed for three days. Now the children are in bed with colds. Eve has been in bed for five days and won't be up for a day or so more. Of course, it is impossible to keep Robin in bed for long, but she is in today.

Fortunately, we planned their joint birthday party for the 21st of this month, as that date suited Mrs. O'Sullivan. Mr. and Mrs. O'Sullivan are in Durban now, on their holiday, and will be away two weeks. The children simply love a party, so I feel I must do that once a year.

We had our first cold snap last week, and everybody has a cold from the sudden change. We kept warm enough, as I have a big fireplace in my room, and I had a fire going on the cold days. I fear I kept it too warm. Do not worry about the children and the open fire, as it is a very big and deep fireplace, with a large hearth in front. Also, the girl has instructions never to leave Robin alone when a fire is going. We can be more comfortable here as far as warmth goes than we have ever been in Johannesburg. I keep my own wood and coal; otherwise, I would have to pay a shilling per fire.

I was writing Father a really nice birthday letter for the 30th of June when I went to bed with my cold and had all my beautiful thoughts congealed. So now I'll have to just say I hope you have a very happy birthday and many, many more of them. We all send you our love and kisses for that day.

Wilfred is still here, and there is a possibility that he will be kept here to teach. This will certainly please me, of course, but Wilfred doesn't like the idea. He didn't come home last weekend, as he was busy at camp, but I am expecting him this weekend. He should have his new uniform this weekend.

I know your black and red outfit looks very smart. I also have my new red hat (felt) to wear with my navy blue suit and my grey suit. I have had a perm this month, which has made an improvement; and I have a new black dress, so new I haven't worn it yet. It is nicely cut and has a very large and very pretty white collar. It has tiny pin-tucks around the hips and across the back of the neck and over the shoulders. I also have two pairs of warm pyjamas for myself, something I have wanted every winter in Johannesburg, but previously I wanted things for my house more, so this is my first winter of real bed comfort. The children have always had them, of course—Robin's two new pairs and Eve's one new pair this winter.

I am in the process of shortening Eve's blue coat, bought in New York City, for Robin to wear this winter. It is a job, as it has such a flared skirt. I bought each of them a new sweater this month—Robin's is green and Eve's is her school pullover, in black and pink.

Mrs. Smith and I got the boss off to Southern Rhodesia yesterday for three weeks. We weren't sorry to see him go either. His nerves were a shade ragged, as he smashed his phone the day before yesterday from pure temper, this being the second offence against the phone. I'd like to turn loose myself sometimes, but most of us have learned a little self-control over the years.

Going back to the book on Hoover, Mother, it can't be a matter of debunking, as those on Washington and Lincoln and others, as Hoover is still living and could sue for libel if all the facts could not be proved. Case after case is given of his business transactions, with very detailed descriptions of each, and none to his credit.

Two of your recent letters have come through uncensored. Perhaps they are tired of reading our personal histories.

I think T.W. did a disgraceful thing, but she certainly feathered her nest by doing it. I don't know how a man could so completely estrange himself from a wife of so many years' standing, shall we say, and from his children. As for K.B., I never thought much of him.

Have I mentioned the pair of pretty pink silk socks for Robin that came through in one of your recent letters? They are being kept for a very special occasion. It is hard to get really pretty socks here.

Bert gave Eve a lovely Bible storybook of Jesus with illustrations that raise up when you open the pages. She also knit a dress, cap, bootees, and panties for Eve's best doll. Eve thinks they are both too marvelous. Eve's grandpa gave her money for a new hat. They are giving Robin a tricycle.

I must stop now, as it is time for the afternoon tea to arrive. Of course, we have morning and afternoon tea served in the office. I have promised cakes this afternoon so must go for them.

Our love and kisses to both our dear ones,

Helen

P.S. Mrs. Smith has just brought out her *Reader's Digest* of November, 1940, the same as the copy you have just sent me, but it was printed in London and it substitutes an article entitled "Cliffs of England Stand" for Anne Lindbergh's article in the American issue. This is interesting, isn't it? The rest is just the same.

Kya Lami
31 Esselen Street
Hospital Hill, Johannesburg
June 14, 1941

My dearest Mother and Dad,

This morning I can thankfully say the children are much better. Eve has now been in bed two weeks with such a severe cold. Robin has been in bed a week with laryngitis and has been running such a high temperature. I spent two days of this week at home with them, as the doctor felt I must. We have such a nice doctor now, a real old-fashioned family doctor. They are so hard to find anymore. He comes and takes lots of time with the children and has infinite patience, as though he has nothing else to do, but I know he has, for he is a very popular doctor. You always feel satisfied with the bill he presents too. You know you have had your money's worth.

I expect Eve to be able to go back to school on Monday, though she will still have her cough, and Robin should be able to go out on Monday if it is not too cold. The trouble with the climate here is that it is cold one day and hot the next. There are no seasons, only sudden changes from day to day. Another thing, it is so invigorating at this high altitude that one does not feel an illness coming on, but suddenly you are very ill. In other words, we are stimulated by the climate and feel good, I think, when we are really not so well.

Wilfred and I had agreed that I should come home with the children as soon as he went up North, but now that the *Robin Moor*[99] has been sunk and that line cannot be considered safe, I would feel too much responsibility in putting Eve and Robin on any ship. I had planned to come by the Robin Line, but it looks like I have waited too long. However, it has meant so much to Wilfred to have us here, as life is pretty grim with him, that, if I had it all to do over again, I would not change my actions. You two have each other, and Wilfred has only me and the children. Too, just between us, he is very much in love with your daughter.

Bert was bridesmaid yesterday to her best friend. She looked simply lovely, more like the bride than the bride. She wore a dusky pink dress with brown suede shoes and gloves and bag, and a dyed brown fox short coat with brown velvet hat

---

[99] Up until May 21, 1941, when the Germans sank the American steamship, *SS Robin Moor*, American vessels had, for the most part, been able to sail under the flag of neutrality. From that point on, however, it was clear that Germany was interested only in world domination; consequently, there was no safe passage by boat.

with the brush around it. The coat and hat were a loan from a friend and are simply gorgeous. Funnily enough, Bert could have married the husband of the girl who loaned her the coat and hat. He has lots of money and she [his wife] has everything she wants. Such is life. I believe Bert is too idealistic for most men. Eve has started talking about Auntie Bert getting married, as she has been anxious to get herself dressed up as a flower girl ever since she saw the flower girl at the wedding we went to.

Eve gave me a very big surprise the other day. She said she would like to read a poem to me from her book of poems—*When We Were Very Young*, by A.A. Milne. She read one poem of five stanzas entitled "Puppy and I," and she was only stumped by the word "I'll." She has heard me read it several times, and she got the book and figured out every word herself as she read it, pointing to each individual word. She spends lots of time with the book, so I am expecting her to read another one any time. She isn't going to have any trouble learning. According to her reports, she is even better in her sums.

Robin is now large enough for the red velvet dress Ann Dixon sent her, and she looks lovely in it. She has two red clips for her hair, and white boots with it. Her hair remains as fair as ever. She is going to have a big nose, while Eve has a very small one. She has broken herself at last of sucking her thumb. What a struggle it was for her.

I am reading *How Green was My Valley* and suggest that you all read it if you really want to enjoy yourselves. Bert says it is such a true picture of the Welsh people. We too often see the people of another country in a romantic light, whereas they are just people like ourselves, only more homely, perhaps, as with the Welsh. It is so easy to get all the books you want to read in a city like Johannesburg. I got this from the library in the building in which I work.

Eve, Wilfred and Robin
Johannesburg, 1941

Wilfred should have his new suit today, so I am crazy for him to get in. I know he will look just too marvelous.

Lots of love to you from all of us,

Helen

Kya Lami
Johannesburg
June 26, 1941

My dearest "Dad,"

For some time I have wanted to write a letter especially for you, as you have been so good about writing to me, even during the time you were tied to the office for such long hours, and now your letter of April 20th, which is the dearest letter I have ever had from you, makes it impossible for me to resist this urge any longer.

As for the war—one's allies one day become one's enemies the next, and so on, until, I can well imagine, we will be biting ourselves before it is all over. In any case, it is useless to discuss it, as the scene changes so rapidly.

I have just noticed on sitting down to write that there were twenty-three days between your letter and a short note from Mother, but they arrived within a day of each other. So you all must not worry if a great deal of time elapses between my letters.

It is strange that you should mention how shy I was as a child, for I had just been trying to write you a letter about that, because it is only now, as I see my childhood and young womanhood in retrospect, with years and distance separating me from the scenes, that I realize and appreciate all the sacrifices you made to give me every opportunity of overcoming my terrible shyness. I certainly had the lion's share of everything in the family—good schools, a trip abroad, a car, and finally a beautiful home, but always a comfortable home thanks to Mother's ability to make a home; and I know all of these expensive things were done to help me, and they did help, but it is only recently that I have completely rid myself of the shackles of shyness and timidity. It was like coming out of the water after a dive—one of my dives—I always stayed under much too long so that there was nothing refreshing about the dive but a great deal of relief on getting from under the weight of the water. The shyness of my childhood became an inferiority complex as I grew older, but recently I woke up to the fact that I was as capable as the next person in many respects, and that where others excelled they had usually given their complete life to one thing and missed much that I had known and enjoyed in just a well-rounded and ordinary life. I am sure that living with Wilfred has helped me, as I feel I have acquired some of his self-assurance, and he claims he has taken on some of my characteristics, which have helped him.

Wilfred has just received his second pip and is now a full Lieutenant. His Major presented him with his pips from the last war, and they are beautiful ones. He did this after hearing Wilfred's little joke on him. The Major has a glass eye, so Wilfred said to a new officer, "You know, our Major has a glass eye." The man said, "How do you know?" Wilfred said, "Oh, it came out during the course of conversation." The nicest part was what the Colonel said when he announced Wilfred's second pip. He came into Wilfred's lecture room and before his class he said, "You perhaps think this course very hard, but I want you to know your instructor also takes courses and passes them with distinction, so he can learn as well as teach, and now I want you to know he is now a full Lt., and furthermore I want you to hear a portion of the letter I have received from the Colonel of the Military College about Lt. Evans: "He is an intelligent, resourceful, and energetic officer." I told Wilfred there wasn't anything more to be said about a soldier who hasn't been at the front and had an opportunity to demonstrate his bravery. Wilfred was interested in the pamphlet on U.S. Army rations and has taken it to camp with him.

Wilfred's leg seems to be all right though the circulation is not as good as in his other leg. His foot is always cold.

Eve is still far from well. She has been sick for about four weeks now. I am beginning to think she has whooping cough, though she doesn't whoop yet. Four of the girls from her class at school have been out with whooping cough. She coughs until she vomits. She has had three bottles of different cough mixtures, and none of them have helped. The doctor doesn't think it is whooping cough. Robin is better and looks as well as ever.

I was so sorry to hear you have had lumbago. Try the Hay Diet.[100] You haven't forgotten it, surely. My boss and his wife eat according to the Hay Diet, and he thinks it is wonderful. She was dying with asthma, and he had stomach trouble and had to take a sedative to sleep, but, for the past four years, they have eaten the Hay Diet, and neither of them has had any trouble since. I told him I preached it to everybody for about two years and made a nuisance of myself, so I didn't want him to get me started again on my evangelistic work. I am glad you have had such a thorough going-over and that they find nothing wrong. I believe more care in your diet is the answer.

Bert was in a train wreck this morning but was not hurt, only badly shaken. She is highly nervous in any case.

We are getting *Time* and *Reader's Digest* regularly from you and look forward to them. I spend most of my evenings reading or mending. I am joining a library this next month and shall read more books. I haven't played bridge in months but

---

[100] An approach to nutrition involving separation of foods into different categories, developed in the 1920s by New York physician, William Howard Hay.

do not miss it anymore. People are not playing so much over here now. Many are busy in the evenings as well as during the day with war work. I have not taken on anything for the evenings, as I feel I must rest some and give the children my time until they are in bed. We have friends here—Mr. and Mrs. Byrne, who have Wilfred and me out a lot on weekends, and, sometimes have me during the week. They have a marvelous place for children but have none of their own, and she has just invited Eve out as soon as Eve can be out—they have dogs and puppies and chickens and just the kind of a place that children love. She thinks it will do Eve a lot of good. Both Mrs. Byrne and Mr. Byrne's people are in England, but they say little, only she simply won't go to see the newsreels now, and I don't blame her.

We also have friends by the name of Gott, and we go there too. Both Mr. Byrne and Mr. Gott served in the last war and are not physically fit to get into this one. One has an arrested case of T.B. and the other heart trouble, and he was an invalid all of last year.

We can't expect our men to come out of these wars as whole as when they went in, but everybody is so brave about it all that it is uncanny. That is the only word I can think of to describe the attitude of the people. And, of course, I must never show less spirit than the rest when I am put to the test.

I have only looked up the old friends in Johannesburg who really counted with me. Both of these girls are lovely, and I do wish you all could know them.

I haven't felt too good lately—had a touch of asthma for two days and then a dreadful cold. I didn't get proper rest on account of the children. The wind is blowing the dust from the mine dumps today, and has been for the past few days, so I think that accounts for my asthma and cold.[101] The weather is bitterly cold just now.

I shall wait until the weather is more settled before I have the polyps removed, as I mustn't have a cold at that time. I shall have it done immediately the weather is favorable.

When Wilfred comes in on weekends, we go to a show or dance, so once a week I step out and enjoy myself even if things have been quiet during the week.

You will get a peep into Eve's mind from the enclosed drawings.

Love and kisses to the two I adore,

Helen

---

[101] In addtion to the inclement weather, Helen, in her usual calm style, omits a description of the cramped and unsuitable room she, Eve, and Robin lived in at *Kya Lami*, sharing it only some ten months later, in her letter of April 10, 1942.

Kya Lami
31 Esselen Street
Hospital Hill, Johannesburg
June 28, 1941

My dearest Mother,

This will only be a short note, as I must get busy as soon as the others get into the office. It is the coldest day I have ever felt in Johannesburg, and everyone is a little slow getting in. My fingers are still stiff from the cold.

Robin's flannel petticoats have arrived just in time, and does she love them. She wanted to be changed three times the first day she had them so she could wear each one. She talks about you as though she knew you. Now it is only fair that you and Father go to Cargille's and have a good picture made for us. It will mean so much to all of us and especially the children in remembering you. By the way, I only paid about 25 cents on the petticoats.

I have telephoned the doctor this morning to come this afternoon and give Robin and me an injection for whooping cough, as I am quite sure Eve has whooping cough. She looks very bad, and I couldn't bear for Robin to go through it too, and it might go very hard with me, so I am doing what I can. I wish to goodness I'd had Eve done as a precaution.

Eve's nose has stopped bleeding since I have been giving her Calsuba in her milk, a form of Calcium.

I wrote Leone about last Mother's Day, and I think I must remember her mother at Christmas time this year. I think it has been extremely nice of her.

I should have sent you the pantie pattern that Eve likes long ago, but will get it off in the next day or so. I am afraid you will have made them all before it gets there though. She can't wear them until summer now.

I must tell you something funny, and you can use your discretion about letting Father know. Eve asked me the difference between a hen and a rooster, and I said, "Well dear, one lays the eggs and the other does the crowing." A few days later I had the doctor over, and he wasn't too popular with the children, so he started drawing pictures to amuse them so he could take temperatures, etc. He drew a dog, a cat, then a chicken. When Eve saw the chicken she said, "My Mommie told me the difference between a hen and a rooster; she said one lays the eggs and the other does the cocking." In my sweetest voice I said, "You mean crowing, dear." Thank goodness he is middle-aged.

I must stop and get to work now.

Love to my two dear ones,

Helen

July 16, 1941

Dearest Mother and Dad,

I have not had much time for writing, as we have been extremely busy in the office for a fortnight, and I have such disturbed rest that I go to bed between 8 and 9 every night unless I go out, and once a week out is a lot for me just now.

I had a letter from Mother yesterday saying you hadn't heard from me for four weeks but others had. I didn't write you during that time because I simply had to get other letters off, and I knew they would all let you know that they had heard from me.

The enclosed letter is from a friend of ours who was Captain of one of the warships at Suda Bay, and I knew it would be of interest to you, as it is a personal story. This man was at our home in Durban at Xmas time. The other enclosure is very common, but it is making the rounds over here and I thought it might amuse you.

The enclosed pictures were taken by Mr. Kingston Russell during his holiday in Southern Rhodesia, and he gave them to me especially to send to you. Mrs. Russell is sitting in the car. These pictures were taken in a small Game Reserve where the animals are comparatively tame because they are never mistreated and left to roam at large. They kill off each other occasionally for food, of course.

Since I read that Mrs. Dungan's home is to be sold, I thought of you all and how comfortable it would be for you and how convenient to town. Would it be a good proposition or not? Taxes are so high in Elizabethton, and the town government so mismanaged, that it makes one chary of owning property there.

You are both dears to insist on me keeping the £12 you sent, and I suppose there is nothing left for me to do but keep it, and I do appreciate it so very much. Right now I feel like trying to buy sleep with it. I am starting on my third day without any sleep day or night—not a wink. I have a bath the first thing in the morning and then keep going on tea and coffee. Eve is looking much better, however, but for some reason her cough is worse these last days. I am keeping her quiet today in bed and see if that helps. I know the biggest help—Mother—but there is just the Atlantic between us, and too many dangers lurking there.

I am glad Mary Alice is getting married. Has Pat Dungan ever grown any? I hope they will somehow be able to give him a start. Mary Alice's picture is very pretty indeed. She seems to be making a very good marriage.

My shoe size is 7½ AAA. I have the same foot as Edna Edens, and, if you could get her to try on shoes for me, it would be a help, because some of the shoes you send aren't comfortable even though they are my size. For instance, a 7½ AAA in the Red Cross shoe is too large for me, and I would have to have AAAA in that make. The white and tan pair by Dickson or Dickenson were the most comfortable shoes I have ever had, but I am sure they were very expensive.

A Vale of Soul-Making (May 1940—Feb. 1943)

Eve appreciated her Birthday card so much, and Robin her slips. I haven't been able to have their party, but they have had very nice birthdays. Did I tell you that we gave Robin a lovely tricycle a bit in advance for her birthday, today. Mr. Evans, Bert, Wilfred, and I gave it to her. It cost £1.15.0, about $7.50 They can both ride it and have lots of fun with it.

I was surprised to hear that Aunt Lula and Uncle Earle have sold their home, and that they got $12,000. Some people have all the luck. It does look like I should get that for mine. I hope you will hold down on the L's. until you get out of the red. I am sure the outside painting was necessary, but they can surely be satisfied for a while. I hope Uncle Earle will build a much cheaper house and salt some of that money away.

I also enclose some drawings of Eve's. Note the STOP street. I was so amused. We never know how much they observe.

I must close now and get to work. Lots and lots of love,

Helen and Babes

[Enclosed letter from a friend to his parents]

Alexandria, Egypt
June 4, 1941

My dearest Mother and Father,

It is quite a fortnight since I wrote to you, but even if I had done so, there were no means of having our letters posted. As soon as I arrived back here, I sent a cable and hope you received it—I was one of the lucky ones to get away from Crete. My mind is still a little confused of what actually did happen, so you must excuse me if this letter is somewhat jumbled up.

For the last month we have been stationed at Suda Bay, and almost without exception they bombed the place daily—they came over in waves, and not a single British fighter to intercept them. Last week they started the "Blitz," and they absolutely blasted the anti-aircraft batteries and troops off the face of the earth.

Most of the fighting was at Canea, only four miles from Suda, so we had our share of bombing. One Sunday we were patrolling the Bay and managed to bring down a plane, but did they give us socks after that. However, none of their bombs hit us, but we had to twist and turn until sunset; the only respite we got was at night. Towards the end, we had to anchor the ships by day and hide in caves. As soon as it was dark, we went back to our ships and did night patrols—that was the only way to keep the men going, and we could not expect the impossible from them.

Well, anyhow, on Monday night I went alongside the wharf for more ammunition, as we only had thirty rounds left, and I was then told of the grave situation and ordered to make for Alexandria as soon as possible, traveling only at night. It was too late to leave then, as I could not have got past the enemy's stronghold before morning, so we anchored and prepared to leave as soon as it was dark. By this time there were only three of our ships left; one left for Alex earlier on in the day, so "Syvern" and ourselves joined forces.

All that day we hid in the caves and were continuously machine-gunned; however, we had no casualties. Just as we were preparing to go back to the ships at sunset, they bombed them heavily, and the ships were ablaze in a few minutes. I understood the gravity of the situation, as the Germans were breaking through, so we decided to march overland to our last port—a distance of forty miles over jagged mountain passes.

We did it alright, but I shall never forget it. The first night we did about fifteen miles, and had to hide as soon as it was light because of the planes machine-gunning us. Later we struck the main road and found the troops on the retreat.

What an experience. Our party soon got mixed up, and we carried on in small groups. We had no water bottles or anything like that, and when we arrived at the wells, it was an absolute fight to get water; as for food, well, we did without—except for what we cadged from the troops. During the day it was terribly hot lying behind the rocks, and at night it got cold high up in the hills, but it was marvelous to see how we pushed on, knowing the Germans were not far behind.

We left Suda Tuesday night and reached Sphakia on Friday morning, when we were taken off the beach by ship—what a walk, but we did remarkably well considering the mountainous country, and only marching by night—of course, we did forge ahead a little by day, but one was continuously diving behind rocks on the approach of aircraft.

I am thankful to be back, but have lost everything—silver cigarette case, gold links, photo frames, camera, and all my clothes. Anyhow, why worry over that? I am safe. There was a parcel for me at Suda, and letters, which I was unable to collect from the Camp Post Office. I suppose the Germans have them now.

I am now staying at a hotel and trying to collect some kit together. Of course, we get £50 to replace ours, but mine was more than that, and to think of the time and labour it took you to knit my socks, Mother. I am quite well and absolutely nothing the matter with me, except perhaps tired feet. Talk about eat and sleep. Well, I never thought I could put away so much. I don't know if any of our men were left behind; it's impossible to find out yet, as some are still arriving and are being sent to various resort camps. Once we met the troops, it was a hopeless mix up, some jumbled lorries, and we soon became separated—it was a case of everyone for themselves. How thankful I am that I have led an outdoor life and am so healthy. Etc.

Love,

Jim

A Vale of Soul-Making (May 1940—Feb. 1943)

Kya Lami
31 Esselen Street, Johannesburg
July 29, 1941

Dearest Folks,

Who do you think is in town? Edith Broadbent. She had lunch with me yesterday, and I am invited out to her friends for dinner tonight. And the husband of these friends was at university in America with Wilfred, went over at the same time, and did the tour around America and all. However, he and Wilfred had a fight over there, so I had never met him until Edith introduced me yesterday. I suppose Wilfred will be very annoyed when he hears I have been there to dinner, but I simply can't keep a fight twelve years ago going. He is manager for Vicks out here and has a beautiful home and has done very well for himself. Edith was all nerves, and her boss made her take a rest, and, fortunately, she left the children behind. She has a good job with Caltex (Texaco) now, traveling. She makes £20 per month plus all her gas and oil, etc., for her car. She started with them at £13 in the office just before I left Durban, so she hasn't done too badly for herself. She was looking like a Grand Duchess yesterday in a black dress, very smart black hat, and short leopard-skin coat.

We had a marvelous weekend. Went to a dance at the Officer's Club, and who should we meet but Stewart Arridge. You remember, they had our house for six months and then went back to England. He is in the R.A.F. and still full of life, but more serious than he used to be. His daughter married the day before he left home, the son of the Polish Minister to England. He and Wilfred were so glad to see each other. They had a big row at one time, but they simply can't help liking each other. Bert went with us to the dance with such a nice Canadian. The next day, Bert arranged for us to see a native dance at one of the mines. I shall send you the pictures we made if they are any good. Our Canadian friend was so enthusiastic over the dance that he took forty dollars worth of ciné film. We then all went to the Country Club for lunch and had Chicken à la King, which I haven't had since leaving home, and a gorgeous hot fruit pie with thick cream. There were other things, but those two were what counted.

August 4, 1941

If I am ever to finish this letter, I must write at home, as Mrs. Smith left last Wednesday on her holiday (three weeks), and I am swamped with work. I like being busy, and I also like running the office myself, as nice as I find Mrs. Smith. For instance, I have just now won her over to the Dewey Decimal system of filing; whereas, if I had been on my own, I would have had it in months ago. Mrs. Smith has been marvelous about showing me the work in the office, and we are really fond of each other. I have perhaps written you that she is a widow with two children who lives with her mother. She has also lost one child of eight after her husband's death. She never complains, though, and takes such an interest in her little boys.

Well, I have been feeling like it must be Xmas time—getting a letter, *Time*, *Reader's Digest*, a lovely linen hanky, four pairs of bloomers for Eve, and my beautiful blue shoes. They are the prettiest shoes I have seen, and they look simply marvelous on my feet. They make my feet look very small. Now if you will try to get me a white pair of shoes, either all white or tan and white, I will be all set up. Then you can let me know what the two pairs come to, and I will see what I can do about sending the money. I think if you have the account made out to me at my address here it will be the best way, and I might have to send the money direct to the store. If it is King's in Johnson City, you will have no trouble making them understand, I suppose. Eve is very thrilled with her panties, and they are what she likes. I had to take the elastic up in the waist, but that was all.

Eve and Robin are over their whooping cough, and they are both looking so well. Eve has beautiful color now and eats well. I have never seen her so pretty. Everyone told me it would do her good, and it certainly has. Today was a holiday, so both of them got their hair washed and curled by Mother. Eve goes back to school tomorrow.

Love to my two dear ones,

Helen

Kya Lami
31 Esseslen Street
Hospital Hill, Johannesburg
August 13, 1941

My dearest Mother and Dad,

I have your letters of June 2nd and 8th and was glad to learn from them that you have heard from me directly and indirectly through others, and that you received the *Outspan*. There is an article in an English magazine on the War Effort in South Africa, which I typed and would love to send it to you, but I can't get the magazine out here. I have seen it in print, but we only have one copy in the office.

Is Helen Hunter going to take up secretarial work? It can be very interesting if you are in the right office. I am so interested in this job that I never look at the clock. I just wish my boss were easier to get along with. We had a big row yesterday, which is nothing unusual. I simply infuriate him because I display a little temper of my own. He considers this his prerogative alone. He has complimented me highly on my work, so I know he would hate for me to go, and I like the work so well that I will perhaps take a lot before I quit. He was trying to get a secretary he had in Durban when I heard of the job, and she told me she wouldn't go back to him for less than £40 per month—about $200. When she said goodbye to me, she acted as though she were sending me to the abattoir.

I haven't received the pair of black shoes and wish they had come along with the blue ones, since those came through safely, but you did the best thing, no doubt, in sending them in separate parcels. Don't worry. I shall take every care of my new shoes. My standbys in shoes are the white and tan pair, which has been half-soled, the black pair with the silk bows, and the blue pair—both received about the time Robin was born, and they, too, have been half-soled and must be redone.[102] All three pairs are really finished, especially since the glaze on the blue pair peeled off the heels and had to be dyed, but I can always excuse my feet by saying I can't get shoes to fit me.

You know I have always worn my shoes out much faster than you, and I must be dressed all the time, working in an office and boarding. Let me know how much the shoes are, in any case, whether I can send the money or not. We are used to the fact that the £ is low, as we hear it every day as a reason for the increase in prices—that, and the increased ocean freight insurance. There are many small things that we pay double for now, and other things twenty-five to fifty percent more. We also have Government bread now, you know, but I consider this good for us. No more of the white bread that I always preached against.

I received the pair of green socks for Eve, and they are such pretty ones too. I also received a pair of pale pink silk ones for Robin; as to another pair of white socks for Robin, I just can't remember. When these things come in your letters, I take them out and give them to the children, and they start using them, and I am apt to forget to mention them. I try to mention everything, because they are all appreciated and always useful, but I may slip up now and then.

Wilfred gets about £3 more per month as a full lieutenant, so we are that much better off. We would be very well off if things were normal, but so would everyone else.

What did you mean by "Uncle Edwin was at camp"? What camp? I always think in military terms these days. I can't write any more this time. I have just received a forty-five-page job to type. How I'll ever get it done with my other work, I don't know.

Love and kisses to you both,

Helen

P.S. Enclosed: story and pictures by Eve

---

[102] At that time it was common to find a small shoe repair establishment in every cluster of shops. Since shoes were not as durable as they are today, and since people generally walked more than they do today, shoes had to be re-soled fairly frequently.

Johannesburg
August 22, 1941

My dearest Family,

    I am enclosing a drawing of Eve's that I think will amuse you. She dictated the story to me without any prompting, and was most careful that I should get it down. At the end of each sentence, she would hesitate and ask me if I had it.

    We got the newspaper clippings of Kathryn Hunter and Mary Alice and enjoyed both. Eve has looked and looked at Kathryn's picture and thinks she is the very prettiest one, and so do all of us. Wilfred thought she looked so pretty and still so much like you.

    We had a great time on Saturday night, the 16th. I gave a cocktail party for Wilfred at Bert's flat—had Bert, Dad, Mr. and Mrs. Burne, Mr. and Mrs. Cade, Mr. and Mrs. Bob Brittain, Asst. Canadian Trade Commissioner, Mr. Lambert out here on business from Canada, Elsa Swan, and Wilfred and myself. Dad then took us all to dinner at his club, and after dinner we went back to the flat and saw some

Carlton Hotel, Johannesburg

ciné films made by Mr. Lambert of the Native war dance we all went to see, also a film of Elsa's of Canada. Everyone seemed to enjoy the affair. I gave the party for Wilfred's birthday, also to celebrate our meeting in August and marriage. Just threw the whole lot in.

    Last night Mr. Lambert had us to the Carlton Hotel, along with others, and showed films he had made of the Victoria Falls and the Game Reserve. They are all in colour and are really splendid. I do wish you could see them. By the way, there is a film on South Africa's war production, called *Sinews of War*, now being shown in America by Fox. I wrote so much about it, as I was invited to the Preview, and it was such a good film of what our War Supplies organization is doing that I would love you all to see it if you get a chance. The Director-General of War Supplies has charge of production plants as well as purchases and supply.

    Eve and Robin have started coughing again. But it is not so bad that we do not get proper sleep. However, I shall be very glad to see the end of this changeable weather, though one really has nothing else the year round in Johannesburg. It has been very warm, and yesterday it turned cold and windy. One day you can go without a coat, and the next you are muffled up to your ears.

    Mrs. Smith will be back the 25th, next Monday, from her holiday. She has been away since the 30th of July. I have kept the office going alone and have done a

A Vale of Soul-Making (May 1940—Feb. 1943) 349

good job of it, but I am tired out. It means slogging away every minute of every day, from 8:30 until sometime between 5:00 and 6:00.

I have taken my blue linen to the dressmaker. She has cut the suit out, and I think it is going to be very nice. I am not taking my other material to her until I see how this suit turns out. I thought the sample of your new dress pretty. What else are you planning to get for this winter? You are so easy on your clothes that you must have a rather nice wardrobe by adding some nice things to it about twice a year, or however often you do. By the way, you were worried about the fur collar on my black coat; it is not at all worn, still good, and still goes out on best occasions.

The war news is not so good just now, but the Russians have put up a good fight. It will soon be our turn again. Wasn't Roosevelt's and Churchill's meeting thrilling? I don't think they should take such chances, though.

Mr. Lambert and Mr. and Mrs. Brittain are sailing for Canada soon. If it were safe, I would have sent the babes to you by them so that they could enjoy proper home life and your good attention. I simply can't have things as I want them for the children under the circumstances.

I am sending Robin to a little play school near us beginning the first of September. There she can learn to play with other children and have companionship during the mornings. I feel she is a lonely little thing, just taking walks with a coloured girl. My girl is thirty years old and has two children of her own who live with her mother. She won't associate with the Natives unless they are very respectable, and in that way I know she won't hang around with a group of Natives on the streets when she is out with Robin. Being coloured, though, she is high tempered and easily offended. The lot of them are a problem at times, and I wish I could be independent of them, but no one is in the country.

Robin got annoyed with Wilfred last Sunday, so she said, "God bless the Germans."[103] I think it is too funny that she should know how to annoy him in return. She is full of devilment these days. I know she would exhaust me if I had to look after her all day. As it is, they pounce on me the minute I get in the evenings and expect me to do one dozen things at once. All of which reminds me, I must stop and go home. I am writing this at the office by staying a little late. By the time they finish with me at home, I am too finished to write a letter.

Bert looked too marvelous last night at the Carlton. She wore a short, pale pink dress, very good-looking, and dark brown shoes, suede, a brown suede bag, and the cutest brown fox fur hat and her brown fur coat. She was so full of life, too,

---

[103] Although I was only three at this time, I remember how politicized our games became as the war continued. One of our favorite skipping-rope songs was "I am a Girl Guide dressed in blue/These are the actions I must do/Salute to the King/And bow to the Queen/ And turn my back on the German submarine."

that she kept us all laughing the complete evening. She was definitely the best-looking woman there. Too bad Mr. Lambert is married, as we all like him so much, and he would be ideal for Bert. He is one of the nicest people you could ever meet.

I must really stop now. I am advertising for a flat but am not taking anything I don't really like and at a price I feel I can manage.

Lots and lots of love to you both,

Helen

Kya Lami
31 Esselen Street
Johannesburg
August 27, 1941

Dearest Mother and Dad,

I know you will be glad to hear that the pair of black shoes arrived yesterday. I was so relieved when I saw the parcel slip, as I naturally worry when anything is on the way under present conditions. They are very pretty and gloriously comfortable. I know I shall get a lot of good out of them. I have them on today with no discomfort, even though they are new. I even walked to work today. I do that quite often, in fact, as it is not too far, taking only about half an hour. Thank you so much. I think they were very reasonable at $5.00. Don't you think I had better try to send the money over for them since I have asked for so many pairs at once? You see, I still want the white ones too.

I am trying to find a flat, as I want to move from Kya Lami, but it isn't easy to find what I want at the price I can pay. The food is still good, but the appearance of the annex, especially, gets worse day by day.

Mrs. O'Sullivan isn't able to get around much, and one doesn't dare mention anything to her, so the only thing to do is get out if you can't put up with things as they are. I have so little time to look around, and just every part of town doesn't suit me because of Eve's school, and my work, and Wilfred's coming in with private cars. We are now so centrally located for everything.

Mrs. Smith is back now, and I am taking a breather. She had a very nice last week, as she met someone she is interested in, and, funny enough, he is from Kya Lami.

Bert and I together are making a very nice white slip for me and a georgette blouse with lots of lace.

Eve wears the *Bundles for Britain* badge all the time. She loves anything like that. It was enclosed in the parcel with the blue shoes.

A Vale of Soul-Making (May 1940—Feb. 1943)

Yesterday morning, Robin said to me, "Mother, I want to get in your bed with you. My bed doesn't feel very fresh." It had just been changed, but anything for an excuse.

How much capital is being paid off now each month on the house; and how much more is there to pay? Wilfred is always asking me this, so please let us know.

The tea has come, so must close and have it with Mrs. Smith. We are having a nice slack time this afternoon, as the boss is away and the work is up.

Love and kisses from us all,

Helen

Room 724
Escom House
Rissik Street, Johannesburg
August 30, 1941

My own darlings,

I have felt like a post office all on my own this week. Eve's lovely winter coat has also arrived; looks just too marvelous on her. The length will be just right for next winter, and that suits me perfectly, as this winter has been short, and it is already too warm for a coat like that. Eve is very thrilled, and, when I saw the price, I wished more than ever that I could be at home with my income. Such a coat could not be bought for less than $15 here at any time of the year.

Of course, we don't have sales anymore except of junk, as they don't know when they will ever be able to get more goods. All imports are on a priority basis now, and rightly so. I could not get a pair of shoes for less than $15 to $20, and then they would be something old and staid-looking, nothing snappy. Bert, of course, can get smart-looking shoes at a reasonable price, but not me with my foot. Eve is going to have the same foot too. I also received the pretty brown linen hanky and shall wear it with my new pink linen dress. I had about six copies of *Time* arrive in the same post. With it all, and best of all, were two letters from Mother.

Night before last, my colored girl walked out in a perfect fury. She was annoyed with the native boys in the boarding house, but just what it was all about I could never find out. She was like a wild woman, so I quickly decided I didn't want her with her temper taking care of the children, so when she said she was going, I said GO. It gave her such a shock that she had a good cry, but I stuck to my decision and she went. I had a great feeling of relief, much to my surprise, and went that evening and made arrangements for Robin to attend a nursery school beginning yesterday. It is run by a Mrs. Brown, a refined English woman, and it is in one of the best parts of town. She has a large house and garden, and lots of strong swings and toys. Eve goes there in the afternoons after her school. They had a lovely time yesterday and were the happiest two imaginable. Robin has her lunch there. It won't cost me much more, only means a little more trouble for me, but it is worth it.

One of the best boarding houses in town is just across the street from Mrs. Brown's place, and I have made arrangements to take the first vacancy there. It is so far above Mrs. O'Sullivan's place, and is very little more, that I feel a perfect fool to have stayed where I am so long. The new place is Fayland's, and it is new—new buildings with all modern conveniences, etc. The lounge is simply beautiful, and one would not be ashamed for anyone to come there to see you. I can't say the same for the place I am in now. When I am out of it, I will tell you a bit more about it. If my life hadn't been happy in every other respect, I couldn't have stood it; it is too depressing for words.

Well, I had a good cry over Mr. Boos. I am sure he died of a broken heart. He was so kind and good-hearted that I am sure Germany, Hitler, broke his heart. When I was at the plants, he came around nearly every week and had a chat with us in the office. He was always full of fun, but a bit nervous, as if he were laughing to cover a hurt, always immaculate in his dress. Now he has joined Mr. Kraemer in the Happy Valley Memorial Cemetery. It is all too terrible.

September 3, 1941

I am just now getting back to this letter and have now received your letter about spraining both your ankles. What rotten luck. To think that you finally took a little holiday and had that misfortune. No doubt you did have a much-needed rest, but I am sure you had a lot of pain too. I am so sorry. The place you went to sounds marvelous, and I only wish I could go to a place just like it.

I have now been working fourteen months with no vacation and several moves with the children and furniture, etc., thrown in. Wilfred and I will take at least two weeks together as soon as my year is up here, and let Bert look after the children. I must get away from them as well as my job.

You will be glad to hear that, in the meantime, I have got the very girl I have been wanting for the children. She is a native, not coloured, and is the wife of the headwaiter at *Kya Lami*. They are both the very best type of native, and she will not have any trouble with the boys employed at the place because of him. I pay her $5.00 more per month, but it is worth it to have peace. She is very quiet but firm with the children. I never liked Elizabeth's manner with them. [104]

---

[104] This is Helen's first mention of Betty, the maid, who was to become an integral part of the family for the next nineteen months. Betty was an educated and capable woman, well liked by the whole family. She spoke four languages fluently—isiZulu, Sesotho, English, and Afrikaans. Note that Helen has adopted the South African use of the term "girl" which she had formerly found so obnoxious.

Robin is continuing with her little school in the mornings, which is $5.00 per month for the mornings. My money has to go for lots of extras because I am at work. Still, we are better off with the job than if I stayed at home and took care of the babes myself. Wilfred had a fit when I told him I was going to try to manage without a girl. It keeps me on the move, and there was always the problem of them being sick a day, and what then?

I cabled you on Monday and said that the lowest figure I wanted to take for the house was $9,500. I was so afraid you might let it go below that before I could get a letter to you that I decided to cable. I don't know whether you ever knew it or not, but right in the midst of the Depression, and when I was having a terrible struggle, I refused $8,000 cash, so of course, with conditions good in America and the loan in good shape, I simply could not think of taking less than $9,500 and am not anxious to sell at that price. I think Welsford is trying to scare you and is perhaps working for L.

I feel quite certain that we can rent for much more than $50 per month, so do not worry about that. Just to ease your mind there, you could ask some other agent what rent you could expect on the place in case you had to get new tenants. We can still hold the place, if we do have to rent at $50, so just sit tight and don't worry one scrap. L., perhaps, thinks I am in a tight place, and he also knows property is the best place to have his money right now. Now that you know how I feel, and that $9,500 is rock bottom, you have nothing to worry about as to responsibility, for I am taking that responsibility, and, if I am wrong, then I can only blame myself.

I sacrificed a lot to hold that house, and L. shall never be the one to have the benefit of that. I am sure he could not build the same house on the same property for less than $12,000, and I doubt if he could do it for that amount at this time of rising prices. What did Uncle Fred's house sell for? Surely Eugene can find this out.

I would love to see the hydrangea, as I always had a personal interest in it. I took it from the potted plant sent Father in the hospital when he was so ill, and planted it on "G" Street; then Ruby Hampton and I moved it to Broad Street. I couldn't have stood it if they had told me I couldn't move it—well, I would just have moved it anyway. It was funny that I could leave everything else but that hydrangea, just because it had been Dad's, and I had replanted it.

Well, we have been lucky, as everything you have listed in your letter as having sent me has arrived. I heard something last night that annoyed me. The South African Government has now passed a law whereby one must apply to the Priorities Board for shipping space on boats to the Union; of course, war supplies have first priority, and then essential industries. To get around this, one merchant in Johannesburg who had just been to New York buying dresses, etc., to stock his store had everything sent by parcel post when he found he couldn't ship it by freight. Of course, the extra cost means nothing to him (that will come off all of us), and war supplies out of the Union must also mean nothing to him. In any case, I have brought it to the attention of the heads here, and I hope something will be done about it. We haven't felt the pinch at all here, and most people here seem determined that we shan't. I am sure our men up North would not feel too pleased to know such things were going on when their rations are cut.

Thanks very much for the $1.00 each for the children's bank accounts. What do they stand at now?

I must wish Mother a happy birthday, and I hope this letter gets there just at the right time to cheer you up on that day. We shall have to really celebrate all our birthdays when next we are together, one after another. We were never much on that, but I think it would be a good idea after our long separation. Bert is celebrating her birthday this coming Saturday, the 6th of September. She is having about sixteen in for cocktails and bacon and eggs afterwards; then we are all going to the Officer's Club to dance. We should have a really nice time. Thank goodness I have someone for the children, so I can really enjoy myself.

Perhaps you did write me about reading *How Green Was My Valley*, and no doubt I got the letter but have just forgotten that. I believe your letters come through for the most part. I am seldom long without one and, when I am, I get two or three at a time.

I must stop now and get home. I am doing this after office, and it is getting late now and the children will be expecting me.

All our love and lots of xxxxxxxx,

Helen

September 13, 1941

My dearests,

I am in the office a bit early this morning, so I shall try to write you two a short letter.

I failed to mention in my last letter that I have received *The Mary Baldwin News Letter* and, much to my astonishment, found a lengthy piece about myself. Thanks very much for sending it in. When I opened the magazine, I said to myself, "Well, I hope someone I know is mentioned." If it hadn't been for the bit about me, and two others, I wouldn't have known a soul. The two other girls mentioned were both older than me, but they have just married—one married a Lieutenant Colonel in the U.S. Army. The man Bert likes is a Lieutenant Colonel, but I think he is enjoying his bachelorhood.

Wilfred was in a very bad car wreck last Saturday but came out uninjured, thank goodness. The other three men in the car were badly injured. The driver got the steering gear through him; one man in the back seat sustained a broken leg and arm, and the other one from the back went through the windshield and was scalped. Wilfred saw the accident coming, so he fell on the floor in front and wrapped his coat around his head and held his little leather attaché case in front of his face. The driver was drunk and speeding. Wilfred didn't know any of them in the car, as he had just got a lift in from camp to Johannesburg with them. The people in the other car were also badly injured, especially a woman who is pregnant. I haven't heard this week of the condition of these people. Wilfred felt sure that two of them would die.

Wilfred then gets into another car, and a wheel comes off of it, and they crash into a pillarbox [a large, solid–red, cast-iron mail box]. There are wrecks every week on this road, and he has felt sure for some time that he would be involved in one finally, as he goes back and forth to camp with so many different drivers.

The film, *Lady Hamilton*, is here now—the one that Roosevelt and Churchill saw together, but it is so booked that one can't get in to see it. You have no idea how far ahead people here can see. They book shows days ahead. Remember when I tried to get into a popular maternity home here with Robin, they told me they were booked for the next ten months, and I said, "Oh, how clever the people of Johannesburg must be." For a table of bridge, you may be asked three weeks ahead. Oh, for a little town, I sometimes think.

I have not had any success so far with finding another place to live. Johannesburg seems to be full—flats, boarding houses, and all. All boarding houses have gone up ten percent on their rates, but our income remains the same. Most places are giving a cost of living allowance, but a certain figure was set for the job I am doing by a board, and that is final.

I feel that I have been doing some very good work in the office lately. I handled the office beautifully for three weeks by myself. My punctuation, etc., seem to suit the old boy, and he is very hard to please, I can tell you. Every detail is a big point with him.

Both Eve and Robin are well and happy these days. In the morning you should see the scattering of the clan. Robin [age 3] takes off in a northerly direction, Eve [age 7] northeast, and I [age 35] come south. This being Saturday morning, the two babes had a lazy morning and were just dressing when I left.[105]

My blue linen suit turned out very nicely, and also the while georgette blouse Bert and I made together. The shade of blue must suit me, as I don't know how many people had a second look at me the two times I have worn it. It looks very tailored and yet feminine, as the blouse is full of lace and the color is light.

I must stop now. This is just a note to let you know we are all right.

---

[105] The customary workweek for office workers in South Africa at that time, and right up into the early 1960s, was Mondays through Fridays 8-5 and Saturdays from 8-12.

The weather is gorgeous, but we shouldn't gloat over it, as we need rain so badly. It has been months and months since we have had anything but two sprinkles lasting five minutes each. Love and kisses from us all.

Helen

Postcard from Helen
Empire Exhibition Johannesburg, South Africa, 1936

Rissik Street, Johannesburg

I walk along here every day, so I thought you would like to see this card. The City Hall is on the right of the trees, and Escom House is far down the street on the right. Bert's apartment in McKay Mansions is also on Rissik Street.

Kya Lami
31 Esselen Street
Hospital Hill
September 26, 1941

Dearest Mother and Dad,
    Mother's letter of the 16th of August came today, censored as usual, which seems very good time to me. It had enclosed a lovely yellow hanky, which makes

the third linen hanky in the last few weeks. I am beginning to have what is known as a supply of hankies, and a supply of anything is practically unknown with me. If I got my washing done only once a week, we would really have to triple our wardrobes. But, as it is, our washing is done every day, and we have a minimum of practically everything, so it makes less packing for our next move. Everything I buy must pass one query: "Can I pack it?" I can pack hankies, so thanks ever so much.

I am very sorry if I have never mentioned the birthday cards Eve and Robin got. They were thrilled with them, and Eve has had me read hers over and over again. They know they mean a great deal to you too. Robin seems to understand so much about Mama Sophia and Papa Harlow. Eve insists she is an American and tries to keep her American accent by practicing it in her reading—all with little success.

Evidently, all of my letters to you don't arrive, as I got your letter telling me to keep the $50 you all sent, and I wrote back thanking you and said again that I hated to take it, but I supposed I must under the circumstances. Please let this go for this coming Christmas, as I think it will be better if we don't send anything, as they need all shipping space so badly. If there are heavy Christmas mails, it will just hold up essential supplies that much. I cannot think of anything we really need, in any case, and a cheerful letter is the best thing we can ever have—and a good picture of you both.

I am so happy your ankles are improving. They treat sprained ankles with massage here, but are there any masseurs around home? One of the young girls at our table is taking the course at the Medical School, which is very near us.

Make no effort to sign L. up on another lease. In fact, if given an opportunity, act reluctant to enter into another lease. If he is asking for so much that you can't get out of the red, flatly refuse. I am sick of the L. family, and I prefer anyone else at less rent. Buck up to him, and I am right behind you. Our holding the house does not depend on him.

I have been going to the hospital twice a day for the past ten days, and it is telling on me. A Miss Lyons who was studying for a matron's post had a breakdown from too much study, and they have her in the observation ward where they are all mental. She depends on me too much, and I must help her if I can, but it is very depressing.

I can't help but think how fortunate we all are in each other that each of us was strong enough to stand the mental stress and strain that we had for such a long time. I have only now realized how close I was to snapping, but thank goodness I never admitted it during the critical time. I think it must have been a complete year that I lost my powers of concentration. Dancing helped me more than anything else during that particular time.

There is a German woman in the ward who has taken a great fancy to me. She is a very sad case. They are Jews, and she can't forget the past, her husband says. When she is normal, she tells me she must control herself, that her family is so good to her, and then she goes off completely the next minute and thinks I am a figure in black, etc. She is beautifully dressed— that is, her gowns and robes are lovely, and her husband and two daughters so nice looking. To think that she realizes her condition and yet can't help herself.

Miss Lyons is not off her head, but she is very depressed. For a woman of forty, she is entirely too dependent on other people, and her problems are the only problems in the world. After seeing these poor creatures, I shall endeavour to be more carefree than ever. Of course, Papa and I usually let trouble overtake us before we will admit it is there. Well, I think you are both bricks because you were marvelous through all that passed—those very sad and difficult years. But how much sadder it could all have been if any one of us had given up and lost our balance.

I must tell you one cute thing from Robin and then go to bed. She said to me, "Mommie, what makes you so stubborn when I talk to you?"

We are all well and are expecting Wilfred home tomorrow. He gets in nearly every weekend.

Our love and kisses,

Helen

Kya Lami
31 Esselen Street
Hospital Hill
October 7, 1941

Dearests,

Well, my [thirty-fifth] birthday is over, and I had such a happy one. You will be glad to know that your birthday letter to me arrived October 1st with the white linen hanky with the blue border. That was certainly well timed and so much appreciated. I had such a surprise this year, as Elsa Swan, a very attractive young girl and friend of Bert's and mine, asked us over for drinks on Tuesday evening before my birthday on Thursday. She said we must toast my birthday.

I only expected a sundowner and then back home, but the party developed with the evening. There were eight people there, and enough men to go round, for a change. After cocktails, Elsa and her brother [Howard Swan, owner of Swan Press] took the party to the Country Club for dinner in the private dining room, which is paneled like the one at the Franklin Club [in Elizabethton].

It was a lovely moonlit night, and the Country Club is the most beautiful place in Johannesburg. After dinner, we all went to the Orange Grove Hotel to dance and got home about one in the morning. Unfortunately, Wilfred wasn't over for all the fun. I don't know when I have laughed so much and felt so gay. Everyone was in high spirits.

Most Americans stop at the Orange Grove Hotel for a month or two when they first come out, until they can buy their furniture, etc. It is full of lions' heads and skins and is very African in atmosphere.[106]

Then, on Thursday, Wilfred came in for the day and sent me beautiful flowers—roses, pansies, forget-me-nots—from the florist. We took Bert, Elsa, and Elizabeth Byrne to the Carlton Hotel for lunch. The Carlton is where the King of Greece stopped when he was here.

Bert gave me a beautiful georgette nightie which she had made, and Elizabeth gave me a nice bottle of perfume to replace one that she she knew Eve had spilled just after I had bought it.

Robin has been in bed today with a cold. She had a temperature and was restless from one o'clock on last night. She seems much better tonight.

Eve is looking forward to receiving her white dresses. She says she may start wearing them now, so they are arriving at just the right time [early spring in South Africa]. I do appreciate your making them for her so very much. She is going to write you herself when they arrive.

The children are very well off for clothes now, except for hats. I am buying them both hats if I can find anything I would have. I want to make Eve a dress, but so far I cannot get a pattern. The town is sold out of patterns. I have a dress pattern for Robin, which I shall have to use over and over, I suppose.

We are not rationed on anything so far. There is plenty of food of every description. There will finally be a scarcity of clothes, etc.; in fact, everything that is imported. However, we have most necessities here. I shall be very glad when we no longer can get silk stockings. That will be one expense cut out. All board and lodging goes up seven and a half percent from November 1st. However, no increase in my pay, or in Wilfred's.

Mother, you can't keep on spending on the Johnson City house at the rate you are now. You must refuse some of L.'s requests. You are only supposed to spend one month's rent per year. He can't expect more.

Bert and Elsa have gone to Durban for five days in Elsa's car. Elsa has a farm [Blackwood] down that way. Wish I could have got off.

Love and kisses,
Helen

---

[106] It was common in those days for the heads of various antelope such as kudu, springbok, and impala to adorn the walls of the huge screened porches of large, older homes, as well as the interiors of hotels and clubs.

P.S. Wilfred is a First Lieutenant. He is teaching maps and compass, the Military Disciplinary Code, and Organization.

Kya Lami
31 Esselen Street
Hospital Hill
October 12, 1941

My dearest Mother and Dad,

Well, I am having a marvelously lazy Sunday morning. I am sitting in bed while I have this chat with you. Wilfred is on maneuvers this weekend, and will be for some ten days, so I am having a good rest. It is really very tiring holding down a job all week, being a mother every morning and evening, and a peppy, cheerful companion every weekend. I don't intend to even leave the boarding house today.

Eve and Robin are getting ready for Sunday school. This, I fear, is largely due to the new hats I bought them yesterday. It is very hard to get Eve to Sunday school. She is evidently not a very gregarious person, as she does not like school either, though she learns very quickly. Their hats are very sweet little straws with ribbon and flowers. They remind me of some Mrs. Alexander used to trim for them. I also bought Eve a new pair of school shoes, the most dreadful-looking heavy black affairs. Her foot has suddenly grown about two sizes. I am going to make Eve one new dress, and then they are well off for clothes for the meantime.

The little picture enclosed was done by Eve for her Auntie Bert's birthday. It is entirely original, as she had no help or suggestions given her. I think it is most amusing.

I have really spoiled myself this month, as I set myself up to a lot of new undies—a new corset which always costs me plenty, three new petticoats, two step-ins, and two brassieres. I really look respectable underneath. When you haven't a house, you can have a few clothes. I was always more interested in my house, when I had one, than in clothes. All spare cash went there, though it was very modestly done. I have also just bought a beautiful fur felt (white) hat with a bit of navy blue ribbon on it. It is a model from London and very "voguish." I shall have some snaps made with it on. It is a hat for the year round in Johannesburg and can be worn with anything. It was very dear, but since I only spent $1.75 on my winter hat, I thought I could have it. The winter hat was always admired and was a definite bargain; so don't feel sorry for me. My new hat was $12.

Having spent all of this money, I am now trying to economize by making my rose linen myself. I spent 3½ hours cutting it out by a Vogue Pattern, and that made me so thoroughly sick of it that I don't know when I'll start sewing it up. It is very complicated and will take infinite patience and work. The main reason I am doing it is that I am so disgusted with my dressmaker. She has made the blue and the white linens up for me, and neither of them feels right. I think I can get a better fit myself.

I find that the last mail for overseas has left which will arrive for Xmas, and I am feeling so ashamed that I haven't got something off for you two at least. Why do I let every Xmas find me wanting? The shipping is such a problem, but, even so, I could have had a little space on some boat, I am sure. Anyway, just now I shall say, do have a Merry Xmas for my sake and your own, and may we all have Peace on Earth by another Xmas. I have in mind some little thing I want to send you, but it will be very late. I hope you will write me to consider some one thing you have already sent me as our Xmas because you have sent so much this past year, and I don't like to always be on the receiving end.

Speaking of being on the receiving end, I must tell you of a letter I received from Bené in Durban. He wrote me that since he has been away from Holland, his home, so long that everyone is a stranger to him, and since he isn't married that he is leaving me and a few other friends what he has. He is about sixty, but there is no reason why he should think of wills, as he has many years before him, but I think it terribly sweet of him to include me. You know, of course, what beautiful things he has—Delft china, oil paintings, rare books, a mink cape, a solid silver tea service, just to name a few things. He says his practice has doubled what it was last year, and, since he has more sense about money now than he used to have, he should have some money too.

He has been generous to a fault in the past. He is a funny little man, very foreign, and I am sure you would wonder at our friendship. He helped me through a very trying time with a bit of gaiety, and he was a perfect gentleman through the whole time, and that is why I think so much of him; and on his side, he found me sincere and really interested in his welfare; whereas many others have used him because he had some money and was unattached. Isn't it strange that I seem to have always taken to people with a different background from my own? It isn't always easy to adjust oneself, but it never fails to be interesting.

It seems that one very important matter was overlooked when Wilfred wound up his affairs and joined up, and that is last year's income tax, which we must now pay—about $175. How would you like to pay that on a year's earnings? Thank goodness, it isn't the English tax, though. Anyway, this certainly spoils the little bit we had saved, but we still have nothing to grumble about. I think Wilfred has done so very well, and I admire him so much for what was a demoralizing time we went through in Elizabethton. I have to laugh about them not giving him a country school even, and now he teaches majors their jobs.

Wilfred puts so much into anything he does. You should read some of the lectures he has written and see the illustrations he has had an artist do for his map and compass lectures. He is never satisfied with just doing a lecture as it is given him, but he enlarges on it by buying books and reading up, and he redoes the whole subject. He has taught himself every subject he now teaches. He is well known now for his work, and has had much notice given him. He still longs to really get in the fight, and I am sure he will have his chance. It is strange, but, when I married, I thought to myself, no wife of an Englishman can escape either sending her husband or her sons to a war. It is a dreadful thought, but that is the price of the Empire, which I believe to be essential for the balance of the world.

I tried to get a darling cottage with a lovely garden not long ago, but I had no chance over a widow who lost her husband in the bombings in England and has her son in Iraq. My war effort just doesn't compare, thank heavens.

Eve and Robin have just returned from Sunday school and are most enthusiastic. They have each a Joseph's coat, which they have coloured in. I shall send you Robin's effort.

Love to our dear ones,

Helen, Eve, Robin

Kya Lami
31 Esselen Street
Hospital Hill, Johannesburg
November 1, 1941

Dearest Mother and Dad,

I did not have a letter from you for several weeks, and then your letter of September 24th arrived before your letters of the 5th and 13th of September, which two arrived on the same day. We must not worry when we do not hear because the delay is usually in the mails and not because you and I do not write.

I was glad to hear that the cable arrived intact. I was not anxious to send a longer one, as my telegrams are so garbled that Wilfred can never make out what I mean. It was signed Evans because the surname must be given, and I would have had to pay for Helen, so don't think anything of that in the future. It is a new ruling since the war, I think. Well, in spite of Welsford Artz, I still want not a penny less than $9,500 for the house. Do not make any special effort on selling it, for L. may come around when prices go up, but he won't be so keen if others come to see it and turn it down.

As well as I remember, he paid $8,500 for that house when he first bought it, and then he finished the upstairs himself. It was just left unfinished by the first owners and builders. I am sure it is now worth the $9,500 that I ask. In any case, it is worth that to me. Tell me frankly how Uncle Earle's home that he has just built for $9,000 compares with it. I am sure they have better bedrooms, and I know that hurts the sale of the house every time, but, taking everything into consideration—Johnson City versus Maryville, etc., ground and all—what do you think?

I was so glad to have news from Aunt Hattie [now age eighty-five], and to hear that she is still lovely. I think she must be a guide for both of us. I suppose one thing that has helped her stay sweet is her good health. I am sure that makes a great difference. I am very disappointed to hear that you do not plan to drive down to Florida with them, and I think it a big mistake. I intend to take advantage of everything offered me for the rest of my life. Why I have ever let anything slip by me, I don't know. I have only realized the last few years that I can't live forever, and I have taken a much keener interest in life. I am glad Father is going, and I know he will love every minute of it. I hope he is going to be away for at least three weeks.

Helen's great-aunt Hattie

I am glad to hear that Virginia is at last taking Ann. Her opportunities in Washington will be so much better. I imagine Ann is very attractive. What a thrill for her to fly to Washington. I suppose it is much the easiest way to send her up alone.

Since the driveway to the house must be fixed, I am glad you are seeing to it. I know the house is a worry to you, as it was to me when I had to deal with L.

I think you must try dressing warmer this winter, and you will find you don't want the house as hot as you usually keep it. I dress in very warm clothes during the winter and can stand the unheated houses as well as the rest of them. I wouldn't like a house as hot again as we used to have. You should keep the heaters closed upstairs until time for the boys to come in the evenings. You could do with a fire in the living room during the milder days, I should think. At least, that is what they would do here.

I was interested to hear that Mr. Smith is getting married. I thought he was a confirmed old bachelor. He is very nice indeed, but somehow I never gave him a second thought, though I worked in the office with him for years. I always thought Ruth Peircy had a soft spot for him. Has she ever married? I suppose the fact that she has had T.B. would frighten men off, but she is so pretty, I think.

I have just this minute experienced the worst earth tremor since being in this tall building. For a very *full* second it felt like every foundation of the building was going. It is a most terrifying thing but over so quickly that everyone forgets them immediately.

My pair of Dickerson shoes are beautifully comfortable and just the right size, so you don't need to worry about that. However, I can take a drawing of my foot, but I don't think it would be of much use to you. I am sorry you are having so much trouble about the white shoes.

You may think Wilfred is lucky to still be in the Union, but he doesn't. You don't know how it galls him. It is very difficult keeping him quiet. You know his disposition; well, it really hasn't changed.

I am glad Father is feeling better since dieting. I like to eat, and eat too much most of the time, and little Robin overdoes it all the time. She simply stuffs herself. When she finds something new that is good, she can't stop until she has a pain in her tummy. Eve is as indifferent as ever about her food.

I shall give Mr. Kingston Russell the message from you. He can be most charming, but this morning he happens to be just everything else but that. I am surprised at how little difference it makes to me anymore. It simply passes over me somehow.

I am glad the bridge club is starting again, for I know how you enjoy it. You must be one of the very few charter members left. I simply can't play anymore. In fact, I think I shall just give even the idea of it up, for it is hopeless without practice.

You hadn't told me that Si had married, and I was so surprised. He should have told Aunt Lula and Uncle Earle before they built if he knew he was going to marry, because I know they would have built a much smaller place. However, as you say, I know it must have been very hard for him to tell them. Having lived with them all these years since Marie's death has not made it any easier for him to marry. I hope he married a nice person, and I think it much better that he should be married, for I always felt sorry for him, and it isn't very nice to be one of those people that others feel sorry for.

What is America going to do now that one of her Destroyers has been sunk?[107] I don't see how she can stay out of it much longer. I am anxious for the next issue of *Time*.

It seems you have not felt well since your fall. I suppose it did more to you than sprain your ankles. Why don't you have some X-rays made? After a fall, one should take Epsom Salts, so I have been told, immediately. It saves one a lot of soreness, it seems. I do hope you will start feeling better and take care of yourself as much as possible.

---

[107] Helen is referring to the sinking of the American destroyer, *USS Reuben James*, sunk by the Germans on October 31, 1941, the day before she wrote this letter.

Wilfred and I are going to have a holiday together. We are so thrilled over it that we are like two children. We leave on the 11th of November at 9:30 p.m. for Knysna. Knysna is in the Cape Province and is where the large Stinkwood Forests are. From there, we go to Plettenberg Bay.

I shall write you while I am away and tell you something about what I am seeing.

We went to a very big birthday party last weekend and had a gay time—about thirty-five there. Our friend, Elsa Swan, has just become engaged to the lad whose birthday it was. She only met him at Bert's party on the 6th of September. It didn't take them long to find out how they felt toward each other. Unfortunately, she had to break a previous engagement with a man up North, and this was most upsetting to her, but then she really can't help it if she has changed in her feelings. She is a most attractive girl—twenty-seven years old, just the age I was when I married, but she appears much younger. By the way, I feel younger than I did at twenty-seven.

I must really close now, as a dozen and one other things must be done.

By the way, Virginia Pollard saw the bit about me in the *Mary Baldwin College* magazine and wrote me a long letter about herself. She has a second husband now. Her boy by her first husband is seventeen, and she has two more—nine and five years old. She lives in Arlington, Va., and teaches voice. Her husband works for the Government. She wants me to visit her whenever I come back to America, and I shall certainly take advantage of the invitation, for I think Arlington and Washington a lovely spot, and it would be so marvelous for the children to see it all.

Love and kisses from us all,

Helen

Room 724
Escomb House, Johannesburg
November 29, 1941

My dearest Mother and Dad,

Well, I am back from my much-too-short holiday. The time I was away simply flew. Anyway, for two weeks I lived like a blinking Duchess and enjoyed myself immensely. Wilfred had more leave than I, so he doesn't get in until tomorrow morning. I am glad he had longer, for he needed the rest more than I did. When I got back, I found Bert exhausted. She said the children were too much for her.

I wrote a bit of my trip on the train going down, so I shall give it to you just as I wrote it.

Our train pulled out of Park Station, Johannesburg, at 9:30 Tuesday night, November 11th, with Bert and Eve to see us off. Just as we were moving out, a soldier and a civilian, both a bit tiddly, grabbed Wilfred's hand and said, "Goodbye, sir. Best of luck!" Though we were definitely headed *South*, they were evidently under the impression that he was on his way *North*. Anyway, the comradeship was good to see and made me feel a little full in my throat. For miles, we had the bright lights of the Reef towns, then all was dark; after a long chat, we went to bed, and Wilfred to sleep, not I. We were up early next morning. We got into Bloemfontein at eight, and Wilfred had a chance to point out No. 1 Harvey Road to me, the address I got from him twelve years ago for my first letter to Africa.

On leaving Bloemfontein, we started on a day with nothing to see from our windows but the high veldt and a clear blue sky. The veldt is nothing and more of nothing. No trees, no grass, no people—except for a very few tiny dorps[108] along the way. This limitless space was refreshingly welcome after nine months in the city, with so many people, so many buildings, and so many cars. During lunch with Wilfred and two other officers, one of them pointed out to me the first mirage I have ever seen. It looked like a very distant small mountain, but, if you looked searchingly, you noticed that it seemed slightly suspended in air, and another thing that gave it the lie was the shimmering heat that danced between us and our false mountain.

After lunch, a wounded R.A.F. came and sat with us in our compartment. He had been wounded through his knee and was on his way to a convalescent home near Knysna. He had been in Egypt for the past four years and hasn't seen his wife in all that time. On my way back from lunch, I looked into one of the open compartments, and there was a young man in uniform with one arm missing. We are seeing so much of this now, either a leg or an arm. With the big drive that is on in Libya now, I am afraid this will be a very sad Christmas in South Africa for so many families, as the casualties will be coming in about then.

Late in the afternoon of our first day on the train, I had a most wonderful experience—I saw the colour effects that I had only seen in paintings of South Africa, and they are so hard to believe. There was a range of four or five very symmetrical granite mountains, one rectangular, one cone-shaped, and so on, and they were lassoed with a heavenly pink light from the setting sun. Slowly creeping up and completely enveloping these mountains before we lost sight of them was a deep and all-consuming purple.

During the night and early next morning, we traveled along the edge of the Great Karroo, which is the greatest sheep country in the world next to Australia. Here they get rain about every ten years. The sheep are mostly the Hammerkop variety, with black heads and white bodies. There are also many ostrich farms

---

[108] "Dorp" is an Afrikaans word for "a small town." However, the word was adopted by the English to describe a small town with little to recommend it.

along the way. We are here just in time to see the cactus in bloom, and the orange flowers are so lovely that the cactus has been used as a hedge for some of the better homes. They also cultivate the prickly pear here; they look like the cactus without the thorns. The natives have been most ingenious and have made their houses of mud and enclosed their kraals with dried Mimosa branches, which keeps the cattle in as well as acting as a fence, since it has about a four-inch thorn covering its branches.

Just about lunchtime on our second day, we got into the country known as the Garden Route. This is considered the most beautiful scenery in Africa, but I don't need to describe it to you, for it is just like home—just like the trip through the Gorge to Linville, etc. The air was bracing and had the same feel as the air in Linville, and especially Blowing Rock. It all made me very homesick, so I think it is best that I live in a part that is so little like home. George is a little town at the foot of the mountains, and there we changed trains and took a local one to Knysna, and, for about two hours, we went through what is known as the lake country, and that is very pretty, then into Knysna, where all the stinkwood furniture is made. That, too, looked like home and the Dixie.[109]

From Knysna, we went to Plettenburg Bay and our very delightful hotel, which was only opened last December. Everything was there for our convenience and comfort, and we had a really wonderful holiday. We bathed in the sea on a very good beach; we danced and had a movie twice a week. I walked around the golf course with Wilfred one day while he played, and we met lots of nice people. In fact, I became very attached to Mary Dean. Her husband is a Naval officer and was also there. She has money of her own and traveled much before she was married. She was terribly interesting, and I am so sorry that she lives in Cape Town and not here in Johannesburg. She and I could talk by the hour to each other.

I am taking Robin and Eve to town this afternoon to have a look at the Christmas toys and to get an idea of what they want most. They are terribly thrilled over the outing.

Do you remember the picture of a baby asleep that I had for so long on my desk when we were in our home on "G" Street? The one with golden hair? Robin looks exactly like that picture when she is asleep.

The babes had a marvelous time with Auntie Bert, but they were glad to see me back, though I am a lot stricter.

Edith Broadbent has just arrived up here and has all the expense and worry of settling here, and, on top of it, she knows Charles is in the big push from now on. I

---

[109] Helen is referring here to the Dixie Chair Company that had been owned by her father, Harlow Dixon, until its liquidation in 1936. She had grown up amidst the twin businesses of lumber and the manufacture of furniture and had a keen eye for quality.

feel so sorry for her and all the other women waiting, waiting for some news or a letter.

By the way, I had three letters from you while I was away, and they meant so much to my holiday. Regarding the one about the shoes, I would suggest that you just make application for an Import License and let them come forward when they can. I am the very person who brought it to the attention of the proper people that merchants in this country were getting merchandise out by sending it all parcel post, and their regulations only affected freight at first. Now parcel post has no preference over freight as far as imports go.

You might state that I cannot get a fit in this country because of the narrowness of my foot, and that I have fallen arches and must have a proper shoe. I knew this would hit me directly one day, but I couldn't see the war effort suffering while merchants stocked their stores.

Have the Vaudills built another house, and who lives in theirs?

Worlds of love from all of us,

Helen

DECEMBER 7, 1941
ATTACK ON PEARL HARBOR

DECEMBER 11, 1941
AMERICA ENTERS WW II AGAINST ALL AXIS POWERS

Room 724
Escom House
Rissik Street
Johannesburg
December 11, 1941

My Dearest Mother and Dad,

Well, at last America is in the war. I am sure the Japanese action has done more to unite the American people than any statesman could have done. Japan seems well equipped for this war and has done so much damage already. I hope it can be stopped very soon. The damage done at Pearl Harbour is heartbreaking, as well as the loss of the two British battleships, *The Prince of Wales* and the *Repulse*. Why can't we be first sometimes, and as sly as our enemies?

I have just received your letter of October 22nd with the pretty blue hanky enclosed. I shall enjoy it very much, and thanks a lot. It looks like hankies will be the extent of what we can send from now on. If we can get this one pair of shoes over, it won't be too bad as, fortunately, you have been resupplying me. Isn't that a blessing? Since you can't send to me, perhaps you can save your money. I have been getting the lion's share lately.

At last I have found another place to live and shall be moving at the end of this month. It is part of a house in one the very best residential suburbs—Melrose. The other part of the house will be occupied by an elderly lady, seventy-one to be exact, who owns the place. I will have a living room, two bedrooms, a study, kitchen, and large breakfast room and bath. It has an adorable garden—a child's dream, in fact. There is a tree house, which is not large enough to be dangerous, but just high enough to be a thrill, two fishponds, an aviary with two budgies already in it, a gift from Bert to the children. There are trees, grass, and flowers, and we are on a very quiet street.

I have considered this move more for the children than for myself, for I will have a very long bus ride back and forth each day; but, to get in a good suburb, that is always true. Unfortunately, I won't get to use my lovely electric stove, as the place is not wired for a stove, and she won't do the wiring because of the expense. However, I have a girl for the drudgery, and I hope she won't kick up a fuss, for a coal stove is hard.

Believe it or not, I again have an outside

Helen with Robin, Eve, and her father-in-law, William Evans, in the garden at 4 Reform Avenue, Melrose, Johannesburg. The house is typically South African, with a pergola and Dutch gable.

lavatory. The way I can manage to run into them is amazing. I suppose these two disadvantages are the reason I have been able to get the place at a figure I can pay. Anyway, the lady is from one of the best families in Johannesburg, and we shall all have congenial and nice people around us and shall not be bumping up against some of the hard customers we have had to see in the past.

Eve, being a sensitive child, has been hurt many times, I am sure, by the people in the boarding house. Since getting back from my holiday and a good rest, I have spent every possible minute with the children and have given Eve, especially, so much attention that I see a great change in her. She had begun to have a sad look about her, but I have almost banished that, and I am sure the house will completely fix that up.

We are going to have a lot of expense, of course, moving the furniture up from Durban and acquiring all the little things that must be bought when you start housekeeping again, but I am sure storage does not help furniture, and we could not go on living in the cramped quarters we were in. I shall feel very good about the children, as the old lady has promised to keep an eye on things for me.

I am really annoyed with you that you are not going to Florida. Changes help to keep one young. I know October and November are simply too heavenly in Tennessee. I have never seen anything so beautiful anywhere else, but I know you need a change. And to think you would turn Father over to Dud Jobe [descendant of Dr. Abraham Jobe, Sophia's grandfather] for two weeks in Florida is unthinkable. I am sure he will enjoy it all immensely, and I hope he takes advantage of everything exciting in Miami. He does love life, and I am glad to see it.

Too bad you are not getting the big dam. I am sure it would have meant a great deal to our section of the country. With inflation around the corner and the world so unsettled, I do not feel too anxious to sell the property in Johnson City, so don't worry about selling it just now.

Please thank Aunt Hattie for the silver card case, which she has given Eve. Tell them all not to forget Robin [now three-and-a-half years old], as she is one of the family too, and a heartbreaker at that. If they could see her, she would win them all. As Eve says, all Robin has to do to make a friend is smile and say hello.

I must stop now and get busy on a rush job.

Love and kisses,

Helen

P.S. Now you are all in the war, the war will finally involve every country and island, I believe. I hope the U.S. will soon make herself felt.

4 Reform Avenue
Melrose, Johannesburg
January 12, 1942

My dearest Ones,

I know it has been such a long time since I wrote, but there has been so much to do that I simply could not settle down to a letter of any description. I am in the office early this morning so have a little time before anyone else comes in.

We are getting nicely settled in the house now, but there has been so much work to do to make it even livable, and there is still considerable work ahead of me; but I shall do it as I can. We can eat and sleep now in comfort, and the finishing touches can come gradually. It is a very sweet little place, and I shall make some pictures right away to send you. Just now we are having so much rain that there isn't much opportunity for pictures.

The $5.00 came the other day from you all and was certainly appreciated. I saw to it that the children had presents from you all on Christmas day, as I received your letter before Christmas about the $5.00. You said to get something practical, but I didn't exactly do that, though. I got Eve a Rap-A-Paint set, which consists of about eight glass pictures that she can fill in with paints for glass. There is also everything to frame them in the set, and she is very enthusiastic about it since she can make pictures for her new room. She likes painting better than anything, and this was such a good set. The girl, Betty, put it in the box with the other toys, and Eve said, "Don't you know better than to put this very nice set in with other toys?" So she measured a drawer space to see if it would take the box, and found it would, and has put it carefully away until I have time to help her with it.

I bought Robin a piano, from you, and she loves it. Unfortunately, Eve is also crazy about it and monopolizes it a great deal, as Wilfred has taught her several tunes on it, such as "I Want to be Happy," "Red Wing," and "My Country 'Tis of Thee," or rather "God Save the King," in this country. Robin got a baby carriage, which she is crazy about, and I dressed her doll in a dress with a zip, which went over in a big way. I dressed Eve's doll beautifully, and it arrived in a playpen. We gave Eve *Pinocchio* and Robin a beautifully illustrated book of Nursery Rhymes. They got a cooking set with a really good small meat grinder, but someone took it. The skillet is iron and can really be cooked in. They got socks and hair ribbons and books to paint in and crayons and two budgerigars, little birds of a lovely blue colour, from Bert. Mr. Evans gave them $5.00, and I bought Government stamps with it.

Did I tell you about Robin when she got the postcard that Father sent her from Florida? I told her it was from Papa Harlow, and she stood by the bed looking at it for a long time, then she started saying, "Now I lay me down to sleep, I pray the Lord my soul to keep." She said this over and over, and of course I realized that her prayers were her chief connection with you.

We do hope the holiday was thoroughly enjoyable. What a pity Mother did not go, as she could have driven both ways, and the expense would have been so little. When I think of how much I have traveled, I feel quite ashamed of myself, but I can tell you I have reached the point that I feel I should like to settle in one house in one town for the rest of my life. I suppose I should always like short trips, however, as a change is good for one.

I am afraid Wilfred is coming down with Tick Fever. He got three ticks on him when he was out on the veldt the other day and feels very depressed and goes hot and cold. He will go into hospital if they find he has fever. Sometimes it is very bad and sometimes not so severe. I do hope he has a light attack. A friend of ours is just getting over it. It is very dangerous to go out camping on account of the ticks.

The boss is not expected back for about five months, but others are carrying on his work, so his absence does not affect my job at all. He has taken this whole thing very badly. The case has not been heard yet, and I am sure he would have been better off if he had let the case come up immediately and not have had this nervous strain. He has been badly knocked up too. [For details, refer to Helen's letter of January 30, 1942].

Eve's jaundice has cleared up, and she has such a good appetite now.

My furniture arrived in good condition from Durban. It cost me $80 to move it, but I had to do something for the sake of the children.

I must get to work now. I think it would be best for you to continue to address everything to the office.

Our love and kisses to you both,

Helen

4 Reform Avenue
Johannesburg
January 22, 1942

Dearests,

I have had every difficulty getting my house fixed up, but things are going some better now. I find the old lady who owns it very mean and difficult, but we have had some very plain words with each other, and she now knows I won't take all of her nonsense. I have a boy cleaning the garden and doing a lot of things that would take Wilfred many weekends, and I don't see why he should spend every weekend working on the place. Betty, my girl, has worked so well and has been a joy and comfort. Sunday, Monday, and Tuesday of this week I was sick in bed with asthma. The first time I have ever had it in Johannesburg, but I think I brought it on by too much heavy work around the house and garden. It seems that I can't do it, so I must just pay to have it done, and when I can't afford it any longer, let it go. Anyway, the boy I have for a few days is so good that my worries are vanishing. He is doing some crazy paving for me, and steps, and lots and lots of cleaning. It is an old world garden and really very pretty, but it must have one good cleaning to give us a start on taking care of it.

We have just received the package from Aunt Nellie and Katye Wray, and what a thrill! Really, we all got such a kick out of Robin's little outfit, and, when I took her out in it, everybody had a look, and another look at her, and then commented on it. I am wondering if Aunt Nellie made it. It looks so well done that I can't believe she bought it in a shop. Now Eve wants me to try to make the same for her. She was thrilled with her pajamas until she saw Robin's dress, etc., then she was all for trying to get into that. I was delighted with my stockings, and the children were crazy about the little toys that I am sure you added. The trouble is, we don't know how to play Jack Rocks. Can you tell us? No one here seems to know the game. I shall write Aunt Nellie very soon.

I just wanted to enclose this clipping, as it supports a statement that I made some time ago, that the riots we had were really trouble between the police and the citizens. We have all had the greatest feeling of insecurity for some time, but thank goodness the government is now taking steps. So many things have happened: railway lines blown up, bombs going off in cinemas, and many murders of girls in uniform right on the streets. The cleanup has come, but there are more for them to put away. Wilfred had to go out to see about a man who had been thrown from his motorcycle by a car at night and had his leg torn off, and, on the way, he had several shots fired at him from ambush, and the doctor's car that followed him had several holes in it.

Must get to work now, as I have a new boss, and I have to make a good impression.

Love,

Helen

Note: As mentioned earliter, at the outbreak of World War II, South Africa had a coalition government known as the United Party. The coalition was between the two European (White) groups: the Afrikaners (South Africans of Dutch, German, and French descent) under Hertzog, who wanted South Africa to remain neutral, and the English under Smuts, who felt that it was necessary to support Great Britain in its fight against Nazism. When conservative Afrikaners found themselves forced into World War II, by virtue of South Africa's being a dominion of the British Empire, some rebelled by aligning themselves with the Nazis inside an organization known as "Die Ossewa Brandwag" (founded on February 4, 1939). So fierce was their opposition to supporting Great Britain that many Brandwag supporters were placed in internment camps for the duration of the war—one being John Vorster, who was later to become a Prime Minister of South Africa. At the end of the war, the Ossewa Brandwag was absorbed into the National Party and ceased to exist as a separate entity. A year before Helen wrote this letter (on February 1, 1941), rioting broke out in Johannesburg, and one hundred and forty soldiers were seriously injured. At that time, however, Helen had her hands full moving to Johannesburg with her two young children to be closer to Wilfred. It's worth noting that, apart from the brief period when Wilfred worked for Westinghouse, neither Helen nor Wilfred had a car. The only home phone they'd had was one in the apartment they lived in when they first arrived in South Africa.

724 Escom House
Rissik Street, Johannesburg
January 30, 1942

Dearest Aunt Nellie and Katye Wray,

First of all I must tell you how thrilled we were with our Xmas parcel from you. It was so very unexpected, for we knew how they had tightened up on exports to South Africa to conserve shipping space. The big thrill was, of course, the red, white, and blue dress, panties, and bonnet for Robin. I simply haven't seen such a dear and original outfit here at any price. I am so vain about showing her off in it that I have asked if I can take her to a friend's wedding tomorrow. Of course, the bride said yes, but if she knew how she is going to be put in the shade by Robin, she wouldn't have been so generous with her invitation.[110]

Eve was so pleased with her pyjamas, and she did need a pair badly—still, I must say her enthusiasm was a bit dampened when she saw Robin's dress. Now I must try to make the same for her. My silk stockings were pressed into use almost immediately with a sigh of relief and a Bless You for your thoughtfulness. Thanks ever so much for everything, and I can tell you it was lots of fun getting it all.

I must admit that I did not have the Christmas spirit this year, and I found it impossible to do anything about it, but Christmas itself passed pleasantly enough for us. Everyone was most kind. I do hope it was a happy time for you with the little ones. I still think of Gene as little, but I know he would be a real shock for me. Can't you send me snaps of Gene and Kay and all of you, in fact? I'd love to have them, and I have never had a picture of the house. Mother tells me Aunt Nellie sent me a lot of pictures at one time, but they never arrived. She thinks it was because the pictures cut the envelope and has told me to wrap all snaps carefully in tissue paper.

---

[110] I believe this was the wedding of their good friends, Dr. Joe Marshall and Elsa Swan.

I am at last settled in a house with my own things around me after having them stored for eleven months, and it is such a pleasure after having other people's taste in decorations. We have a sweet Old World garden with lovely roses, two fishponds, cypresses, and all kinds of shrubbery. Robin has a swing, and there is a little summerhouse for the children to play in. I took the place for the children because it has just the garden I felt any child would love. It is so nice for Wilfred when he gets home on weekends too.

I have put Eve in school at Parktown Convent, which was Wilfred's first school. They take little boys up to seven only. I think the gentleness of the nuns will appeal to Eve. Just now her only concern is that she has a new uniform—always a thrill to her. She loves lots of pretty things.

We all hope that with America in the War it will end just that much sooner. Russia is doing a good job of things, isn't she? Mother sends me *Time*, which allows me to check up on the news we get here.

I do hope Eugene's health is good since his operation, and that things are still going well with him. How are Mr. and Mrs. Clem and Munna?

I would like to know if Aunt Nellie made the dress for Robin. I feel that it is not store bought, as it is so nicely done. I am not too bad at making dresses for the children myself now. I have a Westinghouse Electric Sewing Machine.

I suppose Mother or Father has told you that Wilfred and I had a really nice holiday in November through the Garden Route of the Cape. It was a much-needed change and rest for both of us, as we did not take the children or our jobs with us. The scenery was so lovely and so much like Tennessee and North Carolina that I got real homesick, so I'm sure I did not feel as happy as I would have had the scenery been something completely unfamiliar to me.

Wilfred's best regards to you all, and love and kisses from the children and me.

Helen

4 Reform Avenue
Melrose, Johannesburg
January 30, 1942

Dearest Folks,

I am afraid you have not been getting many letters from me, and I feel so ashamed of myself, as I have been getting so many nice letters from you, and copies of *Time*. Last night I received the issue published about the attack by Japan. I found that we knew practically all that was given there, but it is always nice to check up with *Time* magazine. I have heard it said here that Commander Kimmel was a second Lindbergh. Does the American public think so? I notice that Lindbergh is all out for war now, since it has actually come, and I believe he is sincere. I think he has been sincere in all that he has said and done, and I think she has been too; but I cannot see why they, who have traveled so much, were not more awake to the situation.

I thought you would be interested in the enclosed clipping. I feel very sorry for him, as I am afraid he is now a finished man just because he hasn't taken the whole thing like a man, but has let it wreck him completely. There is little doubt that he has always been a megalomaniac, and a thing like this is too much for his pride. He wanted to crush everybody around him, and did nearly finish Mrs. Smith, but when I came to the office, I stood up to him every time, as Wilfred told me I would have to leave if he noticed I was breaking under the man.

I made him so mad one day by slamming the door in his face that he didn't speak to me for three weeks, and then he told me that if I ever made him that mad again he would fire me. I simply said, "You know I won't mind, as I am a good stenographer and can get another job any day." He said, "Let us drop the subject." And that was that. You can imagine that he had done a lot to bring on all of this from me, as I try to respect any man I work for. [111]

In fact, we are so unsettled in this office, not knowing whether or not he is coming back, that I am taking another job that has been offered me in the organization. This person has been giving me dictation, etc., and yesterday asked me if I would come to his office. He has just joined the organization, but he is a big business man, and I know he will make a good place for himself in the whole set-up, so I am taking my chances with him. I will naturally get the same money, but I am also anxious not to lose any prestige by whom I work for, and I am sure I won't. I also feel that he will be a reasonable man in all of his dealings with staff, etc. It will be a week or two before anything happens, so I will write you later when there is something definite.

I am glad you have received the book on Natal and Zululand. I am invited down to the Swan's place there for Easter, but I very much doubt that I will be able to go, as it will be a big expense for such a short time; but I would love to do it, especially if I could take the children.

---

[111] Helen is referring here to her immediate boss, Mr. Kingston Russell, Assistant to Dr. van der Bijl, Minister of War Supplies in South Africa. Kingston Russell had been charged with "Damaging a Notice Board." *The Star* reported the incident as follows: "Reginald James Kingston-Russell, aged 58, of Tyrwhitt Avenue, Melrose, was remanded in his absence in the Johannesburg Magistrate's Court yesterday until November 27 on allegations of maliciously damaging a notice board, the property of the Johannesburg municipality, refusing to give his name and address, assault, and resisting arrest. The prosecutor, Mr. M.J. Pretorius, said that he had received a certificate to show that Kingston Russell was seriously ill and had gone away to the coast." Kingston Russell was later deemed to have been temporarily insane at the time. "He was fined £1 for injury to property, £5 for refusing to give his name and address," and on the two counts of assault, he was sentenced to fourteen days' imprisonment and suspended for three months.

I am sorry I did not have the Christmas spirit this year, but I felt for one thing that it was terrible to send merchandise out of South Africa when it is going to soon be so hard to get things out here. They are tightening up every day; of course, I knew it was coming before others realized. Even so, there is still enough of everything, and I have bought the material to make something for you, but I will have to get to it when I can, and that looks like it will be some time off.

For anyone to say that it is just like me to have my hair dressed in the latest fashions is too funny because I always spent less on that than any of the other girls and always did it so simply, I think. In fact, I think I made a great mistake by not spending more on such things. I have made a great discovery—my hair will stay set for two to three weeks if done by one man here in town without a perm. I hate perms, as my hair is inclined to frizz, and now I shan't have to have one anymore. I wear it in a simple style and parted in the middle now; it makes me look younger not to have so many set curls. Your hair must be very nice now, and I wish I could see it.

We are so looking forward to the picture. Do I understand there is a picture of you only? How about Father? I asked for a picture of both of you and must have it. It is disgraceful how long it was between pictures with you, Mother. For some reason, every single time I move, the glass gets broken on your picture. You could never guess how many glasses I have had put on that picture. I do hope the one you are sending arrives all right.

I am glad to hear that Virginia Lovett is getting along all right in the business world, so to speak. She must have a very nice job. She is very wise to stay with her mother. Her expenses would increase greatly if she went to Washington, and she would either have to be separated from Richard by leaving him with her mother or would find it difficult to make satisfactory arrangements for him in Washington.

I think you and Father are just sweet to offer to take the children and keep them at your own expense, but I wouldn't think of letting you do that, and now I feel it is much too dangerous for them to cross. Anyway, I don't think I could stand the separation, as I find they and Wilfred mean so much more to me than relaxation and a big time. When Wilfred and I went away, I fretted for the children, though I knew I needed the rest from them. I could hardly wait to get back home.

I will try to get Eve settled to writing the letter to you. I am afraid it hasn't even been tackled yet. You will be glad to hear that Eve is eating everything in sight. She can't be filled, and she is looking so happy these days. I took a house and changed schools all for Eve's happiness, as I could see she was not happy at the boarding house nor at the Government school she was in. You may not approve, because I know the way father feels about the Catholics, but Eve is now at school in a Convent. It costs me $15 a quarter plus dancing, which Bert is paying for, plus a small fee for swimming.

Yesterday was her first day there, and she loved it. The sisters are so gentle and kind, and Eve must have that. At the Government school where Eve was previously, I am afraid the whole atmosphere was too hard for Eve. The class at the Convent was at least half the size as at her other school. With her swimming and dancing extra, I am sure she will be happy. She also has one little friend there that she already knows. Mrs. Maton, from whom I rent, educated her daughter there, and she told me the sisters never tried to proselytize, as the Matons are not Catholics. Her daughter is about my age and has such a sweet manner, and the whole family is very prominent here. Now Eve has a good school and a nice home in the best part of town, and Mother has the bills.

I think I can manage it all if I am careful and forget clothes, etc., which is not hard for me. They mean so little compared with the happiness of one's children and the environment they have. I am going to exercise a little nerve when I next see Wilfred's father and ask him to pay for kindergarten for Robin. The little thing is crazy to go to school, and cries every morning when Eve and I leave her, as she stays all alone. He has plenty and could easily do it. I do not want you to offer it. I want it to come from him. He gets for himself as much as Father makes, and besides that he made $2500 on the stock market last year. As I told you, he gave the children $5.00 together for Christmas and nothing to Wilfred and me. I believe he was very good to Bert at Christmas time, for which I am thankful.

I don't know whether Wilfred is related to Chas. Collingwood, who broadcasts from London. I will ask him when he comes in. We do not have a radio, and I am not familiar with these people of the air.

I am glad you have met Ken Smith's wife and that she is nice. I will always have a soft spot in my heart for all the office crowd at the plants that I was so closely associated with. Could you inquire about Mr. Wampler for me? If he is still there, I'll write to him, for I am sure he would appreciate it and would write me a newsy letter in return. I wonder if Fred Brewer is still there and who is taking Miss Summer's place with him.

It must be too galling to C.T. to have relinquished his place in the sun to A.K. C.T. was very kind and nice to me for a while, but, when I think of his unbounded conceit, I don't think this will hurt him at all, but will do him a lot of good. He was always putting in little cutting remarks about Wilfred after we were married, and I haven't forgiven those. Of course, we'll have to forgive him to some extent, as he tried so hard to marry me. Has Walter Wiley ever married, and isn't he an officer in the Army now that America is in the War? I know it is hard for you to find out about some of these people, but I would like to hear from them again.

I did not notice about Mrs. C. de L. in the papers here. I suppose it was in the paper, however. I imagine de L. was a remittance man[112] from home, as Kenya is

---

[112] A "remittance man" was one who, disgraced at home, lived abroad on money sent from his paternal home.

full of them. They embarrass their families at Home, so they are sent out to Kenya and kept. They of course manage to keep Kenya in the limelight by such things as this.

You are complaining about eggs being 45c a dozen—do you know I must pay from 50c to 75c per dozen all the time for them, and we use two dozen per week. I feel I don't mind the price, for I am fortunate in being able to buy what the children need to eat. The starvation in Europe must be too dreadful for words. Just to have all your food taken away and no way to get more. What a desperate feeling of finality.

Our house is looking very sweet now with all of the curtains up. I want to buy a drop-leaf table and two plain chairs for the breakfast room, and then I'll have enough furniture to go on. I am also selling Robin's cot and buying her a full size bed. Now that I have a chance to sell it, she wants to sleep in it, of course.

We expect a good time this weekend, as Elsa Swan is being married tomorrow afternoon, and we are invited to the church and reception afterwards, and, as close friends, to the groom's house after that, until the train leaves at 7:30 p.m.[113] The petrol ration is making holidays by car very difficult. They have railed their car down so they can use it down there. You are allowed four hundred miles per month unless you are a doctor or traveler, etc. We are taking Eve and Robin to the wedding, as they are so anxious to see it; then Betty will take them home.

The money from Aunt Lula and Uncle Earle has come, but not the money from Uncle Edwin and Aunt Lennie. And, from your letter, I understand the money from Uncle Edwin was sent first. I shall inquire at the bank, but you had better inquire too. I am buying Eve and Robin some clothes with the money from Aunt Lula—Robin a pair of white shoes for the wedding and Eve bedroom slippers and school sweater or pyjamas. I don't know which. Aunt Nellie sent such lovely pyjamas to Eve, and that was just what she needed, only she can do with another pair.

I must stop now. When I really get started, I can't stop, it seems. I have made Eve one school dress and must get busy on another. The colour is beige at this school, with red leather belt. She will still get a lot of wear out of the white dresses on weekends, and the pattern you sent me of the one white dress was just the pattern I needed for her school dress by putting two of the front gores together and making it one big one. The dress was very simple to make with my electric sewing machine. I shall make one more dress for Eve and a blouse for a very good friend of mine, and then I am going to take it easy for a while and play some bridge and go to a few shows, etc.

---

[113] The bride and groom were Dr. Joe Marshall and Elsa Swan, who became close family friends. They owned the dairy farm "Blackwood" in the Midlands of Natal and, later, co-owned several movie houses with Wilfred's sister, Bert.

Love and kisses from the girls to you both,

Helen

> 4 Reform Avenue
> Melrose, Johannesburg
> March 2, 1942

My dearest Mother and Dad,

So far, it is with patriotic fervor that we carry our purchases home exposed to the public view. I almost laughed in the chemist's face the other day when he said to me with a very knowing look, "We still wrap up some things." It was quite apparent that I had not bought any of the "some things," as he certainly wrapped nothing for me. I have been inspecting shopping bags, with an eye to purchase, but they are the ugliest things I have ever seen, and I suspect they were only made for the native trade. When I walk out with my purchases unwrapped, I am always reminded of moving day. For some reason, I resent just any and everybody being able to see my personal possessions. I have often wondered if anybody else feels that way.

I shan't discuss the news, as it isn't good, and we must prepare ourselves for any eventuality. You can know that, if at any time things are really serious with us, I shall be with the children no matter what other duties someone might think I should perform. Furthermore, I have made up my mind to remain at home. Please do not let these remarks agitate you, as the chances are remote, no doubt, but I just want you to know what I'll be doing so you won't wonder about us. So many impossible things have happened that we must consider everything possible.

Our house is looking so nice now, as I have bought new linoleum for the kitchen, and I am gradually fixing up the back of the house. I am getting a new oilcloth for my kitchen table today. The kitchen

Helen, Eve, and Robin

is in green and cream.

The garden is looking too lovely for words, and last night Wilfred and I sat out in the garden in the moonlight. We were looking across the fountain at the outline of the tall pine trees in front, and the whole garden was heavy with the perfume of honeysuckle. The place seemed drenched with peace, and yet we discussed an air-raid shelter.

I shall try to write once a week, but even if I do, you won't get them but about every three weeks, I fear, as that is how I get your letters now.

I am busy every minute now on my new job. I like it ever so much better than the previous one, but, between my work and the children and Eve's lessons every evening, there is no time to myself. After her lessons, I have had sewing to do nearly every night. I usually relax on Friday and Saturday nights, being absolutely fed up with doing my duty by that time. I am glad I do have that feeling, as I might get used to just work and no play.

This past Friday night I went to see *Sergeant York* and simply loved every minute of it. It made me homesick for Tennessee, all right. I am sure that I was the only person in the theatre who was so familiar with the places and people portrayed in that picture. I took Miss Hudson, who lives across the street from me, as they take me into town every morning and deliver Eve at the Convent. It is such a convenience for me, and such a saving, that I wanted to do something nice in return. Before the picture, Bert had us to dinner at her flat in town, so it made a nice evening. I am glad to be in a neighborhood where I want to know my neighbors, which I couldn't say about my previous abode.

Do you remember how I depressed myself going to see Miss Lyons at the hospital last winter? Well, she recovered, left Johannesburg, wrote Bert, and never bothered to write to me. She, perhaps in her unsettled state of mind, decided I had done something to hurt her at some time. Anyway, I had to show her that little bit of kindness, as no one else bothered with

Wilfred, Helen, Eve and Robin

her. Bert went to see her twice, I think, and I went every day or night for about two months.

Have you read *Consulting Room*? I think every woman should read it, so, if you haven't, try to get it. I get most of my reading done going home on the bus in the evenings, as it takes a good half hour out.

Mrs. Maton left on Saturday for a week in Durban, so Bert is going to stay with me this week. I shall enjoy her company.

Wilfred has been in hospital two weeks with colitis but is all right again now. If his diet had been watched, he wouldn't have been in that long. [114]

Eve and Robin are both well and growing so fast. Robin tells the most far-fetched tales just now. Her imagination seems to be working overtime. One thing that is strange is that she is always telling me about playing with little Robert and what he says and does, and Betty says she doesn't know who this child is. She says Robin talks to herself all day while she is playing there alone. I somehow remember Eve talking about playing with a child named Robert when she didn't at all. I want to start kindergarten soon for Robin, for I am afraid she is lonely, and it may be very bad for her.

Did I ever thank you all for the Christmas card? And I just wonder if I have mentioned every hanky you have sent, as we have a nice supply now, which has all come from you.

I am going to write Uncle Edwin and Aunt Lennie, though the money hasn't come, but, since Father sent it, he will have to have it traced. I have written Aunt Lula and Uncle Earle. Any money you send me should be sent to H.D. Evans (Helen Dixon Evans), as that is my legal signature and the other causes trouble each time. I also do business with Barclays Bank and not the Standard Bank, so if you have a choice as to which to send through, you should send through Barclays. I am actually known at Barclays, Rissik Street Branch, where I have an account.

All our love to you both,

Helen

4 Reform Avenue
Melrose, Johannesburg
March 11, 1942

My very dearest Ones,

You have given me one of the big thrills of my life in sending me these marvelous pictures of yourselves. Of course, I remember the picture of Father and

---

[114] This is more evidence of Wilfred's undiagnosed celiac disease. Sadly, the disease was not widely recognized in South Africa at that time. It is often misdiagnosed even today.

always thought it was good and I am so happy to have it, but the new picture of mother was such a wonderful big surprise. It is simply too beautiful for words, and I feel like she could speak to me. Her hair is so lovely, and she looks years younger than when I left. I am so glad it is tinted; it looks like a miniature.

Portrait of Harlow Dixon. Age 58

Everyone says "how beautiful!" Bert is as pleased for me as I am that I have your pictures. Robin is always talking to both of you and has just shown you her new pyjamas tonight. Betty, my girl, is so enthusiastic that she must show and has told her husband to make a trip here to see them. I have to control myself as I want to carry them around with me and show them to everyone, but I know they haven't such good-looking parents, so I feel I would rather be gloating over them.

Anyway, I had two guests last night to meet my Mother and Dad. One was Sister Puller, who was my first and very good nurse with Robin. She hadn't seen Robin since she was five days old, and she thought Robin was simply too wonderful. Robin wore the red velvet dress Ann Dixon sent her, and did look pretty with her very blonde hair. She said her two nursery rhymes for Sister Puller— "Old Mother Hubbard" and "Simple Simon," both quite wrong, as she has never been taught but has picked up pieces of them from hearing them read. She starts out so well on both of them, and it is always a surprise to people to hear the finish.

Going back to the picture of Mother—the dress is so perfect, as it will never date the picture and neither will the style of Mother's hair. I was thrilled right down to your nail polish. I am sure you were thinking of me when the picture was taken, and, of course, Father is sure you were thinking of him.

Portrait of Sophia Dixon. Age 54

I have been having a few guests lately, as I couldn't do anything for people while I was boarding, and are they thrilled with Southern cooking—fried chicken and corn pudding, etc. Since I can only get one pound of flour per month, I am limited in my recipes. I have already finished my flour for this month.

Yes, Melrose is near Parktown North, where I used to live, but there is a very big difference between the two suburbs. Melrose has some of the finest homes in the city, whereas Parktown North is a suburb of poorer homes. Many of the big doctors live in Melrose; in fact, one is our next-door neighbour. Everyone is enchanted with our garden, and the house is clean and presentable. I am living very nicely considering we live on army pay.

I bought the children's winter underwear today, paying $2.50 per vest. I bought four, so that alone was $10. Then Robin had to have two new pajamas and Eve new bedroom slippers. Her slippers are red kid with black fur around the tops and parrots embroidered on the toes. They are lovely, really, and will look nice with her red silk quilted robe from last winter. Bert is giving Robin a new pair of slippers.

Thank you so much for the two pretty green cloths. They are so attractive. If you want to send something small to the children, I suggest hair ribbons, as there is little selection here now, and they love ribbons. I find they stay on better than clips, especially in Robin's hair. Robin received her hanky and was most pleased. I hadn't had any mail from you for about three weeks, and then the pictures, three letters, and four copies of *Time*.

For four weeks now I have been working like mad on my new job, and today my boss said he would ask for an assistant for me. I hadn't complained, but I was glad he could see how much I was doing. I had a girl helping me Monday and Tuesday, also Mrs. Smith gave us a hand, but we can't go on asking favours of other offices. I feel that I am doing better work in this office than I have ever done before. If it were my whole life, I might even be a big success in business, but I just won't let it take any of the time I can have with the children.

The [war] news is very bad for both of us, but I feel that a lot will happen in the next three months.

I am glad some of my letters have come through quickly. Yours still take two months.

My time is so full that I have no ideas for writing. I am sure one needs leisure for that occupation. I had leisure when I wrote the description of the country.

Love and kisses from us all,

Helen

4 Reform Avenue
Johannesburg
April 1, 1942

My Dearest Ones,

Your letter of February 1st arrived the other day and suddenly brought me to the realization that it has been some time since I wrote you. When days are as full as mine, they do fly by.

I see Mother has been enjoying herself buying for the children. The first need in the family was a good winter dress for Eve, and, now that you are taking care of that, I can concentrate on her winter school clothes. Today I bought a beautiful felt hat for her, and I have the school band for it. It was such a bargain that I am terribly pleased. I am going to ask the convent to allow her to wear the school gym and blazer that she has, the only difference being that hers is black and their color is navy blue. I think they will do it because of the war. If they do allow her to wear what she has, I only need to get a school sweater for her. The children and I are terribly thrilled over the clothes that are coming from you and can hardly wait to see them. You should investigate thoroughly what chance you have of sending things to us, or I am afraid you will be disappointed and have things on your hands.

I have never replied, I believe, to the bit you marked in *Time* about La Guardia[115] and the wet handkerchiefs he left behind him in the offices. Personally, I never shed a tear the whole year I worked for my particular demon, nor did I ever feel like it. I used to get blazing mad, and I let him have a taste of my temper a time or two. I have worked so long now that a chief would have a hard time getting tears out of me. Let's say I'm hard.

Anyway, I don't need to worry about that now, as I am working for the most even-tempered man you ever saw. He is all business and to the point and believes in a lot of work, but he never puts you in a flurry, and if you waste his time through an error, he doesn't give you blazes. He seems to let your brilliant moments weigh against your dull ones, as so far he is most evidently satisfied with me, as he is doing all he can to get an increase for me, and a sizeable one at that. I feel I am doing better work for him than I have ever done for anyone, and I know I enjoy it more.

For instance, if I am transcribing a letter he has dictated, and he has left out a point that I am sure should go in, I put it in, he signs it without even mentioning it, and that's finished. I can do this because my mind is on the job every minute I am in the office. He is handing over more and more letters to me to write myself. I

---

[115] Fiorello La Guardia, mayor of New York City from 1933-1945, was a "fiery little man," "a glutton for work," and "a champion of democracy." However, his abrupt manner clearly upset his female workers.

take the minutes of very big conferences; two weeks ago I took one where every manufacturer of a certain industry was represented. They came from all over South Africa. I got along all right too.

Bert has just had two crushing blows. She broke up with her Lt. Colonel for some very good reasons, and then she heard that her other friend was sixty-nine years old, and she had thought he was fifty-eight all the time. That does make a difference to a woman of thirty-eight doesn't it? We had such a good laugh over it, as he had just had her to the Country Club for a dinner dance and had danced every dance and enjoyed the evening thoroughly. Just the same, we both think he is fine and like him just as much as ever. I thoroughly enjoy an evening in his company, as he has such a keen sense of humor.

I have just had an old black felt hat remodeled. I have had it for three and a half years, so I had naturally seen enough of it, and now you would never know it, as it is a very tailored hat with high crown and brim. She also made a dress hat for me with some black fur Elizabeth Byrne gave me and a little bit of black felt. It is very attractive and will look nice with my black winter coat in the evenings for shows, etc. She did this for $5. I have bought two woolen dresses for winter at a great bargain—one is a Paris model, the other Swiss. They are pre-war stock, of course, but good style.

I am having four days off for Easter and am going to have a good rest with the children, and Wilfred, I hope. Of course, the whole organization is not getting this, but somehow they have the idea that I have been putting in some real work.

You asked me if there was a room for Betty at our place. No, and this is the first place we have ever lived where there wasn't a room. She has had to sleep on the screened-in back porch so far, but now Mrs. Maton is building two rooms in the back yard, one for Betty and one for her boy. I am very glad, as I was afraid Betty would finally get tired of not having a room where she could put her things out and have her husband come to see her. She has been going out a lot at night to Jotum [her husband] and also to her aunt. I sometimes sleep quite alone at the place, with only the native boy there who is a useless-looking person. My best protection is a police whistle of Wilfred's. If I ever have any trouble, I shall just blow that, and I can tell you the intruder will be off as fast as his legs will carry him. Bert tries to come out if I am going to be alone, and has been awfully good about that, but she simply can't sometimes when she has made plans to go out.

From what I have read in *Time*, I am terribly worried about the oil and tire business in Johnson City, and I would like to know just what the position is and if you think Uncle Edwin will look after Father if any curtailing is necessary.

I really don't think you should be doing needlepoint unless your eyes are stronger than they were when I left. Your two antique chairs should have needlepoint seats, of course, and they will increase the value of them very much. All my good pieces are antiques. Those two chairs and the chest will go beautifully with what I have. I am sure that you would be amazed to find that anyone could keep house with as little furniture as I have. I sold my bedroom suite when I left Johannesburg to go to Durban, also my dining room table and six chairs, and those I have never replaced, as the price of furniture has gone up by leaps and bounds. It did not matter in Durban, as I had wonderful built-in cupboards and wardrobes, but just now I am keeping my undies, etc., in a suitcase.

Anyway, I feel one does not want too much until life is more settled again. All of this leads to the fact that I am coming home to see you as soon as Wilfred is settled in a job after the war, even if I have to sell my furniture. You can count on that. If I didn't have this definite something in my mind, I couldn't stand this long separation [Helen has not seen her parents for nearly five years], but now that I have definitely decided to do it at all costs (as far as furniture goes), I can settle down to doing my bit toward winning the war. It is very hard to get ahead with expenses we have to pay now. One must just forget savings between that and the cost of living.

I am going to try your recipe for marshmallows and crushed pineapple over the Easter holidays. It sounds good.

Wilfred was transferred on Monday to a camp much nearer and will have to travel only half the distance he has been travelling to come in on the weekends. I am glad he is going to have something that will be easier on him because his work has been very exhausting. He is with the Native Troops now, and it is something he has been working for some time, so I am glad the transfer has finally come through.

Robin asked to kiss you two good-night the other night. She actually said she wanted to kiss Mama Sophia and Papa Harlow, so I suggested your picture, and that seemed to help. If we take a walk along a street she doesn't know, she always asks if you all live in one of the houses. She must feel thwarted in not being able to see you, for she often tells me how she loves you.

Love and kisses from us all,

Helen

P.S. Robin insists on saying the "big prayer," as we call it, "Our Father who art in Heaven," etc., and when it says "Thy will be done," she says, "My will be done," and on through; the "Thy" is "My." She also must say "trespasses" instead of "debts." I have never seen children so keen on their prayers and Bible stories.

4 Reform Avenue
Johannesburg
April 10, 1942

Dearests,

I have had such a big post today: two letters from Mother, a letter from Gladys, and four *Time* magazines. I was torn between this letter and reading these new *Time*s tonight, but you won.

First of all, I am actually at last having my nose operation. I had thought it a very minor operation, but the x-rays taken the other day show sinus infection also, and something else besides the enlarged tissue and polipi. This decision to have the operation has been finally forced upon me by my health. I have continued being very "chesty" ever since my move and never have a full night's sleep, and my breathing is most difficult. I was afraid I could not carry on my work much longer under the circumstances, so I got busy and found a specialist who would also get busy. He is considered the best in the city by someone who works with them all and has seen their work, so I am satisfied about my choice of doctor. He has had overseas training, of course.

I am having the operation in the biggest hospital in the southern hemisphere. It is a huge place and perfectly equipped. My doctor is Afrikaans. The operation will be on the 17th of this month, and I shall write you about two days afterwards, or, if I don't feel like it, Bert will. I shall be in hospital a week and will perhaps take off two weeks after that. They have told me I will need it. He is giving me a general anaesthetic, which is more to my liking, as I haven't forgotten my nose operations in Bristol and Roanoke. I shall have a sister (nurse) with me who is a very good friend of ours. She nursed me with Robin. You will be glad to know I am not alone. Wilfred wants to come over, but he is very nervous right now and waiting around a hospital will not help him any. Wilfred is only thirty-eight miles from here now, and I can now telephone him at no expense [either from the office or from Mrs. Maton's phone]. Before, a call was about 4/-.

Yes, I promised to tell you about my ex-boarding house. Well, I have forgotten it by now, my memory being very short for such things of the past. Anyway, our only window looked out on a brick wall, which was not more than three to four feet away. Just over the wall were practically slum children, and cats that yelled from the top of the wall every night. To go to the lavatory, one had to cross the back yard in full view of the windows to the rooms of the native flat boys in the large block of flats at the back, also in view of the natives living on our premises. Since I only had one room, and the only sitting room to the whole establishment was across the street, I sat in the kitchen at our place, as it was simply a private house that had been taken over as an annex.

The kitchen was the dirtiest place you have ever seen, and I only had a rickety chair that I had to prop up against the wall to sit in. I used to fall asleep because it was warm from the coal stove going, and I'd wake up and suddenly see this horrible place with fresh eyes, and I would get into such a temper about it, but there was nothing I could do because no place wanted children. The boarding houses and the flats with gardens all said no because of the children. Even my present landlady said "no children," but I talked her out of it. Now I wake up in a bedroom all my own, and I look out on the little orchard at the side of my house. The children have their own room; in fact, we have spread out, having living room, study, breakfast room, kitchen, and enclosed back porch, besides the two bedrooms.

Mrs. Maton came in last night for a cup of tea with me and stayed until 11:30, so that completely ruined my intentions of finishing this letter.

I was so proud of Alena Hopkins, and to think she has done it so late, for she must be thirty-five. She had so many setbacks, but it was always her dream.

South Africa realized her position as far as the Japs go, but I certainly do not consider it safe to risk a trip home at this time. We must take our chances here.

Thursday, April 16th

Well, I am just now getting back to my letter. This afternoon I go into hospital, and I am feeling well and happy that at last something is going to be done.

I am so sorry to hear about Aunt Lennie breaking a bone in her foot. I do hope it has been set so she will not have trouble with it. I shall write them very soon. Though I have never received the $10, I do want to thank them for it. Tell Helen and Kathryn that Bert and I do not think they will have any trouble getting married no matter how few boys there are after this war. I hope they marry at about twenty-three, as I feel one has had enough of running around by that time, and I do hope they marry because, since I have married, I think it would be awful to be an old maid, though I didn't think much about it one way or another before I married. Of course, I realize Wilfred and I have been happier than most people are. He came over last night to see me, and left early this morning. He still says he is coming for the operation, so I guess I can't stop him.

I notice in an old letter of yours that you do not want me to go to housekeeping, as you are afraid the children won't get the proper food. Do not worry about that; they are looking much better than when we lived at the boarding house, and Betty, my girl, is a grand cook and simply adores Robin and will see that they are well fed. She certainly has good breakfasts and dinners at night, so I am sure the noon meal is quite all right too; at least, the children seem to be thriving. If it is possible to send anything over, I wish you could send Betty a little present; those things help hold them. She would never stop talking about that if it happened.

Mrs. Smith has been transferred to the secretary of our organization, and I believe he is about as bad as the chief we just got rid of. She says she isn't going to put up with all that all over again; she will just leave. I am thankful I have drawn such a nice man. They asked for me back in the old office to take Mrs.

Smith's place, as it is being kept on in a way, but I said I didn't want to go back, and they have left me where I am.

The war news couldn't be much worse. I think we are getting too used to reverses. It all shows how asleep Britain and America have been. We might employ someone from the other side to run our war effort for us. Nothing you write has been marked out, but I feel like I am going to write something pretty soon that will be scratched.

You will be glad to hear that I had a roll of toilet paper handed to me over the counter the other day, as was, but I had to draw the line there and said I would do without for the duration before I would walk down the street with it unwrapped. Even calling it "bathroom tissue" wouldn't have helped. The chemist wrapped it and assured me he stood to be fined and whatnot. We are rationed on lots of things—soap, toilet paper, to start with—and all stocks of a lot of things have been "frozen," such as light bulbs and all electrical equipment, paint, and I don't know what else. We aren't rationed on sugar, as the production is so big here, but we are rationed on tea to one pound per month. That is quite enough for me, of course, but not for most people. Anyway, it is nearly a dollar a pound. Of course, there is no rubber, and petrol is rationed. [116]

I must stop now and get busy. I came in early to the office this morning to write this. I do hope you don't get this letter and then have to wait about three weeks for the one I shall be writing you in a day or two after my operation.

I do love you both so much and would give oh, I don't know what, to see you. If there weren't so many things between us—like oceans, and Japs, and Germans, I would see you.

Ever your devoted,

Helen

---

[116] What is known as a pharmacy in the United States was called a "chemist" in South Africa. These small stores were privately owned by a pharmacist who would fill prescriptions and often personally attend to customers who needed other products. South Africa's small shops were owned and tended by independent shop owners in the 1940s. These shops were lined up in a row on Oxford Street in Rosebank. I remember the butcher shop with sawdust on the floor and the great carcasses hanging from the rafters; a small general store, owned by a Greek family, that sold milk, candy, and newspapers; the chemist; the baker; the shoe repairer; and so forth. A fifteen-minute walk in the opposite direction brought one to "The Portuguese Gardens"—a flower and vegetable farm with rows of vegetables, a greenhouse, and an irrigation dam—where Helen purchased all of her fresh produce. Such Gardens, as they were known, were owned and operated by Portuguese immigrants, usually from Mozambique.

A Vale of Soul-Making (May 1940—Feb. 1943)

4 Reform Avenue
Melrose, Johannesburg
April 21, 1942

My dearest Mother and Dad,

Well the "op" is over, and I leave the hospital tomorrow. I have been so well taken care of and feel I have been so foolish to put this off for so long. They removed the polyps from the one side and opened the antrum on the other. The antrum washouts are the only painful part of treatment following the operation. It is just marvelous to be able to breathe again and to smell.

I have had just enough visitors but not too many, and I have had some beautiful flowers sent me. The children came to see me with Wilfred, Bert, and Mr. Evans. They are coming again this afternoon with Betty. I shall stay at home and take it easy until I feel quite well. I feel that this rest is going to do me as much good as my "op." When I went into my operation, and when I was coming out from under the anaesthetic, I thought of you two, the ones I used to lean on. I simply could not get any comfort from thinking of those in my life since I have assumed responsibilities.

They select the most marvelous time for my antrum douche— mealtime. Last night a young girl who was up from tonsils saw them doing me and fainted away. She was put back to bed and is just up again now at noon. The nurses think one can stand anything.

We had a complete blackout of the city on Sunday night, and it was most successful. Of course, I didn't get to see anything of it since I was in bed, but those who watched from points of advantage said you couldn't see anything. Since the blackout was from ten to ten-thirty, I was asleep, as my hours for the last five days have been from four in the morning to eight at night. How would you like that? With your new time, perhaps you do get up about that time now.

This letter hasn't much in it, but I know it is the news you want.

Love and kisses to my dear ones,

Helen

4 Reform Avenue
Johannesburg
May 5, 1942

My dearest Ones,

Mother's letter of March 22 just arrived today. Dad's letter to Eve came several days ago, and she is going to answer that. It was such a lovely letter.

I started back to work yesterday and am feeling perfectly well. Mr. Ashworth has tried to make it easy for me, though he is rushed to death. He is so considerate.

I can breathe better and better every day. The operation was perfectly successful, and I feel that I was very silly that I did not do this long ago.

I do hope the box of lovely dresses for the children arrives safely. Please do not worry that you did not send me anything, as I got a thrill out of their new things, and they need the dresses more than anything. They went to a little birthday party yesterday and had a lovely time.

I think Robin must still have been tired from the party tonight, as she spent the supper-hour feeling sorry for herself. She made up one big injury after another. Her persecutions were from physical to mental, and her tormentors were Eve, Betty, and numerous imaginary children, and she enjoyed a good howl after recounting each episode to me. If she were older, I could understand such an outburst, but she is not quite four.

I am elated tonight because of the news that the British have landed in Madagascar. This gives me a brighter outlook about the whole war. At last we are taking the initiative.

I have written Aunt Nellie and Katye Wray and Aunt Lula. I haven't written Uncle Edwin and Aunt Lennie yet, as I hoped their money would come, and I could tell them what I had done with it. I shall write in any case, as I want to sympathize with Aunt Lennie about breaking her foot.

You must get the bank to re-issue the draft for $10. They will do that as a duplicate. We had a draft from Calcutta that had to be re-issued, as we never received it. Wilfred loaned some money to an American couple left stranded out here to go back to America. From New York, the husband finally got a good job in India.

The plants aren't doing much on pay for those who join up. Out here, all the good firms make up the difference between the army pay and the man's salary for the duration of the war. You see, not everybody has felt the pinch as Wilfred and I have. We have managed very well and have no complaints.

I am afraid you all are going to have a real sugar shortage. We are short of lots of things now. I found where I could buy a light globe today, and was I thrilled. The one in my living room had burned out, and I just didn't know where I would get one.

I am glad my vacation letter has been enjoyed. Wish I could always write an interesting letter.

Love and kisses,

Helen

4 Reform Avenue
Johannesburg
May 20, 1942

Dearest Folks,

I posted a letter to Father a few days ago written by Eve; I hope it arrives for his [sixty-fifth] birthday and that this one does too, but I am afraid they will be a little late.[117] Anyway, I do want him to have my very best wishes for his birthday, and I want you both to know that my greatest wish is that none of us will have any more birthdays so many miles apart. I have been away so many years already [almost five years] and it looks like there will be still more years added to them before we can be together. Well, we must just keep our chins up.

Speaking of birthdays, I am going to have a few children in on the 6th of June and celebrate both the children's birthdays then. I am holding my breath until the parcel comes with their dresses. It will be a disappointment if it does not arrive in time for the birthdays, but I am very doubtful. Robin is getting her heart's desire—a doll with real hair and eyes that open and close. She has never had such a nice doll, and that is what she wants. I have already bought it because it is very hard to find much in the way of dolls, and when I saw one that filled all the requirements of this young lady, I took it. I am giving Eve the ring with the ruby stone that was Little Aunt Nellie's. I think she will look after it now. Bert is giving Eve a lovely mirror, brush, and comb set that she won at a dance, and is also making a lampshade for her room.

It has turned very cold in the last few days; in fact, we had a very good snow on Sunday, which is most unusual here. My office is as cold as the great outdoors, and this winter promises to be one of our coldest. The Monday morning after the snow on Sunday, we had no heat at all because a pipe had burst in the building. Today, Wednesday, we also have no heat, but that is only because it is about 2 degrees warmer than Monday. This is one of the older buildings and is not looked after like Escom House, and perhaps won't heat up very well with the system they have in, which is steam but perhaps not capable of heating the place properly. We expect to move to Escom House in a few weeks, though, so I can look forward to being comfortable again. At home we are very comfortable, as we have the kitchen range and a fireplace in the sitting room. Of course, you wouldn't call it comfortable, but anyone out here would. Imagine your bathroom unheated and snow on the ground.

Well, I had a real American evening last night. Edith Broadbent picked me up at the office, so I had dinner with her and another American girl living in the same

---

[117] Since Harlow's birthday was on June 30, this is evidence of just how far ahead one had to plan one's life. Sometime later, a letter written by Sophia took three months to cross the Atlantic.

block of flats. We then went out to bridge with another American woman, and she gave us hot biscuits at teatime, and did they taste good. She also gave us good American coffee. Most people out here don't know how to make coffee. Edith had a simply lovely dinner, and, all in all, I ate too much. It was a good game of bridge, and I did enjoy it, as I simply never get to play. I am going to try to keep up these contacts and play more bridge. I am sure I stay to myself too much.

The American woman who had us for bridge lost her sixteen-year-old daughter a few months back. This girl was by her first marriage. She now has a child two and a half and one nine months old by this marriage. She showed us pictures of her daughter; she was such a lovely-looking girl. I felt so very sorry for her. The child died out here while she was with her mother. She had a young girl, a friend of her daughter's, living with her, or rather staying with her for a while.

I meant to mention that Eve composed her letter herself. I took it down in shorthand as she dictated it to me, then wrote it out for her so she could copy it. Otherwise, I don't know when it would have been finished. She wants to write to Mother, but the child has so little time that I don't know when she will get to it. The drawback is that she and I have so little time together when I can get her down to these things.

Betty is not well, and they want her to go into hospital tomorrow, but her husband won't hear of it. What I would do without her, I don't know. She is not satisfied with the treatment they give at the Outpatients at the Hospital, which is free, and wants to go to a doctor on her own. She will do that, and perhaps he won't think it necessary for her to be off from work. She and her husband together can afford the services of a doctor. This doctor is a native from here who studied medicine in America and married an American negress. I heard that part at bridge last night, and I believe she is simply miserable out here.

Wilfred is doing a very big map of the world to put over our fireplace. I am glad he has this hobby for the weekends. He has done the drawing very well, and I hope he is successful with the painting. It is done on building board.

There is a big to-do on here from the 23rd of May to the 6th of June called Liberty Cavalcade. It has been organized to make money for the war, but so far I hear their expenses have been enormous. They have put up very good structures at the Zoo Lake and wired in a portion of the grounds and have a carnival, etc. There will be lots of small and big things for sale and raffled, etc. To my mind, it is simply crazy to organize such a thing during times like these to make money. They should just tax for what they need. Of course, it is done by the so-called society ladies, or rather originated by them, so one can't expect it to be a real business proposition.

It seems to me that all the wrong people run our world. The crazier your ideas, the more readily they are picked up by the crowd. I can just imagine our enemies wasting their time putting on such a show.

The lunch hour is nearly over and the boss will be in just now, so I must close. He and I are sharing the same office for a few weeks, as he has turned his office over to three chemists doing a special job for him. It does cramp one's style, and I am afraid if it lasts much longer, it will put us right against each other. He is very even tempered, though, and I am certainly much better than I used to be. I know things that used to put me in a fury in the office simply don't bother me now.

All our love and kisses to you both, our dearest ones,

Helen

P.S. I must tell you one little thing that Robin said that amused me. She was looking at a picture of Wilfred in Southern Rhodesia, and she was asking him who built the huts in the picture, and he said he did. Then she pointed to a tree and asked who built that, and he said God did. She said, "Do you mean God Save the King?"

In the prayer the other night, she was blessing all the family and then she added, "God bless the Queen and the Princesses, and God save the King." She is very busy to learn some of her nursery rhymes and has a good ear for them. She also finds rhymes very easy to learn.

A little girl at school was supposed to take the part of "Bo-Peep" in that very long rhyme about Bo-Peep and Boy Blue, and she broke down, so they asked for a volunteer, and Eve held up her hand because she had learned it at home, and she said the teacher said she was good.

4 Reform Avenue
Johannesburg
June 4, 1942

My dearest Mother and Dad,

This is just about the first letter I have attempted during office hours since my change, and I hope I get it written before the conference breaks up and changes my plans. I simply can't wait to tell you of the general excitement caused in our house by the arrival of the lovely parcel of three dresses for the children. To begin with, Eve nearly went crazy over her red, white, and blue outfit and shall wear it to her birthday party of the 6th. She also loves herself in her red dress, and both were shortened to the proper length on the night of arrival; no time wasted with this mother. Robin is terribly thrilled too, and Robin's mother more so, over her dress. It is lovely, but Robin can't wear it until the party on the 6th, which she is sharing jointly with Eve. Robin's dress fits her perfectly, and Eve's dresses are perfect fits also. It simply set them up for the winter.

Everybody envies me these smart clothes of the children's. Edith saw them and was crazy about them, as well as Bert. Eve is coming into town this afternoon with Betty, and I shall try hard to find a red felt hat to go with her red jacket. It is hard to get red, as it is so popular this year, but we are going to try. They must also have their haircuts for the party, and Eve must have her finger measured for the ring. Eve will write you and thank you for the dresses. Of course, she still loves clothes better than anything else.

The money from Uncle Edwin and Aunt Lennie has just arrived today, and I got £2.7.1. for the $10 he sent. I shall write as soon as the party is over and thank them. I am putting the whole amount into a tea set and must add about the same amount to it to get what I want. I know it was sent for the children, too, but I think a beautiful tea set is something that adds to their home and something that can be passed on to them if it is cared for. I have wanted a nice tea set ever since I came out here, as one entertains that way so much of the time, and it is terrible to always feel a little embarrassed by your service. They are very expensive, and by using this money immediately on one, I see my only chance of having it.

I looked around at lunchtime and saw some lovely ones and will decide by tomorrow on one. Everybody here seems to possess a good tea set even if they are starving. It is considered an essential, so I hope you won't consider me extravagant. I can't imagine why I didn't buy it when Wilfred was making good money, except that in Durban we took people out a lot, and here one entertains at home more. Want to have my tea set before I write, as I can be much more enthusiastic over the spending of the money than just the receipt of the money.

I got my doctor's bill this month, and it is Twenty Guineas or £21.0.0. They always add a shilling to the pound; in fact, any of the professions do. As you can see, this is practically $100. I shall manage to pay it off in two months, so that won't be too bad. I haven't had an account from the hospital yet; they don't hold you until you pay here, as has been heard of in Elizabethton. Unfortunately, I have had two colds, but I know I am a lot better, and, when the weather settles down, I hope to feel just fine. I must still do my inhalation every morning and night, and when I leave them off I am not so good. They are a terrible bother too. Anyway, I am so glad it is all behind me, and I know you are glad too.

I had your letter telling me about Helen Hunter landing a job at $25 per week, and I know she must have been thrilled. I am so glad for her and just wish I were there to pick up one at that sum. It seems impossible for my boss to get more for me, though he has boosted me enough and told them they were wasting me on stenographic work, that I should only be used for taking minutes of meetings and for secretarial work, that is, mostly as his assistant: telephoning and making enquiries and writing my own letters, etc. I am doing a lot of it now, but he wants me to have more time for it and give ordinary letters, etc., to a typist.

It is most interesting doing jobs of your own, telephoning Durban, for instance, as I did yesterday, and getting information to pass on to Pretoria. In doing these things on my own, I find I have to make quick decisions on my own, and I do it, right or wrong. If I am wrong, he merely tells me where I am wrong, explains the thing, and I have that much more knowledge to deal with the next thing that comes up. I am sure that if he has his own business after the war he will offer me something good in it.

However, Wilfred and I hope to do something together, and only time will tell what I will be doing, but I doubt if I ever am a housewife again. I like housekeeping just as well as you do, and, when I have to cook, the house stands on end. I think the time I had a dinner party and worked the whole day on it, and a business woman who was a guest stated that any woman should be able to run a house by devoting twenty minutes a day to it, finished me with housekeeping. I felt like taking the food out of her mouth, for it was darned good.

I am carrying out a colour scheme of red, white, and blue[118] for the children's party. The paper decorations are already up and look very nice. The cake is being decorated in red, white and blue, and the candles are red, white, and blue, also the paper napkins. I have done packages of candy (red and white) in red, white, and blue paper, and there will be a toy soldier, sailor, or nurse at each place. I think they will be very thrilled. I am having twelve children, and just as many grown-ups, I'm afraid. I would never mind a children's party if it were not for all the grown-ups that must come along too. Where to put them all, I do not know, but I'll see when they get there. If they can't sit down, they can stand up—I spend twenty minutes a day on my house now. At least they will have a pretty tea set to have their tea out of.

I didn't know it was possible for anyone in America F.B's age to escape service. I thought it was compulsory. F.B. is very ambitious and has had his eyes on the position he now has for years. He had it in mind when I was there. He will hold it down very well too, perhaps even better than Mr. Smith did. Neither of them have the knowledge that Mr. Funcke had. Of course, I was glad to hear that H. had been let out, as I have never forgotten that insulting little beast. When I think of the ones I liked of that nationality, I immediately bring him to mind to counteract any kind feelings I might have toward them. I then have a proper fighting spirit in no time at all. His German girl came over to marry him and had one child when I left; since she is a Catholic, I don't know how many they have now. Rather they are both Catholics. I guess Mr. Wampler is there for life. I am glad they keep him on and that he has that security.

---

[118] Helen was ever the patriot, right down to the decorations for her children's birthday party. In spite of her anger toward the United States, she revered both the British Empire and the American founding fathers.

What a bargain you got in Robin's dress. It would cost over $10 here.

Wilfred's dad is going to pay for Robin to go to kindergarten, as I think I told you in a previous letter. I am waiting for warmer weather, however, and until she can do without her morning sleep. She loves her sleep and her food. She has such a quiet nature, except now and then she has a good fit of temper, which is the funniest thing I have ever seen, but she doesn't know that.

Eve and Robin attend a Church of England Sunday school every Sunday and love it. It is such a beautiful little church that I must take a picture of it and send it to you. It is stone and all covered in ivy. The cleric and his wife, Martha, are a lovely old couple with snow-white hair, and the children love them. Eve and Robin are such affectionate children that they must associate with people that they really love; otherwise it seems to kill something in them. I could always manage halfway as a child. Eve, for instance, is looking forward today to a kiss from her Sister at the Convent, as she always kisses them on their birthday if they tell her, so Eve says. Of course, I would have died if a teacher of mine had kissed me.

Must stop and work. Boss is back.

Love and kisses from us all,

Helen

c/o Director-General War Supplies
Room 435, Escom House
Rissik Street
Johannesburg, South Africa
June 12, 1942

My dearest Aunt Lennie and Uncle Edwin,

I have waited such a long time before writing this letter because I wanted to have the $10 you sent us for Christmas, and spend it, so I could tell you how much fun we had out of it. Now I am just as much in the dark as I have been all these months, as I received through the bank £2.7.1, and I naturally thought it was the proceeds of your $10, but the next day I had a letter from Mother saying they had sent me $15.00 to send Robin to kindergarten, so now I am wondering if the £2.7.1 is the $15 they have sent. It is more like the exchange on $10, however.

Anyway, I spent this money on the day I received it and enjoyed it thoroughly. I bought a most lovely tea set—Planet china, with an old-fashioned flower design. It's something I have been wanting for years and something I can hand down to the children if I look after it properly, which I shall. They must just wait for their share in this money.

If I have spent Robin's kindergarten money, I need not worry, as she has made satisfactory financial arrangements with her grandfather over here. She was very good in her role. In any case, I do want to thank you both for this very generous Christmas gift to the children and me.

Mother wrote me about Aunt Lennie's broken foot, and I am so sorry that you had to go through all that suffering and inconvenience. I have thought, however, that one good thing might come out of it: that having to turn your house over to someone else to do for a while might break you of your habit of doing it all yourself, which must be a very big task the way you insist on keeping it. It is a mixture of admiration for the capabilities of the beautiful housekeepers in the family and chagrin at my evasion of that womanly attribute which I feel when I compare my life with your lives.

I have also heard from Mother about the very good position that Helen has secured in Kingsport as soon as she graduates. You must feel very proud of her. I would like to suggest that she make a study of the Dewey Decimal System of filing. It is used in all public libraries but can be applied to business correspondence as well as books if she gets a thorough understanding of the system. I introduce it wherever I go, and with great success. It will help impress the boss. But in this connection, let me give another piece of advice: don't be so good at filing that you are pushed into that work alone, as there is nothing on earth more boring. She may be starting out as secretary to one man since she is getting $25 per week, but if not, let her keep in mind that that is what she wants to do, because it can be the most interesting work of all office work.

I would also advise her to take any opportunity of taking the minutes of meetings no matter how incapable she feels of doing the work, because it is only in that way that she will get ahead. I never refused to try anything like that which was asked of me, even if I knew I wouldn't do it too well, as I knew that it was all good experience and that one day I would be able to do the job properly. I remember girls at North American [Rayon Factory], who started with me and were just as capable, remaining typists because they didn't have the nerve to try the difficult jobs.

The man I am secretary to now wants to take me off my ordinary typing work and just let me do the minutes of meetings and assist him with interviewing people, etc., and have extra help in the office for the typing. He must convince the big Pooh-Bah first, however, and whether that will be possible or not, I do not know, but of course I hope so, as it will be more interesting.

I had a rather nice birthday party for the children, last Saturday, all in red, white, and blue with the Union Jack, the Stars and Stripes, and the Union flags for decorations (all made in Japan, I am sure). Even my cake was iced in layers of red, white, and blue. These birthday parties seem to mean so much to them, and last year they had whooping cough and couldn't have a party. Robin was given a doll with eyes that open and close, and real hair, which was a request of long standing. Her grandfather Evans told me I was a fool to pay so much for a doll, and I told him I wasn't, as there was a very short time in life that you wanted a doll; it simply couldn't wait.

I gave Eve a little emerald ring that was Mother's and she hadn't had it on five minutes before she lost the stone. It wasn't her fault, and it is now at the jewelers having a new stone put in.

We are enjoying our little house so very much after a year of boarding. The children are looking so well and happy, and I am so satisfied at home that I can't be moved from the place over the weekends.

Tomorrow night we are invited to a housewarming of friends of ours who have just married, and they will show a ciné[119] of their wedding reception. It is all in colour and lovely, as I have already seen it, but they have done considerable work on it since the first showing, and it should be beautiful now. I hope Helen and Kathryn will have cinés made of their weddings; it means so much in the future.

I hope Helen is going back and forth to Kingsport, so she can enjoy her nice home.

Much love from us all to all of you,

Helen

Robin on her fourth birthday with her Shirley Temple doll

4 Reform Avenue
Melrose, Johannesburg
June 19, 1942

My dearest Ones,

So many letters from you, so many *Time*s, money, everything, until I am quite giddy with receiving. It is like Christmas every time a boat comes in now. I don't hear for about three weeks, and I am just getting very despondent and have

---

[119] A ciné is a home movie made with a 8mm or 16mm film in a handheld camera. Owning one of these cameras was rather unusual in those days and thus a popular form of entertainment for family and friends, who would gather at the host's house to watch the home movie.

decided that I will never hear from you again, when mail of all kinds starts pouring in. It usually comes in over a period of three to four days and keeps things humming. By the way, "humming" over here means it doesn't smell good, but, as well as I remember, it has a different meaning at home.

At last all the money matters are straight. The $10 came from Uncle Edwin, or at least so I know now, and the $15 came from you all. I got £2.7.1. and then £3.14.0. about a week later. It was such a relief getting the last amount through my own bank here, where I am known and don't have to identify myself and receive suspicious looks from the teller paying out. I have put the money away for Robin in case she needs it, but she won't, as Mr. Evans is going to pay her kindergarten fee. She is the apple of his eye and stands to get more out of him than any of the rest of the family. She looks exactly like him. You have never seen such a resemblance in your life. He is a very good-looking man, even at seventy, so it won't hurt her at all to look like him.

I know now that I must never mention kindergartens or such things to you all or you will immediately send money. It is far from being my wish that you all should send us one penny. I want you to enjoy what you have yourselves, and the more you have, the more pleased I am. We have quite enough to get along on and are not having a hard life at all.

I couldn't afford to send Robin to kindergarten, but I was quite sure that Mr. Evans would do it since he is so crazy about her. He gives them each a stamp a week for their War Savings Books and they have completed two coupons and have a good start on their third (each). He gave them money for their birthdays, which I put in this.

The children have received their hair ribbons, two each, and are so pleased with them. The broad ribbon in blue and white dot is simply beautiful on Robin. I have never seen her look so pretty. I was glad Father wrote Robin a letter too, because she asked every day after Eve got her letter from Father when she was going to have a letter of her own from Papa Harlow. She was terribly thrilled with it.

I enclose a clipping [See page 376] about Kingston Russell, which closes the case. I believe he is a broken man, and I can't help but feel sorry for him. In that case it was certainly a matter of "Pride goeth before a fall."

I also enclose snaps Bert took on the day of the children's party. Unfortunately, two of their little friends had mumps, and Edith Broadbent forgot to come with Helen and Susan, so the party was small. You will see the afghan Bert crocheted for Robin, also the lovely doll I gave her. I have sent you a lot of snaps of the house and garden, but I feel sure that letter has been lost. It is perhaps the one in between that long stretch when you did not hear, as I have never gone so long without writing. I hope these reach you safely. Too bad my head is off in the one with the children. It is sweet of them. The suit I am wearing is one of the two things I bought for this winter and is very smart, everyone thinks. It is navy blue, and the stripes are in green and red and yellow, I believe. I remade the skirt myself because I didn't like it, and I simply made a perfect job of it. It looks tailor-made, and fits like a glove.

Please do not send flour to me, as the "one pound" I spoke of represents white flour. I can get almost any amount of the brown flour, which can be well sifted and will do for nearly anything. I think your rationing of sugar is much harder, and I am wondering if I would be allowed to send you some. We are rationed to some extent just now, but the new sugar crop will be in the last of this month. Tell me if you would like for me to try to send you some. When I think that you only get between four and five pounds a month, and we use twenty pounds per month, I just don't know how you manage. Of course, I realize that Betty and the children are the big consumers of sugar at our place.

I was surprised to know that Mrs. S.V. Alexander was so old. I think to die of old age is rather dreadful, don't you? I would prefer a heart attack, but I am afraid I have little chance of that. I was sorry to hear of Mrs. St. John's death. I thought she was such a sweet woman, and she had so little out of life it seemed.

I don't know what size socks the children wear, but Eve wears a 12½ shoe (same size) and Robin an 8, I think. Eve has my long narrow foot and Robin a more normal one. Everything you sent fits perfectly, but I think you should leave the hems for me to do as they grow all the time, and it is useless for me to give you any idea now about hems when it will perhaps be some time before you make any more dresses for them.

I know it is only because of the distance that the L.s do not worry me, and I am sorry you must contend with them. I used to nearly despair when I had to deal with them, knowing the precarious state of my finances. If you take anyone else to see the house, you must warn them of what the L.s will do. Your argument with Mrs. Moulton could have been as follows: The L.s once owned the house themselves, so they evidently like it. They only sold it because he thought he was being transferred to New York, and the rayon mills bought it from him. They sold it to me, and Mr. L. has taken great care to live in it ever since, making the plants secure it for him with a three-year lease before they sold it to me.

When I was ready to rent it to Mr. King, of King's Store, because I did not like L., Mr. L. went so far as to go to Mr. King early in the morning on the day I was to hear from Mr. King and tell him that he had a signed lease in his pocket from me, so there was no use for Mr. King to telephone me. Mr. King wanted the house, and it was months before I found out why Mr. King had not telephoned me as promised.

Please keep these things in mind, and if you have someone who really wants it, offer to let them live in it. That is, rent it for three months, subject to buying at the end of that time. I feel sure the disadvantages of the place hit one in the eye on inspection, and that living in it would help sell rather than hurt.

If L. continues to make requests, tell him that you are not making any more improvements at the present and that, if he is not satisfied, you have all decided to move in yourself. He will have no argument against that, and it should keep him quiet. If he knows you want to re-let it, then he may think he is the only one who will pay the rent you are getting now, but if he thinks you are ready to go into it yourself, then he isn't so sure of himself. L. is a bully, and you must show a determined front or there is no end to the way he will annoy you and keep things stirred up.

You must promise that you will take this firm stand, or otherwise I am going to write him a letter that will perhaps make him move along sure enough. I am determined that the house must get out of the red. Our position is much better now than it was when he used to bully me, but I kept it out of the red. He had every reason to think he could make me lose the house then, but he doesn't have reason to think it now. I would suggest that you rather insinuate around that Wilfred and I are doing well financially. L. perhaps thinks because Wilfred is in the army that we are starving. The South African army is much better paid than the English. Perhaps he doesn't know that. I wish they would intern the old devil. I am sure that is where he belongs.

I have had some excitement the last two days. I told Mr. A. to tell the big boss that I was resigning unless I got £25.0.0. That was on the 16th, and he did it. On the 17th the newly appointed Controller of . . . (I prefer to leave that blank), who knows me because he was a member of a committee that I took the minutes of, asked me to come to him as his secretary at £25.0.0. I was amazed that he spoke to me, because his appointment came through the recommendation of our office; however, I wasn't going to turn that down. He then told Mr. A and the bigger boss what he had done, and there was the most awful uproar. The big boss said if the Government could let him pay me £25.0.0., then they could let him pay me £25.0.0. So now I am waiting to see what comes of it.

The man who offered me the new position is Managing director of a firm with branches all over the Union, and it employs seven hundred people, so I felt quite flattered. I do good work, but I have an idea that he also liked the way I dress, for I do dress well in the office now, and he is a man who gives much to dress, and it would hurt his vanity to have a secretary who wasn't well dressed also. I only have four dresses to wear to the office, but they are good ones and I always look nice. I do hope I get the increase, so you won't feel so sorry for me.

I wrote Aunt Lennie and Uncle Edwin about the lovely tea set I bought. Did I write you? It is so beautiful, and it is such a thrill having it. One is scared to death to use china these days, as even the open patterns can't be replaced now, and it may be years before they can be.

How you have kept your lovely dinner set intact so long I don't know. Because you always wash it yourself, I am sure. One does not realize the value of things until one starts acquiring them oneself. I am not through, but the lunch hour is over, and I must get busy on my office correspondence.

Wilfred is home on two weeks leave and is enjoying it so much, and we are enjoying him. His nerves were in bad shape for a while, but he is ever so much better now.

Everyone who comes to see me raves about my handsome parents, and Betty is still very sorry for me that I look much older than my mother.

All my love and kisses from us all.

Helen

Room 435
Escom House
Rissik Street, Johannesburg
June 29, 1942

My dearest Mother and Dad,

Your cable arrived today though you sent it on the 25th. Of course, there are so many priority cables these days that that accounts for the delay, I am sure.

I am sorry you have been worried about me, but I wrote you after my operation while I was still in hospital, and I was only there six days. I wonder now who I gave the letter to for mailing. With the mails so uncertain, I should never have written you that I was going to have the operation, but only have written you afterwards. You can know that Bert will always let you know if anything is wrong and I can't write myself. She is a most conscientious person and very thoughtful.

I am enclosing a letter [see below] from an American friend of mine in the Cape because it gives the experience of the McCarthys, whom we both know. The McCarthys were in our dinner party New Year's Eve two years ago in Durban. It was the night I wore my white dress that I wrote you about. They also used to play bridge with Edith and me in Durban. We know another couple who were on *The City of N.Y.*,[120] and she was drowned while he was saving their little girl. It is all much too risky now. The birth of the baby was in *Time*. Do you remember it? Marjorie Arnold, who wrote the letter, is from Brooklyn and is lots of fun. Her husband Jack is sales manager for Royal Baking Powder out here. They have a factory in Paarl.

---

[120] On March 29, 1942, *The City of New York,* an 8,272-ton motor passenger ship, was sunk by a U-160 off Cape Hatteras on the Outer Banks of North Carolina.

I am enclosing Eve's report card, which I am pleased with, as she was very far behind the standards of the Convent when she entered, and I think she has done well since she started with a handicap.

The Rep Players produced *The Women,* and it was excellently done; the acting was good and the sets beautiful. It has run for three weeks, and usually their plays are only on for a week. I went in a party on Thursday night.

Eve has been in bed for a week with a very bad cold, but she seems much better. Her temperature is nearly normal tonight. It isn't difficult to keep Eve in bed.

My garden is looking clean. I put the finishing touches to it over the weekend. You should see me pruning trees, etc. I love working at such things. You would be thrilled if you could see the big shrubs of gardenias in my garden, the pink, and the white; both are blooming now.

The war news is bad enough for us. There are certainly a lot of worried wives and mothers these days. Edith is very upset, of course, as Charles is in the thick of the battle now. She has had a lot to worry about, but she keeps up appearances and appears bright most of the time. She had heard from her mother and dad, so she is relieved about them to some extent.

I have bought a drop-leaf table from Edith that she wanted to get rid of and which I needed, since I sold my lovely rosewood dining room table. It was very large, though, for the places I seem to get, so I am just as well without it. What I have bought is teak and not beautiful. I hate to buy a piece of furniture that I know isn't beautiful, but I can't hold back forever waiting on just what I want before I buy. Eating on a card table proved nerve destroying.

There is a terrible crime wave on in Johannesburg led by the natives. It is all theft, and at last the police are getting busy. The other night a woman's car stalled near Eve's school and in front of Killarney Court where we used to live, and a native took her bag and fur coat from her while she was stopped.

I must stop now and go to bed, so I'll feel like a day's work tomorrow.

I am glad to know from your cable that you are all well.

All our love and kisses for you two,

Helen, Eve, and Robin

[From Marjorie to Helen]

The Manhattan
Paarl, Cape Province
South Africa
Sunday, June 7, 1942

Dear Helen,

Yes—it's me again, and I did receive your nice long letter and thoroughly enjoyed it, even though I did take so long to answer it. Well, here it is, whatever it is going to be.

Did you and Wilfred get to take that holiday you were looking forward to? And how is Plettenberg Bay? As far as that goes, where is the place? I never heard of it, even. How often do you see Wilfred? "Bill," to us. Is Edith Broadbent up there now, and is she feeling better? Is she working, and how are the children?

I wonder if you know that Rose and Tom McCarthy and little Thomas are back home already? They left here at the end of Feb. Golly, how I hated to see them go, as we got to be very close friends, and I miss her a lot. Well, my dear, it isn't at all safe from here to there, regardless of what the ship carries. They were torpedoed off the Atlantic coast, and were thirty-eight hours in a lifeboat. They visited my mother and dad and sent a newspaper clipping that had all the details in it about their trip.

Rose had instructed little Thomas where to go (at the head of a staircase) in case the boat was hit. Well, they had just gone down to lunch and Thomas was in the children's playroom when it struck. And they all met at the top of the staircase. Then they thought they would go to their room to get their life preservers, and, when they got to their room, it wasn't there. It had been hit direct, and was an open hole.

So they searched around and found some preservers in the children's playroom and donned these. Then they got into a lifeboat, and their other ship sank immediately (*The City of New York*). The wife of the Yugoslav Minister gave birth to a baby in the lifeboat, and a doctor from Brooklyn, with two broken ribs, assisted at the birth. They lost all possessions, and there were quite a few lives lost, and they were very lucky to have been all saved together. Sure did have some experiences, I guess.

When they were picked up by an American ship, Rose gave the new baby its first bath. They sent us a cable when they arrived, and haven't written yet, but gave Mother the clipping to send to us and to say she would write soon. I hope. I sure am glad they were safe, and now I am even wondering if she managed to save her fur cape.

She had everything insured before she left, so she ought to be able to buy a nice new bunch of clothes for all of them. Two other Americans came out here to work at their factory last year, and they are a lovely couple, Lib and Jim Langwill. They are so pleasant, and she is quite attractive. I haven't seen very much of them, as they are in Cape Town and we seldom go there due to petrol [gas], and, when we do go, I like to shop. They were here last Christmas, all of them, the Macs and the Langwills, and it was scorching, as you can remember. However, we had fun and enjoyed ourselves.

Isn't this war something? Whew! We have been entertaining soldiers and sailors that like to come out here for a holiday, and it has been fun. We had some very nice ones, and really felt bad when their visit had come to an end. Not American ones, but English. I also do a little knitting for the Navy (so far have made one pair of socks) but find that my daughter needs more things than the Navy does, from me, I mean.

Well, Helen, just wanted you to know I think of you often, and especially that day we spent at Isipingo beach, which I enjoyed so much. To say nothing of the nice visits we had in Durban. Hope we may have some more in the not too distant future.

Any chance of your getting down this way? Not much chance of my getting up that way either. I mean, while this war is on. So our letters will have to carry us thru. Say hello to anyone I may know that you know, and do write when you get a moment or two. How are your children and do they go to boarding school, or are you near a school?

Loads of love,

Marjorie

435 Escom House
Rissik Street
Johannesburg
July 12, 1942

Dearest Mother and Dad,

I received your letter of May 21st yesterday, and when you say there was a month between the dates of my letters, I feel quite sure you are not receiving all of them. For one thing, you have never mentioned pictures I sent you of this house and garden, and they were sent soon after we moved here. I have sent several times since then good snaps of the children in the garden.

I have been worried about Father's position since I knew he was in the tire side of the Holston Oil, and I am so glad he was so readily fixed up at the plants, as you say—of all places—at the Personnel Department. I can remember when we thought the place was unapproachable. I shall be interested to learn just what arrangements Father makes for the transportation of four thousand eight hundred people. It will certainly be a job, and I have no bright ideas, but I am sure he will since he knows the country and the bus business. What a great pity Uncle Edwin and all did not sell out, but who could foresee what has happened. It shows there is no safe business in the world. One that can survive a depression may not survive a war. I am quite sure I would never have sold out if it had been up to me to decide. I hope the business can hold out until normal days.

I am so very sorry to hear of Aunt Ruth's accident. [Aunt Ruth, one of Dr. Jobe's eight daughters, now seventy-eight, is Sophia's aunt and Helen's great-aunt]. I am afraid it means she is bedridden for the rest of her days. I am sorry to appear heartless, but I do not want you to assume this responsibility. You have had enough gloom in your home, and I want you to feel that you and Father are having a normal and happy life together now. [Harlow is now sixty-five, Sophia is fifty-six, and Helen and Wilfred are both thirty-five years old.]

I am glad for Aunt Hattie's sake that she can be with you for a while and have proper care and nourishing food. I imagine they [Aunt Hattie and Aunt Ruth] are careless about a proper diet when left on their own.

By the way, I steamed my nose before starting this letter, as I must stay in the same room for at least half an hour afterwards. I must steam every night, and, if I do, I have a very good nose, ever so much better, anyway. No asthma anymore, which I was having so much at night, even up here.

You will be pleased to know that I am getting along well with paying off the doctor's bill. I have only £5.5.0. more to pay, roughly $25, which I hope to get off next month. However, I may let it slide another month, as we all have to pay $25 to the government next month to help finance the war. We are able to meet our obligations soon enough, and we do not want for anything. I shall be very cross if you all send any more money out to us, and you also must not send so many and such expensive clothes for the children. They do look nicely dressed these days. I don't know of any children who are better dressed, in fact.

I was very lucky about getting a red and white hand-knitted pullover with long sleeves for Eve to wear during the colder weather with her blue skirt and red jacket. A friend of Bert's knit it for a daughter and found it was too small, so sold it to Bert for the price of the wool, about a dollar. It looks so very nice with her little suit. I bought Eve a beautiful pair of black shoes this month—size thirteen. Can you believe she is such a big girl? I had to set the snaps over to the edge at the waistband of her blue skirt today. She is gaining weight, and I know it would do you good to see her eat after the hours you have spent coaxing food down her.

The hair ribbons have been arriving all right, a red with white dot, a white with red design, and, in your last letter, a red and blue, etc., stripe. The children are thrilled to death, as they have never possessed so many ribbons before. They are well supplied now, so you must let some time elapse before sending them any more. They are going to be quite spoiled with so much, I am afraid.

Wilfred finds he has jumped from the frying pan into the fire. I thought it was a mistake all along, but he wouldn't have known it if he hadn't tried it for himself. He thought he would get promotion, but it hasn't materialized. He was so interested in his other work but not with what he is doing now. He is a quartermaster and should be a captain in that position, but he remains a lieutenant and does the work just the same. It is work that he simply could not be as interested in as lecturing.

I have heard from many sources that Wilfred was the finest lecturer they had. His last class passed one hundred percent because he tutored them at night if they needed it until every man understood the course. Since the examination was set by another officer in the school, the instructors were amazed by the one hundred percent pass.

By the way, I had free hospitalization, so my doctor's bill ends that expense. I went into a free ward at the General Hospital, and I had good attention and enjoyed the experience. They dressed us in the funniest long sleeve, high-neck nightdresses and the most dreadful red bathrobes, all of which depressed Bert to such an extent that she only came twice, but I can stomach a little more than she can.

There were some other very nice people in the ward, and some very queer ones, but all were kind and helped each other when they could. I had a waterbed and was as comfortable as I could be since I had to sit up night and day. Over here, you seem to have to sit up after every operation but tonsil.

My doctor wanted me to go to a nursing home at $60 per week, his words being, "Oh Mrs. Evans, the General is not for people like you. I want you in a nursing home." This speech only made me more determined on my set course. I said, "It will be quite all right for me, doctor, and in keeping with my means." I have no false pride, and I can manage my pounds, shillings, and pence just as well as I used to manage my dollars.

I actually expected to pay something, as I did not want it for nothing, but I knew it wouldn't be much; however, I accepted it free since the specialist charged so much. I would like to know what they would charge at home for the same "op." I feel sure not as much as $100, though.

I have heard that I *may* get my increase, but nothing is official. It will make such a difference if it does come off. I hated to hear that Father had to take less, as I know he is worth so much more. He has been so sensible all along, though, and has taken what was offered and has got on with the job.

A friend of mine here, Elizabeth, is nearly demented, as her husband sits at home while he holds out for a big salary. In the meantime, she keeps things going with her traveling job. He has such big ideas, and is so extravagant when he does have some money, that it is just about as hard for her when he has a job as when he doesn't. I simply could not put up with him, but to leave him has never occurred to her.

I had Edith and a Mr. and Mrs. Coolbaugh for bridge, which I perhaps wrote about in my last letter of June 30th. I enjoyed it very much.

I was just on the point of writing and asking you to send me some bloomer elastic when I found some in a shop yesterday. I had tramped the streets looking for it, and the whole family had their pants pinned up [with safety pins] in hunks. I could only get three yards, but that has made a big difference in our feeling of security. I have been very busy with it over the weekend. I shall go in again tomorrow in disguise, and buy three more yards.

I have a marvelous cookie recipe that takes *no* flour, but it won't do you any good, as it requires a cup of sugar. I make them with Quaker Oats.

Goodness, it's ten o'clock, so I have been writing for two hours, so must close and go to bed.[121]

Love and kisses from us all,

Helen

[Letter from Bert]   July 18, 1942

My dearest Mrs. Dixon,

I have just received your letter, and am replying immediately. I am so sorry you are feeling so distressed about Helen.

Helen made a wonderful recovery from her nasal operation, was out of the hospital within a week. She is wonderfully well, and is enjoying very good health; in fact, she is better than she has been for a long while. The polyp in her nose was affecting her breathing, and since its removal she is feeling the benefit.

I know Helen has written you, but, owing to the irregularity of the mails, some must have been delayed. However, by now you should have received her letters. I would like you to know that you need never worry unnecessarily about her, as I would be the first to let you know if she were ill. We are such a united little family, and all love each other and help where we can. It has been a very great joy to me to have Helen out here, and know my gain has been your loss. However, we will take care of her and our babes. I feel as though I know you so well, as Helen talks to me about you and her father, and your pictures were certainly a very great joy to her; you are both placed in a very prominent position, and the pictures are so life-like.

The babes had a combined birthday party on Eve's birthday the 6th June, and it was really lovely. The colour scheme was carried out in red, white, and blue, which was most appropriate. The cake was white, and we had twelve candles in the above shades, and the filling was also red, white, and blue. We decorated the study with the allies' flags, and one big one in the center of the U.S.A. This

---

[121] Close to this time, Helen finds she is pregnant.

thrilled Eve, as she said it was her country's flag. The frocks you sent them just fitted in with the colour scheme, and they both looked perfectly charming and were delightful little hostesses to their guests. After Robin had eaten so much, she came to me and said, "Auntie Bert, you have not served us with coffee." I do not know where she would have put it, as they had so many lovely things to eat and no restrictions as to how much was good for them.

I am enclosing a few pictures I took of the children at the party, and I know you will enjoy them.

Eve has done very well at school and scored 78%, which I think excellent. She is very diligent and loves her paints and books. I am paying for her to have dance lessons at school, as I think it is so good for them, and gives them self-confidence and poise as they grow older. We spend lovely weekends together, and the children seem to love their Auntie Bert, as I think she rather spoils them. It is only natural for one to do so, as they are so precious to me.

You would adore our little Robin. She is most intelligent and speaks fluently. They are such glorious companions. Robin can say the "Lord's Prayer" by herself, and they "God Bless" everyone they can think of. Papa Harlow and Mama Sophia come next to Mummy and Daddy. Another part of their prayers is "God Bless America and keep "it safed in the war," and God Bless South Africa and keep it "saved in the war." Their prayers are quite a ritual, and I think they try and compete with each other as to who can say the longest one.

I feel as though I have had a long talk to you, and I would greatly enjoy hearing from you if you feel inclined to write me. Helen and I are more than sisters, and she is very dear to me, and whilst she is here do not worry, as I shall help, with the Grace of God, to guard her and hers.

My sincere love and affection to both of Helen's family,

Ever your,

Bert

4 Reform Avenue
Melrose, Johannesburg
July 21, 1942

My dearest Mother and Dad,

You will be glad to know that I am trying to be more systematic about my letters to you now, since I write down each date that I mail you one, so I will have a check on the time lapsing between letters; otherwise, with the way time flies by, I am apt to think it hasn't been so long since I have written, when it has been quite some time. My last letter was written on the 12th.

I did a very good piece of work the other day. I had the minutes of a meeting to take, which lasted an hour and forty-five minutes. It was a very fiery meeting, and it was necessary for me to write the whole time without a break so as to get it as nearly verbatim as possible. When I transcribed my notes, I was simply amazed at how much I had of the whole proceedings. Typed out, it was thirteen pages of foolscap. I got in the very tone of each man's remarks, which was very important because of the heated atmosphere. No one has said it was a good effort, but I know it without being told.

You may be interested to know that I have been offered another job. This is to teach three children and my own for our board and keep and £5 per month. These people live on a big farm in the Transvaal, and this woman is running the farm while her husband is away in the army. They have a governess, but they don't like her. I would be better off financially, and I suppose the children would love it, for they have horses to ride, dogs, chickens, etc., but I am just afraid my nerves would never stand up to five children all day long. I would love to be able to be with mine all day long, but I am also doubtful that my tutorship would be as good as what Eve is getting at her school; there she can have swimming and dancing as extras. Anyway, Wilfred and I plan to go there for this coming weekend as guests, and, after that, I shall know whether I even want to consider it.

I have a junior in the office now to assist me, and my work isn't so hard anymore. For months and months I worked extremely hard, and there was just never an end to it. I like her very much and feel so very sorry for her. She is only twenty-three, and I remember at twenty-three a lot of trouble started coming my way. [At that age, Helen was grieving the loss of her brother; beginning her four-year separation from Wilfred and her long-term emotional and financial commitment to her parents; and was entering the first days of the Great Depression]. She has so much to worry her, as she has one brother who is a prisoner of war in Germany, and another brother who is Missing in Action. She has five brothers in all, and all of them are in some branch of the Service.

Eve and Robin are both well and are having a great time just now with two little friends nearby who have at last recovered from mumps. One child is Eve's age and one Robin's age. Their father has just now joined up, and this is true of quite a few that I know. They have just now felt it imperative to offer their services. These wives are trying to adjust themselves as I did two years ago. I feel very sorry for them, as I know just how they feel until they get used to the idea and are settled into a new mode of life.

I find the old lady in the house with me most difficult at times, but I went through such a time cleaning up the place so I could live in it that I have no idea of leaving until my year is up, and then I am sure she will either want more rent or want me to get out. She is always harping on the fact that she can get £12.10.0 for it instead of my £10.10.0. I told her that she would find anybody paying £12.10.0 very dissatisfied at not having a light in the bathroom or one in the study. Can you imagine such a thing?

A Vale of Soul-Making (May 1940—Feb. 1943)

To add to the ridiculous situation, she has just spent £400 on her side of the house, putting in a kitchen and bathroom and therefore two new electric outlets, but she wouldn't put lights in these two rooms on my side at the same time. Anybody would have thought that I had asked her for something I could take away with me.

The garden is nice, and we have plenty of room, and it is a good neighborhood, so you can see why I am not anxious to move. We had such a stormy scene Sunday before last, but I didn't write you about it because it was all too fresh and irritating at the time. For instance, she has a telephone, and I always pay her three pennies for each call, which is double the charge for a call. However, she must pay a monthly rental, so I consider it only fair to pay her extra. Since I have a telephone at my disposal all day, it is very seldom necessary for me to use her phone. In exchange for this convenience, or at least I considered it so, she used my electric refrigerator, which made it necessary for her to come through my part of the house many times a day.

She also used to allow her boy [man servant] to come through the inside entrance from her part of the house, without even so much as a knock. I had to complain about this for months before it was stopped. Also, for the first four months, she cooked on my stove and took all her baths in my bathroom and never furnished so much as a stick of wood or a lump of coal for the fire. Besides this, she was highly offended if there wasn't a fire going for her to cook on when we were out, and she objected because I asked that her boy build the first fire in the morning instead of Betty doing it. Now she has an electric stove and an electric water heater, so she only uses my refrigerator.

When she said I must share the rent of her telephone if I were going to use it, I reminded her of her advantage of using my refrigerator and also the months she cooked on my stove and never paid a cent for it. She was highly indignant and immediately removed everything from the refrigerator, saying if that was the way I felt about it, etc. I told her to just help herself and take everything out and let us keep ourselves on a separate basis entirely.

She is a person who could accept anything in a most charming manner but can give nothing with any grace. She wants to take everything she can from me. Meanwhile, her daughter has a nice home and spends £17 and £20 for a frock, and has her husband at home, so you can imagine how her tales of being hard-pressed affect me. I really like her daughter, but we can never be on friendly terms with her mother giving her side of the picture to her all the time.

Her daughter gave Eve a beautiful children's book of Greek mythology. We are reading it now, and Eve simply loves it. I, meanwhile, am learning more Greek mythology than I ever knew before. I think it is very advanced for Eve [who is now eight], but she doesn't seem to think so. I read to them every night, and I have read some very good things. Both Robin and Eve loved *Mary Poppins*. I bought *Pinocchio* for them, but they do not care for it so very much.

Mr. Evans is seventy years old tomorrow, and he has invited Bert and me for lunch at his club. We are giving him a picture of Robin framed. I am going to have the same one made up for you all, but coloured, I think. It is an enlargement from a snap, one of the ones I sent you made at her birthday party.

I must stop now and get busy in the office. I think this is all the news, in any case. I had to sign a statement the other day at the bank saying I had received the money Uncle Edwin had sent me. I am glad that is all settled now. Let me know how the Holston Oil is and if they hope to survive these times. I wonder about all of these things and hope for the best. I am also anxious to hear how Father is getting on in his new job and how he likes it.

Love and kisses from Robin, Eve, and your

Helen

4 Reform Avenue
Melrose, Johannesburg
July 30, 1942

My dearest Mother and Dad,

Your letter of the 2nd June along with Uncle Edwin's letter and two issues of the *Time* arrived yesterday at my home address. I also received the Special Service Issue of the *Watuga Spinnerette* from Mr. Wampler. I am wondering if you told him that I was thinking of writing to him. I must write now.

It was so nice getting the snaps of the family. I can't think why you haven't sent these to me before now, as you must know how interested I would be in them. I think everyone is looking well, and I just wished I could see my little family added to the group. We would have swelled the ranks considerably. I am showing these pictures to everybody that I can nab.

I had a most delicious hamburger yesterday at a typically American place. So good that I am going back today for another. Also a piece of apple pie with it. Edith Broadbent asked me there for lunch, but she never showed up; this is most usual for her now. I am sure she forgets her appointments because she is worried all the time, but she tries to appear very bright, and I admire her way of taking things. I invited her with the two children to the children's birthday party and she forgot to come. I never feel the least offended because I know what worry can to do to one's memory.

I feel so disgusted with K.R. for her remark, and I wonder about W.'s sympathies after that. I don't know how anyone can turn against everything they have had instilled in them from birth. I don't want to know such people after the war. Those who have suffered bombings will not forget. Thank goodness the

Germans have quite a lot now that they won't forget. I could not gloat over the destruction in Germany if they had not first caused so much in England, Malta, etc. It is strange, but about a year after I was in Cologne [in 1933] I dreamed a most horrible dream about Cologne: I was standing beside the Cathedral and the whole city was in a half-light, with people running here and there, screaming and falling, sobbing, praying in the streets; the buildings were in half ruins, and it seemed like doomsday. It must have been something like I dreamed, and it is terrible to think of that beautiful city in ruins.

Thank goodness the money of Uncle Edwin's has arrived, as well as the last that you all sent, and all of that is settled. I would suggest that you all not make us any presents unless we have to ask for something, as that will become necessary, I feel certain. For instance, it is only by the greatest good fortune that I finally found some elastic to repair dropping bloomers in the family. However, that situation has been overcome for the present, but I am sure that I shall have to ask for that item some day, as well as hooks and eyes. I finally found them, but only after a search of the town. Another thing is toilet paper. All of these items are so essential, and, when the time comes that we can't get them, they will be appreciated more than anything. Your Christmas present can say something like this: "You can order on me for ___ rolls of toilet paper any time in 1943." This will cause great jubilation in the Evans' household. We are pretty safe as long as we live at No. 4 Reform, as it is a rather leafy place.

Your house at $5,000 is certainly a bargain, and, if you could have started buying when we first moved into it, it wouldn't have been a bad idea, but I don't think you should consider it now.

I am sorry I had to send you such a short cable when I did cable, as you asked for a full one, but here the charge is one shilling a word for a straight cable or nine pence per word for a NLT [Night Letter][122] and you must wire 25 words in an NLT. The cable I sent was 9/6d, and the NLT would have cost me 18/9d, double, so that is why I did not follow your instructions. In America, the long cable is a saving of money, but here it is not, so that is why I shall perhaps always be brief.

It was such a surprise to hear of Margaret Frost's marriage. To me she is still a child. And as far as her sister goes, my only memory of her is throwing mud on me and wiping muddy hands all over my nice dress one day when I was passing there. When I read of her wearing a long white frock to some party given for Margaret, I just wished I could wipe muddy hands on it.

It's a lovely picture of Betty Umbach. Is she really so pretty? How are Mr. and Mrs. Umbach? You haven't mentioned them for some time. I am anxious to see Robin's coat. She will soon be able to wear a lighter-weight coat. Eve has her red

---

[122] A cheaper form of telegram sent for delivery the next day.

jacket, but Robin hasn't anything light except sweaters. I am sure it is pretty in the material you sent us a sample of.

I find my nose improving all the time, and I am so thankful that I had the operation. Everybody rather discouraged the operation, so I had to make up my own mind and do everything on my own. You know how it is when you get older; you just have to look after yourself. It wasn't the money that anyone in the family begrudged me, it was that they didn't think it would benefit me. I simply feel a new person and do not begrudge the doctor a penny of his fee now that I am so much better.

Mrs. Maton was in to see me last night and was as bright and chatty as if we had never had an unpleasant word between us. She is lonely, and I would like to be very nice to her, but, the minute I am, she wants to take advantage of me. She is a queer combination. I, too, find it very lonely out there at times, as the children are in bed so early. I have lived the queer life of having a weekend husband most weekends for the past two years. Between weekends there are just evenings of sewing or reading; and, being alone, I invariably fall asleep before I have done much of anything. Fortunately, Hilda Hudson from across the street and I go to the movies together now and then. They have a beautiful home which reminds me of ours on "G" Street. Hilda reminds me of myself before I was married. She has her own car, so we can go into town or wherever we like. We are going this evening to see *New Wine*. The music alone will be worthwhile.

Robin and Eve are having such fun during Eve's long holidays. They play nearly every day with two such nice little girls their own ages. Just now they have a complete hospital set up on the enclosed back porch, which is lovely and sunny and simply ideal for the winter. Robin's wagon is made up into a bed, and a small suitcase of mine is their First Aid Kit. Eve has made a search of the house for everything that resembles what they use in hospitals. She dresses herself in long black stockings, black shoes, blue dress, white apron, and white cap every day. The things she has thought of show no lack of imagination. I want to mail this this afternoon on my way home, so I won't write more now. I love you both very much and do get homesick for you.

Love,
Helen

4 Reform Avenue
Melrose, Johannesburg
August 26, 1942

My dearest Ones,

At last the mystery of the letter I wrote from hospital has been solved. I enclose it. Though I have looked for it many times since your cable, I only found it yesterday. I am really glad to know it wasn't lost in the mails as we feel more secure about our future letters.

This is my first letter for several weeks as I have been too tired to write. I finally went to the doctor and have been put on drugstore vitamins—"Gelseals." I am feeling better already and have been taking them only three days.

Robin has been in kindergarten about two weeks now and seems to learn a new rhyme every day. She must repeat everything she has learned each night to me. The other night she took off her teacher by frowning and rolling her eyes and repeating this thing the teacher was trying to teach them.

I did appreciate Dad's letter so very much and am glad when he can find time to write himself. I am glad he likes the work at the plant, but he always finds his positions interesting. In fact, he seems more interested now than he ever was in his own business. I certainly appreciated the remarks he made about me and can only say that I think you two deserve to have children you can be proud of. I know I have given you worry in the past because I just now realize how headstrong I was, but I am glad I decided my own fate and need never say my people kept me from doing this and that, as Bert blames her people for not having married.[123] Bert is now busy making her trousseau, with no one in view, but because a fortuneteller told her she would be married very quickly, very soon. I feel so sorry for her pinning her hopes to such a thing. Mr. Evans and Bert are both full of superstitions and feel sorry for Wilfred and me that we are so practical that we only believe what we see.

Wilfred is for the first time interested in coming back. We both feel we would like to live in North Carolina, so we are going to see what can be done with that in mind. I don't care to live in South Africa, as I long for my own people.

Love

Helen

4 Reform Avenue
Melrose, Johannesburg
September 21, 1942

My dearest Mother and Dad,

Your letter of July 2nd has just arrived, and I can say that I also know great relief now that you have finally heard from me and know that I am all right. I have felt so upset that you have written Bert and to Mrs. Maton. That silly Mrs. Maton

---

[123] When she was younger, Bert fell in love with a young man. For some reason her mother disapproved of the man and said: "You will have to choose between him and me." For whatever reason, Bert chose her mother and broke off her relationship with the young man. In later years, Bert became a self-motivated and highly successful businesswoman.

nearly frightened me out of my wits the way she went around the point of telling me she had had a letter from you and not getting to the point of the letter. I am sure people enjoy being dramatic and keeping one in suspense.

Bert wrote you as soon as your letter arrived, and I had written before that. You know of course by now that it takes two months for a letter to get to you. It was terribly silly of me to write you that I was going to have the operation, but I thought the two letters would perhaps arrive together, the one written before and the one after, and that it would give you the feeling that nothing was being kept from you, which I think is very important. That is my great fear, in this separation, that things are being kept from me. I am quite sure they are, too, because I know when I was at home I always had somebody in the family to worry about and now I don't, so a lot must be withheld.

Durban has never been bombed. They did have a scare, but there was nothing to it. They are blacked out all the time, and I am glad, for that reason, that I am away from there.

I am sorry that Uncle Edwin is so worried over his business. He has certainly had his ups and downs in business. It seems you can never be sure of anything in America. I must say that business seems more stable here. It is the uncertainty in America that makes us afraid to risk it again.

I am glad Helen is making such big money, but it may spoil her for a lesser salary after the war. Anyway, she must just face that and be glad she can make it now. That is more than I have ever made. I wish I could be over there for one of those big salaries, but, since Wilfred is still in the Union, I know that it would never have done if I had left and stayed away all these years.

Leone has certainly been lovely to you, and I do appreciate it so much. They do not celebrate Mother's Day over here, so I never think of it, I am afraid. Anyway, it is nice that you are taken to the tea each year of the Mary Cameron Class, and some day yet I'll take you to it, no doubt.

Robin is very anxious for Papa Harlow to know that she quite often has "Papa Harlow Eggs" for breakfast. This is a soft-boiled egg in a cup with toast crumbled up in it and butter. Then last night I cooked a "Mama Sophia Supper"—this was turnip greens with chunks of fat ham and corn bread. Eve ate until I thought she would pop, and so did I, but Robin would not have it except for the corn bread. I told her it was because she was a Springbok (South African) and Eve and I were Americans; this meal was Wilfred's idea, you will be surprised to hear, and he enjoyed it too, though he didn't make the glutton of himself that Eve and I did. It is so hard to get sufficient turnip tops for such a meal, and mustard greens are unknown. Are mustard greens grown or are they the top of some vegetable?

We are very busy in our vegetable garden every weekend now. We have very big cauliflower plants up, about eighteen, and cabbage plants, about twenty-four, and beetroot, spinach, carrots, lettuce, radishes just starting. Eve and Robin planted two seed potatoes themselves that were given to them, and they are doing fine. We are going to put out more potatoes next weekend, as they are so expensive to buy.

I am trying to brown my legs for the summer without stockings, but I don't brown easily, and I only have the weekends for sunshine. However, we moved our clocks up an hour today and we'll get a little more sun in the afternoons, getting out an hour earlier. I am sure my boss is going to be tempted to keep me later because of this change, but I shall not encourage him, as the day is long enough as it is: 8:30 to 5:00 and Saturdays 8:30 to 12:30.

We have only had two rains in eight months now, and we are due for some now and longing for it.

The sox fit Robin perfectly, so the No. 7 is right for her. Of course, Eve grabbed them before she could stop her and stretched them over her foot. She takes an 8½. There were loud screams on both sides over them. Eve still loves things to wear better than anything else. Her request for Christmas is a new blazer for school and new gymslip[124] with new blouses. She is getting them too, as her old blazer is much too tight now, and she will definitely need a larger one next winter. We are cutting down one of Bert's that she only wore a few months. I have bought the blue serge for the gym, and the making is all that is left now. Robin is crazy for such an outfit too, but of course they just wear their gingham dresses to the little kindergarten she goes to. They both had such fits over a lot of empty match boxes over the weekend that I think I shall get Robin a really nice set of blocks for Christmas.

No time for more.

Lots of love,

Helen

4 Reform Avenue
Melrose, Johannesburg
October 15, 1942

My dearest Mother and Dad,

Mother's letter of the 24th of July only arrived yesterday; that is nearly three months! It had not been delayed by the Censors either, as it was not censored. That is the longest it has taken for any letter or parcel. Mother mentions a birthday

---

[124] A gymslip is a sleeveless jumper worn with a shirt and tie. Made from a heavy serge fabric, it was the mandatory winter uniform at Parktown Convent. Since it was worn above the knees and with short white socks, however, it afforded little warmth to the student. It was often worn with the school blazer, which helped provide some warmth against Johannesburg's bitter winters. The blazer had a school badge on an upper left pocket.

parcel that she is sending, but of course it hasn't arrived. I believe she will be allowed to send it, as it is a gift. I sent off a parcel on the 13th and one on the 14th to you all for Christmas, one parcel post, and one book post. I thought I was early enough for Christmas. Now I wonder if they will get there in time.

Anyway, we can't judge those things anymore and will just have to be patient. They accepted both of these parcels at the post office here, as they were gifts. I do hope they come through all right, as I feel sure you will both be pleased with what I have sent.

Bert and I made the nightgown for Mother, and I did the handwork and Bert the stitching, as her machine is set for this work. She said she was so pleased to do something for my mother. This is the gown I mentioned long ago, just now getting finished. I know Mother will want to give it to Helen Hunter, but she mustn't. Mrs. Maton, when she saw me sewing on it and heard it was for my mother, wanted to know if I was going to line it, and Mrs. B., a wit in the office, suggested canvas or sack as being most appropriate. I have a nightie made the same way in pink georgette, but of course it is not so pretty as yours made in chiffon. We simply can't get such materials anymore over here. Bert has bought a few pieces, but she won't be able to get any more.

Betty can make the most delicious pastry now, and I can bake a good cake. You have no idea how proud we are of ourselves. I sift the Government flour for my cakes.

Wilfred has been transferred permanently, or as permanently as the Army posts ever are, to a place one hundred ten miles from Johannesburg. He is a Quartermaster, so now you will know his duties without my going into details. Before this he has been filling temporary posts in different camps, some of them training officer, that is, parade ground work, etc. The post he has been given is a Captain's post, and he should get his Captaincy soon; in fact, he should have had it long ago, but one gets left out sometimes in every walk of life for no good reason. However, I think he is going to get his third pip soon now.

He is anxious for me to come up to live at Warmbaths, which is only three miles from him; it is a health resort, the best in South Africa—one of those places where you drink sulphur water, Ugh! and take mud baths. There is every outdoor amusement there—golf, tennis, swimming pool, bowls, horseback riding. Just everything. The idea is very tempting, and we could afford to do it if he becomes a Captain. In fact, I feel quite sure that I will give up my job when he becomes a Captain, because he can't stand the idea of my[125] working; you have no idea how it hurts him, and the whole thing has been a strain on me, as you can imagine. I have only had two weeks holiday in over two years of working; the other breaks I

---

[125] Helen is now five months pregnant, something she continues to hide from her parents.

had I used to move from Durban up here and have my nose operation. During that time the children have had measles, whooping cough, and yellow jaundice, besides my poor health in Durban all the time. If I don't stop enumerating, I shall start to feel very sorry for myself.

Anyway, I think it will not be amiss for me to give up for a while, and I can always go back to work if I want to. Our big problem is Eve's schooling. We do not think that we would like her to attend the only school in Warmbaths, just a Government country school, because she is so happy at the Convent and is doing so well there, so she would have to continue at the Convent as a boarder, which she is perfectly willing to do, but the expense must be considered. However, Eve as a boarder at the Convent and Robin and myself boarding in a good hotel is no more than just running the house and Eve's fees as a day pupil now. We have put all the figures down, and the new way would actually be some cheaper. Anyway, we are not doing anything until Wilfred has been at his new camp longer and knows more about how things are going with him. Please don't get worried about Eve becoming a Catholic, as there are many Protestant boarders at the Convent.[126]

I know that Mother and I always had difficulty about a powder base. I must tell you my latest find. For years I have used Hind's Honey and Almond Cream as a powder base, but just lately I have started using Crooke's Calamine, and it is so much better. I don't know whether it is American or English, though, so you may have some trouble getting it, but I wish you would try it, as I am sure you would like it. Another discovery I have made is that Vaseline is the worst thing you can put on your lips; it makes them peel and peel. Mother should use a plain white cream lipstick night and day, a thick coating, and then one with color when you go out. The plain one will soften the lips and keep them from peeling. I do this and don't have the trouble I used to have with them peeling and cracking. Nothing like a few beauty hints. Of course, there aren't many women I would tell these beauty secrets to.

October 17, 1942

I don't know what I will do if you aren't allowed to mail the parcel, for I am crazy to have the summer dress Mother described, and also the dresses for the children. I am sure the one she has made for Robin is cute, and I am wondering what has happened to the coat she made for her. Speaking of making a coat for Robin out of Father's trousers and a dress for her out of Mother's dress reminds

---

[129] Parktown Convent was a strict but peaceful haven for Catholics, Protestants, and Jews. As was the custom at the time, however, it was restricted to those who were considered White or of European descent. Many of the students, like Eve and Robin, had fathers who were away at war. Modeled after schools like Roedean in England, private schools of this type were strictly regimented.

me to tell you that we are all making all kinds of things do for us by mending and darning.

October 24, 1942

Well, I am posting this letter today finished or unfinished. You have no idea how many things I have had to do.

More interruptions, so I give up, and will just say that I do hope you both have a very happy Christmas and forget for a few days that there is a war, and remember that though I am far away, I shall be very close to you in spirit at that time.

All our love and a thousand kisses,

Helen and Babes

4 Reform Avenue
December 8, 1942

My dearest Ones,

It is certainly unusual for me to be entirely alone on Sundays, but this afternoon both of the children have gone to play with little friends, Bert is having a good rest at home, much needed, and Wilfred is at camp. Even Mrs. Maton is away; in fact, she has been away for about three weeks with her daughter. I am not a nervous person, though, and sleep with a police whistle under my pillow in case there is a prowler. Anyway, Mrs. Maton is hardly what you would think of as protection. She is Dickie's size and seventy-two. We have been having days and days of rain, but this afternoon I am sitting out on the uncovered part of my stoop hoping to get a few vitamins from the sun while I write. If we are ever going to have a summer, it is now time, but there are really no seasons in Johannesburg. It is nearly always cool.

I have just this week received a lot of mail from you. First of all, I am so pleased you are finally rid of the L.'s. I am sure Mother will find the house hardly any burden at all with the new tenants. Naturally, I am pleased that you are getting $75 rent now. I believe the house account is in the red, so this will help to get it out. Too, with fewer demands for this and that, it can stay in the clear. I am not anxious to sell with the present glutted market in Johnson City. I would not keep the present tenants upset by showing the place. I know its disadvantages, the very ones that Father wrote about; still, it is a house I am proud to own.

Naturally, I have thought of what it would mean to all to own the house you are in if I could sell the Johnson City property, but I do not consider it wise because of its location. Naturally, having ground at the back makes it much better, but it borders on a poor part of town that will not change for years, if ever. The Johnson City property is well located, and I am not interested in exchanging it for other property in Johnson City just now. The property Father mentioned is definitely on the wrong side of town.

Wilfred and I did not go to look over the teaching position, as I decided against it. I thought of all the drawbacks Mother mentioned. The less you have to do with other people, except on a strictly business or a strictly social basis, the better off you are. The in-between propositions do not appeal to me. The war has introduced so much of this half-and-half business.

The bloomer elastic arrived and is greatly appreciated. We haven't had such good quality for ages.

I am sorry to hear about it being necessary for Uncle Earl to have an operation for hernia. I certainly hope it will be successful in every way and that he will look after himself afterwards.

I never heard of Julia Brewer's remark about Monta Vista; I was referring to her remark that she was glad the Germans got to Norway before the English.

I have never heard anything from the Vriesens since their youngest son left South Africa. He spent a night with us before he left, and that was about three months after we first came out here. I am afraid that there has been great sorrow in that family if there is one left to grieve. I remember Frau Vriesen saying to me, "We always try to share others' sorrows and burdens, as we have never had any of our own." Poor thing has now had more than her share, I am sure.

Father wrote that J.T. had never had any promotion since going to the plants, and that was why he was leaving and joining up—more or less. I am surprised to hear that he hasn't advanced, because they were so friendly with the Wolffs. He maybe made himself unpopular with other department heads, as I well remember how he pulled everything out of our department that he could when Mr. Funcke left and Mr. Smith took over. I used to say to Mr. Smith, "Are you going to let him take this and that, and your staff then to do the work?" Mr. Smith was very quiet and easy-going and said, "Let him carry on." He was very grasping and perhaps was over keen for advancement and to gain control. However, I am sorry you have lost them, as they belonged to your crowd and entertained a lot.

The birthday parcel has still not arrived. I telephoned the post office to see if any mails leaving around the first part of August had been lost due to enemy action, but they said no. However, it could have been stolen, since you can't insure it. I shall go to the post office tomorrow to see about it. The notification slip may never have reached me. If it never arrives, we must just consider ourselves lucky that all the rest have, and I appreciate it just the same and thank you for all you have done for us.

I must tell you about the concert at Parktown Convent. Bert and Robin and I went to see Eve in four numbers—a dance, an Afrikaans poem, an English poem, and something else, which I seem to have forgotten. Eve was so beautiful that night with a little added colour to her cheeks and lips. Her costume was a pink satin waist with a blue organdy skirt and yellow stiff net underskirt to make it stand straight out. She wore a band of real rosebuds in her hair and she knew she looked pretty, so her eyes simply sparkled. She was far the prettiest child in her class. She was so decidedly the leader in the dance, and she was so full of poise and self-confidence, that the rest took their queues from her. Her marvelous memory came in well. I expected very little from her dancing and was afraid Bert would be disappointed in her because she has paid for her lessons, but Bert said she was by far the best in her class and was very pleased with her.[127] As I watched her, all of her little life seemed to flash before me, and I couldn't help a few tears. Eve recites beautifully. I am sure she is the artistic type and that it will come out in many ways. Robin is the type that likes to get down and do some good hard work. Robin looks like an Evans, and Eve looks like us.

I am making them each a voile nightie like the one I sent you—Eve's is pink and Robin's blue. I think they will be thrilled. Their Xmas this year will be mostly clothes. Bert is making two dresses for Robin and one for Eve. I have just bought them both new shoes and shall get socks and ribbons, etc. They love to be dressed up.

I am getting string beans, beetroot, and lettuce out of my own garden now. I will have tomatoes, cabbage and carrots later, and pumpkins sometime. I forgot—we also have our own potatoes. The soil is wonderful and, with all the rain, there has been no trouble growing things. Our cauliflower is not going to do well; that is our only disappointment. By Xmas we shall have plenty of peaches too. I am glad to have a few things of my own just now, as prices are so high at Xmas time for all foods. It happens every year.

Dr. van der Bijl has divorced his first wife, an American, and married his secretary, Miss Buxton. Both are attractive women, but Miss Buxton is much younger, my age. It seems terrible for a woman who has given up her people and her country to be left alone when she is about sixty. People should build up so much in their marriage that this can't happen. Miss Buxton is not in such a wonderful position with so many years difference in their ages, and this is her first marriage. There has been a lot of talk, of course, and much more than was warranted, I feel sure. I think through constant association in the office they fell in love, and then there was nothing for him to do but ask for a divorce.

---

[127] As a young woman, Bert taught dance in Cape Town. In 1925, when she was twenty-three years old, Bert was chosen to dance with the Prince of Wales (later King Edward VIII) at a ball in Cape Town given in his honor. A year later, in 1926, Bert's dancing was admired by Anna Pavlova. Years earlier, representatives of the Bolshoi Ballet had tried to recruit Bert—something her father quickly disallowed. It was for these reasons that Helen was anxious to see Bert satisfied with Eve's performance.

This all reminds me of when I was trying to explain marriage to Eve, and I said that when you married a man you must always love him and never love any other man. She looked at me with very big eyes and said, "But suppose you do fall in love with another man, what do you do then?" That really stumped me, and I felt that anybody's answer would be as good as mine.

I must stop now, as this has grown into a very long letter. By the way, I made a nightie just like the one I sent you and got £3.30 for it ($12). Also, I don't want to fail to mention how proud I am of Mother's sales of War Bonds. She is good at selling. I don't know how she is managing to do so much.

Love and kisses to you both,

Helen

8 Reform Avenue
Melrose, Johannesburg
January 7, 1943

My very dearest Ones,

It has been some time since I have been able to sit down and write you a real letter, but I sent the Xmas cards made by Eve, etc., and knew you wouldn't be worried as long as you had something from us. You will understand why I haven't been able to write when I give you some idea of all the changes I have been making.

As you can see from the above address, we have a new home, only two doors from our other place. This move took place on the 2nd of Jan. I can't tell you how delighted we all are with our new place. In fact, I like it better than any home we have had in Africa. It is small and easy to run, consisting of living room, dining room, two bedrooms, kitchen, and bath. There is a large screened-in porch across the entire front of the house, it is burglar-proofed throughout, and every window and door is wired against flies. Besides the front door bell, there is a bell in the living room and dining room to the kitchen.

Our furniture looks most attractive here, and we are as safe as can be. Our neighbours are close on each side, as the garden is small and so prettily laid out, with grass bordered by flowers. We even have a palm tree in the back garden. There is a beautifully built garage where the children keep their toys instead of in the house. There is also an outside laundry. Here we have an electric stove with a slow combustion for hot water.

All of this we get for $4.00 more per month than we paid Mrs. Maton, where we had to cook on a coal stove and be annoyed with her all day. The move came about when she was ready to go to Cape Town for three months and had rented her side of the house. She put up a most dreadful-looking board fence through the garden in three different designs made from scraps of the old summer house she had torn down that was the children's playhouse. She had dug two large pits at our front gate for all the rubbish from the other side. Wilfred and I walked through the garden with her, and he told her she had made the place look like a Native Location by putting up the fence, and, furthermore, she was to close up her rubbish pits before leaving. She went absolutely off her head at this, since I had usually accepted everything and anything because I had no time to look for another place. She said, "You'll leave at the end of the month. I'll have my lawyers put you out." This was the 20th of Dec. Our lease was up at the end of December, and Mrs. Maton and I had not been able to come to terms about us staying on, as she wanted £12.10.0 instead of £10.10.0 per month. I told her I would have some conveniences when I paid the higher rent.

On Christmas day, we received a letter from her lawyers, not demanding that we leave at the end of the month, but giving us one month's notice or the offer of the place until the end of March at the higher rent, and, at the end of March, Mrs. Maton would occupy our side herself. In the meantime, we had found this place, and we got a lawyer who proved to them that we could leave at the end of December. She has now gone to Cape Town for the two weeks instead of her three months. I understand it gave her a terrible shock. Houses are scarce, and she thought she had every advantage. This place is so superior to hers that she is going to be galled every day when she sees us in it. She doesn't know yet where we are living.

This does not end the changes that have taken place. Betty, having been left for over a year on her own, was getting dictatorial. She had another girl staying with her for two weeks, and when I had had all of it I could stand and said she would have to go, Miss Betty said she would go too. Of course, she is a wonderful servant but just beyond herself because of the authority she had had, so I made up my mind I would have to come home for an indefinite period and either settle Betty or get a new girl. This threat of hers was also in December, but when she was paid at the end of the month, she made no move to leave, though I never asked her one way or the other.

On the 1st, I came home on eighteen-days' holiday. Just to make a break, so she can more gracefully take orders from me, I told her several days after the 1st that I was going to give her a week's holiday with pay. That break will smooth things out, I am sure. During that time I shall do my own work, as this little place will be easy to keep. The children are both home on their long holidays, so we don't have to run to schedule, and I am sure they will help as much as they can, especially Robin, who is very domestic. Eve is sweet about errands, but she doesn't like to dirty her hands.

After my holiday, I am resigning and shall stay at home indefinitely. Wilfred has wanted me to do this for some time, and I must admit I am pretty well exhausted.[128] Since I have come home, and after I was more or less settled in this new place, I have had a sleep every afternoon, and I have to be waked for supper, and then I feel I had rather do without it than get up. It is too wonderful to be able to write you this letter at night and not feel at all tired. It was hard for me to give up, as I am so used to driving myself, and, in order to calm my nerves and make myself give up to the new order of things, a nice home and rest, I have been reading *The Importance of Living* by Lin Yutang. I could not have picked up a more helpful book when it comes to relaxing and enjoying the everyday things about us.

I must not resign until after my holiday; otherwise, I do not get it. I need only give twenty-four hours notice then. Of course, Mr. Ashworth knows of my decision, and he is terribly upset by it. Every time he interviewed somebody for the job, he would call me in afterwards and say, "But she isn't like you." That seemed to be all he was looking for, my twin someplace. He and his wife invited us as a family to their home during Xmas. I could hardly get the children to leave with any grace at all, as they have a swimming pool, and Eve and Robin went in with their four boys. Robin was jumping in over her head and thinking nothing of it. Eve went in a few days later at a public pool here and suddenly began to swim. I must take her again, in a day or two, while she has her confidence in herself.

I want to send you Eve's exam book for the year so that you can see what work she is doing and just what she did on her final tests. Her average was 91%, which made her either second or third in her class. This was a big come-up from 78%, which was her average for the first half of the year at the Convent. Her grandfather Evans was so pleased with her that he bought her the school blazer. I had previously made it a gift from you all and him, but he gave me another Pound, so he could give it entirely. She has changed from a rather annoying child to a wonderfully sweet little girl just in this year at the Convent. The whole family here is in agreement that she must continue her schooling there, regardless of everything else. Robin is already wanting her school to reopen, so we can't cut down there either. I think Granddad Evans will look after both school fees if we can't, since I have stopped work, and remember: he has the money to do it.

He would have bought the house we are living in, but he thought the price was very much out of line, and I had to agree with him. Property is sky high here now, and there is a lot changing hands.

I had three of my neighbours in to tea this morning, as I haven't been able to be very neighbourly previously, and I was afraid to delay having them, as I am so apt to get into a groove and just enjoy my children and house quite on my own. I had

---

[128] This is something of an understatement, since Wilfred is still away in training for war, Helen has two children, a full-time job, no car, no home phone, a problem with her sinuses, is eight months pregnant, and is just finalizing her fourteenth move in six years.

Mrs. McCullum, who took Mrs. Maton's flat furnished. She is an evacuee from India. I want her to meet some of her neighbours. She started out with a poor impression of me because Mrs. Maton had her ear at the start.

I saw our First Division arrive here on Tuesday, but it upset me, as I could only think of those they left behind them. I met up with old Mrs. Broadbent, trying to find her way around Johannesburg on her own, as they were expecting Charles to come in. I was glad I wasn't working and could take the time to take her to the place to meet him in case he arrived. Of course, Edith was as thoughtless of her as ever. Whether he arrived or not, I have not heard as, unfortunately, I have no phone and neither has Edith. You can't get them anymore.

I wrote you that I made a hit with Wilfred's Commanding Officer. Well, it turned out to be the worst thing that could have happened. The man has been given a bigger post and had promised Wilfred a major's job when he was transferred, and then I came along. According to Wilfred, I became an obsession with the man. He could talk of nothing else. He tried to arrange parties for me and tried to get my address to come to see me, and, finally, when he was quite drunk one night, said something to Wilfred that no husband could stand for.

When he left them for his new post, he asked Wilfred if he would like to come with him, and Wilfred merely said, "No, sir," and saluted. You can imagine how much good this has done Wilfred. My meeting the man was all Wilfred's idea, as he thought the family touch of wife, etc., would be beneficial. I must explain to you that the man was fascinating, but fascinating as the devil would be.

Next day

At this stage, I heard a familiar whistle at the gate and Wilfred was home unexpectedly. He does like our new home, and, fortunately, will have a long weekend with us.

I have just received a letter from a friend of mine from here, visiting in Southern Rhodesia, to tell me she is coming back to get a divorce. While she was nursing her mother who was dying of cancer, a blonde (divorced with two children), age thirty-eight, simply took her husband from her. My friend is one of the prettiest and loveliest women you could ever meet. She is well read and interesting, but, unfortunately, has never been able to have children. Her husband is a handsome man, but you would also consider him a most sane and sensible man. They were ideally happy together until this woman came along. She must be older than Marjorie. Marjorie says she is a businesswoman with money of her own. I wish I could give some helpful advice, but a thing like this stumps me. Marjorie said she gave them a free rein, hoping Howard would recover and simply kept quiet, but it hasn't helped. No one could be more attractive and feminine than Marjorie, but what can she do? This follows right on the death of her mother, too.

I really must close now, as Wilfred will be coming in. He had to go to Pretoria today on army business. He is President of a Court Martial being held there.

I hope you know how much I love you two and how I long to see you.
Love and kisses from,

Helen

8 Reform Avenue
Melrose, Johannesburg
January 26, 1943

My own dears,

This red typing looks rather childish, but the blue is worn out completely, and I see the red is perfectly good, so no doubt all my letters will be in red for some time to come. This stationery is a little queer too, but I feel I should use anything I have on hand in the way of paper, for we really have a shortage. The other day I went to town and there was no toilet paper and no toothpaste to be had in the whole town. They have promised to relieve the toilet paper situation, but not the toothpaste. Bert is good at scrounging around and knowing the little, out-of-the-way places, and she finally bought three rolls of paper for me, their last three. She also sold me a tube of toothpaste. We can use salt and soda for our teeth, which will be economical and is very good for the teeth, I believe.

Well, it has been like Christmas around here, and I don't know where to begin to tell you about it. First, the money arrived—SIX POUNDS, which, I can tell you, is a goodly sum and has been spent on the things we want and need most. In a day or two after the money arrived, two boxes from you found port at last. We have now received a dress for me, a dress (floral glaze) for Eve, and a pink dress for Robin plus a coat for Robin, the red white and blue dress or pinafore with panties and bonnet to match for Eve, the apron for Betty, Cleanex, which carried us over the days we had no toilet paper, and there is still some and what a treat it is. I was so thankful to finally see these parcels because I had entirely given them up as lost. I really think we have been extremely lucky, as I have now received every parcel you have sent.

Everything is simply lovely, and we all had a marvelous time trying on and admiring ourselves and each other. Yes, and the books for the children arrived, with the balloons. You could not have made a better selection. Eve has read every prayer and learned some of them and now says a grace at table for us, or rather Robin and Eve say it in unison. Of course, they loved "The Night Before Christmas" with the pictures, and this has been read several times. Your parcels were five and a half months on the way. They must have been all over the world if it isn't that they had to wait in New York such a long time before being shipped.

Anyway, the summer dresses arrived for our first hot weather, and we have already been enjoying them. I have never seen Eve look so good as in the floral dress. The red, white, and blue I must alter, and right away, as she is crazy to wear it. Our wardrobes have been considerably freshened up by these arrivals. I like my outfit very much indeed, and it is just the right type of thing for Johannesburg because it is cool but tailored. We couldn't thank you enough for all these lovely things, and I am so glad your money and time were not wasted and that we have the benefit of what you have done because you love us. Just for fun, I shall tell Betty that she must write to you and thank you for her apron. Right now she is on holiday. I gave her two weeks off, as she seemed worn out, and it is customary here to give them leave each year. I have a friend of Betty's for the two weeks, and everything is going along just the same as with Betty.

I would have done my own work for two weeks while Betty was away if it were not that I am home to have a rest, and I couldn't have one if I were doing the housework. Unfortunately, my nose operation was not a complete success, and the doctor wants to redo a portion of it, but not the sinus, which was the big op. What he has to do now is only cauterize my nose in his rooms. For months we have been waiting for me to be free of a cold so that he could do it, but I haven't been without a cold for a very long time, and it is also giving me trouble again with my chest and sleepless nights. I am still on my Vitamins, but my blood pressure is low, and I seem a little subnormal altogether, so I must have this rest. I find it very hard to settle myself and not do things that hurt me, especially as I have just moved. You know all the things there are to do in settling a new house; also, I am sure there are two years mending and darning staring me in the face.

The quiet work does not hurt me, but it is the other work that really appeals to me. Wilfred and Bert have such fits every time I lift some little thing, or dig a little in the garden, that they make me feel like an invalid. When I am chesty at night, they can always give me the reason why I am, for they saw me do something during the day that I am not supposed to. I have certainly been cursed with a second-rate nose all my life.

Don't write and ask Bert anything about me, because she would say I should not have written you this and worried you, but I know that you know me so well that there has to be some reason when I give up. However, do not get the idea that I am more ill than I am, as I am not. You know only too well the struggle I have nearly always had to have a nearly normal life and still live with my nose.

Mother's short letter of Nov. 5 arrived at the same time as the parcels and a letter from Father dated 4th Aug. I was terribly upset to learn that you had to leave 814 Broad Street because it will take a long time to feel at home in another place, as you have been there so long and were so comfortable there. To think you have been living some other place for a month or two, and I don't even know where.

The only good thing about it all is that you won't have roomers, and I hope Mother won't have a furnace to keep going.[129]

I have thought for a long time that the house and roomers were too much work for her. It would have been too much for me, I know. How about that little shingle house beside Wolf's and back of Curtis's house? It is tiny but would be so easy to run, I should think, and it used to rent for about $15 per month. Did I tell you that I could only get this place I am in for six months? I feel pretty sure the owner is going to want it at the end of that time herself. It seems to me you might rent part of your furniture to somebody who is in temporarily, except they seldom take care of it as you would. I do hope you are comfortably fixed up by now and are happy in your new place.

I must tell you some of the things I have done with the money you and Uncle Edwin and Aunt Lennie sent. I bought a silver-plated hot water jug, which is so essential to the *calm* serving of tea. It is a lovely thing. I bought three dining room chairs, not too wonderful to look at right now, but they won't be too bad when I have finished with them, as I am going to dress them up so their previous owner wouldn't know them. I have bought out Mrs. Maton's half of the lawn mower we owned together. She is furious, as this is an item you can't buy today. She has just now discovered me as a business woman, as, before, I let her pull off all her little deals because I had no time to argue with her, and I was not in a position to be firm.

Eve and Robin had a big treat from you by going to the *Sleeping Beauty* pantomime.[130] There is always an Xmas panto, and it is always expensive, so they wouldn't have seen it otherwise. I hope you don't mind that I spent most of the money on practical things.

Poor Betty had everything stolen from her room the night before she was to leave on her holiday. She was very upset, of course, and it has made me a little

---

[129] While Sophia and Harlow had only lived on Broad Street in Elizabethton for about twelve years, Sophia had lived in the small city of Elizabethton for most of her life. Since Sophia's grandfather, Dr. Abraham Jobe, had purchased one hundred forty-three acres in Elizabethton back in 1845, Sophia's family had enjoyed its connections with the town for ninety-eight years. Sophia's father, Dr. E.E. Hunter (Dr. Jobe's son-in-law), had made substantial contributions to the development of the town, including acting as contractor for the now-famous covered bridge. This deep-rootedness must have made Helen's aversion to Elizabethton and many of its residents all the more poignant for Sophia.

[130] Panto, or pantomime, has for centuries been popular in England and in Commonwealth countries. Based on famous children's fairy tales, the pantomime is generally performed during the Christmas and New Year seasons. Pantos include songs, slapstick comedy, cross-dressing actors, sing-alongs, and shout-out phrases. While the children take the panto at face value, adults in the audience are kept laughing both at the risqué double-entrendres and at the innocent confusion of the children, who fail to see most of the jokes.

nervous about the house, but the Civic Guards look after my house twice every night, and I hope we'll have no more trouble. This house is completely burglar-proofed, but still, you never know how they might manage to get in, and, too, one does not want to have a fright.

Betty was sleeping out, which she should not do, so it is really her fault. They dropped the apron you sent her. I was so glad she did not lose that because it had only arrived the day of the burglary. She had an awful lot of clothes that I didn't dream she possessed when she made out her list. On top of that, I discovered by her husband's Post office Savings Book, that was also dropped, that they have Two Hundred and Twenty Pounds saved up,[131] so she could afford the loss better than I could.

I am enclosing Eve's last report, which we are so proud of. She came either second or third in her class, and we feel this is particularly good, as she was so behind when she entered Standard I.[132] There are two Grades and then they start in the Standards. Just what it compares with at home, I do not know, but I will send you some of her work to see. She starts Standard II tomorrow. Robin is already back at her school and has been put into Grade I, so she has actually started her schooling at four-and-a-half years. She is very keen on learning, but it seems early to me.

Bert leaves this week for three weeks holiday at a little seaside resort south of Durban. There will be other friends of hers there, so I think she will enjoy herself. She has let her flat for two months and will come out to stay with me when she returns. She said she would pay me the rent of her flat, which will be a little boon to me as Bert is little expense because she eats like a bird, and I can give her just what we would have, in any case.

There is much more I would like to write about, but I must get to bed now, so will save it for another time.

Lots and lots of love to my dear ones so far away,

Helen

---

[131] While domestic workers earned modest wages, they had room, board, and uniforms all provided, and very little expense for transportation, so it was possible for them to save if they were frugal. However, this does not account for the costs of keeping their children, who had to live miles away, usually with grandparents, in food, clothing, and accommodation.

[132] Standard 1, in South Africa, is the same as third grade in the United States.

8 Reform Avenue
Melrose
Johannesburg
February 7, 1943

Dearest Mother and Dad,

This is a midsummer Sunday afternoon and painfully quiet, as Wilfred did not come in this weekend, Bert is on holiday, and the children are having their nap. Dad always visits us on Sunday mornings, so I shall be rather lonely for the rest of the day.

I had two *Time* magazines from you this week, and Xmas card and wedding announcement from Elizabeth Swan, but no letter from you yet. In one *Time* I found the clipping of Aunt Ruth's passing; however, I did not mourn, as I knew it came as a relief to her as well as those who nursed her. I am glad Aunt Nellie stayed with Aunt Hattie, and I hope Aunt Hattie will visit around the family for a while. It should do her good. Aunt Hattie is the last of her generation in our family, and I am sure all will want to be kind to her and try to cheer her up.

I can't tell you how all of South Africa has felt over the tragic death of our General, Dan Pienaar.[133] I wonder if anyone received that news with dry eyes. We all feel very proud of Roosevelt for flying to Casablanca. It is wonderful that these men of such prominence and long past the years of devil-may-care will take such chances with their lives. The older I get, the busier I want to be. I think Field Marshal and Mrs. Smuts have a most wonderful life; they are so busy, they do not have time to note the passing of the years.

Bert has asked me to ask you to send her five yards of floral glaze material like Eve's dress. She wants to make a housecoat for herself. The best colour on her is a light blue if you could get that to predominate. If you have a housecoat pattern to send that you do not want, or cut a paper pattern from yours, it would be a help, as we can seldom get a pattern out here. We cannot buy the material she has asked for either. She will send you the money, as we can send small amounts, I believe. It would be wise to send the thread, as she might never match it and could only buy one reel if she did.

I would like for you to send me No. 620 Kodak films now and then, as we can't get them any longer, and I'd like to send you snaps of the children and our different home. Also of our three kittens, who are simply too cute for words. Can you imagine me allowing the children to acquire three kittens and all females?[134] I

---

[133] Major General Dan Pienaar was a magnetic military figure in South Africa during World War II. Popular with all races, his untimely death at the age of forty-nine stripped South Africa of a man who might have saved the country from the tragedy of apartheid.

[134] Eve remembers the two of us dressing the kittens in little outfits and wheeling them about in a doll's perambulator.

have never seen them enjoy anything more, though. The children would enjoy a stick of chewing gum now and then in a letter. We can't get that, so I told them I would ask you, and they are terribly thrilled.

When I meet up with the two women who have taken the two apartments of Mrs. Maton's house, I do not get a chance to tell my story about her, as they are so full of her themselves after only a month or less for the one on my side. That I put up with her for a year shows more patience than you know. I know I make a big mistake in letting things slide until I have had just too much, and then I let go in such a big way that there is no mending. It would be far better to make it understood that you are never going to be imposed upon.

I would particularly appreciate a copy of the *Ladies' Home* Journal or *House and Garden* now that I am home and trying to be domestic. If I found one to buy, it would be a year old. I seem to do nothing but ask for things in this letter, but all of these things would give us much happiness.

We feel that Robin has real talent for dancing, and I think she will go to Eve's teacher at the Convent next quarter. If anything, she gets blonder all the time, and the pink dress you sent makes her look very blonde.

Love and kisses from us all to you dear ones,

Helen

Eve, Wilfred, baby John, Helen, and Robin in Johannesburg

7
Affairs are Now Soul-Size
March 1943 ~ October 1943

Affairs are now soul-size.
The enterprise is exploration into God.

~ *Christopher Fry*

7

On February 28, 1943, Helen gives birth to baby John. Two weeks later, Wilfred leaves his little family in Johannesburg in preparation for going into battle in North Africa. This picture was taken on the day of his departure for North Africa, one month after John was born. It is the only picture ever taken of our entire family that survives.

Helen is at home alone. She has made fourteen moves, mostly alone, since her arrival in South Africa five-and-a-half years earlier. She is now left with a procession of maids who abandon her one by one because of the amount of work they are expected to do with a baby in the house.

This means that Helen has no one to help her with the baby and her two young children. She must wash by hand and hang out the laundry and diapers, she must keep a fire burning in the small coal stove to ensure a sufficient supply of hot water, she has no car so must walk to the store to buy groceries and carry them home, and she is ill, saying, "I just don't feel up to scratch at any time."

With Wilfred up north in Egypt, the end of Helen's life finds her enjoying her friendly neighbors who pop in on her, making sure that she is all right. Occasionally, of course, they find her somewhat lonely—but as determined as ever in her optimism. Remaining firmly planted in the reality of day-to-day living, Helen finds joy wherever she can—particularly in her exquisitely beautiful baby son and in her loving husband, Wilfred, who, ten years after their marriage, despite being away in Egypt, "has never stopped courting" her. She tries to continue to work and keep house, slow to admit that the load is too heavy to bear.

Wilfred, who has now been away from home for three years, wants everyone (meaning his in-laws, Sophia and Harlow) to be as happy as he and Helen are. But, almost presaging all that she is about to sacrifice, Helen reluctantly gives up her charming kittens, the first of many losses.

From Helen [age 36] 　　　　　　　　　　　　Braemar Maternity Home
　　　　　　　　　　　　　　　　　　　　　　　　Johannesburg
　　　　　　　　　　　　　　　　　　　　　　　　March 2, 1943

My dearest Mother and Dad,

There is so much news to give you that it is hard to know where to begin, but I feel sure you will agree with me that nothing can be more important than the fact that you have a brand new grandson—John Kevren Evans, born Sunday, the 28th of February, at 10:45 a.m. in the Braemar Maternity Home. He is a little thing, only 6 lbs. 14 ozs, but he is well and strong, and we are all thrilled and happy about him.

So far the Evans family thinks he looks like me, but that is because he is only two days old. I heard it with Robin too: "Look at the nose, just like Helen's." Since this is my last baby, I shan't bother to explain that all babies have flat noses because I won't have to hear it again anyway. John has hair the colour of mine, whereas his sisters were bald. He has lovely skin and nice colour and opened his eyes the minute he was born. I had my usual easy time, about 2½ hours in all. I got to the nursing home only an hour before he was born, as I had to dress. Bert had to do last-minute packing for me, and Wilfred had to telephone the doctor, the nursing home, and order a taxi from town, which is five miles away.

I must interrupt about baby to tell you we have just had the worst earth tremor I have felt here. It was really frightening, as I could hear the plaster falling in the walls and my water danced in the bowl on the washstand. For a second, I just wasn't sure that the building was going to hold together. It is an old place to begin with, but I have a very delightful room with some antique chairs that I would love to buy. It is a bedroom like one would have at home, done all in blue, and, since I am one floor up, I just look out on the tops of some lovely trees. I have a northern exposure, which is like having a southern exposure at home. I have a private room, as one wants privacy at this time and my nerves need a rest. My doctor is a woman gynecologist, Dr. Janet Robertson, one of the best known in the city. Though she only arrived a half hour before the baby was born, I saw her stop to pray, so you can know the type of person she is at heart, though, in the work-a-day world, she is very brusque and full of swear words when she is angry. She is a type that people unburden on. She is a widow with an adopted daughter.

I hope you like the name of John Kevren, as I selected it. I like John because it is plain and manly, and I have liked Kevren ever since I heard it. I knew that Kevren was a family name in Wilfred's family, but I didn't know that his great uncle was John Kevren until I had decided on the name. This uncle was a good man who was dearly loved by Wilfred as a boy and of whom Mr. Evans cannot say enough. A name was hard to select, as we were always running into names of my old beaux. Bert and I liked Richard, but Wilfred hadn't forgotten Richard H.

There was no John outstanding in my mind but Father's father. Robin has announced that she is going to call him Kev.

I know you will forgive me for not telling you about John before this, for I knew it would be impossible for you not to worry during times like these. I certainly missed all the sewing you did for Robin and Eve. I did John's, just the minimum, but enough. Bert has knitted many beautiful things for him. I shall only have to buy rompers later on, and we get beautiful Madeira ones here for so little.

Let me relieve your mind about my finances because that will worry you, I know. I saved every penny I could from the time I knew there would be another one, and I have $400 to see me through. This amount will enable us to live nicely for some time, plus what Wilfred can allot us. He gives us the very maximum he can from his pay. It is good to feel secure and know that you do not have to look to someone for assistance.

We can all feel very thankful for John Kevren's life, as he was born with the cord tied tightly around his neck. Dr. Janet said if he had been my first he would have been stillborn. What an awful thought. It is because he was born quickly and with ease that we have him here.

March 3

I was interrupted yesterday and could not finish, though I started writing at five o'clock in the morning. Wilfred left today for the camp where they are assembling our new Sixth Armoured Division for overseas service. He is going as Navigation Officer. That was his special subject when he was lecturing, you will remember. This turn of affairs was a shock to me, of course, and is no doubt the reason John arrived two weeks early. I want tò be brave like the others, for I have never seen such bravery among women as displayed here. I have had Wilfred here for two-and-a-half years, so I cannot complain.

I do not expect Wilfred to go immediately, but he can be sent any day, and I must prepare myself for it. I heard this ten days before John arrived and was taken very ill and was never quite well again until now, and I am feeling very well indeed. I am so thankful the baby was born before Wilfred's leave was over and before there was the possibility of his not seeing the child. Wilfred has been told by the Colonel that he will get his captaincy, so I think it is certain enough now for you to make any birth announcement in home town paper as Capt. and Mrs. Evans. There are people in Johnson City who would be interested too.

Your letter of January 1st arrived February 27, and, since I have not received any of your December letters (with stockings), it came as a great shock to me. You see, I do not know what Father is doing in Bristol, and I suspect dirty work from L. at the plants. I know how you are going to miss Elizabethton and your activities there. I long so much for us to be reunited under happy and pleasant conditions. If the seas were safe, no one could keep me here now. Why must we both be lonely on opposite sides of the globe?[135] [136]

Helen

8 Reform Avenue
Melrose, Johannesburg
March 8, 1943

Dearest Aunt Lennie and Uncle Edwin,

Maybe you will understand my delay in writing to thank you for the $10 sent for our Christmas when you know we now have a son, born Sunday, the 28th of February. I have already written Mother and Father, of course, but this letter may reach you before theirs, so I don't know who will have the news first. His name is John Kevren, and he is just a little fellow—6 lbs.14 ozs., but he is well and strong. We go home day after tomorrow, which I am looking forward to, as Wilfred is at home on embarkation leave, and I want to be with him as much as possible before he leaves.

However, I have enjoyed my rest at the Nursing Home very much, and I have often thought of a remark of Aunt Lennie's when she was in hospital with Kathryn: "I have looked forward to this, as it is a real holiday." It is true, for suddenly there is nothing more you can do about anything, and you can rest and be lazy with a clear conscience, and everybody aids and abets you in the matter. I have had a lovely quiet room and the very best attention. I have a very prominent woman gynecologist and like her very much. When I saw all three of my children in my room for the first time, I really felt I had a family.

Your Christmas present was certainly appreciated and was spent on all kinds of things that we needed most. I bought one real luxury with the money that came from you and Mother and Father, and that was a plated silver hot water jug.

---

[135] This is a moment of abject loneliness for Helen. She is home with a new baby. She is ill. She has no one to turn to. Wilfred is on his way north. This is beyond the usual immigrant's experience of missing home. Helen is in dire need, yet she rapidly pulls herself together with her usual grace and fortitude.

[136] Two days after Helen wrote this letter, on March 5, 1943, Essen, Germany (home of the Vriesens), was subjected to one of the heaviest raids of the war. Over four hundred residents were killed, nearly sixteen thousand injured, and fifty thousand were made homeless. It has been three years since the last correspondence between the Vriesen and the Evans families, and eleven years since Wilfred had lived there.

Mother writes me about how very attractive and popular Helen and Kathryn are. I do wish I could see them at this age, as I think young girls are so lovely, and life is so exciting for them.

Love and our best wishes to you all,

Helen

8 Reform Avenue
Melrose, Johannesburg
April 8, 1943

Dearests,

I have taken a long time between letters, as my last to you was written in the Nursing Home, but I know Bert has written you quite a few. You can imagine that my time has been full, but I think I will have more time now, as things are settling down; however, I will have to divide my time for correspondence between you all and Wilfred now. Bert goes back to her flat in a week's time, and Betty has given notice that she is leaving at the end of the month, so we are going to feel a little lost when we are left a small family of four—John, Robin, Eve and myself.[137] I guess Betty thinks the work too much now with John's nappies; however, I wish she had given her notice before I gave her a holiday. You will be surprised at how much we pay the natives out here, as I pay Betty $4.00 a week.

Thank goodness and thank you, two pairs of stockings have arrived—but not the last and thinnest pair that you wrote about. I can feel well dressed now. I am also enjoying the dress you sent me very much, as I have never been able to wear it until now. I also had another summer dress that I had not worn when I bought during last winter because I liked it so much. Thankful I am that they were in the house and not in the trunk in the garage, where most of my clothes were stored.

I have had to give up my three kittens. I sent them to the Society for Preventing Cruelty to Animals, and they dispose of them in a humane way. I can still see them about, for they were lovely and so playful, but I had to reduce the size of my family. I now have a puppy that is far more trouble than the three kittens, and I only keep her because Wilfred got her for me for protection, and she will be wonderful protection when she is grown up. She is a purebred Doberman Pinscher and worth a lot of money. Her father cost $500 and is privately owned, and her mother is from the police kennels.

---

[137] Baby John is just five weeks old, Wilfred is in Egypt, and Helen's health is increasingly fragile. By this time, Betty had been part of the family for nineteen months.

I do hope I get to see Pete Hendrickson and Bill Toncray, but I haven't seen any American troops in Johannesburg. If I were living at the coast, I might have a chance to see them.

The sheering on your nightgown was done by threading the bobbin of the sewing machine with the sheering elastic and the needle with thread; then it is a matter of adjusting the tension. It is not supposed to be good for the machine, however. So far, I have never done it on my electric machine.

I would like you to send me some teats for John's bottles. We use the same wide-mouthed one as we used for Eve. I only have two and have not been able to find any more. I also have two bottles only and would like another if you can pack it well. You know I want Pyrex only. As for Eve and Robin, the only scarcity is socks.

John has been very lucky in presents, as his Grandfather Evans gave me Five Pounds to buy a pram for him, and Mr. and Mrs. Ashworth (he is my ex-boss) gave me the most beautiful hand-knit shawl with crocheted border, of Shetland wool. They cost about $15. Also a lovely Angora cardigan, which costs about $5.00. This morning Mrs. Ashworth delivered a box of grapes, a present from Mr. Starck, who happens to be one of the wealthiest men in S.A. The grapes are direct from his fruit farms in the Cape and are the export variety, which are the largest you have ever seen. John has had many other presents and we have had callers galore, nearly as bad as with Eve in Elizabethton. Everyone likes a newborn baby.

John is thriving beautifully and is lovely and strong just like Eve and Robin were as babies. He is only five weeks old, but he holds his head up and smiles and coos and pushes himself with his feet. He weighs about nine pounds now. He is very fat and healthy looking. He is just about to settle down to getting me up once a night, but at the most only twice a night for half an hour each time, so if one goes to bed early it is not too much of a strain.

I shall write to Aunt Lula and Uncle Earle as soon as I can, also Aunt Nellie about the dress she sent Eve, and Robin and me hankies, which were much appreciated. Robin's was in such a cute container and gave her a big thrill.

Robin wears a 10½ shoe and Eve a 13½. Eve needs white socks for school; in fact, I prefer white socks for both of them, as they go with everything. Try to get a heavyweight sock, as you have sent some thin ones that are through after two wears. Also, I would like some white darning cotton, as I can't get it and mine is finished, so the socks they have are going from bad to worse. Send some black while you are sending, as it might come in useful as Eve has blue socks. She loved the navy blue ones you sent her; they are very pretty, and will look well with her new navy blue gym that I am trying to make her. I bought Robin a pair of new brown school shoes which she thinks are marvelous, and I told her they were from you, as I hadn't spent all her Xmas money from you. I also bought Eve new bedroom slippers that are most attractive, and I told her they were from you as well. Robin got new slippers too, but they were from Christmas money Mr. Evans had given her.

I must stop now, as I want to take John to Dr. Janet's baby afternoon. I am not going so much for advice as to show him off, I'm afraid.

Lots of love from us all,

Helen

8 Reform Avenue
Melrose, Johannesburg
May 8, 1943

My dearest Mother and Dad,

I get less time than ever now for writing, but just know that no news is good news, and I shall do the best I can about writing. Every opportunity I get, I sleep, as John is not the placid baby that Robin was, and as for Eve, you had her, and I really know nothing about how she behaved. John is getting much better, however, and I hope in another two or three weeks he will sleep the night through, from ten o'clock to six, anyway.

We heard yesterday that Wilfred had reached his destination, and for this much we are very happy. Wouldn't it be funny if he met some Elizabethton boys?

Isn't the news in North Africa marvelous? The newspaper stated yesterday that, with the Mediterranean practically our pond, we can expect fewer mails to and from the Union. I should think that would be affected considerably.

I enclose a picture of us all (John's first picture) taken the morning Wilfred left home after his embarkation leave. We didn't get in much of the garden, as we had to get right against the fence to get any sun, as it was early in the morning and the house cast a shadow over the lawn. We have a very pretty little garden, and I am sorry we couldn't get it in with the last film we had, or are likely to have.

Mr. Evans entered a billiard match of the different clubs in the city; there were one hundred sixty-nine entries, and he has won, until he plays in the finals Tuesday night. We are all very excited about this, as he is seventy-two years old, and each time he has played he has been at the table for three hours with strong lights on him and a large gallery of spectators. We do hope he wins the final, as it would mean so much to him, and he would get a gold medal that he would give to John. The tournament was organized to raise money for the Dan Pienaar Memorial Fund.

My new girl is very dumb but does try very hard. I told her to go to the shops to get a pound of ox liver for the dog, and she came back with cold sliced ox tongue. I asked her if she thought that was dog meat; she felt so bad over it that she wanted to take her own money and go back for the dog meat. Of course, I wouldn't let her. She is conscientious and honest, I believe, so I shall overlook a lot. I have to train her to cook, and you know how little I know about it myself, so it isn't easy.

I must stop now, as the fire in the grate is dying out, and since it is a cold, wet night out, I do not want to get chilled.

Bert comes out at least twice a week and has proved a wonderful friend. She is making me go to her flat for this weekend, and she is taking care of John. It will be heavenly to sleep there a night undisturbed.

Love from myself and the children,

Helen

> 8 Reform Avenue
> Melrose, Johannesburg
> May 16, 1943

My dearest Mother and Dad,

Now I am the one on the anxious seat, as I haven't heard from you in weeks. However, I am trying to calm myself with the thought that it is either because you are moving or because of the shipping situation.

I had my first letter from Wilfred on Thursday from up North. He was busy making himself comfortable in the desert with four petrol tins and a wooden box.[138] It sounds like the lap of luxury, doesn't it? He was complaining that there were no letters for him when he arrived, but I expected it to take them much longer to go up than it did, so I did not post early enough. We have a very cheap Air Mail Service between here and the Middle East—only 3d a letter postcard, which goes sealed, and on which I can get a long letter by typing it. This is the same postage as I put on a letter to you.

I shall perhaps repeat myself a lot, as I won't know whether I have written you or Wilfred a thing.

In case I haven't told you, Robin is making remarkable progress in reading now. She loves it and will read as long as you will listen. She doesn't wait until she has had it at school but tries any page in her reader and with success.

John is growing beautifully and is a real good baby on the whole now. He still has me up several times at night, and the nights are getting very cold now for that foolishness. Bert took care of him last night, and I slept at her flat. She does everything anyone could to give me a hand and see that I have rest. I hope you will write and thank her. Even you could not have done more for me than Bert has

---

[138] Wilfred was stationed in the desert in Khataba, northwest of Cairo, which had been set up as a staging area for tanks and other equipment for the South African Sixth Armored Division. Tank training, however, did little to prepare South African soldiers for deployment in Italy, where the action was guerilla warfare rather than tank warfare.

done. Of course, she loves John too, just as much as I do, I believe, so it is not all sacrifice, but she is taking the bitter with the sweet.

My health has been very bad. I had reached the stage of having an attack of asthma every night, and I took Ephedrine twice every night. The whole thing naturally left me exhausted the next day, and we had decided I couldn't stay on in my house, though the landlady had said I could have it for as long as I liked; the house sits low, and we thought that affected me.

Last Wednesday, I went to a masseur who put me on an alkalizing diet of fruit and vegetables and gives me treatment twice a week, which consists of ultra violet rays, massage, etc., and I haven't had an attack of asthma since my first treatment. I am simply a new person. She recommends parsley tea for kidney trouble. If you would like to try my diet, let me know. I am sure it would make anyone feel better, if done for a while. Thank goodness, I went to her instead of wasting money on doctors. I paid a doctor in Durban $75 to do something for my asthma, and he did not help me one little bit. This has also brought my waistline back to normal.

Isn't the war news marvelous? See what the Americans and the English can do together.

Must close now.

Love and kisses from us all,

Helen

P.S. Tell Uncle Edwin I have a Doberman Pinscher puppy whose father cost $500. I couldn't have a better watchdog, as he will tell you. I already have a plaque on the gate: "Beware of the dog." That is a joke, so far, of course, as she is so young.

May 26, 1943

My own Dearests,

I have just had a marvelous post from you consisting of three letters and three *Time*s, also a letter from Gladys. The letters were dated February 13, 1943; February 24, 1943; and March 13, 1943.

If I had only written you yesterday, as I planned to, an accident would never have happened. I was just ready to sit down to write when my landlady popped in and asked me to drive out to some Tea gardens for tea. We were just leaving when Robin returned from school, so she came with, as well as Mrs. Grant's little girl. We had tea at a very pleasant place and then drove to Morton's Riding School, where Mrs. Grant keeps her two horses.

As we were ready to leave, one of her horses appeared, all saddled, and another horse she does not know. She put her child up on her horse and made toward the strange horse with Robin. The boy leading her horse called to her not to put the child on the horse, as it was dangerous, but she still went on. I called to her and told her not to put Robin on, but at that minute she threw Robin onto the horse and the horse stood on his hind legs. She held on to Robin and tried to pull her off, and as she pulled her off, the horse kicked them both with his back legs. She was hit in the stomach and winded, and Robin was hit on the shoulder. I am so thankful it was not her face or stomach.

Robin is in the Children's Hospital with a broken collarbone and suffering from shock. They are going to x-ray her shoulder and arm today to see if there is anything else wrong. I left her in a large ward of poor little mites who had all kinds of breaks. She was so good it was frightening. I can see her today at 2:30 and can find out today at 12:00 what the specialist has found out on examination. The specialist is Dr. Greenberg, who is considered good.

Mrs. Grant is such an impulsive person that she is always getting into trouble. She feels terrible about the whole thing and claims she did not hear us call her, but this I do not believe. She will pay the expenses, she says, but, just the same, Robin will have a lot of suffering to endure and will miss her schooling, just as she is getting along so well. We have so much to be thankful for, though, and this I shall keep in mind.

I do not like it that Father is working from six to six, as that is more than I could do when I am well. I think he must have some relief from such hours. I think, since he is working such hours, he is doing as much as the men in the front line trenches, and I am very proud of him. I think we can be very proud of the men in our little family, with Wilfred at the front and Dad working from six to six, and we're bringing up another man for the future generation. John Kevren is such a good baby now and doing so well. He has the most endearing smile you have ever seen. He has a lovely baby carriage now, very modern. The outside is peach and the inside is upholstered in blue leather. It is beautifully sprung and like a bed.

I am pleased about the rental of the Johnson City property and that there have been no losses in rent. How much in the red is the property, and how long do you think it will take to get even now? Have the trees and shrubbery done, and, if any is lost, replace it when you can afford it, as the place may yet be our home one day. It would be paid off about the time Eve and Robin should have a nice home to entertain their friends in. Eve is determined to go back to America. South Africa to her is not home but just a sojourn. Why she takes this attitude, I do not quite understand, as I try to make this home to them.

As you know by now, all of your parcels to me have been received, except the stockings enclosed in a *Time* magazine. I do need a pair of shoes, something with a sensible military heel. Do not send black, as I simply can't bear it anymore. I do not want brown either, but a nice tan or one of the colors you wrote about. I have a nice pair of white sandals, so I do not need that type of shoe. I want a plain winter shoe but not lace up. I would like something with a large tongue and strap perhaps.

I would like them bought with Eve's money, and I can repay her here by buying war stamps for her. I think some of the children's money should be put into War Bonds or stamps for them. Do this with most of their savings. The government should have use of all idle money at this time.

Your new flat sounds too spacious for words. I hope you are settled now. Out here, you can't move a tenant as long as they pay their rent. I couldn't be in a more suitable house. My neighbors are simply wonderful to me, and I know everybody in the block.

I went to see *Desert Victory*, the campaign in Egypt and Tunisia, and, for the most part, the strategy used in the battle of El Alamein. You must see it if it comes to Bristol. It is a wonderful film of the actual fighting. Of course, it is hard to think of Wilfred as well as the others in that desolate expanse of desert.

I am glad to know Aunt Kate is well off, and I hope she will enjoy it now. She has denied herself enough in her lifetime, I think.

May 29, 1943

I have waited to finish this letter until I had a complete report on Robin. It is only a fractured clavicle on the left and a badly swollen and strained right arm. She was in hospital two days, and we have her home now. Last night I had no sleep between Robin and John, but I slept this afternoon as a friend came in and looked after them. I expect to have a good night tonight, as I am alone with the children.

Bert is so highly strung that she upsets the household when she is here. Last night, Robin had a fit of hysteria, and I could not calm her until I got Bert to bed and had her on my own. Today I have had her up and dressed and taking a pride in getting about, but yesterday Bert stayed at home and pampered her, and she cried all day and would not be touched, even.[139] I know you think it queer that I live alone, but it is best, as Bert is so bossy that I feel like a child again. I give her her way for peace, and I did not know until last night how fed up I was with having someone else run my family and me. Before I knew it, I lost my temper so completely, and so terribly, that I am still ashamed of myself. I was wondering today what had happened to me, and why, and two of my neighbours came to me and said, "With all of Bert's marvelous kindness, she is keeping you and the children upset because she is so highly nervous." And that sums it up, but it took a remark from the outside to make me see what was wrong.

Three copies of *Time* came to my new address of No. 8 today, so I am glad to know you know of my move by now.

Wish I had time to write more, but I am so busy.

---

[139] To be fair about Bert's compassion for Robin's hysteria, Helen did not realize at the time that the doctors had put a half-inch thick rubber strap around Robin's clavicle so tightly that it cut through the skin, creating a thick scar, still visible today, some seventy years later.

All my love to you two dear ones,

Helen

June 11, 1943

Dearest Ones,

Father's Air Mail letter of the 22nd March and Mother's Surface Mail letter of the 27th March arrived on the same day; however, Father's letter was marked INSUFFICIENTLY PREPAID AIR MAIL SERVICE. I am afraid the Air Mail service is a washout, though, even when fully paid. When I enquired at the post office here on the first of June, because I wanted to send Father an Air Mail letter for his birthday the 30th of this month, they informed me that there was no difference in the time it took the Air Mail and the Surface Mail from South Africa. I believe the Air Mail service from North Africa is another matter. It would naturally be good to keep the troops satisfied. The service between Wilfred and myself is very good, taking only from seven to ten days. The fee to America is just over $1.00 per half ounce.

I see from your letters that you are both worried about me, but your worries are absolutely groundless, and I wish you would just relax and enjoy yourselves as much as you can. I shall tell you exactly what I have to live on, and you will see that I am not under any financial strain. By Wilfred's being Up North, he has no mess fees and is only allowed $25 while in the field per month; the rest comes to me, which is about $170 to $175 per month. Since I rent my garage for $5.00 per month, my rent comes to $50. My food bills have not gone up very much, since I do not buy any tinned goods but fresh vegetables and fruit, which I get from the gardens only two blocks away. The vegetables are very cheap and the fruit is not bad. Meat is still under American prices, so you can see I am not badly off.

The tinned goods are expensive, but it is foolish to buy them when I can have fresh beans, peas, cabbage, etc., the year around. Just now, I am paying less than five cents for a cauliflower large enough for one meal, and a cabbage is the same price. It would be a poor show if I could not stand on my own feet when I am thirty-seven years old, or nearly that. The children are well fed and look it. Even Eve has a nice colour now and does not have a week or two in bed every now and then, as she used to have. She is really quite strong now and eats as much as I do, or rather a deal more, now that I am on a diet.

Day before yesterday, I bought a lovely coat for myself while I still had a little of the money I had saved. Since my burglary, I had been reduced to wearing an old coat of Bert's, the same as I wore all the time I was pregnant because of its loose fit. I found that people were still giving me seats on the buses, and they actually tried to claim me as a new case at the Maternity Home when I returned for $5.00 they owed me, so I decided I must have a nice coat. It is a wrap around with attractive big pockets and a colour that is good with browns or black. It is just a good weight for this climate. [140]

I paid $40 for it and am terribly pleased. It is a Fairweather, and, if I see my finances will stand it, I am buying a suit a little later. Now are you convinced? You know me. I never spend unless I have it. It may sound strange to you, but Wilfred is as set on this policy as I am, so we never in our married life had any bills to worry us.

My treatment for asthma is proving so very beneficial now. I am just now feeling the full benefit of my diet and Violet-ray and massage. I am so thankful that I went to a masseuse and did not go to a doctor for injections, which only introduce more poison. My skin is lovely; it is so good that I hate to cover it with powder and rouge. Imagine me with natural colour. And do not think that comes from TB; that fear is groundless. My only complaint is asthma, and I can't even complain of that now—so what am I to talk about?

Your flat looks so convenient according to the plan you drew, and I am sure it looks attractive with your furniture. I think you should ask for your dining room suite from Uncle Edwin, as they have certainly had most of the wear out of it, and, if you leave it with them much longer, they will feel it is theirs. It would give such an air to your place, and I want you to have it. It is one thing I should love to have one day, as, to my mind, it is the prettiest suite I have ever seen. So will you hold on to it for me? I am managing with a drop-leaf table now, as my dining room here is very small, and, moving around as I have been doing, I never know whether or not I will have a dining room for a full suite of furniture.

Our very nice parcel arrived with your two letters, and Eve is finding the yellow cardigan beautifully warm. I must say it reminded me of the green one I had a fight with Mary Swan over as far as length goes, but Eve just tucks it under. I am saving the blue one of Robin's until warmer weather, as she has heavier ones for just now. It is so pretty that, of course, she is dying to wear it now, but Bert had just made her one, and I had just bought her one. My belt is ever so attractive and looks so good on one of my woolen dresses. I shall certainly find some use for the pink material you sent.

Robin's arm will be out of the sling on the 16th, so we haven't much longer to wait. She doesn't suffer with it now very much, but she needs a lot of rest, and sleeps the whole of every afternoon as well as the nights. She is playing out in the garden now with a little boy of two-and-a-half who is safe enough, I think. I am afraid the older children will be too rough. The hospital bills came to $40, but that

---

[140] While Helen had initially focused on how the robbery affected Betty, she only now admits to her own substantial loss resulting from the fact that, like Betty, she had stored many of her clothes in the garage. This is one of Helen's many attempts to shield her parents from her difficulties.

is not worrying me, as I am passing them on to Mrs. Grant. They do know how to charge here. This is for two x-rays and two days in hospital.

I hear from Wilfred regularly and had a letter yesterday. He is giving courses in desert navigation, just as he did down here, and it is so much in demand that he has a night class as well as his day classes. He is also Information Officer, lecturing on current events and strategy. I am glad he is busy and has little time to think of his discomforts. I send *Time* on to him now, as he always looked forward to its arrival. He has been congratulated on his work by his Colonel as he has passed out his first class already, and they made a wonderful showing when they marched out into the desert with only compass points to go by.

John weighs twelve and a half pounds in the nude, and is a beautiful baby. He looks such a real boy already. You cannot cuddle him, as he is only interested in sitting on your lap if you hold him up, so he can have a good look around. I have two boxes of Pablum, which will see me through until he can eat oatmeal. The C.C.D. sugar I use is the nearest thing to Mead's Dextri-Maltose that you can get. He gets orange juice and prune juice or carrot juice every day.

I am enjoying my little family so much, and like being at home so much better than the office. With the scarcity of good stenographers, I could probably make $150 per month if I went back to work and could therefore afford a white nurse, but I am going to enjoy John myself and am only interested in having enough to live on, which I have. A friend of mine wants me to hold her part-time job for her during August. It is only two afternoons a week and one morning, and for this she gets $25, so I am doing this for the month of August, as I will not have to neglect my family to do it. The job is keeping open the office of the Camp Fire Girls in America. The friend is the wife of a Lieutenant Colonel in the Indian army. She is an evacuee from India.

Eve had a nice birthday, as she got a watch from her Auntie Bert and Grandfather. Wilfred and I gave her two pairs of flannel pyjamas and two pairs of socks. To find those two articles was a miracle. Then your parcel arrived just a day or two before her birthday, so she really did well. We all love the things you sent us and do appreciate them so much. There was no party, but we are taking the children and two or three friends to see *Pinocchio* when it is on at the end of this month. I have read the book to them and they are crazy to see the picture.

Bert gave Robin the *Water Babies* when she first had her accident, and Robin loves it. It is an old English favourite with the children. I do not remember it from my childhood. Bert is so very good to the children.

John sleeps in his pram at night, too, as it is so comfortable, and more cozy than his big cot. We are already having cold weather. His pram is one of the best ones I have ever seen. It is beautifully sprung and upholstered.

I shall draw you a plan of my little house below.

Affairs are Now Soul-Size (Mar. 1943—Oct. 1943)

We all send bushels of love to our two dear ones,

Helen, Eve, Robin, and John

8 Reform Avenue
Melrose, Johannesburg
July 4, 1943

My own dearest Ones,

Well, I don't notice the English doing any celebrating today; however, I decided to have a few of them in to tea this morning and do a little celebrating on the quiet. I didn't mention that I was celebrating the 4th but I was, and they helped me do it. It is a miserable day, really, rainy and cold. I have a lovely open fire going, and I always find that cheer enough for me. I just hope you all will have coal this coming winter for fires. I think Lewis should be considered a traitor to his country and be put in confinement for the duration. Do the miners have a case? Aren't they as well paid, and better, than workers in other industries?

I simply can't believe that you won't receive the long letter I wrote you from the Nursing Home just before I wrote Uncle Edwin and Aunt Lennie. I also wrote Uncle Earle and Aunt Lula in the Nursing Home but will write again. I shall be furious if you never receive that letter, as it will be hard to rewrite it. Also, Bert wrote you eight letters in all at that time, with three days between each. You simply must receive some of those. They concern John and me, of course. I have had letters from Aunt Kate and Gladys, which I appreciated so much and shall answer when I can, but my days are so very full. Too, my neighbours drop in often, as they are afraid I will be lonely, and much of my time is taken up that way. They are the nicest neighbours I have had since coming to South Africa.

John was born about two weeks early on Sunday morning, February 28, at 10:30 o'clock. Naturally, I was thrilled that he was born in February, since it is the birth month of Lincoln and Washington, and I was also thrilled that he was born on Sunday. Wilfred and Bert were both at home with me, and it took them both working at top speed to get me packed and off to the Nursing Home in time. We had a taxi take us the five miles to the Nursing Home, and they took me straight to the theatre and onto the operating table in my clothes. The doctor, a lady doctor, did arrive in time, but since she is short and dumpy and had done a lot of running to make it, she was slightly winded upon arrival. John was born with the cord tied tightly around his neck, and it was only because he was born with such ease that we have him today. He only weighed 6 lbs. 14 ozs., but all the babies there were on the small side. I think the war can be blamed.

Wilfred saw John last when John was four weeks old, though John was eight weeks when Wilfred actually left for the North. We had always planned to have another baby, but, of course, I had thought we would have him after the war.

Anyway, it is just as well that he is here and gets over his first months while father is away, as father is very jealous of my time, and of course babies must come first. I am being very possessive now, as I am sure father is going to be very possessive of this son when he gets home.

John is a beautiful big baby now. He is fed on D.C.D. Sugar in his milk. It is the nearest thing to Mead's Dextri-Maltose that we can get now. He has orange juice, carrot juice, and prune juice as well as Pablum. You can't buy Pablum any longer, but I secured two packages from a friend of mine in Durban who bought a case when her baby was born and had two left over. These will see him through the early months, and then he can eat oatmeal. Edith Broadbent loaned me a splendid book on baby care and diet, and I go by it. I also have the privilege of taking the baby to my doctor every Wednesday afternoon for advice, weighing, etc. We have only been twice, though, as it is difficult since I do not have a car. A friend who had the same doctor for her baby took me in once in her car.

John gave me a time for a while, as he would wake four and five times every night, but now he sleeps from six to six, and life is worth living again. I can't wait for the films to arrive, so we can take some pictures to send to you and Wilfred.

Wilfred is in a camp just out of Cairo. He went up in April. He has been instructing in desert navigation ever since he has been there. He has so many [students] that he must have evening classes. I have a feeling that he is doing very good work and must be rewarded sooner or later by another pip, which will make him a Captain. He should have had it long ago, but the army is unpredictable. I enclose a clipping from our newspaper, which will give you an idea of how Wilfred and the rest live when they are in the desert. He has written me when visibility was about one foot. I hope he can come out of it with his health, but one wonders how any of them do. I think he will write to you all soon, as he has mentioned to me in a recent letter that he wanted to. He is very pleased with John, and he will be happy when he gets your letters about John, which I have forwarded to him. He wants the whole family to be as happy as we are.

In Aunt Kate's letter she mentioned that she felt disappointed that I had not named my son Robert, but thought it was because I had a Robin. Wilfred suggested the name of Robert, and I thought Robert Kevren would be a pretty name, but I felt that it would hurt me too much to say Robert every day, as it would be a constant reminder of the greatest tragedy of our lives. As it is, I find myself often calling Robin "Robert." I selected the name John Kevren merely because I thought it nice and manly, and it just happens that I hit upon an uncle's name. This man was a very good and righteous man and loved by all the family.

I am looking forward to the arrival of the last parcel you sent off with films, chewing gum, and two dresses for John, also the nylon stockings. I simply can't feature myself the proud possessor of a pair of nylons at this time. I shall certainly look after them and know they will be an agony to me, really, just as my tea set is.

I paid about $20 for my tea set a year ago, and now it is worth $60, so you can imagine my torture when I use it. I must use it every time I have anyone in, too, as I broke the handles off of every other cup I have the morning after I got home from the Nursing Home. We cannot get cups and saucers at all, nor pots and pans, and I only have the minimum. This past week I broke my one and only Pyrex baking dish and glass salad bowl.

Thank goodness for the flannel petticoats you made for Robin, as they are coming in handy for John. You can't buy a vest in town, and his were ruined in the Nursing Home by improper washing and have drawn up terribly; however, he is warm now in the flannel petticoats. Diapers are now $10 a dozen when you can find them, but I bought enough to do John, long ago, thank goodness. It is much better not to send money to me until you have written and asked if I want the money or some article. Since this has always been an import country, except for the export of gold, you can imagine that we are without quite a few articles.

Grandpa Evans with Eve, John, and Robin

You should see the empty shelves in some of our biggest shops. There is still a lot in the stores, but when you look for essentials, you find they haven't them so often. Wilfred is sending me twelve tubes of toothpaste from Cairo, as we haven't had any for six months now. We can now get toilet paper occasionally, but, for a long while, there was none and no substitute but newspaper. I hope you will manage to have enough with your food ration cards. Please study your diet and see that you have the essentials. For instance, canned baked beans have no value, and you should not bother to buy them and waste your coupons. We have a raw lunch every day—lettuce, slaw, tomatoes, watercress, radishes, carrots, etc. Eat plenty of fruit fresh or stewed, and you will see the difference in the way you feel, I am sure.

Robin does not have to report to the Children's Hospital any more from last Wednesday. This has taken so much of my time, as, for about two weeks, we went every day for dressings after they discovered the terrible cuts and bruises she had from her appliances, or rather after I discovered them. Mrs. Grant is paying the bill, which I have had greatly reduced. I did not feel like helping her out by asking for a reduction, but I did not want any more unpleasantness with her, since she owns the house, and it is always possible for the landlord to make it uncomfortable for the tenant. Robin is just now turning somersaults, so you can see she is perfectly all right now. She is always playing hospital and casualty with her dolls now.

Bert knit the most beautiful sweaters and full suits for John as a present—about three carriage suits, and four other sweaters and caps and booties. She has also given him a pair of rompers, Madeira ones. She is always doing something for him. In fact, to her, he is just like her baby. I try to share him with her and let her feel he is hers too. Mr. Evans gave John Five Pounds for a perambulator, but, of course, I am managing to get more out of it. I bought a pram from a friend and fixed it up myself, and it is lovely. I shall buy a high chair with the rest of the money.

I do appreciate the money you are sending Eve and Robin and shall let you know what I do with it. I also think it awfully kind of Aunt Lennie and Uncle Edwin to send John and me $5.00 and, when it comes, I shall let you know how I spend it.

I have had the *Ladies' Home Journal* but not *Better Homes and Gardens*. I hope it comes soon. I have never received the third pair of rayon stockings either. I really wish you had kept the nylon stockings for yourself, as I know you have many more occasions that justify such stockings being worn than I have. It is the most unselfish thing I can imagine anyone doing.

I have just this week made myself a blue skirt to wear with one of the jackets dropped by the burglars who stole my clothes. It was one of the suits I bought last year and wore at the children's birthday party. I believe you have a picture of me in it minus head. I am not too badly off as I now have the two suits I bought last year, and the grey woolen dress I bought in Durban, and a new coat. My new perm is very flattering and has made me feel like a new person. It was worth all I paid for it.

Yesterday, I took Robin and Eve to see *Pinocchio*, and they were thrilled to death. I enjoyed it too. Eve wants to see it again, so I shall let her when it comes to the local cinema out our way.

I do have a *big* family now. They take all of my time, and, with three, you simply concentrate for the moment on the one who needs you most just then. This week Eve was in bed two days with a cold, then Robin got it, and so it was Eve with me the first of week, and then it was Robin and so on.

Wilfred has done some sightseeing in Cairo and climbed Cheops, the highest pyramid, I believe. I am glad he is getting something out of it all. He has been in the army three years today. We have hardly ever had a normal life, as we started with the Depression and now we have had this interruption of three years already of his business life as well as our family life. I do think it is remarkable that we have managed to bring up three children this far; it somehow gives me faith in the future. If we have managed through these ten years, we will surely be able to manage with our family from here on.

This has been written through a Sunday afternoon of interruptions from all three. The girl is off, and I have been on my own with the three of them. I now have my third girl since Betty left. It looks bad for me. The first one was good riddance, the second one I was sorry to lose, and now this third one hits somewhere in between the other two.

According to the newspaper I got yesterday, the war has ceased—and the only noteworthy news is the election in South Africa. I think it is quite certain that Smuts will win without any difficulty. I have the paper delivered every day except Sunday. I am also getting a telephone, which will help to keep me in touch with the world. I am very fortunate that I am getting it.

Love and kisses from us all to both of you. I am sorry you heard about John from others and did not get your letter, or rather letters, first, so you could tell the news. I feel that Father is especially pleased by his letter. Anyway, you both made me happy with your letters, and they have gone on to Wilfred.

Helen

> 8 Reform Avenue
> Melrose, Johannesburg
> July 18, 1943

My dearest Mother and Dad,

I have an idea that you are not getting all of my letters, so I am keeping the dates that I write, and I shall give the date of my last letter each time. This time my previous letter is dated the 4th of July. I seem to get all of your letters, though they come in a mixed order.

I haven't heard from Wilfred now in three weeks, and I was hearing regularly every week, and I often don't hear from you all for three weeks, so I have my waiting to do too. I know you write, but there are so many ways for delays to occur these days.

The news is good, isn't it? I feel that our first landing party in Sicily was one of the hardest moves we had to make, as it was the initial step for invasion. Let us pray that all continues as well as it has started.

The children had a lovely joint birthday party given them on Saturday, the 10th of July, at Bert's flat in town. Mr. Bunny Brown a bachelor friend of Bert's, gave it to them. Rather, he has been married twice but is divorced, and his two children died. He is the most generous soul you could meet, and he gave them a wonderful party.[141]

There were ten children in all at the table, plus John in somebody's arms throughout the party. There was a large birthday cake for Eve, and a little smaller one for Robin, with nine and five candles respectively. There were professional cakes and, besides being beautiful, they were good. They also had pink ice-cream, lemonades with colored straws, and each child got a chocolate bunny with marzipan carrots in its lap, and each got a darling pink marzipan pig. There were scones and tarts and other sweets, and every child reported a marvelous time. One little boy said it was the best time he had ever had in his life.

They played spin the plate and hide the thimble, so times haven't changed much since we were children. Mr. Brown's pleasure was in looking on and seeing so many children happy. He is not a flame of Bert's, but he does these things for everybody he meets and likes. He is fifty-six years old but looks much older. He gives me different little gifts, always in the food line, and usually things I can't get, so I won't enumerate. The children have always had a party, and I am so glad the routine was not broken into this year, as I didn't feel that I could do it except in the most simple way and with about half the number they had. The party cost him at least $15.

I am enclosing a clipping of interest, as I did not get my Army pay for two months after Bill left. Of course, we are never stranded, as Mr. Evans can always come to the rescue and did. It was annoying, though, and had the effect of making wives think their husbands had left without providing for them, which was the intention of course.

Your money for the children's birthday has not arrived, but I bought Robin a beautiful dress from you and will pay myself back when it arrives. It is of Madeira embroidery; the material is light blue, and it has white collar and cuffs and the embroidery is in white. It is simply lovely and was not more than what you have sent her. Unfortunately, they do not make these dresses in larger sizes, and this is the last I shall be able to buy for her. They are more or less inexpensive, and the other ready-mades from America and England had terrible prices on them.

I am starting right away to make some dresses for both Robin and Eve, but more especially Robin, as so much of what she has was handed down from Eve, and they are all wearing out at once, it seems. I gave Robin a bracelet, as that is what she wanted. It was inexpensive but rather attractive, and she is crazy about it. She simply adores her dress, and it looks so attractive with the coat you made her with the blue collar, being just the same shade of blue as that collar.

---

[141] Bunny Bown's kindness and generosity continued for some years, particularly at Easter, when he would remember to bring chocolate Easter bunnies for us and take us for rides in the countryside around Johannesburg in the dickey seat (rumble seat) of his car.

John, I think, must now be the best baby in Johannesburg. He sleeps every night from six o'clock to seven the next morning. In that way I get a good night's sleep. I am sure he would never have settled down if Bert had stayed here. She is so full of nerves that they vibrate through the house when she is in it. If she sleeps here a night, he will wake during that night, so this is not my imagination. I knew he would settle down and be as good as Robin was if I could only be on my own, so I had to insist on Bert's going back to her flat. John is getting more blonde all of the time and shall have Robin's colouring, I think. He is really lovely and is now the prettiest of my three babies. When he was born he was certainly the ugliest of the three, but not now.

You all would love all of the children, and I do wish we could be with you. They are good children and lovable. South Africa, to Eve, is just a sojourn. America is really her home. This feeling is so strong in her that I am sure she will make America her home one day. I have promised her the house in Johnson City for her own, so we can't sell it. The price of property here today is simply ridiculous. It is better to rent.

I am still in love with my little house and garden. I must find time to do some gardening just now. I must take my bulbs out, and plant them in boxes, and get them ready for transplanting. I am learning a little about gardening all the time now. Of course, it is a disgrace out here not to know a lot about gardening. I have just had a garden boy for two days cutting down a very high hedge in the back, which kept the sun from my clothes' lines. It had been allowed to grow into trees, actually, and now I have enough wood to do me a year. He told me quite a lot of useful things about my garden.

I had a very interesting letter from Bill [Wilfred] some time ago and shall quote part of it that may interest you:

"I have been in Cairo and down the Nile to Hel Wan. The trip was intensely interesting, as I came in from the desert north of Cairo and went down to Cairo along the Rosetta branch of the Nile. The canal system is amazing, so are the variegated smells. All down the Nile, one crawls through throngs of Gyppos on diminutive donkeys or men driving towering piles of alfalfa from beneath which twinkle four little donkey hoofs. The scenes are literally biblical. When a hut falls down, they merely build one with Nile mud. The result is the impression that all of Egypt is falling down, which would worry me not at all.

The centre of Cairo is, of course, a modern town, and is, I suppose, the most cosmopolitan city in the world today. I visited three of the most famous of their mosques, and the inlaid and glasswork is indescribably lovely. They are many-domed, and under each dome is a tomb. The altars are done in ivory and gold. One-piece carpets of about 200 x 200 ft. are of russet. I'm all for livening up churches, but the Egyptians have ideas far in advance of mine.

Also went down into the Muski Bazaar, which is not a building but a street, such as one sees as being typical of old Cairo or places in Palestine. I called in at an old perfume shop, which Smuts has twice visited. It was doubly interesting as, coming down the Nile, I had passed through the gardens where the flowers for this particular firm are grown. There were a thousand perfumes there, and I was in a whirl after smelling a few dozen of them. I bought a small bottle of concentrated Jasmine, which I am sending off in a day or so. The bottle looks frightfully cheap, but I can assure you what I paid for the contents would shake you.

From Cairo I went south to Hel Wan, the South African base camp, which was merely a repetition of the upper Nile, yet fascinatingly interesting. Coming back, I came through Mena and visited the pyramids of Ghiza. I hired a camel and went out to the Sphinx and climbed all over the great Pyramid of Cheops. Cheops is about 420 feet high. I climbed 200 feet inside to the highest tomb. There we struck out over the desert and so home."

I shall also quote something rather amusing because of the way Bill has written it: "I'm so sleepy I can hardly keep my eyes open, and I'm as sore as a boil. Played polo on Egyptian donkeys this afternoon, using pick handles for mallets. You would have rolled with laughter at the incidents. The donkey I was riding went suddenly mad with the urge to procreate. He kicked and hee-hawed until I went over his head, then he made for the lady of his choice who was sedately supporting a major. She woke up to the situation as he bore down on her, disposed of the major, and went hell bent for leather for the tents. Don Juan thundered screaming after her (Curtain.)"

I am taking a job, but it is such a little one that it is really a scream. Anyway, I get £2.00 twice a month for it, or $8.00. I work from 2 – 5 p.m. one day a week in an ophthalmic surgeon's office. His regular nurse must be relieved one afternoon a week, and he loves work so much he is there every day, so that is where I fit in. He is very well known in the city, and I shall find the work interesting.

I do not start until the middle of August, but I went the other afternoon to find out something about it and learned, for one thing, that children are sometimes born with cataracts, or they can develop by the age of two. The surgeon is a man of sixty, and his nurse has been with him for twenty-two years, so he must be rather nice to work for. I shall work one week on Wednesday afternoon and the next week on Saturday afternoon. Don't you think it an ideal job for me? I am still going to do the Girl Guide job in August, and that pays me £5.00 for three afternoons per week.

I have had a letter from Uncle Edwin, written, however, before you got the news about John. I hope to get some letters off this week to the family.

I have just had a terrible time with help. Week before this last I had no girl turn up on Monday or Tuesday, then an agency sent me one on Wednesday, and she didn't come back on Thursday. I suppose because I had her do the washing. Then

Friday, I took one on who presented herself at the door, and she has been with me since. You can imagine the work I had to do with the three children, cooking, doing everything for John, building fires, etc. I nearly finished myself and have felt tired all the week, so, this afternoon, I sent the girl to the park with the three and slept all afternoon and feel much better for it.

We have a lovely new park out our way, and the children love to go there because there are swings and slides, etc., and a wading pool for summer, also sand piles. They have a huge sand pile here at home, but, of course, the one at the park is more fun. One always has trouble with help here when one has a young baby. I think it must be the baby's wash, as that is the only extra John means to them, as I look after him myself.

This girl is spotlessly clean about herself and the house, so I hope she is with me for some time. She always dresses in a white coverall and white cape, and they are *white*. Some of my girls have not been tidy even though they were good. Betty, for instance, became very slovenly before she left, and she had been such a clean girl. It sounds like I was a bad influence, but I wasn't, as I was always after her, but nothing helped at the end. I had finally reached the point that I hoped she would leave because she was too dirty.

Sister Murdock is giving me five more treatments for the price of the course of ten that I paid her for; that is, I am getting fifteen treatments instead of ten. I think it very nice of her. I have never had an attack of asthma since going to her; however, she wants to see my head and chest completely clear before I leave her. If we had only known about diet when I was a child, what suffering I would have been saved. It is actually merely a matter of two *green* vegetables a day, and plenty of fruit, and no condiment or sugar. I think I always over-ate, and that started my trouble.

I am worried about your ever being able to send me shoes now that you are rationed to three pairs a year. Can you get them to make an allowance for me—or what? I desperately need a pair of walking shoes, just the most comfortable thing you can find, if you can get them for me. I tried to have a pair half-soled and they said the tops wouldn't take the sole, so you can imagine my predicament. I have been to every shoe shop for a pair, but there isn't a thing in town that I can wear. All I care about is comfort now. Of course, I don't want a shoe that looks like it was for someone of seventy-five, but there are youngish styles in comfortable shoes now. As I have said, I would like a light tan, or, if you can't get that, blue or black. However, I am trying to get away from black, as it no longer looks good on me. I do not like black during wars either. We *need* bright colours.

I took Eve and Robin to see *Pinocchio*, and they loved it. I enjoyed it too and am going to let Eve go again when it is on at our local cinema, the Odeon. What a name for a picture show! By the way, I have just been informed by the management of the Odeon that I will be issued with a pass for myself and any friends any time I want to go to that particular cinema. Isn't this a bit of luck? We know these people, but I never thought they would do this for me.

I had Edith and Charles Broadbent for dinner this past Wednesday night. He is back from up North. He was up for a year. I also had Joan Hale, so we had bridge after dinner, and I did enjoy it, though I know very little about it any more, and they are all good players. It is Joan Hale's mother that I am doing the one afternoon a week for. Her mother is a perfect dear, and, imagine, she has been working in one place for twenty-two years, and her father and grandfather were rolling stones, so she must have some of that in her, and yet she has stayed put all these years. Her husband died many years ago when Joan was a child, so Mrs. Hale has had to bring her up by herself. Joan, I suppose, is nearly my age now. They have a flat together.

I must stop and get to bed, or I shall undo all the good I gained from my afternoon's sleep.

Our thoughts and love and kisses are yours,

Helen

8 Reform Avenue
Johannesburg, South Africa
July 20, 1943

My dearest Gladys,[142]

Your letter and one from Aunt Kate came in with Mother's and Father's letters congratulating me on the arrival of John Kevren. Thank you so much. It is good to know you are interested and even a little envious. Why don't you go ahead and have another? I am having a grand time with my lovely baby. Of course, it took a while for him to settle down, and I must admit I had plenty of disturbed nights, but now, at four and a half months, he sleeps from six at night to seven in the morning without a sound from him. That gives me plenty of rest, and caring for him during the day is just a pleasure. I thought the other morning that I wished I knew I would have a baby to bathe every day for the rest of my life, as to me it is great fun. I may well be occupied along that line as, the other day, Robin asked me if I would work for her when she was grown and had her babies, as she wouldn't know how to look after them. The nerve of this coming generation!

I think Pat's calling you "an old timer" is a scream. As good-looking as he is, and with such an early interest in the ladies, I think you will have your hands full. I remember I was interested in little boys at Pat's age too, but, for some reason, Eve doesn't seem to notice them. It is perhaps because she goes to school at the

---

[142] Gladys was one of Helen's cousins, daughter of her Aunt Lula and Uncle Earle.

Convent and does not see any boys, and the only one she plays with is only five. Robin says she is going to marry John, so you see how serious the whole matter is in our family.

I simply can't believe that Barbara is getting married—or rather, is married by now. I can still remember your mother feeding her a hard-boiled egg as a baby on the side porch, which was always so cozy and comfortable.

I have moved from No. 4 to No. 8 Reform Avenue and like it much better. This is, in fact, the coziest and most comfortable house I have had in South Africa. I have a living room, dining room, kitchen, two bedrooms and bath, and a very large screened porch. None of the houses have steam heating, but my open fireplace in the living room keeps it warm, and I have electric heaters for the two bedrooms. I can really be warm here in the winter, but in most houses over here, you just take the winter as the good Lord sends it.

You sound like you can really work, talking about moving a cord of wood, and ironing. I had my hands full last week, as my native girl did not turn up on Monday or Tuesday. Wednesday, I had a girl from the employment agency, but she didn't come back on Thursday because I gave her a big washing to do. Friday, I employed a girl at the door and put her to ironing and she is still with me. However, I had the housework and children for the whole week, and, I can tell you, it is too much when there are three and one is a baby. I made fires, washed nappies (diapers), cooked, cleaned what I could get to, and, in the main, survived together with my children.

What these girls want is the housework without the washing and ironing. They have been very spoiled, as some people employ them just as nurse girls, and perhaps they have only one child to look after, at that. Housekeeping is harder over here. For instance, I have an electric stove and electric refrigerator, but I don't have a vacuum cleaner, and floors are not so nice as at home and must be polished on hands and knees once a week to make them look like anything.

I had a parcel from Wilfred today containing Jasmine perfume from Cairo and twelve tubes of toothpaste. Both articles are unprocurable here, so you can imagine how welcome it all was. He is also going to send me six rolls of toilet paper, which is just the last word in a thoughtful present, as that too is not to be had.

Two weeks ago I took the children to see *Pinocchio* and they loved it, as I had read the book to them about a year ago. Last Saturday they jointly celebrated their birthdays with eight little friends. The party was given for them by a friend of ours with plenty of money but no children. He lost his two, and loves all children. It was a lovely affair. I introduced our old favourites of "Spin the Plate" and "Hide the Thimble," and the children thought them great fun. One little boy said it was the best time he had ever had in his life (five years of age).

I was quite ill before and after John's birth, but had no trouble at the actual birth or while I was in the nursing home for ten days. He was born during a great upheaval with us, as we were notified that Wilfred was going North just before he was born, and about six weeks after he was born Wilfred left, so I had just too much worry at the wrong time. Now I am feeling quite well again, and everybody says I am looking fine.

The news is good, and I just live for the end of this long struggle we are engaged in. Wilfred has been in the army three years this month, which is a lot of time out of one's life. I am glad Wayne has not been called.

My kindest regards to Wayne.

Lots of love to you, dear,

Helen

8 Reform Avenue
Melrose, Johannesburg
August 11, 1943

Dearest Ones,

I see that I have been very dilatory about writing, as the last date I have set down is the 18th of July. Anyway, I am honest, and I hope this will let you know when letters are missing, or when it is just that I have not written. Why you have only had one letter from me and one from Bert since John's birth, I do not know. When I think of my very long letter from the nursing home not arriving, I feel that I shall never write a very long letter again but more short ones. I am sure if the one letter you received from me had been the long one, you would have said you had a nice long letter from me. Bert wrote you eight letters at that time with three days between each. Bert has never received the letter from you about your dream, nor the Christmas card you mentioned.

I am sure Father is looking forward to a stay in Louisville, and I wish you had decided to go with him. I would love such an opportunity myself, as it is beautiful country. I don't know how things are in Bristol, but here you could rent your apartment for four months and be free to do what you liked with that burden off the budget.

I am sorry to hear about Kathryn's fall in the swimming bath [South African term for a swimming pool] and hope she is quite all right by now.

Hope Helen Hunter takes her engagement more seriously than I ever took one. Wilfred and I never became engaged for that reason. I told him that if I liked him well enough at the last minute, I would marry him, and that is how I settled down to bringing up a family of three. I hope they don't have to let the affair drag along too long, as I have always been sorry that I did not marry Wilfred when I first met him, and he feels the same way about it.

Have I told you that I have this little house for two more years, if I want it that long? It is all signed up, and I feel very settled, except for the idea of coming home, which is always present.

I have heard from Uncle Edwin and Aunt Nellie about John, and Aunt Nellie says I will see changes in everyone, but you say you have not changed much. I do want to come home before the changes in all of us are a shock. My hair has reached that stage that I wish it would go white completely, as it is most uninteresting as it is. I am a perfect size 16, and weigh 123 lbs.[143] I am not wrinkled, as I seem to have your type of skin; however, this dry climate is very trying on the skin. The children just about drain my strength, so I don't look fresh as I might if I didn't have them. I wouldn't want to live without them, though, and John is just the most marvelous thing that has ever happened to us.

We do not have ration books, as you have, and I think this is because this is the rich man's country, and the stores must depend on the few for most of their trade. The stores ration one, though; for instance, one small box of matches at a time, one lb. of white flour per month, two candles at a time (these are used in the natives' rooms), one pair of pyjamas, or one of any piece of underwear. Of course, if you have the time and can find another store with pyjamas, you can buy as many pairs as you like. The price of underwear has doubled, and materials also.

Bert has given me a piece of cyclamen material, which will make a lovely dress. I have a large straw hat to wear with it. The dress I had for the hat was stolen. I saw a movie of myself in my cyclamen outfit at a wedding (in colour), and I must say it looked good.[144] I am thrilled over having it replaced. Bert has also given me a black suit of hers. The coat is nice and fits me perfectly, but the skirt is not so good, so I had thought of a plaid or checked skirt to wear with the coat. She has two new tailored suits that are very smart. She needs clothes more than I do, as I am very much at home just now.

My servant question does not improve. The last one gave me such cheek that I was dying to slap her face. She took an hour to get Robin from school, and that should take half an hour, so I told her I would not have her loafing on the way while I was at home doing her work, and she said, "What have you been doing?" I told her not to dare ask me that and she repeated it twice. I telephoned the police, and they came and gave her a straight talk, and she had the impudence to cheek them. He told me I could not get rid of her without paying her a month's wage in

---

[143] This is a 17 lb. weight loss since Helen last mentioned her weight in September of 1938.

[144] Elsa Swan, wife of Joe Marshall, was a keen photographer who made many home movies. I remember seeing the movie a friend, using Elsa's ciné camera, had made of Elsa and Joe's wedding. Sadly, all of these were lost many years ago when the Marshall's lovely thatched home, "Blackwood," in Tweedie, Natal, burned to the ground.

lieu of notice, which I could not afford to do. I told him to ask her where she worked before, and she refused to tell and simply shook like a leaf when this was asked.

You can imagine how I felt about having her in the house. I thought, if I had to sit with her a month, I would get plenty of work out of her, so I started, and by the next morning she had decided she wanted to leave with only pay for the days she had worked. She was also unkind to the children, and I was glad to see the back of her. They think I am so dependent on them that they believe they will get by with everything, but, if it breaks me, they won't run away with me. I had to do my work two days this time before I got another one. I'd had to go to the expense of a wash girl to try to keep the peace, but I don't know that that makes much difference. The big trouble is our men being away, and I am only one of many having the same difficulties with them. They have made so many laws to protect the native, that we now need some laws to protect ourselves from them.

I am sorry you are having all the trouble over John's parcel, and I can tell you the things had better be big if he is going to get in them. He is all of 17 lbs. now. He is five months and has eight ounces of milk per four feeds, and three ounces of orange juice, two tablespoons of Pablum, vegetables, and apple sauce every day with four drops of Halibut Oil. He is better than the breast-fed babies I have seen on the baby afternoon at the doctor's rooms. He learned to growl a few days ago, and we had this for two days running.

Wilfred has been on a course and made the highest marks ever attained, with 100% on one paper and 98% on another. He has a good brain, and he is ambitious, and will drive himself to the limit to come out well. He said he was the only one to work through the heat period in the afternoons.

If you can enclose snaps in an envelope, they would be appreciated, as we can't buy them, and must take them from one garment to another that needs them more. Also more elastic if you can get it. Children's socks, when you can get them, are $1.00 a pair and the worst-looking things you have ever seen.

We enjoyed the clipping about Aunt Hattie. After I had read it to the children, Eve wanted to know if they had advertised Aunt Hattie in the paper. I said yes, it was something like that.

I got Eve to talking about America the other day and was amazed at the things she remembers. She asked me if I remembered those long stairs in Mama Sophia's house, and I said yes. She said, "I used to go halfway up those stairs and lie down on a step and that was my bed and the steps below were my house and the steps above me were my house." She said, "One day I lay down on that step halfway up, and I pretended to read a book, and I fell down those steps." Did she? She also sat down and made out a list of her toys for me to ask about, and, on it, were the pink wicker carriage, the rocking horse, the big house, the ironing board and iron, and other things I can't remember just now. She talked about you all in a way that made me know she really remembers you. She remembers her trip to Nashville too. Robin is extremely jealous that she has never seen America and known you all, as Eve has.

I must stop now and go to bed, as it is quite late. As you see, I simply can't write a short letter.

My love and kisses to my two dearest ones,

Helen

8 Reform Avenue
Melrose, Johannesburg
South Africa
August 20, 1943

Dearest Aunt Lula and Uncle Earle,

I wrote quite a few letters from the Nursing Home in April, and one was to you, but from all reports from home, you have not heard from me, and neither did Mother and Father get the long letter I wrote them about John. John is beside me in the garden, lying in his perambulator, playing with a brightly-coloured hanky of mine. He is a lovely big chap, weighing 17 lbs. or more by now. He is a marvelously good baby and nothing but a pleasure in the home. Of course, it took him a while to settle down after we got home from the Maternity Home; in fact, it took him about two or three months, and during that time I had to pile of out bed at two o'clock, four and six, and, for your amusement, I must tell you how I managed it. I would hear this young cry of my wee one and think I simply could not get up again, especially at four o'clock, and then I would think: "Aunt Lula could do it. She always got up early. Nothing was ever too much trouble for her." And out I would get. It must make you feel rather good to know you have been a help and inspiration to me over all these years, and right over on the other side of the world. Now John sleeps from six o'clock at night until seven the next morning, so I don't have to call on your energy to see me through.

I want to thank you again for the $5.00 you gave the children for Christmas. Mother has banked it for them at home where they each have a little bank account. They are both very keen on their bank accounts in America, as they are very afraid of going to America and not having any money since we have told them the money is different. You have been most generous in remembering the children every Christmas. I really feel that it is too much with all the grandchildren you have of your own to give to, and I think you should not do it. Anyway, it is appreciated by us all.

I have had a very nice letter from Gladys about John, and have answered it. I hope she received it. She told me about Barbara's approaching wedding. She has married very young, but a young marriage can be the most successful one, I think.

The older people get, the harder it is for them to adjust themselves to each other. I hope she will be very happy indeed.

Wilfred is experiencing the most dreadful heat where he is in North Africa—128°F in the shade. He has just been on a military course where he made the highest marks ever attained. He said he did it by being the only man to study during the hot period of each day. Speaking of Wilfred reminds me of something he said to me several times: "I am sorry I never knew your Aunt Lula better, as I am sure she is a person I could like very much."

Robin and Eve are both out this afternoon, visiting different friends. This is unusual, as they nearly always play together or with the same friends. They are in different schools, however: Eve going to Parktown Convent and Robin to a nearby kindergarten. Robin's kindergarten takes them through the first three grades of school, as well as being a kindergarten, and Robin [age 5] is now in the First Grade.

I have been having no end of trouble with help, having had seven girls since John was born. Now the gossip of the neighborhood among the natives is that it is too much work here for one girl since I have three children. You can imagine how this infuriates a good old American. The trouble is, I think, that I live in a neighbourhood where my neighbours keep from two to six servants. I thought I was fortunate in getting a small house I could afford in such a good locality, but I don't know whether I was or not. I have done it all alone for a week at a stretch to show them, but I am afraid they are not impressed. Anyway, a new one started yesterday, and she is good, so I hope all is well.

Much love from us all to all of you,

Helen

8 Reform Avenue
Melrose, Johannesburg
August 20, 1943

Dearest Aunt Nellie,

Thank you so much for your letter about John Kevren, my latest love. It seems from your letter that you, too, did not receive the letter I wrote you from the Nursing Home in March. I wrote you then announcing John's arrival and to thank you for the hankies, which arrived for Christmas, and were so much appreciated by all. Robin's hankies came in such a sweet folder, and she was very thrilled with the folder as well as her three handkerchiefs. It simply makes me sick that Mother and Father did not receive their letter from the Nursing Home announcing John, as it was a very long one in which I tried to answer every question that I thought might come to their minds. Aunt Lennie's and Uncle Edwin's letter seems to be the only one of the lot that arrived.

Affairs are Now Soul-Size (Mar. 1943—Oct. 1943)

What a lovely child Kay is. I am so glad you enclosed the newspaper clipping of her. She and my Robin are something alike except that Robin is not so feminine-looking as Kay and has lost her sweet baby look just now. John is going to be like Robin, very blonde. It is surprising how much blondness is coming out in our family now.

I was sorry to learn of the death of Judge Maxey, and Aunt Margaret's feeble state of health. Judge Maxey, however, has had a very long and, I should think, rather full life. The grandchildren of his adopted daughter must have afforded him a great deal of pleasure, as they seem to be doing well.

It is nice that you have had the Clems and Ronnie with you. I am not surprised to hear of Munna's delicate health. It just surprises me that she is still with us, as she seemed so frail when I knew her fifteen years ago. Have you been to Texas since I came out here? I really can't remember. I hope Mother does have a visit with you while the family is away in Texas, as it will no doubt do you both a lot of good. I wish I were close by, so I could do the same.

We also have Nurses' Aides here, but, of course, I have never had the time to take the course and do that work. The office kept me fully occupied, and now home and the children demand all of my time. I have had seven girls since John Kevren was born, and, part of the time, no girl at all. The latest arrival started yesterday, and she is good, so I hope all goes well. Here, at home, you always find out after they have left what they have been up to. I discovered that one had been chopping up my chopping block for kindling. A friend asked me what I did about it. I said, "Well, since I must chop the kindling wood now, I continued on the chopping block, as I found it the easiest way."

The last girl to leave left at twelve o'clock Sunday morning because, she said, the work was too hard. I told her I wouldn't pay her unless she stayed a day or two, until I could get another girl, but nothing would stop her. She just went out and packed up her clothes and marched off. I looked at Bert and Bert looked at me and I laughed and said, "Bert, no lover has ever taken my breath way as little Edith has just now."

To have three children and a small income in any country is a crime. My swanky neighbours have from two to six servants, so I may be driven to live in another suburb where the other people manage with one. I do like our street, though, as it is friendly and they are people like myself. We visit together and go to cinemas together, etc., and in these days of little petrol one must have congenial neighbours.

I am glad Lora Nellie has done so well in her nurses' training and that you can be so proud of her. Which is the prettier of the two girls now, Lora Nellie or Josephine? What is Josephine doing? I believe Edward is married. Of course, I still think of him as a child. It is wonderful how Annie ever managed to bring up her three children, but I was always sure you helped her a lot. Anyway, she deserves great credit.

I am sorry to hear that Eugene is getting grey, as well as Elizabeth, but none of them, I am sure, have changed as much in that respect as I have. I have a very fashionable white streak that didn't have to be bleached for me by the beauty parlour. However, I have a young figure, like a girl of sixteen. I suppose my figure is better than it has ever been. I weigh 123 lbs. I don't know whether it is the climate or the difference in food, but I have never been inclined to put on fat since I have been out here. Of course, lately, I have been on a fruit and vegetable diet for my asthma and that has taken the pounds off of me, and it also cured my asthma.

All being well with my domestic, I am starting in a physical culture class in the city next week with a friend of mine nearby. They go at it for an hour, but I shall perhaps last fifteen minutes, for a start. Anyway, I think it will be good for me, and she simply loves it, and says she feels on top of the world afterwards.

I hear regularly from Wilfred, and that keeps me contented. His letters take about ten days. He only complains of the heat—128°F. in the shade—and the dust. I can tell that home and family have never seemed so marvelous to him as just now.

My very fondest love to one I have always loved, and every good wish for Eugene and his family.

Helen

8 Reform Avenue
Melrose, Johannesburg
August 29, 1943

Dearests,

It has been some time since I have had a letter from you, but I received a *Ladies' Home Journal* and three *Time* magazines this last week. My last letter to you was dated the 11th of August, but on the 20th August I wrote to Aunt Lula and Aunt Nellie, and they will no doubt let you know they have heard. I wish I had more time for letters, but I'll just tell you how today has gone, and so go so many of my days.

Wilfred's father was here by the time John was bathed this morning, and he stayed until twelve o'clock or later; Elizabeth Byrne telephoned and asked if she could come for lunch. She only left when she saw Edith Broadbent and her children arriving at four o'clock. I could see Edith didn't want to go home, as Charles has just left for the North for the second time, so I said, "Stay for supper and I'll make hot biscuits" (I really said scones), so she immediately took me up. Then Hilda Hudson came in and stayed until suppertime. The girl is off on Sunday afternoons, so I was busy. You may think that this only happens on Sunday, but last Monday was just the same round of people. They think I can't go out on account of John, so they all come to see me. This really goes on all the time with me. Maybe it is because I live in a little house that doesn't frighten anyone away. I have often wondered if our place on "G" Street didn't frighten people to some extent.

Since I last wrote, I have had more trouble with servants. I now have No. 8, Lizzie by name. I think I am settled with her, but I have had so much trouble that I don't want to make any predictions. I have had to swing the whole show several times lately, and with a young baby that is not easy. The last one walked out twelve noon Sunday, two weeks ago. She said the work was too hard, and even though I refused to pay her for her week's work, she went. A month's notice on either side is customary and legal.

Wilfred and I had our tenth wedding anniversary on Thursday. He wrote to a florist in town and had the most wonderful flowers sent out to me on that day. It was a lovely surprise, and there were so many that the house is filled with them— sweet peas, violets, jonquils, larkspur. Wilfred has never stopped courting me, which means a lot to a woman, I think. I also got four letters from him this last week, which is a great improvement in that respect. Did I tell you he has been on a course and made the highest marks ever attained? He made 100% on one paper and 98% on another.

John is sitting up unsupported now. He is strong and has beautiful rosy cheeks. He sleeps in my bedroom, and Eve and Robin share a room. John is acquiring new noises, which he often practices during the night, so I only wish I had a room where he could be on his own.

I started my job of one afternoon a week on the 14th. I have been three times and really enjoy it. I am supposed to act as an assistant to this ophthalmic surgeon by putting drops in eyes and handing instruments to him for small operations performed in his rooms. He invited me to watch him remove three cysts from an eyelid, but I got sick and had to leave. I like making appointments, collecting money, and the bookwork part of the job. I also forgot to give him tea on my first afternoon, which is a cardinal sin out here.

I feel sure I'll have a letter from you this week that I can answer. A letter must have come with the magazines but is being censored.

How is the house account getting along? Is it out of the red yet? How much is still owing on it?

Could you send me some sewing machine needles? I have none and can't get them and have three dresses cut out to make for the children. You could send them in a letter, if they were stuck into some material. Too bad about John's little dresses. Have you ever found out what is the trouble? Thanks for the chewing gum and the magazines. Old and young were both pleased. I always send the *Time* magazines on up to Wilfred.

I am tired tonight so won't write more now.
My love and kisses to you both,

Helen and Babes

8 Reform Avenue
Melrose, Johannesburg
September 16, 1943

My dearest Mother and Father,

I think you two are the naughty ones about writing, as I have had three *Time* magazines but no letter since I wrote you on the 29th of August. I am trying to be better about writing, and this is my reward. Never mind. I refuse to worry. Do you know what I always start thinking when I don't hear? That you are on your way out here. Have you ever heard of such an optimist? If I weren't inclined this way, I couldn't take all I have had to take.

Well, isn't the news wonderful? The capitulation of Italy brings us that much nearer our goal. We were terribly excited here, but only New York celebrated the news in a worthy manner. There was no demonstration here; we just talked and looked happy for a day or two.

I have just had an interesting letter from Wilfred, as he is just back from visiting the battlefields of El Alamein. Men were with them who were in the battle, and they made the battle live again, he said, by telling little incidents, which happened during that time. He bathed in the Mediterranean both morning and evening and wrote our names in the sand along the beach. They returned by way of Alexandria, and there he had a wonderful meal at the famous Pastrandi's. He said they went in just as they came out of the desert, had a real whiskey, which he followed with a divine omelette, and then fish, fish, and fish with tartar sauce and salads. Followed by a red wine, Turkish coffee, and a packet of Lucky Strikes. He says he smoked them one at a time, but I hardly believe it. Replete with food, he then took a Ghari [a horse-drawn carriage that became popular in Egypt due to the British influence in the late nineteenth century] and rode

Wilfred holding whip in a ghari, Alexandria, Egypt

around for half an hour and felt at peace with the world. I can imagine how he appreciated these things after months in the desert on army rations.

After having had nine girls in three months, I have an old girl who started on the 3rd of this month and who seems to be satisfied and is very good. She knows how to manage John, and Robin is so sweet to her that she may become attached to the two children and *want* to stay with us. If they don't rather adopt you as a family, you can't hold them. There must be a little feeling there. Eve more or less ignores all of them, so I can't count on her for help in holding them. I have had to stay very close to home during this unsettled time, as I didn't want to trust John to their tender mercies.

I went to a dance at the Officers' Club with Hilda Hudson the first Saturday of this month. She had to sell tickets for the dance, and I helped her. Then we danced with spare men. It did me a lot of good to get out and find I was not utterly unattractive to men. I have been asked to come the first Saturday night of every month to help entertain, which I shall perhaps do. The nice thing about it is that you do not have to put up with any nonsense because you are completely independent of the men, having your own car, and not having been taken by anyone.

Bert silently disapproved of this outing, but my other friends were all for it; in fact, my going to a dance caused quite a stir in the neighbourhood. I wore my hair in my new style, which I copied from a magazine giving hairstyles. This style was marked "Fortyish," yet everyone thinks it makes me look younger. It consists of a fringe of small curls across my forehead, which comes out of a high wave across my head. The rest is in a plain roll around my head.

Anyway, you shall see it soon, as yesterday two *Time* magazines arrived, and the one with the cover of Mussolini contained a roll of films. I shall immediately get busy making snaps of John, Eve, Robin, and myself and the house. If Judy, our dog, can behave herself, she will also be in the picture, but she is seldom in repose. She was a little off-colour, and I gave her a Bob Martin Condition Powder. She was supposed to have a course of three a day for three days, but after the very first powder she tore the linoleum out of the laundry and ripped it into shreds all over the back garden, then raced and raced madly around the palm tree. When she isn't this way, it is time for me to worry about her, and when she is this way, she is a nuisance.[145] I am reminded every day now why you didn't take to a pet for us as children. We thought it was hard, but Mother is the one with all the trouble of feeding them and doctoring them, etc.

---

[145] My strongest memory of Judy was her habit of getting a firm hold of my right foot and the pedal of my tricycle while I was riding. It did not matter how fast I pedaled, she would run next to me, her head circling faster and faster without her ever giving up. Eventually, I would be the one to give up in despair.

Eve is crazy for a bicycle now, and I am reminded of Helen Hunter saying she never lived until she got her bicycle. The price of bicycles here now is too dreadful, as they haven't been imported for some time, and the demand is greater than ever because of the petrol shortage. I want her to have one, though, as I think she wants it as much as I wanted a pony as a child, and I still think it was a mistake that we didn't have a pony. A bicycle is a much more reasonable request than a pony, too, as there is some difference in the upkeep.

I do hope there are letters from you this mail and not just magazines. You must not get as bad about writing as I am. I really think that, for once in your life, you have more time than I have. You have several times said that you felt you should be doing something to help the war effort by getting a job or something. I think you should just take life easy and play bridge as much as you like and enjoy yourself. There are so many years that mothers drive themselves that, when their family is grown, they should take it easy. I don't expect to be very helpful after I have reared my family.

I have a wonderful set-up now in my domestics. The wash girl and the house girl are of different tribes and can't talk to each other. In fact, it seems that Esther, the house girl, can't speak the language of any of the native servants around us, so there is no screaming across the back fence, which is usually a favourite pastime. She approved of John, but he is the only one who gets to see her toothless mouth. Otherwise, her lips are firmly compressed.

John seems to have taken everything out of me. He is too blooming for words, but I just don't seem to feel up to scratch at any time. I am going to my doctor to see what can be done, but you know how one puts off the doctor. Anyway, Bert has heard a lot of complaints from me, and, as you know, she loves to believe in the supernatural, we shall call it, and I am just as far the other way. Well, we had ructions the other day when she asked me if I would let her take me to a Christian Science Healer. Really, that is the last place I can imagine myself ending up. She goes to séances, you know, and believes in fairies. She brought a book out to prove it to me. Eve and Robin don't think I am a bit nice because I haven't this imagination. I sometimes wonder if I am being anything like Mrs. Everett, who wouldn't let her children imagine anything. I hope not. In spite of this big difference between us, Bert and I get along together beautifully, on the whole.[146]

---

[146] It is possible that the book Helen is referring to is *The Coming of the Fairies*, by Arthur Conan Doyle. Doyle, and others, had been hoodwinked by a series of 1920 photographic hoaxes perpetrated by the cousins, Francis and Elsie Griffiths. Later, the young cousins found themselves in the embarrassing position of having convinced many, including Doyle, creator of the famous detective Sherlock Holmes, of the veracity of what had begun in 1917 as an adolescent prank.

I have just finished a dress for Robin and one for Eve. I am making myself a white tailored blouse next; then, more dresses for Robin. Eve has nothing to hand down to her just now. They are desperate for socks, as they have tender feet and they get rubbed if they go without. Robin's foot is about 7" long, and Eve's 8." I spend days darning socks that I itch to throw away because I know they will have another hole the very first time they are worn because they are that rotten.

I go to my funny little job tomorrow afternoon. That will be the last day for this month. They are very pleased with my work, and I do enjoy it. On Saturday, I noticed that Wednesday afternoon is packed with patients, so I shall have a hectic time.

Did I write you about being invited out for bridge with some of the best players in Johannesburg, also "social lights," and I beat the socks off of them. I have never played such bridge; of course, I had the cards or I couldn't have done it. However, on several hands I played, they commented that it was brilliantly played. Everyone had to pay me when the afternoon was over. I made a great effort to go that afternoon, so it did me a lot of good to play so well. I didn't even have a servant at the time, and Elizabeth Byrne came to look after John and the children.

This coming Saturday, Bert is taking us all to the Ballet. I am anxious to see Robin's reaction to the dancing, as she has never seen a dancing display, and she is so keen on dancing. That will be the thrill I get out of it. Eve is all keyed up, but she saw the Ballet last year and knows what to expect.

All our love to you two. We speak of you so often, and you are constantly in my thoughts.

Your,

Helen

8 Reform Avenue
Melrose, Johannesburg
September 29, 1943

My dearest Ones,

I have had so much mail from you in the last few days that I shall mark your letters paragraph by paragraph and answer them as they come, so the important things may not be first at all in this letter of mine but just as they were written by you. I have four letters from you, Eve has one, and your parcel arrived, as well as numerous copies of *Time* and *Better Homes and Gardens*.

Do let me thank you for the parcel first of all, as it contained so many essential things. Your letter must have made the Censor weep, as the parcel came through post-haste. Do you know I was spoon-feeding John his milk when the bottles arrived? Three nipples came and you marked four on the outside of the parcel. The children were so thrilled with their socks, and I was so relieved to have that situation bettered. I did appreciate my notepaper, which I shall use for special occasions, and the tissues were so welcome. We haven't seen tissues here in ages. Of course, the darning cotton was too welcome for words. Could you enclose a card of snaps in a letter sometime if you can still get them? They can't be bought here, and, since I am making the children's clothes, I find it difficult not having them, for I have never worked buttonholes, though I am going to have a try.

Before I forget it, I addressed my last letter to you of Sept. 16th to 809 instead of 804 Cumberland St. You may get it all right, but if you haven't received it, please inquire. Bert has had one of her letters to you returned. It was addressed to your old address in Bristol, Tennessee. I think it rotten of those people not to forward your letters to you. I feel sure all the trouble about your not hearing from us has been there. Bert has never received your letter about your dream.

I am so terribly sorry to hear of Mrs. S.'s death, and I know you have felt it, as you seemed to see so much of her. You and I could be so much comfort to each other if we could only be together. Since the S. children did ask for their father's body to be moved, I am glad T.W. had the decency to comply with their request. Personally, I think she did a dreadful thing in marrying him when she was supposed to be a friend of the family. I don't know how people can be so heartless.

The first I have heard of Aunt Kate's position is that you think she will leave. Are the Mahoneys your cousins, and what is Aunt Kate's position—housekeeper? If the Mahoneys have been satisfied to eat what their cook has cooked for six years, I personally would leave her to it and take it easy around the place. She will never be able to change the ways of a cook of six years standing. I wouldn't do this work if I had a comfortable income without it. I think she should try to enjoy life a little. What other funeral did you send flowers to besides Mrs. S's? Was the wedding present for Barbara?

You sew so well you should be able to make yourself an attractive wash dress. Here we would jump at a dress like mine for $14.95. You should see what we are offered at that price: sleazy material, no cut or design at all. Just the plainest housedresses. I look at them and wonder if anybody is ever going to buy them.

I am glad you have at last heard from me and have received three of Bert's letters.

I am so sorry to hear that Aunt Nellie and Eugene are not well. I hope they will get to the seat of their trouble and do whatever is necessary. Do you think Eugene might have T.B.? Some people have dry T.B. and do not cough. Why doesn't he go to a specialist in Asheville where they have seen so much of that trouble and would know in a minute if he has it? He simply must not let a thing like this go on. If he must, have a year's rest, it seems to me. Mr. Clem can well afford it and, by doing it for them, would only be insuring his daughter's future. Your next letter said you have been over and they were better.

I haven't tried John's suit on him yet, but he will have to wear it right away, as he will soon be too big for it. Friends came to see us with their nine-month-old baby, two months older than John, and the two weighed the same, but John was a head taller than she was. He weighs over twenty pounds. We put them on the floor together and John looked her over and then made a lunge for her hair, which was very inviting-looking black fluff. He gave it a good tug and set her off crying. It was so indicative of their futures. The suit is so pretty, and Bert wanted to put it on for the pictures we made of John on Sunday, but I thought you would like to see him in something we got here.

I have heard no more from the Colonel since my letter, which would put off any man except one with a rhino hide. Yes, the Colonel is married, but his wife lives in the country and runs his farm. He has grown children and grandchildren. He has always had a weakness for the ladies. I was just supposed to be a new conquest.

The news of poor little Ann's accident upset all of us. What a dreadful thing to happen and how sickened you must all have felt. I do hope she will be perfectly all right. Where is the hole in her head? What part of the head? Give my love and best wishes to her and all her family. I am sure Aunt Kate and Mrs. Alexander were very upset. The Elizabethton paper can give the strangest account of things that I have ever read. "Dixon girl" sounds too dreadful. I can never show one of their clippings over here. It is also too bad the Alexander side of the family is the only one worth mentioning.

It is good to see the house finances in good condition. I know the house is a bother to you, and I do appreciate what you do on it. I leave everything about it to your judgment. I hope that money from that house will give us a start in business that will enable us to give it back to you. I have always considered the house yours, but I have seen Wilfred's ability in business, and I want to give him a chance of a good start after the war, if possible. Wilfred has had a partnership offered him in a well-established insurance business, and we want to investigate that thoroughly. The man who owns it wants to retire, and he only has a daughter to leave it to, so he wants her to run the office and to take in a partner for the contacts. He has spoken to Wilfred about it. Wilfred would be very good at this, as he can approach anybody and will know a lot of people after the war. It is plant and mercantile insurance, not life.

I will get Wilfred's picture off right away now. I am afraid I just haven't mailed it.

I am glad you thought Eve's letter good and also her handwriting. She did not do well in school this term, and I think it is because she does not understand her teacher. I have been to see Reverend Mother about it and hope, during this next term, she will be able to make up the past low marks and pass into the next Standard.

I have sciatica, according to Sister Murdock. Anyway, I have felt rotten for such a long time, and yesterday I could stand it no longer so went to her to see if she could do anything for me. Her treatment did help, and I have been easier today. I have kept in bed today, except for attending to John, and have kept as warm as possible. I am confident I have had a bad internal chill. If I could have a week in bed with no responsibility, I feel I would be all right again, but how to get that I really don't know. Anyway, I have started doing something for myself. I wish I could find a doctor that would give me faith in the medical profession again. I am glad they have discovered the root of Eugene's trouble and that they are now treating him. It is also good to know that Aunt Nellie is quite all right again.

Well, I think about the biggest news of your letters is that you are taking a bookkeeping course from the University of Tennessee.[147] I really can't tell you how much I admire you for doing this. I hate to think of you ever going out to work, but I am glad to think of you being prepared to do a job that would be congenial and not degrading if it should be necessary for you to work. How are your eyes? I am always worried about your sewing for us, as your eyes seemed so weak before I left. Maybe they have strengthened, as mine have.

My hearing has also improved since coming here. I think it was a purely catarrhal condition. How is Father's hearing? You all never write of being ill, and that makes me very suspicious sometimes, because I don't see how you can manage to never be ill. I am glad you have a policy for that now; however, I am the one who needs such a policy. We have spent a good $400 on my health in the last few years. I can assure you that I am doing everything possible to build myself up. I study our food, and I lead the quietest life possible. I am selling Judy, my dog, as she gets on my nerves. The President of the Doberman Pinscher Club of Johannesburg is coming this weekend to see Judy and will advertise her for me. I hope to get $20 to $25 for her. She is worth about $125, but I can't claim her pedigree. She is too rough with children, and I am afraid to have her around John. If they only knew it, I am on the point of giving her away.

I am so very sorry to hear about Mrs. Umbach. You must all give her encouragement, no matter whether you mean it or not, as one gives up so readily when in poor health, and especially if you have cancer or anything else so incurable. She is such a fine sweet woman, and it seems so unfair for her to have

---

[147] Sophia's report card from the University of Tennessee reads as follows: "This is to advise you that you passed the first class of Industrial Accounting with the grade of A-Good. The second class in Accounting will begin Tuesday, Oct. 12, 1943—same time and place. Important that you attend." I do not know if Sophia ever entered that class. Sophia was fifty-six at this time. However, Sophia finally entered the workforce in her sixties when she worked in the Medical Library at Duke University.

to end her days full of dread and suffering. It takes a lot of courage to face a slow death. I, too, hope I go quickly. Mrs. Umbach is fortified with religion and has more there to hold on to than some of the rest of us would have if faced with the same thing. I hope God will be merciful.

I couldn't ask for a better baby than John is now. He is good at night and good all day long. He eats well and takes to every new food introduced. How you had to coax Eve with her food. I, too, marvel at how you brought up Eve and looked after Mama Hunter [Sophia's mother] too. You never gave me enough responsibility when I was at home. I am always thinking about it and wondering why you shielded me so much. You should have required more of me all through the years, as it was impossible for me to appreciate what you did for me, as I had never tasted the other side. I had so little responsibility that it is a wonder I didn't break down under it when it came to me.

It did make me do a foolish thing in Durban. Wilfred wanted to take a big furnished house at a reasonable rental, but I simply wouldn't do it, but put him in a flat at $5.00 less per month, just because the house looked so big to me that I didn't think I could run it. He has never forgiven me for that, as he loved that house. It is the one we had for one Christmas and could have had permanently a month later. I said it was on the wrong side of town, and, later, when he found the American Consul lived in a big house in the same block, I thought he would murder me. I'll never take him to another flat or boarding house, as he is like a caged lion in either. What he is going to be like after the wide-open spaces of the desert, I don't know. He needs plenty of room.

Mr. Evans did not win the medal in the billiard tournament but did win the silver cup (second) and has given it to John.

I think I wrote you before that Bené is getting a divorce. It didn't last any time. He is difficult, and I shouldn't like to be the woman trying to make a success of marriage with him. He married a woman with money, and a very good-looking woman too, I believe, beautifully dressed and all that. She would have to be all of that to appeal to Bené, and such things mean a little too much to him. He is always perfectly groomed. I doubt if he would have left me money; it would most likely have been some of his objects d'art.

I hope Helen will not have to wait too long to marry. I don't believe in that when you find the right one. It sounds like she has picked a very suitable husband, and I hope Kathryn will do likewise. Tell her I hope she will have a few years of marriage without babies. It is not wise to start your responsibilities so early. How old is Helen now? I suppose she is twenty-one or twenty-two. I am pleased to hear of her promotion. Is she working in Johnson City or Kingsport?

I have just received your fifth letter today; also a slip from the post office saying I have a parcel with nine shillings and nine pence duty. This is sure to be the shoes, and how pleased I am to get them. I am glad you couldn't get white, as I am better off for white shoes than anything else. I have held back on the last pair you sent me in white and have never given them hard wear. I shall go to the post office tomorrow to get my shoes. When I got the slip today, I couldn't go out, as it was raining, and I must be careful with this sciatica. Since they are cream kid, they should look nice with my new coat. They make a simply perfect birthday present and are arriving practically on the day [October 2]. I call that good, with the irregularity of the mails. I am afraid I haven't even said happy birthday to you for your October birthday, but I do hope it will be a happy one. I have several invitations for mine, and, if I feel well, I should enjoy it very much.

Bert has invited me to have tea in town with her that morning and lunch with Dad at his Club, then I do my job in the afternoon for a few hours, and Hilda has asked me to go to the Officer's' Club to dance, and Bert has invited me to see a play which is starring a friend of Bené's, whom he had to lunch with me when he was up here at Christmas time. She is supposed to be excellent and may come to America to go on the stage. I am sure I shall not feel like a dance, but I may feel like the play—*Servant of God*.

Wilfred does not have his Captaincy yet and may not get it, the way it is being held back. Wilfred has no insurance. He never felt secure with Sears or Westinghouse and that is why he did not take out a policy. Though he did so well with Westinghouse, there were politics to play all the time to stay in, and one never knew which side was *the* side. One must feel certain of a specified income before you can know what size policy you can afford. However, if anything should happen to Wilfred on Active Service, I would get a pension of at least $125 per month. I could not expect more from any policy we would have taken out.

I am glad you have bought the War Bonds for Eve and Robin. I told them about them, and they feel like millionaires. I am very surprised at how much money they had. Eve is especially anxious to be rich. Robin has $25 in War Saving stamps, and Eve has $30 over here.

I have written until I am about dilly, but I had to get on top of this flood of letters from you. I hadn't heard for some time, you know, and then it came like Christmas mail. I also have a slip from the P.O. saying they are holding a letter or something for me to open, as they think it contains a dutiable article. So there is even something else.

I haven't heard from Wilfred since the last letter I wrote you.

I noted Dr. Staley's death but no mention of grandchildren. Haven't Shirley and T.F. any children? I wonder if she is still beautiful? I imagine so, as she had the looks that would last. I hope you see her, so you can tell me. She is a very sweet person. I really must say cheerio and get some sleep.

I love you both so much and hope you are well and happy.
Your,

Helen

October 7, 1943

Dearest Folks,

You, my sweets, certainly gave me a marvelous birthday. My shoes and stockings arrived in time for my birthday. They are so beautiful that my friends have come especially to see them. My feet and legs haven't been so well dressed in years. I have never seen more beautiful shoes, and I really can't thank you enough for such a big thrill. No other present could have pleased me so much, for they were two things I couldn't buy, no matter how much money I had.

I had a lovely birthday and thought so many times during the day that the fuss should be made over my mother and not me. The news of Wilfred's captaincy came in my birthday letter from him. This means so much to him and is a big lift financially. He will be able to give me £5 more per month. Wilfred's father gave me £1, or $5.00. Bert gave me a housedress, talcum powder, and bath salts, and Hilda gave me perfume and six hankies. Elizabeth Byrne sent me a four-pound sirloin roast, and Eide Hawkins came over with a big cake. Elizabeth has seen such hard times that she believes in being most practical even though she was born to be just the other way. Bert and I went to see *Servant of God*, which starred a girl Bené had to lunch with me one day. The play was written by a South African, produced and played by a South African. We have some very good productions here.

You wrote me some time ago that you and Uncle Edwin were sending some money. It has never come, and you haven't mentioned it since. I believe it was to be for Robin and Eve's birthday, and for John from Uncle Edwin.

Must stop for now, my dears. We love you two so very much and only wish we could be with you.

Helen

Helen with baby John in Johannesburg

8 An Open Boat
October 1943 ~ December 1943

'Tis thus with people in an open boat,
They live upon the love of life, and bear
More than can be believed, or even thought,
And stand like rocks the tempest's wear and tear.

~ Lord Byron

8

Helen knows she is very ill but has not yet been diagnosed with the condition that will finally take her life. She carries on bravely in the face of significant challenges. Unable to care for three children, she finally places Eve and Robin as boarders at Parktown Convent, all while suffering from agonizing pain. Often alone with baby John, she continues the running of the house with its coal stove, living without a car, doing laundry by hand, walking to the store and the market for supplies, and dealing with the separation from Wilfred who is in combat in North Africa and Italy.

With Wilfred up North and Bert at work, and her parents in America also on war rations, Helen now turns to her father-in-law. Despite his rather taciturn nature, Mr. Evans shows his caring by paying Helen's substantial hospital bills, by continuing to visit, and by talking over plans for the whole Evans family to live together in the countryside after the war is over. And, despite their differences in style, beliefs, and temperament, Bert is Helen's constant ally, devoted friend, and surrogate mother to Eve, Robin, and John.

True to her personality, Helen does not dwell on her hardships. She continues rather to reassure, show competence, and find joy wherever she can. Perhaps most remarkable of all, Helen, who has been in hospital receiving radium treatments, continues to write long letters to Sophia and Harlow, reminding her parents, "Our happiness is all within ourselves, so it really does not matter where we are." Then, like a flame that brightens before it is extinguished, Helen finally gets help and relief—a reliable maid and Wilfred's return with the Africa Star after seeing action in Egypt and Italy.

Helen's letter to her parents [age 36]   October 27, 1943

Dearests,

It has been a while between my letters this time, and I'll own up to it. My last letter was written about the fifth of this month, thanking you for my shoes and stockings, which, so far, I have only worn once.

I know this letter will arrive about Christmas time there. I am not at all pleased with what I am going to write about, but, when you read it at Christmas time, you can read it with the assurance that I am by that time in better health than I have known for several years. For the past three weeks I have only known hospitals, operating rooms, etc., so how can I be expected to write about anything else, for what else do I know?

To begin with, I have never been well since John was born, and, for the months of August and September, I practically gave up, for I was in constant pain, like labour pains, though, of course, not so severe. I found myself becoming an invalid. It was only with the help of aspirins and my willpower that I ever did anything. I got worlds of cheap advice from well-meaning friends, but only Elizabeth Byrne gave me sound advice.

The doctor I had with John said I was in fair condition but needed building up—I found her very slap-dash all along. Bert tried, with the best intentions, to take me to a Christian Science Healer, and, when I wouldn't go, she went on my behalf. I took this move as an indication that she thought it was all mental with me, which annoyed me intensely; however, I doubt now that that was in her mind, as she is becoming very interested in the topic. She is now reading the life of Mary Baker Eddy, the *Eddy Bible*, together with the *Bible*, etc. I think a real Scientist is a very cheerful person, and that I admire, but I do hope she does not go to the point of dismissing doctors.

Heaven only knows, I have had very little faith in doctors for years, as I have spent enough on them with little in return; but fortunately for me, I have a doctor now that I have the utmost faith in—he is Dr. G. Drury Shaw. Elizabeth Byrne preached him to me for literally months; she said he was considered the best gynecologist south of the Equator. Finally, when I realized I was growing worse every day, and when I was in constant pain, I telephoned for an appointment. Then, I announced I was going to him, and the turmoil that followed—Bert said he charged one of the big shots at her office $500 for his wife's confinement, that he was the most expensive man in town. Others said—you know it will mean an operation if you go a Specialist. I felt so weak I thought I couldn't face an operation, and, as for my finances, I had $25, and that to run the house on the rest of the month. Nothing stopped me, however, and I went on the 6th of this month. He found immediately upon examination that my womb was misplaced; also that I would need curettage. On the 9th, I had a lovely injection in my vein and immediately blanked out, and he did this much at least for me. I have not had a talk with him, so whether he did more I do not know.

I stayed in the hospital, and, exactly a week later, I went back to the operating theatre and had my first treatment of radium. I had to nurse my little packet of radium from 8:30 one morning until 5:00 the next morning. He let me out of hospital for three days, and, exactly a week after my first radium treatment, I had my second. The original plan was to repeat it exactly a week later, but now I am home for a rest, and there will be two weeks before the last treatment; then I hope all I have to do is eat and sleep and rest to be 100% again.

Dr. Shaw is a kind-looking man, and he looked strong enough to carry my burdens, so I have dumped them on him and haven't worried a scratch. I asked him what he would charge for the operation, and when he named the most reasonable figure of $50, I nearly collapsed on him. I have now had much more done than originally intended, so I can expect his fee to go up. It will cost about $250, I believe, when it is all over, as I will have had the operating theatre four times and an anaesthetic that many times. My hospital bill is already $100.

Wilfred's father has been a trump when it came to a time of need, and has told me he will pay everything, and he absolutely becomes furious if I even talk about the bills. I feel that, after all, since I haven't the money, it is only right, as he has a grandson to carry his name on, and he simply worships John. I don't want you all to make any offers, as you did quite enough for Wilfred and me in America, and Mr. Evans has made a lot of money on the stock market.

I am having the best care and attention; I couldn't get better anywhere, and my doctor is highly qualified. I feel that he will always do the best he can for his patients, as he became a gynecologist because his first wife died in childbirth, and he blamed the doctor. He was a general practitioner at the time.

You must be wondering, by now, what I did about the children. I put Robin and Eve in the Convent as boarders, and they simply love it; they don't know whether they like home or the Convent better. I am so glad they are happy. Robin is the youngest there and the pet of all the older girls, I understand. Mother Assistant asked Bert to compliment me on the way I had brought up Eve and Robin, as they are the two best-behaved children they have ever had at Parktown Convent.

Robin goes to school and study hour and everything that the others do, and I was able to borrow two dresses for her (uniforms rather) so she thinks she is really a big girl now. They are allowed to come home this Sunday for the day. As for little John, we left him with Esther, the native girl. She is the old, reliable type and adores John. He has improved right along, getting fatter and browner, so I know he has had good attention. Bert and Dad were here every night, and Bert bathed John then and made his milk mixture for the day. I thought I was indispensable, but I found out I wasn't.

I am sorry not to send you two any presents this Christmas, but I can't go shopping, and I don't feel that I should when Dad is spending so much money on me. I am afraid I won't even write the cards that I wrote last Christmas, as all that takes my strength, and I must conserve it. You'll understand, I know.

I received your letter of August 9th while in hospital. (While I think of it, the radium treatment is to cure some ulcers I have.) I am glad you are hearing from me.

I am going to try the frozen dessert of oranges, lemons, and bananas this Sunday for the children. It is hard to make a dessert with no white flour and no cream, since cream is against the law.

I saw *Mrs. Minever* some time ago and simply loved it.

I am glad Ann Dixon is all right now.

I shall be sending you some pictures right away that we made with your roll. They were made just before I went into hospital. John did not have to be propped up at six months. He sat well then by himself. Does Dorrette still not hear from Fred? It is a good thing she has the baby to take her time and attention.

Bert still comes out every evening, but Dad has gone back to his boarding house. My friends have been lovely to me. Elizabeth Byrne was in constant attendance. I really think she was frightened after she saw what she had let me in for, as she felt solely responsible for me going to the doctor. When I told her the one "op" wasn't the end of it, she was nearly frantic and said, "Well, for the Lord's sake, don't peg out, as the family would always hold me responsible." Though she is hard up, she has sent me stacks of new magazines (we get them now) and the most beautiful flowers about four times.

John and his Auntie Bert

May you have a happy Christmas, and my best wish is that day will find peace reigning over the world. It may take longer than that, but not much longer maybe.

My love to my two sweet ones and hugs and kisses from the babes. Must have my afternoon sleep now—two hours.

Helen

An Open Boat (Oct. 1943—Dec. 1943)

Parktown Convent

Note: Parktown Convent was a well-endowed private girls' school run by Catholic sisters of the order of the Holy Family. With over four hundred students, K-12, it was both a boarding and a day school for girls (boys were admitted as day scholars in the first two grades). Some boarders came from as far away as Bechuanaland (Botswana), Northern Rhodesia (Zambia), Southern Rhodesia (Zimbabwe), the Belgian Congo (Democratic Republic of Congo), and Nyasaland (Malawi).

In 1942, Parktown Convent was situated on large, beautifully manicured grounds, containing four tennis courts, a hockey field, two netball fields, a swimming pool, three spacious wooded play areas, large lawns, and several quadrangles. The buildings included separate housing for the nuns and students, classrooms, a large performance hall, and a chapel.

The program offered was strong in academics and in the arts. Elocution, drama, dance, music, the visual arts, physical education, and sports were emphasized.

Located in Parktown, one of the best suburbs in Johannesburg, the Convent was built as a result of the vision of Reverend Mother Ambrose Farren, who was criticized for building a school so far from the center of town. The project was not an easy one, as the materials for the structure had to be transported to the site by ox wagon. The foresight of Reverend Mother is to be marveled at, since she started building her dream school in 1905 (in response to the gold rush of 1886) when the City of Johannesburg was only nineteen years old.

A sad moment occurred in May, 2013, when the school's great hall (not shown in the photograph), built in 1935, with its art deco finishes, burned to the ground. It was the same hall where Helen and Bert had watched Eve dance in 1942.

Dearest Mother,

Your letter of August 23 arrived before I sealed my letter. In it you gave me the news that Father has gone to Burlington, N.C., to work. For weeks I have worried over his job in Bristol [where Harlow worked for the bus company]. I knew you all were worried. It simply breaks my heart that you all must know such insecurity at this time in your lives. It is the rotten economic system, or no system, in America, and for that reason I hate the land of my birth, and I have kept Wilfred from returning because of what it did to us. We would have been back long ago, but I have always said no, because I'll never forget what it did to us for five years at least. My dream is to get myself in a position to ask you out here, and know I can give you security. Just now I feel so weak I don't know how I can ever accomplish anything, but I won't always feel this way. I do admire you two. Aunt Nellie's news is good. I can't bear to hear about Uncle Edwin. We are so mortal. I love you.

Helen

November 15, 1943

My dearests,

This is just a note tonight to enclose the pictures of the family that you made possible. The one of me with the three children looks very grim, but I really don't look like that.

I also enclose a Christmas card made by Eve. She did it at home by herself, and I found it among her things the other day. The front is completely original, but I can see she has copied from some card on the inside. I think it very sweet, and I am sure you will.

I have Eve and Robin home with me now. They came home yesterday, as I am through with hospitals now.

John has not been sleeping well, but I hope I have discovered the trouble and that all will be well tonight. He has cut his two lower front teeth but was not upset.

Can't write more tonight, as I am dead for sleep.

Will write soon.

Love,

Helen

November 27, 1943

My own dearest Parents,

According to the last date I have put down, my last letter to you was written on the 27th of October. I just hope I didn't record the note with the snaps in it and that it really hasn't been so long since I have written. For about ten days after my last bout in hospital, I didn't feel too good, and then, when I was able to do, I had Bert sick for about a week, and then we brought the children home from the Convent, and my hands have been very full. Now, by the goodness of God, we are all well and happy and are preparing for a three-week's holiday in January. We plan to all go to a friend's farm in Natal.[148] It is in a beautiful spot and not near the sea but in the mountains. The children will love it, I am sure.

John is now crawling all over the place just as Eve used to. Speed, about a mile-a-minute. I sat with him in the front garden yesterday and let him go. He was in the flowerbeds and everywhere, but he put everything in his mouth. I decided if I could put a muzzle on him I could give him his freedom and free my mind of all worry.

I am very sorry that you have had so much to do in connection with the house in Johnson City lately, and that you had to buy a stoker. If L. had moved his when he moved, the other people would not have expected that luxury. Anyway, it is an asset and, who knows, we may live there one day ourselves. Eve talks about her house in Johnson City, and Robin wants to know if Eve is going to let her live with her. Eve is growing very beautiful, and I feel that when she is eighteen and more she will perhaps almost be famous for her beauty. I hope to help her grow up to be as good as she is beautiful, and then she will give us all much happiness.

I enjoyed Father's letter from Burlington, giving us so much news about his surroundings. It is good, too, to know how highly he regards me, and it is made perfect by my great admiration and love for both of you.

The children have received their letters from Father, and Eve has been busy on an Xmas card for him. I will see if she has finished it and get it off. She will also write while she is home on her Xmas holidays.

Well, great news: your Xmas parcel has already arrived and we are all delighted. My blue shoes fit perfectly, and I hardly know myself with so much good-looking footwear. I didn't have the desire to buy any clothes when I had no shoes that were nice; now I shall get something. I do hope you and Father will manage without the coupons you gave up to me. It was certainly sweet of you. Eve's dress is beautiful and the colour suits her nicely. Robin's undies are adorable, and she would never have had such nice ones if it hadn't been a present. I am putting John's romper on him tomorrow, and I know he will look sweet. I like the peach colour for him. Whenever you send him things, send on the big side,

---

[148] Helen is referring to the large dairy farm, "Blackwood," situated in the Midlands of Natal, home of their friends, Dr. Joe Marshall and his wife, Elsa, whose wedding she, Wilfred, Eve, and Robin had attended some years earlier. Sadly, this trip never materialized. In the years to come, however, Joe and Elsa were to prove themselves sterling friends of the family.

as he is so fat. I suppose he weighs 25 lbs. now. He is a lovely baby. He also stands now, and has two teeth, but not the right ones. He is cross-cutting them.

The church paper I sent was Church of England.

What seems to be Eugene's trouble? Isn't it perhaps overwork? Men often upset their constitutions by worry over the responsibilities they have assumed. This may be Eugene's whole trouble, and just a calmer outlook on life might give him renewed strength. He is much too young and much too necessary to let illness have a part in his life. If everyone could accept things as Father does, they would live to be a hundred. I am sure it took Dad some years in the Christian Faith to acquire the calm outlook he now has.

Bert and I have just discovered why she hasn't received any of your letters to her. She picked up the tag off my parcel and noticed you had written her Box No. as 1164, whereas it is 1167. The box number is that of New Consolidated Goldfields, so of course the post office had no way of tracing Bert when they found the letters were not for 1164. She is making enquiries.

Wilfred's tent mate has just arrived from Up North and brought us all presents from Wilfred—leather handbags for all, and $25 in mine and $5.00 in each of the children's. The bags are extremely nice, and the money comes in so nicely for Xmas. He says Wilfred is well and happier than he has ever been in the army.

I hope Father has found an apartment for you in Burlington by now. I do hate to see you moving around so much and hope you can be settled there as long as you like. I am amazed at the high income tax you are paying. You certainly can't get anywhere with such a tax.

Wilfred did not go North as an instructor, though he has held some classes in navigation since he has been up there. He is Supply Officer in "Q" Services. He sees that the ammunition, gasoline, etc., get fed to the right places. I haven't sent the picture of Wilfred off yet, but will try to get that done right away.

I am making a sweet blue and white flowered gingham dress for Robin that keeps on reminding me of Aunt Kate for some reason. I think she had a similar gingham many years ago.

You should send me a roll of film sometime. I know you are enjoying the pictures of John made with my only roll. I think I have told you how I got it. Yes, I am sure you know that story.

When you send me a parcel worth over £2, about $10, I have to get an import permit for it. I had to get it for this last one, so keep that in mind, as they are sometimes held up for ages. Fortunately, I know my way around and got one quickly.

Wilfred has been all over Egypt—Cairo, Alexandria, Port Said—and has visited some of the battlefields. He sent me two snaps in his last letter, and he does look well.

I have given up my funny little job, relieving once a week, since Wilfred can give me more now. He thought it silly, as the pay was so little. The pay was good for the amount of work I did.

Will you find out from Kathryn when Ward Belmont was founded? An American woman here told me she went to Ward Belmont, and she claims to be eighty-five. I find it hard to believe she's that old, and this would just be a check. [Ward Belmont, a prestigious finishing school in Nashville, Tennessee, was founded in 1865.]

I really must go to bed, as I have had a busy day and am very sleepy now.

My deepest love to you, and love from the babes too,

Helen

8 Reform Avenue
Melrose, Johannesburg
December 17, 1943

My Darlings,

At last you two dears are together again, and I am so happy for both of you. I imagine that Burlington is rather nice; in any case, you are living in the state that I like best. Why don't you two go to Nags Head on your holiday and stay with Allie Grice (Mrs.). I'll bet she can still give all the low-down on Wilfred's and my love affair there. I'm afraid her description of events would be exaggerated and highly colourful. What she might have to say does not change the fact that it stands out as the most wonderful week of my life; the only time I have been absolutely happy. For a week I did not know the time of day, the day of the week, nor the month of the year.

Our second Christmas parcel has arrived and what a surprise it was to us all. Eve and Robin have gone out tonight to dinner and a Christmas tree and won't be home until ten o'clock. They wore their new dresses, new hair ribbons, new socks, all from you, and new shoes from Bert. They both looked simply lovely, and Eve looked more grown-up than I have ever seen her. She gave me a shock by announcing that she was going to dance tonight with Peter Keeble—who is twelve.

Back to our box from you. I was simply delighted with the pair of stockings; they are terribly nice, and the pair of pillowslips are just what I need, and they are such lovely ones. John's new suits look most grown-up. He is very well off now for clothes from just what you have sent him. I am glad you have sent them large, as he is such a big boy. He has five teeth at nine months, pulls himself up to the furniture and stands, and crawls all over the house. Everyone notices how he wants to grow up. He sees Robin and Eve playing and riding the tricycle, etc., and he is most annoyed that he can't do it too. He was simply wild when he couldn't even sit up. This is not just a mother's imagining, but others have seen it too. By the way, I was so glad to get the new socks that were in the box too. We loved all the things and they are most appreciated by us all.

Eve and Robin are getting a big surprise for Christmas. I have bought them a bicycle. It is a 24" and will fit Eve; however, Robin will have to wait and grow into it. They are hard to get and expensive now, but I wanted Eve to have it when she was so crazy for it. She will simply go mad Christmas morning when she sees it. Wilfred sent them $5.00 each for Christmas, and I sold Judy [the dog] for $20, so I thought while the money was in hand I had better get it. The man took Judy in five minutes, and I realize I could have had more for her, but I was so afraid I would not get rid of her that I put my price low. It has been so peaceful without her. As Robin said, "Now the garden is ours."

Bert has sold all of the lovely nighties she made, over a year or so, at the most exclusive department store here. They simply jumped at the things. She got $35 for her negligee and the same price ($35) for her sets of nightgown and bed-jackets. She has sold them three of these sets. She sold them one gown like yours for $15. She is now making a gown and negligee to match and will get $55 for it. Not too bad when she keeps a responsible position going at the same time. She makes $150 per month now at her job. The head of the underwear department is a French woman, and she simply loves Bert's designs and her work is perfect. Just between us, Bert can make the $55 set in two days because she can work so fast. I have never known anybody who can accomplish like Bert can.

I am simply feeling like a new person these days. It is wonderful to feel well and happy. I have a good girl now too, and that makes a difference in life. She is most conscientious, as yesterday, being a holiday, I had a shoulder of lamb for lunch and there was a great deal left. I told her to take it off the table, but I just said, "Take it," and she thought I gave her the whole thing to eat. They always go to their room to eat, and she had her brother there, so they ate it, and as they ate they realized how much there was and decided it wasn't meant for them, and she came to ask, and was so upset when I told her it was not for her, but for our supper, that she came in and offered me 2/6, about 50 cents. I tried and tried to make her feel all right about it, but she is still on the subject today. Since I wouldn't take her money, she wants to go to the butcher to buy me some meat.

Wednesday afternoon I had a table of bridge, my first afternoon bridge in three years. I had Elizabeth Byrne, Edith Broadbent, and my next-door neighbour, Mrs. Crewe. The Crewes are from India where he was in the Government service. When he retired, they came out here. She has a most beautiful garden. Elizabeth and Edith are both on holiday until the New Year. Edith is going to Nelspruit for Christmas; it is a beautiful spot where all the citrus fruit is grown.

I have bought Robin and Eve lovely histories of the United States; Robin's is most beautifully illustrated. Oh, I nearly forgot to mention the book of Bible stories. Eve took the book and settled herself for the complete afternoon and practically read it through. Now she is reading aloud to Robin. She was so thrilled with that book that she actually paid no attention to her dress until the following day. She adores Bible stories, which reminds me of something funny. While Robin was a boarder at the Convent, she was taught the Creed, so she says that at night along with about four prayers she has learned, but she does considerable mumbling on all of them. However, when she comes to the word "Pontius Pilate," she says "Conscious Pirate." I think it so sweet that I can't correct her.

Eve, you will be pleased to know, did very well in her end of the year report from school. She came sixth in her class of thirty-one pupils and is promoted to Standard III. The schools here start with Grade I, Grade II, and then Standard I, etc. I am very pleased with Eve, as I had no time to give her on her lessons.

I do hope you all are liking your new home and that your Christmas will not be lonely. Dad, I never thought you would get Mother so far from Elizabethton. I should think she would find it a real experience. Our happiness is all within ourselves, so it really does not matter where we are. I am expecting Mother to confess that she actually likes Burlington better than Elizabethton.

Our very dearest love to our two American Sweethearts,

Helen and her gang

Sailing to Byzantium
January 1944 ~ June 1944

O sages standing in God's holy fire
As in the gold mosaic of a wall,
Come from the holy fire, perne in a gyre,
And be the singing-masters of my soul.
Consume my heart away; sick with desire
And fastened to a dying animal
It knows not what it is; and gather me
Into the artifice of eternity.

~ William Butler Yeats

9

Saturday, January 22, 1944, Helen writes excitedly to her parents. Wilfred is home! As she composes the letter, Helen is preparing to go to a dance at the Officers' Club in Johannesburg with Wilfred who, much to her delight, will be wearing his Africa Star ribbon.

Preparations for the dance are considerable. The maid has been alerted to care for the three children; John has been tucked into his crib, and Robin is on the bed watching Helen's every move as she sits before her three-mirrored dressing table, manicuring her nails, rolling her hair, and powdering her nose before donning her long, white satin halter-neck gown which complements her "very young figure." Eve, who had not seen all the preparations, is stunned by her mother's beauty as she enters the living room with her handsome officer husband. A fairytale queen? An angel?

Other memories of those precious months crowd in. On a visit to the Officers' Club for lunch one day, Helen leaves the building on a brief errand. Wilfred calls Eve and Robin to the second-story window to watch her as she crosses the street below. As the three gaze at her, Wilfred exclaims, "There goes the most wonderful woman in the world!"

At home, Wilfred is filled with the excitement of new possibilities. At thirty-seven, he has various kinds of work experience behind him, but the most exciting career of all has been his years in the army. He is thrilled by the idea of becoming a navigation instructor. His enthusiasm for teaching is boundless, as demonstrated by the large map of the world he had constructed before leaving for North Africa. He finds the map and sets it up on the dining room wall. He has painted every country a different color—Germany is white with black spots. After grace at the table, he turns meal times into exciting geography and literary lessons for the whole family. I well remember his having us learn the Latinate version of "Twinkle, twinkle little star":

> Scintillate, scintillate, globule vivific,
> Fain would I fathom thy nature specific,
> Loftily poised in ether capacious,
> Strongly resembling a gem carbonaceous!

Some may call it a nonsense rhyme, but Wilfred, seeing it as a gateway for a child's understanding of Latinate roots in the English language, takes pains to make sure we understand the meaning of each word.

With few sources of entertainment other than reading and the occasional movie or concert, it was customary back then for children to recite poetry or to sing for visitors. I imagine that the recitation of "Scintillate, Scintillate," coming from a five-year old, made for a charming moment's entertainment.

Somewhere there is a picture of our family taken out in the country north of Johannesburg. Eve and Robin are wearing their summer school uniforms, so it was probably an Outing Sunday from Parktown Convent in February 1944. Wilfred is holding baby John. Helen must already have been suffering from an unknown illness, but she looks well. Bert probably took the picture. It was a time of dreaming of a brighter future with Wilfred home on "important military business" and Grandpa Evans having done well on the Stock Market. There were plans to build a house for the family and a cottage for Grandpa Evans on the sizeable property. But these dreams were not to be fulfilled. Destiny had other plans for each of us that no one could have imagined on that sunny Sunday morning.

By March it becomes clear that the game is up, and Wilfred and Helen both know it. It has been fifteen years since they met and almost eleven years since their marriage. The couple has put everything into making their union work, both for themselves and their little family. But Helen's journey has been too hard for her to survive. There is no clear record of the two months Wilfred and Helen spent together with baby John while Eve and Robin were back at boarding school, but the poignancy of their situation must at times have been overwhelming. They are finally reunited and able to spend every other Sunday with Eve and Robin and every evening together with their wonderful baby son, but both know that Helen is dying.

Ever the master of the gracious thank-you letter and courageous acceptance of her fate, Helen's last letter is one of appreciation for all that is blessed in her life. Writing to her Aunt Nellie, she says, "This past year has been a dead loss to me as far as what I have to show for it in a material way. But I have had two of the biggest things of my life happen to me during this past year—I found my God as I had never known Him before, and I had the most beautiful and perfect son born to me."

With Helen dying, Sophia's presence is deemed essential. Finally, aided by Senator Roger Gant, Sophia receives congressional and military authorization to travel by flying boat from New York to Lisbon, and from there to Johannesburg, South Africa. With the help of U.S., British, and Belgian Air Forces, Sophia embarks on an eighteen-day odyssey. While D-Day and the subsequent Battle of Normandy rage below, Sophia flies halfway across the world. She arrives in Johannesburg, South Africa, nine days before Helen dies on Saturday, June 24, 1944, at age thirty-seven.

Sailing to Byzantium (Jan. 1944—June 1944)

8 Reform Avenue
Melrose, Johannesburg
January 22, 1944

My dearest Mother and Dad,

Well, I have the most wonderful news for you—Wilfred is home. He flew down about two weeks ago to do a job here in the Union. In fact, he is going to be stationed here in Johannesburg and will be able to live at home. I didn't know anything until he telephoned me from Pretoria. I am sure you can imagine our excitement. I can't tell you what it has done for me; everybody says I look like a new person.

He is one of the very first to come back with the Africa Star, which is only given to men who have seen action. It has been announced in the Press that there have been commando raids on the Italian Coast,[149] so I think it is all right for me to tell you that he took part in some of those raids. Thank heavens I didn't ever know he was in action until it was all over, and he was safely back home. He has had many thrilling experiences, also hardships in the form of heat, etc. He is in a rather important work here.[150]

Wilfred and John, age one

I have received three letters from you in the past two weeks and also the box of dresses for the children and socks. I think the dresses are the prettiest they have ever had, and so think the Evans family. Their grandfather Evans nearly burst with pride when he saw them all dressed in their new togs. I say the children are very well off for clothes now thanks to you and the present of $10 from Uncle Edwin. That box arrived before your letter saying it was a present from Aunt Lennie and Uncle Edwin. I shall write and thank them very soon. I must tell you to send socks a little larger for the children; however, they are well supplied now, so don't send any more. John's suit is simply beautiful; he is too handsome in it. A size 2 fits

---

[149] Italy had capitulated on September 8, 1943.

[150] The nature of Wilfred's "important work" back in Johannesburg has never been disclosed. However, his familiarity with Germany, his fluency in the German language, and his knowledge of surveying and astronomy might have been part of the reason for his having been sent back to South Africa.

him now. The other suits you sent I have had to turn over to a shop for sale, as a one-year is too small. By the time you want to send again he will need a size 3, I suppose. I have had the greatest waste in his first suits because when they are too small there is nothing to do about them.

I am enclosing Eve's school report. Robin is starting at the Convent with Eve on the 26th of this month, which is the beginning of the school year over here. She will have to settle to serious work now. Robin says she doesn't know why Eve likes to pass every year, as she only gets harder work in the next standard.

Robin, as a boarder, age 5 (top row, second from left) with her first grade classmates at Parktown Convent

Wilfred, Hilda Hudson, her boyfriend, and I are going to the Officer's Club in town to dance tonight. You will remember I went with Hilda once when Wilfred was away. I shall be very proud of my captain husband with his ribbon. Wilfred met many boys from Tennessee while he was away but none from home.

I bought a beautiful tailored suit yesterday in navy blue. The idea of Bert's coat with a new skirt sounded all right, but I looked like I had on handed-down clothes and felt depressed, so I thought I had better do something about it. I paid $40 and have something that I shall feel well dressed in when I go into town. I am also having a suit made in mauve linen with Italian quilting on collar, cuffs, and pockets. I am paying $10 for the making, and I think it is going to be lovely, as they do beautiful sewing at this firm of dressmakers.

I seem to be clothes conscious, and I am, as I haven't done anything about clothes for two years now. My latest idea is just too wonderful. In the smartest shop in town, I saw a dinner dress composed of plain long black skirt, flared, with separate bodice of black and aquamarine sequins, just like your material. The bodice was simply snug-fitting to hip length, with short sleeves held up by inner padding or epaulet nicely done. I can't remember the neckline, but I think a cowl front would be the easiest. Now I wonder if you could make the bodice, one for you, and one for me. I can make my skirt. My hip 36", waist 30", bust 34" measurement. I am terribly keen on this and do hope you still have the material. I shall draw what I have in mind—as much as possible. If you don't understand my explanation, maybe you could send enough for a blouse, and I'll have it made. This is old material, and the scent of your perfume will convince the customs.

Bert has just had a cheque for $22 for nighties she has made, and they have swamped her with orders. Now she is running out of the shirring or sewing elastic since it can't be had here. Can you do everything possible to get it for her, and send it in small lots all the time? The colours most needed are white, pink, and blue. Aunt Kate could try in Bristol. This is terribly important to Bert, and I can help when I have time, and make something out of it too. I could make money all right, if it were not for the children, but my hands are full with them, but they are my pleasure. I have just had to refuse a position at $150 per month as private secretary to the newly appointed Food Controller. He is from Cape Town but will be in Pretoria in this job, but I couldn't move to Pretoria nor consider travelling back and forth every day—an hour each way by train. Anyway, I felt honoured that my work was so well known that it was offered to me. That is what Bert makes.

Eve, John, and Robin

My health is marvelous now, and I feel impatient to be most active again, but Wilfred is dictating these days, and he says that since I have had an illness, I am going to take it easy or as much as possible with our family, and he is now trying to make arrangements for me to have a few weeks' holiday on my own, without a single child. What success he is going to have I do not know.

Do not worry about my hospital and doctor bills, as they are all paid, $400 in all. I was certainly a liability in 1943, but watch me as an asset in 1944.

The New Year has held only good for us.

I am glad Burlington people have been so kind to you, and I want you both to be happy there. I wish Father would not work such long hours. It is not a gain in the long run to wear oneself out. I overdid things too long and speak from experience. I would stick to eight hours a day, unless it was absolutely necessary to do more. I know Mother misses Aunt Kate as much as Aunt Kate misses her. What is holding her in Bristol? Why doesn't she try Burlington for a change?

I certainly hope the sale of the house has gone through and that you can have that off your mind, as I can see it has been a great worry. We have been unfortunate in tenants. I can only wish them to be tenants in Johannesburg for a while; then they would appreciate that house and what has been done for them. I hope, if you have bought War Bonds, that they are in your name and not mine, so there will be no tie up if we want to cash in on them. I want this money to be a means of bringing us all together permanently. I, like you, feel a visit would only be unsettling.

Love from us all to our sweethearts,

Helen

Helen's Last Letter [age 37]

8 Reform Avenue
Melrose, Johannesburg
March 4, 1944

My dearest Aunt Nellie,

Your lovely Christmas parcel arrived yesterday and was a big thrill to me; however, Eve and Robin won't have their presents until tomorrow (Sunday) when they come home for the day from the Convent. They are boarders this term, as I found I had too many children. John, on his own, is quite enough to manage. We thought this the only thing to do until I get my strength back to some extent from my operations last year. Enough of that side of my life.

I must tell you how intrigued we all are with the cut-out which lights up in the dark. I hope Robin will be allowed to have it beside her bed at school. [While toys were not tolerated at Parktown Convent, for some reason the nuns made an exception for the glow-in-the dark cutout from America. It a was a novelty for everyone back then.] Isn't she a wee thing to be at boarding school? The children always love new hair ribbons and socks. Socks have been nearly unprocurable here, so they are certainly welcome. I do like my hair ornament and hope I shall soon have an occasion to wear it. John's suit is a beautiful thing, and is fortunately on the big side. I have had a most awful waste in suits being too small for him; some have only been tried on once. His suit looks like some of your sewing.

Sailing to Byzantium (Jan. 1944—June 1944)

I do admire you for the many things you accomplish. This past year has been a dead loss to me as far as what I have to show for it in a material way. But I have had two of the biggest things of my life happen to me during this past year—I found my God, as I had never known Him before, and I had the most beautiful and perfect son born to me. He is blonde like Gene was, and just as chubby and quick.

Mother says she has never seen Eugene looking so well as when she last saw him. I was so happy to hear this, as I knew he had not been well for some time.

Are you happy in your work? Mother thinks it a wonderful job, but I should think it hard to leave Eugene's lovely home and go to live in one room, because I know what lovely surroundings mean to you. I am sure you are filling a very necessary position in America's War Effort, though.

It is wonderful having Wilfred back from the Middle East. He is stationed in Johannesburg and is living at home now. I would love a letter from you just about you and yours. It would be nice to have some pictures of you, Katye Wray, Eugene, and the children. Surely you have some you could have developed. Kay is just a few months younger than Robin, isn't she?

John:
"The most beautiful and perfect son"

Mr. Evans has bought twenty acres of land North of Johannesburg; the best residential section of Johannesburg is all North. It is about fourteen miles from the heart of town. We are planning to build there in the very near future, a typically South African country house of whitewashed brick walls and thatched roof. Mr. Evans will retire and manage the place, as we intend to farm to the extent of our own needs at least. It has a most heavenly view of distant mountains. There are few places with a view around Johannesburg.

I am glad Mother no longer has the care of the Johnson City property. We always had such trying tenants in the place.

I do thank you, Aunt Nellie, for sending us such a lovely box, and I know with what loving thoughts each thing was bought.

My love to Eugene, Katye Wray, and the children, and heaps for your dear self.

Helen

> WESTERN UNION
>
> APRIL 21, 1944
>
> THINK YOUR PRESENCE WOULD SPEED HELENS RECOVERY USE ANY MONIES BELONGING US FOR PERSONAL SAFETY SUGGEST PLANE=
> WILFRED EVANS

> WESTERN UNION
>
> MAY 6, 1944
>
> IMPERATIVE YOU COME I MAY BE INVALID FOR MONTHS HOME WITH NURSE AFTER SEVERAL WEEKS IN HOSPITAL WITH SEPTICEMIA SUGGEST PLANE= HELEN EVANS

[Copy]

GLEN RAVEN COTTON MILLS
Glen Raven, N.C.
May 10, 1944

Senator Robert R. Reynolds
Washington D.C.

Dear Senator Reynolds,

Confirming telephone conversation with you this morning, relative to securing passage to Johannesburg, South Africa, for Mrs. Harlow S. Dixon of Burlington, N.C., beg to give you the following information and statement from Mrs. Dixon.

Mrs. Dixon urgently desires passage to go to the bedside of her daughter, Mrs. Helen Dixon Evans, who is critically ill of Septicemia and whose recovery is very doubtful unless she receives excellent attention and is relieved of the care and concern for her three young children. This daughter is the only child left to Mrs. Dixon, as her only other child, a son, was lost in the U.S. Marine Corps in Nicaragua.

Mrs. Evans and her husband have lived in Johannesburg for the past seven years. Her husband is Capt. W.V.C. Evans of the Colony [sic] of South Africa Tank

Corps, Branch of the British Army. Capt. Evans was with the British Forces in North Africa and is now stationed in North Africa [sic] on active duty. Mrs. Evans until her illness was secretary (in the Directorate General of) War Supplies of Colony of South Africa.

Last report (of Mrs. Evans) is that her recovery is very doubtful and that she will be an invalid for months and perhaps for the rest of her life even if she recovers.

We therefore urge your good offices on their behalf to bring the supreme satisfaction of knowing that she will be permitted to render every assistance to her daughter, her only surviving child.

Very truly yours,
(SG'D) Roger Gant.

From DR. PHILIP BAYER

94 Lister Building
Jeppe Street
Johannesburg

THIS IS TO CERTIFY THAT: Mrs. Evans wife of Captain Evans is suffering from cancer of the uteri. It is essential for her to receive H.11 treatment immediately. As recent results show that several cures have been reported by this form of treatment.

I strongly recommend that the H.11 be sent out by Military plane, and if the necessary permission could be obtained I would immediately cable to the Standard Laboratories, Sunbury on Thames.

Signed Philip Bayer, MD

[Handwritten]
Package to be sent to Major Fish, S.A.A.F.
Air Liaison Officer
High Commissioner's Office
London

Signed J.M. Watt, Lt. Colonel
May 5, 1944

[Copy]

UNITED STATES SENATE
Committee on Military Affairs
May 13, 1944

Lt. Col. Leigh C. Parker
Deputy Assistant Chief of Staff
Priorities and Traffic
Air Transport Command
War Department
Washington D.C.

My dear Colonel:

I have before me your letter of May 11th in regard to the application of Mrs. Harlow Dixon of Burlington, North Carolina, for air transportation to Capetown, South Africa. I regret exceedingly to learn that this seems to be almost impossible and that her application, so to speak, was virtually declined.

Enclosed herewith I am sending you a letter I have just received from Mr. Roger Gant, a friend of mine in Burlington, in the interest of Mrs. Dixon. I would appreciate it if you would read this letter carefully and reconsider her application and let me hear from you at your earliest possible convenience.

Of course you can appreciate Mrs. Dixon's anxiety to reach her daughter's bedside before death.

With assurances of my esteem, I am
Very sincerely yours,

(Sg'd) Robt. R. Reynolds
U.S.S.
Extra Report Delivery
Pennsylvania Hotel

AIR ATTACHÉ
BRITISH EMBASSY
WASHINGTON, D.C.
May 16, 1944

Dear Sir,

The Air Attaché here has received a request from the United States Priorities authorities for assistance in moving a Mrs. HARLOW DIXON from America to Johannesburg. The United States Navy have apparently stated that they can get her to Lagos.

Mrs. Dixon does not qualify for priority, but I think that the case is unusual and perhaps merits our assistance on a "top of the non-priority list" basis, or possibly at Priority "D." The journey is on compassionate grounds with strong backing from influential political quarters. I enclose extracts from correspondence on the subject. The Embassy are anxious to help so far as we can, and apparently they rather owe the Americans a passage of this nature as they have previously helped us out with a similar case.

I have said that I am not at all happy about a passage via Kisumu or Khartoum but that we could help her from Lagos to Leopoldville without great difficulty. I have therefore signaled Consul General Leopoldville asking him if he can obtain a S.A.B.E.N.A. passage from there to Johannesburg. If he can help and if the Navy do get her to Lagos I would be most grateful if you could help over the Lagos - Leopoldville stage on the S.A.B.E.N.A. charter.

Yours sincerely,
R.J. Poland

[Handwritten]
Sir Andrew Jones
Resident Minister's Office
Achimota
Accra
Gold Coast Colony

Mr. Herschel, (J.L.C)
These are the papers relating to Mrs. Harlow Dixon. I feel that the circumstances warrant a Priority "C." Will you please advise her as to the best route to take.
June 6

[Handwritten]
Dear Vice Consul,

The bearer of these papers, Mrs. Harlow Dixon, is anxious to get to Johannesburg as quickly as possible for the reasons stated in the second enclosure. There are prospects of her getting away tomorrow by a U.S. plane. Will you kindly use your influence to enable her to obtain a seat in the train to Johannesburg if there is no aircraft by which she can travel.

    Sincerely, Malcolm (?)
    6/6/1944

Telegram to Sophia from friends:

WESTERN UNION

    WE HAVE ALL FINGERS CROSSED BETTING ON YOU.
    BON VOYAGE. FRANCES LEONE JOSEPHINE.

SOPHIA'S JOURNEY

Following is Sophia Dixon's account of her eighteen-day wartime journey from Burlington, North Carolina, to Johannesburg, South Africa. While the Battle of Normandy raged below, Sophia Dixon flew, courtesy of the U.S., British, and Belgian authorities, from New York to Lisbon and from there to South Africa.

Left Burlington with Harlow for New York on May 28, 1944. Much to attend to in N.Y., and, without Harlow to help obtain the necessary visas, it just couldn't have been accomplished. Duncan Mackenzie is due full credit for making Harlow accompany me, and in many ways rendered the most valuable assistance. Roger Gant [Senator], with all his influence in Washington and with Sen. Reynolds, made my trip possible. I can never forget these two men, and their wives, for their untiring efforts and great sympathy.

Harlow and I arrived with many other passengers at LaGuardia airport in time for the routine questioning and checking, and I was off to the flying boat about 10:00 on the morning of May 30, 1944. No one was permitted to go to the boat except the passengers, and we were all carefully checked out. I was momentarily upset to find, when I arrived at LaGuardia field, I wasn't on the list, and it took several minutes to get this corrected.

Sophia's passport picture, 1944

We weren't assigned any particular seats on the plane, so I cast my eyes around for the most desirable-looking companion and made a happy choice in a Mr. Boyd, who proved kind and most helpful. After we became talkative and right well-acquainted, he said, "I stood behind you with my wife in the Pan American office in N.Y., and as my wife is later to meet me in London, I told her to look at you, how correctly dressed you were for traveling, and I wanted her to arrive in London looking as well groomed. I knew you were a widely traveled woman." This would never do to leave him under such an impression when I expected to call on him for help many times, so I told him it would be my first trip out of America.

Carefully strapped into our seats, and shown where our life preservers could be found, we were off on a clear bright morning—over N.Y. and out to sea. It is shocking how quickly a great elevation is reached, and one is soon flying above the clouds.

All on board the clipper were government men, diplomats, or war workers. There were three girls going to Madrid to work at the American Embassy, there was a courier carrying the diplomats' mail pouch—and withal a very congenial crowd.

Bermuda was to be our first stop. However, before reaching there, I sighted a submarine on the surface, and when I called the attention of others on the plane to it, everyone was peering out the window, and finally someone went forward to the pilot and reported it; so signals were exchanged and we found it was one of the Allies' subs. This was about the only excitement aboard except for food and drink, and there was plenty of both.

We landed in Bermuda at 4 o'clock in the afternoon, expecting to have tea and an early take off, but, to the joy of all, except myself, some plane trouble developed, and we were sent by lovely launches to a very nice hotel—The Belmont Manor. Had it not been for my anxiety to be with Helen, I too could have relaxed at the expense of Pan American, and could have enjoyed what thousands do, or long to do, for their vacations.

After dinner, which I had with a Swiss courier, I went in a launch with three others to another island, Hamilton. There proved to be absolutely nothing of interest, so we soon returned to our hotel, where other guests were dancing and swimming, but I soon retired and was up the next morning (May 31st) to enjoy the lovely flowers and a stroll through the gardens. The people I met interested me quite as much as the scenery. I had an interesting conversation with Mrs. O'Brien, a Canadian woman, who formerly wrote for *Look* magazine and has lived in Bermuda for the past fifteen years. She haunts the hotels, especially Belmont Manor, where many notables have stopped, and she usually manages an interview. King Carroll and Lapescu being quite interesting guests.

We left the hotel at 5:15 p.m on May 31st, expecting to take off at 7 o'clock, but another plane landed and damaged the wing of our plane, so repairs and tests delayed us until 8:30. We were not served our dinner on the plane until 11 p.m., so we were very late getting settled for the night. At 1 p.m. on June 1st we landed at Fayal Island, in the Azores. The black sand on the shores and the dirty children playing in it were not a nice introduction, but, after passing through customs and turning in our passports, we were taken to a very nice hotel for Pan American guests and had a nice lunch, and we all felt quite refreshed for our take off at 3 p.m. (June 1) for Lisbon.

There is nothing new to relate about the flight across the Atlantic—just billows of clouds and a great expanse of blue water, an occasional boat, but they all look so very, very small from our altitude.

Arrived in Lisbon at 11 o'clock at night in a downpour of rain. There were so many passengers that we were an endless time passing through customs, and, even though late, several of us decided to drive to Estoril to the Palace Hotel, and it was well worth the effort, for the food was marvelous, and the hotel gardens were the most beautiful and most colorful things one could imagine. The morning of June 2nd (in Estoril and Lisbon) was bright, and I spent my time, after a late breakfast, wandering through these gardens. I had no desire to dash into Lisbon and do any sightseeing. I knew the trip ahead was hard.

We left Lisbon at 9 o'clock on the evening of June 2nd, just before sunset. I never beheld any painting more beautiful. It will be a lifelong memory. On June 3rd, before dawn, we arrived in Dakar, West Africa. On account of a strong tail wind, we were three hours ahead of schedule and cruised around for an hour before landing. After breakfast of bacon and eggs, which I feared were cold storage, we were driven on a sightseeing tour. However, there was nothing of particular interest to be seen, and I was rather relieved to take off again. There was rain and rough flying for a while out of Dakar, but I had become quite seasoned and there was no ill effect. We landed at Boloma, Portuguese Guinea, for lunch, but, on account of the heavy rain, we had lunch on the plane.

All along the route we lost a few passengers and would then pick up new ones, but really I felt I had lost a friend when Mr. Boyd remained behind in Dakar. But every place I felt I needed help, someone was there.

Our next stop was Fish Lake, in the afternoon of June 3rd, and, when I was met at the plane by Lt. Murphy, he announced that he thought he was meeting Mrs. Roosevelt. They had just been told to get ready for a woman, and he says that is the way she is usually announced. It must have been a great disappointment, but he couldn't have been nicer to our first lady than he was to me. We drove all over the native quarters in a jeep, and then I was assigned to a guest house—well screened—and you just have to travel through this country where there are no screens to know how this is appreciated. At Fish Lake I met several people—Missionaries (returning to the U.S.), and one N.Y. newspaper correspondent who had had her passport taken from her because she entered France without a visa, and she was being sent back to the U.S. She was on her ear about the whole thing.

From Fish Lake I took off at 9 a.m. for Roberts Field, landing there at 9:45 a.m. with the distressing news that they had no idea when I could get a plane out. I was given a room in the Officers' Barracks and was frightened to death that night when I found I was absolutely alone. All the men went to a picture show. One whole side of my ground floor room was just screened in. Across the river, quite near the barracks, I could hear the natives with their weird music and singing. I thought of Lena Whittaker, and how she would die of fright. Lizards were climbing up the screen trying to get into my room, and finally one almost succeeded when it got into a mended place in the wiring, so I did something I never thought was possible—I mashed it with my foot. The barracks had one big washroom for all these men, and I just slipped in when possible. Imagine my relief and surprise when I was called over the phone and told I could get a plane for Accra at 10 o'clock on the morning of June 5th.

There were two stops en route to Accra. We arrived in Accra at 6:15 p.m., June 5th. From Roberts Field to Accra, I traveled on a British plane, with bucket seats and loaded with freight; there were only two other passengers.

All the way, from New York to Liberia, there was one negro passenger, and was he black! He was a Senator from Liberia, and he wore a black and white striped shirt—the same one all the way—stopped at all the best hotels, ate in the same dining rooms, and at the same time we did. However, he was most retiring and inoffensive.

On arrival in Accra, on the British plane, I was transferred to the American airport and met by Major Cattrell. He wanted to take me to dinner, but I declined, and he took me to the American Red Cross hostess house where I was most comfortable. On the morning of June 6th, the Red Cross furnished a car, and Mr. Gray and I drove miles to see Sir Andrew Jones, who had been notified by the British Embassy in Washington to assist me in getting to Johannesburg. I also had a letter from the British Ambassador to deliver to him. I found he had made the following arrangements for me to leave Accra June 18th by plane for Leopoldville and leave Leopoldville (in Belgian Congo) on June 27th and travel by train to Johannesburg. This is a five-day journey. I accepted this but told him I was going to make a great effort to get away sooner. Mr. Gray and I talked to *B.O.A.C.* about my passage (Sir Andrew Jones had given me a priority C for plane travel), and I was told to secure an exit permit and some additional visas. This took time and hard work but was accomplished through the assistance of Mr. Gray (Red Cross).

JUNE 6, 1944
D-DAY, BATTLE OF NORMANDY

(Eve's 10th Birthday)

I was in Accra the day of the invasion [D-Day, June 6th] and cried, and rejoiced as well, at the great undertaking.

I really was overcome with joy when *B.O.A.C.* called me about noon on June 7th and told me to report at the airfield at 2:30. This trip was only to Lagos, however, and I had no idea when I would be able to get another plane. I was most unhappily located in Lagos, where I was sent to State House. The guests were actors, who entertained troops at the various camps, and they were so foreign and cheap I felt defiled. Much to my relief, I received a call by phone, June 8th, saying I could get a plane at noon. On arrival at the airport, I found my only traveling companions were five American service men: 1st Lieutenant Richard Middleton, Los Angeles; Capt. Leslie Durant, Manchester, N. H.; Maj. Forrest Campbell, St. Louis; a Corporal; and a Private. They were on leave and were going to Johannesburg from Khartoum, and had been on their way sixteen days.

(In Lagos I saw many large lizards sunning themselves on the walks. The male ones are the prettiest.)

At 3 o'clock in the afternoon we arrived at Douala, French Equitorial Africa. You just drop down out of the sky in these little places, hardly knowing why, except that you are always sprayed as you leave the plane, also as you re-enter (we called it de-lousing), your passports examined, also all inoculation certificates checked. Then they offer you the most terrible things to drink. I had to be like a camel; when I found something I dared drink, I took an extra amount to keep from famishing.

I can scarcely describe my overnight stop at Douala. We were taken to a terrible place, just rooms over a place where food and drinks were served, and I seemed to be the only woman around. I sat with the American service men until they had drunk too much, and then I went to my room without any supper. I left an early call at the desk, for next morning we were to leave for Stanleyville, but no one called, so I got up before day and got the boys up so we wouldn't miss our plane. Tried to eat a breakfast cooked by a native that I saw shining shoes and hadn't washed his hands afterwards. This was really the black spot of the trip.

Leaving Douala (on the Congo river) on the morning of June 9th, we landed in Stanleyville, in the Belgian Congo, about five the same afternoon. Stanley, who begot the Belgian Congo, would never recognize this country now. I found here the best accommodations since leaving Accra. One would hardly expect a room with private bath and shower in the heart of Africa, but such I found—and how heartwarming. I should give a few moments here in recognition of the virtues and achievements of the noble missionaries, but, since this is just a short account of my flight to South Africa, I shall pass on; but one cannot forget the important role of Livingstone and Stanley in the opening up of Africa.

In the early morning of June 10th, we left Stanleyville, and our next stop was Juba, in the Sudan, and here I had to secure another visa, and I borrowed the money from Maj. Campbell, for I didn't want to cash a ten dollar check and have money with me that I possibly would never have an opportunity to use. It was here I began to dread the yellow fever carrying mosquito, and for days I kept my legs and arms saturated with a preparation I had secured on the west coast of Africa that was supposed to be effective for several hours. I know it must have been, for I believe I came through without a bite.

In the space of a few days I flew over swamps, bush, desert, rolling land, vast lakes, and meandering rivers that Livingstone, Stanley, and others had given the better part of their lives to explore. Names like Kenya, the Congo, the Sudan, the

Nile, and Tanganyika ceased to be colored places on the map and became realities racing by at 10,000 feet.

When I purchased my ticket in Accra for Vaalbank Dam, I was told I would be routed the most direct route, so I was greatly surprised when I realized, on the afternoon of June 10th, that I was flying directly north. I called the attention of Lt. Middleton to this fact and he looked out the plane window and said, "Things are growing strangely familiar," so at our first opportunity we asked an officer what our next landing would be and he said we would land at Khartoum in thirty minutes to spend the night.

I never saw such downcast men, and I was equally perturbed. The soldiers were back at their starting point after about eighteen days of travel. They didn't dare report back to camp for fear their leave would be cancelled, so they remained at hotels and took off with us at 5 o'clock the morning of June 11th, hoping finally to reach Johannesburg.

The hotel at Khartoum was located right on the bank of the Blue Nile. A very nice hotel indeed. Meals well prepared and nicely served by Indians in long white robes with red fezzes and broad red bands about their waists. I never endured such intense heat in my life as I felt when I stepped off the plane in Khartoum; it was breathtaking. My room at the hotel was lovely—very large, with private bath and a large electric fan directly over my bed, which kept going all night, and even at that my gown got so wet I had to take it off to dry. There were long sand bags at each door, and I got the idea they were there to keep the snakes out but later found out they were for the dust storms.

As I sat in the lobby waiting for the plane passengers to assemble, two men especially attracted my attention. They were so well groomed, and I was more than delighted when I found they were to be fellow travelers right to Johannesburg. They were both from Washington—Mr. Herbert Fales, who is in the foreign diplomatic service, and Mr. Eldon P. King, a government man, who seemed to be constant companions. They were finally of great assistance to me.

From Juba to Khartoum we were flying over the desert sands for hundreds of miles; everything was perfectly barren.

The Pan American flying boat could be heated quickly, but not so with the British planes, and I suffered greatly from the intense cold. The meals we had on *B.O.A.C.* were box lunches, stored on the plane, and were mostly unappetizing; however, we landed often and could get fair meals.

Regardless of the time we were awakened at our hotels, we were always served a wonderful pot of tea and wafers. When we took off very early in the morning, this was often all we had until our next landing.

After Khartoum, our next stop was for lunch at Laropi. Having heard and read much of Lake Victoria, it was quite a thrill to land on this beautiful large lake and have tea at Port Bell—this is in Kenya Colony. Here we took on some new and interesting fellow travelers. Among them, Mr. and Mrs. Awre from Cairo, who came through Johannesburg and were truly kind and thoughtful of me. This was some of the most interesting part of my trip.

In Kisumu, June 11th, we were comfortably located at a hotel again. I was fortunate enough to have a private bath and good meals, but the early take off (6 o'clock) on the morning of June 12th caused me to pack so quickly I left behind a dress and princess slip, which I was unable to recover. Traveling directly south, and with a feeling I was nearing Helen and her family, my heart grew somewhat lighter and the scenery more interesting. The sands of the desert are monotonous, but, from Kisumu south to Mozambique, the land is rolling, and there are thousands of native huts. We flew so high, the cold was intense, and it didn't warm me up in the least when I saw in the distance Mt. Kilimanjaro, but the scene is unforgettable. (Tanganyika, Kenya, and Uganda produce coffee.) The natives show some initiative by growing coffee on the slopes of Kilimanjaro, but, after viewing their huts and the surrounding territory, you wonder how they exist.

In the vicinity of Kilimanjaro the valley is rich with palm and banana groves. In a tropical surrounding such as this, to behold a mountain snow-covered seems infinitely improbable and unreal. The natives have made furrows down the mountainside to irrigate their crops. These gradually reach quite a depth by natural erosion, but the elephants often trample down the banking, and the tribesmen must repair the damage. Kilimanjaro is about 19,500 ft. high (I believe) and looks like a huge cake with the icing running down the sides.

We stopped for lunch at Mombasa, Tanganyika; in the afternoon of June 12th, we passed over Zanzibar and Pepper Islands. Someone on the plane remarked that Zanzibar was nothing but dirt and flies, but from the air it was truly beautiful, and the coloring of the water around was gorgeous—so varied. On Pepper Island, and Zanzibar as well, there are groves of cloves, trees of spice and fruit, tea, cocoa, coconuts, and oil palms.

We made a short stop at Dar-es-Salaam, Tanganyika. Here you find black waiters wearing scarlet and yellow jackets over long white robes and rows of Indian shops and swarms of Indian children. Every trifling experience in a wholly new country strikes with the force of novelty, and is always strange and vivid.

When we landed at Lindi, Nyasa [Lake Nyasa] for mail, the plane passengers were given a lovely launch ride. Soon after our take off, there was a gorgeous rainbow reflected in the water as we ascended. It was veiled by a billow of white clouds. I shall never forget this sight.

We were treated to a beautiful sunset as we landed at Mozambique, Portuguese East Africa, for the night. We were taken to Hotel Do Lumbo. This is neutral territory (or supposed to be, but one doesn't feel like it); therefore, the five American service men I had been so interested in were not allowed to enter. Undaunted, though, they told me they would yet find a way to Johannesburg. We were called in time to take the plane at 2:30 in the morning, but for some reason we didn't leave Mozambique until 3:15 on the morning of June 13th.

We were rewarded for being up so early by a beautiful sunrise, and took off in the blazing glory of a rising sun. The sun's rays, tipping the rolling clouds, turned them to a bright rose. At 8:45 we stopped at Beira for breakfast. This is still in Portuguese East Africa. For lunch, we landed at Lourenco Marques.

The trip on the East coast of Africa is an interesting and colorful one, little talked about, perhaps, but such ports as Mombasa, Dar-es-Salaam, Zanzibar, Mozambique, and Lourenco Marques stretch around the coast like a pageant. Along the stretch of a single coast there is represented the work of three European powers as colonizers. The Portuguese at Mozambique and Lourenco Marques, the British at Mombasa, and the Germans at Dar-es-Salaam ("Haven of Peace"), for, although Tanganyika is no longer German, the old German buildings still remain.

It is on the East coast one gets a glimpse, by air, of Darkest Africa in the country where the natives live in their heavily thatched huts beneath the coconut palms. Lourenco Marques is only ninety miles from the Game Reserve. Gasoline shortage made it impossible to make this trip, but later I did have the privilege of seeing colored movies made by Mr. Dunham. The pavements are of elaborate mosaic patterns. The market square has a bandstand, and there are little tables around which people sit and drink wine. It is a great holiday resort, with a racetrack, bullfights, and soccer as diversion.

Starting so early from Mozambique (Portuguese East Africa), too early in fact for breakfast, we landed at 8:45 for breakfast at Beira, and lunch at Lourenco Marques—with only a short time for sight-seeing.

Arriving the same afternoon (June 13th) at Durban, in the rain, the plane cruised all over the city and we had a wonderful view. We were to fly next morning at 6:45 for Vaalbank Dam, but the weather was too bad, so I had to go by rail. Mr. Fales and Mr. King managed to get me a reservation on the train at 3:40 (June 14, 1944). Arrived June 15th at Johannesburg.

Sophia arrived in Johannesburg nine days before Helen died. In the stoicism typical of Helen, Sophia's description of her wartime journey to Africa never mentions her dread of her daughter's impending death or the anxiety of possibly arriving too late. The following telegrams and final letter tell the end of the story.

POST OFFICE TELEGRAPHS   June 20, 1944

CRUSHED BEYOND ALL DESCRIPTION OVER YOUR DEAREST HELEN. HER
SINCERE CHRISTIANITY SHOULD FORTIFY YOU AND OTHERS TO BEAR IT.
OUR HEARTS AND THOUGHTS ARE WITH YOU. WE LOVE YOU DEARLY. EARL
CHARLIE EUGENE EDWIN HUNTER AND FAMILIES

POST OFFICE TELEGRAPHS   June 21, 1944
ELIZABETHTON TEN

MRS. HARLOW DIXON
8 REFORM AVE
MELROSE JOHANNESBURG UNION OF SOUTH AFRICA

OUR THOUGHTS AND PRAYERS WITH ALL

RUBY EDNA DEMA FRANCES ELVA JOSEPHINE LEONE GROSSMAN

[Note from Sophia Dixon to Harlow Dixon on the day Helen died]

Johannesburg, June 24, 1944

Harlow dearest,

In writing to all the family in the same letter, I am sure you know how hard it is. But I want to add this little note to tell you how I love you and how dreadfully I miss you.

Could we have been together through this terrible trial, I know we could have been a great comfort to each other.

One of the very last things I ever said to Helen was, "Helen, I want you to know how deeply your father and I love you," and she said, "Don't I know," and looked into my eyes with those big blue eyes swimming with tears.

Really sweetheart, can life ever be the same again?

Sophia

Afterword

Helen's song sings its own beauty,
Her life and letters a simple blending of
Birth, love, and death—
The three cords that bind us
To each other—and to the invisible world beyond.

And so, back to the riddle: "How is it possible for two people to continue to love one another for fifteen years despite finding themselves living apart for eight of those years, suffering though four more, and happily settled for only three?"

The answer, of course, lies in the power of love and loyalty to overcome the combined toll of reticence, separation, financial stress, prejudice, and war. Then too, after reading Helen's letters, one gains a strong sense of the invisible powers of destiny, character, perseverance, and humor at work in their lives. Helen and Wilfred's love grew in spite of the difficulties they faced—maybe even because of them.

Their growth was possible because of their inner qualities. Helen's inner qualities we can glean from her letters: Love, loyalty, courage, positivity, frugality, resourcefulness, conscientiousness, an interest in everything, an abiding sense of humor, and a willingness to reach out to experience the world by moving beyond the shyness that had inhibited her in childhood. At one point Helen says, "I have had no fights within myself. No inclination to take an easier path." That attitude remained true of her even as her health failed. In her last year of life, after demonstrating her flexibility by establishing a home in fourteen different places, Helen took on yet another job. Then, in her final letter to her Aunt Nellie, she mentions her spiritual growth: "I have found my God . . ." We have no details—only the sense that she has a feeling of completion.

Wilfred's gifts to the relationship were different. He brought the excitement of far-away places—South Africa, Southern Rhodesia (Zimbabwe), England, Wales, America, Germany, Egypt, and Italy; academic brilliance; and fluency in five languages. He was a dedicated student of farming, philosophy, business, geography, and current affairs. He endured a brush with Nazism, served in World War II, and was recognized both through his business and war endeavors for his willingness to put learning, knowledge, and commitment ahead of his personal comfort. He also brought perseverance and commitment. A less dedicated soul might have left the marriage in the first three years. But he stayed by Helen's side in spite of daily insults from family and neighbors. He also showed love and forgiveness. In a letter to her parents, Helen writes, "Wilfred has asked me to write and say that he would like to forget the bad feelings of the past . . . he wants us just to consider that we were all in an impossible situation." And, finally: Romance. As Helen says, "Wilfred has never stopped courting me." With her wry sense of humor, she tells her parents ". . . just between us, he is very much in love with your daughter."

Through these letters to her adored parents and through the children they bore and loved without reservation, Helen and Wilfred's legacy lives on. Eve became an architect, eurythmist, and a poet. She designed the first buildings of the Emerson Waldorf School in Chapel Hill, which she helped to found. John became a highly successful businessman, and Robin became a professor of English literature at Linfield College, a small liberal arts college in Oregon. They were shepherded into adulthood by the love and dedication of their father, the Whitley family, and their ever-devoted Auntie Bert.

Helen and Wilfred's grandchildren—Tom, Simon, Leigh-ann, Bronwyn, and Vanessa—and their great-grandchildren—John, Dixon, Adrienne, Rhys, Finley, Henry, Simon, and Liam—have, through this book, the opportunity to know Helen Dixon Evans as the extraordinary woman she was.

Helen's legacy for future generations may be summed up in her own words, written four years before her death: "Please don't ever think of my life as a sad one, because I do not consider it so, as I still get a big kick out of everything, and whatever happens is just a broadening experience."

Timeline

Aug. 14, 1906	Wilfred Victor Collingwood Evans born in Johannesburg, South Africa
Oct. 2, 1906	Helen Hunter Dixon born in Elizabethton, Tennessee, USA
1923 – 1924	Helen attends Mary Baldwin College in Staunton, Virginia
1925 – 1928	Helen studies at Virginia Intermont
Summer 1928	Helen on grand tour of Europe
1925 – 1929	Wilfred studies Agriculture at North Carolina State University
April 30, 1929	Helen's brother, Robert (Red) Dixon, a U.S. Marine, is killed in Nicaragua
May 1929	Wilfred graduates from North Carolina State University
Aug. 1929	Helen and Wilfred meet at Nags Head, North Carolina
Aug. 1929	Helen invites Wilfred to her parents' home on "G" Street in Elizabethton, Tennessee, USA
Aug. 1929	Wilfred returns to Africa; starts first tobacco research station in Marandellas, Southern Rhodesia (now Zimbabwe)
Sept. 1929	Dow Jones Industrial peaks at 381.17 (a level not reached again until 1954)
Oct. 29, 1929	Wall Street Crash
1929 –1939	The Great Depression
Winter 1929 –33	Helen and Wilfred correspond, Wilfred from Southern Rhodesia and Germany, and Helen from Elizabethton, Tennessee, USA
Sept. 1929 – 36	Helen secretary at The American Rayon Corporation, Elizabethton, Tennessee

Dec. 1931	Wilfred contracts blackwater fever in Marandellas
Jan. 1932	Wilfred leaves Southern Rhodesia and sails from Cape Town to Germany; to study German, he lives with Prof. and Mrs. Vriesen in Essen
Feb.-Aug 1932	Wilfred is Secretary to the Reverend Right Honorable Count von Korff
Sept. 1932	Wilfred, now fluent in German, moves to Munich to study philosophy at the University of Munich
1932	Dow Jones bottoms out at 41.22
1932	The Dixon family, severely impacted by the Great Depression, moves from "G" Street to Broad Street, Elizabethton, Tennessee
Early 1933	Wilfred's sister, Bert, sails from South Africa to Germany, visits the Vriesens in Essen and Wilfred in Munich; the Evans family, living partly in London and partly in Cape Town, has not been financially hurt by the Great Depression
Aug. 1933	Helen sails to Germany
Aug. 26, 1933	Helen and Wilfred marry in Essen, Germany
Oct. 1933	Helen returns to the United States
Late 1933	Wilfred escapes from Germany, sails for England and the U.S.
1933 – 1936	Dixon and Evans families live together on Broad Street, Elizabethton, Tennessee. Unemployment in the U.S. now reaches 24.9%; Wilfred, in spite of all efforts, remains unemployed until 1937; Helen, the main support of the family, continues her secretarial work at the North American Rayon Corporation
June 6, 1934	Helen Eve Collingwood Evans is born, Elizabethton, Tennessee
1936	Harlow Dixon liquidates the Dixon Furniture Company
1937	Wilfred moves to Nashville, Tennessee, works first as Janitor/Porter at Sears, and later as head of Refrigerator Department

Timeline

	Helen moves to Nashville, Tennessee; works as a secretary
	Wilfred offered job as Representative in the Union of South Africa for Sears International
Oct. 1937	Helen, Wilfred, and three-year-old Eve sail for South Africa, via Southampton and London, England
May, 1938	Kiki Vriesen visits Helen, Wilfred, and Bert in Johannesburg, South Africa
July 16, 1938	Myfanwy (Robin) Collingwood Evans is born in Johannesburg
August, 1938	After nine months, Wilfred leaves Sears International and takes a position with Westinghouse in Johannesburg
August, 1939	Wilfred becomes Branch Manager of Westinghouse, Durban, South Africa
Sept. 3, 1939	Britain and France declare war on Germany
Sept. 6, 1939	South Africa enters World War II as an ally of Britain
July 4, 1940	Wilfred signs up as World War II volunteer, is transferred to Johannesburg-Pretoria area where he begins his training; Helen, Eve, and Robin remain in Durban some five hundred miles away
July 1940	Wilfred begins service in the South African army as a Sergeant
August, 1940	Helen works as filing clerk at the Dunlop Rubber Company in Durban
October 1940	Wilfred promoted to Second Lieutenant
Feb. 1941	After a seven-month separation from Wilfred, Helen moves with Eve and Robin to Johannesburg where she has been appointed secretary to Kingston Russell, Assistant to the Minister of War Supplies; Helen and the children live in a boarding house while Wilfred continues to live at camp outside Johannesburg
June, 1941	Wilfred promoted to Lieutenant
Dec. 7, 1941	Japanese attack Pearl Harbor
Dec. 8-11, 1941	America enters World War II

Jan. 1942	Helen moves with Eve and Robin to Melrose, an upscale suburb of Johannesburg where she rents part of a house belonging to Mrs. Maton
Jan. 1943	Helen moves with Eve and Robin to a single-dwelling in Melrose, creating her fourteenth home since moving to SA; Helen resigns from the Ministry of War Supplies
Feb. 28, 1943	John Kevren Collingwood Evans is born
Mar. 1943	Wilfred promoted to Captain, leaves Johannesburg to prepare for action in Egypt and Italy
Oct. 1943	Helen enrolls Eve and Robin as boarders at Parktown Convent, a private girls' school, which Eve has been attending as a day scholar; Helen hospitalized; has first radium treatment; Bert stays overnight after work to help with baby John
Jan. 1944	Wilfred home with special wartime duties; receives the Africa Star; the first time he has lived at home in three and a half years
April 1944	Helen hospitalized in Johannesburg General Hospital
May 28, 1944	Sophia leaves Burlington, North Carolina, to be at Helen's bedside; flies to Africa from New York
June 6, 1944	Battle of Normandy
June 15, 1944	Sophia arrives in Johannesburg, South Africa
June 24, 1944	Helen dies

South Africa, 1940

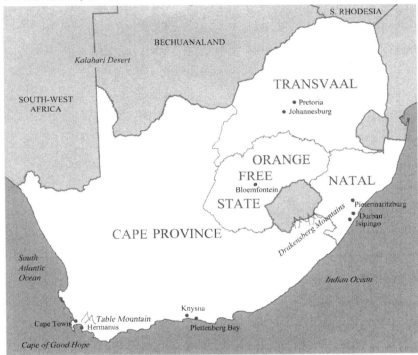

Places mentioned in the letters

FAMILY TREE
ANCESTRY OF FAMILY MEMBERS MENTIONED IN LETTERS

HELEN HUNTER DIXON

Paternal

Great-grandfather: Thomas O. Dixon (b. 1818)
Great-grandmother: Lucy A. Dixon (b. 1826)

Grandfather: John Thomas Dixon (b. 1847)
Grandmother: Helen Virginia Dixon (b. 1847) (Mama Dick)

Father: Harlow Shaw Dixon (b. 1877)
Father's Brother: Hunter Dixon (b. 1879) (Kate)
    Sons: Thomas (Unmarried)
            Gordon (Virginia): Ann

Maternal

Great-grandfather: Dr. Abraham Jobe (b. 1817)
Great-grandmother: Sophronia Poteet (b. 1826)

Grandfather: Dr. E.E. Hunter (b. 1845)
Grandmother: Mollie Jobe Hunter (b. 1851) (Mama Hunter)
    Sisters: Hattie (b. 1856)
              Ruth (b. 1864)
              Nine other siblings

Mother: Sophia Hunter (b. 1886)
    Siblings: Walter Hunter (Lena): Hildred
               Fred Hunter (Unmarried)
               Earl Hunter (Lula): Gladys and Marie
               Charlie Hunter (Elizabeth): Harris
               David Hunter (Nellie): Eugene
               (Katye Wray, née Clem): Gene and Kay
               Nellie Hunter (Died age 12)
               Edwin Hunter (Lennie): Helen, Kathryn

Harlow Dixon marries Sophia Hunter (1905)
    Children: Helen Hunter Dixon (b. October 2, 1906)
                Robert Edward Dixon (b. November 8, 1908)

WILFRED VICTOR COLLINGWOOD EVANS

Father: William Evans (b. 1872)
Three sisters

Mother: Eva Agatha Hudd (b. 1875)
Four brothers
One sister

William Evans marries Eva Agatha Hudd in Wales (1898)
Leave Wales for South Africa, 1902

Children: Alberta (Bert) Theodosia Hudd Evans (b. 1902)
Wilfred Victor Collingwood Evans (b. 1906)
Thelma Evans (b. circa 1911)

Wilfred Victor Collingwood Evans marries Helen Hunter Dixon (August 26, 1933)

Children: Helen Eve Collingwood Evans (b. June 6, 1934)
Robin Myfanwy Collingwood Evans (b. July 16, 1938)
John Kevren Collingwood Evans (b. February 28, 1943)

530

Sophia's Journey

Leg	From	To	Distance mi	Date	Aircraft	"Airline"
1 to 2	New York	Bermuda	780	30-May	Boeing 314	Pan Am
2 to 3	Bermuda	Azores	2050	31-May	Boeing 314	Pan Am
3 to 4	Azores	Lisbon	1060	1-Jun	Boeing 314	Pan Am
4 to 5	Lisbon	Dakar	1730	2-Jun	Boeing 314	Pan Am
5 to 6	Dakar	Bolama	250	3-Jun	Boeing 314	Pan Am
6 to 7	Bolama	Fish Lake (Lake Piso)	435	3-Jun	Boeing 314	Pan Am
7 to 8	Fish Lake (Lake Piso)	Roberts Field	90	4-Jun	Douglas?	?
8 to 9	Roberts Field	Accra	700	5-Jun	DC 3?	?
9 to 10	Accra	Lagos	260	7-Jun	DC 3	?
10 to 11	Lagos	Douala	465	8-Jun	?	SABENA
11 to 12	Douala	Stanleyville (Kisangani)	1100	9-Jun	?	SABENA
12 to 13	Stanleyville (Kisangani)	Juba	530	10-Jun	?	SABENA
13 to 14	Juba	Khartoum	740	10-Jun	?	SABENA
14 to 15	Khartoum	Laropi	830	11-Jun	Short Empire	BOAC
15 to 16	Laropi	Port Bell	235	11-Jun	Short Empire	BOAC
16 to 17	Port Bell	Kisumu	150	11-Jun	Short Empire	BOAC
17 to 18	Kisumu	Mombassa	435	12-Jun	Short Empire	BOAC
18 to 19	Mombassa	Dar es Salaam	195	12-Jun	Short Empire	BOAC
19 to 20	Dar es Salaam	Lindi	220	12-Jun	Short Empire	BOAC
20 to 21	Lindi	Mozambique	355	12-Jun	Short Empire	BOAC
21 to 22	Mozambique	Beira	510	13-Jun	Short Empire	BOAC
22 to 23	Beira	Lorenzo Marques (Maputu)	450	13-Jun	Short Empire	BOAC
23 to 24	Lorenzo Marques (Maputu)	Durban	285	13-Jun	Short Empire	BOAC
24 to 25	Durban	Johannesburg	315	14-15 Jun	Train	SAR
Total Mi.			14170			

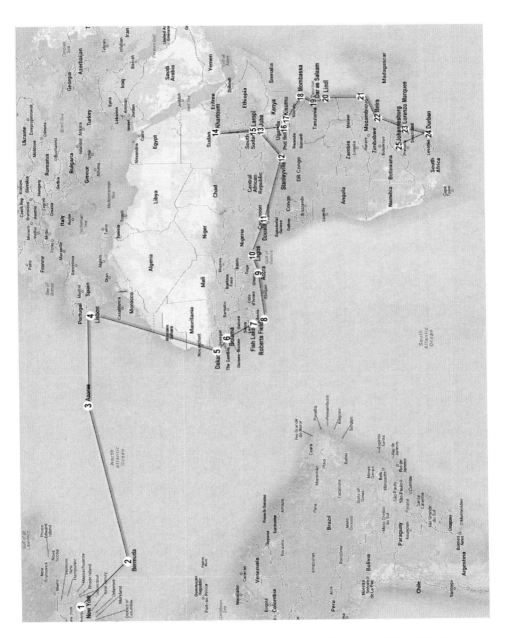

Sophia's Journey from the United States to South Africa, 1944

ACKNOWLEDGEMENTS

Many people have helped bring these letters to life. My older sister, Eve, not only discovered and saved the first set of letters but constantly encouraged and saved me from getting lost. Her memories of our mother, father, aunts, uncles, cousins, and grandparents on both sides of the family have been essential for the completion of the story.

My mother's cousin, Kathryn Hall, and her husband, Ben Hall, have been wonderfully kind, generous, and hospitable as they welcomed us back to Tennessee—a world my sister, my brother, and I came to know only as adults. Kathryn and Ben are poignant reminders of the many other American relatives we never knew in person.

I am also indebted to my distant cousin, Bill Hunter, who has spent decades researching the descendants of and the life and times of Johannes Jager (my great-great-great-great-great grandfather), who came to America from Switzerland and changed his name to John Hunter back in the eighteenth century. Bill Hunter's perseverance over the years inspired me to persevere with this project for the last many years.

I consider Kristin Parker an honorary family member for her depth of devotion to the task of helping to transcribe many of the letters. Others who feel like family are the Wilsons, who own the mansion built by my great-grandfather, Dr. E.E. Hunter, on Riverside Drive in Elizabethton, Tennessee.

Then there was the extraordinary kindness of Mary Ransom, who traveled to North Carolina State University in Raleigh to research my father's years in school there. We had heard the family stories of his brilliance and enthusiasm for learning but had not been able to document his time at North Carolina State University until Mary's visit to the university library.

I have also benefited enormously from the able assistance of Cathren Murray, who organized and scanned dozens of family photos; from Linda Olds, who read and discussed the early versions of the text with deep empathy; from the proofreading skills of my sister, Eve, and my friends, Miriam Lacey, Robert Hamilton, and Fred and Judith Shipley. Colleagues in several departments at Linfield College have helped me in different ways—David Groff encouraged me to take this project seriously as long ago as 2004, and Jean Caspers, Diane Welch, and Patrice O'Donovan helped me with various questions I have had regarding copyright and mid-twentieth century health practices. Lendie Bliss deserves special mention for her dedicated and remarkable skills in genealogy research.

In preparing the text for publication, I have had the good fortune to have Michal Wert's expertise in formatting and proofreading the book and Bettie Denny's fabulous talent as artistic director. Both Michal and Bettie have spent countless hours refining, conferring, and making an incalculable impact on the quality of the final text. It was through Michal's and Bettie's devotion to the book that I came to believe that I had more than a family story. Without the extraordinary support of these two friends, this book would not exist.

In the last phases of reviewing the text, I have had the benefit of the editing skills of Chris Nordquist. Working with Chris has been a joy, since she is not only an exacting and capable editor but also a deeply sensitive human being. I always emerged from our sessions feeling that she was responding to the book at the deepest level possible. If this book is ever used as an academic text, it will be thanks to Chris, who is responsible in large measure for encouraging me to write and append the many footnotes in the text.

Over the years, I have enjoyed a great deal of support from my family and friends whose gentle inquiries have kept me on task. Chief among these were my niece, Leigh-ann Sprock; my brother, John; and my dear friends, Liz Jagla and the late Pamela Harris, who would, on occasion, beg me to tell my mother's story at one of her wonderful parties. Her enthusiasm lives on.

Finally, there has been the moral support of my sons, Tom and Simon Lawton, and my ever-devoted husband, Keith, whose cheerful fires, hot meals, knowledge of World War II, and extensive computer skills have kept me and the project on track.

(Note: Any errors or omissions are mine alone.)

Robin Lawton

HELEN AND WILFRED'S CHILDREN

From left: Eve, John, and Robin (editor)—all now live in the U.S. with their families.

ABOUT THE EDITOR

Robin Lawton and her husband, Keith, emigrated from South Africa to the United States in 1973. They live on a small vineyard in Yamhill County, southwest of Portland, Oregon. Robin is a Professor Emerita of Linfield College, where she taught for twenty-five years. They have two grown sons, Tom and Simon.

Made in the USA
San Bernardino, CA
10 June 2015